READINGS IN

CANADIAN

FOREIGN POLICY

CLASSIC DEBATES AND NEW IDEAS

READINGS IN

CANADIAN
FOREIGN POLICY

CLASSIC DEBATES AND NEW IDEAS

SECOND EDITION

DUANE BRATT
CHRISTOPHER J. KUKUCHA

OXFORD
UNIVERSITY PRESS

OXFORD
UNIVERSITY PRESS

8 Sampson Mews, Suite 204, Don Mills, Ontario M3C 0H5
www.oupcanada.com

Oxford University Press is a department of the University of Oxford.
It furthers the University's objective of excellence in research, scholarship,
and education by publishing worldwide in

Oxford   New York

Auckland   Cape Town   Dar es Salaam   Hong Kong   Karachi
Kuala Lumpur   Madrid   Melbourne   Mexico City   Nairobi
New Delhi   Shanghai   Taipei   Toronto

With offices in

Argentina   Austria   Brazil   Chile   Czech Republic   France   Greece
Guatemala   Hungary   Italy   Japan   Poland   Portugal   Singapore
South Korea   Switzerland   Thailand   Turkey   Ukraine   Vietnam

Oxford is a trade mark of Oxford University Press in the UK
and in certain other countries

Published in Canada by Oxford University Press

Copyright © Oxford University Press Canada 2011

The moral rights of the author have been asserted

Database right Oxford University Press (maker)

First Published 2011

Library and Archives Canada Cataloguing in Publication

Readings in Canadian foreign policy : classic debates and new ideas /
editors, Duane Bratt & Christopher J. Kukucha.—2nd ed.

ISBN 978-0-19-543781-2

1. Canada—Foreign relations—Textbooks. I. Bratt, Duane, 1967–
II. Kukucha, Christopher John

FC242.R43 2011   327.71   C2010-906633-2

Cover image: Veer/Ocean Photography

This book is printed on permanent (acid-free) paper ∞.

Printed and bound in Canada

2 3 4 — 15 14 13

CONTENTS

PREFACE

The first edition of *Readings in Canadian Foreign Policy: Classic Debates and New Ideas* was a pleasant surprise. Its formula of combining classic articles with newer, more issue-specific ones appealed to students, instructors, and researchers alike. When Oxford University Press approached us about writing a second edition, we had specific ideas about how to improve upon the first collection. The result is a larger text with a number of new original articles and pedagogical features.

Part 1, our theoretical section, has the fewest changes. The original articles by John Holmes, David Dewitt and John Kirton, and Stephen Clarkson all remain in the collection. Each of these classic articulations of the three mainstream perspectives (middle power, principal power, and satellite) is complemented by updated contributions from Tom Keating, John Kirton, and Brian Bow and Patrick Lennox. Additional theoretical perspectives are provided by Claire Sjolander and Kathryn Trevenen (feminism), and Mark Neufeld (Gramscian). Two historical chapters were also added at the beginning of this section: John Kirton identifies the 10 most influential books in Canadian foreign policy and Adam Chapnick offers an important historical review of the period from 1945 to 1968.

Parts 2 and 3 continue to examine the external and domestic determinants of Canadian foreign policy. Previous selections by Don Barry (Canada–US relations), Paul Gecelovsky (prime minister), and Chris Kukucha (provinces) remain, but have been updated to include information from the years of the Harper government. The chapter by John English on the role of Parliament has been joined by an update by the editors on minority governments. New to this edition are chapters from John Kirton (G8/G20), Andrew Cooper and Whitney Lackenbauer (Indigenous diplomacy and the United Nations), Douglas Ross (NATO), Patrice Dutil (DFAIT), and Stéphane Roussel and Jean-Christophe Boucher (Quebec).

Parts 4, 5, and 6—the issue-specific sections—have been completely revamped. The security section begins with a historical analysis of Canadian defence policy by Kim Nossal. This is followed by new chapters by Duane Bratt (Afghanistan), Monica Gattinger and Geoffrey Hale (Canada–US border), and Rob Huebert (Arctic). In the trade and economic issues section, Elizabeth Smythe has updated an original chapter on Canadian investment policy, with new chapters by Robert Wolfe (trade) and Stephen McBride (the 2008–9 financial crisis). In the final section of the volume, focusing on social considerations, there are updated chapters by Nelson Michaud (values), Heather Smith (environment), and David Black (Africa). They are joined by a new chapter on Canadian aid policy by Stephen Brown and a harrowing first-person account by Maher Arar of his torture in a Syrian prison after being renditioned there by US authorities. To put Arar's story into context, the editors have written a brief introduction on the role of human rights in Canadian foreign policy.

Beyond these significant changes to the content of the second edition, there are also some new pedagogical features. The section introductions and bibliographies remain (and have been updated), but they have been joined by lists of key terms and dates in Canadian foreign policy.

ACKNOWLEDGEMENTS

As noted in the first edition, we are fortunate to participate in a community of scholars that is diverse and collegial. Despite obvious differences, there is an ongoing commitment to dialogue and quality of research. We hope this continues in the future. Particular thanks must be extended to Kim Nossal, the dean of Canadian Foreign Policy, who agreed to contribute a previously published article on the evolution of Canadian defence policy at the project's late stages.

As with the first edition of this book, our experience at Oxford University Press was once again extremely positive and professional. Sponsoring editor Caroline Starr first approached us about doing a second edition and from that moment on, developmental editor Allison McDonald guided us through the rest of the process. Thank-yous are also extended to Jennifer McIntyre, the copy editor, and Christine Escalante, the production coordinator.

Besides the staff at OUP, we are also indebted to the anonymous reviewers who provided excellent advice on how to improve the first edition.

Finally, both of us are fortunate to be surrounded by people who provide the required support and inspiration for a project such as this.

Chris Kukucha

I want to thank Duane for yet another positive collaborative experience. I also want to extend my love and appreciation to my wife, Renee, and my sons James and William.

Duane Bratt

I want to acknowledge the sabbatical that I received from May 15 to December 30, 2009, from Mount Royal University. This gave me the time, in the crucial stages of this project, to complete my required tasks. Once again, my collaboration with Chris could not have gone more smoothly. I also want to recognize the patience of my wife Teresa and my children Chris and Dorothy as I went through another book project. Finally, I wish to take this opportunity to publicly welcome Chris's new wife Stephanie to the family. By now, you know what you are getting with your new father-in-law.

PERMISSIONS

Maher Arar, 'Maher Arar: Chronology of Events, September 26, 2002 to October 5, 2003'. Source: www.maherarar.ca/cms/images/uploads/mahersstory.pdf. Kerry Pither, *Dark Days: The Story of Four Canadians Tortured in the Name of Fighting Terror*.

Don Barry, 'Managing Canada–U.S. Relations in the Post-9/11 Era: Do We Need a Big Idea?' CSIS Policy Papers on the Americas (November 2003), by the Center for Strategic and International Studies, Washington, DC.

Adam Chapnick, 'Canadian Foreign Policy, 1945–1968', from 'Victims of Their Own Success? Canadians and Their Foreign Policy at the Onset of the Cold War', *Zeitschrift für Kanada-Studien* 30, 1 (2010): 9–23.

Stephen Clarkson, 'Conclusion', in Clarkson ed., *An Independent Foreign Policy for Canada?* Copyright © 1968. Published by McClelland & Stewart Ltd. Used with permission of the author and the publisher.

Andrew F. Cooper and P. Whitney Lackenbauer, 'The Achilles' Heel of Canadian Good International Citizenship: Indigenous Diplomacies and State Responses', *Canadian Foreign Policy* 13, 2 (2007).

David B. Dewitt and John J. Kirton, *Canada as a Principal Power: A Study in Foreign Policy and International Relations* (Toronto: John Wiley and Sons, 1983), 13–20.

John English, 'The Member of Parliament and Foreign Policy', in Fen Osler Hampson and Maureen Molot, eds., *Canada Among Nations 1998: Leadership and Dialogue*. Copyright © 1998 Oxford University Press Canada. Reprinted by permission of the publisher.

Monica Gattinger and Geoffrey Hale, 'Borders and Bridges along a Multidimensional Policy Landscape: Canada's Policy Relations in North America', a summary of *Borders and Bridges: Canada's Policy Relations in North America* (Toronto: Oxford University Press Canada, 2010).

John Holmes, 'Most Safely in the Middle'. International Journal 39, 2 (Spring 1984), 366–88. Reprinted by permission of the Canadian Institute of International Affairs.

Rob Huebert, 'Canadian Arctic Sovereignty and Security in a Transforming Circumpolar World', *Foreign Policy for Canada's Tomorrow* no. 4. Canadian International Council: Toronto, 2009.

John J. Kirton, 'The 10 Most Important Books in Canadian Foreign Policy', *International Journal* 64, 2 (Spring 2009).

Christopher Kukucha, 'Dismembering Canada? Stephen Harper and the Foreign Relations of Canadian Provinces'. Originally published in *Review of Constitutional Studies* 14, 1 (2009). Courtesy of the Centre for Constitutional Studies.

Kim Richard Nossal, 'Defending the "Realm": Canadian Strategic Culture Revisited'. Originally published as 'Defending the "Realm": Canadian Strategic Culture Revisited', *International Journal* 59, 3 (Summer 2004): 503–20; updated for this volume.

Stéphane Roussel and Jean-Christophe Boucher, 'The Myth of the Pacific Society: Quebec's Contemporary Strategic Culture', *American Review of Canadian Studies* 38, 2 (August 2008), 165–87. Reprinted with permission.

Heather A. Smith, 'Unwilling Internationalism or Strategic Internationalism? Canadian Climate Policy under the Conservative Government', *Canadian Foreign Policy* 15, 2 (2009).

Claire Turenne Sjolander and Kathryn Trevenen, 'Constructing Canadian Foreign Policy: Myths of Good International Citizens, Protectors, and the War in Afghanistan', in J. Marshall Beier and Lana Wylie, eds., *Canadian Foreign Policy in Critical Perspective*. Copyright © 2010 Oxford University Press Canada. Reprinted by permission of the publisher.

Robert Wolfe, 'Canada's Adventures in Clubland: Trade Clubs and Political Influence', from J. Daudelin and D. Schwanen, eds., *Canada Among Nations 2007* (Montreal and Kingston: McGill-Queen's University Press, 2008), 181–97.

CONTRIBUTORS

Maher Arar is a Syrian-born Canadian citizen who was sent to Syria by the United States as an alleged terrorist. A public inquiry in Canada fully exonerated Arar of all charges and ordered the Canadian government to pay him a $10.5 million settlement.

Donald Barry is professor in the Department of Political Science at the University of Calgary.

David Black is professor of political science and director of the Centre for Foreign Policy Studies at Dalhousie University.

Jean-Christophe Boucher is assistant professor and Canada research chair in international security at the Quebec Institute of International Studies, Université Laval

Brian Bow is associate professor of political science at Dalhousie University.

Duane Bratt is associate professor of political science in the Department of Policy Studies at Mount Royal University.

Stephen Brown is associate professor at the School of Political Studies at the University of Ottawa.

Adam Chapnick is associate professor of defence studies at the Royal Military College of Canada.

Stephen Clarkson is professor emeritus in the Department of Political Science at the University of Toronto.

Andrew F. Cooper is the associate director and a Distinguished Fellow at the Centre of International Governance Innovation.

David B. Dewitt is the associate vice-president research, social sciences and humanities, at York University.

Patrice Dutil is associate professor in the Department of Politics and Public Administration at Ryerson University.

John English is university professor of history and political science at the University of Waterloo.

Monica Gattinger is associate professor in the School of Political Studies at the University of Ottawa.

Paul Gecelovsky has held academic appointments at the University of Lethbridge, the University of Western Ontario, and the University of Windsor.

Geoffrey Hale is an associate professor in the Department of Political Science at the University of Lethbridge.

John W. Holmes (1910–88) served in the Department of External Affairs in the late 1940s and the 1950s and was later the head of the Canadian Institute of International Affairs.

Rob Huebert is professor of political science and associate director of the Centre for Military and Strategic Studies at the University of Calgary.

Tom Keating is professor in the Department of Political Science at the University of Alberta.

John J. Kirton is professor of political science and director of the G8 Research Group at the University of Toronto.

Christopher J. Kukucha is associate professor in the Department of Political Science at the University of Lethbridge.

P. Whitney Lackenbauer is associate professor in the Department of History at St Jerome's University.

Patrick Lennox is the author of *At Home and Abroad: The Canada–U.S. Relationship and Canada's Place in the World*, and co-editor of *An Independent Foreign Policy for Canada? Challenges and Choices for the Future*.

Stephen McBride is a professor in the Department of Political Science, McMaster University.

Nelson Michaud is professor of international relations and associate director of the Groupe d'études, de recherche et de formation internationales at L'École Nationale d'Administration Publique in Québec City.

Mark Neufeld is associate professor in the Department of Political Studies at Trent University.

Kim Richard Nossal is Sir Edward Peacock professor of international relations in the Department of Political Studies at Queen's University.

Douglas Alan Ross is professor of political science at Simon Fraser University.

Stéphane Roussel is professor of political science and Canada research chair in Canadian Foreign and Defence Policy at the Université du Québec à Montréal.

Claire Turenne Sjolander is professor at the School of Political Studies at the University of Ottawa.

Heather A. Smith is associate professor of international studies at the University of Northern British Columbia.

Elizabeth Smythe is associate professor of political science at Concordia University College of Alberta.

Kathryn Trevenen is assistant professor in the Institute of Women's Studies and the School of Political Studies at the University of Ottawa.

Robert Wolfe is professor at the School of Policy Studies at Queen's University.

PART I

STUDYING CANADIAN FOREIGN POLICY: VARYING APPROACHES

WHAT IS CANADIAN FOREIGN POLICY?

Historically, Canada has attempted to define its foreign policy in both explicit and implicit terms. *Canada in the World*, the 1995 government white paper on foreign policy, for example, stated that 'domestic policy is foreign policy. Foreign policy is domestic policy.'[1] Lester Pearson, on the other hand, famously suggested that 'foreign policy is domestic policy, but with your hat on.' Ottawa's 2003 *Dialogue on Foreign Policy*, however, clearly articulated three main 'pillars': ensuring global security and the security of Canadians, promoting the prosperity of Canadians and global prosperity, and projecting Canada's values and culture.[2] These three pillars were reinforced in the 2005 International Policy Statement, released by Paul Martin's Liberal government, which stated that its foreign policy would rest on 'three core priorities—prosperity, security, and responsibility'.[3] This volume will examine the relevance of these statements in the context of security, trade, and social issues. This text will also argue that most studies of Canadian foreign policy tend to focus on one aspect of a state's external relations, such as international developments, the domestic policy process, or the role of individuals. In the Canadian case, therefore, there is a need to adopt a more holistic framework in evaluating foreign policy. As Kim Nossal has made clear, 'foreign policy is forged in the nexus of three political environments—international, domestic, and governmental. It is within these three spheres that the sources, or the determinants, of a state's foreign policy are to be found.'[4]

In addition to accepting that Canadian foreign policy is a nexus, it is also essential to consider issues of system, process, and change. In terms of systemic issues there is the obvious understanding that international developments have an impact on Canada's global relations, and that these external variables can take many forms. For most western developed states, including Canada, foreign policy is guided by certain ideational assumptions regarding the international system, namely realist and neo-liberal institutionalist perspectives. These perspectives accept the reality of a state-centric competitive anarchic international system in terms of both political and economic relationships. At the same time, however, cooperation is still possible at the international level in the form of regimes and other institutions, which allows for an evaluation of both absolute and relative gains. It is important to note, however, that this does not restrict Canada's ability to pursue issues related to its own self-interest. Neo-liberal institutionalism is based on the understanding that sovereignty and economic protectionism are realities, and Canada has demonstrated repeatedly that these options will be embraced in the formulation of Canadian foreign trade policy. Neo-idealism also accepts liberal efforts to engage civil society and promote greater democratization.

Non-state actors are also influenced by many of the same realist and neo-liberal systemic considerations, especially corporate and sectoral interests. At the same time, however, many also have very different 'structural' assumptions that are instead guided by gender, class, or ethnicity. These 'critical' approaches challenge the basic core organizing principles of the modern state system, and represent alternative international structural interpretations. It is important to understand that these considerations can also shape the foreign policy of states, namely in the form of non-traditional factors not usually accounted for in realist or neo-liberal frameworks.

In addition, Canadian foreign policy is influenced by 'process' issues, which can include domestic institutional factors such as constitutional and judicial realities; the role of the prime minister, provincial premiers, cabinets and executives at both levels of government; federal and provincial legislatures; bureaucratic interests; and intergovernmental relations linked to international affairs. At the same time, however, process factors must also examine non-institutional inputs. Sectoral actors, for example, consist of industry associations, specific corporations, individual executives, advisory groups, and consultative links with federal government departments or officials. In addition, societal interests—which are typically treated as secondary considerations in studies of Canadian foreign policy—incorporate organized labour, environmental groups, First Nations, civil society, and a wide range of other non-governmental actors. Finally, ideational issues focus on how 'dominant ideas' are transferred, or entrenched, at both levels of analysis, contributing to exploitive relationships related—but not limited—to ideology, class, gender, ethnicity, and culture.

To fully understand process-related issues, however, causal relationships must also be explored, especially in terms of state autonomy. Specifically, there is a need to evaluate the international and domestic activities of institutional, sectoral, societal, and ideational actors. Additionally, these observations must account for the transnational activity *between* states that contributes to policy convergence. Finally, international pressures related to treaties, financial markets, and global capital can also lead to limitations of domestic autonomy, although this will vary greatly from sector to sector.[5] What is also missing, however, is the acknowledgement that domestic actors can have a direct impact on the international system. The institutional policies of central and non-central governments, for example, are often transferred between levels of analysis as states consult, negotiate, and implement agreements.

Finally, any discussion of foreign policy must incorporate a review of 'change' that moves beyond traditional discussions of state autonomy. In other words, 'change' must identify developments that represent a pattern of relations that are significantly different from previous relationships. This could include shifts in power-based capabilities, re-interpretations of regime-based norms and standards, and/or membership in international institutions. In order to fully evaluate outcomes, however, it is useful to also engage critical interpretations of foreign policy. In fact, tangible benefits can be gained by including these issues in rational, realist, or neo-liberal approaches. In terms of trade policy, for example, issues of class are relevant to the role of organized labour and civil society's backlash to neo-liberalism within the state, while also being relevant to the obvious economic disparities between the developed and developing world. Gender-based NGOs and social movements also place pressure on states at both the international and domestic levels, although liberal feminists would take a much different view of the neo-liberal patriarchy than would those with a socialist or more critical perspective. Ethnic and cultural issues present further challenges in terms of neo-liberalism's insensitivity to non-western-oriented economic considerations and issues of collective rights. All of these social issues are relevant to questions involving state autonomy and the level of analysis problem, in terms of structure, process, and change.

HOW IS CANADIAN FOREIGN POLICY STUDIED?

Traditional frameworks

Chapters 3–5 in Part 1 outline the traditional frameworks for analyzing Canadian foreign policy. Maureen Appel Molot, in a seminal article, points out that the vast majority of the thinking about Canadian foreign policy has been preoccupied with Canada's place in the world—its role, status, position, influence, and power.[6] There are three different images that have prevailed: Canada as a middle power, a principal power, or a satellite power. The dominant image is of Canada as a middle power. Historically, middle powers were perceived as situated below the great powers of the United States, Russia, the United Kingdom, France, China, Germany, and Japan. The middle power perspective assumes that Canada has an important role to play both in multilateral and bilateral regimes and in institutions because of its wealth, geographic location, and human capacity. Initially, Canada's functional role in strong multilateral regimes was viewed as a way of constraining the _realpolitik_ of great power rivalry by providing an alternative rules-based mechanism for ensuring world order.

Several authors have adopted this approach when examining the evolution of Canadian foreign policy. The most prominent observer of Canada as a middle power was John Holmes.[7] His classic discussion of being 'safely in the middle', in Chapter 3, touches on a number of traditional themes. Tom Keating, a contemporary expert on middle power, focuses more on the principle of multilateralism and reflects the increasing tendency of some scholars to question the utility of categorizing states as middle powers due to the ambiguity of this standing in the contemporary international system. Specifically, Keating argues that Canadian policy-makers have repeatedly relied on both economic and security regimes to fulfill a wide range of foreign policy objectives. Keating, however, also suggests that Canadian support for international regimes is not unconditional. In response to both international and domestic pressures Ottawa has pursued unilateral and selected bilateral arrangements in its external relations. At the same time, what becomes apparent over time 'is that these alternatives are deviations from the norm, are short-lived, and are frequently combined with complimentary multilateral activities'.[8] Keating provides a brief update to the middle power approach by examining the 'new multilateralism' and its impact on Canada. In particular, he assesses the challenges to Canada's commitment to multilateralism due to the desire by some in Canada to forgo aspects of multilateralism in favour of closer bilateral ties with the United States. Nevertheless, Keating concludes that Canada 'recognizes the necessity to secure a broader base of support for multilateral cooperation and the institutions that sustain it'. Kim Nossal and Andrew Cooper have also addressed Canada's traditional role as a middle power.[9]

An alternative image is that of Canada as a principal power. Canada has many capabilities—abundant natural resources, high levels of technology, well-educated people, a high standard of living, and membership in exclusive groups like the G7/8—that rank it far ahead of other middle powers. Principal power theorists argue that Canada is able to pursue its own policies in the international system with relatively little interference/The first to acknowledge this position was James Eayrs, who wrote in 1975 that the rising importance of oil-producing states, the increasing significance of natural resources in the global political economy, and the declining economic status of the United States all increased Canadian power.[10] Norman Hillmer and Garth Stevenson also adopted this approach in 1977 when they suggested that Canada was not a 'modest power'.[11] It was David Dewitt and John Kirton, as noted in Chapter 4, who argued most strongly in favour of Canada being labelled a 'principal power' because of the decline in status of the United States. Although they were writing almost a decade after Eayrs they also cited a decrease in American hegemony that portrayed Canada as an 'ascending power' whose 'star was on the rise'[12] in comparison. Kirton reflects on the theoretical legacy of his book. He also provides additional evidence of the principal power thesis by highlighting Canada's abundant natural resources (water, oil, potash, uranium, etc.), declarations by other major powers that Canada is one of them, trade agreements, its military deployment to Afghanistan, and its role in the G8 and G20. Although the popularity of the principal power approach has declined in recent years it still serves as a core foundation for studying Canadian foreign policy.

Another alternative image, and the opposite of the principal power approach, is that Canada is a peripheral-dependent/satellite country. In this conception, Canada moved seamlessly from existing as a British colonial dependency to being pulled into the orbit of the American empire. The origins of the satellite model date back to the 1920s when

Archibald MacMechan complained that Canada was becoming nothing more than a 'Vassal State' of the United States.[13] A.R.M. Lower also echoed this sentiment in the 1940s when he described Canada as a 'subordinate state' or 'satellite' to its American neighbour.[14] The satellite approach gained increasing momentum during the 1960s when several observers argued that Canada was adopting policy decisions that were deferential to the United States, especially in terms of military and security issues. Although George Grant touched on many of these themes in *Lament for a Nation*,[15] the most prominent voice of the satellite movement in terms of Canadian foreign policy came from Stephen Clarkson. For Clarkson the problem was largely one of leadership; senior officials were not willing to distance themselves from American influence.[16] The answer, as described in Chapter 5, was to aggressively protect Canadian sovereignty by promoting greater government intervention in the economy through the establishment of mechanisms such as the Foreign Investment Review Agency (FIRA) and the National Energy Program (NEP). More recent contributors sympathetic to this argument include Stephen McBride, John Helliwell, and Alex Michalos.[17] Stephen Clarkson has recently re-entered the debate by suggesting that institutions such as the North American Free Trade Agreement (NAFTA) and the World Trade Organization (WTO) have imposed a 'supraconstitution' that constrains 'authority that was once the exclusive preserve of domestically elected legislatures'.[18] Clarkson presents a brief retrospective of *An Independent Foreign Policy* as an addendum to Chapter 5. Brian Bow and Patrick Lennox, in honour of the fortieth anniversary of *An Independent Foreign Policy*, brought together a new generation of Canadian scholars to reconsider Clarkson's thesis.[19] Based on the conclusions of this book, Bow and Lennox provide an update to Chapter 5.

As previously mentioned, Maureen Appel Molot argued that the traditional approaches to the study of Canadian foreign policy—especially the middle, principal, and satellite models discussed in the preceding three chapters—are no longer adequate for a number of reasons. Not only do the traditional methods fail to evaluate the complexity of Canadian foreign policy in terms of a holistic analysis of system, process, and outcome, but they also suffer from the following weaknesses:

a) They are atheoretical, with only implicit ties to IR theory.
b) The approaches fail to focus on domestic politics and/or international/domestic linkages (the level of analysis problem).
c) Problems and opportunities related to Canadian foreign policy are largely scrutinized through the lens of state autonomy. Other more critical approaches are required.
d) There is no real discussion of economic issues (trade and finance).

In addition, non-institutional actors, both sectoral and societal, are usually ignored. For these and other reasons, David Black and Heather Smith have called for the application of non-traditional models in the study of Canadian foreign policy. In particular, they argue, there is a need for models that explore 'the interaction between state, society, and global levels of analysis'.[20]

Non-traditional models

One of the main non-traditional models is feminist analysis. Feminist analysis explores, in the words of Deborah Stienstra, 'how gender relations are shaped and how they, in turn, shape Canadian foreign policy'.[21] Stienstra's article, which was written in the mid-1990s, was particularly critical of the fact that, despite an increase in the application of gender-based analysis in the study of international relations, it has not been extended to examining Canadian foreign policy. This was a groundbreaking study that added to the voice of a group of scholars led by Sandra Whitworth, Heather Smith, Edna Keeble, and Claire Sjolander that critiqued Canada's international role from a feminist perspective.[22] Specifically, it is argued that 'women and gender issues have been excluded from the study of Canadian foreign policy' because the 'feminine is devalued in the way that people think'.[23]

In Chapter 6, Claire Turenne Sjolander and Kathryn Trevenen use feminist analysis to evaluate Canada's military operation in Afghanistan. By examining government speeches from 2006 and 2007, Sjolander and Trevenen argue that Ottawa has tried to depict Canada as a 'good international citizen' and as a protector of the 'weak'. This 'evoke[s] a moral position based in Canada's perceived tradition of upholding ideals of equality, multiculturalism, and human rights at home, and how they function by mobilizing powerful ongoing justifications and stories of gender as nation.' However, the result of this official narrative is to 'blur the realities of Canada's involvement in Afghanistan and function to limit debate about the justifications and ongoing feasibility of the mission.'

A second critical perspective is Gramscian structural analysis and 'dominant-class' theory, which is reviewed by Mark Neufeld in Chapter 7. Antonio Gramsci (1891–1937) was an Italian socialist, activist, and political theorist. His prison notebooks, not published until the 1950s, were filled with critical commentary about socialism, capitalism, communism, and fascism. Robert Cox and Stephen Gill have applied many of Gramsci's ideas to the study of world politics.[24] Of particular importance is the Gramscian notion of hegemony whereby the institution and maintenance of a world order serves the interests of the dominant social class in a wide range of states. Gramscian hegemony, then, is not based on coercive force, but on consent gained through intellectual and moral leadership. Neufeld uses the Gramscian approach to assess the Chrétien government's efforts in the 1990s to 'democratize' Canadian foreign policy and to promote democracy abroad. Neufeld argues that this emphasis on domestic democratization 'can be understood, in terms of the national formation, as a form of passive revolution designed to strengthen hegemony domestically.' Internationally, the purpose of democratization is to prevent 'the creation of an effective counter-hegemonic bloc.' Whether home or abroad, Neufeld concludes that '"democracy" may represent little more than an alternative means of consolidating and perpetuating unequal relations between people and communities.'

PLAN OF THE BOOK

This book is structured with three primary goals in mind. The first goal is to illustrate that the setting of Canadian foreign policy exists at the intersection of the international, state, and societal levels of analysis. The second goal is a thorough examination of the stated purposes of Canadian foreign policy, namely physical security, economic prosperity, and the promotion of Canadian values. The third goal aims to draw attention to some of the weaknesses in the Canadian foreign policy literature and to offer a critical, or more holistic, approach to studying Canada's global relations.

Part 1 develops the various mainstream and critical approaches to the study of Canadian foreign policy identified in this introduction. Before delving into the theoretical debates discussed above, Part 1 provides some context through two historical chapters. Chapter 1, written by John Kirton, assesses the scholarly attention to Canadian foreign policy by identifying the most influential books on the subject. Many of the authors that Kirton recognizes are contained in this volume. Chapter 2, written by Adam Chapnick, describes the major events of Canada's foreign relations from the end of World War II to 1968. Since international relations scholars use history as our laboratory to test theories, it is important that students have a basic understanding of how Canada's role in the world has evolved since World War II.

Part 2 examines the constraints and opportunities facing Canada in the international environment through an examination of Canada–US relations and three important international organizations (G8/G20, the United Nations, and the North Atlantic Treaty Organization). In 1983, the *International Journal* hosted what has become a classic debate on the domestic sources of Canadian foreign policy between Kim Nossal and Cranford Pratt.[25] Therefore, Part 3 examines the major domestic actors that shape, make, and implement Canadian foreign policy: the prime minister, parliament, bureaucracy, and the provinces. Part 4, the first of three issue-specific sections, examines Canada's pursuit of international peace and security through a historical analysis of Canadian defence policy, its military operation in Afghanistan, the security of the Canada–US border, and its Arctic security strategy. Part 5 examines Canada's pursuit of economic prosperity through international trade clubs, Canada's international response to the 2008–9 global financial crisis, and investment. Part 6 begins with Nelson Michaud's examination of culture as a variable in Canadian foreign policy. Selections that analyze Canada's efforts to promote its values abroad in the areas of environmental protection, foreign aid, African development, and human rights complete the section.

Key Terms

Feminism
Gramscianism
Middle Power

Principal Power
Satellite

Notes

1. Canada, *Canada in the World: Government Statement* (Ottawa: Canada Communications Group, 1995), 4.

2. Department of Foreign Affairs and International Trade, *A Dialogue on Foreign Policy: Report to Canadians* (Ottawa: Communications Services Division, 2003).

3. Canada, *Canada's International Policy Statement, A Role of Pride and Influence in the World* (Ottawa: Government of Canada, 2005), 5.

4. Kim Richard Nossal, *The Politics of Canadian Foreign Policy*, 3rd ed. (Scarborough, ON: Prentice-Hall, 1997), 7.

5. George Hoberg, Keith G. Banting, and Richard Simeon, 'The Scope for Domestic Choice: Policy Autonomy in a Globalizing World', in Hoberg, ed., *Capacity for Choice: Canada in a New North America* (Toronto: University of Toronto Press, 2002), 252–99.

6. Maureen Appel Molot, 'Where Do We, Should We, Or Can We Sit? A Review of Canadian Foreign Policy Literature', *International Journal of Canadian Studies* 1, 2 (Spring-Fall 1990), 77–96.

7. John W. Holmes, *Canada: A Middle-Aged Power* (Toronto: McClelland and Stewart, 1976); John W. Holmes, *The Shaping of Peace: Canada and the Search for World Order, 1943–1957* (Toronto: University of Toronto Press, 1979).

8. Tom Keating, *Canada and World Order: The Multilateralist Tradition in Canadian Foreign Policy*, 2nd ed. (Don Mills, ON: Oxford University Press, 2002), 23.

9. Kim Nossal, *The Politics of Canadian Foreign Policy*; Andrew F. Cooper, *Canadian Foreign Policy: Old Habits and New Directions* (Scarborough, ON: Prentice-Hall, 1997); Andrew F. Cooper, Richard A. Higgott, and Kim Richard Nossal, *Relocating Middle Powers: Australia and Canada in a Changing World Order* (Vancouver: UBC Press, 1993).

10. James Eayrs, 'Defining a New Place for Canada in the Hierarchy of World Powers', *International Perspectives* (May–June 1975): 15–24.

11. Norman Hillmer and Garth Stevenson, eds, *A Foremost Nation, Canadian Foreign Policy in a Changing World* (Toronto: McClelland and Stewart, 1977).

12. David B. Dewitt and John Kirton, *Canada as a Principal Power: A Study in Foreign Policy and International Relations* (Toronto: John Wiley and Sons, 1983), 38.

13. Archibald MacMechan, as cited in Nossal, *The Politics of Canadian Foreign Policy*, 61.

14. A.R.M. Lower, as quoted in Phillip Resnick, 'Canadian Defence Policy and the American Empire', in Ian Lumsden, ed., *Close the 49th Parallel Etc: The Americanizaiton of Canada* (Toronto: University of Toronto Press, 1970), 99.

15. George Grant, *Lament for a Nation: The Defeat of Canadian Nationalism* (Toronto: McClelland and Stewart, 1965).

16. Stephen Clarkson, ed., *An Independent Foreign Policy for Canada?* (Toronto: McClelland and Stewart, 1968).

17. Stephen McBride, *Paradigm Shift: Globalization and the Canadian State* (Halifax: Fernwood, 2001); John Helliwell, *Globalization and Well-Being* (Vancouver: UBC Press, 2002); Alex C. Michalos, *Good Taxes: The Case for Taxing Foreign Currency Exchange and Other Financial Transactions* (Toronto: Dundurn, 1997); Alex C. Michalos, 'Combining Social, Economic and Environmental Indicators to Measure Sustainable Human Well-Being', *Social Indicators Research* 40 (1997): 221–58.

18. Stephen Clarkson, *Does North America Exist? Governing the Continent after NAFTA and 9/11* (Toronto: University of Toronto Press, 2008) and Stephen Clarkson, *Uncle Sam and US: Globalization, Neoconservatism, and the Canadian State* (Toronto: University of Toronto Press, 2002).

19. Brian Bow and Patrick Lennox, eds., *An Independent Foreign Policy for Canada? Challenges and Choices for the Future* (Toronto: University of Toronto Press, 2008).

20. David R. Black and Heather A. Smith, 'Notable Exceptions? New and Arrested Directions in Canadian Foreign Policy Literature', *Canadian Journal of Political Science* 26, 4 (December 1993): 745–75.

21. Deborah Steinstra, 'Can the Silence be Broken? Gender and Canadian Foreign Policy', *International Journal* 50, 1 (Winter 1994–5): 126–7.

22. For other examples of gender analysis in Canadian foreign policy see Claire Turenne Sjolander, Heather A. Smith, and Deborah Stienstra, eds, *Feminist Perspectives on Canadian Foreign Policy* (Don Mills, ON: Oxford University Press, 2003); Edna Keeble and Heather A. Smith, *(Re) Defining Traditions: Gender and Canadian Foreign Policy* (Halifax: Fernwood, 1999).

23. Keeble and Smith, *(Re)Defining Traditions*, 20.

24. Robert W. Cox, 'Gramsci, Hegemony and International Relations: An Essay in Method', *Millennium, Journal of International Studies* 12, 2 (Summer 1983): 162–75; Stephen Gill, *American Hegemony and the Trilateral Commission* (Cambridge: Cambridge University Press, 1990); Stephen Gill, ed., *Gramsci, Historical Materialism, and International Relations* (Cambridge: Cambridge University Press, 1993).

25. Kim Richard Nossal, 'Analyzing Domestic Sources of Canadian Foreign Policy', *International Journal* 39, 1 (Winter 1983–84), 1–22; Cranford Pratt, 'Dominant Class Theory and Canadian Foreign Policy: The Case of the Counter-Consensus', *International Journal* 39, 1 (Winter 1983–84): 99–135.

1

THE 10 MOST IMPORTANT BOOKS ON CANADIAN FOREIGN POLICY

John J. Kirton

In many ways the scholarly study of Canadian foreign policy has become a rich, robust, and rapidly growing field. It is now well over a century old, if one dates its inauguration from the publication of Goldwin Smith's *Canada and the Canadian Question* in 1891, a book that understood that Canada's relationship with the United States was properly part of, or even at the centre of, the field.[1] From 1945, when many of today's scholars start their scrutiny, to 1995, the detailed bibliographies compiled under the auspices of the Canadian Institute of International Affairs recorded works of all kinds as relevant to the subject. Since then, the explosion of material has been too vast for this careful bibliographic compilation to be published in print, especially as the internet has arrived to help others take on the task in electronic form.

Since 1970, courses on Canadian foreign policy have become staples of universities' undergraduate curricula across Canada, accompanied by selective forays into the United States and beyond. These courses have been mounted and delivered in the first instance by the doctoral students produced by John Holmes, with some help from James Eayrs, at the University of Toronto over many years. More recently, the 4000-member International Studies Association has created a separate Canadian Studies section that has been nourishing, expanding, and honouring its senior scholars since its inception. There are now over a dozen articles reviewing the state of the Canadian foreign policy field![2] There are also several that reflect on its connection with, and theoretical inheritance from, international relations as a whole. All signs thus suggest that the study of Canada foreign policy has gone prime time on a global scale.

But amidst this proliferating scale, scope, and self-reflection, there remains an unanswered question: Is Canadian foreign policy really a self-contained scholarly field with an intellectually coherent, progressive research tradition, defined by seminal books of creative inspiration and continuing relevance at its core? There are good reasons to doubt that it is, especially in contrast with the larger field of international relations in which it properly resides. Here foundational works such as those by Thucydides, Hans Morgenthau, Robert Keohane and Joseph Nye, John Ruggie, Kenneth

Waltz, and Alexander Wendt are used, disputed, or at least recognized and referred to by all. In contrast, the study of Canadian foreign policy has long been an endeavour involving those from many disciplines, starting with history and law. It has also been one to which practitioners from government, the media, research institutes, and the business community contribute a great deal. And it has always had its 'second solitude', an important French-language literature centred in Quebec, which has long enriched the few who have been able or willing to read it on the other side of Canada's great linguistic divide.

To determine whether there is a coherent field of Canadian foreign policy based on broadly recognized, intellectually generative foundational works, this study identifies and justifies the impact of the top 10 most important books on Canadian foreign policy of all time. Part 2 focuses on books rather than journal articles as the probable source of the foundational centerpieces, given the small number of journals, especially peer-refereed ones, focused on the subject over many years. It further aims at works of enduring importance, reducing the 'recency bias' that would otherwise propel today's biggest hits, most prolific scholars, curricular fashions, and policy favourites to the top of the list. It thus sets aside the standard mechanical metrics of citation indices and Google hits to probe the content of the 'top 10' and explore how they shaped thinking, research, and teaching for many years in the past—and probably will for many years to come. This is thus the list of Canadian foreign policy's finest wines that have aged well enough to be continuously copied, adapted, and selectively consumed directly by the dedicated purists in the profession today.

Given the diverse and fast-moving shape of the field, it is unlikely that all scholars currently teaching and researching in it will agree with every book on the list. Those raised as realists, liberal institutionalists, world systems political economists, or constructivists in the diverse field that Canadian foreign policy has become, and those from different generations, geographic regions, genders, and language groups, will have their own special selections. But virtually all should recognize the works on this top-10 list, accept most as clear choices or credible candidates, and be able to mount a considered case to explain why the personal favourite that has been omitted is better than one or more of the ones that have made it on. In addition to representing the personal picks of someone who has taught and researched Canadian foreign policy for more than 30 years, this list should thus serve as the beginning of a debate about what the field is, based on what its best books are. Others are welcome to suggest and justify their own 'blasts from the past' in the years ahead.

THE KEY SCHOLARS IN CANADIAN FOREIGN POLICY TODAY

If a book is to be important its innovative ideas should stand at or near the centre of the field today. It is thus useful to begin by identifying somewhat systematically the top 10 scholars of Canadian foreign policy, what books appear most often on the syllabi of the undergraduate courses on the subject across Canada, and from where both groups draw their central intellectual inspiration.

The best available published evidence about the top 10 scholars of Canadian foreign policy comes from the TRIP survey of international relations faculty in 10 countries, published in February 2009. Although it specifically asked respondents to '[l]ist four IR scholars whose work has had the greatest influence on Canada's foreign policy in the past 20 years,' the answers provide a reasonable indication of scholarly importance, especially if influence on government policy and the public's thinking are taken as a responsibility of the scholars' role. See Table 1.1 for the results.

These results show a strong representation of political scientists whose teaching and research has concentrated on Canadian foreign policy over two or three decades, and who have authored most of the textbooks available today. It also shows some reasonable balance by theoretical tradition, generation, gender, and region, especially in its inclusion of two scholars who live and work outside Canada.

The most notable imbalance is the slender representation of francophone Quebecers, only one of whom appears on the list.

Amidst this diversity a strong historical footprint appears: the intellectual legacy of John Holmes and James Eayrs looms large in the work of first-ranked Kim Richard Nossal, third-ranked Denis Stairs, and sixth-ranked John Kirton. Several others, such as fourth-ranked Andrew F. Cooper, have been substantially influenced by their work.

Table 1.1 Most important scholars in Canadian foreign policy

Scholar	Most influential Rank (share %)	Most used Rank (share)	Combined Rank (share)
Both lists			
Kim Richard Nossal	1 (46)	3 (4)	1 (4)
John Kirton	6 (12)	2 (5)	2 (8)
Tom Keating	7 (11)	5 (3)	3 (12)
Andrew F. Cooper	4 (20)	9 (1)	4 (13)
Stéphane Roussel	9 (6)	8 (2)	5 (17)
Most influential only			
Janice Stein	2 (35)		
Denis Stairs	3 (29)		
Jack Granatstein	5 (13)		
Jennifer Welsh	7 (11)		
Claire Sjolander	9 (6)		
Joseph Nye	9 (6)		
Thomas Homer Dixon	9 (6)		
Most used only			
Duane Bratt		1 (6)	
Christopher Kukucha		1 (6)	
Fen Osler Hampson		3 (4)	
Brian Tomlin		5 (3)	
Norman Hillmer		5 (3)	

Notes: 'Most influential' is the response to the question, 'List four IR scholars whose work has had the greatest influence on Canada's foreign policy in the past 20 years', in answer to the survey whose results were reported by Richard Jordan and his colleagues.[5] 'Most used' refers to those authors whose books appeared as core works most often on the syllabi of undergraduate courses on Canadian foreign policy taught in Canada in 2008–9. The author is grateful to Zaria Shaw for conducting this survey of 25 courses and the compilation of its results from the 42 books being used. TRIP Survey of International Relations Faculty of 10 Countries: http://irtheoryandpractice.wm.edu/projects/trip/Final_Trip_Report_2009.pdf.

To identify which scholars' books are actually used in undergraduate classes on Canadian foreign policy across Canada, a survey was conducted of all relevant syllabi available on the Web. The results, also reported in Tabe 1.1, show the importance of *Readings in Canadian Foreign Policy,* edited by Duane Bratt and Christopher Kukucha in 2007, and the volumes of the *Canada among Nations* series, appearing with a different but overlapping set of editors every year.[6] Yet it also shows the importance of monographs produced as textbooks by Kim Nossal, John Kirton, and Tom Keating, and of five co-authored works from Brian Tomlin and Fen Osler Hampson. While no research work is sufficiently central to rank highly on the list, the selections in the Bratt-Kukucha reader provide a strong indication of the most important scholars and books from the past for the field today. Here there is a strong reliance on works by Stephen Clarkson, John Kirton, and Cranford Pratt, with two contributions each, and by John Holmes, Tom Keating, Maureen Appel Molot, Claire Turenne Sjolander, and Mark Neufeld, whose writings fill out the opening section of the book. Among the small set of five scholars who are listed as both 'most influential' and 'most used,' Kim Nossal also appears in the Bratt-Kukucha reader.

To enrich these systematic surveys with direct reputational data, several of the leading scholars in the field, currently active in both Canada and the United States, were asked over the past two years to identify their choice of the two most important books. In their answers, there was only one work written by a journalist, Andrew Cohen's *While Canada Slept.* There were two from longtime career practitioners, Allan Gotlieb's *The Washington Diaries,* and Michael Hart and William Dymond's *Decision at Midnight.* There were also several historians, led by Jack Granatstein, Norman Hillmer, and C.P. Stacey. There were none from lawyers or economists. The field for

political scientists has become a largely self-contained, autonomous scholarly one.

There was a high degree of consistency, both in the scholars and in their books selected. The list was led by Nossal; followed by Holmes, Eayrs, and Kirton; then Stairs and Cooper; and finally Clarkson, Charles Doran, Michael Tucker, and Michael Hawes. These results are quite consistent with those who were judged as producers of, or whose work lies behind, the most influential and most-used books today. With this foundation, it is time for judgment to be exercised in selecting the top 10 books, listed in chronological order below.

THE TOP 10 MOST IMPORTANT BOOKS IN CANADIAN FOREIGN POLICY

1. R.A. Mackay and E.B. Rogers, *Canada Looks Abroad*
2. James Eayrs, *The Art of the Possible: Government and Foreign Policy in Canada*
3. Stephen Clarkson, *An Independent Foreign Policy for Canada?*
4. John Holmes, *The Better Part of Valour: Essays on Canadian Diplomacy*
5. Bruce Thordarson, *Trudeau and Foreign Policy: A Study in Decision-Making*
6. Denis Stairs, *The Diplomacy of Constraint: Canada, the Korean War and the United States*
7. Peyton Lyon and Brian Tomlin, *Canada as an International Actor*
8. Charles Doran, *Forgotten Partnership: US–Canada Relations Today*
9. Andrew F. Cooper, Richard Higgott, and Kim Richard Nossal, *Relocating Middle Powers: Australia and Canada in a Changing World Order*
10. Kim Richard Nossal, Stephane Roussel, and Stéphane Paquin, *Politique internationale et défense au Canada et au Québec*

Note: It was agreed at the outset that this list would exclude works produced either alone or with co-authors or co-editors by John Kirton (the author of this article) or by David Haglund and Joseph Jockel (co-editors of the *International Journal*).

1. R.A. Mackay and E.B. Rogers, *Canada Looks Abroad,* (Oxford: Oxford University Press, 1938)

Published in 1938, this was the launch volume of the *Canada in World Affairs* series produced by the Canadian Institute of International Affairs. Successive volumes in the series provided a detailed description of the subject through to J.L. Granatstein and Robert Bothwell's *Pirouette: Pierre Trudeau and Canadian Foreign Policy* in 1990.[8] But more importantly, MacKay and Rogers's outline of the policy options for practising, and the underlying logic for analyzing, Canadian foreign policy created the classic trilogy that has defined the field ever since.[9] Its option of the 'league' outlined the liberalist-internationalist approach of Canada as a middle power that has dominated the study, if not the conduct, of Canadian foreign policy to this day. Its option of 'North America' (Canada) as a small, isolated state close to the US alone offered what became the satellite approach. And its option of 'empire' presented Canada as a country consequential for the global balance of power, and thus a foremost nation or principal power, as the later complex neo-realist approach would claim.

2. James Eayrs, *The Art of the Possible: Government and Foreign Policy in Canada,* (Toronto: University of Toronto Press, 1963)

In the two decades following the Second World War, the fusion of policy-makers and scholars created a consensus on the concept of Canada as a middle power. But it produced no autonomous scholarly logic to show how this, or any alternative, might be correct. The first career-long scholar in the field, recognizable as a social scientist by the standards of today, was James Eayrs, whose influence has been profound. Eayrs wrote largely as a historian in his multi-volume series, *In Defence of Canada*. He also wrote more as a critical journalist in such works as *Northern Approaches, Diplomacy and Its Discontents,* and *Fate and Will in Foreign Policy*. But it was his masterful *The Art of the Possible: Government and Foreign Policy in Canada* that stands out as perhaps the single most influential work in the field to this day. Published in 1963, it set the field's continuing focus and framework on the making of Canadian foreign policy. It systematically identified and explored the external, societal, governmental, and individual determinants of Canadian foreign policy, introducing to the field the levels of analysis that Waltz had pioneered in the study of international relations as a whole.[11] Nossal, Kirton, and Thordarson are intellectually direct descendants of Eayrs, while Denis Stairs and Douglas Ross are enriched as well by *In Defence of Canada*.

3. Stephen Clarkson, ed., *An Independent Foreign Policy for Canada*, (Toronto: McClelland and Stewart, 1968)

Soon after Eayrs established the field as a social science, there erupted a plethora of normatively inspired, policy-oriented books arguing that Canada was or should be a multilateralist middle power, or that it was and should not be a dependent satellite of the United States. From this deluge, the single work with the most enduring impact is George Grant's 1965 *Lament for a Nation*.[12] But the one book from the energetic 1960s that re-established and enriched Canadian foreign policy as a social scientific field, as well as having a significant policy influence, was Stephen Clarkson's 1968 collection, *An Independent Foreign Policy for Canada?* In addition to the remarkable insights in its individual chapters, its concluding analytical synthesis defined a logically coherent framework for capturing the content of Canadian foreign policy. Its outline of an independent foreign policy offered several key concepts for what was later codified as the complex neo-realist perspective. It did so long before James Eayrs wrote his 1975 article, which is widely viewed as the inspiration for this approach.[13]

4. John Holmes, *The Better Part of Valour: Essays On Canadian Diplomacy*, (Toronto: McClelland and Stewart, 1970)

It was at the end of this period of great intellectual innovation that John Holmes, the epitome of the diplomat-turned-scholar, arrived on the scholarly scene in full force. Along with Eayrs, he is the most influential author in the field to this day. His two-volume work, *The Shaping of Peace: Canada and the Search for World Order,* written at the peak of his career, is the *In the Defence of Canada* for those who think Canadian foreign policy is in essence not about defence and war but about diplomacy and peace, based on international institutions, with the United Nations at the core.[14] Indeed, with Eayrs the realist, Clarkson the critical political economist, and Holmes the liberal internationalist, the three wise men had all taken their place on the playing field. Holmes, however, was ultimately not a historian, as Eayrs had been intellectually at the start. Rather, he was a policy commentator and essayist of consummate skill, as displayed in *Life with Uncle* and *A Middle-Aged Power.* His best collection was his first, *The Better Part of Valour,* published in 1970. In its wonderfully readable way, it offered the core insights of the liberal internationalist perspective that those with 'tidy minds' could later arrange into a theory that could co-exist and compete with the theories and interpretations that Eayrs and Clarkson would create.

5. Bruce Thordarson, *Trudeau and Foreign Policy: A Study in Decision-Making,* (Toronto: Oxford University Press, 1972)

It was not only at or near the political economy department of the University of Toronto that the scholarly field of Canadian foreign policy was formed. Thanks to Peyton Lyon, Brian Tomlin, and Lester Pearson (when he left political life), Carleton University's Norman Paterson School of International Affairs was active at an early stage. Carleton's first work of enduring scholarly consequence, in keeping with the generational revolution of the time, came from one of its students, Bruce Thordarson, in 1972: *Trudeau and Foreign Policy: A Study in Decision-Making.* It offered three case studies of key decisions at the outset of the Trudeauvian era— an advance from Eayrs's seminal study of the single Suez crisis in 1956. It examined external, societal, and governmental determinants across the levels of analysis more systematically than Eayrs had in 1963. Far more convincingly than the biographical vignettes that adorned *In Defence of Canada*, it concluded that it was not international fate but individual will that mattered.[15] And it connected causes directly to effects, showing how Trudeau's personal belief system drove changes in Canadian foreign policy itself.

6. Denis Stairs, *The Diplomacy of Constraint: Canada, the Korean War and the United States,* (Toronto: University of Toronto Press, 1974)

It was, however, Denis Stairs who really brought the Eayrsian and Holmesian inheritances together in *The Diplomacy of Constraint: Canada, the Korean War and the United States* in 1974. This was the quintessential case study, an approach pioneered by John Holmes and expanded by his graduate students in their seminar at the University of Toronto for many years. Stairs's book was a multi-dimensional marvel, relying both on documents, when available, and on specialized oral interviews. And it invented the concept—the 'diplomacy of constraint'—at the core of the liberal internationalist theory of Canadian foreign policy, as the foundation on which the entire edifice could deductively be built.

7. Peyton Lyon and Brian Tomlin, *Canada as an International Actor* (Toronto: Macmillan, 1979)

Carleton reappeared at the end of the 1970s in the form of Peyton Lyon and Brian Tomlin's *Canada as an International Actor* in 1979. The book certified Lyon's status as a true scholar, as distinct from the recently retired foreign service officer with policy convictions that he had been when he wrote *The Policy Question* in 1963. The book introduced Brian Tomlin, who pioneered the use of quantitative methods in the field, even if he was to move to more mainstream methods with great skill in his later work. The 1979 book was a productive fusion of quantitative and qualitative methods that showed, whatever the predispositions of the senior author, that Canada was more than a mere middle power with only modest relative capability in a changing world.

8. Charles Doran, *Forgotten Partnership: U.S.–Canada Relations Today,* (Baltimore: Johns Hopkins University Press, 1984)

Canadian foreign policy has long been a subject of more than merely local interest. Non-Canadians have made important book-length contributions, notably William T.R. Fox, Annette Baker Fox, Melvin Conant, John Sloan Dickey, Jon McLin, Roger Frank Swanson, and Joseph Nye Jr., in his co-authored work with Robert Keohane, *Power and Interdependence,* in 1977. But the stand-out contribution is Charles Doran's *Forgotten Partnership: U.S.–Canada Relations Today,* published in 1984.[16] It offered an integrated argument that articulated the core concepts and relationships for the model

of special partnership that extended the liberal internationalist theory to Canadian foreign policy toward, and with, the United States. Along with only William Fox, who wrote *The Super-Powers: The United States, Britain and the Soviet Union* in 1944 and *A Continent Apart: The United States and Canada in World Politics* in 1985, Doran was a leading scholar of international relations whose insights in his *The Politics of Assimilation: Hegemony and Its Aftermath* enriched his study of Canadian foreign policy in his several subsequent books devoted to this subject alone.

9. Andrew Fenton Cooper, Richard Higgott, and Kim Richard Nossal, *Relocating Middle Powers: Australia and Canada in a Changing World Order,* (Vancouver: University of British Columbia Press, 1993)

The end of the Cold War, the Soviet empire, and the Soviet Union forced students of Canadian foreign policy to consider whether their inherited ideas remained relevant for the new age. Many concluded they did. Tom Keating updated the liberal internationalist middle power argument in *Canada and World Order* in 1993 and 2002, and Stephen Clarkson the peripheral dependent satellite one, after his *Canada and the Reagan Challenge* in 1980, in *Uncle Sam and Us: Globalization, Neoconservativism and the Canadian State* in 2002 and *Does North America Exist? Governing the Continent after NAFTA and 9/11* in 2009. But Andrew F. Cooper and Kim Richard Nossal innovatively came together with an Australian colleague, Richard Higgott, to ask the question in a comparative context, in a way that was embedded in new concepts of international relations. The resulting *Relocating Middle Powers: Australia and Canada in a Changing World Order* inspired a subsequent cascade of conceptual innovation by Cooper and Nossal to enrich the field for the new age.[17]

10. Kim Richard Nossal, Stéphane Roussel, and Stéphane Paquin, *Politique internationale et défense au Canada et au Québec,* (Montreal: Les Presses de l'Université de Montréal, 2007)

The final work on the top 10 list is *Politique internationale et defence au Canada et au Quebec,* by Kim Richard Nossal, Stéphane Roussel, and Stéphane Paquin. It is the only book to survive the strong bias against recent volumes that cannot yet prove that they will stand the test of time. This book is the most recent version of Nossal's English-language *The Politics of Canadian Foreign Policy,* a work that modernized the Eayrsian focus on the making of Canadian foreign policy and has served as a core textbook since its first publication in 1985. The current version infuses the distinctiveness of Quebec and represents the first major fusion of anglophone and francophone scholarship in the field. It thus shows that there is, at long last, a single field of Canadian foreign policy, reflective of the rich diversity that the subject itself contains.

John Kirton has been teaching and researching Canadian foreign policy at the University of Toronto for over thirty years and is the author of Canadian Foreign Policy in a Changing World *(Toronto: Thomson-Nelson, 2007).*

Key Terms

Middle Power
Realism
Satellite

Notes

1. Goldwin Smith, *Canada and the Canadian Question* (Toronto: Hunter, Rose, 1891).

2. These started with Michael Hawes, *Principal Power, Middle Power or Satellite?* (Toronto: York Research Programme in Strategic Studies, 1984); Maureen Appel Molot, 'Where do we, should we, or can we sit? A review of Canada's foreign policy literature', *International Journal of Canadian Studies* 1–2 (Spring 1990), 77–96; Denis Stairs, 'Will and circumstance and the postwar study of Canadian foreign policy', *International Journal* 50 (Winter 1994–5), 9–39; and Daizo Sakurada, 'The contending approaches to Canadian foreign policy and Canada–US relations: A reinterpretation of literature', proceedings of the sixth Tsukuba annual seminar on Canadian studies, 1995, 50–70.

3. Axel Dorscht and Gregg Legare, 'Foreign policy debate and realism', *International Perspectives*, November–December 1986, 7–10; Axel Dorscht, Tom Keating, Gregg Legare, and Jean-François Rioux, 'Canada's international role and "realism"', *International Perspectives* (September–October 1986), 6–9: Axel Dorscht, Ernie Keenes, Gregg Legare, and Jean-François Rioux, 'Canada's foreign policy', *International Perspectives* (May–June 1986), 4–6; John Kirton, 'Realism and reality in Canadian foreign policy', *International Perspectives*, January–February 1987, 3–8;

David Haglund and Tudor Onea, 'Sympathy for the devil: Myths of neoclassical realism in Canadian foreign policy', *Canadian Foreign Policy* 14 (Spring 2008), 53–67.

4. Paul Gecelovsky and Christopher Kukucha, 'Canadian foreign policy: A progressive or stagnating field of study?' *Canadian Foreign Policy* 14 (Spring 2008), 109–19.

5. Richard Jordon, Daniel Maliniak, May Oakes, Susan Peterson, and Michael J. Tierney, 'One discipline or many? TRIP survey of international relations faculty in 10 countries', Institute for the Theory and Practice of International Relations, College of William and Mary, Williamsburg, VA: February 2009.

6. Duane Bratt and Christopher Kukucha, eds., *Readings in Canadian Foreign Policy* (Toronto: Oxford University Press, 2007).

7. Notably Brian Tomlin, Norman Hillmer, and Fen Osler Hampson, *Canada's International Policies: Agendas, Alternatives and Policies* (Toronto: Oxford University Press, 2008).

8. J.L. Granatstein and Robert Bothwell, *Pirouette: Pierre Trudeau and Canadian Foreign Policy* (Toronto: University of Toronto Press, 1990).

9. Douglas Ross, *In the Interests of Peace: Canada and Vietnam, 1954–1973* (Toronto: University of Toronto Press, 1984).

10. James Eayrs, *Fate and Will in Foreign Policy* (Toronto: Canadian Broadcasting Corporation, 1967).

11. Kenneth Waltz, *Man, the State, and War: A Theoretical Analysis* (New York: Columbia University Press, 1959).

12. George Grant, *Lament for a Nation: The Defeat of Canadian Nationalism* (Toronto: McClelland and Stewart, 1965).

13. James Eayrs, 'Defining a new place for Canada in the hierarchy of the world', *International Perspectives*, May–June 1975, 15 and 24.

14. John Holmes, *The Shaping of Peace: Canada and the Search for World Order, 1943–1957,* volumes I and II. (Toronto: University of Toronto Press, 1979, 1982).

15. James Eayrs, *In Defence of Canada: Peacemaking and Deterrence* (Toronto: University of Toronto Press. 1972).

16. By way of disclosure, although I, along with David Haglund and Joseph Jockel, received my doctorate at the Johns Hopkins University School of Advanced International Studies, I had graduated with a Ph.D. supervised by Roger Frank Swanson before Doran arrived to lead the Center of Canadian Studies there.

17. Andre F. Cooper, *Canadian Foreign Policy: Old Habits and New Directions* (Scarborough: Prentice Hall Allyn and Bacon Canada, 1997).

2

CANADIAN FOREIGN POLICY, 1945–1968

Adam Chapnick

The question of whether foreign policy has been, or indeed should be, determined by interests or values has dominated recent analyses of Canada's role in the world. It is an intriguing issue, characterized aptly, albeit provocatively, by the former Canadian ambassador to the United States, Allan Gotlieb, as a clash between realists and romantics.[2] It has no definitive answer. Typically, foreign policy practitioners in Ottawa have preferred caution to bold international initiatives, but there have been sufficient exceptions to justify entire books meant to promote and demonstrate the contrary.[3] Moreover, both approaches have some basis in Canada's post-Second World War history. The first decade favours Gotlieb's realists, while the second is more consistent with the vision of his romantics.

The typical starting point for Gotlieb's realists is Canada's so-called golden age, the period generally understood to have begun shortly after the end of the Second World War during which international circumstances, the domestic political environment, and popular attitudes at home were all compatible with the pursuit of a Canadian foreign policy that served a widely accepted definition of the national interest to an unprecedented extent.[4] By the mid-1950s, in spite of the acclaim brought to Canada when its former secretary of state for external affairs, Lester B. Pearson, accepted the Nobel Peace Prize, that age was coming to an end. The opportunities to exert a consistently disproportionate role in world affairs were more limited, just as Ottawa became saddled with unrealistic, popular expectations to demonstrate Pearsonian-like leadership abroad.[5]

Unable, or unwilling, to admit Canada's relative decline publicly, from the late 1950s through the 1960s, successive Conservative and Liberal governments took their country's self-proclaimed middle power role too seriously, or so the realists maintain.[6] To them, the period from 1957 to 1968 was a time when rhetoric flourished, and increasing numbers of Canadians believed that they had no national interests other than world peace. Such romanticism was nurtured by the political leadership, with one prime minister even announcing with pride, 'so far as Canada is concerned, support of the United Nations is the cornerstone of its foreign policy.'[7]

To the romantics, even if 'the post-golden age may not deserve the laudatory epithets' of the previous period, it nonetheless 'entrenched the essential continuity of Canadian internationalism . . . [T]he accumulated Canadian distinction and prestige were too good to be either ignored or resisted.'[8] Ottawa's commitment to selfless, value-laden participation on the world stage in the 1960s—and its success in promoting its worldly agenda—was hardly different from the approach and effectiveness of Canada's political and diplomatic elite twenty years earlier.

Regardless of which interpretation seems more plausible, by 1968, pride in the previous decade's accomplishments seemed to disappear, replaced by condemnation of an era alleged to have been characterized by excessive national self-confidence and blindness to global realities. Almost immediately upon taking office, Prime Minister Pierre Elliott Trudeau called for a foreign policy review. The resultant white paper, *Foreign Policy for Canadians*, rejected his immediate predecessors' approach to international engagement. As historian Robert Bothwell has explained, Trudeau's government contended that Canadian foreign policy 'had become the handmaiden of a misguided devotion to international institutions. Along the way, Canada's national interest had been lost, or at least submerged, and Canada had earned itself the reputation of an international busybody.'[9] Academic differences over whether Trudeau was right persist to this day.

While making no claims to comprehensiveness, nor to any greater insight than those of the historians and political scientists who have attempted this exercise before, the rest of this chapter seeks to summarize Canada's foreign policy experience between 1945 and 1968. It does so by dividing the nearly quarter century into three phases: the early postwar (1945–53), which favours Gotlieb's realists; the time of transition (1954–7), which provides evidence suitable to either interpretation; and the age of romanticism (1957–68), which speaks for itself. While coming to no specific conclusions, it is more sympathetic to the realist point of view, if only because, as Lester Pearson once said, 'The true realist is the man who sees things both as they are and as they can be.'[10]

CANADIAN FOREIGN POLICY IN THE EARLY POSTWAR PERIOD, 1945–1953

The Second World War stimulated a dynamic transformation of the international power structure that had significant implications for Canada's external status and standing. The changes began with the fall of France in 1940. To that point, while the Canadian government had been committed to the global conflict alongside the British and French militaries, the national contribution had been relatively insignificant and unimpressive.

Prime Minister William Lyon Mackenzie King brought his country into the war united, if also unprepared, and initially his primary concern was keeping obligations to a minimum.[1] When France fell, however, Canada became Great Britain's most significant wartime ally. Ottawa's engagement with the conflict and its influence upon it—in both economic and military terms—necessarily increased.

France's decline was followed by a series of fundamental changes that overtook Europe and Asia during the Second World War. Leading states like Great Britain saw their economies depressed and their fiscal infrastructure devastated. Other former and future powers, like China, Japan, and Germany, were left in political disarray. As a result, for a short period in the late 1940s, those states whose geography had shielded them from the destruction of the conflict, like Canada, emerged disproportionately strong and capable of exerting unusual influence on international developments.

Also strengthened by the outcome of the war was Ottawa's most significant economic and military ally, the United States. Moreover, in the 1940s Washington was open to cooperating with like-minded nations to consolidate an international anti-communist network.[12] Canada was among the United States' most valuable partners both in the Cold War and in the development of a new global economic order, and the State Department, along with its executive leaders, was therefore more apt to include Ottawa in high-level discussions than it had been in the past or would be in the future.

The end of the Second World War also coincided with the creation of a new system of global governance. Between 1943 and 1947, at a time when much of the developed world was shifting its focus to reconstruction, Canada was able to play a significant role in the founding of a series of critical multilateral organizations, including (chronologically) the International Monetary Fund (IMF), the International Bank for Reconstruction and Development,

the United Nations, the General Agreement on Tariffs and Trade (GATT), and what is known today as the North Atlantic Treaty Organization (NATO).[13] Certainly, the Canadian negotiators were taken seriously because of their abilities, but one cannot deny the opportunities that were created by the difficulties experienced by Canada's allies and associates.

Finally, from the more narrow perspective of global security, although a majority of North Americans felt relatively safe prior to the Second World War, with the launch of the first atomic weapons on Hiroshima and Nagasaki in August 1945, the international community encountered a danger that left no person entirely secure. At a time when only the United States had mastered atomic technology, those in the possession of the materials necessary to build the bombs became disproportionately important. Canada, the only allied power with an active uranium producing and refining industry, again found itself in a position of influence.[14]

In summary, changes at the global level that began with the fall of France in 1940 and extended into the early postwar period provided an opening for states like Canada to exert unusual authority on the world stage. There was room for countries who were unaccustomed to playing a major role to act boldly if they so chose. Nonetheless, not every state that would soon be called a middle power embraced the opportunity.[15] In this context, one must consider issues and events at the national level that facilitated Ottawa's specific effort.

The first, and perhaps the most significant, was the state of the Canadian economy. Although there were initial challenges in the immediate postwar period, after 1946, real GDP in Canada rose every year during the next decade (and indeed into the early 1970s). Consumption increased, as did business investment. Oil and gas reserves were discovered in Alberta, and national projects like the TransCanada Highway created jobs and stimulated an already vibrant domestic market. Growth rates into the early 1950s were also impressive, allowing for new government spending and enterprise.[16] Canada's economic strength lent it international credibility, while the stability that strength provided gave Ottawa freedom to concern itself with matters beyond the country's borders.

The federal government's control over its often disgruntled provinces was also unusually strong. In 1941, Mackenzie King used his wartime powers to impose a series of tax rental agreements that provided the federal government with overwhelming control over the national economy. In exchange for their cooperation, the provinces received unconditional transfer payments. Tax rentals were not replaced by tax sharing until 1957 and by tax collection agreements in 1962.[17] Until then, intergovernmental relations rarely ventured into the realm of foreign policy, leaving Ottawa with one less factor to consider as it developed and implemented its global strategy.

Not only did the federal government and the provinces demonstrate a degree of unity in their outlook on external relations (if only because the provinces were otherwise occupied and constrained), so did Canada's political parties. The period that followed the conscription crisis of 1944 was one of refreshing parliamentary cooperation on the world stage. The Liberal prime minister, Mackenzie King, invited the Conservative's House leader, Gordon Graydon, and the Cooperative Commonwealth Federation's leader, M.J. Coldwell, to join the Canadian delegation to the United Nations' founding conference in San Francisco. Representation during subsequent meetings of the UN General Assembly through the early years of the Cold War was also multipartisan.[18] This civilized environment enabled the federal government to consistently advance a clear vision of Canada's role in the world. In January 1947, Secretary of State for External Affairs Louis St Laurent pledged that 'in its external relations the government in office should strive to speak and to act on behalf of the whole of Canada and in such manner as to have the support of all the Canadian people regardless of party affiliation at home.' What has since become known as the Gray Lecture remained the standard statement of the nation's foreign policy principles for at least a decade.[19]

Canada spoke with one voice in world affairs, and its government had a coherent grand strategy.[20] As St Laurent explained, ever since the battles of the Second World War had ended, his country had become an active player in the conflict against communism on the side of political liberty, the rule of law, and the values of humanity. No longer could Canadians remain isolated in North America; in the postwar world, they had both a duty and a responsibility to promote their international interests, as well as those of their allies. Ottawa was a secondary power, and could not be expected to contribute to the same extent as some of its global peers. But it would do what it could, and would likely exert its most significant influence through multilateral organizations and institutions.

The government advanced this vision effectively because its relationships with the media and the public service were exceptionally strong. For a brief period in Canada's national history, all three groups largely agreed on the importance of active participation on the world stage and of cooperating to spread their message to the widest possible audience. As historian Patrick Brennan has explained, for the journalists, 'getting the story straight necessitated the closest of contacts with the establishment that formulated and implemented foreign policy.' Moreover, he has noted, 'admiration for the brainpower and dedication [within the Department of External Affairs] . . . was eclipsed only by the degree of respect and affection the press, and especially the top-ranked men, had for [Lester] Pearson.'[21]

The Department of External Affairs and its related public service agencies were populated by a selfless group of internationalists whose talents and acclaim were appreciated beyond Canada's borders. Louis Rasminsky was a leading voice in the creation of the International Monetary Fund and the World Bank. Hume Wrong was treated with the utmost respect as Ottawa's long-time ambassador in Washington. Norman Robertson was on America's short list to become the United Nations' first secretary-general, and John Read was one of the original nominees to the International Court of Justice in 1946. At a time when foreign ministries were playing a significant role across the western world, Canadian diplomats were well prepared to make a difference.[22]

Finally, members of the public were supportive of global engagement without demanding direct input into the process. They expressed pride in their country's achievements during and after the Second World War while permitting their external representatives the freedom to operate without overt concern for the domestic political ramifications of their initiatives.[23] The mandarins acted accordingly, balancing pragmatism with idealism while never losing track of Canada's national interests. Once politics re-entered the equation in the mid-1950s, the national foreign policy process deteriorated.

Until then, as John Holmes has argued (and as St Laurent had predicted), Ottawa's most significant contributions to world affairs arose primarily out of its participation in international institutions.[24] Canada's functional principle—the philosophical basis of Canadian international engagement from the middle of the Second World War onward—meant that the country could make its most significant difference in the world when engaged in issues for which it had pre-existing expertise as well as an interest in active participation.[25] A corollary to this principle was that strategic effect would come more easily in areas that concerned the great powers the least. It therefore made sense to show initiative in the development of the International Court of Justice, in global reconstruction efforts (through the United Nations Relief and Rehabilitation Administration), and even on such mundane issues such as the composition of the UN secretariat.[26] As a non-great power, it was in Ottawa's interest to function within an international system of rules and regulations. As a nation whose economic prosperity was unusually dependent on foreign trade, it made sense for Canada to establish constructive working relationships with members of the developing world. And blessed with an able diplomatic corps, the Canadian government understood that its global initiatives stood their greatest chance of implementation within multilateral institutions developed primarily by Canada's leading wartime allies.

The fast-growing Department of External Affairs was similarly active in the evolution of the British Commonwealth. In 1950, Canada helped establish the Colombo Plan, the first formal development assistance program for Africa. During the Korean War (1950–3), the Canadian military made a notable, albeit not exceptional, contribution as part of a British Commonwealth division.[27] Finally, an effective relationship with India facilitated Lester Pearson's diplomatic success during the Suez Crisis. In every case, Ottawa recognized the importance of counterweights. There was never any doubt that the United States was Canada's most important ally—at Washington's request, Ottawa did not recognize Communist China after Mao's victory over the nationalists in 1950; it supported hot pursuit into Chinese territory during the Korean War; and it negotiated a series of bilateral and binational defence agreements, including 1957's North American Air Defence Command—but the benefits of diversification were rarely forgotten either. [28]

Nor did the Canadian government neglect its broader international responsibilities and obligations. Support for the military during the Cold War reached its peak during the Korean conflict.[29] The Department of External Affairs expanded dramatically throughout the first postwar decade. Ottawa's commitment to international development, although limited, increased in importance as decolonization progressed. Canada contributed on time and disproportionately to the UN's operating and supplementary budgets throughout the 1940s and 1950s. The quality of Canadian personnel was similarly impressive.

Finally, it was rare for the political leadership to promise more than it could deliver. As St Laurent explained, Canada always kept 'in mind the limitations upon the influence of any secondary power'. The senior members of his Department of External Affairs were aware that 'no society of nations can prosper if it does not have the support of those who hold the major share of the world's military and economic power'. There was 'little point' in a country of Canada's stature 'recommending international action, if those who must carry the major burden of whatever action is taken are not in sympathy'.[30]

THE FOREIGN POLICY TRANSITION, 1954–1957

Between 1954 and 1957, Canadian foreign policy underwent an ironic transition. Ottawa was recognized publicly for its global achievements. The romantic assessment of its ability to make a difference on the world stage, held by an increasing number of national analysts and commentators, appeared to be justified. And yet, from a strategic perspective, the government's efforts to effect global change caused it to depart from the recipe for influence that had served it so well over the previous decade.

In 1954, Canada accepted a seat on an exclusive subcommittee of the United Nations' disarmament commission. The position placed it on relatively equal footing with four of the five great powers. (Only China was excluded.) The following year, the federal government co-sponsored a resolution praising the establishment of the International Atomic Energy Agency.[31] These actions might well have represented global leadership, but they also constituted a significant change in foreign policy. Back in 1946, when the Soviet Union introduced an unhelpful resolution on disarmament, the Canadian delegation to the UN had declined to respond publicly. Its reasoning was made clear in a subsequent publication. Ottawa did not 'consider it appropriate that a population which had never had armed forces which might constitute a threat to the peace of the world should take the lead' on nuclear issues. Such issues, noted the Department of External Affairs' 1946 report on the UN, were best left to the United States.[32] Less than ten years later, the national attitude was different. The political leadership no longer deferred automatically to Canada's great power allies.

There were grounds for this more optimistic approach to policy-making. The death of Joseph Stalin in 1953 created an improved international context in which an increasingly moderate and conciliatory Soviet Union seemed open to compromise and de-escalation of the Cold War. In 1955, Paul Martin (Sr), the federal cabinet minister who led the Canadian delegation to the UN while Secretary of State for External Affairs Lester Pearson was away in Moscow, lobbied successfully for an agreement among the great powers to admit 16 new members to the UN General Assembly. His efforts ended a long-standing impasse between the United States and the Soviet Union.[33] In the new global environment, it seemed as if Canada could and would make a difference. At the same time, however, Martin's actions broadened traditional understandings of the Canadian national interest. Certainly, the new United Nations better reflected the contemporary geopolitical environment, but it also empowered the international community to counter the inclinations of Canada's greatest ally, the United States.[34]

Martin's successful initiative inspired Canadian analysts to expect more from their country. Not much later, the 1956 Suez Crisis amplified the public pressure on the government in Ottawa to be noticed abroad. In January 1957, as the United Nations Emergency Force became operational, a writer for *Saturday Night Magazine* proclaimed 'a kind of break-through to new levels of responsibility for Canada in the world'. To Maxwell Cohen, Lester Pearson's Nobel Prize–worthy intervention and assistance in establishing the first modern international peacekeeping force—the United Nations Emergency Force—marked 'a turning point in the Canadian world role inside and outside the United Nations'.[35]

Indeed it did, but not for the reasons that Cohen suggested. As historian Trevor Lloyd has documented, rather than launching it, the Suez Crisis *concluded* an exceptional period in the practice of Canadian external relations.[36] Whether the 1954–7 period should be considered the end of the realists' golden age or the prelude to a decade of romanticism is therefore unclear. It is more certain that what followed was a period of adjustment and romantic thinking, enabled, if not encouraged, by a changing set of global and domestic circumstances.

ROMANTICISM AND CANADIAN FOREIGN POLICY, 1957–1968

Although many in Canada failed to realize it, the world in 1957 was a different place than it had been when Germany and Japan surrendered in 1945.[37] The international power structure, which seemed so fluid at the end of the war, had solidified. The Cold War had entrenched the United States and Soviet Union as superpowers within a bipolar system. Beneath them, the nations of Europe, whose economies had been so ravaged by the total war of the early 1940s, had recovered and begun to unite, and the relative strength and influence of countries like Canada consequently diminished. Although recent research notes that Canada's strong *British* ties remained evident into the 1960s, there is no doubt that Canadians were less *European* in 1957.[38] Moreover, the symbolic and historical links to the Commonwealth began to eclipse the real ones.

The old British Empire was no more and, just as the return of Europe had affected Canada's position in world affairs, so too did the 'rise of the rest'. In the words of historian Paul Kennedy, the admission of 40 former colonies to the United Nations in the 1960s meant that 'the old UN system . . . with its majority of votes in the North, would never be the same again.'[39] It did not take long for Canada's influence in the General Assembly, where the non-aligned movement came to dominate, to weaken. Certainly, as a so-called middle power, Ottawa still served as a reliable, non-colonial western ally in the Cold War. But its opinions were often less important than those of states such as India, whose influence over the non-aligned community caused the superpowers to take notice. At the Geneva Conference of 1954—meant to finalize the resolution of the Korean War and deal with a pending crisis in Indochina—Canada was not consulted before its allies, at India's insistence, appointed it to serve on international commissions on supervision and control (ICSCs) in Vietnam, Laos, and Cambodia. Caught in the awkward position of having been volunteered for an assignment for which it was not prepared, Ottawa concluded that it had no choice but to accept, regardless of whether serving on the ICSCs advanced Canada's own national interests.[40]

The Geneva experience was indicative of an evolution in the US approach to international relations which affected Canada significantly. More aggressive and less consultative, Washington under Dwight Eisenhower, John F. Kennedy, and Lyndon Johnson struggled to understand Ottawa and its concerns.[41] Moreover, as the size of the US economy and defence industry expanded, so did the discrepancy in power between the United States and its associates. The incentive to take Canadian opinions seriously decreased in conjunction with Canada's declining ability to play a significant role in US foreign policy initiatives.

The global governance system upon which Canada depended so strongly also faced challenges in the late 1950s and early 1960s. A trend towards greater regionalism in Europe limited the impact of the GATT negotiations until an agreement to lower tariffs was finally reached in 1967.[42] In 1958, the new French president, Charles de Gaulle, came to see NATO differently than its ruling elite. The conflict led to France's withdrawal from the organization's integrated military command. The great powers chose to work outside of the United Nations to deal with the escalating situation in Vietnam. The United Nations failed to deter Washington's disastrous Bay of Pigs invasion in 1961, and the Security Council's actions to quell an ongoing crisis in the Congo were less effective than supporters of the organization might have anticipated, or hoped.[43]

Nuclear proliferation also contributed to the changing nature of the international power dynamic. Whereas the postwar period began with a single nuclear-armed state, by 1964 the Soviet Union, Great Britain, France, and China had all joined the nuclear club. In the United States in particular, Eisenhower's New Look—an approach to continental and European defence that relied heavily on the nuclear deterrent—alienated Canadian moderates.[44] Ottawa could still lobby actively for disarmament, but Canadians now had to present their case to multiple actors, none of whom had sufficient incentive to listen.[45]

Finally, as the postwar period evolved, the impact of the foreign ministries across the western world decreased. Improvements in information technology provided global leaders with more immediate access to both each other and the general public. Announcements and speeches that used to be the purview of foreign ministers became responsibilities of heads of government, and personal, summit-level diplomacy gained a new prominence. In Canada, the replacement of the long-governing Liberals with John Diefenbaker's inexperienced group of Progressive Conservatives increased the challenges facing an intermediate-sized power.[46] The new Canadian government lacked competent ministers with foreign policy experience. The sudden death of Diefenbaker's first appointee as secretary of state for external affairs, Sidney Smith, meant that after having a single representative in the portfolio for close to a decade, in 1959 Canadians welcomed their fourth foreign minister in just over three years.

The domestic situation was also tenuous. Consumption spending declined significantly in 1957 and 1958, and exports stagnated. By 1961, unemployment was more than double what it had been four years earlier.[47] The economy began to recover in 1962, but by then Canadians had grown even more tightly attached to their social programs, and increasingly determined to expand the size and scope of the welfare state regardless of the impact on federal allocations for foreign affairs and defence. The provinces—whose constitutional responsibilities included social policy—gradually reasserted their power in negotiations with their federal partners, and spending that might once have been dedicated to international security was redirected towards priorities at home.[48] Parliamentary debate during the Suez Crisis—the Conservatives accused the Liberals of abandoning Great Britain during its gravest time of need—effectively ended the anti-communist Cold War consensus that had largely determined the direction of Canadian foreign policy since 1945. In 1957, Prime Minister Diefenbaker chose not to attend a bipartisan dinner celebrating Liberal rival Lester Pearson's Nobel Prize. His Progressive Conservatives further undermined any plans to strategize about Canadian interests from a long-term perspective by using potentially damaging anti-American rhetoric in their efforts to sway voters to their side.[49] 'It's me against the Americans, fighting for the little guy',[50] argued Prime Minister Diefenbaker during his failed campaign for re-election in 1963. Pearson's more centrist Liberals, equally afraid of losing public support, reduced their emphasis on international relations altogether, insulating them from specific criticisms but also leaving them unable to effectively redefine a unifying vision of Canadian foreign policy for the future.[51]

The great triad of the early postwar period—the media, the civil service, and the federal government—also crumbled. By the mid-1950s, a new generation of reporters had embraced a more combative approach to political journalism.[52] The Conservative government looked upon its public servants as what Diefenbaker called Pearsonalities, and the bond between the executive and the mandarins was never the same.[53] Beginning with the establishment of the Royal Commission on Government Organization in 1960 (the Glassco Commission), the Department of External Affairs encountered public criticism for its organizational and administrative attitudes and 'general distrust of outsiders'[54] which affected departmental morale and, in time, capabilities.[55] The mandarinate was not all to blame. Neither Conservative Howard Green (1959–63) nor Liberal Paul Martin Sr (1963–8) were as effective in advancing Canadian interests as their predecessor as secretary of state for external affairs, Lester Pearson, had been. Green was hard-working and dedicated, but his strong will deprived Ottawa of

some of the flexibility it needed to play an effective global role. His advocacy of disarmament won him accolades from certain elements of the Canadian population—particularly those who believed that 'the celebration of idealist optimism could win over the fixation on "effectiveness"'[56]—but his romantic determination to collaborate with like-minded countries at the UN regardless of the views of Ottawa's great power allies ensured that the world body's resolutions had limited impact.[57]

Green was, according to defence analyst Joseph Jockel, the 'decisive voice' in reneging on Ottawa's commitment to participate in NORAD's 'Operation Skyhawk' in 1959, leaving Washington frustrated and dismayed. The following year, the secretary of state for external affairs' opposition to nuclear weapons created irresolvable tension with Minister of National Defence Douglas Harkness. The dispute, and Diefenbaker's unwillingness to settle it, left the Conservative cabinet deadlocked on the pressing issue of Canada's NORAD (and NATO) obligations for over two years.[58] Harkness's resignation failed to clarify the Conservative government's security policy, and contributed to the Liberals' return to power in 1963.

The new prime minister, Lester Pearson, placed the much more experienced Paul Martin in charge of foreign affairs. Nevertheless, the naked ambition of the former and future candidate for the Liberal Party leadership hardly benefited Canada's global credibility. Martin was successful at times—he was instrumental in organizing a UN peacekeeping expedition to Cyprus, for example—but he often aimed too high, as romantics often do, and as a result drew attention to his country's limitations as much as he did to its strengths. As Robert Bothwell has rightly pointed out, 'Some thought [Martin] had difficulty distinguishing small points from larger issues. Some were uneasy at his ability to reinterpret the record in his own favour. Many of them would have agreed with the American official

Bill Bundy, who when asked to summarize his impression of Martin said that he was 'pas sérieux', someone not to be taken seriously.'[59] Martin's miscalculation of the power of, first, Blair Seaborn and then Chester Ronning to mediate between the United States and the People's Army of Vietnam in the mid-1960s underlined his overconfidence in his own, and Canada's, power to effect change in US policy. By the later 1960s, he was struggling to maintain the full confidence of Pearson's cabinet and less able to advance dramatic initiatives.

In spite of the challenges, Canada's record during the 1957–68 period was not without its achievements, and these successes help explain why romantics see a continuity of Canadian foreign policy accomplishments throughout the period that followed the golden age. Ottawa continued to be an active supporter of the United Nations, and its participation in new peacekeeping missions in Lebanon, the Congo, Yemen, West New Guinea, and Cyprus enhanced its reputation as a leading player in global peace support operations.[60]

Canada also remained active within the British Commonwealth, with Prime Minister Diefenbaker drawing positive attention to his country when he criticized South Africa over its policy of apartheid at the Meeting of Commonwealth Prime Ministers in 1961. At the time, no other white Commonwealth leader was willing to demonstrate the same courage. Diefenbaker's relations with Britain were less successful—his foolish call to divert 15 per cent of Canadian trade to Great Britain in 1957 and his vocal opposition to London's efforts to join the European Common market in 1960 alienated British political leaders—but his outspoken advocacy of human rights and his commitment to official development assistance through the Colombo Plan drew accolades from some of Canada's smaller partners and allies.

Under Lester Pearson, Canada and the United States resolved an awkward dispute over power generation on the Columbia River System. Subsequently, confronted with provincial demands that none of his predecessors had been forced to contemplate, Pearson faced down the foreign policy challenges that accompanied the Quiet Revolution in Quebec through a combination of ad hoc policies and clever diplomatic negotiation. His efforts enhanced Canada's relationship with a number of developing francophone countries in Africa, even if they were less well received in Charles de Gaulle's France. Finally, in 1965, Ottawa and Washington completed the Auto Pact, a major victory for Canadians that came about in spite of massive American disappointment in the Canadian prime minister's outspoken criticism of US policy in Vietnam just months earlier.

Perhaps most important to a general understanding of Canadian foreign policy in the post-1957 period—and therefore worthy of somewhat more detailed analysis here—is the publication of a seemingly innocuous diplomatic report on the state of the Canadian–American relationship, *Canada and the United States: Principles for Partnership*, in June 1965. The work appeared during a time of significant cultural upheaval in North America and beyond. The 1960s witnessed the coming of age of the baby boomers: the sons and daughters of the veterans of the Second World War. This exceptionally large demographic cohort had the numerical power to be a force in global politics at a young age and a natural inclination to challenge authority. Access to a growing number of publicly funded universities gave them a platform to air their concerns. And with the US war in Vietnam growing in intensity, and American investment in Canada increasing concurrently, they had an ideal target. In the words of two Canadian historians, by the mid-1960s in Canada, 'anti-Americanism had become the national sport.'[61]

The impact on discussions of foreign policy was immediate. A book published by CBC journalist

James M. Minifie in 1960, *Peacemaker or Powder-Monkey: Canada's Role in a Revolutionary World*, which blamed Canada's close relations with the United States for depriving Ottawa of the international influence that it had exercised so effectively during the Suez Crisis, spawned a virtual industry in Canada dedicated to ending Ottawa's perceived deference to American geopolitical initiatives. Minifie and his followers advocated neutrality as a recipe for independence and counselled (romantically) a return to global leadership that should have come naturally to a well-regarded non-colonial power.[62] By 1965, then, Canadian–American relations had been deteriorating for a number of years, and a binational study of how to improve them was a laudable political undertaking.

The authors of what became known as the Merchant-Heeney Report were good choices on paper, but ill-suited to the mood of the time. A former US ambassador to Canada, Livingston Merchant, and a former Canadian ambassador to the United States, Arnold Heeney, were part of an older, conservative generation of foreign policy practitioners. Their argument that, in the case of bilateral disputes, both countries would be better served if resolutions were negotiated 'in private, through diplomatic channels',[63] ignited a storm of protests and divided Canadians along generational lines. Heeney's colleagues, mandarins who had served during the golden age, understood and supported the report's pragmatism. New Canadian nationalists, including a future foreign minister—Lloyd Axworthy—were furious. One of them, a philosophy professor at the University of Toronto, condemned 'the bankruptcy of this approach to world affairs'. Others argued only somewhat less emotionally for a new approach to Canadian foreign policy that was less dependent on the aims and interests of the United States.[64]

The debate had not been resolved by 1968 when Pierre Trudeau came to power, but the new prime minister's electoral victory—along with Egypt's abrupt dismissal of the United Nations Emergency Force in 1967—was a symbolic turning point nonetheless. Old ideas that had defined Canada's place in the world for over two decades seemed initially to have little place in Trudeau's Ottawa. It was time for a new foreign policy, one that placed Canada first, regardless of allies' criticisms or concerns.[65]

* * *

At least initially, Trudeau combined the realism and romanticism of his predecessors. He sought to redefine Canadian national interests, but he did so in a way that appealed to the public's sense of moral righteousness and de-emphasized the significance of the United States to Ottawa's international conduct.[66] As a result, there was no clear winner in the realists versus romantics debate, only a new opportunity to revisit the question of what did, and should, motivate Canada's behaviour on the world stage.

Just over 40 years later, not much has changed.

Key Terms

Functional Principle
The Golden Age of Canadian Foreign Policy
The Gray Lecture

Notes

1. See, for example, Nelson Michaud's chapter in this volume as well as Michael Hart, *From Pride to Influence: Towards a New Canadian Foreign Policy* (Vancouver and Toronto: UBC Press, 2008), 320–35; Michael Byers, *Intent for a Nation* (Toronto: Douglas & McIntyre, 2007), 6–16, 215–41; Steven Kendall Holloway, *Canadian Foreign Policy: Defining the National Interest* (Peterborough: Broadview Press, 2006), 5–18; Roy Rempel, *Dreamland: How Canada's Pretend Foreign Policy Has Undermined Sovereignty* (Montreal and Kingston: McGill-Queen's University Press, 2006,) 1–7, 151–75; Jennifer Welsh, 'Are Interests Really Value Free?' *Literary Review of Canada* 14, 9 (November 2006): 1–5; and Denis Stairs, 'Myths, Morals, and Reality in Canadian Foreign Policy', *International Journal* 58, 2 (Spring 2003): 239–56.

2. Allan Gotlieb, 'Romanticism and Realism in Canada's Foreign Policy', *Policy Options*, February 2005, 16–27.

3. See, for example, the contrast between Adam Chapnick, 'Peace, Order and Good Government: The "conservative" Tradition in Canadian Foreign Policy', *International Journal* 60, 3 (Summer 2005): 635–50; and Costas Melakopides, *Pragmatic Idealism: Canadian Foreign Policy, 1945–1995* (Montreal and Kingston: McGill-Queen's University Press, 1998).

4. For a more complete assessment of the golden age, see Adam Chapnick, 'The Golden Age: A Canadian Foreign Policy Paradox', *International Journal* 64, 1 (Winter 2008–9): 205–21.

5. Peyton V. Lyon, 'The Evolution of Canadian Diplomacy Since 1945', in *De Mackenzie King à Pierre Trudeau: quarante ans de de diplomatie canadienne*, ed. Paul Painchaud (Quebec: Les presses de l'université Laval, 1989), 13–33, specifically 21; and Trevor Lloyd, *Canada in World Affairs 1957–1959* (Toronto: Oxford University Press, 1968), 8.

6. On middle powers, see Adam Chapnick, 'The Middle Power', *Canadian Foreign Policy* 7, 2 (Winter 1999): 73–82; and Chapnick, 'The Canadian Middle Power Myth', *International Journal* 55, 2 (Spring 2000): 188–206.

7. John Diefenbaker, quoted in Canada, Department of External Affairs, *Report of the Department of External Affairs 1957* (Ottawa: Queen's Printer, 1958), 2.

8. Melakopides, *Pragmatic Idealism*, 52.

9. Robert Bothwell, *Alliance and Illusion: Canada and the World, 1945–1984* (Vancouver and Toronto: BC Press, 2007), 278.

10. L.B. Pearson, *Democracy in World Politics* (Toronto: S.J. Reginald Sanders and Company, 1955), 121.

11. C.P. Stacey, *Canada and the Age of Conflict*, vol. 2, *1921–1948: The Mackenzie King Era* (Toronto: University of Toronto Press, 1981), 272–4, 281. On King and national unity before the war, see J.L. Granatstein and Robert Bothwell, '"A Self-Evident National Duty": Canadian Foreign Policy, 1935–1939', *Journal of Imperial and Commonwealth History* 3, 2 (January 1975): 212–33. On Canada's unpreparedness, see Adrian W. Preston, 'Canada and the Higher Direction of the Second World War, 1939–1945', in B.D. Hunt and R.G. Haycock, eds., *Canada's Defence: Perspectives on Policy in the Twentieth Century* (Toronto: Copp Clark, 1993), 98–102.

12. Allan P. Dobson and Steve Marsh, *US Foreign Policy Since 1945*, 2nd ed. (London and New York: Routledge, [2001] 2006), 29.

13. Tom Keating, *Canada and World Order: The Multilateralist Tradition in Canadian Foreign Policy*, 2nd ed. (Toronto: Oxford UP, [1993] 2002); Adam Chapnick, *The Middle Power Project: Canada and the Founding of the United Nations* (Vancouver and Toronto: UBC Press, 2005); Kathleen Britt Rasmussen, 'Canada and the Reconstruction of the International Economy, 1941–1947', PhD Dissertation (University of Toronto, 2001).

14. Robert Bothwell and William Kilbourn, *C.D. Howe: A Biography* (Toronto: McClelland and Stewart, 1979), 168–9, 213.

15. On the differences, for example, between Canada and Australia at the end of the war, see Chapnick, *The Middle Power Project*, 143–4.

16. Kenneth Norrie, Douglas Owram, and J.C. Herbert Emery, *A History of the Canadian Economy*, 3rd ed. (Scarborough: Thomson Nelson, 2002), 374–9.

17. Ibid., 347, 396.

18. John English, '"A Fine Romance": Canada and the United Nations, 1943–1957', in *Canada and the Early Cold War, 1943–1957*, ed. Greg Donaghy (Ottawa: Department of Foreign Affairs and International Trade, 1998), 77.

19. St Laurent, quoted in Chapnick, 'The Gray Lecture and Canadian Citizenship in History', *American Review of Canadian Studies* 37, 4 (Winter 2007): 448. See also Hector Mackenzie, 'Shades of Gray? "The Foundations of Canadian Policy in World Affairs" in Context', *American Review of Canadian Studies* 37, 4 (Winter 2007): 459–73.

20. David Pratt, *The Ross Ellis Memorial Lectures in Military and Strategic Studies: Is there a Grand Strategy in Canadian Foreign Policy?* (Calgary: Canadian Defence and Foreign Affairs Institute, 2008).

21. Patrick H. Brennan, *Reporting the Nation's Business: Press–Government Relations during the Liberal Years, 1935–1957* (Toronto: University of Toronto Press, 1994), 142, 143. Pearson left the foreign service to become Louis St Laurent's secretary of state for external affairs in 1948. On Pearson's abilities, see John W. Holmes, 'The Unquiet

Diplomat—Lester B. Pearson', *International Journal* 62, 2 (Spring 2007): 300, 302.

22. For more detail, see J.L. Granatstein, *The Ottawa Men: The Civil Service Mandarins, 1935–1957* (Toronto: University of Toronto Press, [1982] 1998).

23. Robert Bothwell and John English, 'The View from Inside Out: Canadian Diplomats and Their Public', *International Journal* 39, 1 (Winter 1983–4): 65. See also, Chapnick, *The Middle Power Project*, 149; John W. Holmes, *The Shaping of Peace: Canada and the Search for World Order, 1943–1957*, vol. 2, (Toronto: University of Toronto Press, 1982), 332–3; and Arthur Andrew, *The Rise and Fall of a Middle Power: Canadian Diplomacy from King to Mulroney* (Toronto: J. Lorimer, 1993), 32. Polls from the period confirm Canada's support for internationalism as well as evidence of their relative ignorance of world affairs. On internationalism, see Canadian Institute of Public Opinion, 10 January 1945, cited in *Public Opinion Quarterly* (Spring 1945): 106–7; on the lack of sophisticated understanding, see Gallup Poll #186, May 1944, in which 50 per cent of respondents declare themselves either not familiar with or undecided on whether the United Nations had been making progress. Cited at www.library.carleton.ca/ssdata/surveys/doc/gllp-49-may186-cbk [1 August 2008].

24. Holmes, *The Shaping of Peace*, 2 vols (Toronto: University of Toronto Press, 1979, 1982).

25. On Canada's functional principle, see Chapnick, *The Middle Power Project*, 23–4; and Chapnick, 'Principle for Profit: The Functional Principle and the Development of Canadian Foreign Policy, 1943–1947', *Journal of Canadian Studies* 37, 2 (Summer 2002): 68–85.

26. Canada, Department of External Affairs *Report of the First Part of the First Session of the General Assembly of the United Nations* (Ottawa: King's Printer, 1946), specifically 28.

27. In historian Robert Bothwell's words, 'The Canadian contribution to the war was large enough to be noticed, though not enough to weigh decisively in the balance when important American interests were at stake.' See his *Alliance and Illusion*, 89.

28. On the related ideas of 'the diplomacy of constraint' and 'defence against help', see Denis Stairs, 'The Diplomacy of Constraint', in Norman Hillmer, ed., *Partners Nevertheless: Canadian–American Relations in the Twentieth Century* (Toronto: Copp Clark, 1989), 214–26; and Donald Barry and Duane Bratt, 'Defence Against Help', *American Review of Canadian Studies* 38, 1 (Spring 2008): 63–89.

29. Canada had largely demilitarized after the Second World War but rebuilt its armed forces aggressively in response to the UN's call to engage in Korea. The Canadian military remained relatively strong through the 1950s and into the 1960s.

30. Louis St Laurent, *The Foundations of Canadian Policy in World Affairs* (Toronto: University of Toronto Press, 1947), 33.

31. Canada, DEA, *Report of the Department of External Affairs 1955* (Ottawa: Queen's Printer, 1956), 8. On Canada's significant role in the IAEA, see Duane Bratt, *The Politics of CANDU Exports* (Toronto: University of Toronto Press, 2006).

32. Canada, DEA, *The United Nations 1946: Report of the Second Part of the First Session of the General Assembly of the United Nations* (Ottawa: King's Printer, 1947), 37.

33. On Martin's experience, see Greg Donaghy and Don Barry, 'Our Man from Windsor: Paul Martin and the New Members Question, 1955', in *Paul Martin and Canadian Diplomacy*, ed. Ryan Toughy (Waterloo: Centre for Foreign Policy and Federalism, 2001), 3–20.

34. Tom Keating, *Canada and World Order: The Multilateral Tradition in Canadian Foreign Policy*, 2nd ed. (Don Mills: Oxford University Press, [1993] 2002), 103; and John Holmes, *The Shaping of Peace*, vol. 2, 346. For more idealistic assessments, see Canada, DEA, *Canada and the United Nations 1954–55* (Ottawa: Queen's Printer, 1956), 30; and John Hilliker and Donald Barry, *Canada's Department of External Affairs*, vol. 2, *Coming of Age 1946–1968* (Montreal and Kingston: McGill-Queen's University Press, 1995), 122.

35. Maxwell Cohen, 'A New Responsibility in Foreign Policy', *Saturday Night*, 19 January 1957, 28. On UNEF, see Michael K. Carroll, *Pearson's Peacekeepers: Canada and the United Nations Emergency Force, 1956–67* (Vancouver and Toronto: UBC Press, 2009).

36. Lloyd, *Canada in World Affairs 1957–1959*. Lloyd's analysis of the end of the so-called golden age remains as valuable as anything that has been written since. For more contemporary analyses, see Andrew Cohen, *While Canada Slept: How We Lost Our Place in the World* (Toronto: McClelland and Stewart, 2003); and Robert Greenhill, 'The Decline of Canada's Influence in the World—What is to be done about it?' *Policy Options*, February 2005, 34–9.

37. On the romantic impulse, see Cohen, *While Canada Slept*. For the most fervent defence of the romantic interpretation of this period, see Melakopides, *Pragmatic Idealism*. Prime ministerial speeches from the late 1950s and early 1960s express similar sentiment. See Arthur E. Blanchette, ed., *Canadian Foreign Policy, 1955–1965: Selected Speeches and Documents* (Toronto: McClelland and Stewart, 1977).

38. On the British connection, see Phillip Buckner, ed., *Canada and the Age of Empire* (Vancouver: UBC Press, 2004).

39. Paul Kennedy, *The Parliament of Man: The Past, Present, and Future of the United Nations* (New York: Random House, 2006), 121.

40. Holmes, *The Shaping of Peace*, vol. 2, 203; Bothwell, *Alliance and Illusion*, 197.

41. John Herd Thompson and Stephen J. Randall, *Canada and the United States: Ambivalent Allies*, 4th ed. (Athens and London: University of Georgia Press, [1994] 2008), 199.

42. On Canadian trade policy during the period, see Michael Hart, *A Trading Nation: Canadian Trade Policy from Colonialism to Globalization* (Vancouver and Toronto: UBC Press, 2002), 204–68.

43. On the Congo, see Kevin A. Spooner, *Canada, the Congo Crisis, and UN Peacekeeping, 1960–64* (Vancouver and Toronto: UBC Press, 2009).

44. Thompson and Randall, *Canada and the United States*, 197–8.

45. The lobbying itself, taking place at the same time as Canada was accepting nuclear weapons as part of its NATO obligations, was a prime example of the country's romanticism. See, for example, 'Statement by General E.L.M. Burns, representative of Canada on the First Committee of the United Nations, 30 October 1961', cited in Blanchette, *Canadian Foreign Policy, 1955–1965*, 57–62.

46. On the problems with new governments, see George C. Perlin, *The Tory Syndrome: Leadership Politics in the Progressive Conservative Party* (Montreal and Kingston: McGill-Queen's University Press, 1980).

47. Norrie et al, *A History of the Canadian Economy*, 381.

48. The exception to this argument is spending on foreign aid, which increased dramatically. Given how little of the federal budget was allocated to aid in the first place, however, these numbers are relatively unimportant. On the challenges with the provinces, and the romantic face placed upon them, see, for example, 'Statement issued by the Secretary of State for External Affairs, Mr. Paul Martin, 23 April 1965', cited in Blanchette, *Canadian Foreign Policy, 1955–1965*, 409–10.

49. Norman Hillmer and J.L. Granatstein, *For Better or For Worse: Canada and the United States into the Twenty-First Century* (Toronto: Thomson Nelson, 2007), 194; Hilliker and Barry, *Canada's Department of External Affairs*, 135.

50. Quoted in Hillmer and Granatstein, *For Better or for Worse*, 208. Beginning in 1961, the newly formed New Democratic Party was no better.

51. See, for example, Bothwell, *Alliance and Illusion*, 260–3.

52. Brennan, *Reporting the Nation's Business*, xi.

53. Hilliker and Barry, *Canada's Department of External Affairs*, 134–43; H. Basil Robinson, *Diefenbaker's World: A Populist in Foreign Affairs* (Toronto: University of Toronto Press, 1989), 6–9; and Adam Chapnick, *Canada's Voice: The Public Life of John Wendell Holmes* (Vancouver and Toronto: UBC Press, 2009), 94–102.

54. Gilles Lalande, *The Department of External Affairs and Biculturalism*, vol. 3 of *Studies of the Royal Commission on Bilingualism and Biculturalism* (Ottawa: Queen's Printer, 1969), 14.

55. Hilliker and Barry, *Canada's Department of External Affairs*, 198–208.

56. Melakopides, *Pragmatic Idealism*, 58.

57. Canada, Department of External Affairs, *Report of the Department of External Affairs 1960* (Ottawa: Queen's Printer, 1961), v, 11, 14. See also Peyton Lyon, *Canada in World Affairs 1961–1963* (Toronto: Oxford University Press, 1968), 280. For more on Green specifically, see his speeches in Blanchette, *Canadian Foreign Policy 1955–1965*.

58. Joseph T. Jockel, *Canada in NORAD 1957–2007: A History* (Montreal and Kingston: McGill-Queen's University Press, 2007), 52–66.

59. Bothwell, *Alliance and Illusion*, 217.

60. Martin, 'Peacekeeping: Some Prospects and Perspectives', cited in Blanchette, ed., *Canadian Foreign Policy 1955–1965*, 46–52.

61. Hillmer and Granatstein, *For Better or for Worse*, 230.

62. James M. Minifie, *Peacemaker or Powder-Monkey: Canada's Role in a Revolutionary World* (Toronto: McClelland and Stewart, 1960).

63. Quoted in Chapnick, *Canada's Voice*, 168.

64. Charles Hanly, 'The Ethics of Independence', in *An Independent Foreign Policy for Canada?* ed. Stephen Clarkson (Toronto: McClelland and Stewart, 1968), 27. See the rest of the Clarkson collection for an indicative sample of the new nationalist views of the time. For a retrospective analysis, see Brian Bowe and Patrick Lennox, eds., *An Independent Foreign Policy for Canada? Challenges and Choices for the Future* (Toronto: University of Toronto Press, 2008), and in particular, the editors' introductory chapter. For a sampling of popular views, see Editorial, *Toronto Daily Star*, 13 July 1965, 6; Bruce Hutchison, 'The Prickly Neighbors', *Winnipeg Free Press*, 22 July 1965; and James Eayrs, *Diplomacy and Its Discontents* (Toronto: University of Toronto Press, 1971), 49–58.

65. For an excellent summary, see John Holmes, *Canada: A Middle-Aged Power* (Toronto: McClelland and Stewart, 1976), 8–19.

66. Most striking was the result of his foreign policy review, *Foreign Policy for Canadians*, which included six books detailing Canada's foreign policy priorities, none of which focused on the United States.

3

MOST SAFELY IN THE MIDDLE

John W. Holmes

Medio tutissimus ibis.

—Ovid

It seemed like sound advice for Canada when we were launched after the Second World War into the giddy world of international diplomacy: 'You will go most safely in the middle.' There was enough of Mackenzie King in it to carry the cabinet and enough forward motion for an impatient body of foreign service officers and a public that seemed more anxious than Mr King to accept rather than avoid commitments. He probably sensed all along, however, a Canadian disinclination to pay much for status or to maintain the requisite armed forces for an aspiring major power. Mr King did not much like the classification 'middle' power. As far as status was concerned, he regarded it as somewhat demeaning to be ranked with, say, Mexico, but he had little zeal for the entangling responsibilities such as, for example, membership in a United Nations commission to seek the peaceful reunification of Korea. In any case, the idea that Canada was a middle power did gain wide acceptance. What we

had considered ourselves before is hard to say, our preference for smallness when contributions were in order conflicting with the sense of bigness that came from being the second largest country in the world. The ambiguity has persisted.

What has become of the middle power and its role in the past 25 years? At the end of the fifties we seemed to have got it neatly defined. The term 'middle power' had been conceived in the first place as a way of explaining to the world that Canadians were of greater consequence than the Panamanians but could not take on the obligations of the Americans, or even the French. It was useful in encouraging a wallflower people to get responsibly involved in keeping the peace and unleashing the world economy while at the same time warning them that they should not expect to wield the influence of a 'great' power. Canada's early forays into international diplomacy encouraged confidence that we were needed and, if we did not set our sights too high, that we could impinge. Mackenzie King's conviction that we should keep our noses out of distant problems because we had no distant interests was turned upside down. That became our qualification for intermediary therapy in the United Nations and elsewhere. So 'middle' power took on an unexpected meaning. Altogether it fitted very well a country that was recognizing that it could best work through combinations and through international institutions; there were three major associations (the United Nations, the Commonwealth, and the North Atlantic Treaty Organization) and many minor ones that fitted our needs aptly. The variety, furthermore, made us more confident of the freedom of movement we had come to cherish in a long history of groping for our own place in the sun.

/ The high point had come in 1955 and 1956 when our accomplished leaders, Paul Martin Sr. and Lester Pearson, with wide if not universal international acclaim, led the lesser powers in the General Assembly in revolt against great power arrogance over the issues of new members and the Suez. The replacement, shortly afterwards, of this skilled team by the inexperienced Conservatives slowed us down but did not substantially alter the concept. The satisfactions, however, diminished, and as new issues—the rise of the Third World, nuclear escalation, continental economics, provincial claims in foreign policy—began to press us harder, one could see that 'middlepowermanship', while still a valid concept, did not tell us much about how to handle 90 per cent of the agenda that crowds the day of a foreign service officer.

It was really only after the so-called golden decade of the middle power had passed that we began to grow self-conscious about it. Having been as guilty as any in analyzing and defining this mystic role, I became worried by the mid-sixties over the glorification and formalization of a kind of diplomacy that was really just common-sensical and not as unique as we were hinting. At a conference in Banff in 1965 I asked: 'Is there a future for middlepowermanship?' The irony would, I thought, be grasped by a generation who

knew Stephen Potter. The term 'brinkmanship' had been coined by James Reston to deflate John Foster Dulles, but it was then incorporated into the language as if Dulles had said it himself. I should have listened to Charles Lamb: 'Clap an extinguisher on your irony, if you are unhappily blessed with a vein of it.' The mood in the land was earnest. A new breed of scholars was now adding greatly to our sophistication in terms of foreign policy but seeking somewhat too arduously to define the indefinable. The word 'middle-powermanship' began to buzz. Editors and politicians needed something to cling to, and in a time of increasing uncertainty the illusion gained ground that the multifarious range of international involvements could be subsumed in a succinctly definable 'foreign policy'.

There was already an anxiety to cling to what seemed fleeting glories. More regrettable was the consuming interest in what one might, if one still dared, call rolemanship. For scholars it was less seductive than for politicians. There was nothing wrong in the efforts, scientific or intuitive, to draw a bead on Canada in world politics and economics, provided the abstractions were restrained and not pressed too far. Middlepowermanship got boring, however, and by the end of the sixties a new prime minister proclaimed a revolt. He questioned whether the national interest had been adequately served in all the strenuous 'helpful fixing'—another term that was drafted ironically but interpreted solemnly—that went with middlepowermanship. Pierre Trudeau's grasp of foreign policy and diplomacy was dubious, but he was posing a question being widely asked by an 'attentive public' disenchanted with formulae too oft repeated. The 'role of a middle power' was under critical review. The idea had become increasingly associated with 'peace-keeping', and attitudes to that proud Canadian function were soured by the expulsion of the United Nations Emergency Force (UNEF) from

Egypt in 1967 and the embarrassment and frustrations of trying, as a member of three international supervisory commissions, to control the peace in Indochina at war.

It was certainly time for a review, but it is unfortunate that the role of the middle power had become confused with 'do-goodism', constantly misconstrued in a debate over 'nationalism' and 'internationalism'. The idea gained ground that somehow the national interest of Canada, particularly its economic interests *vis-à-vis* the United States, had been sacrificed because Lester Pearson was off at the United Nations for a few days a year. A much greater number of public servants and cabinet ministers, among them the redoubtable C.D. Howe, had been guarding our trade and commerce than those few engaged in the high-profile acts in New York or Geneva. Canada had been drawn into accepting responsibilities for world order because it was wanted. Canadians had not gone looking for distinguished service, although in general they welcomed the challenge. If there was any soliciting of such assignments it was tentative. The determination to play as effective a role as was possible for a middle power was based on a very hard-headed calculation of national interest at the end of a war in which too many Canadians had been killed following a depression in which too many Canadians had starved. It was a firm rejection of the prewar assumption that Canada could escape disaster by dancing on the periphery. It was taken for granted that there was no national interest greater than the preservation of a world in which Canadians could survive and prosper. Collective defence and collective law as the best means of serving and protecting Canada itself were better understood by those who had passed through the thirties and forties than by later generations who, nurtured on the new 'victimization' school of Canadian history, took a more claustrophobic view of the national interest.

It was of course always arguable ad hoc that some national interest had been ill defended, but it was intellectually slipshod to see this in either/or terms. The same simple thinking was evident in the simultaneous debate over the efficacy of 'quiet diplomacy', associated persistently with feckless middlepowermanship. That quiet diplomacy had quite often failed to move other powers, especially the United States, was easy to prove, but it did not follow that loud shouting would have moved a mountain either. It was still not widely recognized that there are no sure ways and means for a middle power to get its way at all, that abstractions are to be handled with care, and that a more discriminating look at specifics is a better way to further the national interest and avoid despair.

The attack on classical middlepowerism came from two directions. There were those on the right who thought all Canada's energies should be directed to selling apples and reactors. The more articulate critics on the left did want Canada to play a grand peace-inducing role in the world but thought that we were hindered by our alignment. They saw 'uncommitment' as a means to a worthy end. Then almost inevitably 'independence' came to be seen as an end in itself. In particular that meant independence of the United States, partly, it was thought, because we could not be regarded as objective actors in world diplomacy if we were allied to one of the superpowers, and partly because the close economic tie was believed to be intimidating us from foreign policies that would serve specifically Canadian ends and help to keep the world in balance. The independentist school of thought strayed from the Canadian tradition of regarding independence functionally. We had pursued self-government but not independence from Britain for the simple reason that our national interests seemed better served that way. We needed Britain as counterweight and the prestigious Foreign Office to conduct Canadian diplomacy on the cheap. Independence was a Yankee word that even Mackenzie King rejected. In practice we acted independently when we wanted to and joined a team when that was more useful. The new nationalism was based on a persistent misreading of the postwar period, popularized regrettably by a great Canadian historian, Donald Creighton. The assumption that the Canadian government had embraced 'continentalism' with enthusiasm when they had broken with the shackles of the British is an anti-American version of our history based ironically on the tenets and mythologies of certain American scholars. It is essentially anti-Canadian also because it assumes Canadian incompetence. Since our historians have been able to delve into postwar Canadian as well as American files, the record has been very considerably revised, but 'Canada as victim' lingers on in textbooks to which students are still subjected. It suffuses also much masochistic comment on our foreign policy, which does not accord us even middle power status.

In all this clamour the pursuit of the national interest got derailed, and the role of this middle power confused. That Mr Trudeau has worked his way eventually to his predecessor's concept of the basic national interest would seem to have been proved latterly by his dedication to reconciliation between North and South and the restoration of the dialogue between East and West. He was, nevertheless, responsible initially for setting Canadians off on a few false scents and for leaving the impression that there occurred in the early seventies a profound change in Canadian foreign policy. The Pearson–Martin years of the sixties were written off as more of the same old middlepowermanship, although with less spectacular results. The extent to which change has been attributable in fact more to the turning earth than to policy planning in Ottawa has been ignored. Already during the Diefenbaker regime it was clear that the configuration

of power in which this middle state had flourished was becoming unhinged.

The world has changed and we along with it. The intensification of economic competition in the world at large, the price of oil, nuclear escalation, the banking crises, the relative decline of both the United States and Canada in the world economy, and the rigidifying of East–West as well as North–South relations have profoundly affected the states of North America. They have altered our predicaments and challenged the rules and habits by which we have played. If we seek the causes for patterns of change in Canada–US relations, for example, I suggest that we are more likely to find them in these alterations than in the philosophical stance and the Weltanschauung of Mr Trudeau. Because Pierre Trudeau is one of the few statesmen around with a sophisticated philosophy and a reasonably consistent prospect of the world, Canadians, and other peoples as well, tend to see him as causal rather than influential. That is even more true of his critics than his admirers. When I say that he is reasonably consistent, I am aware of perceived contradictions in his attitudes to nuclear weapons or economic protectionism, but his philosophy does embrace paradox. He must be a politician as well as a philosopher, and he is constrained by the will of cabinet colleagues and the Liberal caucus. His Weltanschauung of 1983 is not that of 1968, and he is probably more willing than most prime ministers (male or especially female) to admit that he has changed his mind—although not much. That his views, his beliefs, and his prejudices have considerably influenced Canadian foreign policy is undeniable. He has certainly changed the style.

My main point, however, is that Canadian policies in recent years have been determined more by what has happened in Washington or Houston, Brussels, or Tegucigalpa, than by what has been decided or sought in Ottawa. I suggest, although without total conviction, that Canadian policies would not have been very different if there had been another Liberal leader or a longer Conservative government during these years. The range of Canadian foreign policies is considerably more restricted by basic geopolitical, economic, and cultural factors than critics and opposition spokesmen assume, and the room for radical change is circumscribed. I am not hereby proclaiming, as do our archaic Marxists, that Canada is a bound victim of American imperialism. We have considerably more room for manoeuvre than most middle powers, but even superpowers have a limited range of choice in these intervulnerable times.

The reason for the undue attention to Trudeauism is probably to be found in the prime minister's stance on foreign policy when he came to office. Foreign policy was not his major preoccupation, and at least until recently it has not been. His views on the subject were highly academic, reflecting those widely held by many other professors at that time. His exposure to the contradictions of actual policy-making was limited. In fact he revealed a certain lack of understanding of what foreign policy, diplomacy, and the foreign service were all about. He was impatient of the diplomats because they had to obtrude certain inescapable facts of international life on his visions. He mistakenly thought embassies abroad were engaged simply in reporting on the world scene and could be replaced by more subscriptions to *Le Monde* or the *New York Times*. Among his many misjudgments was his insistence that Canadian policy had been too reactive. In his innocence he failed to see that, however energetic and imaginative Canada could be in the world, it could not hope to shape in advance the circumstances to which it would have to respond.

For these reasons Mr Trudeau wanted a brand new foreign policy for Canadians. We and our allies were led to expect radical change. Attracting most attention were his questioning of Canada's commitment to NATO and its failure to establish

relations with the Beijing government. He set in motion a review that culminated in the white paper, *Foreign Policy for Canadians*—in fact a collection of many-hued brochures on various aspects of foreign policy in which loyal civil servants sought to distil what they thought the prime minister would want, tempered by the advice given during the review by 'the people' (mostly politicians and professors). It was time for a thorough review of postwar policies in a changing world, and the effort was worthwhile. The white paper suffered, as it was bound to suffer, from the fact that no government can discuss its relations with other countries in complete candour, as one might in a post-graduate thesis. Beneath the inevitable circumlocutions were pockets of sound advice. It was a learning experience for the PM and all concerned; but the booklets are primarily of interest now as indicators of the philosophical base from which Mr Trudeau set out to learn about foreign policy.

To his credit he did listen and learn to a greater extent than his critics have allowed. Within a year he had accepted the argument that NATO was a good thing and that Canada should withdraw not all but only half its forces from the European theatre. He soon found out that events in faraway Africa would require him to play the mediatory role expected of Canada in the Commonwealth, whether he sought to save the world or leave it to others to patch up. He proved to be a good diplomat and decided that the Commonwealth was also a good thing.

He learned too that his favourite project of recognizing the People's Republic of China was more complex than just standing up to the Department of External Affairs and the Yankees; it would involve extended and fancy diplomatic negotiation by his best professionals before a satisfactory formula could be reached. The professionals were not opposed to recognizing Beijing, but they did not want their prime minister to fall on his face. They had to make sure at an uncertain time that Canadian recognition would not be rejected by the Chinese. The satisfactory result was attributable not only to his policy and the eventual acceptance by Beijing of a clever formula covering the Taiwan problem, but also to the coincidence of a shift of Chinese policy toward more normal international relations. Washington was less upset because of the new China policy being conceived by Henry Kissinger. Mr Trudeau deserves credit for making a commitment about China before an election and sticking to it, but recognizing Beijing was not a new policy. Canadian governments since 1949 had stated that intention but had always been stalled by some temporary obstacle. There was more in the way of a new will and new circumstances than new policy.

It is not surprising, however, that the impression was left that we were being ushered into a revolutionary change in direction. When the world proved intractable and perversely went its own course, policy did not look all that new. So there was a tendency, not so much by Mr Trudeau as by his devotees, to offer a somewhat rearranged version of what had gone on before in order to simulate contrast. Previous leaders, as mentioned earlier, were portrayed as having been too intent on international high jinks to protect the store. Those in Washington and elsewhere who had actually faced the formidable C.D. Howe in his defence of Canada's industrial program or Lester Pearson's polite but really quite resonant diplomacy were puzzled, but no matter. The conviction of a new national stubbornness was an essential element of Trudeaumania—even if it was not really a part of Trudeau's own philosophy.

A man by profound conviction anti-nationalist, concerned with broader issues than trans-border bargaining, was made to seem like a red-hot nationalist when nationalism was in the wind. Canada's so-called 'economic nationalism' of the

seventies, whether wise or unwise, was in fact attributable not to the PM's philosophy but to the threat of American 'economic nationalism' as perceived in the import surcharge and the domestic international sales corporations (DISC) legislation of 1971. It was a reactive policy. The misinterpretation has persisted, particularly in the United States, and it is little wonder that American business circles, rallied by the *Wall Street Journal,* have of late ascribed the disease they call Canadian economic nationalism to the anti-American vagaries of this exotic Canadian leader. In this confusion they are, of course, stoked by their admirers in Calgary now that anti-nationalism has become trendy. Mr Trudeau is a nationalist in the sense that he wants to strengthen the Canadian fabric. He wants Canada to be influential abroad as a model of internal internationalism, of peaceful living together. He has said many times that a failure of Canadians to maintain our kind of federation would be viewed with dismay throughout the world because most countries now have to consolidate more than one language and tribe. He emphatically rejects the kind of nationalism that is simple anti-Americanism. He is more inclined to take Canada's independence for granted than to make a false goal of it—and that is healthy. As Harald von Riekhoff has pointed out, 'Trudeau's reasoning is . . . most firmly linked to the global society paradigm and has less of the traditional state-centric orientation.'[1] The middle power is seen as the model power.

There was detectable a new will, or a new stubbornness, in certain aspects of foreign policy. Or was it renewed will? In 1945 it had been largely an alteration of will rather than a whole new philosophy of foreign policy that led Canada into its new era of world diplomacy. A new impulse was perhaps required. Lester Pearson had reluctantly agreed in the early sixties to accept nuclear weapons because we had promised our allies to do so. His stated intention was, however, to negotiate decently with NATO to get out of that role. That process was delayed and Mr Trudeau pressed it to a conclusion. Lester Pearson had hoped to transfer at least some of the forces in Europe to Canada, which, he had always insisted, was part of the NATO front. Mr Trudeau showed a stronger will to defy criticism and act, but he scaled down his original intentions regarding NATO very considerably and emphatically accepted the importance of the treaty as an element of detente, and of Canadian participation in it. Mr Pearson had always wanted to recognize Beijing but never had adequate support in cabinet or the country to act boldly. Mr Trudeau made his pledge before the election and had to go through with it.

A clearer example of this new will of the seventies, frequently cited, was the Arctic Waters Pollution Prevention Act of 1970 in which the government, responding to a chauvinistic hullabaloo over the northern voyage of the American tanker *Manhattan*, proclaimed unilaterally a 100-mile zone which the coastal state would police and defied the International Court of Justice to intervene. It was said that this bold act differed from the previous habit of Canadian governments to go for a compromise. There is some truth in this. The act may have been attributable in part to the easier confidence of a man who had been less exposed to the corrosive game of international compromise, but it was also in the spirit of traditional functional middlepowermanship. It was in fact a compromise with the domestic demand for the claiming of Arctic sovereignty *tout court*. It claimed precisely what was needed for practical purposes without grandiloquence. It asserted the right of a lesser power not only to challenge but also to push along international law when the great powers were intransigent—reminiscent somewhat of Paul Martin's defiance over new members of the United Nations in 1955. It was certainly successful, for the Americans and others were soon proclaiming

an analogous principle in the 200-mile economic zone favoured at the United Nations Conference on the Law of the Sea. It launched the Trudeau administration on its most effective and laudable international enterprise, a leading and highly constructive role in the most important contribution to world order since San Francisco. It was the culmination of efforts, which had actually begun during the Diefenbaker regime in 1958–60, to adapt the historic maritime laws to a new age. It was 'helpful fixing' of the highest order, a worthy contribution to international structure in which, furthermore, the Canadian national interest has been somewhat more than decently advanced.

The rejection of the grand enterprise by the Reagan administration was a disastrous blow, but instead of submission in Ottawa there has been firm resistance accompanied by quiet diplomacy. In the classical tradition of Canada's United Nations activities there have been persistent efforts, not by hortatory rhetoric but by unobtrusive collaboration with other middle powers, to seek out the compromises that might enable the Reaganites to return to the fold. The helpful fixers—our old associates the Scandinavians, the Australians, etc.—have been labelled, even by the Americans, as 'the good Samaritans'.[2] Plus, *peut-être, c'est la même chose*. It has not yet achieved the desired goal, but the strategy is long range. The constructive leadership and brilliant diplomacy of the Canadians in the whole evolution of the United Nations Law of the Sea has enabled survivors like me to insist that their fixing is as helpful as it was in the golden decade; it is just that now it is performed in exhausting nocturnal negotiations beyond the television cameras. They serve alike the national and the international interest, mindful of the wise admonition of an eighteenth-century essayist, William Shenstone: 'Laws are generally found to be nets of such a texture as the little creep through, the great break through, and the middle-sized are alone entangled in.'

So where does all this leave the role of a middle power in the eighties? Those who think foreign policy is simple proclaim confusion and inconsistency, and, of course, decline. Those who realize the complexities might more charitably detect a learning experience not only for the prime minister but for all the citizenry. We have been aided by an expanding crop of political scientists and historians, cutting through the mythologies and, of course, occasionally creating new ones. In accordance with the times, the debate became excessively ideological in the late sixties and early seventies. The ideologies were usually imported and hard to fit to the real facts of a middle power that had been pretty successfully defying a great capitalist power for a couple of centuries, and which had also been an imperialist power of sorts in its own right. The political scientists and historians are by no means untinged by ideology, but the more clinical approaches are bearing fruit, as we rise for snatches of air above the fog of clichés. There has been unhappily a new fog of unintelligibility that keeps the masses unconverted, but one must in this case believe in the trickle-down theory.

There is abroad in the land a new pragmatism, often mistakenly identified as conservatism because it rejects the simplicities of the left as well as those of the far right, and is too often obscured from editors and speechifiers by their dedication to partisan combat. The persistent effort to identify the major parties with certain foreign policies is perverse. The extent to which foreign policy is determined more by the changing scene than by changing ministers is shown in the fact that in 1984 the Conservatives are seeking election on the grounds that the Liberals have messed up Canada's relations with the United States. That is one of the grounds on which the Liberals ousted the Conservatives in 1963. Is it perhaps also of some significance that the leaders of all three political parties say that they are cleaving to the middle ground in the Ovidian tradition even though they are tempted to please variant audiences with immoderate pitches.

It may be counted as progress that the role of a middle power is now seen in a more discriminating way. History has provided the scholars with many more case studies than they had when our world was new. There is a groping for different terms. James Eayrs sees Canada as a 'foremost power', and John Kirton and David Dewitt call it a 'principal power'. Those terms are in themselves interesting because they challenge the more popular assumption that Canada has sunk in the international pecking order. Our power is, of course, infinitely broader and stronger than it was in the golden decade, but there is more competition. The concept of power is regarded more searchingly. The nuclear power of the super-players is increasingly seen as inapplicable, deluding them into assumptions about the extent to which they can manage the world. Distinctions are being made between military, economic, and diplomatic influence. Canada's claim to be an effective middle power in security questions was made in the forties on the strength of its major contribution to the allied forces during the war. After we had demobilized, however, we were ourselves reluctant to sustain the military strength required to maintain that kind of clout in the United Nations or NATO. The stark contradictions became apparent with the call to support the United Nations cause in Korea in the summer of 1950. When we had to match our high-flown rhetoric about the United Nations and collective security with deeds, the Canadian public realized that the barracks were bare. Our medium-rare reputation in the United Nations now depended on the skills of our diplomacy rather than the might of our arms. We were propelled for a short time into high-level company because we had been one of the three atom powers of 1945, but we soon realized that when you are not a major contributor to the problem you can't make very convincing offers to deal with it. In any case the influence we had in arms control circles rested less on our own nuclear capacity than on the diplomatic prowess and reputation of two generals turned ambassadors, McNaughton and Burns.

It was in any case Canada's economic capacity that first gave it recognition as an important actor and which has proved much more enduring. The military capacity we could offer was for peacekeeping rather than peace-enforcing, and it was important not for its quantity but for its quality, especially technological. Our particular kinds of middling power have had to be assessed in terms of their applicability. We have our wheat and our diplomacy and certain skilled and bilingual soldiers to offer, but military power in the abstract has really mattered little to our role as a middle power. It can be argued, in the abstract of course, that our influence in NATO would be increased from fair to middling if our military contribution was increased, but when one gets down to concrete decisions it is harder to see that there would be much difference. It is true, of course, that if we had no armed forces and were non-aligned, we would almost certainly get shorter shrift from all our allies. Whether that immaculate position would give us greater moral strength in world affairs is the subject of persistent debate, with the skeptics still dominant in Ottawa.

From the beginning Canada's approach to the role of a middle power was functional. We had demanded our due place in allied decisions on *matériel*, where we counted, during the war and made our first pitch for appropriate representation in postwar bodies over the United Nations Relief and Rehabilitation Administration on the grounds that we would be a major supplier. The issue was distorted by our ill-advised campaign to get a special place on the Security Council, not as a great power but as a middle power deserving attention for military merit. God knows what would have

happened had the cabinet grasped the financial and manpower implications of maintaining that heady status. After the Korean enterprise, when the Security Council tacitly abandoned its pretensions to maintain a workable system of universal collective security and devoted itself to 'helpful fixing', the irrelevance of military force to a special status in its deliberations or to sustain across-the-board middle power became obvious. It had nothing to do with the strength of Canada's voice in the International Monetary Fund, the General Agreement on Tariffs and Trade (GATT), or the International Wheat Agreement where we mattered a good deal more.

Judging our power by its applicability ad hoc should save us from delusions. It might enlighten (without entirely discouraging) those who see foreign policy largely as a simple matter of taking resonant stances on wickedness in a naughty world. We have too much debate about stances and too little about method. It is the cynics rather than the do-gooders who profit from that situation. Economic sanctions, whether against the Soviet Union or South Africa, are considered as moral gestures, but they ought to be carefully calculated as means to some definable end. Otherwise we risk the kind of reverse suffered over the pretentious sanctions against the USSR over Afghanistan. A successful foreign policy requires concentrated attention. Denouncing villains is sloppy diplomacy. In most issues the problem is not identifying the villain but coping with the predicament. Some of the time we are all more or less guilty.

When Prime Minister Trudeau initiated his peace campaign in the autumn of 1983 he was wise to furnish himself with specific proposals worked out by the professionals with long direct experience of the realities of arms control negotiations. The early successes of Canada as a middle power were attributable to our skill in producing sound ideas for the general rather than just the Canadian interest. That is the way to be listened to. In various international institutions our representatives, whether they are our scientists in the World Meteorological Organization or the United Nations Environment Programme or our engineers or our diplomats, are still being constructive without getting headlines. That is how the international infrastructure is laid. The Canadians agree or disagree with the Americans and balance the national and international interest ad hoc. What they do is sensational only in the long haul and largely ignored by the media for regrettable but understandable reasons; so the perpetual disparagers hold sway. The more dogged nationalists repeat their irrelevant slogans about Canadian foreign policy being an echo of Washington's, revealing thereby their essential anti-Canadianism and their ignorance of the substance of a modern foreign policy. The anti-nationalists on the right display, as they did in imperial days, their lack of confidence in the intelligence and capacity of their own people, by advocating simple docility to a greater power. But in real foreign policy there is such a long agenda, so many ways of succeeding or failing, and these generalizations are almost always wide of the mark. Pleading the rights of a middle power as such is one of the generalizations that will rarely get us far. Applying pressures surgically has got us a good deal. The public has to think functionally, and in this it is now getting some good leadership from a new crop of scholar analysts—at least when it can get the gist of what they are saying.

How useful is it then to talk still of the role of a middle power? The hierarchies, such as they were, are breaking down and the categorization of states shifts. Countries are what they are for all kinds of historical, geographical, and other reasons. Each is unique, and all bilateral relationships are special. Cuba or Israel often act like great powers, and South Africa is treated as one by its enemies. Aside from the somewhat anachronistic categorization

of five great powers in the Security Council, there is no fixed classification of states in the United Nations. Countries pay their dues in accordance with individual assessments based largely on economic factors. Membership in the so-called 'Western European and Others' group assures Canada of a reasonable chance for election to the Security Council or other bodies. We still have the advantage of not being tied too tightly to any bloc in multilateral diplomacy, an attribute traditionally associated with our kind of middlepowerism. Loyalty to collective NATO agreements and perceptions of basic common interests properly limit our freedom of action somewhat. So does a sense of respect for the feelings of Commonwealth or francophone associates and the large neighbour. Our greater need for an open world economy restricts our instinct for protection. There is, however, much more flexibility in our situation than is usually assumed. No country has an 'independent foreign policy'.

In the beginning Canada had regarded blocs as obstacles to sound decision-making, and we have always rejected the idea of a conformist NATO or Commonwealth voting bloc, as distinct from a consultative group. As the number of members of United Nations bodies has increased we have come to realize the importance of blocs in overcoming the anarchy of multilateral negotiation. They work best, however, if the membership shifts in accordance with the subject, as has been the case pre-eminently in the United Nations Conference on the Law of the Sea. As one of the coastal states we often opposed our major allies while paying due respect to their concern for certain strategies on which we too depend. On other issues we worked with other partners. We accept the validity of the Group of 7 as a voting and bargaining instrument while protesting against the kind of across-the-board voting on political issues that is a major cause of stalemate in the General Assembly. On the Law of the Sea we are a major power because of our fish and nickel and enormous seacoast, and we can confidently act as such. In nuclear matters our endeavours are better conceived as lateral rather than frontal, except in the matter of the proliferation of uranium or reactors. Although we could hardly expect to settle, for example, the Soviet–Chinese border dispute, in other conflicts there is quite often something we can do in good company if we retain a due sense of proportion.

Ours is not a divine mission to mediate, and the less that far-too-specific verb is used the better. It is the mission of all countries and in particular all statesmen and diplomats, with the probable exception of Albanians, to be intermediaries or to seek out compromises in the interests of peace. Our hand is strengthened by acknowledged success, but it is weakened if planting the maple leaf becomes the priority. Whether or not the role of a middle power is now an exhausted concept (or just a boring one), the fact is that the world still needs a good deal of the kind of therapy we thought of as 'middlepowermanship'.

Our idea of the role of great powers is just as much in need of review. It is doubtful whether the great, and especially the super-, powers ever had as much sway in the managing of the globe as is implied in current theory. In the early postwar years the United States had the economic and military wherewithal and the residual authority that went with it to act almost as a surrogate United Nations while some kind of world order was being established. This was done with widespread if not universal, and certainly not formal, assent from the world community. It did not 'run' the United Nations, however. It could influence the voting and often, though not always, block by rough or smooth means what it did not like. It was never able to 'control' the votes of a majority because to get support it had to make concessions. It is well not to exaggerate the erstwhile power of the United

States now that we are concerned with diluting it. The world must cope with an American administration that wants to revive the past. Aside from Mr Reagan and friends there seems to be wide agreement that the United States cannot count any more on the kind of authority it once had. By the same token the United States cannot be counted upon for that kind of management or for the residual resources. It was never the ideal arrangement, but what is now to be feared is that there will be no management at all.

The obvious alternative to unilateralism is multilateralism, but the latter is, as the painful lessons of over 40 years make clear, extraordinarily difficult to achieve. Hence the fears that beset us all as a familiar framework of power crumbles. In inveighing against the abuses of power, great, middle, or small, we tend to forget the responsibility that goes with each gradation of power. The transition from superpower dominance to a healthier distribution is not going to be accomplished simply by demanding that the supers surrender. What, if anything, the Russians are doing about it in their bloc heaven only knows. The Americans, on our side, tend too simply to see this as letting their allies supply more funds and troops while they go on making the decisions as demanded by their system of government. The rest of us want first of all to share in the decision-making but have to struggle with the paradoxes between something like cantonal democracy and the veto. Middle powers and the lesser greats have to show leadership in accepting wider responsibilities even when that means risking American displeasure. That kind of foreign policy requires positive thinking. There is everything to be said for persuading the superpowers and their proxies to withdraw from Central America, the Middle East, and all of Africa, but that is only a beginning. Something still must be done about the endemic problems of El Salvador, Lebanon, Afghanistan, Grenada, and Chad. We have been arguing that these problems may be ascribed to domestic causes rather than to foreign conspiracies and that means they will not be solved simply by American or Soviet or Cuban withdrawal. They threaten the security of Canadians or New Zealanders as much as they do that of Texans or Ukrainians.

/ If there is still a point in Canadians seeing ourselves as a middle power in the eighties, it may be to discipline ourselves. When we found a mission as intermediary mediums we began to get some grip on our Canadian capabilities. When a definition that was analytical and descriptive came to be seen as prescriptive we got a little frenetic. However we still need guidelines to cling to and knowing one's strength remains a sound principle. If we are now more discriminating and calculating in our estimates of our own as well as others' powers, so much the better. Skepticism about spreading our good offices too wide may have induced a sense of proportion about the number of rescue missions, crusades, or moral interventions a country of 25 million can conduct at one time. We have to contend with the persistent feeling of other countries that we are smug, self-righteous, and officious. Our moral majority may want the government to pass judgment on every misbehaviour in the world, and no doubt they will feel better if we do so, but it is the surest way to undermine the beneficent role of a middle power. It is furthermore a kind of cop-out by some well-intentioned people whose attention might better be directed to the baffling contradictions we face over policies that hit closer to home. If one were to judge from questions in the House of Commons one might conclude that Canadian foreign policy was largely a matter of deciding what to do about El Salvador and South Africa.

The middle power that is a major power in the world economy is caught in dilemmas not unlike those of a major military power, and they require hard thinking. It is not only a question of deliberately using power. There is also the inescapable question of withholding it. Canada cannot help, for example, being a food power of decisive proportions and a producer of a wide array of mineral resources. It is not difficult to reject as immoral the idea of using food as a weapon to gain political ends, but if food is so scarce that it has to be rationed, on what bases do we make it available and to whom? That is the kind of issue we face in a rudimentary way with our none-too-plentiful energy supplies in the International Energy Agency. How much greater our problems will be if, with our broad territory and small population, we have to feed the new billions of Asians and Latin Americans. The experience of economic sanctions over Rhodesia and Afghanistan has led us to the too simple conclusion that they don't work and that's that. But the concept of sanctions is inseparable from the trading and aiding that are recognized as high priorities of Canadian foreign policy. We will grapple with these issues more safely in the middle of international institutions. The United Nations system remains of central importance because we of all countries need international disciplines, but where our vote really matters now is not in the Assembly or Security Council but in GATT or the International Monetary Fund or the World Bank, which are at least as important parts of the United Nations as is the General Assembly. Those are the places where, for example, we register our differences with the United States over Nicaragua or Grenada in votes on loans that count. Our positions on the increase of financing for the Fund or the International Development Association are not decisive but they can be marginally so.

The distinguished British scholar, Denis Brogan, told Canadians 30 years ago, 'The very fact that Canada is now one of the treasure houses of the world makes the naive isolationship of the inter-war years . . . impossible. A uranium producing country cannot be neutral.'[3] That means not privilege but responsibility for a middle power. One thing that has changed is that the role of a middle power costs more, not just financially but politically. Helpful fixing in the postwar period impinged much less on the priorities of the electorate. When the big international issues now are resources and coastal waters, defence spending, Asian imports, and non-tariff barriers—the things on which our future depends—the ridings will be less quiescent. Our idea of foreign policy has been stretched, and it is no longer true to say that it is not a major issue in elections. Public awareness of the long-range view for a middle power is more essential than ever.

It was in the setting of the wide international community that Canada first saw itself as a 'middle' power. Like all other countries Canada was adapting itself to the shift of power from Europe to the United States. There was never a question, as legend has it, of a conscious decision to transfer allegiance from the British to the American protector. Canadian governments worked hard to restore the triangular balance in which we had felt comfortable, to bring Europe and America together in alliance, and to create the international institutions in which we could be ourselves. It was a giant step out of the colonial mentality. Although American power was more nearly omnipotent then than it is now, we had not become so much obsessed by it. Increasingly one feels that Canadians see their foreign policy only in the context of American foreign policy. The fact that it would be seen in better perspective if we compared it with those of other countries our size, with our European allies, with Australia, or with Mexico, is ignored in the single-minded concentration on what Reagan or Shultz, Mrs Kirkpatrick or Dan Rather, are up to. It is not a matter of being pro- or anti-American; the obsession is common to both.

If the Americans have come to dominate our foreign policy, it is not, as nationalists have thought, by arm-twisting and threatening sanctions. We have let the American media capture us for their debate. The danger is not that we support their policies; we associate ourselves just as often with the critics. It is rather that our minds are on what the United States is or should be doing, not how we, with our very different kind of role to play in the world, should be acting. It is irresponsible. Statements by politicians and others often imply that our foreign policy consists simply of approving or disapproving of American actions. When we criticize the Russians for shooting down airliners or take action against them over Afghanistan, this is persistently described as supporting or not supporting the Americans, as if we were helping them out in their private struggle with the Russians and not pursuing our own quarrel with aggressors in the broad company of the United Nations and NATO. By treating NATO as a United States–dominated organization, we and the Europeans have only helped to make it so and dimmed in the process the moral strength of the alliance. Surely the lesson of Canadian experience of middlepowermanship is that we can be a stronger world citizen and a stronger ally if we act in accordance with our own wisdom. The colonial tradition dies hard. It was reported (incorrectly, I hope) that one of our major political parties had been unable to reach a position over Grenada because it did not know whether to follow Mr Reagan or Mrs Thatcher. That is a kind of 'middle' policy that I thought we had long since abandoned. As Norman Snider wrote recently in the *Globe and Mail*, 'Canadians would be better advised to suppress all those neo-colonial urges to jump up and salute at the most powerful English-speaking nation around and continue to do their own thinking.'[4]

It is unfortunate that the excesses of the nationalists of a few years ago helped to discredit the kind of healthy, self-respecting nationalism that Canada needs to combat the cringing anti-nationalism, the idolatry of foreign gods, from which we suffer at present. Surely there is a middle way here that is more sensible and safer and in our own best tradition. Is it so demeaning in a churning world to maintain our peculiar reputation for good sense, moderation, a will to see all sides of a question, and an instinct for compromise? Must we call that mediocrity?

Key Terms

Functionalism

Foreign Policy

Helpful Fixer

Middle Power

Notes

1. 'The Impact of Prime Minister Trudeau on Foreign Policy', *International Journal* 33, 2 (Spring 1978): 268.
2. Leigh S. Ratiner, 'The Law of the Sea: A Crossroads for American Foreign Policy', *Foreign Affairs* 60 (Summer 1982): 1015.
3. 'An Outsider Looking In', Canada's Tomorrow Conference, Quebec City, 13–14 November 1953.
4. 'Rethinking our Allegiance', *Globe and Mail*, 3 December 1983, L9.

UPDATE

MULTILATERALISM RECONSIDERED

Tom Keating
January 2010

'One senses among Canadians that support for the UN and other multilateral institutions remains strong in the abstract, but that it is shallower than it used to be in real terms.'[1]

Introduction

The Canadian government's involvement in and commitment to multilateralism is under review. The volume and frequency of critical commentaries about international institutions and the value of multilateral diplomacy has increased noticeably. So too have disparaging comments about the value of multilateralism for the pursuit of Canadian foreign policy objectives. In one sense this is perhaps unsurprising as there are many problems with international institutions, and multilateral diplomacy frequently deviates towards acceptance of some form of least offensive solution. It is also more than obvious that since the 1990s successive Canadian governments have decided that investment in foreign policy, let alone multilateral institutions and practices, has not been a high priority. While the declining commitment has been developing for many years, the Harper government has taken particular pride in acknowledging and applauding these trends and been more forthright in turning away from multilateral commitments and rejecting multilateralism as 'a weak nation strategy'. In its place one hears calls for a more robust (read: military) foreign policy with closer alignment with the United States. Both the diagnosis and the prescription bear closer scrutiny. John Holmes was wise to remind us that '(i)t is obviously foolish to argue stubbornly that multilateralism is always best'.[2] We should, however, also be careful of abandoning a good idea. Multilateralism was never going to be the answer to the world's problems, but in a world of more than 190 states, thousands of private corporations, and countless transnational non-governmental organizations, some means of bringing them together under some commonly recognized and accepted principles seems worth the effort.

The challenge to multilateralism has been brewing for some time. The American government's decision to abandon efforts for a compromise at the United Nations (UN) in the Spring of 2003 and to invade Iraq with a 'coalition of the willing', set off, yet again, commentaries on the condition of the UN, on the idea and practice of multilateralism, and subsequently on the value of both as cornerstones of Canadian foreign policy. Multilateralism has been maligned in Canada and more extensively in the wider international community.[3] Within Canada, multilateralism has been criticized for failing to support Canadian interests and for a preoccupation with form over substance. The Canadian government has also been criticized during the past 10 to 15 years for failing to support its rhetorical commitment to multilateralism with tangible resources.[4]

Despite this, the Canadian government continues to provide some support for multilateralism and for the principal institutional forum for multilateralism, the UN. Support for a more inclusive form of multilateralism has been evident in recent meetings of the International Monetary Fund (IMF) where it has been reported that Canadians have a 'newfound activism' and 'are fronting for the G-20'. (McKenna, 2006:B3) There is also support for multilateralism from some quarters. Glen Hodgson, chief economist at the Conference Board of Canada and a former chief economist in both the Department of Finance and the IMF, has said, 'Canada is an advocate of multilateralism not because we are Boy Scouts, but because it serves our national interests.' (*National Post*, 2002:A17) A *Globe and Mail* editorial states that 'There is an advantage in being the world's clubbiest country, for it allows us to act as a moderator and bridge among nations. But membership has its responsibilities.' (Toronto *Globe and Mail*, 1994:A28) Indeed, for *Globe and Mail* columnist, Jeffery Simpson, Canada's continued attachment to multilateralism is self-evident: 'Canada's instincts, by contrast, are those of a modest-sized international player. They nudge Canada toward solving world problems through international laws, diplomacy, treaties and multilateralism. Canada doesn't have any power, military or otherwise, so how else would it see the world?' (Simpson, 2003:A21)

In the late summer of 2005, the Canadian government committed its unwavering support to the United Nations and the extensive reform measures proposed by UN Secretary General Kofi Annan. More specifically, the government strongly promoted the doctrine of Responsibility to Protect and a UN Peacebuilding Commission. Both of these proposals would legitimate extensive UN involvement in the domestic affairs of member governments. As such they were representative of what then Prime Minister Paul Martin referred to as the 'new multilateralism' in his foreword to Canada's 2005 foreign policy statement. 'We seek nothing less than a new multilateralism, in which the real and pressing needs of people are addressed. Canada has always contributed to and benefited from multilateralism. We believe strongly in finding cooperative solutions. But we also recognize that we must be ready to change with the times and lead where we can, especially where multilateral institutions are acting too slowly or are not up to the task.'[5] Support is also apparent in the former prime minister's strong support for the G20 and an L20. This can be seen in the decision to merge the G8 and the G20 in June 2010 when Canada will be joined by South Korea in co-hosting the first formal G20 summit. The 'new multilateralism' identified by Prime Minister Martin is not completely new, as there have been comparable murmurings within Canadian policy circles since the early 1990s. As discussed by the prime minister, the 'new multilateralism' suggests both a more interventionist set of international institutions as well as the possibility of moving beyond these institutions to intervene, if and when, the institutions fail to act. From this vantage point, the 'new multilateralism' challenges both past practice on the part of foreign policy-makers in Canada and long-standing principles of international order.

Canadian support for a multilateralist foreign policy can be traced back many years. Most significantly, it emerged as a cornerstone of Canadian foreign policy during and in the immediate aftermath of the Second World War. At the time multilateralism was the lesser evil of the likely bilateral options, under the colonial wing of a fading British Empire or as part of the emergent American superpower's sphere of influence. In certain respects, the latter was unavoidable, but multilateral institutions were expected to help restrain the embrace.

Multilateralism was, however, more than just a way of securing a degree of Canadian independence in a world dominated by more powerful players. It was also favoured as a desirable way of organizing international politics, and was an approach that not only allowed a space for lesser powers to have some input, but also sought to insure that political principles and practices at the international level would be developed in a manner that would support peace, order, and good governance while protecting the sovereignty and interests of lesser powers. Multilateralism was, as a result, viewed as a foreign policy orientation that would acknowledge and support the sovereign equality of member states, guaranteeing them both a voice (commensurate with some notion of contribution) and protection from absorption by more powerful states. The multilateral system was in this respect as much a realist approach as it was an idealist one.

Canadian support for multilateralism rested on several important assumptions. Perhaps foremost among these was an assumption that multilateralism was not only compatible with Canadian sovereignty and independence, but would actually reinforce these, pressed as they were by the power and proximity of the United States. It is misleading to argue, as some have done, that successive governments' support for multilateralism necessarily entailed an abnegation of interests as if this was some sort of altruistic gesture on the part of the Canadian government for the good of the international community. Indeed, it was the ability of multilateral initiatives and processes to serve Canadian interests in such an effective manner that enabled multilateralism to achieve such prominence in the discourse and practice of Canadian foreign policy.

On the other hand, it is wrong to conclude that the support for multilateralism has been nothing more than the blind pursuit of narrowly defined national interests under a façade of community-spiritedness. It is apparent that over time and across issues that Canada's multi-lateralist foreign policy has also made a constructive contribution to world order. One of the principal strengths of multilateralism, both as a foreign policy orientation and as a guide for managing world order, is its ability to promote the involvement of a multiplicity of players in a process that provides good opportunities for interests to be pursued and secured in a manner that is widely accepted as legitimate by the participating states.

As a result, countries such as Canada that have such extensive multilateral connections and commitments have, in the words of John Holmes, 'a greater responsibility for making the system work'. Over the past five decades Canadian foreign policy has often been dedicated to doing just that. Starting from the recognition that the country's interests required a stable international system in which Canadians had both opportunities and the necessary capabilities to inject their own views, policy-makers favoured institutions that would guarantee Canada a voice. The support of successive Canadian governments for an institutionalized world order based on principles such as state sovereignty, liberal trading practices, and regional security arrangements reflects what Hedley Bull once described as a Grotian view of the world.[6] This is a view that privileges order above other values, in part because order served Canadian interests, but also because order allowed for the pursuit of more substantive goals. These efforts may in part be seen as a sacrifice of principle and a commitment to process over end results. Yet in an environment where the failure of process can also generate a failure to achieve the desired results, a concern for process was not inappropriate.

This approach was based on a belief that the process was not independent of the outcome in two critically important ways. First, that the process of global governance was instrumental in shaping the outcome and certain processes would tend to favour outcomes more likely to meet Canadian objectives than would others. Second, that the process itself was a critically important part of global politics and to encourage particular processes encouraged a particular form of global politics. It was not so much a matter of form replacing substance as much as a view that form *was* substance. What has been generally true of Canadian foreign policy is perhaps indicative of the place of lesser powers in an anarchic system dominated by great powers. As Holmes wrote, 'foreign policies of middle powers are inevitably directed not only at the substance of an issue but also at the means by which they can affect the resolution of that issue. The machinery of world politics is their special concern.'[7] Since the early 1940s Canadian officials have devoted a considerable amount of skill and effort to keeping the multilateral machinery working.

For a country of Canada's stature, size, and demography, multilateralism continues to make good sense. It seems at some level obvious that the Canadian government should seek out and support a multilateral framework of international institutions and rules that would provide a degree of order in an otherwise anarchic system, especially an order that is so much in accord with Canadian values and interests. Yet what at one level seems so obvious becomes less clear as one considers both the changing character of that multilateral framework and the

rules, attitudes, and practices of the country's closest and most important foreign policy partner, the United States.

One of the most significant developments affecting multilateralism has been the clear and
at times explicitly vehement opposition to multilateral processes and agreements displayed on
occasion by the US government. This is not to deny the fact that the US government has been
under some pressure (both at home and abroad) to try, or to be seen to be trying, to seek
multilateral support for its policy preferences and to seek to bring multilateral agreements in
line with American interests. One of the distinguishing features of the immediate post–Second
World War environment was the strong US government support given to international institutions. This support has declined dramatically. Part of the explanation for this lies in the
unique circumstances that shaped American foreign policy in the 1940s. Other reasons can be
found in changing political coalitions in the United States, shifting perceptions and realities
of American power, and the growth of ever more intrusive international institutions. The
effect has been to make the US government at times skeptical of the value of international
institutions and less committed to using them or making them more effective. While George
W. Bush's administration was particularly critical of these institutions, it is misleading to see
this as simply a reflection of the whims of those presently in power in Washington, for the
attitudes are more widespread and deeply seeded in the United States.

The tensions in American foreign policy create a particular difficulty for Canada. For
many years, working in support of multilateral institutions was fully consistent with maintaining good relations with the United States. Recently, however, Canadian and American
interests have frequently clashed in international institutions over issues such as environmental agreements, the International Criminal Court, and the UN's role in Iraq. International
institutions need the support of dominant powers such as the United States, and countries
such as Canada need institutions that are able to exert some influence on the United States.
This was one of the primary motivations of Canadian foreign policy in the 1940s and there is
no compelling evidence to suggest that this motivation should be any different today, though
the task itself may require a different strategy. In the short term, gaining American support
will likely mean changing multilateral institutions more than changing American foreign
policy. It will mean ensuring that multilateral institutions are not used to isolate the United
States and that sincere and constructive efforts are made to reconcile American interests with
the work of these institutions.

American attitudes are, however, subject to change depending on the way the political
winds are blowing. The election of Barack Obama and the appointment of Susan Rice as US
ambassador to the UN is a marked contrast from George W. Bush and John Bolton. In one of
her first statements, Rice stated, 'If ever there were a time for effective multilateral cooperation
in pursuit of US interests and a shared future of greater peace and prosperity, it is now.'[8]
Whether this marks a full turn in US foreign policy must await the test of time.

So too do political winds change in Canada. For as the American government seems to be
moving back to a more multilateralist approach, some have noted a move away from support
for multilateralism on the part of Canadian officials. 'A headlong retreat is now underway

from multilateralism and from what could be called a missionary or idealistic foreign policy.'[9] This may seem somewhat exaggerated, but there have been indications of shifting priorities beyond those already mentioned. Among these is an inclination to turn away from the UN when it does not serve immediate objectives as occurred at the time of the landmines treaty and the NATO-led war against Serbia. John McDougall for one has suggested that the more recent Canadian military deployments to places such as Kosovo and Afghanistan "have to be regarded as departures from the classic peacekeeping model . . . and service in them is better regarded as an extension of membership in NATO and Canada's allegiance to the US than as an expression of Canada's traditional UN peacekeeping commitment'. He further states that these 'commitments seem to be more about shoring up its partnership with the US than keeping faith with its longstanding tradition of international peacekeeping.'[10]

Other developments in the global arena and in the conduct of Canadian foreign policy have had an effect on the practice of multilateralism and the responsibilities of international institutions. There has been a substantial increase in the number of multilateral agreements and institutions, and in jurisdictional reach. But these developments are not restricted to trade and are not simply a function of the process of economic globalization. There has also been a proliferation of agreements in other areas such as the environment that act as a constraint on national policies as they seek to impose globally determined standards and practices. It has been estimated that the number of international treaties has more than tripled since the early 1970s and that the number of institutions has increased by two-thirds since 1985. This development poses strains for many governments, but especially for a committed participant such as Canada, whose government has sought to maintain the country's internationalist credentials, not only by signing on to these agreements but by encouraging many of them. Yet as these agreements encroach more directly on domestic affairs, support becomes exceedingly difficult. Nowhere is this better illustrated than in the Canadian government's response to the Kyoto Protocol. After years of failing to make any serious effort to meet its obligations under a series of Liberal governments, the Harper government walked away from the protocol. It was a decision that led some to cite Canada as one the world's major threats to international law.[11]

The greater caution, if not outright opposition, to multilateral agreements is, in part, a reflection of the changed character of global politics and the increased demands for more substantive forms of governance at the regional and international levels. These developments are best reflected in the expanding agendas of international trade and financial institutions. They also reflect a more substantive view of the global order, one that goes beyond the procedural norms of earlier periods and demands more substantive policy changes by states in areas that previously fell within their domestic jurisdictions.

Finally, they reflect an attempt on the part of states to address significant social and economic problems with international level agreements. An examination of the sources of these developments lies beyond the scope of this discussion paper, though it is worth noting that while some lie beyond the Canadian government's control, others have been supported or encouraged by the government. Additionally, some fall directly within the control of the government and result from explicit government policies. On their own, and especially in combination, these developments have created a new set of circumstances that affect the role of multilateral processes and institutions in global politics and in the conduct of Canadian foreign policy, making it at the same time more difficult both to manage and to support.

There has been a tendency for much of multilateral activity in recent years to challenge the sovereignty and capacity of states as the principal political agents. One of the most important areas of activity for Canadian foreign policy-makers has been in advancing a rules-based system governing relations among states. Over time these rules have evolved from procedural rules into more substantive ones that challenge the sovereignty and capacity of states as they seek to regulate relations within states, between governments and their citizens. In addition, under emerging practices of global governance, international and regional institutions are assuming increased responsibility for the security and welfare of individuals in various parts of the world. This alters the context in which states must operate.

These practices are also expanding the responsibility of the institutions through which global governance is being conducted. It often appears, however, that the aspirations of these institutions are not in line with the political will and the concomitant resource contributions of member governments. To date, both international governmental organizations (IGOs) and NGOs have repeatedly demonstrated that they lack the capacity to provide welfare and security to people in need. Not only do they lack the necessary resources to make a difference but they also often lack the interest, the political will, the legitimacy, and the long-term commitment. Thus, what is problematic, in much of the advocacy and activity surrounding new approaches to global governance, is the tendency to assume that institutions do indeed possess the capacity and will to act. Yet the capacity of institutions is, at best, a limited one, influenced by competing interests and the commitment of supporters. Even the best IGOs and NGOs encounter donor fatigue and a flagging of volunteer spirit. To raise expectations beyond what one is prepared or able to deliver might create a 'false sense of security' and thereby prevent the pursuit or acceptance of a less severe alternative. It might also severely undermine the long-term support not only for specific institutions, but also for the very process of multilateralism. This is certainly evident from a Canadian perspective as falling levels of support correspond to increased demands for action and increased efforts on the part of institutions to take on more responsibilities.

As one embarks on a campaign for global governance one must be sensitive to the limits of both ends and means. For a country such as Canada that has relied extensively on multilateralism and international institutions, these developments carry special significance. Perhaps foremost among these factors is the importance of considering the role that states are to play in securing global order. Governance issues are arguably among the most important facing the international community. They also remain critically important at the national level. In the absence of effective governance at the global level and given the pressing demands that encumber states as a result of globalization, emergent international norms, transnational threats, and democratic pressures from within, states around the globe are facing significant challenges to their sovereignty.

While the new multilateralism in Canadian foreign policy has done much to further these trends, there are also indications that the government recognizes the necessity of securing a broader base of support for multilateral cooperation and the institutions that sustain it. For example, Prime Minister Martin promoted the idea of a League of Twenty (L20), based on the Group of 20 (G20) Finance Ministers, that includes states such as China, India, Brazil, and Indonesia, among others. The L20 proposal reflected a concern for the lack of representation in the Group of 8 (G8) and other international financial institutions. The 'breadth of membership is crucial', Martin stated, 'for we have learned a fundamental truth about policies to promote development: they will work only if the developing countries and emerging markets help shape them, because inclusiveness lies at the heart of legitimacy and effectiveness.'[12] The same can be said of other arenas of global governance. For a country such as Canada, that sees value in the process as well as the content of multilateralism, it will be important to keep this in mind.

Key Terms

Multilateralism
New Multilateralism

Notes

1. David Malone, 'UN Reform, A Sisyphean Task,' in Cooper and Rowlands, eds., *Canada Among Nations*, 2006, p.100.
2. John Holmes, *No Other Way: Canada and International Security Institutions* (Toronto: Centre for International Studies, University of Toronto, 1987).
3. See for example, Frank Harvey 'Addicted to Security: Globalized Terrorism and the Inevitability of American Unilateralism', *International Journal* 59, 1 (Winter 2003–4): 27; Michael Hart, *From Pride to Influence: Towards a New Canadian Foreign Policy* (Vancouver: UBC Press, 2008).
4. See for example, Michael Ignatieff, 'Canada in the Age of Terror: Multilateralism Meets a Moment of Truth', *Policy Options*, February 2003, 14–18.
5. Rt Hon. Paul Martin, Prime Minister of Canada, May 2005.
6. Hedley Bull, *The Anarchical Society* (Toronto: Macmillan, 1977).
7. John Holmes, *The Better Part of Valour* (Toronto: McClelland and Stewart, 1970), viii.
8. Stephen Kaufman, 'United States "Ready to Lead Once More" at United Nations', August 14, 2009. Retrieved January 3, 2010, from www.america.gov/st/peacesec-english/2009/August/20090814134131esnamfuak0.685 1007.html.
9. Richard Gwyn, 'Headlong Retreat is Now Underway from Multilateralism', *Guelph Mercury*, October 17, 2006, A9.
10. John McDougall, *Drifting Together: The Political Economy of Canada–US Integration* (Toronto: Broadview, 2006).
11. George Monbiot, 'Real Villain is Not the US,' *Manchester Guardian Weekly*, November 12, 2009, 18–19.
12. Paul Martin, 'Notes for an Address by the Honourable Paul Martin to the Royal Institute of International Affairs', London, 24 January 2001 (Ottawa: Department of Finance Canada, 2001). Available at www.fin.gc.ca/news01/01-009e. html.

4

THREE THEORETICAL PERSPECTIVES

David B. Dewitt and John J. Kirton

Despite their differences over themes, interpretations, and values, scholars of Canadian foreign policy share an implicit interest in a single set of fundamental questions about Canada's behaviour in international affairs. These questions have been developed through public debate concerning Canada's role abroad.

The first debate centred on whether Canada should use its new formal freedom from the United Kingdom, attained in the 1931 Statute of Westminster, to sustain the League of Nations, enhance Canada's position as a North American nation, or support Britain in maintaining a broader global balance of power.[1] Although support for this last alternative was reflected in Prime Minister W.L. Mackenzie King's September 1939 decision to enter the Second World War and in Canada's substantial contribution to the Allied cause, the end of the war saw a new debate between those preferring a retreat to quasi-isolationism and those urging active international participation commensurate with Canada's new material strength.[2] The victory of the latter group gave Canada two decades under prime ministers Louis St Laurent, John Diefenbaker, and Lester Pearson during which the precepts of liberal internationalism evolved. The 1968 election of Prime Minister Pierre Trudeau's Liberal government began a new debate about whether Canada was reverting to the isolationist and continental instincts of the interwar era, modifying its internationalist traditions to reflect new circumstances, or defining a new approach to Canadian behaviour abroad.[3]

Out of this debate has emerged the need for a more explicit, rigorous, and comprehensive analytical framework for the study of Canadian foreign policy. By drawing upon the literature of Canadian foreign policy, general foreign policy analysis, and international relations, it is possible to identify the most fundamental questions about Canada's international behaviour.[4] Based on the thesis that a country's external activities and international presence are related to its size and capabilities—population, resources, and specialized skills and knowledge—a central challenge for students of international affairs and foreign policy has been to determine the relationship between these attributes and international behaviour. In the Canadian context, a postwar issue has been whether Canada's attributes are sufficient to propel it from its former status as a minor actor through small- and middle-power ranking to a more prominent place in the community of nation-states. In the shadow first of the United Kingdom and more recently of the United States, Canada has been perceived as a regional power without a region, and recognized as a middle-range partner in the Western coalition. One set of questions relating to this issue concerns Canada's historic position, or *rank*, in the hierarchy of the international system; the next questions provide the explanatory focus for Canada's *activity*, *association*, and *approach to world order*, examining the relative significance of *external*, *societal*, and *governmental* determinants.

THE CENTRAL QUESTIONS OF FOREIGN POLICY ANALYSIS

INTERNATIONAL PRESENCE
Rank

Virtually all students of foreign policy begin their explorations with a perception of a state's historical experience. Formulated into models that may try to account for the past, these evolutionary myths are partly the inherited results of exposure to particular historical traditions, partly ideological or philosophic orientations conditioning one's interpretations of evidence, and partly crude summations of easily measurable attributes. Yet in most cases, they are grounded in an underlying conception of whether the state's capacity to pursue its national interests—most basically, self-help

in a competitive international system—is being diminished, maintained, or expanded over time.[5]

What is Canada's place in the international system relative to that of other states? The concern with defining Canada's position was heightened by its leading international stature at the end of Second World War, when a newly emerging world order was being shaped out of the ruins of global conflict. Canada's ability to influence these efforts was seen as being linked directly to its ascribed status. In the study of international relations, this focus on a state's rank has been sustained by mounting evidence of the salience of national capabilities in determining foreign policy behaviour.[6]

The question of rank includes the state's relative capability, as measured by a standard set of objective attributes such as population size and distribution, indigenous fuel supplies, and size of standing armed forces. It is also concerned with the position that it ascribes to itself and that it asserts internationally, and with the acknowledged status ascribed to it by other international actors.[7] It includes the consistency of these elements across varying international systemic configurations, geographic regions, substantive issue areas, and critical power resources.[8] And it is based on the state's maintenance of minimum levels of performance in meeting the basic requisites of statehood—notably security, sovereignty, and legitimacy.[9]

INTERNATIONAL BEHAVIOUR
Activity

The importance of a state's international ranking—both ascribed and achieved—is based upon the hypothesized relationship between rank and externally oriented behaviour.[10] The primary aspect of a state's behaviour is the activity it directs toward other actors in the international realm.

Concern here centres on the *degree* of a state's activity, or the simple volume of interaction it has with its 'targets' abroad; the *variety* of this activity, or the similarity across time, issues, and targets in the volume and intensity of action; and the *diffusion* of this activity among targets abroad.[11]

Association

Association is the intersection of one state's external activities with those of another, and includes the question of *initiative*—the extent to which the state maintains its membership in an existing group, participates in forming a new or altered group, or acts without direct reference to any group. It embraces a country's *commitment*—the time, resources, and effort expended to produce similarity between the country's own position and the group position. And it contains the element of *focus*, or the extent to which the central target of the country's activity lies within or outside existing or emerging groups.[12] Characterized by degrees of conflict and cooperation, association can be measured by the extent to which a country's activity is similar in time, content, and target to that of other states.

Approach to world order

Also relevant is a state's attempt to foster a global order in which relationships are organized into regimes and institutions that promote a particular distribution of political power and economic resources.[13] The first aspect is the *degree* to which the state considers that order should be registered in a comprehensive, well developed, interrelated, and autonomous network of international organization and law. A subsequent aspect is that of *scope*, that is, the extent to which a state seeks to ensure that international order, at all levels of institutionalization, has the full, active participation of all members of the state system, and embraces a

broad range of subjects. A third aspect is *transformation,* the extent to which a state supports moderate specific alternatives or more permanent alterations in the structure of existing and emerging regimes and organizations.

DETERMINANTS OF INTERNATIONAL BEHAVIOUR

External determinants

To explain a country's particular pattern of activity, association, and quest for order, most scholars focus on the stimuli that a country receives from states and organizations abroad, whether or not these are directed at it. Their initial interest centres on the *relative salience* of this external environment—the extent of variation in a state's foreign policy behaviour caused by these states and organizations as compared to the variations explained by forces at home.[14] A further concern is the *scope* of relevant external determinants—the number and range of states and international organizations with a direct impact on a state's foreign policy behaviour. A third issue deals with a state's *sensitivity* to external stimuli—the immediacy, directness, and specificity with which external events and conditions affect the decisions of leaders and the behaviour they authorize.[15] Finally, interest centres on *actor relevance*—the identity of those particular major powers, groupings of middle and smaller powers, and leading international organizations that have the most salient, wide-ranging, and immediate impact on a state's foreign policy behaviour.

Societal determinants

A similar set of questions arises in regard to domestic influences on a state's international behaviour.[16] The *relative salience* of domestic organizations is of fundamental concern, as is the issue of the *scope* of societal actors—the extent of differentiated, specialized, and autonomous non-governmental institutions that have a direct impact on foreign policy behaviour.[17] Further aspects are the *sensitivity* of the government to these organizations and the *relevance* of particular actors, notably parliament, political parties, interest groups, labour, media, business communities, and provincial governments. Also of importance is the country's profile of population, resources, and technology, and the impact of these critical factors on the structure and activity of societal actors.

Governmental determinants

The final set of questions addresses the influence of the executive branch of a state's central government on foreign policy-making and ensuing behaviour.[18] The central questions remain the relative overall *salience* of governmental factors, the *scope* of institutional differentiation and autonomy, the state's *sensitivity* to its foreign policy process, and the *relevance* of specific governmental actors.[19] Attention is directed at the relevance of the prime minister and his or her closest associates, the government's foreign office, and especially the domestically oriented departments and agencies responsible for critical changes in the state's pattern of growth in population, resources, and technology.[20] The complexity of the modern state requires that attention be given to the central foreign policy's coordinative structures and processes in attempts to define autonomously and implement overarching conceptions of the national interest.[21]

Table 4.1 provides a schematic overview of the seven basic foreign policy questions and the predictions of each of the three theoretical perspectives.

Table 4.1 Theoretical perspectives on Canadian foreign policy: Predictions based on ideal types

Foreign Policy Questions	Liberal Internationalism	Peripheral Dependence	Complex Neo-realism
1. Rank	middle power	small, penetrated power	principal power
2. Activity			
Degree	active participation	low interaction	global involvement
Variety	responsible participation	undifferentiated interactive	interest-based involvement
Diffusion	multiple participation	imperial-focused interaction	autonomous bilateral involvement
3. Association			
Initiative	combination	adherence	unilateralism
Commitment	consensus	acquiescence	divergence
Focus	constraint	support	diversification
4. Approach to World Order			
Degree	moderate institutionalization	existing institutionalization	revised institutionalization
Scope	multilateralization	hegemony and marginal universalism	concert
Transformation	reformation	marginal redistribution	modification

Table 4.1 *continued*

Foreign Policy Questions	Liberal Internationalism	Peripheral Dependence	Complex Neo-realism
5. External Determinants			
Relative Salience	moderate	high	low
Scope	moderate	low	high
Sensitivity	moderate	low	high
Actor Relevance			
United Kingdom	moderate	high	low
United States	moderate	high	low
USSR	moderate	low	high
China	moderate	low	high
Large European States and Japan	moderate	low	high
Non-European Middle Powers	high	low	moderate
Small European States	high	low	moderate
Other Small States	high	low	moderate
NATO	moderate	low	high
United Nations	high	low	moderate
6. Societal Determinants			
Relative Salience	moderate	low	high
Scope			
Institutional Differentiation	moderate	low	high
Institutional Autonomy	moderate	low	high
Sensitivity	moderate	low	high
Actor Relevance			
Parliament	high	low	moderate
Parties	high	low	moderate
Associational Interest Groups	moderate	low	high
Labour	moderate	low	high
Media	low	moderate	high
Business Community	low	moderate	high
Provincial Governments	low	high	moderate
Critical Capabilities	resources and technology	resources	population, resources, and technology
7. Governmental Determinants			
Relative Salience	moderate	low	high
Scope			
Institutional Differentiation	moderate	low	high
Institutional Autonomy	moderate	low	high

Table 4.1 *continued*

Foreign Policy Questions	Liberal Internationalism	Peripheral Dependence	Complex Neo-realism
Sensitivity	moderate	low	high
Actor Relevance			
Prime Ministerial Group	moderate	low	high
Department of External Affairs	high	low	moderate
Foreign Service Departments	low	moderate	high
Other Domestic Departments	low	moderate	high
Agencies and Crown Corporations	low	moderate	high
Central Foreign Policy			
Co-ordinative Structures	moderate	low	high

THE COMPLEX NEO-REALIST PERSPECTIVE

Preoccupied with the powerful challenge that peripheral dependence presents to liberal internationalism, students of Canadian foreign policy have devoted relatively little attention to the possible relevance of a third interpretive perspective, one derived from the realist theory that has dominated the study of international relations as a whole. As expressed in the major work of its most popular proponent, Hans Morgenthau, classic realism highlights the ceaseless interplay among great powers preoccupied with maximizing their military security by manipulating the balance of power to secure a fragile stability within an international system characterized by anarchy.[22] It portrays this central theme of the history of international relations as a cyclical pattern in which the short-term stability produced by a balance of power is followed by a breakdown of this equilibrium, leading to war and the creation of a new transitory balance. It focuses almost exclusively on the small set of great powers involved in arranging the balance, the military security interests that motivate their activity, the conflictual quest for

advantage relieved only by temporary military alliances, and the structure of the resulting balance of power as the only form of order that a context of anarchy allows.

Given the fundamental fact of anarchy, states are portrayed as giving predominant weight to external determinants, as each is preoccupied with monitoring and adjusting to shifts in the balance abroad. Neither societal nor governmental processes are given significance as determinants, since they are forced by the requirements of the security dilemma to be aggregated in advance, within the impermeable shell of the sovereign state, as 'factors of national power' and 'quality of leadership', respectively.

This standard realist portrait has had little appeal to students of Canadian foreign policy, for several reasons. Generally, it seemed intuitively irrelevant to the dilemmas of a newer country, beset internally by regional and ethnic cleavages and foreign penetration, preoccupied by a full array of nation-building imperatives, and confronted externally with the necessities of managing interdependencies in collaboration with like-minded but vastly more powerful neighbours. More precisely, preoccupation with security dilemmas, military interests, and the instruments of force appeared secondary to practitioner and scholar alike. For both, armed conflict had been an intermittent, somewhat discretionary concern, always conducted in association with larger external powers, and aimed centrally at sustaining the systems of deterrence within which the primary tasks of foreign policy were pursued.

Realist precepts seemed to be further contradicted by the fundamental features of Canada's historic emergence as a nation. Until well after the First World War, Canada's external *vision* had been affected by a profound and practical attachment to a stable and benign British imperial system.[23] During the interwar period, in a deliberate effort to distinguish themselves from the United Kingdom and the central European system, Canadian leaders eagerly embraced a North American identity defined by the very absence of power politics and by the invention of a uniquely cooperative and peaceful form of international relations.[24] After the Second World War, the very tenacity with which American leaders adopted realism as a justification for their policy of global containment engendered skepticism on the part of Canadian leaders, armed with the legacy of distinctive visions and experienced in detaching themselves from the doctrines and accompanying demands of their imperial leaders abroad.

To the attitudes of heritage was added an accident of history. It was the fate of the modern phase in the study of Canadian foreign policy to emerge at a time when the dominant actor in the international system, the United States, was itself moving beyond the immediate demands of the security dilemma, and when the precepts of realism were beginning to lose their intellectual appeal.[25] At the outset of the 1960s, the emergence of an apparent bipolar stability, confirmed by the outcome of the Berlin and Cuban crises, provided American scholars and their Canadian counterparts with the vision of a system in which security was assured in the short term,

rendered permanent by the new nuclear balance, and superseded by the tasks of enhancing abroad a range of values formerly perceived as subordinate.[26] In such a mood, there was little incentive to continue debates about Canada's precise role in North American defence and nuclear deterrence or general concerns about its place in a North Atlantic alliance.[27] Realism seemed to have little to offer the student of Canadian foreign policy.

As America's global dominance faced new challenges in the late 1960s, so too did the precepts of standard realism. The emerging dynamics of global politics provided an empirical foundation for a renewed interest in a realist theory considerably more complex, as were the dilemmas it addressed.[28]

The 'complex neo-realist' perspective begins by accepting the fundamental premise of standard realism: the primacy of politics. It sees separate states pursuing distinctive interests in an international milieu in which no natural harmony of interests exists. Its new contribution is the emphasis it places on the prevalence of international order—tentatively defined by the convergence of the interests of principal actors leading to an emerging stable global system, but still grounded in the values of an internationally predominant power.[29] Most importantly, it highlights the complex constellation of interests and values that states and non-state actors in such an ascendant, system-defining position are able to pursue.[30]

Complex neo-realism thus focuses on the role of hegemonic powers in ensuring, defining, and extending international order in a system in which universal values remain secondary, in which a common security calculus and interest in balance provide no substitute, and in which leadership is required to transform convergent interests into stable order.[31] It sees the history of international relations characterized by the rise to positions of international primacy of a succession of hegemonic powers, with periods of balance among roughly equal powers as relatively rare, temporary, and particular to periods in which one state has lost its hegemony before another has emerged.[32] And in the critical transition from balance to hegemony, it highlights the way in which order may be defined by a concert of principal powers.

Collectively substituting for states exercising individual hegemony, such 'principal powers' are not merely the familiar great powers of realist theory.[33] Rather, they are principal states in three senses. First, they are the states in the international hierarchy that stand at the top of the international status ranking, collectively possessing decisive capability and differentiated from lower-ranking powers by both objective and subjective criteria. Second, they act as principals in their international activities and associations, rather than as agents for other states or groupings, or as mediators between principals. And third, they have a principal role in establishing, specifying, and enforcing international order.

At the heart of a state's position as a principal power is its possession of surplus capability: a margin of strength in a broad array of sectors well beyond that required to meet the basic requisites of statehood and the minimal performance expected of modern states.[34] Surplus capability relieves principal powers of the tyranny of responding to short-term security dilemmas and provides them with the luxury of basing their international behaviour on the outcomes of political debates within their societies and on the definitions provided by their state apparatus. Surplus capability thus provides such states the discretion to act autonomously, on the basis of internal choices, on a global stage. Such choices derive not from an exclusive or predominant concern with security but from a multiplicity of values in which priority is given to those political interests that integrate, assign weights to, and provide coherence to specific concerns of military, economic, social, and cultural spheres.[35] This configuration

of internal values is embedded in a historically evolved and distinctive array of specialized capabilities, which channels the external activity of a principal power and renders it competitive with those of its counterpart.[36] Surplus and specialized capability together enable principal powers to define the characteristics of international order in a way that disproportionately reflects their distinctive values and to extend that order, and hence their values, into member states throughout the international system.[37]

Traditionally, scholars of Canadian foreign policy have not conceived of their country as having the capabilities or performing the functions of a principal power. Yet, led by key individuals within the state apparatus, they have begun in the past two decades to develop from themes that move in that direction.[38] The first such theme, developed from 1960 to 1968, was a thrust toward globalism, especially significant because of the intent to employ aid as an instrument to advance specifically Canadian interests worldwide, on a bilateral basis. Canada extended its formal diplomatic presence to all regions and major capitals in the world, dealt with quite distinctive cultural groupings, and supplemented conventional diplomacy by the deliberate use of such new techniques as cultural relations and development assistance.[39]

The most dramatic manifestation was the programmatic and geographic expansion of Canada's development assistance. Constituting the major division between the distributive thrust of liberal internationalism and the globalist thrust of complex neo-realism, this transition was initiated in the 1960s when significant Canadian aid began to be deployed in specific francophone countries for the domestic political purpose of meeting the challenges to Canadian foreign policy from Quebec and France.

A second major theme, which emerged from 1968 to 1971, advocated an interest-based initiation of external behaviour. Rejecting the reactiveness that they thought characterized Canadian foreign policy in the Pearsonian approach, dissatisfied domestic critics and officials of the new Trudeau government sought to ensure that the Canadian government would be capable of discerning future trends at home and abroad, identifying their impact on Canadian interests, and formulating policies in advance, enabling Canada to withstand the impact of forces from abroad and thereby to maximize its self-determined interests. This emphasis presumed both a direct focus on national interests as the basis for policy calculation, and the initiation of policies and programs having little direct dependence on the international situation at the time.[40] In its initial form, this theme of internationally projected values offered the image of a 'new' Canada whose policies—concerned with such values as bilingualism, ethnic relations, federalism, techniques of parliamentary government, income redistribution, and environmental protection—provided an example for other states to emulate and a foundation for Canadian behaviour abroad. After 1973 it was enriched by an emphasis on a third major theme: the way in which unique Canadian assets—deriving from its small, diverse, skilled population, its extensive resource base, and its developed technology—gave Canada a more active role in defining a new international order based on these values.[41]

The emergence of these major themes of principal-power capability and behaviour is logically based on a series of premises and precepts that address the seven central questions of foreign policy analysis from the perspective of complex neo-realism. In application to Canada's post–Second World War foreign policy experience, this begins with a view, similar to the other perspectives, of an international system characterized by the disappearance, over the years 1945 to 1957, of the United Kingdom's hegemonic legacy and its replacement by an American hegemony. However,

in contrast to liberal internationalism and peripheral dependence, complex neo-realism sees the key factor as the erosion of the hegemonic position of the United States from 1968 onward.[42] Canada's international experience is seen as one of secular, sustained development, reflected most profoundly in its steadily increasing ability to define, advance, secure, and legitimize distinctive national interests and values in a competitive process with adversaries and associates.[43]

In response to the question of international rank, the complex neo-realist perspective portrays Canada, particularly since 1968, as an ascending principal power in an increasingly diffuse, non-hegemonic international system.[44] Placed in the context of the most prevalent global configuration—a top tier of eight powers, with an average of seven involved in the central, European-based system, and nine on a global basis if the central and peripheral systems are combined—Canada is argued to be part of the classically defined 'top tier' group.[45]

In addition to a location in this configuration, principal powers have three specific characteristics. The first is a rank roughly comparable to other states in the top range, unexcelled by states outside it, and closer to those within than to outside states immediately below.[46] The second is a set of organizations and instruments sufficient to help deter significant direct assaults on its homeland and to provide a strategic presence abroad. The third consists of special rights in determining and preserving international order in political, military, and economic spheres, together with distinctive values and sufficiently strong influence to attract the attention of other principals and to help define the orientation of some lesser states.

With these criteria, the complex neo-realist argument asserts that Canada's objective capability—grounded in the relative size, breadth, and diversity of its natural resources, advanced technology, and skilled population and in other standard calculations of national power—places it predominantly within the top tier of the system.[47] Canada's designated rank is reinforced by its involvement in groupings composed of members drawn exclusively or predominantly from this top tier.[48] While acknowledging Canada's lack of independent nuclear and conventional military deterrence, complex neo-realism recognizes that Canada's military capability at home and abroad directly contributes to strategic stability in several critical regions. Moreover, it assigns Canada a prominent position within the top tier in defining and managing global regimes in major-issue areas and leadership within a distinctive grouping or network of lesser states on such questions.[49]

The degree, variety, and diffusion of Canada's external activities provide the initial indication of aspects of its international behaviour that characterizes it as an emerging principal power. The degree of Canadian activity is expressed by the maintenance of permanent political involvement in virtually all regions, sectors, and forums of world politics. Such global involvement is registered in the consistently high volume of interactions in which Canada engages with a large number of actors abroad. Grounded in a need to continuously manage a state's immediate, direct, durable interests, global involvement arises when several relatively stringent conditions are met: the existence of societal actors sufficiently powerful to influence behaviour and critical security interests or commitments; the presence of a full range of concerns and values that give the international behaviour additional significance; the recognition that behaviour is based at least partly on state-specific interests, vulnerabilities, and values, rather than universal doctrines; and the desire of partner countries to maintain the involvement.

From these conditions, the variety of activity is defined as one of interest-based involvement predicated on the distinctively national interests and values previously identified as the touchstone of Canadian participation. Canadian policy and behaviour are likely to exhibit some inconsistency over time and across issues as officials also seek to make their contributions in the context of past efforts while maintaining congruence with the accumulated expectations and interests of others. Such activity may appear as a large number of highly complex patterns quite distinct from one another, irregular and seemingly unpredictable as a variety of interests and decision strategies compete.

As a further consequence of Canada's global behaviour, the diffusion of activity is seen as a tendency toward autonomous bilateral involvement. Reflecting the need to develop and maintain direct ties worldwide, distinctive effort is made on specific state-to-state relations while relatively less involvement occurs with international organizations having universal membership. In this mode, new and multiple membership, concern with balance across affiliations, and stress on fluidity assume lesser prominence. Priority is given to employing the state's resources in servicing the particular interest of each specific bilateral relationship. In practice, this suggests a fuller and more equal association with a larger number of non-universal organizations and, more importantly, the development of direct bilateral relations with groups and actors beyond the Anglo-American sphere. More specifically, in this thrust bilateral diplomatic representation on a resident basis is given and received with most actors, posts acquire a 'multiprogram' character, regular visits by heads of government increase, and joint organizations are formed with regional bodies and individual countries.

From the complex neo-realist perspective, this tendency toward global, interest-based, bilateral activity is supplemented by associative behaviour characterized by a set of competitive orientations: a predisposition toward unilateral initiatives, a divergence in policy commitment, and a diversification of focus away from any associated imperial state. Emphasizing unilateral initiatives, Canada's diplomatic behaviour does not necessarily concentrate on inducing other states to act, does not require their active cooperation, passive support, or subsequent imitation for success, and is therefore not heavily dependent on calculations of their likely behaviour for its initiation. In short, this diplomatic behaviour is not a heavily context-dependent attempt to preserve or engender cooperative arrangements, but rather a self-motivated effort to operate within the confines of the existing system to national advantage. A desire to act primarily with equivalent states on the one hand, and to maintain relatively exclusive spheres of influence on the other, reinforces this emphasis on selective involvement of other actors as dictated by each issue.

The second competitive tendency, divergence, is reflected in actions in which relatively little effort is made to ensure consistency with the actions of other states and in which dissimilar actions often result. Positions may be taken at variance with those of members in existing groups, and sometimes this exercise of leadership will initiate a new grouping. Little emphasis is given to offsetting the weight of a given bloc or eroding bloc cleavages. As a result, Canada often adopts positions on major issues discrepant with those of traditionally associated states.

The third and most significant competitive tendency is that of diversification, manifested in active efforts to concentrate behaviour on actors other than an associated imperial power or its groups, with the aim of obtaining alternative sources of resources such as information, markets, investment, and general political support. In particular, it involves a deliberate attempt to forge relations and assume compatible positions with other states that are roughly equivalent in status or even more

powerful and thus capable of serving as a substitute for, or rival to, the traditional imperial power. Diversification rests on the following beliefs: that in the absence of such action, existing behavioural domination by the prevailing imperial power would continue; that this is not in Canada's interest; that Canada has the power to force a more acceptable balance by itself; and that this effort can be sustained even in the face of active opposition from the imperial power.

In overseas relations, the rivalry induced by diversification is constrained somewhat by the fundamental responsibility of all major powers to preserve a general balance of power and reduce the likelihood of war. However, these tasks are performed by individual as well as collective actions, rest on negotiated settlements among equals more than on compromises forwarded or facilitated by other parties, and provide only an overarching framework in which major power interests are pursued in a competitive fashion. Within this framework, diversification engenders the establishment of cooperative relationships with other major or emerging powers as an alternative to its affiliation with an associated imperial power. At that point the process may extend into an intensive and increasingly competitive relationship in which Canada becomes involved in the internal political processes of its new partner, incompatible interests become apparent, and diplomatic conflict results. Alternatively, the continuation and reinforcement of a close, cooperative relationship may result in an effort at counterweight, in which the new partner is deliberately invoked as an ally directly against the preferences of the previous imperial power.

Canada's pursuit of diversification within North America breeds an emphasis on arm's-length diplomacy. Bilateral relations with the United States resemble those between any two sovereign states with unified governments: formally equal while differing in objective, formulating national positions in advance, guarding information, and seeking to outmanoeuvre adversaries, link issues, and dominate policy implementation. Within Canada itself, the corresponding value of an autonomous society prompts a reliance on strategies that prohibit outright further American penetration and actively reduce the existing American presence.

In an emerging principal power, in the complex neo-realist view, the defence of national interests and the promotion of distinctive values engender a strong incentive to follow and promote a detailed conception of world order compatible with its purposes. The first manifestation of this incentive is an active effort to revise the existing patterns of international institutionalization. Believing that such frameworks preserve old values and inhibit emergent powers from securing equality with their established counterparts, these states reduce their verbal and material support for the standard set of international institutions, seek to forge alternative organizations or informal groupings, and forge alliances with new states that have attained success within the existing order. Moreover, efforts to promote a well-developed, highly autonomous, and fully consistent structure of international law are reduced, on the grounds that such constructions introduce rigidities that impede the process of revision.

A second component of a complex neo-realist approach to world order is the promotion of principal-power concerts through the creation of groupings in which effective participation is restricted to states within the top tier, and more particularly to states with a rank equal to or greater than one's own. Premised on the recognition of Canada's principal-power rank and claims, this tendency is directed at strengthening the distinction between groups made up exclusively of principal powers and mixed groups of principal and lesser powers. In addition, it increasingly transfers important questions from the latter to the former in the interests of a more rapid and realistic

revision and more effective management of the international order.

Modification of the existing international order in keeping with its distinctive interests and values is the third criterion of a principal power's approach to world order. Accepting the basic legitimacy of those structures that allowed it to ascend to principal-power status, Canada devotes few resources to conducting direct, comprehensive assaults on the formal framework of existing institutions. Yet, in an attempt to reinforce its new position, it seeks to forge alliances with those who have successfully manipulated the existing system and who are likely candidates for major-power status in the near future. And in an effort to register the particular contribution it can make to the management of the global system and to secure the support of emerging powers who sustain its position, it forwards distinctive conceptions of what a new international order should be.

Implicit in complex neo-realist writing is the assumption that these action tendencies and doctrines are sustained by an external environment rather more open and less concentrated than in the classical formulation. This configuration, when combined with Canada's principal-power status, reduces to a low level the overall salience of the external environment, disperses its influence across a wide number of states, and endows a multitude of states with a noticeable, if minor, impact on Canadian behaviour. Thus complex neo-realism assigns the 'imperial' actors—the United Kingdom and the United States—a significantly reduced role in providing a stimulus, framework, and referent for Canadian behaviour. At the same time it allows the major European powers, and Japan, the Soviet Union, and China, a relatively high impact, not only by providing a broader affiliation to balance Canada's relations with the United States but also in serving as comparable, autonomous actors in their own right.

The significant weight attached to the positions and initiatives of these major states reduces to a moderate level the significance of the smaller European and overseas middle powers as associates of Canada in international diplomacy and as a factor when Canada undertakes autonomous action. Within this sphere, attention shifts from states with a historical relationship with Canada to those with similar socio-cultural attributes or convergent population, resource, and technology characteristics and to those emerging into the major-power realm. Finally the United Nations, as the institutional codification of an increasingly obsolete pattern of international relations, declines to a moderate position as an influence on Canadian behaviour, while the North Atlantic Treaty Organization (NATO), a more restricted body with a direct role in security and in defining systems, experiences an offsetting increase.[50] Moreover, a much greater influence is enjoyed by such new, restricted-membership, task-specific bodies as la Francophonie, the Namibia Contact Group within the Security Council, the Organization for Economic Cooperation and Development, the International Energy Agency, the London Suppliers Group on nuclear materials, and the Western Economic Summits held since 1975.

A complex neo-realist orientation perceives the domestic environment as being marked by the emergence of highly salient, ongoing disputes over foreign policy issues, grounded in the interest of autonomous major organizations throughout the national society. The high importance of domestic organizations rests in the first instance on the likelihood that the country's possession of a surplus margin of capability allows for and prompts an effective debate within society about the purposes for which that power should be employed. Furthermore, the existence of routine global involvements by societal organizations increases the number of actors whose primary interests are affected by foreign affairs, who possess direct, specialized international expertise, and who thus have legitimate, divergent perspectives about the best course to pursue. Moreover, the stress on national interest and initiative emphasizes the desirability of considering domestic sources and taking the time for domestic actors to mobilize, organize, and debate. Together these factors produce a domestic process that, in conformity with a pluralist conception of politics, contains a highly developed set of differentiated institutions, each autonomously defining and pursuing specific interests among societal competitors and organizations in the external and governmental realm. Thus, Canada's international behaviour becomes highly sensitive to such societal factors.

The depth and durability of these societal interests give the overtly political and directly accessible institutions—Parliament and the party system—only a moderate role in influencing government behaviour. In contrast, associational interest groups, labour, the media, and the business community all enjoy a high degree of influence, in keeping with the precepts of interest-group theory. Finally, provincial governments possess a moderate degree of influence. The result is a highly dispersed and evenly balanced process, in which all types of institutions and especially those organizations whose strength is based on population, resource, or technological capabilities, have substantial impact.

Within the executive branch of the federal government, complex neo-realism predicts the existence of a decision-making process resembling bureaucratic politics, but one in which strong central coordinative mechanisms operate to produce overall order. The decision-making process of government is viewed as highly salient in foreign policy behaviour, resulting from the vigorous debate taking place among a well-developed constellation of organizational subunits capable of registering their missions with considerable speci-ficity. Within this constellation, a relatively moderate influence is assigned to the Department of External Affairs and its career foreign service officer corps; a high degree of influence, in contrast, is assigned to other foreign service departments and domestic departments. Exercising dominant influence are those within the prime ministerial group and in the central foreign policy coordinative structures closest to it, given their role in defining overarching values and the overall national interest. Indeed, great emphasis is placed on the emergence of a large, highly specialized, and tightly controlled set of such coordinative structures as a

means for integrating and transcending the multitude of powerful competing missions within the government and competing interests within domestic society. Therefore, Canadian foreign policy behaviour is argued to be, in the context of complex neo-realism, highly sensitive to key governmental actors but durable, interrelated, and comprehensive nonetheless.

These three theoretical perspectives on Canadian foreign policy provide our entry into the study of Canada's postwar international behaviour. Determinations about the usefulness, accuracy, and validity of each one must be made in the context of the empirical record, not on an *a priori* basis.

Notes

1. R.A. MacKay and E.B. Rogers, *Canada Looks Abroad* (Don Mills, ON: Oxford University Press, 1938). See also Robert Bothwell and Norman Hillmer, eds., *The In-Between Time: Canadian External Policy in the 1930s* (Toronto: Copp Clark, 1975). The most authoritative history of this period is contained in C.P. Stacey, *Canada and the Age of Conflict*, vol. 1, *1867–1921* (Toronto: Macmillan, 1977), and *vol. 2, 1921–1948* (Toronto: University of Toronto Press, 1981).

2. John W. Holmes, *The Shaping of Peace: Canada and the Search for World Order, 1943–1957*, 2 vols. (Toronto: University of Toronto Press, 1979, 1982). On the move toward the war and its legacy, see James Eayrs, *In Defence of Canada*, 4 vols. (Toronto: University of Toronto Press, 1964, 1965, 1972, 1980).

3. See Dale Thomson and Roger Swanson, *Canadian Foreign Policy: Options and Perspectives* (Toronto: McGraw-Hill Ryerson, 1971); Peter Dobell, *Canada's Search For New Roles: Foreign Policy in the Trudeau Era* (Don Mills, ON: Oxford University Press, 1972); Peyton V. Lyon, 'A Review of the Review', *Journal of Canadian Studies* 5 (May 1970): 34–47; Lyon, 'The Trudeau Doctrine', *International Journal* 26, 1 (Winter 1970–1): 19–43; James Hyndman, 'National Interest and the New Look', *International Journal* 26 (Winter 1970–1): 5–8; and Kal Holsti, *Proceedings of the Standing Committee on External Affairs and National Defence*, Statement no. 7, 19 July 1971.

4. The most influential framework provided by students of general foreign policy analysis is presented in James N. Rosenau, 'Pre-theories and Theories of Foreign Policy', in R.B. Farrell, ed., *Approaches to Comparative and*

International Politics (Evanston, IL: Northwestern University Press, 1966), 27–92. For a view of the development and application of this framework, see Patrick McGowan and Howard Shapiro, *The Comparative Study of Foreign Policy: A Survey of Scientific Findings* (Beverly Hills, CA: Sage Publications, 1973); and James N. Rosenau, ed., *Comparing Foreign Policies: Theories, Findings and Methods* (Toronto: John Wiley and Sons, 1974).

5. The prevalence of such myths and models in the social sciences is noted, by specific example, in Larry Ward et al., 'World Modelling: Some Critical Foundations', *Behavioral Sciences* 23 (May 1978): 135–47. The major traditions in Canadian historical writing are discussed in Carl Berger, ed., *Approaches to Canadian History* (Toronto: University of Toronto Press, 1967); and Berger, *The Writing of Canadian History: Aspects of English-Canadian Historical Writing: 1900 to 1970* (Don Mills, ON: Oxford University Press, 1976). A brief portrait of the implicit models in the writing on Canadian foreign policy is offered in John W. Holmes, 'After 25 Years', *International Journal* 26, 1 (Winter 1970–1): 1–4.

6. Kal Holsti, *International Politics: A Framework for Analysis*, 3rd ed. (Englewood Cliffs, NJ: Prentice-Hall, 1977), 390; Maurice East and Charles Hermann, 'Do Nation-Types Account for Foreign Policy Behaviour?' in Rosenau, ed., *Comparing Foreign Policies*, 269–303.

7. The best treatment of the classic formulations of relative capability, position, and status is provided in Martin Wight, *Power Politics* (Harmondsworth, England: Penguin, 1979). For modern extensions and applications, see Klaus Knorr, 'Notes on the Analysis of National

Capabilities', in James N. Rosenau et al., eds., *The Analysis of International Relations* (New York: Free Press, 1972); Knorr, *The Power of Nations: The Political Economy of International Relations* (New York: Basic Books, 1975); and Ray Cline, *World Power Trends and US Foreign Policy for the 1980s* (Boulder, CO: Westview Press, 1980). Recent applications to individual states include Ezra Vogel, *Japan as Number One: Lessons for America* (Cambridge, MA: Harvard University Press, 1979); and Wolfram Hanrieder, 'Germany as Number Two? The Foreign and Economic Policy of the Federal Republic', *International Studies Quarterly* 26 (March 1982): 57–86. Yet to appear is a piece in this tradition arguing the case for 'Canada as Number Seven'.

8.   See K.N. Waltz, *Theory of International Politics* (Reading, MA: Addison-Wesley, 1979); Charles Pentland, 'The Regionalization of World Politics: Concepts and Evidence', *International Journal* 30, 4 (Autumn 1975): 599–630; William Zimmerman, 'Issue Area and Foreign Policy Process: A Research Note in Search of a General Theory', *American Political Science Review* 67 (December 1973): 1204–12; William C. Porter, 'Issue Area and Foreign Policy Analysis', *International Organization* 34 (Summer 1980): 405–28; A.F.K. Organski, *World Politics*, 2nd ed. (New York: Knopf, 1968); and W.W. Rostow, *The World Economy* (Austin: University of Texas Press, 1978).

9.   Following the treatment in Joseph Frankel, *International Relations in a Changing World* (Don Mills, ON: Oxford University Press, 1979), 8–27, security is defined as the possession of defined, externally recognized boundaries unlikely to be changed in the short term by outside force. Sovereignty is defined as the capacity of the central government to enforce its jurisdiction and preserve the identity of its major societal institutions, and legitimacy as its ability to attract regularly high degrees of voluntary compliance from its citizenry.

10. The three basic categories of externally oriented behaviour are formed by viewing state behaviour at progressively higher levels of analysis: activity (acting state), association (state in interaction with other states), and order (system of interacting states). Each of these categories is divided in turn by the three stages of behaviour offered in events data analysis: emission, transmission, and reception or impact. See J. David Singer, 'The Level of Analysis Problem in International Relations', in Klaus Knorr and Sidney Verba, ed., *The International System: Theoretical Essays* (Princeton, NJ: Princeton University Press, 1961), 77–92; and Charles Hermann, 'What Is a Foreign Policy Event?' in Wolfram Hanrieder, ed., *Comparative Foreign Policy: Theoretical Essays* (New York: David McKay, 1971), 295–321.

11. Diffusion is defined more specifically as the number of, balance among, and intensity of relations with the targets of Canadian action abroad. Analytically, the impact of Canadian behaviour on a target transforms Canadian 'activity' into 'relations'. It thus leads to the next level of analysis—association—in which attention is directed at the internal character of a pattern of relations (or a 'relationship').

12. Analytically, because the overall focus of Canadian behaviour is directed at the distribution of power in the international system and can affect that distribution, it gives rise to the subsequent concern with order, or the structure of the international system that a given distribution of power yields.

13. The basic concept of world order is discussed in Hedley Bull, *The Anarchical Society: A Study of Order in World Politics* (New York: Columbia University Press, 1979). See also Robert Tucker, *The Inequality of Nations* (New York: Basic Books, 1977). For a current debate on regimes, see *International Organization* 36 (Spring 1982), entire issue.

14. The importance of systemic attributes, such as the actions of individual states on a state's international activity, is argued in James Harf et al., 'Systemic and External Attributes in Foreign Policy Analysis', in Rosenau, ed., *Comparing Foreign Policies*, 235–50. Evidence that the relative status and salience of external actors has a particular impact on Canadian foreign policy behaviour is contained in Don Munton, 'Lesser Powers and the Influence of Relational Attributes: The Case of Canadian Foreign Policy Behaviour', *Études Internationales* 10 (September 1979): 471–502. Salience includes the concept of vulnerability, which refers to 'the relative availability and costliness of the alternatives that the actors face'. It is defined as 'an actor's liability to suffer costs imposed by external events even after policies have been altered' and is measured by 'the costliness of making effective adjustments to a changed environment over a period of time'. Robert O. Keohane and Joseph S. Nye, Jr, *Power and Interdependence: World Politics in Transition* (Boston: Little, Brown, 1977), 13.

15. Compare the concept of sensitivity as degree and speed of costly impacts from, and responsiveness to, outside events, including social, political, and economic contagion effects, 'before policies are altered to try to change the situation'. Keohane and Nye, *Power and Interdependence*, 12–13.

16. For an introduction to the literature on domestic sources of foreign policy, see Henry Kissinger, 'Domestic Structure and Foreign Policy', *Daedalus* 95 (Spring 1966): 503–29; James N. Rosenau, ed., *Domestic Sources of Foreign Policy* (New York: The Free Press, 1967); McGowan and Shapiro, *Comparative Study*, 107–32; and Peter J. Katzenstein, ed., 'Between Power and Plenty: Foreign Economic Policies of Advanced Industrialized States', *International Organization* 31 (Autumn 1977).

17. For societal determinants, a further breakdown of scope includes the concepts of institutional differentiation

and autonomy derived from Samuel Huntington, *Political Order in Changing Societies* (New Haven: Yale University Press, 1968), and the discussion of penetrated political societies in Rosenau, 'Pre-theories and Theories'. On the dual nature of the influence relationship between domestic and governmental actors in the Canadian case, see Denis Stairs, 'Publics and Policy Makers: The Domestic Environment of the Foreign Policy Community', *International Journal* 26, 1 (Winter 1970–1): 221–48; and Stairs, 'Public Opinion and External Affairs: Reflections on the Domestication of Canadian Foreign Policy', *International Journal* 33, 1 (Winter 1977–8): 128–49.

18. See Richard Snyder, H.W. Bruck, and B.M. Sapin, eds., *Foreign Policy Decision Making* (New York: Free Press, 1962); Graham Allison, *Essence of Decision: Explaining the Cuban Missile Crisis* (Boston: Little, Brown, 1971); McGowan and Shapiro, *Comparative Study*, 65–106; and, most usefully, Stephen D. Krasner, *Defending the National Interest: Raw Material Investments and US Foreign Policy* (Princeton, NJ: Princeton University Press, 1978); Alfred Stepan, *The State and Society: Peru in Comparative Perspective* (Princeton, NJ: Princeton University Press, 1978); and Eric A. Nordlinger, *On the Autonomy of the Democratic State* (Cambridge, MA: Harvard University Press, 1981).

19. 'A principal task of research is to determine the extent to which any particular state (a) is procedurally neutral and allows an autonomous and competitive process of interest aggregation to present binding demands on the state, (b) is a class instrument in which the full range of its coercive, administrative and legal powers is used to dominate some class fractions and protect others, or (c) achieves some degree of autonomy from civil society and thus contributes its own weight to civil society.' Stepan, *State and Society*, xii–xiii.

20. These three groups emerge from most empirical analyses of a state's foreign policy apparatus; for example, I.M. Destler, *President, Bureaucrats and Foreign Policy: The Policy of Organizational Reform* (Princeton, NJ: Princeton University Press, 1972).

21. These coordinative structures and processes are staffed by what Stepan terms the 'strategic elite' and depend for their efficacy on the 'ideological and organizational unity of that elite'. Stepan, *State and Society*, xiii.

22. Hans Morgenthau's classic work is *Politics Among Nations: The Struggle for Power and Peace* (New York: Knopf, 1948). Other classic works in the realist tradition, broadly conceived, are E.H. Carr, *The Twenty Years' Crisis, 1919–1939: An Introduction to the Study of International Relations* (New York: St Martin's Press, 1939); Raymond Aron, *Peace and War: A Theory of International Relations* (New York: Praeger, 1967); and Bull, *Anarchical Society*.

23. Carl Berger, *The Sense of Power: Studies in the Idea of Canadian Imperialism, 1867–1914* (Toronto: University of Toronto Press, 1970).

24. Don Page, 'Canada as the Exponent of North American Idealism', *The American Review of Canadian Studies* 3 (Autumn 1973): 30–46.

25. John H. Herz, 'Rise and Demise of the Territorial State', *World Politics* 9 (July 1957): 473ff; and Herz, *International Politics in the Atomic Age* (New York: Columbia University Press, 1959). See also the criticisms summarized in Stanley Hoffman, *The State of War: Essays on the Theory and Practice of International Relations* (New York: Praeger, 1965).

26. This broadening of the concepts of security and national interest and the introduction of a more prominent role for values and moral considerations were led by Arnold Wolfers, *Discord and Collaboration* (Baltimore: Johns Hopkins University Press, 1962).

27. For example, R.J. Sutherland, 'Canada's Long-Term Strategic Situation', *International Journal* 17 (Summer 1962): 199–233; James Eayrs, 'Sharing a Continent: the Hard Issues', in J.S. Dickey, ed., *The United States and Canada* (Englewood Cliffs: Prentice-Hall, 1967), 55–94; Klaus Knorr, 'Canada and Western Defence', *International Journal* 18 (Winter 1962–3): 1–16; and Melvin Conant, *The Long Polar Watch: Canada and the Defence of North America* (New York: Harper and Row, 1962). From an earlier period, see the great classics, J.B. Brebner, *North Atlantic Triangle: The Interplay of Canada, the United States and Great Britain* (Toronto: Ryerson, 1945); 'A Changing North Atlantic Triangle', *International Journal* 3 (Autumn 1948): 309–19; and Harold Innis, *Great Britain, the United Nations and Canada* (Nottingham, England: University of Nottingham Press, 1948).

28. For the best summaries, see Keohane and Nye, *Power and Interdependence*; and Stanley Hoffman, *Primacy or World Order: American Foreign Policy Since the Cold War* (New York: McGraw-Hill, 1978).

29. Wight, *Power Politics*, 30–40; and Jeffrey Hart, 'Dominance in International Politics', *International Organization* 30 (Spring 1976).

30. Hans Morgenthau, *The Purpose of American Politics* (New York: Knopf, 1960); Arnold Wolfers, 'Statesmanship and Moral Choice', *World Politics* 1 (January 1949): 175–95; and Wolfers, *Discord and Collaboration*. While this broader conception of interests and values follows many of the recent extensions of realist thinking, it does *not* embrace the globally derived, universally common, or inherent 'cosmopolitan values', argued in John H. Herz, 'Political Realism Revisited', *International Studies Quarterly* 25 (June 1981): 182–97, and suggested in Stanley Hoffman, *Duties Beyond Borders: On the Limits and Possibilities of Ethical International Politics* (Syracuse, NY: Syracuse University Press, 1981). Essentially, our argument

asserts that balance-of-power dynamics do not usually prevent a state from acquiring a position of hegemony, that such states have 'milieu' goals, and that such goals are partially determined by a historically engendered conception of national values.

31. The major works that provide the basis in the general literature for our complex neo-realist model are George Liska, *Imperial America: The International Politics of Primacy* (Baltimore: Johns Hopkins University Press, 1967); Raymond Aron, *The Imperial Republic* (Englewood Cliffs, NJ: Prentice Hall, 1974); and David Calleo, *The Imperious Economy* (Cambridge, MA: Harvard University Press, 1982). Equally important is a stream of literature focusing on the dynamics within and between states, which give rise to processes of hegemony. See, in particular, Nazli Choucri and Robert C. North, *Nations in Conflict: National Growth and International Violence* (San Francisco: W.H. Freeman, 1975).

32. See A.F.K. Organski, *World Politics*, 364–7; and Wight, *Power Politics*, 30–40.

33. On great powers, see Wight, *Power Politics*, 41–53.

34. The concept of surplus capability is drawn from Charles Kindleberger, 'Dominance and Leadership in the International Economy', *International Studies Quarterly* 25 (June 1981): 245. In our formulation, it is not only an absolute criterion based on internal capability but also a criterion relative to domestic demands, external security threats, and ultimately the demands for creating international order that are bred by different external distributions of power.

35. Collectively, a particular configuration of interests and values is termed 'the national interest'. The traditional, security-focused concept of national interest has met with considerable skepticism from scholars of international politics, for reasons well summarized in James N. Rosenau, 'National Interest', in David L. Sills, ed., *International Encyclopedia of the Social Sciences*, vol. II (New York: Crowell, Collier, and Macmillan, 1968), 34–40. Our concept derives from subsequent efforts to defend and refine the concept, such as Joseph Frankel, 'National Interest: A Vindication', *International Journal* 24 (Autumn 1969): 717–25; Donald Neuchterlein, *National Interests and Presidential Leadership: The Setting of Priorities* (Boulder, CO: Westview Press, 1978); and, especially, Krasner, *Defending the National Interest*. In our conception, the national interest is a set of premises, perceptions, and policy-relevant priorities that is durable (extending for a minimum of, say, five years), comprehensive (in embracing interests from several issue areas or sectors of society), interrelated (in specifying the relationships among interests), internally prioritized (in providing a particular scale of order or weighting to components), and general (in relating directly overarching values that structure the scale of priorities). In process terms, 'the national interest' is seen in broad foreign policy declarations, doctrines, or the calculus underlying seminal decisions when these endure beyond the electoral cycle, actively involve a number and range of government departments, require extensive interdepartmental interaction, engender interdepartmental conflict or major efforts at harmonization, and stimulate more than formal authorization, monitoring, or servicing activities from the chief executive group or central coordinative structures. Thus 'the national interest' embraces both 'interests', which are specific to societal sectors and government departments and affected by decision in a direct and immediate way, and 'values', which are general to society and the state and produced by the chief executive group and central coordinative structures. Because society lacks unified control and central coordinative structures, interests are primarily the preserve of society, while values reside primarily in the state.

36. The concept of specialized capabilities is drawn from Choucri and North, *Nations in Conflict*, 14–43.

37. In short, they present the possibility of leadership, as conceived in Kindleberger, 'Dominance and Leadership'.

38. In addition to the works cited in the introduction, our presentation of complex neo-realism draws on the following literature in the Canadian foreign policy field: Hyndman, 'National Interest and the New Look'; Ivan Head, 'The Foreign Policy of the New Canada', *Foreign Affairs* 50 (January 1972): 237–52; 'Dossier Canada', *Politique Internationale* 12 (Summer 1981): 181–302; A.E. Gotlieb, 'The Western Economic Summits', Notes for Remarks to the Canadian Institute for International Affairs, 9 April 1981, Winnipeg; and Charles Doran, 'Politics of Dependency Reversal: Canada', Paper prepared for the International Studies Association Annual Meeting, 21–24 March 1979, Toronto.

39. Note the co-existence of the two themes in the prescriptions of Reid in 'Canadian Foreign Policy, 1967–1977'. Distinctive cultural groups included, most notably, the francophone countries and the People's Republic of China.

40. See Clarkson, ed., *Independent Foreign Policy*, 253–69; and Hyndman, 'National Interest and the New Look'.

41. See Head, 'Foreign Policy of the New Canada'; and James Eayrs, 'Defining a New Place for Canada in the Hierarchy of World Powers', *International Perspective,* May/June 1975: 15–24.

42. More particularly, we see the United States acquiring hegemony from 1945 to 1960 and exercising stable, virtually unchallenged 'high' hegemony from about 1960 through 1967.

43. Robert Bothwell, Ian Drummond, and John English, *Canada Since 1945: Power, Politics and Provincialism* (Toronto: University of Toronto Press, 1981).

44. 'Canada is a large power; to call us a "middle power" is inaccurate . . . As an immigrant country, with a barely developed national resource base to our economy, and a rapidly adapting capability in technology and processing, we are to some extent only now beginning to reach our true potential.' A.E. Gotlieb, 'Canada–US Relations: The Rules of the Game', Christian A. Herter Lecture Series, The Johns Hopkins School of Advanced International Studies, 1 April 1982, Washington DC, 4, 10. The term 'principal power' is used by Marc Lalonde, 'Le Canada et l'indépendance énergétique du monde libre', *Politique Internationale* 12 (Summer 1981): 206.

45. A.F.K. Organski and Jacek Kugler, *The War Ledger* (Chicago: University of Chicago Press, 1980), 43.

46. For an illustration of this calculation, see Gotlieb, 'Western Economic Summits'.

47. For an example of a national capabilities presentation, see Peyton V. Lyon and Brian W. Tomlin, *Canada as an International Actor* (Toronto: Macmillan, 1979), 56–76.

48. Such groupings include the Western Economic Summit, the Namibia Contact Group, and, less clearly, the four-power Caribbean Consultative Group, the 1970 uranium cartel group, the initial London Suppliers Group on nuclear materials, the executive directors of the International Monetary Fund, and historically, the United Nations Atomic Energy Commission.

49. These groupings include states in the Commonwealth and francophonie, particularly those from the Caribbean and Africa and, less clearly, small and middle powers from the North Atlantic region. One very stringent measure of such states is the group that Canada has represented at one time as an executive director on the International Monetary Fund: Norway, Iceland, Ireland, Jamaica, Guyana, Barbados, and the Bahamas. From this perspective, the standard observation of Canada—as a 'regional power without a region' because of the dominating presence of the United States—overlooks the three major poles of Canada's regional sphere: as a transcontinental and trans-Atlantic power, beginning with Confederation in 1867 and culminating in the admission of Newfoundland into the Dominion in 1949; as a northern power, symbolized by the Arctic Waters Pollution Prevention Act of 1970 and conceptualized in Franklyn Griffiths, *A Northern Foreign Policy* (Toronto: Canadian Institute of International Affairs, 1979); and as a Caribbean power, based on this historic Canada–West Indies trade and currently registered in Canada's leading role in development assistance in the region.

50. More precisely, within the United Nations, greater emphasis is given to the Security Council and to the new generation of organizations and special conference groupings created in the 1970s to deal with new 'global' issues.

UPDATE

CANADA AS A PRINCIPAL POWER 2010

John J. Kirton
Revised, May 6, 2010

Introduction: Canada as a Principal Power 1983

In *Canada as a Principal Power: A Study in Foreign Policy and International Relations*, published in 1983, David Dewitt and I argued that Canada was emerging as a principal power in a more diffuse international system, as identified by a new complex neo-realist theoretical perspective on Canadian foreign policy. At the time, the work seemed significant on several counts.

First, the suggestion that Canada could be a principal power broadened the scholarly and policy debate beyond the traditional duelling dichotomy of Canada as a middle power or satellite (Granatstein 1969). Inspired by James Eayrs's (1975) brilliant but breezy insight, it recaptured and modernized the intellectual richness of the initial trichotomy of policy patterns and options that had been present at the creation of the systematic study of Canadian foreign policy in R.A. MacKay and E.B. Rogers *Canada Looks Abroad* in 1938 (Hawes 1984, Bratt and Kukucha 2007, Kirton 2009).

Second, *Canada as a Principal Power* was arguably the first fully theoretical work on Canadian foreign policy, in that it offered three competing, logically interrelated sets of specified concepts covering all the major dimensions of the behaviour and determinants of Canadian foreign policy and capable of empirical application and disconfirmation. While others had offered core concepts, notably Denis Stairs's (1974) *The Diplomacy of Constraint*, or systemically explored the determinants of key decisions, as in Bruce Thordarson's (1972) *Trudeau and Foreign Policy*, only in 1983 did a comprehensive theoretical, empirically testable edifice arrive.

Third, that theoretical edifice was explicitly grounded in the larger theories of international relations and foreign policy, rather than treating Canadian foreign policy as a subject of merely local conceptualization and concern. While earlier international relations concepts such as 'middle power' and dependency theory had enriched the study of Canadian foreign policy, *Canada as a Principal Power* explicitly drew on the major modern international relations theories from within the realist, liberal institutionalist, and political economy/world systems traditions and was designed to be used for a study of Canadian and comparative foreign policy.

Fourth, as subsequent scholars correctly recognized, this theory was a systemic one (Tomlin et al. 2008). It argued that Canada was emerging as a principal power in, and because of, a more diffuse international system. Its systemically grounded theory flowed from the two most influential international relations works of the time. First, Kenneth Waltz's (1979) *Theory of International Politics,* with its stark emphasis on the structural significance of relative capability among major powers, and second, Robert Keohane and Joseph Nye Jr's (1977) *Power and Interdependence*, with its new emphasis on sensitivity and vulnerability in an era when systemic interdependence as a parallel component of the structure of the international system was taking hold. The work sought to pull the study of Canadian foreign policy beyond an idiographic concern with individuals, histories, and biographies, to become part of, benefit from, and contribute to the large community of international relations scholars. It also began to move the study of Canadian foreign policy from the supply-side driver of relative capabilities as the key cause of a country's international behaviour to the demand-side driver of vulnerabilities, with a richer conception of both the supply and demand sides than those traditionally at work.

Canada as a Principal Power received considerable critical acclaim upon publication. But it did not immediately inspire a host of other scholars or doctoral students to develop or apply its theoretical innovations in major works (Molot 1990). In part this was due to bad timing. James Eayrs's initial insight in 1975 that Canada was now a 'foremost nation', and the full-blown 'principal power' claim to which this gave rise, seemed sensible in the energy-short, détente-bathed mid-1970s. However, it proved to be incorrect and implausible in the mid-1980s as Canada suffered from a severe recession, as Ronald Reagan seemed to restore the United States' hegemonic primacy, and as the superpower Soviet Union expanded into Afghanistan. These events seemed to make the diffusing international system of the 1970s disappear into a new world of tight Cold War bipolarity, as the closed, insensitive, and invulnerable billiard ball-like polities of conventional realism returned.

Moreover, the primary Canadian audience, somewhat correctly, saw that the book closely charted, and was theoretically inspired by, the doctrines and doings of the governments of Prime Minister Pierre Elliott Trudeau that had started in 1968 but that had disappeared, amidst the disgrace of a bandwagoning public, in 1984. Nor were they designed to be normative, and thus useful to the ongoing policy and political practice in which too many scholars of the subject are involved. It thus easily fell out of favour, especially when some scholars of Canadian foreign policy in the cash-strapped 1990s turned their talents to producing short policy-oriented papers on the problems of the moment.

More importantly, the book's complex concepts were not easy to comprehend and digest. Additionally, *Canada as a Principal Power* did not fully develop the conceptual insights that logically flowed from its theoretical foundations. It took another quarter of a century for one of the co-authors to do that, in *Canadian Foreign Policy in a Changing World,* published in 2007. With that elaboration and its application to 25 years of evidence after the theory was first offered, it is now possible to assess how theoretically valuable and empirically prescient and accurate *Canada as a Principal Power* has been. While that assessment must ultimately come from the co-authors' colleagues, the basic case for the defence is offered below.

Theory 2010

The fully elaborated argument, flowing from the 1983 foundations, rests on five central elements, some of which were implicit or obscured in the original work.

The first is the central argument, that Canada is not in and of itself a principal power. Rather, it is a principal power only in a changing world defined by the severe, sustained, and probably irreversible decline of the United States as a system-dominant power; by the diffusion of its 'released' relative capability to a diffuse set of rising powers rather than a single challenger; by the emergence of a new, expanded top tier of principal powers; and by the location of Canada in that top tier rather than the one below. This elaboration makes clear that this is a systemically grounded theory, and imposes four specific systemic conditions—decline, diffusion, top tier expansion, and Canadian inclusion—that must exist if the argument of Canada's emergence and establishment as a principal power is to prove true.

The second element was to specify an anchor of invariants for starting to explain and predict how Canada, or any other country in this system, would behave once these systemic conditions and the societal and governments determinants within the country changed. With sovereign, exclusive, territorial states in a structurally anarchic system as a starting point, it argued that Canada, like all countries, has six essential national interests—survival, sovereignty, security, territory, legitimacy, and relative capability—from which its foreign policy flows. This theory was able to give pride of place to the recurrent national unity challenge as a survival threat to Canadian foreign policy, allowed people to measure how well Canada was doing in defending its national interests compared to all the other polities in the present or past, and helped us conclude from the evidence that Canada could be the most successful country in the world since the Westphalian system first arose way back in 1648. Such success as a state allowed Canada as a nation increasingly to seek and secure its distinctive national values, a concept first theorized and then empirically identified as anti-militarism, environmentalism, multiculturalism, openness, globalism, and international institutionalism. The theory entered into and drew from the new debate about whether Canadian foreign policy does or should derive from interests or from values, and from which ones in each case.

The third element, coming at the systemic, societal, and state levels, was the concept of neo-vulnerability (Kirton 1993). Joseph Nye's initial concept of vulnerability, probably inspired by the OPEC oil shock of 1973, was based on a deliberate state action aimed at and designed to hurt a target state. The concept of neo-vulnerability extended Nye's insight to include and emphasize how non-state, indeed non-human, activities and processes that were unintended and untargeted could spread anywhere to afflict even the most powerful polity, whose unilateral, protectionist, or isolationist policy changes could not remove or reliably reduce the vulnerability to national interests and distinctive national values (as well as mere preferences) that thus arose. These new security threats were conceptualized and identified in 1993 as terrorist, ecological, and drug- and health-related (Kirton 1993). Immediately after the chapter specifying them went to press, terrorists associated with Al Qaeda hit the twin towers in New York City and killed nearly 3000 Americans on 11 September 2001. By September 2005, the United States had 'lost a city' to Hurricane Katrina, in a physical realization of what had only been the constructed imagination of nuclear war gamers in the city-trading deterrence age. By the classic calculus of the 'body count', the world's most capable principal power, the United States, had become the most vulnerable one, while the least capable principal power, Canada, remained, despite the Air India tragedy, the least vulnerable one.

The fourth theoretical element was the explicit articulation of the parsimonious but powerful principal power paradox. It stated that as states gain in relative capability they become less policy-takers and more policy-makers within the international system, with the result that external determinants have less salience in shaping their foreign policy and societal and governmental determinants higher salience in doing so. This logic united the cause-and-effect components of the seven basic questions of foreign policy analysis on which the three theoretical perspectives of liberal internationalism, peripheral dependence, and complex neo-realism were based. Given the argument that Canada was emerging as principal power, this pointed to a future in which individual determinants within the governmental ones—even ultimately the beliefs and skill of an individual prime minister—could actually matter in the making of Canadian foreign policy and its results for Canada and the world. This element restored democratic policy accountability and human agency to a systemically rarefied world in which the leader of Canada was previously only a rationally confined calculator of systemic determinants, or socialized out of the Canadian political system if, as with John Diefenbaker in 1962, he or she failed that stark systemic test. The principal power paradox also predicted a future in which a Canada doing so well in defending its national interests could focus in its foreign policy on forwarding Canada's distinctive national values as the foundation for a new world order. Pierre Trudeau successfully started this tradition in the late 1960s, and under Prime Minister Paul Martin Canada asserted its vision of itself within the international community in the 2005 *International Policy Statement—A Role of Pride and Influence in the World.*

The fifth element was to advance beyond the trend of Canada emerging, declining, or staying the same, to specify a threshold or a level at which Canada would actually arrive as a principal power in a changing and much changed world. Specifying thresholds, like making point predictions, is a difficult task, and securing further clarity here is a task that remains. But the theory contained so many components that could be used to trace and test the dynamics, and thus the ability of Canada to secure its desired approach to world order, that by 2007, in *Canadian Foreign Policy in a Changing World*, I concluded that Canada had now emerged as a principal power in a much changed world. Those focused parochially on Canada's new prime minister, Stephen Harper, had their doubts. But those focused on a changing world saw a broader picture. With the United States afflicted by possible political and military defeats in Iraq and Afghanistan as well as by a global financial crisis, and with China, India, and Brazil gaining economic and political influence, in part through the new G20 summit, the specified systemic conditions for this bold assertion appear to be materializing.

Evidence 2010

Canada as a Principal Power was constructed on the premise that the facts do matter, despite whether or not commentators in downtown Toronto like what their prime minister in Ottawa is doing. The ultimate test of the work is whether it accurately predicted an actual or potential future for Canadian foreign policy, or predicted the major alternatives if the systemic conditions unfolded in an empirically different but theoretically well defined way. Amidst the many empirical applications to be made before a definitive conclusion can be reached on this point, a few fundamental facts stand out to suggest that this empirical test might have been met.

The first concerns objective capability and the long list of critical components of power or performance on which Canada stands number one in the world. These include uranium production, potash, fresh water, coastlines, temperate forests, and liveable and multicultural cities. Canada is first in the production of hydroelectricity and third in natural gas, prompting Prime Minister Stephen Harper to assert Canada's intentions of being a 'clean energy superpower'. Canada's position in the specified top tier of seven to nine powers is bolstered by its second place rank in territory, and in having, thanks to Alberta's tar sands, at least the world's second largest oil reserves. Canada's objective capabilities in terms of resources, population, and technology suggest a principal power ranking.

The second fact concerns the asserted position and acknowledged status. Prime Minister Kim Campbell's 1993 statement that Canada is a major power, and Prime Minister Harpers' declaration abroad that Canada is an emerging energy superpower, make the 1983 claim that Canada was emerging as a principal power look modest. In 2006 in London, British prime minister Tony Blair presented Canada as a major superpower in the energy field.

To Canadians themselves in Calgary in 2007, Blair predicted that Canada will become one of the most powerful countries in the world. Among current leading commentators outside of Canada, in 2008 Fareed Zakaria concluded that 'Canada is becoming a major power'. He described Canada as a benign neighbour of the United States, with better broadband, health care and automotive manufacturing, a troop contributor to the American-led, UN-endorsed mission in Afghanistan, and a core part of the global British Empire in its illustrious past (Zakaria 2008: 29).

The third fact concerns activity and association. Canada now has six full bilateral free trade agreements and is negotiating one with Europe—the largest market in the world—in a Trudeauvian diversification dream finally come true. Moreover, since 1990, Canada has become a highly war-prone country, going to war ever more expansively and always winning, or at least not yet losing. Canada's longest engagement in Afghanistan remains to be won.

The fourth fact concerns the approach to world order. Canada has not only advanced highly authentic and ambitious conceptions, but achieved them as well. Under the agency of Prime Minister Paul Martin, Canada advocated for and secured the Responsibility to Protect principle, the antithesis of Article 2(7) of the UN Charter and anchor of the Westphalian system, now collectively affirmed by the leaders of virtually every country in the world. As Canada's finance minister in 1999, Paul Martin invented the Group of Twenty (G20), a group of systemically significant states that leapt to leaders' level summit meetings in 2008 in response to the American-turned-global financial crisis and the financial vulnerability it entailed. The G20 is now the central forum for global economic governance, working alongside the more established Group of Eight (G8). In 2010, Canada will chair the G8 major market democracies' summit, and co-chair the newly institutionalized G20 summit meeting. Its place at the centre of global governance is well entrenched.

Conclusion

Any serious theory lives on in the mind of its creator, its predictions constantly challenged by new observables, frequently beleaguered by self-doubt. In that spirit, it is important to note two possible threats, beyond the globally existential issues of nuclear and climate vulnerability, that could dislodge Canada from its now established principal power perch. The first, from faraway Afghanistan, is the first war that Canada could, having fought for so long, actually lose, with consequences for the country that can only be predicted by going beyond Canada to the comparative foreign policy realm.

The second threat touches on national unity, the core component of the first national interest of survival. It is the haunting reminder from René Lévesque's important article 'For an Independent Quebec', in *Foreign Affairs* in 1976, that federal government policy constituted 'demographic genocide' for Canada's francophone population. Canada prides itself on a multiculturalism founded by francophones and that includes the First Nations population as part of the essence of this distinctive national value. How Canadian foreign policy can solve that compounding problem is a challenge of the first order.

The theory put forth in *Canada as a Principal Power* is still relevant today in explaining Canadian foreign policy. In 2010, Canada has emerged as a principal power, particularly in the energy field. As Canada continues to shift from being a policy-taker to a policy-maker in the international system, Canadian politicians will play an increasingly influential role in international affairs, promoting distinctive Canadian national values and interests in the world.

Key Terms

Complex Neo-Realist Perspective
Principal Power

References

Bratt, Duane, and Christopher Kukucha, eds., (2007). *Readings in Canadian Foreign Policy* (Toronto: Oxford University Press).

Eayrs, James. (1975). 'Defining a New Place for Canada in the Hierarchy of the World,' *International Perspectives* (May/June): 15–21.

Granatstein, J.L. (1969). *Canadian Foreign Policy Since 1945: Middle Power or Satellite?* (Toronto: Copp Clark).

Hawes, Michael. (1984). *Principal Power, Middle Power or Satellite?* (Toronto: York Research Programme in Strategic Studies).

Keohane, Robert, and Joseph Nye. (1977). *Power and Interdependence: World Politics in Transition* (Boston: Little, Brown).

Kirton, John. (1993). 'The Seven-Power Summit as a New Security Institution,' in David Dewitt, David Haglund, and John Kirton, eds., *Building a New Global Order: Emerging Trends in International Security* (Toronto: Oxford University Press), 335–57.

Kirton, John. (2007). *Canadian Foreign Policy in a Changing World* (Toronto: Nelson Thomson Canada).

Kirton, John. (2009). 'The Ten Most Important Books on Canadian Foreign Policy', *International Journal* 64 (Spring 2009): 553–64. (Also reprinted in Duane Bratt, and Christopher Kukucha, eds., *Readings in Canadian Foreign Policy: Classic Debates and New Ideas* (Oxford University Press: Canada, revised edition, 2011).

Mackay, R.A., and E.B. Rogers. (1938). *Canada Looks Abroad* (Oxford: Oxford University Press).

Molot, Maureen. (1990). 'Where Do We, Should We, Or Can We Sit? A Review of Canadian Foreign Policy Literature,' *International Journal of Canadian Studies* 1, 2 (Spring–Fall 1990): 77–96.

Stairs, Denis. (1974). *Diplomacy of Constraint: Canada, The Korean War and the United States* (Toronto: University of Toronto Press).

Thordarson, Bruce. (1972). *Trudeau and Foreign Policy: A Study in Decision-Making* (Toronto Oxford University Press).

Tomlin, Brian, Norman Hillmer, and Fen Osler Hampson (2008). *Canada's International Policies: Agendas, Alternatives, and Policies* (Toronto: Oxford University Press).

Waltz, Kenneth. (1979). *Theory of International Politics* (Don Mills: Addison-Wesley).

Zakaria, Fareed. (2008). *The Post-American World* (New York: W.W. Norton & Company, 2008), 182.

5

THE CHOICE TO BE MADE

Stephen Clarkson

In most cases disagreements over Canadian foreign policy appear to revolve round matters of fact.
Continentalists believe that our membership in
NATO increases our political influence, while
Nationalists reject the link between the Atlantic
alliance and Canada's international effectiveness.
Yet only part of the dispute is really concerned with
'hard facts'. The major points at issue are questions
of evaluation and interpretation. We can establish
as facts what amounts of money and manpower we
devote to our NATO commitments, but this does
not *prove* Continentalists right in their contention
that our contribution of guns and troops increases
Canada's power in West Europe or Washington.
Nor does it *prove* Nationalists' contrary thesis that
the influence we may have is not worth the cost
that would better be devoted to peace-keeping
through an international police force. In both cases
the authors are really invoking the support of conflicting assumptions to which they make the tacit
appeal that political influence through collective
action is desirable in Continentalists' view (insignificant in Nationalists'), that the communist
threat is serious (or unreal), that the Atlantic area

is more (or less) important to Canada than the
under-developed world, and so on . . .

TWO ALTERNATIVES

Once we recognize this, we can see that the key to
the often confusing debate on what Canadian foreign policy should be can be found in the underlying clash between two opposing foreign policy
theories. Each theory contains a complete, if
implicit, explanation of the world situation and of
Canada's role in it, including a view of the American
relationship and a statement of objectives for Canadian diplomacy. Let's follow current fashion and
call the contending theories 'quiet' and 'independent'. By the 'quiet' foreign policy approach I mean
the official policy as expressed in statements, the
government's practice as seen over the last five
years and the image projected by our diplomats in
their execution of this policy. Although is referred
to throughout this book as an 'independent' foreign policy has not been systematically articulated
as a coherent doctrine, I shall present briefly what
appear to me to be the major positions of each

theory in order to crystallize their differences and so make possible a choice between these opposing approaches to Canada's foreign policy.

THE INTERNATIONAL SITUATION
Quiet approach

As in the late 1940s and 1950s, the world is still polarized along ideological lines between the forces of Communism and the West. Despite the splits in the Marxist-Leninist bloc, the defence of the free world is still the major priority. Revolution is a continuing threat to world stability, especially in the under-developed continents of Asia, Africa, and Latin America. This makes it all the more important to contain Communism in Vietnam and Cuba lest the whole 'third world' fall to the Reds like a row of dominoes. The United States is the only power able to pursue a containment policy on a world-wide basis. Its allies must support this effort.

Independent approach

The stabilization of Soviet and European communism has reduced the former Communist military threat to the West, turning the Cold War into a cold peace. The major world problem is no longer the East–West ideological confrontation but the North–South economic division of the world into rich and poor. Revolution is less a Red menace than an aspect of achieving the urgently needed socio-economic transformations in the under-developed world; in any case it is no direct threat to our society. Naive American impulses to save the world from Communism are misguided, out of date, and a menace to world peace. The breakdown of the monolithic unity of both the Communist and Western blocs gives middle powers like Canada greater margins for independent manoeuvre.

CANADA'S NATIONAL INTERESTS
Quiet approach

As a Western, democratic, and industrial country, Canada's national interests are essentially similar to those of our continental neighbour and friend, the United States, which is still the arsenal and defender of the free world. Worrying about national unity is of far less importance than pulling our weight in the Atlantic Alliance. Collective security is the only defence against new Hitlers or Stalins; we must not forget the lessons of 1939 and 1948.

Independent approach

A less ideologically but more socially concerned view of the world shows that Canada's national interests coincide more with general progress than with the maintenance of the United States's superpower status. Our external economic and political interest in trade with Communist countries diverges from American restrictions against 'trading with the enemy'. Canada's internal political divisions and our national identity crisis create another urgent national task for our policy: reinforce Canada's sense of bicultural personality.

INDEPENDENCE
Quiet approach

Foreign policy independence is an illusion in the present-day world unless it is defined as head-in-the-sand isolation. We might just as well try to cut Canada off from North America and float out into the Atlantic. Independence must also mean a narrow and harmful anti-Americanism.

Independent approach

Far from being illusory, independence—being able to control one's own socio-economic environment—is an essential condition for the healthy development of the nation-state. Independence means neither isolation nor anti-Americanism, unless making up our own minds on the merits of individual foreign policies is considered un-American.

INTERDEPENDENCE
Quiet approach

Relations of interdependence are the situations within which middle powers must normally operate. Alliances and supranational organizations provide Canada with the best way to exercise influence and be useful in day-to-day international affairs. Ties of interdependence also guarantee weaker powers against arbitrary action by the strong, both by binding the super-powers to listen and by giving the small a forum within which to unite their forces.

Independent approach

Obligations freely undertaken in cooperation with other countries are perfectly legitimate if they improve both the national and the world situation, for example, IMF or GATT. Interdependence can create new opportunities that can be exploited to further the national interest commercially and increase our influence diplomatically. Fulfilling our many international commitments is the staple of our diplomatic activity and the means of building our influence. But we must be ready to use this credit when initiatives are needed. Too much interdependence can become glorified dependence.

INTERNATIONAL OBJECTIVES
Quiet approach

In the light of this analysis of the international situation and our national interests, we should strive to defend the status quo, nurturing our influence in Washington and helping maintain the solidarity of the Western alliance as the expression of our commitment to internationalism and the defence of democracy. Our order of priorities should be the American relationship first, then the Atlantic Alliance, finally the developing countries. All our actions should keep in mind the central importance of collective actions as the appropriate activity of a middle power.

Independent approach

Given the more relaxed international environment and our internal need for a more distinctive foreign activity, Canadian objectives should outgrow our anti-communism to embrace the aims of international equality and socio-economic modernization. This may entail more economic sacrifice and more tolerance of revolutionary change, but an enlightened nationalism requires re-evaluating our aims in terms of the most pressing needs of the whole world and will refuse to hide behind any alliance apron strings. Accordingly the 'third world' should now come first in our priorities as the affairs of the Atlantic community can more easily take care of themselves. Our American relationship should not prejudice these international priorities.

OVERALL FOREIGN POLICY STRATEGY
Quiet approach

Our general strategy should be affiliation, or close alignment and cooperation, with our super-power neighbour to achieve maximum diplomatic power by our influence on the Western bloc leader. We can only enjoy this influence by accepting the American foreign policy framework and restraining our urge to criticize the Americans. This then gives us access to the inner corridors of US power.

Independent approach

Canada is too unimportant in Washington's world-view for us to have significant direct influence on American foreign policy. Our strategy should be to act directly in a given situation after making an independent evaluation of the problem. Except for continental matters of direct Canadian–American concern, influence on Washington would normally be a secondary objective. Even then our power to affect Washington's policy will depend on our international effectiveness, not our allegedly 'special' relationship.

TACTICS TO IMPLEMENT THE STRATEGY

Quiet approach

'Quiet diplomacy' describes the foreign policy method most appropriate to implement an affiliation strategy. It puts special emphasis on confidential, friendly contacts with our allies, primarily the Americans, so that any differences that may arise are ironed out before they can reach crisis proportions and come out in the open. American views should be anticipated and taken into consideration as part of our own policy-making. Publicity is to be avoided as are public declarations of criticism by our leader. Rather, our role should be to seek common ground between those in disagreement.

Independent approach

Communications between our diplomats and those of other countries are by definition quiet. Carrying on our routine diplomatic business will therefore be unobtrusive. But there is no reason to make quietness a cardinal feature of our foreign policy, for this is to renounce in advance one of the most effective of a small power's bargaining

tools, the use of exposure and public pressure to strengthen our position against a big power. If we have something to say and want to be heard, we must speak up. In dealing with the State Department, which has dozens of importunate allies to cope with, not to mention its enemies, the demure may earn some gratitude from harried American diplomats. It does not follow that the 'smooth' diplomat will get more response than his 'raucous' rival.

FOREIGN POLICY STYLE

Quiet approach

Our international style for quiet diplomacy should be that of the discreet professionals who operate outside the glare of the TV lights and the prying eye of the press in close harmony with the diplomats of our allies, unobtrusively husbanding our stock of goodwill and influence. This would maintain our credit as a responsible friend in Washington, preserve our special access to inside information and so maximize our ability to affect American policy-making when we do disagree privately with it.

Independent approach

A hush-puppy style may be proper for our diplomats but is not the manner that our political leaders should adopt if they want to reinforce the Canadian identity. Without having to bang their shoes on the United Nations podium they could adopt a more assertive stance that makes clear Canada's existence as a bicultural nation with a unique set of policies. It is unrealistic not to be concerned with the 'public relations' aspect of our foreign policy, since the way we present ourselves in the world—our international image—has a direct bearing on our international effectiveness.

To this extent it is true that the posture of independence is a vital part of the policy.

THE AMERICAN RELATIONSHIP

Quiet approach

As it is this relationship that gives Canada special influence through our geographical, political, and psychological proximity, nurturing the American relationship should have highest priority. We should not question the ultimate goals of the United States that has, after all, world-wide responsibilities for the defence of the free world. In addition we must realize that Canada cannot survive economically without the goodwill of the Americans upon whom we depend for our high standard of living. It would be 'counter-productive' to try to influence American policies by publicly opposing them. This would only reinforce the extremist elements advocating the policies we opposed.

Independent approach

Our relations with the United States are 'special' because of the disparity of our power and the degree to which we depend on American trade and capital inflows. We should for this reason devote careful attention to our relations, especially if we are planning international moves of which they do not approve. The huge military and political power of the US should make us particularly critical of American policies however well-intentioned the Average American may be. Our well-being is not a product of bounteous concessions made by the US but of economic development considered to be to both countries' advantage. Our relationship should be governed by this awareness of mutual benefit. There is no evidence that independent actions strengthen extremism in the US. If we really wish to influence American public opinion, we have to make it clear what policy we advocate. There is no better way than actually pursuing it.

RETALIATION

Quiet approach

We are so dependent on the American economy that we cannot afford to do anything that might annoy them such as taking some foreign policy initiative that displeases Congress or the Administration. The price of independence would be a 25 per cent drop in our standard of living. . . . We are, after all, the little pig that must be eternally vigilant lest the big pig roll over. . . . We cannot increase this risk by provoking it to roll deliberately. In such areas as the Defence Production Sharing Agreements we gain enormously from being able to bid on American defence contracts. The share of the US market we have won pays for our own purchases of American war material at prices cheaper than we could produce it ourselves. We cannot afford the luxury of independence, whatever our conscience might say, since independent actions might jeopardize these arrangements.

Independent approach

The possibility of retaliation is present in all international relationships. It is true that we are more vulnerable to American than the US is to Canadian retaliation, but we must not forget that retaliation is a reaction of last resort showing that all milder negotiation has failed. By being willing to use the whole armoury of diplomatic weapons—bilateral and multilateral, informal and public—we could reduce the dangers of retaliation conjured up by the all-or-nothing approach of quiet diplomacy. We must realize that as the little power, we have important advantages. We can concentrate our whole attention on defending our interests in the continental relationship, which, from the

American point of view, is but one of dozens of issues of greater importance. We have important hostages in Canada, the very subsidiaries that are the instruments of US political and economic pressure. We can also use the threat of mobilizing public opinion to strengthen our hand against possible intimidation and economic blackmail. Our goodwill and our favourable image in the United States as a long-standing friend is a further asset we should not ignore.

INTERNAL IMPACT OF FOREIGN POLICY

Quiet approach

The internal implications of our diplomacy are negligible and should remain so. Foreign policy should be practised to achieve specific external goals and not to boost the national ego. If Canadians have an identity problem, they should cure it themselves, not resort to artificial stimulation. Similarly we should not let our concern for internal problems of biculturalism distort our foreign policy. External affairs and internal politics should be kept in their proper places. Quebec should not drag foreign policy into its federal arguments with Ottawa.

Independent approach

It is impossible to dissociate external from internal policies if only because external relations are carried out by all branches of government—finance, commerce, defence, and citizenship are involved and even the provinces, quite apart from external affairs. Foreign policy must in any case be seen as only one aspect of the government's total network of policies. We cannot afford *not* to exploit the nation-building potential of our foreign policies, since the way others perceive us—dynamic and bicultural, or ineffectual and

divided—can strengthen, or undermine, our own national identity. Similarly, if we accept French-Canadian desires for cultural equality and Quebec's demands for greater self-control, our foreign policy should reflect and reinforce Canada's new binational politics.

The 'quiet' approach to our foreign policy is not an extremist absurdity, however unlike most nations' foreign policy doctrines it may appear. It is the rationale of Canadian diplomacy. The over-riding concern for kid-glove relations with our American neighbours was articulated in 1965 by the Merchant-Heeney Report with all the hallmarks of official policy. The feeling of economic dependence is not an opposition charge but a situation acknowledged by the prime minister himself.[1] The surprisingly unsophisticated cold warrior analysis complete with the domino theory of Asian communism is heard time after time from our diplomats, both senior officers and newly inducted recruits. In our discussions with these foreign service officers during our ULSR seminars, we found them cut off from the Canadian public whose views they take to be adequately expressed by *Globe and Mail* editorials or questions posed in the House of Commons. More disconcerting is the professionals' scorn for the amateur that colours their attitude toward the value of the public's opinion. Quiet diplomacy is enshrined as the conventional wisdom of our federal political establishment.

INDEPENDENCE YES, QUIET DIPLOMACY NO

However accepted this doctrine may be, I would submit that it is no longer suitable for Canadian foreign policy in the late sixties. It is inappropriate, first of all for the reasons stated in the 'independent' replies to the 'quiet' positions summarized above: its view of the world is ten years out of date; its understanding of Canada's international needs and capabilities is hopelessly circumscribed.

'Quiet' foreign policy is also unacceptable in a mass democracy. If, to be effective, our quiet foreign policy must be carried on in complete secrecy so that even its successes should not be known lest they compromise further success, . . . how are the voters ever to know whether the policy is justified? Are they simply to accept the protestations of diligence and sincerity by the minister of External Affairs or the prime minister and the assurances of our diplomats, all claiming to plead impartially in their own cause? Until all the files are open . . . we cannot know for sure. But even then how would proof be certain? To be sure that the quiet approach had been the more effective it would be necessary to show what results the independent approach would have produced in exactly the same circumstances— an obviously impossible condition. We cannot wait 50 years for the files to be open, even if they did promise final proof. Quiet diplomacy has been practised long enough for the onus to be on its defenders to demonstrate their case. The record does not lend them very strong support. Such a diplomatic success as Pearson's constructive role in the 1956 Suez crisis is an example of independent initiative, well conceived at an appropriate time . . .

When the defenders of quiet diplomacy expound on our influence in Washington, their argument raises more doubts. To start with they are hard put to provide empirical evidence of Canada's power to make Washington act in the way we want. They go on to insist that this putative special influence in Washington is the basis for Canada's power in other countries who take us seriously, because they assume we have a unique path to American waiting chambers. But they then warn that we should not actually try to use this influence for this would undermine this special position and so our international status. Strange logic, a sophisticated rationalization for inaction. Influence is

like credit: it has to be used to exist. The quiet diplomatists manage to underrate Canada's real power to act by exaggerating our potential influence.

The alternative to quiet diplomacy is not 'raising a row'; it is developing an independent foreign policy. Independence means above all striving for maximum effectiveness. Those times when Canada has been most clearly effective it has acted directly, achieving negotiations in Korea or the exclusion of South Africa from the Commonwealth. This means neither that it acted alone nor against a big power. Kicking Uncle Sam in the shins or twisting the lion's tail has no necessary part in any of Canada's more independent actions. Canadians are not even aware that our enlightened aid program toward Tanzania was pushed forward despite Dar-es-Salaam's rupture of relations with Britain. Such acts are satisfactory because they are effective. They are effective because the Canadian initiative itself contributed directly to achieve the particular goal. They achieved this goal because in these situations the Canadian government acted flexibly; not out of deference or automatic loyalty to another power. To act flexibly means to make up one's own mind— to be independent.

To make independence the standard for our foreign policy is not to opt out of the many undramatic areas of collective diplomacy in which Canada makes a continuing major contribution at a supranational level. Nor does independence imply anti-Americanism, however much the bogey of 'making a row' is raised. Deciding policies on their own merits may well lead to disagreement with American policy. Still there is no reason to inflate such policy disagreements to disastrous proportions unless the defendants of quiet diplomacy really believe the Americans to be the most vindictive politicians on earth. . . . we have followed a line directly counter to American policy on a problem of the highest sensitivity, Cuba, and still not suffered retaliation. The point is that if we diverge it is not for the sake of a quarrel but to practise what we feel to be the correct policy, after due consideration of the Americans' reasons. It is hard to believe that a more assertive Canadian foreign policy would be countered in Washington by a concerted anti-Canadian policy. The more truculent General de Gaulle has become, the gentler has been the Americans' treatment of France. With so much direct investment in Canada, it is unlikely that the Americans, in Baldwin's phrase, would want to get rid of a blemish on the finger by amputating the arm.

Independence also requires realism in our conception of the American relationship. Our interactions with the US are so intense and multitudinous at all levels of political, economic, cultural, and personal contact that we should make a fundamental distinction between our foreign policies on one hand and our American policies on the other. While pursuing what we consider to be the best policy abroad, it is in our interest to place the strongest emphasis on the maintenance of good neighbourly relations with the US. In all matters of mutual concern, whether financial investment, tariff policy, resource development, or cultural interchange, the policies of both countries toward each other must continue to be formulated in close consultation. We clearly have an essential unity of self-interests with the Americans in our continental partnership. But partnership requires equality, and equality implies independence. . .

An independent foreign policy is an ethically just policy. Continentalists attack the critics of quiet diplomacy for being 'ostentatiously on the side of virtue, regardless of practical consequences'. One can heartily agree that a 'tub-thumping moralistic approach' is distasteful and that a disregard for practical consequences is irresponsible. Yet an argument for independence is not *moralistic* for raising *moral* problems. Nationalists argue that an independent approach is necessarily more ethical

for it requires an autonomous calculation for every policy of the probable consequences both for Canada and for those our policy will affect. It is the defenders of quiet diplomacy who are open to the charge of moralism if they cling dogmatically to a moral judgment of American policy made twenty years ago.

An independent foreign policy also presupposes responsibility. As only a free man is considered responsible for his actions, only a nation which makes its own decisions can be considered in charge of its destiny and can expect its citizenry to believe in its integrity. And like the youth who can only develop maturely if they liberate themselves from parental controls, the nation-state can only achieve full expression if it is master in its own house, able to act in the community of nations as a fully responsible entity.

THE PROBLEM OF REFORM

If independence is more desirable as an overall guideline for our foreign policy, why is quietness still the guiding light of Canadian diplomacy? Not from American pressure. Nor for lack of international scope, particularly in the under-developed world. The conclusion must be that the problem is here at home. Yet we can hardly blame public opinion. The opinion polls, for all their inaccuracies, indicate that the general public's views have been consistently more nationalist on foreign policy issues like Vietnam, the Dominican Republic, and China than the government.[2] All the major parties have, at the very least, strong wings in favour of a more independent diplomacy. Predominant editorial opinion, church statements, students groups, and academic protests complete the general picture of a public opinion that increasingly rejects quietness.

It would be superficial to conclude with facile exhortations to the leadership to change its policy. The conditions are so favourable for an independent foreign policy that the persistence of a quiet approach indicates more fundamental problems are involved. If we are to make some proposals for reform we must assess the underlying reasons for this anomalous state of affairs. These are threefold and interconnected: a decision-making structure that isolates the government from public participation and control, an elitist ideology for the civil service that legitimizes this insulation, and a leadership that perpetuates this situation.

The foreign policy-making process is almost completely sealed off from the normal give and take between public and government. Even members of Parliament have no significant access to this 'closed circuit'. In a recent article surveying the problems of the Department of External Affairs, the undersecretary of state for external affairs, Marcel Cadieux, deals quite extensively with his relationship with the minister. Yet, with the exception of consulting university specialists, he makes no mention of the contribution that members of the public, parliamentarians included, can make to the formation of the nation's foreign policy. 'Without public understanding', he concedes, 'we can hardly hope to develop Canada's role in world affairs.'[3] He doesn't seem to feel that the public has any greater part to play than to stand and wait, deferentially yet comprehendingly, in the spectators' boxes.

It is institutional security from criticism that makes quiet diplomacy the natural ideology of the diplomatic caste. It gives a theoretical justification for the handling of all business by routine bureaucratic channels. If foreign policy is the private domain of the administrator, he or she need not take seriously clamour, interest group opinion, or, God forbid, parliamentary interference. Public discussion of foreign policy problems is fine and even desirable, our diplomats will hasten to profess, so long as it does not disturb their professional activity.

The crucial link in this combination of institutional isolation and bureaucratic elitism is its endorsement by the leadership. Paradoxically the Liberal leaders bring an unprecedented background of experience to their handling of foreign affairs. Yet Mr Pearson, the Nobel Prize winner, has turned the 'unobtrusive oil can' tactics, which led to his own international successes in the mid-fifties into a dogma which frustrates the continuation of this early record. Mr Martin, for all his concern for his public image, is unable to convey to the nation a convincing and unambiguous understanding of what Canada can achieve internationally and has not been able to transmit the growing public concern for foreign policy questions into revised governmental policies. Nor has he shown any sign of opening the major issues of foreign policy, such as the decision to renew the NORAD agreement, to public debate in parliament. Institutions, ideology, and leadership: we have here a troika of conditions that require basic reforms and changes. Yet remedies cannot be solely of relevance to our foreign policy. We face a general problem of Canadian democracy—the responsiveness of governmental policy and the civil service to public scrutiny and control. Reforms needed in this area of public policy are needed in other branches as well:

> All bureaucracy is conservative, but the conservatism of diplomatic bureaucracy is in a class by itself. The ethos of diplomacy is an ethos of suspicion—suspicion tempered by skepticism, snow tempered by ice. The foreign service officer is a nay-sayer in statecraft, the abominable no-man of diplomacy. His mission in life is to preserve the status quo from those who propose to alter it.[4]

. . . [T]he problem of foreign policy change is the problem of subjecting bureaucratic inertia to some reasonable form of public control.

LET THE PUBLIC IN

The first step is to open the process of policy-forming so that the expression of expert, informed, and articulate opinions can have a major impact on foreign policy-making. Yet in this age of McLuhan, our channels for public participation in politics are still using a Walter Bagehot technology. Gallup polls give irregular insights into public views on simplified issues, but their findings are ignored unless politically exploitable. A partial solution is to put the measuring of attitudes on a regular and scientific basis, possibly by a research institute that would, by continuous sampling, make 'what public opinion wants' no longer a subject for guesswork. More important, structural change such as the activation of the parliamentary committee on foreign affairs . . . could institutionalize the public scrutiny of foreign policy in a way compatible with the parliamentary system. To be meaningful the committee would need a full-time research staff and would have to be able to require testimony from expert and interested groups as well as diplomats. While such a watchdog committee could not actually make policy, the defence committee hearings on tri-service unification have proved that basic public issues can be brought out into the open for thorough airing. The hearings would also provide our diplomats with a link to articulate opinion; they would start to see themselves as public servants rather than tight-lipped agents.

Another by-product would be important, if intangible. Coverage of the committee hearings by mass media would help give the public a sense of being involved in this hitherto exclusive area of policy. Other ways should be initiated to increase the public's interest in foreign policy.

If our foreign activity is to have the strength of public participation, the public must be sufficiently informed. Never have ordinary people been so exposed by instant communications to international events, so bombarded with journalistic commentary and academic debate. Never have they had such a high level of education to absorb this information. But the data on Canadian foreign policy with which the public could come to policy conclusions is not made available. The change that is needed here is less quantitative than qualitative. To make public opinion aware of Canada's foreign policy problems, mass media and newspaper reports must relate their analysis of foreign affairs to Canadian external activity.

CIVIL MASTERS OR CIVIL SERVANTS?

To change from a quiet to a more independent approach to our foreign policy will require a transformation of the values of the practitioners, the diplomats in the Department of External Affairs. So long as the personnel of external affairs maintain a secretive, distrustful attitude toward the public, an independent foreign policy is doubly stymied. An informed, alert public opinion cannot be developed if extensive, relevant information is not made regularly and easily available. As long as external affairs maintains its Mandarin mystique explicitly tied to quiet diplomacy and anti-communism, the civil servants would be likely to block the implementation of an alternative foreign policy, even if the government should desire it.

To change our diplomats from civil masters to civil servants will require a change in their ideology. A partial measure is to modify the environment they enter when they are recruited into the service so that the values they absorb conform to the desire of the public and the views of the leadership. In France, for example, recruits to all branches of the upper civil service receive three full years of practical and theoretical training at the National Administration School where they absorb the dynamic, nationalist values of the French state and so start their career as activist, not conservative, civil servants. The excellence and dynamism of the French civil service is one of the principal reasons for the impact of de Gaulle's foreign policy in Europe. Rather than have our new diplomats absorb willy-nilly the smug, conservative attitudes of the established bureaucracy, an introductory training program—needed in any case to improve technical and linguistic competence—could give them an awareness of the role that the political leadership wants Canada to play and a consciousness of the challenge of achieving these goals in a democratic framework.

To prevent the diplomats from becoming cut off from public and informed opinion they need continual 'professional retraining' just as any doctor or engineer. Sabbatical leaves for research and senior staff officer courses are needed if our international crisis managers are to keep up intellectually with the rate of change of the crises they are entrusted to manage.

LEADERSHIP FROM THE TOP

No change in our diplomats' value system and no structural reform will be very productive without a third innovation: dynamic leadership. The muddling through of the quiet approach will continue until Canada's leaders realize that determination and a clear articulation of political objectives are needed to turn potentiality into reality. Canada is wealthy, strong, and developed. It does not need the mountain-moving voluntarism of Mao Tse-Tung. It simply needs a leadership that can make it clear to the public—if not in a little *Red Book* at least in a *White Paper*—what role Canada can play and how its objectives are to be achieved. This would give a sense of direction to the unusual talents in our diplomatic service and harness the force of public opinion behind this effort.

PARTNERSHIP WITH QUEBEC

It is finally necessary to remove the uncertainty overshadowing the future of confederation. Although Quebec nationalism has made a major contribution to the development of a more independent Canadian activity, particularly in starting an aid program to the French-speaking African states, the open diplomatic warfare between Ottawa and Quebec that broke out in conjunction with de Gaulle's visit to Quebec is rapidly becoming self-destructive.

It is time to come to some firm decision whether or not Quebec can satisfy its international aspirations as a special province in the federation acting both through Ottawa and autonomously in its areas of provincial jurisdiction. This is essentially an issue for Quebecers to decide, though their compatriots can reasonably urge that the debate be fair and full before any irrevocable step is taken. It is for the French-Canadian intellectuals to spell out the costs and benefits of special status in the federation versus complete separation. Their English-speaking colleagues can point out, however, why they would like Quebec to stay in the effort to develop a new foreign policy. Not only does Quebec's wealth add strength to Canada's foreign power but, more importantly, Quebec's culture and technology makes it possible for the total Canadian international effort in the underdeveloped world to have a unique impact. But the only finally convincing argument is the demonstration that Ottawa can mount a foreign policy that would be more independent and more effective than the foreign role that Quebec could play by itself, as a single state. Quiet diplomacy has failed to provide this proof.

It is our belief that an independent foreign policy could give this proof to French and English Canadians alike by, first, rejecting its lingering anti-communism and downgrading the Cold War alliances while, second, redirecting its resources and redefining its priorities to a determined support for the political, economic, and social needs of the developing countries—both through its multilateral diplomacy in international organizations and by directly making Canada a 'great power in foreign aid'.[5]

THE PUBLIC SHOULD CHOOSE

We need more open diplomats, we need more public participation in policy-making. But most of all we need to choose: between the quiet, continental foreign policy we have followed in the main over the past decade and an independent foreign policy.

Key Terms

Continentalists
Independent Diplomacy
Nationalists

Quiet Diplomacy
Satellite

Notes

1. Interview published in *Maclean's*, July 1967, 52.
2. Unpublished paper presented to the ULSR by Roman March, Carleton University.
3. Marcel Cadieux, 'La Tache du Sous-Secrétaire d'Etat aux Affaires extérieures', *International Journal* 22, 3 (Summer 1967): 527.
4. James Eayrs, *Fate and Will in Foreign Policy* (Toronto: Canadian Broadcasting Corporation, 1967), 50.
5. A phrase coined by Escott Reid in a speech to the Kiwanis Club, Toronto, 27 September 1967, when he argued that Canadian aid should be expanded from $300 million to $1 billion in five years.

UPDATE: THE CHOICES THAT WERE MADE AND THOSE THAT REMAIN

Re-reading 'The Choice to be Made'—the conclusion to the book, *An Independent Foreign Policy for Canada?* that I edited four decades ago after organizing a year-long process of discussions between many Canadian diplomats and a cross-disciplinary group of younger academic colleagues—gave me a strange feeling. *Plus ça change.* And much has changed in Canada's international, continental, and domestic context. *Plus c'est la même chose.* And much also remains the same in our seemingly eternal debate about Canada's role in the world.

THE CONTEXT: *PLUS ÇA CHANGE*

Let's pass in review how things were back then, what's happened since, and how they are now in the three scales that condition the country's foreign policy: the global, the continental, and the domestic.

GLOBAL BALANCE OF FORCES

Forty years later, the global balance of forces then is almost unrecognizable compared to today. Then, in the late 1960s, the Cold War standoff between East and West seemed frozen forever.

Although some non-aligned countries in the developing world kept their distance from both camps, Canada, which was on the flight path for long-range bombers and intercontinental missiles between the Soviet Union and the United States, had no choice but to support the Pentagon's strategy, however mad—and the Mutually Assured Destruction on which the United States' second-strike nuclear-retaliation doctrine was, literally, mad. Even when outrage at the United States' imperialist efforts to force its will on Vietnam had Canadians demonstrating by the thousands outside American consulates, Ottawa dissented from Washington's policy at its peril, since the fear of US economic retaliation was the ever-present subtext of Canada's international disagreements with Uncle Sam.

Since then, with the collapse of the Soviet Union, the United States passed from being the hegemonic entity of the West—its capitalist partners had supported Washington's construction of a liberal global order after the Second World War—to being the hegemonic entity of the world: in 1995, the launch of the World Trade Organization (WTO) created a global economic order using a made-in-the-US rule book to which almost every country willingly subscribed.

Having been invited, on Pierre Trudeau's watch, to join the Economic Summit, the exclusive club of the seven most powerful states, Canada had been an actively contributing participant as the new trade regime was negotiated. Although its relative power in the global hierarchy declined with the rise of China, India, and Brazil, Ottawa occasionally managed to take the lead in brokering multilateral agreements such as the International Criminal Court and the treaty banning anti-personnel landmines, even in the face of Washington's opposition.

Now, following 11 September 2001, when the United States subordinated its economically hegemonic role to its militarily imperialist persona, which unilaterally and arbitrarily tried to spread American values in the Middle East by force, poles of resistance have sprung up. The future economic colossus, China, is even threatening America's sense of energy security by buying a share in Alberta's oil resources.

Based as it was on evident misinformation and miscalculation, Washington's rogue behaviour in Iraq generated such dismay among the Canadian public that the country's political elite was obliged to back away from its default position of supporting the United States. And, even though Paul Martin vowed to repair the relations with the George W. Bush administration that he felt had been imprudently broken by his predecessor, Jean Chrétien, he was impelled by the public's distaste for Rumsfeld militarism to decline support to the US National Missile Defense program.

CANADA'S POSITION ON THE CONTINENT

Much has changed in Canada's political economy position in North America. In the late 1960s, Canada was striving to find ways to reduce the bleeding caused by its US-owned economy by constructing a more nationally focused market that would be less vulnerable to damaging American actions.

Since then, a decade's experimentation with a more nationally focused industrial strategy flamed out in the early 1980s with the ambitious but disastrously timed National Energy Program. John Turner's self-immolation in the 1984 federal election handed power to Brian Mulroney who, having sworn to give Washington the benefit of the doubt, proceeded to join with then-President Ronald Reagan to sign a declaration of economic disarmament called the Canada–United States Free Trade Agreement (CUFTA). CUFTA locked Ottawa into a set of rules designed to subordinate the country's resources and manufactured production to the needs of the American economy.

Once Washington had established precedents to foreclose Canadian economic autonomy, it expanded the continental scope of what Ronald Reagan called the economic constitution of North America by including Mexico in this integrative régime. With the North American Free Trade Agreement (NAFTA) extending the WTO's massive and intrusive rules, Canada found itself saddled with an external constitution that sounded the death knell of an independent Canadian capitalism capable of competing with the United States. Canada's wealth remains dependent on pumping oil (for which the US thirst is insatiable), developing other economic niches (which are complementary but not competitive with US industries), hewing wood (which the US resists buying beyond the point that threatens rival US forestry interests), and, probably, drawing water (that is, diverting water southwards, an issue that is already on the agenda in the Great Lakes and southwestern states).

Now, following close to two decades of border-lowering economic integration, Canada has been hit with Washington's latest strategic doctrine, a 'war on terror' focused on a border-raising, national security priority. Whereas Canadian leaders were able to dissent over the American position on Iraq, they have no freedom to diverge over its border policies because, in the Bush administration's view, security trumps trade. If Ottawa does not satisfy Washington that the Canada–US boundary is secure against terrorists—meaning that its immigration policies, its anti-terrorism secret policing, and its passport control processes meet with the approval of the Department of Homeland Security—the economic arteries that now flow from North to South will be blocked.

CANADA'S DOMESTIC SCENE

By 1968, the federal and provincial governments had put in place the health care system that was to become, with the Canadian flag, a defining element of Canada's national identity.

Since then, the relatively generous system of social-policy support for the unemployed, the poor, single parents, and the aged, which had been nurtured during the Trudeau years, came under attack by neoconservative budget slashing. The public's passion for health care, however, convinced politicians to restore those financial cuts. Meanwhile, Trudeau's immensely popular Charter of Rights and Freedoms gave millions of non-British and non-French immigrants a sense of security that theirs was not a second-class citizenship.

Now, differences between Canadian and American values grow ever greater. In sharp contrast to the fundamentalist conservatism espoused in the White House, the US Supreme Court, and the Congress, the Canadian government has followed the Canadian Supreme Court's lead by legalizing same-sex marriage and decriminalizing the possession of marijuana. These attitudinal differences underpin the continuing debate within Canada over its own foreign policy.

THE DEBATE: *PLUS C'EST LA MÊME CHOSE*

Canadian attitudes have changed little; Canadians remain anxiously obsessed with how to get along with their one and only neighbour in the face of its sometimes laudable but often destructive behaviour. As they look overseas, they remain worried about their standing in the rest of the world and how best to contribute to resolving its most urgent issues.

Interested academics, along with a limited number of journalists and civic-minded citizens, study how to understand these problems. The analytical and normative positions resulting from this consideration continue to fall into two distinct schools of thought, generating a debate that seems as irreconcilable as it is eternal.

Because its global, continental, and domestic context has changed, so too have the goalposts for the debate about Canada's foreign policy choices moved. Because the Cold War's demise has relieved Ottawa of the imperative to support the United States on the major issues, the foreign policy field it faces is considerably broader. But because the WTO and NAFTA have tied one hand behind the government's back and because there are very few economic sectors that remain under Canadian ownership and control, the field is also much shorter. Nevertheless, there are still two main schools of thought, two teams, as it were, which rally their supporters to propound opposing positions.

CONTINENTALISTS

A century ago Canadian imperialists expounded the view that the Dominion of Canada's prime goal should be to retain its connection with the British Empire in order to guarantee its military security, its economic well-being, and its cultural identity. They reflected the interests of exporters who shipped their produce to Great Britain, importers who shipped consumer goods back across the Atlantic, the banking community that financed this commerce, and the intellectuals whose careers depended on nourishing their links with Oxford and Cambridge in the 'mother country'.

At that time, nationalists who wanted autonomy from the Empire looked to the United States as a progressive haven, relations with which could help burnish the Dominion's prospects as a self-sufficient and fast-growing, but more autonomous, society.

Four decades ago, the pattern had shifted: pro-British imperialists had become pro-American continentalists. Those wanting to extend relations with the United States were the dominant resource and manufacturing corporations for which continental integration promised economic salvation. Continentalists, as 'The Choice to be Made' explained, admonished Canadians to support US foreign policy whether it was right or wrong. As the hearth of freedom in the Cold War, Washington should not be criticized. Furthermore, Canada's influence in the world depended on proving its influence in Washington's corridors of power. Being on the inside—pulling our own weight, being seen as sound—was the precondition for being effective in international forums. Even when we disagreed with Washington, we were advised not to speak our mind lest we risk being punished. Continental integration should be accelerated, they argued, since the interdependence of the two economies provided Canada with some insurance against Washington's arbitrary action; if it tried to punish Canada, the United States would really be harming its own interests.

Since then, the same logic pushed Ottawa to negotiate CUFTA and NAFTA and abandon the previous strategy of developing a self-standing economy.

Now, in the aftermath of 11 September 2001, Canadian continentalists have made the same arguments. Ottawa should support US military policy in Iraq and the National Missile Defense not because these are sensible policies but because Canada might be punished for not toeing the American line. Canada's global influence depends on being seen as insiders in Washington where our advice is heeded. Criticizing American policy, they argue, will only alienate our American interlocutors and be self-defeating.

NATIONALISTS

The economic nationalist position has long been ambivalent. While admired by some for its great social, technological, and intellectual achievements, the United States was also seen as a threat to

Canadian security. Interdependence really meant a dependence that shut down the possibility for creative action abroad. Rather than practising 'quiet diplomacy', nationalists felt that Ottawa should develop a public diplomacy that spoke its mind. This could be valuable itself in buttressing Canadians' sense of their bilingual and multicultural identity.

Since then, nationalists have been mainly on the losing side of the debate. While they could take some comfort from Pierre Trudeau's occasional forays on the world scene and from Brian Mulroney's defiance of both Margaret Thatcher and Ronald Reagan over apartheid in South Africa, they had to mourn their two defeats over free trade and resign themselves to the country's economic-policy castration and consequently to its ever-closer and dependent integration in the American system.

Lloyd Axworthy's surprisingly successful ventures in low-cost niche diplomacy—the International Criminal Court and the land mine treaty—proved the nationalist view that public diplomacy could produce effective foreign policy. But the Department of Foreign Affairs and International Trade had been too drained of funds, personnel, and morale from years of neoconservative budget-cutting for Axworthy's muscular 'damn-the-torpedoes' approach to continue under other leadership.

Now, the nationalists enjoy a clear, if temporary advantage. The American application of unilateral, pre-emptive war in Iraq has proven such a patent disaster that 'ready-aye-ready' solidarity with George Bush has almost no traction outside the boardrooms of the Canadian Council of Chief Executives (CCCE). Even the CCCE has been consternated by Washington's blatant disregard of its NAFTA commitments in defying dispute panel rulings that remanded US countervailing and anti-dumping duties levied against Canadian softwood lumber exports. Other examples of Washington's

unprincipled protectionism, most glaringly, its prolonged ban on imports of Canadian beef, make continentalist arguments a hard sell. Nevertheless, Canada remains locked into its external constitution, just as its negotiators intended. Advocates of greater autonomy have few power levers at their command.

In the final analysis, the Canadian foreign policy debate between continentalists and nationalists remains just as unresolvable as that between the ideological right and left in domestic politics. The two schools are rooted in different value systems and support opposing corporate and citizen interests. Deploying actual evidence has little effect. Turning to the reforms advocated four decades ago, it is clear that much of what I recommended then has actually been implemented. White papers have been written on foreign policy issues, Parliament's Standing Committee on Foreign Affairs and International Trade has held hearings across the country on the major issues facing Canada and produced substantial reports, and public opinion polls are constantly commissioned in order to take the electorate's pulse.

The mandarinate—the diplomatic elite which kept its foreign policy cards close to its vest—has vanished and its place of dominance over Canadian foreign policy has been assumed by trade policy analysts inspired by an equally exclusive and arrogant ideology. It was the reverse takeover of the old Department of External Affairs in 1982, when the trade commissioners were moved to Sussex Drive from the Department of Industry, Trade, and Commerce, which led to Canadian foreign policy being hijacked by a mania for free trade agreements. Similar to the old Ottawa mandarinate in their anti-democratic elitism, but inspired by a messianic and economics-based faith in neoconservative market deregulation, they drove out considerations of Canada's national interests as a global power in order to hitch the country to America's destiny.

Now that the future of the United States seems decidedly less rosy; now that India, Brazil, and even Mexico are moving up the power hierarchy behind China; now that many Canadians have taken the future into their own hands by operating across national borders in non-government organizations that are directly coping with pandemics and rebuilding failed states, the continentalist–nationalist debate has taken on a renewed relevance. If the United States has become a rogue imperial power whose policies exacerbate rather than remedy global warming, expand rather than contain nuclear proliferation, provoke rather than stifle terrorism, and speed rather than slow the spread of HIV/AIDS, there is a powerful argument to 'go around' the United States, as former Defense Secretary Robert McNamara recently urged the international community.

Many foreign policy choices have been made over the past four decades, but many still remain to be made day by day and year by year. Given the ineradicably deep gaps separating the normative positions of continentalists and nationalists, what choices Ottawa should make will continue to be debated. Forty years from now, it would be surprising if the debate had been definitively resolved. With luck, students and scholars in the middle of the twenty-first century will conclude that the choices made in this period contributed to averting the social, economic, and environmental disasters that were facing both Canadians and the world during this century's first decade.

UPDATE

THE 'INDEPENDENCE' DEBATES, THEN AND NOW: FALSE CHOICES AND REAL CHALLENGES

Brian Bow and Patrick Lennox

The advent of the Obama era in American diplomacy seemed to bring with it much hope for a more ambitious and proactive Canadian foreign policy. Unshackled from George W. Bush's 'with us or against us' mindset, and inspired by Barack Obama's promise to rebuild America's reputation abroad through multilateral engagement, Canada might have been expected to try to reinvigorate a stagnant foreign policy that had gotten bogged down in—and devolved almost exclusively into—the bloody counter-insurgency in southern Afghanistan. But the Harper government instead turned its focus inward, and Canadian voters seemed not merely acceptant, but generally approving.

Through most of this decade, most Canadians were confident their country was on steady ground, but worried that the United States under the Bush administration was headed for trouble (particularly, but not only, in Iraq). So there were frequent calls for Canada to break away from the United States and pursue a more 'independent' foreign policy. These calls fell silent in late 2008 and early 2009, however, with the election of a popular new president and the onset of the ongoing global recession. International political challenges were multiplying, but Ottawa was caught up in the petty intrigues that go with minority government, and the

Canadian public wanted its leaders to focus on getting the country's financial house in order. To the extent that Canada has actually had a foreign policy over the last couple of years, it has mainly centred on efforts to try to limit casualties until the clock runs out on our commitment to Kandahar, to negotiate bilateral trade or investment agreements wherever that seemed relatively easy, and generally to follow America's diplomatic lead on global finance, climate change, the Honduras coup, and reconstruction in Haiti.

The debate over whether Canada can and should pursue an 'independent' foreign policy, in other words, has faded into the background for now; but it is only a matter of time before it erupts again. It is a natural, possibly inescapable, side effect of Canada's unique position in the world, which is always simmering on the edge of Canada's political consciousness, and flares up from time to time into a full-blown existential crisis. Because Canada is profoundly dependent on the United States for its prosperity, its security, and its capacity to have a significant impact on the wider world, Canadians recognize a need to stick close to the Americans, to try to influence them, and to avoid provoking them. However, because of that very same dependency, because there are subtle differences between Canadian and American political cultures, and because Canada doesn't face the same global strategic challenges that the US does, Canadians also have an impulse—particularly in times when the two countries seem to be going in markedly different directions—to try to increase self-reliance, to find new international partners, and to make a show of pursuing different priorities.

In the 1960s, the war in Vietnam raised doubts about Canada's traditional commitment to work closely with the US, and prompted Canadian nationalists to demand a more 'independent' foreign policy. But proponents of the traditional approach pushed back, arguing that striking an independent posture would bring few tangible gains and might come at a high price, in terms of lost influence and lost economic advantages. Stephen Clarkson summarized this wide-ranging debate in terms of a dichotomy between the proponents of 'quiet diplomacy' and the advocates of 'independence'. His characterization of the debate gives us a good sense of the battle lines in 1968, and we can see strikingly similar divides in the more recent debates about how Canada ought to relate to the Bush administration, particularly in the controversy over whether or not Canada should support the US-led invasion of Iraq.

But, as we argued in our 40-years-later revisiting of the 'independence' debate, Clarkson's stark dichotomy over-simplified and distorted the original debate, and pulled our attention away from other, more crucial challenges for Canadian foreign policy.

In Clarkson's summary, the proponents of quiet diplomacy are portrayed as inflexible, timid, and generally out of step with the major historical developments of the day. They are so caught up in the Cold War rivalry that they cannot see the emergence of a new global order in which Canada might play new roles and have new partners. The advocates of independence, on the other hand, are wonderfully clever and brave, having apparently figured out not only how to resolve all of the inherent dilemmas haunting Canadian foreign policy-makers, but how to do so in a way that would satisfy Canadians' moral convictions, and even reconcile the clashing priorities of Canada's various regions and ethnic groups. Setting aside the question of whether the 'independentists' of the late 1960s really had all the answers, it's important to be clear that their 'quiet diplomacy' rivals weren't nearly as hidebound and morally bank-rupt as Clarkson made them out to be. Most of those arguing for maintaining Canada's trad-itional partnership with the US didn't like the Vietnam War any more than their critics did, but judged that Canada could have more of an impact on what happened in southeast Asia—or virtually anywhere else in the world—by sitting down at the table with the Americans and trying to nudge them in the right direction, rather than by trying to act alone. Canadian lead-ers could be critical of the US from time to time, as Pearson was in his Temple University speech, but only where there was a real impasse, and only within the context of a generally close and collaborative relationship.

When we fast-forward almost 40 years to the war in Iraq, we find the Chrétien government facing a similar choice. But Chrétien, unlike Pearson, chose to go with the flow of public opin-ion, mounting the soapbox and loudly proclaiming Canada's 'independent' stance. Chrétien's decision was of course very popular with voters, and did much to burnish his otherwise-dubious foreign policy legacy, but it was not without costs. The break over Iraq raised ques-tions in the US about whether Canada was really a reliable ally and a close friend to the US, which made American policy-makers less receptive to subsequent Canadian appeals for con-sideration on lumber quotas, beef restrictions, and border controls. There was no clear-cut and direct 'retaliation', just as Clarkson's independentists would have expected, but there was still a price to be paid, just as the proponents of quiet diplomacy worried there might be. Moreover, since Chrétien felt compelled to offset the break over Iraq by increasing Canada's commitment to Afghanistan, we could also see at least some of the casualties suffered there in recent years as another part of the indirect costs of our foreign policy independence. Critics of the quiet diplomacy approach might argue that it has been discredited by Canada's experi-ence in Afghanistan, since our close collaboration with the US, and all of the sacrifices made in the dusty hills of Kandahar province, do not seem to have done much to secure Canadian influence in Washington. The evidence on that score is mixed, however, and the earning of 'diplomatic capital' in Afghanistan was clearly undercut by lingering recriminations over Iraq.

Clarkson was right in arguing that the divide between proponents of quiet diplomacy and advocates of independence was not so much a philosophical one, but rather one based on dif-ferent hunches about the answers to *factual* questions: Does the US reward Canada for taking a collaborative approach to foreign policy? Does it punish Canada for challenging the US on foreign policy issues? Does Canada have the capacity to act alone? Are there other potential international partners for Canada, and could Canada reconcile these new partnerships with its economic interdependence with the US? When and where does 'doing well' by working closely with the US conflict with our impulse to 'do good' by acting on Canadian values?

Unfortunately, recent iterations of the 'independence' debate are still driven mostly by hunches and loaded anecdotes, because we have not made much progress over the last 40 years in finding solid answers to these pivotal questions, building from well-developed theor-ies, and anchored in systematic empirical research. We seem to think we already know, intui-tively, everything there is to know about Canada–US relations, so study of the relationship has been set aside in favour of other, more 'exotic' places and problems, and a once-lively field of research is becoming an academic backwater. Given what is at stake for Canada, there is a clear and pressing need for greater efforts to understand the nature of the bilateral relationship, the inner workings of American government and society, and the way that the two countries relate to the wider world. And that understanding can only come through substantial investment of resources, and a more intensive and sustained engagement between academics, policy-makers, and the general public.

But there are some things that we do know. Canada can make up its own mind about whether or not to stand beside the United States, but it can never really stand 'shoulder to shoulder' with the global colossus that lives next door. There is a certain sense of partnership and mutual obligation which sustains the old idea of a 'special relationship' between the two countries, but there is also Canada's profound dependency on the US for both its security and its prosperity. There is a clear hierarchy in the bilateral relationship, and all of our philosophical debates over the best 'approach' to managing our relations with the US must be predicated on a clear-eyed recognition of the underlying material reality that fundamentally limits and directs our choices.

We should be clear here that there *are* choices to make, and they are important ones. Over the last 40 years, successive Canadian governments (and the people who vote for them) have chosen to allow the country's capacity to exercise an effective foreign policy to rust out. Our military, our development aid programs, and our foreign service are all underfunded, politically neglected, and at least a little bit demoralized. It should be obvious that choosing not to make these investments now will come at some cost to Canada further down the road, whether one considers oneself a proponent of quiet diplomacy or an advocate of independence. Without the means to fight, to aid and support, or to innovate and lead, Canada can neither win a seat at the table with the US nor act alone. Thus while the 'independence' debate will always be with us, the crucial debate for today is probably the much more fundamental one over whether this country is serious about having a foreign policy at all.

Key Terms

Independent Foreign Policy
Quiet Diplomacy
Special Relationship

6

CONSTRUCTING CANADIAN FOREIGN POLICY: MYTHS OF GOOD INTERNATIONAL CITIZENS, PROTECTORS, AND THE WAR IN AFGHANISTAN

Claire Turenne Sjolander and Kathryn Trevenen

We are not daunted by shadows because we carry the light that defines them—the light of freedom and democracy, of human rights and the rule of law. . . . Our role in Afghanistan is Canada at its best and the Canadian people are proud to stand with you. (Prime Minister Stephen Harper, quoted in Blanchfield, 2007: A3)

Canada has a noble tradition of helping the world's needy. There are few countries more needy than Afghanistan. . . . Afghans cannot rebuild their society unless they can be confident their efforts won't be wrecked by terrorists and insurgents. Canadian forces are helping give them the security they need. The forces are also playing humanitarian roles, delivering aid supplies, medical treatment and other services. Because of international help, Afghans can now vote freely in elections, send their children to school and go about their daily lives. Women are regaining some of the rights erased by the fanatical Taliban regime. As Mr. Harper put it, these are things worth standing up for. What Canada is doing in Afghanistan is 'in the very best of the traditions of this country . . . stepping up to the plate, and doing good when good is required. (*Globe and Mail*, 2006: A16)

Nowhere is Canada making a difference more clearly than in Afghanistan. Canada has joined the United Nations-sanctioned mission in Afghanistan because it is noble and necessary. Canadians understand that development and security go hand in hand. Without security, there can be no humanitarian aid, no reconstruction and no democratic development. Progress will be slow, but our efforts are bearing fruit. There is no better measure of this progress than the four million Afghan boys and two million girls who can dream of a better future because they now go to school. . . . Like the North Star, Canada has been a guide to other nations; through difficult times, Canada has shone as an example of what a people joined in common purpose can achieve. (Canada, 2007a)

Portrayals of Canadian soldiers who 'carry the light' of freedom and democracy, who fund and build schools for orphans, and who do 'good when good is required' play a central role in defining the Canadian imaginary. These portrayals respond to the idea that Canada is a morally virtuous international actor, that it protects the rights of women and children at home and abroad, and that Canadian forces have a disinterested and 'noble tradition of helping the world's needy'. As Canadians, we are used to thinking of our armed forces as primarily concerned with the work of peacekeeping and, in so doing, as representing the best of what Canada has to offer to the world.[1] In these national narratives, Canada indeed imagines itself as a 'north star' guiding other nations.

In this chapter, we argue that the Conservative government's representations of the war in Afghanistan during its first two years in office depend on and continually reiterate two main national narratives: the first portrays Canada as a 'good international citizen', a noble and disinterested multilateral international actor; the second depicts Canada as 'protector' of the weak. We examine how these narratives evoke a moral position based in Canada's perceived tradition of upholding ideals of equality, multiculturalism, and human rights at home, and how they function by mobilizing powerful stories of gender and nation. In portraying Canada as a good international citizen, government speeches have largely focused on the development work that the Canadian troops have been doing in Afghanistan (such as reconstruction projects, including building schools), and on the humanitarian reasons for intervening—reasons often supported by pointing to

the situation confronting women and children. These representations blur the realities of Canada's involvement in Afghanistan and function to limit debate about the justifications and ongoing feasibility of the mission. The narrative of Canada as the moral protector of the 'weak' functions in a similar way to police the parameters of debate. As protector of Afghan civilians (notably women and children), and as combat soldiers (who are really peacekeepers), the image of the Canadian military—and thereby of the Canadian state—as protector becomes one against which political opposition is difficult to articulate.

This chapter examines the narratives used by the Conservative government through an analysis of government speeches in 2006 and 2007 discussing the Afghanistan mission. While Canada's intervention in Afghanistan hardly ended in 2007, and as of the early spring of 2009 is committed to continue until 2011, the 2006–7 period provides a useful examination of a particular period in Canada's Afghan war. While Canada first intervened in the conflict in Afghanistan in the weeks following the events of 11 September 2001, it was not until early 2006 that Canadian forces found themselves directly involved in a sustained and costly combat mission, no matter what Canadians believed about the nature of that mission. In early March 2006, for example, Strategic Counsel, a market research firm, conducted the first of a series of surveys on Canadians' opinions toward the Afghanistan mission. This poll revealed that Canadians were overwhelmingly likely to identify peacekeeping rather than combat as the primary role of Canadian troops in Afghanistan (with 70 per cent of Canadians, and 76 per cent of Quebecers, identifying peacekeeping as the primary focus of the mission) (Strategic Counsel, 2006: 21).[2] The reality on the ground in Kandahar had begun to suggest otherwise, however. From the initial deployments of 2001–2 until the move to Kandahar in late 2005, eight Canadian soldiers had been killed in Afghanistan: four in April 2002 as a result of a 'friendly fire' incident at the hands of a US fighter jet; two in October 2003 when their vehicle hit a roadside bomb outside Kabul; one in January 2004 as a result of a suicide bomber; and the eighth in November 2005, the victim of a traffic accident outside Kandahar. By contrast, 36 Canadian soldiers and one Canadian diplomat were killed in Afghanistan in 2006, and a further 30 perished in 2007. By mid-April 2009, 117 Canadian troops had lost their lives in Afghanistan. Of those killed in 2006 and 2007, only five died as a result of friendly fire or other accidents—the others perished in combat.[3] This number of fallen Canadian troops represented the largest death toll for Canada's military since the Korean War—and the numbers were diligently reported to a public long unaccustomed to news of death from the front.

The return of Canadian troops to the southern province of Kandahar, beginning in late 2005, clearly heralded the start of the most dangerous phase in Canada's military operations in Afghanistan. By early 2006, Taliban insurgents were beginning to mount major offensives against NATO troops, with Kandahar province—and thereby Canadian soldiers—as one of the primary targets for such action. In early 2006, as well, a new minority Conservative government led by Stephen Harper had come to power in Ottawa—a coincidence with respect to developments in Afghanistan that nonetheless permits the marking of a departure from the previous phases of the mission.

That the deployment of Canadian troops back to southern Afghanistan coincides both with a significant increase in fatal attacks *and* a change in government in Ottawa provides reason enough for a particular focus on this phase of Canada's Afghan mission. One additional factor motivates our interest in the period after 2005, however. The year 2006 marks the start of the period during which Canadian public opinion became increasingly aware—and increasingly critical—of Canada's involvement in Afghanistan. While the souring of Canadian opinion on the mission is at least in part related to the increase in battle fatalities, the growing negative assessment of the war became, in and of itself, a source of pressure on the Canadian government—and a factor increasingly important to the framing of the discourses on the war presented by that government.

A total of 66 speeches on the topic of Canada's involvement in Afghanistan were collected for the period between 31 January 2006 and 31 December 2007. The speeches retained for analysis were those of official representatives of Canada's Conservative government: Prime Minister Stephen Harper, defence ministers Gordon O'Connor and Peter MacKay, foreign affairs ministers Peter MacKay and Maxime Bernier, as well as ministers of international co-operation Josée Verner and Beverley Oda. In addition, the speeches of senior public officials acting on behalf of Canadian ministers of the Crown (speaking in their absence) were included. While the media coverage of these speeches, as well as of comments made by government officials to the press, is crucial to examine in the construction of Canada's foreign policy in a time of war, such a systematic assessment is not attempted in this chapter. Rather, the messaging provided by those speaking in the name of the Canadian government is the focus of this analysis, for this messaging allows us to assess the extent to which the main narratives of Canadian foreign policy are deployed and reiterated by the government itself.

CANADA AS THE GOOD INTERNATIONAL CITIZEN

In order to understand the construction and functioning of the good international citizen/peacekeeper narrative, we first need to examine the context in which it operates. During the first days of the Harper administration, the government painted Canada's security interests starkly against the image of the terrorist attacks of 11 September 2001. As the Minister of National Defence, Gordon O'Connor, had argued in his first speech in February 2006, Canada's 'mission to Afghanistan is in our national interest. On September 11th 2001, terrorists attacked North America and Canadians were killed. Let me be clear: when terrorists attack Canadians, Canada will defend itself. That's why we're in Afghanistan' (O'Connor, 2006a). The continental context (as well as Canada's partnership with the United States) was emphasized. By 2007, however, reference to 9/11 begins to fade from the government's speeches, replaced by an emphasis on the multilateral institutions to which Canada belongs. Softer and more altruistic messages become the norm in response to an increasingly skeptical Canadian public. A 2007 Strategic Counsel report obtained by the *Globe and Mail* emphasized the importance of so doing, recommending that the Canadian government place the emphasis on 'rebuilding', 'enhancing the lives of women and children', and 'peacekeeping' in communicating with the Canadian public in order to change negative perceptions of the Afghan mission (Freeman, 2007: A1).[4]

The softening of the government rhetoric through minimal reference to 9/11 allowed government officials to emphasize more altruistic motivations for the Canadian involvement in Afghanistan. This should not be interpreted to mean that the Harper government has argued for an exclusively 'altruistic' explanation of our role in Afghanistan, however. Rather, the government has made a strong link between Canada's security interests and the broader goals of helping Afghans, as a February 2007 speech by the Prime Minister illustrates:

Canada's involvement and sacrifices in Afghanistan serve our national interests and values on several levels. It's not just about foreign aid, though that's part of it. It's not just about doing our duty with the United Nations and our NATO allies, though that too is part of it. And it's not just about living up to our beliefs in freedom, democracy, human rights and the rule of law, though that most certainly is part of it too.

But as Chris Alexander [deputy special representative of the United Nations secretary-general for Afghanistan and former Canadian ambassador to Afghanistan] has frequently pointed out, global security hinges on success in Afghanistan. If we fail in Afghanistan, if that country relapses into anarchy and once again becomes a haven for extremists and terrorists, the world will be manifestly more dangerous. Afghanistan is the front line of the international security challenge of the modern, post-Cold War world. We must build a successful alternative there in order to defeat extremism and terrorism everywhere. (Canada, Office of the Prime Minister, 2007)

Harper begins by recalling the selfless motives behind intervention: foreign aid, duty to the values and goals of the UN and NATO, defending Canada's belief in freedom, democracy, human rights, and the rule of law. But he also links the Afghan mission to Canada's security interests—Afghanistan is the 'front line' for contemporary security challenges, and these are as relevant to Canada as they are to any other member of the international community of states. By connecting Canada's security interests, at least as constructed by the Conservative government, to the more altruistic goals of freedom, democracy, and aid, Harper has effectively covered all bases. Under this formulation, even Canada's 'national interests' are morally defensible—they are about making the world a less dangerous place.

By arguing that 'we must build a successful alternative there in order to defeat extremism and terrorism everywhere', Harper appears to address both disinterested and interested motivations—Canada wants to help others at the same time as it strives to keep itself safe. This formulation, however, offers a simplistic view of Canada's so-called 'self-interest' and functions to limit true debate on the justifications for intervention in Afghanistan.

The disinterested motivations alluded to in even Harper's self-interested speeches point to the first narrative that the government has drawn on to explain and justify the Afghan mission. This narrative mobilizes conceptions of Canada's role as an enlightened middle power, concerned with multilateralism and peacekeeping. It portrays Canada as a good international citizen, more concerned with helping others than with advancing its own self-interest. Central to this narrative is the image of the Canadian peacekeeper.

As Sandra Whitworth has argued, this image of Canada as peacekeeper is a central myth in the Canadian imaginary. In this myth, 'Canada is an altruistic and benign middle power, acting with a kind of moral purity not normally exhibited by contemporary states' (Whitworth, 2003: 76). Although Canadians are now in Kandahar in a combat mission that evolved out of the American invasion in 2001, the government continues to capitalize on the public perception that the Canadian military is first and foremost a peacekeeping force, acting under the auspices of the United Nations. [This perception has meant that as the Canadian participation in Afghanistan evolved from Kabul to Kandahar, public debate has not seemed to fully acknowledge that the Afghanistan mission is part of a war, not a result of an established consensus to create a peacekeeping force. In particular, many government speeches highlight the argument that Canada is in Afghanistan at the invitation of the democratically elected Afghan government. While this was true in 2007, it was certainly not the case in 2001 when the invasion took place; framing speeches around the Afghan government's request presents the mission in Afghanistan as if it is similar to other 'muscular peacekeeping' missions that begin with a clear invitation from the government.]

This construction of Canada as a good international citizen, a peacekeeper (even if self-interested), is not neutral, however. Central to this myth of Canada as a peacekeeping 'good citizen' is a portrait of Afghanistan as backward, uncivilized, and helpless in the face of internal strife. Following Sherene Razack, we question the racial logic that informs narratives depicting peacekeepers as subduing unruly and savage Third World people. In *Dark Threats and White Knights*, speaking to the US intervention in Afghanistan and Iraq, Razack contends that:

[E]mbedded deep within the conceptual foundations of the Bush administration's notion of a life-and-death struggle against the 'axis of evil' is a thoroughly racial logic. Disciplining, instructing, and keeping in line Third World peoples who irrationally hate and wish to destroy their saviours derives from the idea that Northern peoples inhabit civilized lands while the South, in Chinua Achebe's words, 'is a metaphysical battlefield devoid of all recognizable humanity into which the wandering European enters at his peril.' . . . [C]olour-line thinking was certainly in evidence in the American invasions of both Afghanistan . . . and Iraq . . . , invasions justified on the ground that it was necessary to drop thousands of bombs on Afghanis and Iraqis in order to save them from the excesses of their own society. . . . Oil, the free market, and the historical support the United States has given to the Taliban and to Saddam Hussein, among other despotic regimes, all disappear under 'smart' bombs. Once the smoke clears, peacekeepers walk in. (Razack, 2004: 7–8)

The Canadian government draws on this same racial logic to stifle debate on the Afghan mission. Government speeches foreclose any notion that non-military methods could have led to a democratic Afghanistan (or that negotiating peace with the Taliban and rival factions should—or even could—be the primary goal of foreign intervention), and always imply that ousting the Taliban was first and foremost a humanitarian project, one that nonetheless could employ any means necessary. Throughout the operation of the narrative of Canada as a good international citizen, Canada's motives remain unquestioned and unquestionable. Although the prime minister and other ministers refer to Canada's undefined 'security interests' throughout their speeches in 2006 and 2007, Canada's role as good international citizen gets the most detailed elaboration. The ministers of defence and foreign affairs stick to three key messages throughout their speeches on Afghanistan.

The first is that Canada is participating in an international coalition in Afghanistan. Maxime Bernier, minister of foreign affairs, explains that 'Canada currently has troops in Afghanistan because it made a commitment to the international community. We are there under a UN mandate. We are there at the invitation of a democratically elected Afghan government, with thirty-six other countries, including Australia, the Netherlands, Germany, Italy, France and the United Kingdom' (Bernier, 2007).

The second message is that the Afghan people themselves support the mission and have requested Canadian help. Bernier argues that 'Canadian soldiers, diplomats and humanitarian workers are in Afghanistan to defend the universal values of respect for basic human rights, as enunciated by the Afghans themselves in their constitution' (ibid.). Finally, Bernier drives home the point that, at its foundation, the Afghan mission is about helping Afghans:

[O]ur mission in Afghanistan is about helping people rebuild their lives after years of oppression. It is about ensuring they have the resources to realize their aspirations. It is a stabilization mission. A development mission. It is our most important mission—a mission that promotes freedom, democracy, human rights and the rule of law. (Ibid.)

The minister of national defence, Peter MacKay, reiterates the connections between stabilization, development, and the work that the Canadian military is doing. In an address titled 'The Hard Questions', MacKay explains:

Security enables good governance and development, and good governance and development reinforce security. The three are indivisible. The Canadian Forces are fighting with other countries in Afghanistan to allow for permanent and self-sustaining development. We are seeing developmental progress that reinforces our security successes. Here again, the military is just one part of a team working in Afghanistan. (MacKay, 2007e)

He asserts the same connections in an earlier speech, arguing that 'the Afghanistan Compact outlines a three-pronged approach to stabilizing Afghanistan: security, governance and development—three fronts closely intertwined and mutually reinforcing. Governance and development are dependent on security, but security cannot be maintained without governance and development' (MacKay, 2007d).

In all of Harper, Bernier, and MacKay's statements above, military intervention—'security'—is inextricably linked to development and good governance, conveying the message that Western military intervention is the only way that Afghanistan can create a democratic government. MacKay makes this logic clear in an address in March of 2007. He maintains that:

[only if there is security in Afghanistan can development workers and humanitarian assistance specialists get on with their tasks of helping Afghans through economic development, education and reconstruction projects. Only if there is security can the fledgling steps in democratic governance and the rule of law be consolidated and extended. And only if there is security, can human rights in Afghanistan be grounded and protected in law and enforced in public. (MacKay, 2007a)]

Here, history and context are both erased—Afghanistan is portrayed as a country that can only be 'tamed' by a strong Canadian military effort and no mention is made of the long history of foreign military and colonial intervention that shaped contemporary Afghanistan's many conflicts and divisions.

The Canadian government also frequently refers to the professionalism and skill of its military. In the same speech, MacKay stated that, 'thanks to the skills, professionalism and courage of our soldiers, the nascent peace stretching over most of the country has now been extended to large parts of Kandahar province' (ibid.). Again, MacKay makes the links between security and development: 'we are now consolidating those security gains and using this opportunity to increase our focus on bettering the lives of civilians, pushing ahead with reconstruction projects, building schools, encouraging small businesses and implementing governance programs' (ibid.). The narrative of Canada as good citizen depends on the assumption that Canadians are better equipped than Afghans—equipped not only with material resources like military hardware and development dollars but also with *moral* resources such as courage and professionalism.]

Importantly, in the representation of the Canadian military as good international citizen in Afghanistan, the *actual* tasks performed by the military are less important than the public perception of the 'appropriate role' of that military. It is not necessary for Canadian policy-makers to actually use the word 'peacekeeping' in defining the nature of Canada's mission in Afghanistan, nor does the 'selling of the mission' depend on the explicit use of such a phrase. What is important is the place of peacekeeping in the Canadian imaginary; as Whitworth noted earlier, and as Lane Anker has argued: "'Peacekeeping" represents a defining aspect of Canadian identity, reflecting fundamental values, beliefs and interests. . . . Public support for a strong Canadian role internationally is largely rooted in our proud history of peacekeeping. In fact, many Canadians regard peacekeeping as the most positive contribution that Canada makes to the world' (Anker, 2005: 23).[5] The image of Canada as a good international citizen, through its narrative focus on building schools, on democratic governance, on humanitarian assistance, on the rule of law, and on the promotion of individual freedom, reinforces a perception among Canadians that its military engages in tasks that are peaceful, or that 'make' peace. This morally unquestionable position combines with a portrait of Canada as a protector of the weak to render Afghanistan as an abstract and ahistorical canvas on which to write the story of Canada's national virtues.

CANADA AS PROTECTOR

While the narrative of Canada as the 'good international citizen' depends on many national myths relating to Canada's perceived historical role as middle power, peacekeeper, and moral conscience, it also works in harmony with the second narrative frequently mobilized by the government relating to Canada's role as 'protector'. This narrative of

Canada as protector of the weak complements the narrative of Canada as a moral citizen by creating a model of the stern but righteous father who must protect his family. Here, Afghan women and children, in particular, become the object of Canada's concern.

Canada's paternal role involves both the soldiers and the government that directs them. In a speech to the troops in Kandahar in May 2007, Harper tells the military:

Because of you, the people of Afghanistan have seen the institution of democratic elections, the stirring of human rights and freedoms for women, the construction of schools, healthcare facilities and the basic infrastructure of a functional economy. Still, you know that your work is not complete. You know that we cannot just put down our arms and hope for peace. You know that we can't set arbitrary deadlines and simply wish for the best. And you must also know that your hard work is making a real difference to real people and their families. (Harper, 2007b)

Foreign Affairs Minister Peter MacKay echoes these sentiments: 'perhaps the single most noticeable difference in that country is that women are now not only permitted to start and operate a business, but they can also vote, they can sit along[side] male counterparts in government, they can simply walk the streets unharassed—activities that were unheard of under the brutal Taliban regime' (MacKay, 2007b).

In almost all of the speeches delivered by the prime minister, the defence ministers, and the foreign affairs ministers in 2006 and 2007, women's rights, schools, and health care are evoked as primary concerns for the military mission. Like the comments linking security to development, these speeches argue that the oppression of women and children is a primary reason for Canada's presence in Afghanistan. First, Canada's military will liberate Afghan women from the oppression of the Taliban, and then they will deliver the necessary development aid required to put girls in schools and women in government. In 2007, many government ministers pointed to progress for women in Afghanistan as proof of Canada's beneficial role in the country. Returning to his 'Hard Questions' address, we find Peter Mackay arguing that:

we are supporting women who, under the Taliban regime, were forbidden to go to school, to work or to vote. Their voices were silenced, and to drive home that point, they were beaten for unimaginable things, such as for wearing shoes that made noise on the pavement as they walked. We are building a future for children, so that they can all be educated, have access to medical care, and have the freedom to grow up in a climate of security and hope rather than in fear. (MacKay, 2007e)

Josée Verner, minister of international co-operation, was particularly positive about the mission's impact on women. Her speaking notes for a breakfast during International Development Week in 2007 reflect this optimism:

[W]omen in Afghanistan suffered terribly under the Taliban regime. Previously, they were teachers, doctors, journalists, and homemakers. Then, overnight, they lost the right, not only to practise their profession, but also to leave their homes. Girls did not go to school. Now, things are gradually changing. With Canada's support, Afghanistan adopted a new constitution that recognizes equality between women and men. As a result, in recent elections, 25 per cent of the seats in Parliament were filled by women. We are working with the Government of

Afghanistan, our Canadian partners, and civil society on several fronts, to ensure that women and girls in Afghanistan are actively involved in rebuilding their country. (Verner, 2007)

Verner's speaking notes reveal two interesting claims. The first is that women in Afghanistan lost their rights 'overnight' under the Taliban regime. While no one would challenge the claim that the Taliban ruthlessly targeted women and radically restricted their basic rights and safety, this attack on women did not happen overnight, nor did it entirely originate with the Taliban. As organizations such as the Revolutionary Association of Women of Afghanistan, Human Rights Watch, and Amnesty International have all documented, widespread abuse and oppression of women took place under different warlords and regional governments in Afghanistan before the Taliban, and continues today (Human Rights Watch, 2002). The claim that women suddenly lost their rights dehistoricizes women's situations in Afghanistan and makes them an object of rescue. As a homogeneous group of suffering women, Afghan women become an unquestionable reason for intervention and Canada as protector becomes particularly suited to the task. As other scholars have argued, this justification for the war in Afghanistan begs the question of why the international community didn't intervene to help Afghan women before the 9/11 attacks (see, e.g., Rawi, 2006). It also highlights the strategic importance of the 'rescuing women' argument, an argument that doesn't seem to be helping the thousands of women in Darfur who are currently being killed and raped.

Chandra Mohanty's discussion of Western feminism's colonizing impulse and ethnocentric universality identifies three principles often assumed in feminist work on women in the Third World

and here reflected in the Canadian government's portrait of Afghan women. The principles are, first:

the assumption of women as an already constituted, coherent group with identical interests and desires, regardless of class, ethnic or racial location, or contradictions that implies a notion of gender or sexual difference or patriarchy which can be applied universally and cross-culturally. The second analytical presupposition is evident on the methodological level, in the uncritical way 'proof' of universality and cross-cultural validity are provided. The third is a more specifically political presupposition underlying the methodologies and the analytic strategies, *i.e.*, the model of power and struggle they imply and suggest. (Mohanty, 1997: 175–6; also see Mohanty, 1991)

These analytic strategies construct a uniform representation of an average Third World woman who 'leads an essentially truncated life based on her feminine gender (read: sexually constrained) and her being "Third World" (read: ignorant, poor, uneducated, tradition-bound, domestic, family-oriented, victimized etc.)' (ibid., 176). They also constitute the counter-image of the independent, educated, and empowered Western woman.

Mohanty's analysis of the colonizing impulse in some Western work on the 'Third World woman' is important in the context of the war in Afghanistan because it reveals the homogenizing effects the government narratives have. Instead of recognizing the heterogeneity of subjects it reports on, Canadian government representations erase the complexity, flexibility, and moments of agency found in Afghan women's experiences. Mohanty explains that by using 'Third World women' as a stable category of analysis, some Western accounts 'assume an ahistorical, universal unity between women based on a generalized notion of their subordination' (ibid., 182). This perspective on subordination means not only that the Canadian government fails to recognize the agency of Afghan women, it also gives them a reason to step in and 'save' them from oppressive cultures. As Gayatri Spivak further argues, it is through this produced imbalance in power and agency that 'imperialism's (or globalization's) image as the establisher of the good society is marked by the espousal of the woman as *object* of protection from her own kind' (Spivak, 1999: 291).

The importance of critically assessing representations of Third World women in the West lies in part in the portrayal of women as the helpless, passive, or innocent casualties of patriarchal cultural traditions, religions, or governments. Portraits of Afghan women during the war against the Taliban regime disclose the dangers in such a narrow representation. During the war, Afghan women have often been portrayed by Western media and governments as part of the reason for armed intervention— they had to be saved from the brutal oppression of the Taliban. Again, that the Taliban enacted policies violently repressing women's rights, education, and activities is not in contention. But by evoking the 'innocent' female victims of the Taliban as a reason to intervene *after* 9/11, the coalition perpetuated the practice of using the category 'women' as part of a self-serving foreign policy. Representing any group of women as a coherent category carries this danger. Although appeals to 'women's rights' or 'Afghan women's suffering' are understandable at times (when trying to mobilize money, media attention, or government resources, for example), they can inadvertently abet counter-attempts by the Taliban to generate an equally general category of the opposite sort. By mobilizing and exploiting the image of Afghan women as helpless victims of their religion, country, or culture, Western coalition governments simultaneously increased the stakes of attempts to control Afghan women and regulate their activities. It is thus necessary to question and complicate the coherence of these categories by attending to complex realities that exceed the generality invoked, while simultaneously working to build effective alliances. To complicate these categories we not only need to attend to the history and heterogeneity of Afghan women's experiences, but we also need to disrupt the power of the narrative of Canada as 'protector' of the weak.

LIMITING DEBATE: THE IMPACT OF NARRATIVES

Demonstrating that the government uses particular narratives to sell the war in Afghanistan seems like a fairly obvious point to make. Of course the government tries to spin its policy, and of course wars will be portrayed in ways that make the 'home nation' look just and righteous. In this case, however, these narratives not only offer a justification for the mission in Afghanistan, they also try to eliminate debate about the mission by mobilizing moral arguments. By evoking an image of Canada as a just international citizen with a particular moral compass and as a protector of women and children, the government implies that any critic of the mission is therefore content to sacrifice democracy and let women suffer. The narratives forestall discussion of Canada's strategic alliance and shared interests with the United States, the complex history of conflict in Afghanistan, the role that Canadian made armaments play in conflicts around the globe, and the many times when Canada and the international community have ignored (and continue to ignore) the widespread oppression faced by women.

In the context of this moral outrage, critics of the war become the 'real' enemy. In his 'Hard Questions' speech Peter MacKay makes this link clear:

> Canada understands that there are real risks involved in helping the Afghan people achieve these gains. Without a doubt, we will continue to stand by our brave Canadian soldiers and our fallen heroes. We believe that each and every soldier serving in Afghanistan is leaving a proud legacy, and we honour their commitment. However, what we face is the Taliban still working to generate doubt and fear. They would like nothing better than Canada and other NATO countries to withdraw from Afghanistan. They know that the Canadian court of public opinion has tremendous influence. They are very aware of our domestic discussions on this issue, and they will try to exploit our debate for military gain. They can't beat us on the battlefield. That is the only way this cunning adversary can win. This is the enemy that our brave men and women in uniform face. (MacKay, 2007e)

Public debate, in this passage, becomes the ally of the Taliban and the enemy of Canada's commitment, soldiers, and legacy. Under these conditions, any questions about the war are framed as a betrayal of Canada's national character.

By mobilizing ahistorical moral outrage to justify the mission in Afghanistan, the government also ignores criticisms from NGOs, government agencies, and the military itself regarding the dangers of having soldiers trying to deliver development aid as they are fighting a war. The contradictions (both theoretical and practical) between the narrative of Canada as good international citizen and protector and the realities of combat are covered over by this layer of moral outrage and certainty. In this way, the deaths of Canadian soldiers (and never the deaths of Afghans) become the ongoing justification for continuing the mission. The narratives of the good international citizen, committed to multilateralism and peacekeeping, and of Canada as protector of the weak combine to foreclose the public space for debate on the purposes and legitimacy of Canada's intervention in Afghanistan. As the *Calgary Herald* insisted two days following the death of Captain Nichola Goddard in Afghanistan:

> Those who complain of the meaninglessness of a soldier's death do not grasp how utterly vain such a death would be if Canada abruptly left Afghanistan because of it and the seeds of democracy languished, unwatered, in the volatile climate there. We will pay a far greater tribute to Goddard and to the other Canadian soldiers who have lost their lives there if we finish what they started. (*Calgary Herald*, 2006: A30)

The lessons of the 2006–7 period of Canada's military intervention are simple: the government's deployment of the narratives of good international citizen and protector of the weak framed Canada's intervention in Afghanistan in such a way that it became nearly impossible to reach any other conclusion than that of the *Calgary Herald* editorialist—and democratic debate in Canada became all the poorer for it.

Since 2007, of course, the circumstances in Afghanistan have not improved, and the Harper government has repeatedly reiterated its intention to withdraw (at least militarily) by 2011. The prime minister has even gone on record to state that the war in Afghanistan is now unwinnable (CNN, 2009). Despite these apparent changes in the government's orientation towards the war, the justification for Canada's presence continues to be articulated around the mythologies of Canada as good international citizen and protector.

Opposition to the war is muted. The window on public debate over the mission in Afghanistan opened a crack, however, with the news in early April 2009 that the Afghan government was prepared to adopt a law effectively sanctioning marital rape. 'Canada continues to call on the Afghan government, in the strongest of terms, to honour its human rights treaty obligations under international law, including respect for the equality of women before the law', Prime Minister Harper responded. 'We cannot state strongly enough our concern for the rights of women in Afghanistan' (Canada, Office of the Prime Minister, 2009). If the prosecution of the war leads to outcomes that clearly undermine Canada's good international citizen and protector roles, is Canada's participation in the war politically sustainable?

Notes

1. As an article posted on the Department of National Defence website notes, despite the evolution of the role the Canadian Forces have been called upon to perform, Canadians overwhelmingly cite peacekeeping as a key contribution of Canadian foreign policy. As the article points out, this is in part a reflection of the lack of understanding of the actual tasks performed by the Canadian Forces: 'Notwithstanding this lack of awareness of operations, when asked what the most positive contribution that Canada as a country makes to the world, "peacekeeping' remains the most frequent selection. Almost nine in ten Canadians, in fact, report that "promoting world peace" is the most important foreign policy objective for Canada' (Anker, 2005: 27).

2. The poll question read: 'What do Canadians perceive to be the purpose of our troops in Afghanistan—peacekeeping or combat?' The survey of 1000 Canadians was conducted between 9–12 March 2006, with an overall margin of error of 3.1 per cent.

3. It should be noted that many Canadian deaths in Afghanistan have occurred as a result of improvised explosive devices (IEDs). These are reported as such rather than as combat deaths (deaths as a result of a military offensive or enemy attack) by the Canadian military. Having said this, the Canadian military does classify the vast majority of Canadian deaths in Afghanistan as combat-related, on the assumption that IEDs are not traditionally found in non-combat zones.

4. The 16 July 2007 Strategic Counsel poll revealed that 81 per cent of Canadians, including 79 per cent of Quebecers, felt that the possible negative impact on the rights of women and children needed to be taken into consideration when considering if Canadians should stay in Afghanistan beyond 2009 (see Strategic Counsel, 2007: 16).

5. Despite the key role peacekeeping plays in defining the Canadian imaginary, it is important to note that by 2006, for example, Canada ranked fifty-fifth out of 108 as a UN peacekeeping country based on its commitment of equipment and military personnel (United Nations Association in Canada, 2007).

References

Anker, Lane. (2005). 'Peacekeeping and public opinion'. *Canadian Military Journal* 6(2): 23–32.

Bernier, Maxime. (2007). 'Notes for an address by the Honourable Minister of Foreign Affairs, to the International Conference on Canada's Mission in Afghanistan'. Montreal, 19 September. Retrieved from www.canadainternational. gc.ca/canada-afghanistan/speeches-discours/sp_mfa_190907.aspx.

Blanchfield, Mike. (2007). 'PM shines light on "Canada at its best": Harper touts rebuilding of Afghanistan'. *Calgary Herald*, 23 May: 23.

Calgary Herald. (2006). 'Our resolve honours soldier'. 19 May.

Canada, Office of the Prime Minister. (2007). 'Prime Minister Stephen Harper announces additional funding for aid in Afghanistan', 26 February. Retrieved from http://pm.gc. ca/eng/media.asp?id=1555.

———. (2009). 'PM joins world leaders in supporting NATO's commitment to Afghanistan', 4 April. Retrieved from http://pm.gc.ca/eng/media.asp?category=1&id=2509.

Canada. (2007). Speech from the Throne, 17 October. Retrieved from www.sft.ddt.gc.ca/eng/media.asp?id=1364.

CNN. (2009). 'Canada's Harper doubts Afghan insurgency can be defeated', 2 March. Retrieved from www.cnn.com/2009/WORLD/asiapcf/03/02/canada.afghanistan/index.html.

Freeman, Alan. (2007). 'Change tune on war, PM told', *Globe and Mail*, 13 July.

Globe and Mail. (2006). 'Harper's ringing words on the Afghanistan mission', 14 March.

Harper, Stephen. (2006a). 'Prime Minister stands by Canada's commitment to Afghanistan', 17 May. Retrieved from http://pm.gc.ca/eng/media.asp?id=1165.

———. (2006b). 'Address by the Prime Minister at the Canada–UK Chamber of Commerce, London, UK', 14 July. Retrieved from http://pm.gc.ca/eng/media.asp?id=1247.

———. (2007a). 'Announcement of additional funding for aid in Afghanistan', Office of the Prime Minister, 26 February. Retrieved from http://pm.gc.ca.

———. (2007b). 'Prime Minister Stephen Harper speaks to Canadian troops during visit to Afghanistan', 23 May. Retrieved from http://pm.gc.ca/eng/media.asp?id=1667.

Human Rights Watch. (2002, December). 'Afghanistan: "We want to live as humans"'. *Repression of Women and Girls in Western Afghanistan* 14(11).

MacKay, Peter. (2007a). 'Notes for an address by the Honourable Peter MacKay, Minister of Foreign Affairs and Minister of the Atlantic Canada Opportunities Agency, to the Standing Committee on Foreign Affairs and International Development', 20 March.

———. (2007b). 'Notes for an address by the Honourable Peter MacKay, Minister of Foreign Affairs and Minister of the Atlantic Canada Opportunities Agency, to the Vancouver Board of Trade', 11 April.

———. (2007c). 'Notes for an address by the Honourable Peter MacKay, Minister of Foreign Affairs and Minister of the Atlantic Canada Opportunities Agency, to the Pugwash Conference', 7 July. Retrieved from http://w01.international.gc.ca/minpub/Publication.aspx?isRedirect=True&publication_id=385287&Language=E&docnumber=2007/27.

———. (2007d). 'Notes for an address by the Honourable Peter G. MacKay, PC, MP, Minister of National Defence, for the Diplomatic Forum, St Andrews-on-the-Sea, New Brunswick', 10 September.

———. (2007e). 'Notes for an address by the Honourable Peter G. MacKay, PC, MP, Minister of National Defence, to the Chateauguay Chamber of Commerce: "The Hard Questions," Chateauguay, Quebec', 17 October.

Mohanty, Chandra. (1991). 'Cartographies of Struggle: Third World Women and the Politics of Feminism', in Chandra Talpade Mohanty, Ann Russo, and Lourdes Torres, eds., *Third World Women and the Politics of Feminism*. Bloomington: Indiana University Press, 1–47.

———. (1997). 'Under Western eyes: Feminist scholarship and colonial discourses'. In Padmini Mongia, ed., *Contemporary Postcolonial Theory: A Reader*, pp. 172–97. London: Arnold.

O'Connor, Gordon. (2006). 'Speaking notes for the Honourable Gordon J. O'Connor, PC, MP, Minister of National Defence at the Conference of Defence Associations Institute Annual General Meeting', 23 February. Retrieved from http://www.forces.gc.ca/site/newsroom/view_news_e.asp?id=1860.

———. (2006a). 'Speaking notes for the Honourable Gordon J. O'Connor, PC, MP, Minister of National Defence, for NATO Parliamentary Association Meeting. Quebec City, Quebec', 17 November. Retrieved from www.forces.gc.ca/site/newsroom/view_news_e.asp?id=2145.

Rawi, Mariam. (2006). 'Women in Afghanistan today: Hopes, achievements and challenges'. Speech delivered to the University of South Australia by a member of the Revolutionary Association of the Women of Afghanistan (RAWA), 27 April. Retrieved from www.rawa.org/rawi-speech.htm.

Razack, Sherene. (2004). *Dark Threats and White Knights: The Somalia Affair, Peacekeeping and the New Imperialism*. Toronto: University of Toronto Press.

Spivak, Gayatri Chakravorty. (1999). *A Critique of Postcolonial Reason: Toward a History of the Vanishing Present*. Cambridge, MA: Harvard University Press.

Strategic Counsel. (2006). *A Report to the Globe and Mail and CTV: Perceptions and Views of Canadian Armed Forces Troops in Afghanistan*, 13 March. Retrieved from www.thestrategiccounsel.com/our_news/polls/2006-03-13%20GMCTV%20Mar9-12%20(Mar13)%20Afghanistan%20-%20Rev.pdf.

Strategic Counsel. (2007). *A Report to the Globe and Mail and CTV: The State of Canadian Public Opinion on Afghanistan, Conrad Black*, 16 July. Retrieved from www.thestrategiccounsel.com/our_news/polls/2007-07-16%20GMCTV%20July%2012-15.pdf.

Verner, Josée. (2007). 'Notes for a speech by the Honourable Josée Verner, Minister of International Cooperation, at the breakfast at the Board of Trade of Metropolitan Montreal, International Development Week 2007, Montreal, Quebec', 6 February. Retrieved from www.acdi-cida.gc.ca/cidaweb/acdicida.nsf/En/RAC-25111126-LSX?OpenDocument.

Whitworth, Sandra. (2003). 'Militarized masculinities and the politics of peacekeeping: The Canadian case', in Claire Turenne Sjolander, Heather A. Smith, and Deborah Stienstra, eds, *Feminist Perspectives on Canadian Foreign Policy*, 76–89. Toronto: Oxford University Press.

7

DEMOCRATIZATION IN/OF CANADIAN FOREIGN POLICY: CRITICAL REFLECTIONS

Mark Neufeld

Countries are 'more' or 'less' democratic . . . cross-national (diachronic) comparisons indicate that Canada always appears high on a list of nation-states on this criterion.

Jackson and Jackson[1]

The logical link between competitive capitalism and political freedom has not been established.

C.B. Macpherson[2]

INTRODUCTION

Democratization, no less than globalization, has become a watchword for world politics at the end of the twentieth century. Indeed, the relationship between capitalism and democracy constitutes one of the central intellectual questions of our time. Here, Canadian foreign policy will be examined as a test-case of democratization in a context of globalizing neoliberalism. I will argue that the recent 'democratization' of Canadian foreign policy should be seen as the latest Canadian contribution in support of a US-led capitalist world order, as well as an example of 'passive revolution' designed to shore

up a crumbling domestic hegemony. I will begin by presenting evidence for the centrality of democracy for current Canadian foreign policy, both as a goal of policy as well as a means for creating and implementing that policy. I will then offer an interpretation of this phenomenon drawing on the neo-Gramscian framework.[3] I will conclude with some reflections on the lessons the Canadian case holds for those committed to a truly democratic counter-hegemonic project, and for our understanding of the relationship between globalization and democracy.

DEMOCRACY AND CANADIAN FOREIGN POLICY

Even the most casual observer of Canadian foreign policy cannot fail to be struck by the high profile achieved by the issue of democracy in recent years. The ruling Liberal Party's 1993 election handbook, *Creating Opportunity: The Liberal Plan for Canada*[4]—better known as the 'Red Book'—affirmed that democracy should be both i) a source and ii) an objective of Canadian foreign policy. This view was re-affirmed in the report of the Special Joint

Committee created by the Chrétien government to review Canadian foreign policy, following its consultation with NGO representatives and concerned individuals during the spring and summer of 1994, and in the government's tabled response to that report.[5] I will take these two issues in turn.

Democracy as a source of Canadian foreign policy must be seen in connection with the government's stated commitment to consult with Canadians about the future direction of foreign policy. In addition to the hearings held by the Special Joint Committee noted above, the major manifestation of this commitment has been the activities of the Canadian Centre for Foreign Policy Development, created in 1995 in response to the 1994 Special Joint Committee review, and dedicated to ensuring 'that the voice of Canadians [will] be heard' in the foreign policy process.[6] Operating with a budget of $1.5 million per year, the main activity of the centre has been the convening of annual 'National Forums on Canada's International Relations', beginning in 1994. Involving a series of meetings across the country with select representatives of NGOs, academe, media, business, and labour, as well as government officials, the National Forum has produced a series of reports and recommendations on Canada's foreign policy, on a variety of themes.[7]

The commitment to consult continues to figure prominently in official foreign policy discourse. Canada's foreign minister, Lloyd Axworthy, speaks approvingly of the role played by the National Forum, and other formal and informal consultations (including a web-page 'suggestion-box')[8] in 'maintaining a high level of support for Canadian foreign policy and activities abroad, and in setting priorities, particularly important in a time of resource constraints'.[9]

Democracy is also increasingly represented as the goal of Canadian foreign policy. Democracy as a major foreign policy objective is regularly framed in terms of the shift from traditional 'peacekeeping' to 'peacebuilding', with the latter involving the promotion of a broad range of commitments including respect for human rights, economic development, the rule of law, and political democratization. More specifically, peacebuilding is understood to promote stability in target countries or regions by providing the 'technical underpinnings' of a 'social infrastructure' which includes 'a civilian police force, free and vocal media, and an impartial judiciary'.[10]

In addition to these official programs and activities, it is also worth noting the creation, in 1988, of the state-funded 'International Centre for Human Rights and Democratic Development', an 'independent and non-partisan organization which initiates, encourages and supports the promotion, development and strengthening of democratic and human rights institutions and programmes as defined in the International Bill of Human Rights'.[11] The activities of the Centre include both public consultation with Canadians[12] as well as providing support for 'democratic development' beyond Canada's borders, and reflect once again a concrete example of the Canadian state's commitment to democracy in terms of both process and goal of Canadian foreign policy. Clearly, the current emphasis on democracy as both a source and goal of Canadian foreign policy is more than simple rhetoric. What is not necessarily self-evident, however, is its significance. In order to clarify this issue, a short digression into the area of critical International Relations (IR) theory, and its application to Canada's place in the world order, is required.[13]

CONCEPTUALIZING CANADIAN FOREIGN POLICY: A NEO-GRAMSCIAN FRAMEWORK

The key to understanding Canadian foreign policy in the postwar period is the notion of Canada as a 'middle power'. Following Robert Cox, Canadian 'middlepowermanship' can be understood in terms of its contribution to the hegemonic order of *pax americana*.[14]

> 'Hegemony' is used here in the Gramscian meaning of a structure of values and understandings about the nature of order that permeates a whole society, in this case a world society composed of states and non-state corporate entities. In a hegemonic order, these values and understandings are relatively stable and unquestioned. They appear to most actors as the natural order of things. They are the intersubjective meanings that constitute the order itself. Such a structure of meanings is underpinned by a structure of power, in which most probably one state is dominant but that state's dominance is not sufficient by itself to create hegemony. Hegemony derives from the ways of doing and thinking of the dominant social strata of the dominant state or states insofar as these ways of doing and thinking have inspired emulation or acquired the acquiescence of the dominant social strata of other states. These social practices and the ideologies of 'hegemonic order. Hegemony frames thought and thereby circumscribes action.[15]

The regulative ideal of 'middle power' has been central to the formulation, implementation, and, above all, legitimation, of Canadian foreign policy.[16] Attention should be paid to both the international level as well as the level of domestic politics, which together comprise the global order. At the international level, middlepowermanship directed the Canadian state to play the role of 'help-mate' to the United States as the latter worked to construct a world order—*pax americana*—consistent with the needs of the dominant classes of the core states. In general terms, the Canadian state did this by supporting the US

agenda within a series of multilateral fora, including the North Atlantic community, and the Bretton Woods and UN systems. More specifically, the notion of 'middle power' oriented the Canadian state to a role supportive of the hegemonic global order in two critical senses: i) by fulfilling an important role of facilitator and mediator, Canada helped to defuse potential conflicts which, if not addressed, might have undermined the stability of the global order;[17] and ii) by showing itself willing to sacrifice short-term national interests for the greater good, Canada helped to reinforce the notion that the global order was, in fact, not a narrowly 'American' order, but one which truly represented the ' common interest'.[18]

Middlepowermanship was equally relevant to the construction of hegemony at the domestic level, both materially and ideologically. First, through its stability-reinforcing role of facilitator at the international level already noted, the Canadian state helped to create the conditions for stable, managed economic growth. It was this growth upon which the compromise of the liberal welfare state—the cornerstone of hegemony within core states like Canada—depended. Secondly, the image of 'middle power', with its attendant emphasis on Canada as a responsible member of the international community, was crucial in creating a domestic consensus in support of extensive involvement in the support of the international order, without which Canada's ability to play the 'helpful fixer' would not have been possible. Finally, and perhaps most importantly, in representing Canada's selfless activism in the international realm as the natural expression of Canadian society as a whole, middlepowermanship reinforced the notion that the social order within Canada's borders was an essentially just one, and deserving of widespread public support.

In sum, in its original formulation the regulative ideal of 'middle power', like the global order it served, was framed in terms of dominant class interests and in tune with a hegemonic global order. What is equally significant, however, is that this understanding of 'middlepowermanship' did not go uncontested. Indeed, beginning in the 1960s, public questioning of the traditional assumptions about the international order by emerging oppositional social groupings led, outside of elite circles, to a substantive redefinition of the notion of 'middle power'. Pratt has referred to this social grouping, which arose in the context of declining hegemony and which remains active into the present context, as the 'counter-consensus'.[19] What distinguished the members of the counter-consensus was their rejection of the principal assumptions informing elite discourse about the global order, and their criticism, in politico-normative terms, of the militarism associated with the Cold War as well as the workings of the international economy, which they saw as systematically disadvantageous to the Third World.

Radicalization and expansion of the social base of the counter-consensus through the 1970s and 1980s, most recently in the context of anti-free trade struggles, led to increased emphasis on the links between disarmament, economic development and wealth re-distribution, environmental policy, and democratization at the global level with radical change at the domestic level. In this respect, the counter-consensus could be understood as forming part of an emerging counter-hegemonic bloc.

Of particular importance for the discussion here is the fact that the counter-discourse of the counter-consensus gave new meaning to the regulative ideal of Canada as a middle power. Significantly, the links of the earlier notion of middle power to support for an American-led hegemonic order were severed. Rather, middle power was recast to signify the influence enjoyed by a country like Canada and the potential such influence offers to effect radical progressive change in terms of disarmament, economic development and wealth redistribution, environmental policy, and democratization of the foreign policy-making process.

> The outline of a global community, in which the planet's resources could be managed by institutions practising fairness and stewardship, is coming into view . . . People who sense the power and creativity of our time now demand a safer, saner world in which governments, using the levers in hand, generate the production of the goods of life, not the weapons of death. As this constitutes an enormous challenge to Canada, this land so blessed in space, resources, technology, ability and reputation throughout the world. The rise of middle-power influence with the end of superpower enmity provides Canada with an unprecedented opportunity to work for the development of global security structures.[20]

It is not hard to appreciate how this oppositional understanding of middle power was fundamentally incompatible with dominant class interests, both domestically and internationally. It is not at all surprising, therefore, that concerted efforts would be made to counter the redefinition offered by the counter-consensus.

Initially, official spokespersons countered calls for progressive activism in Canadian foreign policy by advancing a far more restricted, 'limitationist' notion of middle power. This limitationist notion of middle power, which first achieved prominence in the Mulroney years, was also a regular feature of official discourse in the early years of the Chrétien government following its election in 1993.[21] The Liberal government statement, *Canada in the World*, for example, repeats the pattern established in the 1980s by twinning traditional affirmations of 'exceptionalism' in Canada's foreign policy record—

Canada's history as a non-colonizing power, champion of constructive multilateralism and effective international mediator, underpins an important and distinctive role among nations as they seek to build a new and better order . . .

—with thinly veiled admonishments to limit expectations of progressive action in the future—

While Canadians strongly support an active foreign policy, they also have a realistic view about the challenges ahead and the constraints—especially financial constraints—that we face. . . . [Accordingly] We will not do everything we have done in the past, nor shall we do things as we have done before.[22]

Similarly, calls for the promotion of Canadian values such as human rights in *Canada in the World* were coupled with public statements which sought to distance government policy from that orientation by downplaying the importance of human rights records in determining Canada's trade relations.[23]

It soon became clear, however, that this strategy would not be successful. Put simply, beyond its questionable utility as a guide for state action in the international area, it was highly unlikely that a limited conception of middle power would ever satisfy the demands of the counter-consensus. From the perspective of state managers, what was required was a re-invigorated notion of middle power that would serve simultaneously to guide Canadian foreign policy in its goal of maintaining a global order consistent with the needs of capital as well as re-establish the legitimacy of Canadian foreign policy in the eyes of its counter-consensus critics. Ironically, the resources to formulate such a re-invigorated policy were to be found in the discourse of the counter-consensus itself.

THE 'DEMOCRATIZATION' OF CANADIAN FOREIGN POLICY: PASSIVE REVOLUTION IN ACTION

And they call it democracy . . .

Bruce Cockburn

Gramsci's notion of 'passive revolution' provides a useful guide to understanding the 'democratization' of Canadian foreign policy.[24] As with many of Gramsci's key concepts, more than one reading of their meaning is possible. Passive revolution, for example, can be understood as the way in which the capitalist class rose to ascendancy in places such as Italy and Germany where, in contrast to France where the old feudal classes were overthrown by an ascendant bourgeoisie, no dominant class was able to establish hegemony in Gramsci's sense. As such, it has been argued that 'passive revolution . . . is particularly apposite to industrialising third world countries'.[25]

There is a second reading possible, however, which sees passive revolution as equally applicable to national formations in which hegemony has been achieved. Here passive revolution is understood as the normal response of the hegemonic class to an organic crisis. In the words of Roger Simon, Gramsci suggests that the passive revolution

is not only an interpretation of the Risorgimento but also of 'every epoch characterised by complex upheavals'. Whenever the hegemony of the bourgeoisie begins to disintegrate and a period of organic crisis develops, the process of reorganization which is needed to re-establish its hegemony will to some extent have the character of a passive revolution. . . . Passive revolution is involved whenever relatively far-reaching modifications in a country's economic structure are made from above, through the agency of the state apparatuses, without relying on the active participation of the people.[26]

Crucial to any understanding of passive revolution is the attendant notion of *'trasformismo'*—the co-optation of the potential leaders of subaltern social groups through the strategy of 'assimilating and domesticating potentially dangerous ideas by adjusting them to the policies of the dominant coalition'.[27] In the Canadian case, the leaders to be co-opted were those active in the social movements which formed the core of the counter-consensus. And the 'dangerous idea' to be assimilated and domesticated was the conjoining of 'democracy and foreign policy'. Indeed, calls for democracy had been central to the re-formulated notion of middle power advanced by the counter-consensus. Critically, many members of the counter-consensus accepted that Canada was a well-functioning democracy, with one important exception. That exception was the domain of foreign policy. Accordingly, as evidenced by the terms and recommendations of what was, arguably, the most sustained effort of the leaders of the counter-consensus to contribute to such a redefinition of the notion of middle power—*Transformation Moment: A Canadian Vision of Common Security*[28]—the democratization of the foreign policy-making process was a central concern:

> Democratic governance is an essential requirement of human security. Only when people can define for themselves what is in their best interest, and choose for themselves how to pursue it, can they create the just societies that human security depends upon. In Canada and around the world, people are increasingly demanding the right to decide for themselves how to run their lives, organise their societies, look after their needs. Even in the long-standing

democracies, there is a growing demand for citizens themselves to be accorded greater responsibility for running their own lives. . . . The Citizens' Inquiry itself was a response to this demand.[29]

The proposed reforms dealt with Parliament and its role:

> Parliamentary reforms should be made to democratise Canadian foreign affairs and defence policy, including, at a minimum, changes to ensure that: any placement of Canadian forces on active service requires parliamentary approval within ten days; all treaties (bilateral and multilateral) entered into by Canada must be approved by Parliament to enter into effect; and all collective security agreements—whether new or renewals—must be approved by Parliament to enter into effect.

Democratization was to extend beyond parliamentary reforms, however, to include greater public participation in the policy-making process, including 'more open access to government information' and 'regular public hearings'.[30]

> The Canadian government should publish an annual 'security policy' green paper for consideration by the Standing Committee on External Affairs and International Trade and the general public. In addition, the government should establish procedures for regular consultation between the Privy Council secretariat responsible for integrated security policy and the Parliament, provincial governments, and the Canadian public.[31]

One cannot but be struck, in light of these recommendations, by the degree to which official policy has accommodated the form—if not the intent—of the calls for the democratization of foreign policy-making. From parliamentary reforms to annual reviews by Foreign Affairs on the promotion of democracy abroad to regular 'national forums', both the general discourse as well as specific recommendations have been adopted. It is hardly surprising, therefore, that many of those consulted in the national forums have responded warmly to the government's initiatives to 'reach and include a wider range of civil society in policy discussions'.[32]

That it is only the form, and not the substance, of democracy that has been adopted must, however, also be recognized. As one realist critic noted, the link between the national forums and substantive democracy is a rather tenuous one:

> The National Forum of March 1994 was widely billed as an example of how to democratise foreign policy. . . . But let us not delude ourselves—or insult the taxpayers who picked up the tab for flying the participants to Ottawa, putting them up in local hotels, and feeding them fine wine and food; this was not an affair of, or for, the demos. On the contrary; this was an elite gathering, strictly for Canada's conferencing classes.[33]

Nor are these public consultations 'neutral' as regards the parameters set for discussion. At the Toronto meetings of the Third Annual Forum in 1996, for example, participants, drawn from a cross-section of NGOs and business along with government representatives, were subjected to a plenary session featuring reflections on how to use 'our information edge' to enhance Canada's 'soft power' in the globalizing world economy.[34] Thus prepped, they were then divided into working groups and assigned themes for discussion. The theme assigned to Working Group 1 was the following: 'Canadian Content, Sovereignty and Competitiveness in the Global Information Infrastructure'. Interventions expressing the concern that

this formulation of Canada's place in the global communications order was hardly neutral, that a discussion framed in terms of 'Canadian Content, Participatory Democracy and Social Justice' might lead to different kinds of policy recommendations, were duly noted and then systematically ignored.[35]

Neither are 'national forums' neutral with regard to their impact on participants. Most significantly, potential critics from within the NGO community are transformed into 'stakeholders'. As Nossal notes, '[u]nquestionably, stakeholder politics is an excellent tool of political management for state officials. It ensures that those primarily affected by a policy area will have an opportunity to have their say, to comment on proposed policy changes, to register their objections or to offer their ideas. It thus not only protects state officials against future claims by stakeholders; it also binds the stakeholders more tightly to the policies eventually adopted.[36]

In sum, the 'democratization' of Canadian foreign policy-making can be understood, in terms of the national formation, as a form of passive revolution designed to strengthen hegemony domestically. The degree to which it can serve to strengthen and even re-establish hegemony internationally will be discussed in the following section.

PROMOTING POLYARCHY: THE CANADIAN CONNECTION

> It is paradoxical that in relations between civilizations it is not the democracies of the West but the Communists—professed materialists, who, concealing their reactionary and enslaving goals, exploit the truth that man does not live by bread alone, nor defend himself solely by arms. . . . Much might be accomplished . . . if provision were made for the exchange of university lecturers and students in history or politics or philosophy, and for visits of editors and newspapermen. In addition to sending Western

machines, it would be important to make read-ily and cheaply available to students in Asia some of the works of the leading thinkers whose insights have shaped Western civilization. Lester B. Pearson, *Democracy in World Politics.*[37]

In this section, I take up the question of what one US scholar has termed 'democracy promotion'.[38] In an important contribution to the neo-Gramscian analysis of world order, William Robinson has argued that US foreign policy now seeks to pro-mote a limited form of democracy as part of the effort to replace coercive means of social control in the South with consensual ones. By the mid-1980s (and thus before the collapse of the Soviet bloc), he argues, there was an explicit shift in US policy from the promotion of authoritarianism to the promo-tion of democracy. The shift in policy is more than simple rhetoric; it correlates with the creation of a 'democracy promotion' apparatus involving 'new governmental and quasi-governmental agencies and bureaus, policy studies, and government and private conferences, to draft and implement "dem-ocracy promotion' policies and programs".[39]

Robinson distinguishes the limited notion of democracy—polyarchy—from that of the sub-stantive notion of 'popular democracy'. Unlike the latter, which concerns itself with outcome as well as process, polyarchy

> argues that democracy rests exclusively on pro-cess, so that there is no contradiction between a 'democratic' process and a social order punctu-ated by sharp social inequalities and minority monopolization of society's material and cul-tural resources. Thus, under the polyarchic def-inition, a system can acquire a democratic form without a democratic content or outcome.[40]

It is the former, represented by the 'rule of law' and elite-managed 'free and fair elections', which must

be instituted in order to prevent popular move-ments from achieving the latter.

The means to achieve polyarchy is a new form of aid complementary to the traditional forms of economic aid (to promote the development of capitalist market relations) and military aid (to repress social dissent). The new form of aid is that of 'political aid', and departs significantly from the traditional notion of government to government aid. Its objective is for 'US and local elites thoroughly [to] penetrate not just the state, but civil society', in order to exercise control not from above but from below and from within.[41]

As Robinson notes further:

> This explains why this new political interven-tion does not target governments per se, but groups in civil society, such as trade unions, political parties, the media, and women's, stu-dent, and other mass organizations. In coun-tries subject to US 'democracy promotion' programs, civil society is the target of penetra-tion as the locus of a Gramscian hegemony. As two Project Democracy consultants explained: 'The new policy instrument—aid to friendly political organizations abroad—[. . .] helps build up political actors in other polities, rather than seeking to influence existing ones'.[42]

It is no surprise, given this understanding of dem-ocracy, that 'democracy promotion' was instituted, first and foremost

> in those counties where social movements, scattered protests, and pressures for democratic change had begun to coalesce into mass national democratization movements, such as in the Philippines, Chile, Nicaragua and Haiti.

The immediate purpose of US intervention in these national democratization movements was to gain influence over them and try to shape their outcomes in such a way as to pre-empt more radical political changes and fundamental challenges to the socioeconomic order. Beyond this immediate purpose, 'democracy promotion' was aimed at advancing the agenda in intervened countries of the transnational elite—consolidation of polyarchic political systems and neo-liberal restructuring.[43]

Robinson's intervention represents a significant contribution to the growing neo-Gramscian literature on globalization and democratization, and provides a useful backdrop against which to measure both the extent of the Canadian state's complicity in—and the distinctive character of Canada's contribution to—democracy promotion.

The case of Haiti provides a good illustration of the first. To begin, it is worth noting that promoting democracy in Haiti was given high priority by the Chrétien government. As Foreign Minister Axworthy explained:

. . . following the restoration of democracy in Haiti, the lack of a trained civilian police force was seen as a threat to the fragile state. Canadian and international support for police training, as well as programmes to train the coast guard, judges, and grassroots organizations are all part of building an infrastructure for peace. While the situation remains delicate, our ongoing efforts give hope that a sustainable democracy can be achieved in Haiti.[44]

Indeed, the Canadian government played the major role in sustaining the UN operation in Haiti since its inception in 1994, both financially and in terms of personnel (peacekeepers, human rights monitors, and RCMP officers).[45] It is estimated that by the end of 1997, the Haiti mission cost Canada nearly $450 million out of the Department of National Defence budget alone—a figure that does not reflect other costs in support of democratic peacebuilding from the budgets of the Canadian International Development Agency (CIDA) and the Department of Foreign Affairs and International Trade (DFAIT) for RCMP officers and judicial reform.[46]

Following Robinson, there is little mystery as to the kind of democracy that was to be extended to Haiti. What does require explaining is why democracy promotion in Haiti was made such a priority by the Canadian state? The answer must be sought, of course, in a constellation of factors including US efforts to encourage the establishment of satellite democracy promotion institutions in its G7 partners,[47] specific pressures emanating from the Canadian Haitian community, as well as concerns about a wave of Haitian refugees appearing on Quebec's (Montreal's) doorstep. Between the international and the local, however, was the expectation that democracy promotion as a goal of Canadian foreign policy, like democracy as a source of policy, would prove to be highly popular with important segments of the counter-consensus.

Nor was this expectation unreasonable. Along with the democratization of the foreign policy-making process, a central part of the re-definition of middle power offered by the counter-consensus was the promotion of democracy as a central objective of Canadian foreign policy. In *Transformation Moment,* for example, this goal was formulated in terms of an expanded view of Canada's traditional peacekeeping activities:

Peace-keeping has been by far Canada's most useful military contribution to international security since World War II . . .

No country has contributed more to the global success story that peace-keeping has become. . . . The need for peace-keeping is likely to remain and even to grow for many years to come. The nature of peace-keeping operations is expanding and now includes many non-military as well as military operations, including such tasks as election-monitoring, civil policing, and even temporary national administration. . . . This expansion of roles promises to make peace-keeping an even more important contribution to global security in the future.[48]

Once again, therefore, the discourse of the counter-consensus provided the very resources of legitimation for Canada's support of polyarchy abroad, even as the latter was undertaken in the hope that critics would be transformed into stakeholders.[49]

If Canadian efforts in Haiti underscore the consistency of Canadian foreign policy objectives with those of the United States, Canadian initiatives in multilateral fora also stressed the continuing importance of middlepowermanship for understanding the unique contribution the Canadian state makes to the democracy promotion enterprise. Canada's central role in the creation of the 'Unit For the Promotion of Democracy' (UPD) within the Organization of American States (OAS) serves as a good example. Following Canada's entry into the OAS in 1989, it soon became, in the words of one observer, 'more American than the Americans in leading the rallying cry for democracy and free markets in the hemisphere'.[50] The creation of the UPD was one of the Canadian government's first initiatives. In addition to diplomatic support, the Canadian government provided funding for the UPD and former Canadian ambassador in the region, John Graham, was appointed as its first director. Canada's efforts were continued in its successful lobbying effort within the OAS for the 'Santiago Commitment to Democracy and the Renewal of the International System', adopted at the twenty-first General Assembly of the OAS in Santiago in June 1991. The declaration committed member governments 'to adopt efficacious, timely, and expeditious procedures to ensure the promotion and defence of representative democracy'.[51]

The significance of Canada's success is that it was achieved despite the understandable reservations of other member governments given the history of American intervention in the region under the guise of liberal democratic principles. In this, it can be argued, Canada played the invaluable role—which only a middle power can play—of using multilateral forums to legitimize emerging norms and institutions as representative, not of the interests of the dominant state but of the 'universal interest'. This is no less important for the success of democracy promotion as a hegemonic project than it was for other dimensions of *pax americana*.[52] In sum, while it is no doubt the case that the 'promotion of polyarchy is a policy initiative that is becoming internationalized under US leadership',[53] the dependence of the United States on second-tier core states such as Canada fulfilling their functions as legitimizers—not to mention taking a lead role in contexts where US activism would do more harm than good—must not be overlooked.

CONCLUSION

For those looking for easy labels, Canada is more than a middle power. We are a global middle power, called on to play an international role in the pursuit of global interests.

Lloyd Axworthy[54]

There is no better evidence of the abandonment of the limitationist notion of middle power and the embrace of the discourse of the counter-consensus than this affirmation of Canada's global vocation by its current foreign minister. Nor is this commitment to international activism merely rhetorical.

Canada's foreign policy efforts to 'improve international governance through, *inter alia,* democratization, respect for human rights, and the peaceful resolution of disputes'[55] makes a valuable contribution to the legitimation and stabilization of the current world order, as the manufacture of 'a uniquely Canadian identity and a sense of Canada's place in the world'[56] serves simultaneously to reinforce hegemony in domestic terms. The 'democratization' of Canadian foreign policy also stands as a sobering example of how 'passive revolution' poses a major threat to efforts to articulate a framework of ideas which can serve the creation of an effective counter-hegemonic bloc.

None of this is to suggest, of course, that current elite strategies are guaranteed to be successful. Indeed, there are good reasons to conclude just the opposite. To begin, there is little chance that core states will establish stable hegemonic orders in dependent states based on polyarchic forms of democracy.[57] The reason is that successful hegemonies never rest on practices of ideological legitimation alone. Following Gramsci, hegemony also depends on the leading group making real and significant concessions to subaltern groups. In the North, for example, stable hegemonic orders have been the product of ideological legitimation in combination with social welfare provisions. In dependent states, however, such concessions do not accompany the polyarchic forms of democracy being instituted. Despite the ideological potency of the discourse of democracy, rule is not based on consent. Rather, 'the role of coercion remains central, despite the implementation of various liberal-democratic shells'.[58]

In terms of the stabilization of hegemony domestically, Canadian elites are bound to be no more successful. First, the continuing violation of basic human rights in dependent states where polyarchic forms of democracy have been instituted (unavoidable given the ongoing need for coercion of economically marginalized sectors of society) should give even the least radical groupings within the counter-consensus pause; it is but a small step to the question of what kind of democracy are core states promoting abroad that sees human rights violations increase after 'democracy' has been established?[59]

Secondly, even if *trasformismo* is successful in co-opting the less radical elements of the counter-consensus, it is unlikely that hegemony will be strengthened greatly in the wider Canadian society. The 'democratization' process is accompanied by neo-liberal restructuring designed to withdraw the very social welfare concessions upon which a stable hegemony rests. Accordingly, it would seem more likely that overt resistance by the working class will increasingly characterize Northern social formations like Canada's, ideological cooptation of some middle-class elements in the counter-consensus notwithstanding.[60]

A final point is the lesson contained within the successful elite appropriation of the counter-consensus's discourse of democracy and its operationalization as polyarchy in support of globalizing neo-liberalism. Largely, this was possible because, while often employed in counter-consensus discourse, the meaning of—and corresponding institutional arrangements for—a non-polyarchic form of democracy were never spelled out. Accordingly, a condition of a successful counter-hegemony is rigorous intellectual elaboration of a critical understanding of democracy appropriate to the current global(izing) context.[61]

In conclusion, it is undoubtedly true that democracy 'matters both as a source and objective of foreign policy': democracies do 'make foreign policy differently' and they do 'make different foreign policies'.[62] It is also true, however, that dependent on the context, 'democracy' may represent little more than an alternative means of consolidating and perpetuating unequal relations between people and communities. As such, the differences between formally democratic and non-democratic foreign policies may be less significant than might appear at first glance. The real questions in evaluating the significance of democracy as a source for, and objective of, Canadian foreign policy are 'what kind of democracy is being instituted?' and 'what role does that democracy play in supporting and perpetuating what remains a markedly unjust and violence-prone global order?' Answering these questions will take us a good way toward understanding the much-vaunted link between democracy and globalization.

Notes

In the writing of this paper, I benefitted from the comments of Cranford Pratt, Franklyn Griffiths, Stephen Clarkson, David Black, Jean Kirk Laux, Denis Epp, and William Robinson. I also acknowledge the financial assistance provided by the Social Sciences and Humanities Research Council.

1. Robert J. Jackson and Doreen Jackson, *Politics in Canada: Culture, Institutions, Behaviour and Public Policy,* Second Edition (Scarborough, Ont: Prentice-Hall, 1990), p. 25.

2. C.B. Macpherson, *Democratic Theory: Essays in Retrieval* (Oxford: Oxford University Press, 1973), p. 149.

3. As enunciated by Robert Cox and others. See Stephen Gill, (ed.) Gramsci, *Historical Materialism and International Relations* (Cambridge: Cambridge University Press, 1993).

4. For an introduction to the Neo-Gramscian school, see Randall German and Michael Kenny, 'International Relations Theory and the New Gramscians,' *Review of International Studies 24,* no. I (January 1998), pp. 3–21.

5. See Canada in the World: Government Statement (Ottawa: 1995).

6. Canadian Centre for Foreign Policy Development, Annual Report (1996/1997), p. 1.

7. The most recent, for example, focuses on the themes of i) peacebuilding, ii) international communications, and iii) child protection. See the 1996 *National Forum on Canada's International Relations Report* (Canadian Centre for Foreign Policy Development).

8. At www.dfait-maeci.gc.ca.

9. L. Axworthy, 'Canada and Human Security: The Need for Leadership,' *International Journal*, 52 (Spring 1997), p. 195.

10. 'Canada and Human Security,' p. 186. Haiti is regularly held up as a prime example of Canadian peacebuilding efforts.

11. International Centre for Human Rights and Democratic Development Annual Report 1996–97, p. 3.

12. A recent seminar featured leaders of Canada's business community discussing the role of business in promoting human rights abroad. See 'Globalization, Trade and Human Rights: The Canadian Business Perspective: A Summary Report of the Toronto Conference,' (Montreal: International Centre for Human Rights and Democratic Development, 1996).

13. While not the focus of this paper, there is a clear meta-theoretical dimension to the notion of critical IR theory. I have tried to sketch out the general parameters of critical theorizing elsewhere. See Mark Neufeld, *The Restructuring of International Relations Theory* (Cambridge: Cambridge University Press, 1995).

14. See R. Cox, *Power, Production and World Order: Social Forces in the Making of History* (New York: Columbia University Press, 1987). See also Robert Cox, *Approaches to World Order,* T. Sinclair (ed.), (Cambridge: Cambridge University Press, 1996).

15. 'Multilateralism and world order,' in *Approaches to World Order,* pp. 517–18.

16. For greater elaboration of the notion of 'middlepowermanship' in neo-Gramscian terms, see M. Neufeld, 'Hegemony and Foreign Policy Analysis: The Case of Canada as Middle Power,' *Studies in Political Economy* 48 (1995), pp. 7–29. See also M. Neufeld and Sandra Whitworth, 'Imag(in)ing Canadian Foreign Policy,' in Wallace Clement (ed.), *Understanding Canada: Building on the New Canadian Political Economy* (Montreal and Kingston: McGill-Queen's Press, 1997), pp. 197–214.

17. It will be remembered that the Pearsonian innovation of 'peacekeeping' was prompted by the desire to regulate a conflict between core states during the Suez crisis. Specifically, the Canadian peacekeeping contribution allowed for a resolution of the potentially destabilizing rift between France and Great Britain, on the one hand, and the United States on the other. In short, it can be argued that from the beginning the principal function of peacekeeping has been to contribute to the maintenance of order and stability within the hegemonic spheres—a goal very much in keeping with the 'national interest' of a non-superpower.

18. It can be argued that Canada's political leadership was not always completely consistent in this regard. One of the corollaries of middlepowermanship was the principle of functionalism, according to which countries, such as Canada should be allotted a seat at the table in international

organizations to the degree to which they contributed. This principle, while achieving some success in deterring the great powers from appropriating all decision-making power to themselves, clearly contradicted liberal international principles of global governance (*i.e.*, the formal equality of all states) by arguing, in effect, that there should be a further differentiation between secondary and less powers. The cost of advocating a principle of global governance which hardly lent itself to the claim of representing the ' common interest' was that at the first meeting of the UN General Assembly, Australia, and not Canada, won a seat on the Security Council. See Tom Keating, *Canada and World Order* (Toronto: McClelland & Steward, 1993), chapter 1.

19. Pratt defines the 'counter-consensus' as 'internationally minded public interest groups', which exist in substantial number, and which have traditionally been 'peripheral to decision-making in Canadian public life'. Within this group, Pratt includes church-related organizations like Project Ploughshares, the Canadian Council for International Co-operation, Oxfam, the Canadian Catholic Organization for Development and Peace, Ten Days for World Development, the Inter-Church Committee on Human Rights in Latin America, and the taskforce on the Churches and Corporate Responsibility, as well as secular organizations such as disarmament, peace, or Third World solidarity groups. One should also include organized labour, as well as extraparliamentary opposition groups such as the National Action Committee. See Cranford Pratt, 'Dominant class theory and Canadian foreign policy: the case of the counter-consensus,' *International Journal* 39 (Winter 1983–4), pp, 99–135.

20. *Transformation Moment: A Canadian Vision of Common Security. The Report of the Citizens' Inquiry into Peace and Security,* (Co-published by Project Ploughshares and the Canadian Peace Alliance: March 1992), p. 6, emphasis added.

21. Interestingly, under the Liberals the term 'middle power' itself has been resurrected. In early November 1993, for example, the new foreign affairs minister, Andre Ouellet, promised a foreign policy review with explicit reference to the tradition of 'middlepowermanship': 'It's clear Canada's foreign policy must be reviewed in the context of the end of the Cold War . . . It also has to be reviewed in the context of Canada's capacity, as a middle power, to play an important role at the United Nations'. The *Toronto Star* (Friday November 5, 1993), emphasis added.

22. *Canada in the World* (1995), pp. 8, 9.

23. In this regard, note Foreign Affairs Minister Andre Ouellet's insistence that 'to try to be a Boy Scout on your own, to impose your own rules on others when indeed nobody else is following it is absolutely counterproductive and

does not lead to any successful future.' *Globe and Mail* (Tuesday May 16, 1995), p. A 11.

24. See Antonio Gramsci, 'Notes on Italian History,' in Quinton Hoare and Geoffrey Nowell Smith (eds.), *Selections from the Prison Notebooks* (New York: International Publishers, 1971).

25. Cox, 'Gramsci, hegemony and international relations,' in *Approaches to World Order,* p. 129–31.

26. Roger Simon, *Gramsci's Political Thought* (London: Lawrence and Wishard, 1982), pp. 48, 49.

27. Cox, 'Gramsci, hegemony and international relations,' p. 130.

28. *The Report of the Citizens' Inquiry into Peace and Security* (March 1992) (see note 20). The inquiry, which held a series of public meetings across the country, was organized by the Canadian Peace Alliance. Its fourteen cosponsors reads like a virtual 'Who's Who' of the counter-consensus, including the Assembly of First Nations, the Canadian Council for International Cooperation, the Canadian Council of Churches, the Canadian Labour Congress, and the National Action Committee on the Status of Women.

29. *Transformation Moment,* pp. 52–53.

30. *Transformation Moment,* p. 53. Significantly, the report called as well for 'reforms to the mandate and oversight of Canada's intelligence agencies to ensure Canadians do not become targets of surveillance just for participating in the political process,' p. 53.

31. *Transformation Moment,* p. 4.

32. 1996 *National Forum Report,* p. 1.

33. Nossal, 'The Democratization of Canadian Foreign Policy: The Elusive Ideal,' in Maxwell A. Cameron and Maureen Appel Molot (eds.), *Democracy and Foreign Policy: Canada Among Nations 1995* (Ottawa: Carleton University Press, 1995), p. 39.

34. According to the 1996/97 Annual Report of the Canadian Centre for Foreign Policy Development, Ann Medina, a prominent Canadian journalist, was paid $7000 to develop this theme as a background paper for the 1996 National Forum. It is worth noting that the paper was not ready until after the forum ended, depriving it, for good or for ill, of any real impact on the work-group discussions. It was subsequently published, however. See Ann Medina, 'Canada's Information Edge,' *Canadian Foreign Policy* 4, no. 2 (Fall 1996), pp. 71–86.

35. See the summary of the discussions of Working Group I in the *National Forum Report.*

36. Nossal, p. 38, emphasis added.

37. (Toronto: S. J. Reinald Saunders and Co., 1955), pp. 92, 93.

38. See William Robinson, 'Globalization, the world system, and "democracy promotion" in U.S. foreign policy,' *Theory and Society* 25 (1996), pp: 615–65. See also W. Robinson,

Promoting Polyarchy: Globalization, US Intervention, and Hegemony (Cambridge: Cambridge University Press, 1996).

39. Robinson, 'Globalization,' p. 623.

40. Robinson, 'Globalization,' p. 625.

41. Robinson, 'Globalization,' p. 643.

42. Robinson, 'Globalization,' p. 643.

43. Robinson, 'Globalization,' p. 644.

44. 'Canada and Human Security,' p. 186.

45. Canada's RCMP has been given the mandate of training Haiti's 5000-member National Police force so that it may function with respect for democratic norms.

46. See Tom Keating, 'Promoting Democracy Abroad: Assessing the Practical and Ethical Implications for Canada', paper prepared for the 'Workshop on Human Rights, Ethics and Canadian International Security Policy', sponsored by the Centre for International and Security Studies, York University, Toronto, November 21–2, 1997. Significant as well was the establishment of the 'Lester B. Pearson Canadian International Peacekeeping Training Centre' (PPC) by the Canadian government in Nova Scotia in 1994. It is funded from the budgets of the departments of national defence and foreign affairs and international trade. The central organizing framework for the PPC is that of the 'New Peacekeeping Partnership'. This term is applied: to those organizations and individuals that work together to improve the effectiveness of modern peacekeeping operations. It includes the military; civil police; government and non-government agencies dealing with human rights and humanitarian assistance; diplomats; the media; and organizations sponsoring development and democratization programmes. (from the 'General Information Packet' of the PPC).

47. See Robinson, *Promoting Polyarchy*. It should be noted that the post–Cold War transition in Central! Eastern Europe also provided an opportunity for the United States to press its OECD allies to adopt 'democracy and human rights' as a common agenda. It was the traditional role of 'middlepowermanship' as a legitimizing discourse—exceptional among OECD countries—and the resulting concern to neutralize the critique of the counter-consensus, however, that explains why the democracy agenda has been embraced so enthusiastically by Canadian state managers and even members of the Canadian business elite. On Eastern Europe, see Jean Kirk Laux, 'From South to East? Financing the Transition in Central and Eastern Europe,' in Maureen Appel Molot and Harald von Riekhoff, *Canada Among Nations 1994: A Part of the Peace* (Ottawa: Carleton University Press, 1994), pp. 172–94. For an example of the democracy agenda reflected in the discourse of Canada's business elites, see the public address of Thomas d'Aquino, president of the Business Council on National Issues (BCNI): 'Globalization, Social Progress, Democratic Development and Human Rights,' delivered at the annual general meeting of the 'Academic of International Business,' September 27, 1996.

48. *Transformation Moment*, pp. 68–9.

49. For background, see Robinson, *Promoting Polyarchy*, pp. 364–65. Unfortunately, Robinson neglects to discuss the role played by Canada in this regard.

50. See Keating, 'Promoting Democracy Abroad,' pp. 5–6.

51. See Tom Farer, *Collectively Defending Democracy in a World of Sovereign States: The Western Hemisphere's Prospect* (Montreal: International Centre for Human Rights and Democratic Development, 1993). See also Keating, 'Promoting Democracy Abroad,' pp. 5–6.

52. Indeed for some Canadian foreign policy analysts, multilateralization is, in international terms, the very essence of democratization. See, for example, James Rochlin, 'Markets, Democracy and Security in Latin American,' in Cameron and Molot, *Democracy and Foreign Policy*, p. 265.

53. Robinson, 'Globalization,' p. 653.

54. Lloyd Axworthy, 'Entre mondialisation et multipolarité: pour une politique étrangère du Canada globale et humaine,' *Études internationales* 28/1 (March 1997), p. 112.

55. 'Canada and Human Security,' p. 184.

56. 'Canada and Human Security,' p. 185.

57. William Graf, 'The State in the Third World,' in Leo Panitch (ed.), *The Socialist Register* 1995: *Why Not Capitalism?* (London: Merlin Press, 1995), p. 155.

58. This may also go some way in explaining the tensions reported in Haiti between the Mounties, who wanted to 'train civil police officers' who would respect democratic norms as is required in a functioning polyarchic democracy, and American representatives who, less sensitive to the ideological dimension of the exercise but more realistic as to the nature of polyarchic rule in dependent states, sought to train Haitian police as though they were 'a military style force.' See Keating, 'Promoting Democracy Abroad'.

59. The Philippines is a case in point. Amnesty International reported a significant increase in human rights violations following the collapse of the Marcos regime.

60. As Graf notes, this is a process which has its parallels in developing states as well: The ruling coalition has been fortified, in the neoliberal era, by the addition of many sectors of the middle classes. For to the extent that the middle classes have not been decimated by austerity and conditionalities, they have, in large measure, abandoned their former opposition to authoritarian military governments that led them to form alliances with labour and the poor and have been co-opted, via the provision of formal liberal democracy, into centrist and conservative parties where they have melded with the ruling coalition to

preserve the existing distribution of economic power. See William Graf, 'The State in the Third World,' p. 155. See also William Graf, 'Democratization "for" the Third World: Critique of a Hegemonic Project,' *Canadian Journal of Development Studies. Special Issue* (1996), pp. 37–56.

61. For an initial foray into this area, see M. Neufeld, 'Democratic Socialism in a Global(izing) Context: Toward a Collective Research Programme.' Paper submitted for the Lelio Basso Prize for Economic and Political Alternatives.

62. See Cameron and Molot, *Introduction to Democracy and Foreign Policy*, p. 1.

SELECTED BIBLIOGRAPHY

COMPREHENSIVE TEXTS

Byers, Michael. 2007. *Intent for a Nation.* Vancouver: Douglas & McIntyre.

Cohen, Andrew. 2003. *While Canada Slept: How We Lost Our Place in the World.* Toronto: McClelland and Stewart.

Cooper, Andrew F. 1997. *Canadian Foreign Policy: Old Habits and New Directions.* Scarborough, ON: Prentice-Hall.

Eayrs, James. 1963. *The Art of the Possible: Government and Foreign Policy in Canada.* Toronto: University of Toronto Press.

English, John, and Norman Hillmer, eds., 1992. *Making a Difference? Canada's Foreign Policy in a Changing World Order.* Toronto: Lester.

Granatstein, J.L., ed., 1986. *Canadian Foreign Policy: Historical Readings.* Toronto: Copp Clark Pitman.

Hart, Michael. 2008. *From Pride to Influence: Towards a New Canadian Foreign Policy.* Vancouver: University of British Columbia Press.

Holloway, Steven Kendall. 2006. *Canadian Foreign Policy: Defining the National Interest.* Peterborough, ON: Broadview Press.

James, Patrick, Nelson Michaud, and Marc J. O'Reilly, eds., 2006. *Handbook of Canadian Foreign Policy.* Lanham, MD: Lexington Books.

Keating, Tom. 2002. *Canada and World Order*, 2nd ed. Don Mills, ON: Oxford University Press.

Kirton, John. 2007. *Canadian Foreign Policy in a Changing World.* Scarborough, ON: Nelson Education.

Mackay, R.A. and E.B. Rogers. 1938. *Canada Looks Abroad.* Oxford: Oxford University Press.

Michaud, Nelson, and Kim Richard Nossal, eds., 2001. *Diplomatic Departures: The Conservative Era in Canadian Foreign Policy, 1984–93.* Vancouver: UBC Press.

Munton, Don, and John Kirton, eds., 1992. *Canadian Foreign Policy: Selected Cases.* Toronto: Prentice-Hall.

Nossal, Kim Richard, Stéphane Roussel, et Stéphane Paquin. 2007. *Politique international et defense au Canada et au Québec.* Montréal: Les Presses de l'Université de Montréal.

Nossal, Kim Richard. 1997. *The Politics of Canadian Foreign Policy*, 3rd ed. Scarborough, ON: Prentice-Hall.

Tomlin, Brian W., Norman Hillmer, and Fen Osler Hampson. 2008. *Canada's International Policies: Agendas, Alternatives, and Politics.* Don Mills, ON: Oxford University Press.

Tucker, Michael J., Raymond B. Blake, and P.E. Bryden, eds., 2000. *Canada and the New World Order.* Toronto: Irwin.

Tucker, Michael. 1980. *Canadian Foreign Policy: Contemporary Issues and Themes.* Toronto: McGraw-Hill Ryerson.

Welsh, Jennifer. 2004. *At Home in the World: Canada's Global Vision for the 21st Century.* Toronto: HarperCollins.

Canada Among Nations, an annual edited volume, is organized around a timely theme. It is a product of the Norman Paterson School of International Affairs at Carleton University, and is currently published by McGill-Queen's University Press.

ACADEMIC JOURNALS

Articles on Canadian foreign policy can be found in many peer-reviewed academic journals around the world. That being said, however, there are two journals that specialize in the study of Canadian foreign policy. The Canadian International Council, founded in 1928 as the Canadian Institute for International Affairs, is Canada's oldest association for the discussion of international events and Canada's place in the world. The CIC publishes the *International Journal*. *International Journal* is a quarterly journal that has published since 1946 and has been the starting point of many of the most important debates in Canadian foreign policy. *Canadian Foreign Policy*, which was started in 1995, is published by the Norman Paterson School of International Affairs at Carleton University. This particular journal includes articles from practitioners, academics, and media representatives, as well as roundtable discussions, documents, and book reviews.

LITERATURE REVIEWS AND PERSPECTIVES ON CANADIAN FOREIGN POLICY

Black, David R., and Heather A. Smith. 1993. 'Notable Exceptions? New and Arrested Directions in Canadian Foreign Policy Literature', *Canadian Journal of Political Science* 26, 4 (December): 745–75.

Blanchette, Arthur E., ed., 1994. *Canadian Foreign Policy 1977–1992: Selected Speeches and Documents*. Ottawa: Carleton University Press.

———. 1980. *Canadian Foreign Policy 1966–1976: Selected Speeches and Documents*. Ottawa: Carleton Library.

———. 1977. *Canadian Foreign Policy 1955–1965: Selected Speeches and Documents*. Ottawa: Carleton Library.

Granatstein, J. L. 1969. *Canadian Foreign Policy Since 1945: Middle Power or Satellite* Toronto: Copp Clark.

Hawes, Michael K. 1984. *Principal Power, Middle Power or Satellite? Competing Perspectives in the Study of Canadian Foreign Policy*. Toronto: York University Research Programme in Strategic Studies.

Molot, Maureen Appel. 1990. 'Where Do We, Should We, Or Can We Sit? A Review of Canadian Foreign Policy Literature', *International Journal of Canadian Studies* 1, 2 (Spring–Fall): 77–96.

Nossal, Kim Richard. 2000. 'Home-Grown IR: The Canadianization of International Relations', *Journal of Canadian Studies* 35 (Spring): 95–114.

Stairs, Denis. 1994. 'Will and Circumstance and the Postwar Study of Canadian Foreign Policy', *International Journal* 50, 1 (Winter): 9–39.

MIDDLE POWER PERSPECTIVES

Axworthy, Lloyd. 2003. *Navigating a New World: Canada's Future*. Toronto: Vintage.

Andrew, Arthur. 1993. *The Rise and Fall of a Middle Power*. Toronto: Lorimer.

Chapnick, Adam. 2009. *Canada's Voice: The Public Life of John Wendell Holmes*. Vancouver: UBC Press.

———. 'The Canadian Middle Power Myth', *International Journal* 55, 2 (Spring): 188–206.

Cooper, Andrew F. 1997. *Niche Diplomacy: Middle Powers after the Cold War*. Toronto: Macmillan.

Cooper, Andrew F., Richard A. Higgott, and Kim Richard Nossal. 1994. *Relocating Middle Powers: Australia and Canada in a Changing World Order*. Vancouver: UBC Press.

Dewitt, David B. 2000. 'Directions in Canada's International Security Policy: From Marginal Actor at the Centre to Central Actor at the Margins', *International Journal* 55, 2 (Spring): 167–87.

Holmes, John W. 1976. *Canada: A Middle-Aged Power*. Ottawa: Carleton Library; Toronto: McClelland and Stewart.

———. 1970. *The Better Part of Valour: Essays on Canadian Diplomacy*. Ottawa: Carleton Library; Toronto: McClelland and Stewart.

Hynek, Nik, and David Bosold, eds., 2010. *Canada's Foreign & Security Policy: Soft and Hard Strategies of a Middle Power*. Don Mills, ON: Oxford University Press.

Pratt, Cranford, ed., 1990. *Middle Power Internationalism: The North–South Dimension*. Montreal and Kingston: McGill-Queen's University Press.

PRINCIPAL POWER PERSPECTIVES

Dewitt, David B., and John J. Kirton. 1983. *Canada as a Principal Power: A Study in Foreign Policy and International Relations.* Toronto: John Wiley and Sons.

Eayrs, James. 1975. 'Defining a New Place for Canada in the Hierarchy of World Powers', *International Perspectives* (May–June): 15–24.

Hillmer, Norman, and Garth Stevenson, eds., 1977. *A Foremost Nation, Canadian Foreign Policy in a Changing World.* Toronto: McClelland and Stewart.

Hampson, Fen Osler, and Maureen Appel Molot. 1998. 'The New Can Do Foreign Policy', pp. 23–55 in Fen Osler Hampson and Maureen Appel Molot, eds., *Canada Among Nations 1998: Leadership and Dialogue?* Don Mills, ON: Oxford University Press.

———. 1996. 'Being Heard and the Role of Leadership', pp. 3–20 in Fen Osler Hampson and Maureen Appel Molot, eds, *Canada Among Nations 1996: Big Enough To Be Heard?* Ottawa: Carleton University Press.

Hampson, Fen Osler, Michael Hart, and Martin Rudner. 2000. 'A Big League Player or Minor League Player?', pp. 1–25 in Fen Hampson, Michael Hart, and Martin Rudner, eds., *Canada Among Nations 1999: A Big League Player?* Don Mills, ON: Oxford University Press.

Kirton, John. 2002. 'Canada as a Principal Summit Power: G7/8 Concert Diplomacy from Halifax 1995 to Kananaskis 2002', pp. 209–32 in Norman Hillmer and Maureen Appel Molot, eds., *Canada Among Nations 2002: A Fading Power.* Don Mills, ON: Oxford University Press.

———. 1999. 'Canada as a Principal Financial Power: G7 and IMF Diplomacy in the Crisis of 1997–99', *International Journal* 54, 4 (Autumn): 603–24.

Lyon, Peyton, and Brian Tomlin. 1979. *Canada as an International Actor.* Toronto: Macmillan of Canada.

SATELLITE POWER PERSPECTIVES

Bashevkin, Sylvia. 1991. *True Patriot Love: The Politics of Canadian Nationalism.* Toronto: Oxford University Press.

Bow, Brian, and Patrick Lennox, eds., 2008. *An Independent Foreign Policy for Canada? Challenges and Choices for the Future.* Toronto: University of Toronto Press.

Clarkson, Stephen. 2002. *Uncle Sam and Us: Globalization, Neoconservatism, and the Canadian State.* Toronto: University of Toronto Press.

———. 1985. *Canada and the Reagan Challenge: Crisis and Adjustment, 1981–85.* Toronto: Lorimer.

———. ed., 1968. *An Independent Foreign Policy for Canada?* Toronto: McClelland and Stewart.

Doran, Charles. 1996. 'Will Canada Unravel?' *Foreign Affairs* 75 (September/October): 97–109.

Grant, George. 1965. *Lament for a Nation: The Defeat of Canadian Nationalism.* Toronto: McClelland and Stewart.

Hampson, Fen Osler, and Maureen Appel Molot. 2000. 'Does the 49th Parallel Matter Anymore?', pp. 1–27 in Fen Osler Hampson and Maureen Appel Molot, eds, *Canada Among Nations 2000: Vanishing Borders.* Don Mills, ON: Oxford University Press.

MacLeod, Alec. 2000. 'Hobson's Choice: Does Canada Have any Options in its Defence and Security Relations with the United States', *International Journal* 55, 3 (Summer): 341–54.

Molot, Maureen Appel, and Norman Hillmer. 2002. 'The Diplomacy of Decline', pp. 1–33 in Norman Hillmer and Maureen Appel Molot, eds, *Canada Among Nations 2002: A Fading Power.* Don Mills, ON: Oxford University Press.

CRITICAL APPROACHES

Beier, J. Marshall, and Lana Wylie, eds., 2010. *Canadian Foreign Policy in Critical Perspective.* Don Mills, ON: Oxford University Press.

Howard, Peter, and Reina Neufeldt. 2000. 'Canada's Constructivist Foreign Policy', *Canadian Foreign Policy* 8, 1 (Fall): 11–38.

Keeble, Edna, and Heather A. Smith. 1999. *(Re)Defining Traditions: Gender and Canadian Foreign Policy.* Halifax: Fernwood Publishing.

Neufeld, Mark. 1995. 'Hegemony and Foreign Policy Analysis: The Case of Canada as a Middle Power', *Studies in Political Economy* 48: 7–29.

Roussel, Stephane, and Charles-Phillipe David. 1998. 'Middle Power Blues', *American Review of Canadian Studies* 28 (Spring/Summer): 131–56.

Sjolander, Claire Turenne, and David Black R. 1996. 'Multilateralism Re-constituted and the Discourse of Canadian Foreign Policy', *Studies in Political Economy* 49 (Spring): 7–36.

Sjolander, Claire Turenne, Heather A. Smith, and Deborah Stienstra, eds., 2003. *Feminist Perspectives on Canadian Foreign Policy*. Don Mills, ON: Oxford Univsity Press.

Stienstra, Deborah. 1994. 'Can the Silence be Broken? Gender and Canadian Foreign Policy', *International Journal* 50, 1 (Winter): 103–27.

PART II

EXTERNAL FACTORS AND CANADIAN FOREIGN POLICY

Canadian foreign policy is greatly affected by two different aspects of the international environment: 1) the international system in which Canada must operate (geography, anarchy, polarity, etc.); and 2) Canada's place in that international system. The first aspect of the international environment comprises sets of variables that are givens, 'in the sense that every foreign policy maker must confront them without being able to challenge them easily or rapidly'.[1] The second aspect of the international environment was discussed in the articles on middle power, principal power, and satellite power in Part 1. Part 2 focuses on the different external actors that Canada confronts in the international system. Canada's relationship with these external actors provides it with a number of constraints and opportunities in conducting its foreign policy.

This history of Canadian foreign policy, since the end of the Second World War, has been the tension between bilateralism[2] and multilateralism. From pre-confederation until 1945, Canada's foreign policy was a balancing act between two different bilateral relationships: the United Kingdom and the United States. Since 1945, it has been a balancing act between a bilateral relationship with the United States and a multilateral impulse through international organizations. At times, Canada has sought to distance itself from the United States, as with the Third Option initiative of the early 1970s, but at other times Canada has sought greater collaboration with the Americans, as with the decision to pursue a comprehensive trade agreement in the 1990s. This section explores this tension by focusing on Canada's relationship with the United States and the United Nations.

Canada's geography, security, economy, and culture are all inexorably intertwined with those of the United States. Over $2 billion annually in trade, and half a million people daily, cross the border. There also exists a vast collection of ties between family, friends, interest groups, sports leagues, and businesses on both sides of the border. These connections have been formalized in a number of different institutions including the International Joint Commission (IJC), the Permanent

Joint Board on Defence, NORAD, and the North American Free Trade Agreement (NAFTA). Further complicating matters is the power imbalance that exists between Canada and the United States. While the United States is the world's only superpower with great wealth and military might, Canada is a medium-sized country with only roughly 10 per cent of its neighbour's population and economic size. Given the massive multi-disciplinary, but asymmetrical, relationship that exists between Canada and the United States, it is safe to say that no international issue is more fraught with dangers for the Canadian government.[3] When prime ministers become too close to American presidents, as in the cases of Louis St Laurent and Dwight Eisenhower or Brian Mulroney and Ronald Reagan, they are criticized for abandoning Canadian autonomy. However, when they become too distant, as happened with John Diefenbaker and John Kennedy, Pierre Trudeau and Richard Nixon, or Jean Chrétien and George W. Bush, they are criticized for abandoning Canadian security and economic interests.

Don Barry explores the complexity of the bilateral Canadian–American relationship in Chapter 8. Ottawa and Washington have traditionally avoided linkage, as Robert Keohane and Joseph Nye wrote in 1977, because of the large number of non-state actors, the huge volume of interactions, the complexity of the relationship, and the absence of military coercion.[4] However, since 9/11 a 'big idea' has been promoted by different groups on both sides of the border that would explicitly link greater security integration (what America wants) with greater economic integration (what Canada wants). This 'big idea' meshes two of Canada's key foreign policy objectives: physical security and economic prosperity. Barry concludes, like Keohane and Nye did 30 years ago, that the 'sheer size and complexity' of the relationship would make negotiation of the 'strategic bargain' difficult to achieve and that Canada, as the weaker of the two parties, would therefore be negotiating from a position of weakness.

A second set of external factors exist as international organizations. Canada is a great supporter of international organizations and belongs to most universal organizations (United Nations, World Bank, World Trade Organization, International Monetary Fund, International Criminal Court), regional organizations (North Atlantic Treaty Organization, Organization of American States, North American Free Trade Agreement), and historic/linguistic organizations (Commonwealth and Francophonie). Tom Keating has argued that Canada's interest in multilateral institutions has been due to both external sources (Canada's middle power position, trade dependency, and as a counterweight to the US) and domestic sources (activist Canadian politicians and officials, public opinion, and civil society).[5] Canada's role in its three most important international organizations (G8, UN, and NATO) is explored in this section.

In 2010, Canada simultaneously hosted the G8 in Huntsville, Ontario, and the G20 in Toronto, Ontario. It is possible that this will be the last gathering of the G8 as it will be replaced by the G20. Canada has jealously guarded its inclusion in the G8, but over the years the G8 has seemed an anachronism due to the rise of the BRIC countries (Brazil, Russia, India, and China). It was significant that when the global financial crisis hit in

2008, it was the G20, and not the G8, UN, or IMF, that became the key international forum. Ironically, former prime minister Paul Martin was a key catalyst for the formation of a G20.[6] Given the changing roles, responsibilities, and membership of these ad hoc (but important) international clubs, Canada's role in the G8 and G20 needs to be assessed. John Kirton, in chapter 9, provides such a discussion.

Since its creation, the United Nations has figured prominently in Canadian foreign policy. However, the UN is more than just the Security Council and the General Assembly; it also includes the specialized agencies (World Health Organization, International Labour Organization, etc.) and issue-specific conferences. In chapter 10, Andrew F. Cooper and P. Whitney Lackenbauer move beyond the key organs of the UN to examine aspects of Canadian diplomacy at the United Nations through their case study of aboriginal politics and Canadian foreign policy.

NATO is the symbol of the Western alliance and Canada has been a charter member. Doug Ross, in chapter 11, traces the evolution of Canada's involvement in NATO. In the process, Ross focuses on two main issue areas: 1) NATO's changing mandate from Cold War deterrence of the Soviet Union to its post–Cold War operations in the former Yugoslavia and Afghanistan; and 2) NATO's changing nuclear weapons doctrine.

Notes

1. Kim Richard Nossal, *The Politics of Canadian Foreign Policy*, 3rd ed. (Scarborough, ON: Prentice-Hall, 1997), 8.
2. This has also been called continentalism or regionalism.
3. For a historical account see Lawrence Martin, *The Presidents and the Prime Ministers: Washington and Ottawa Face to Face: The Myth of Bilateral Bliss, 1867–1982* (Toronto: Doubleday, 1982).
4. See Robert O. Keohane and Joseph S. Nye, *Power and Interdependence: World Politics in Transition* (Boston: Little, Brown and Company, 1977).
5. Tom Keating, *Canada and World Order: The Multilateralist Tradition in Canadian Foreign Policy*, 2nd ed. (Don Mills, ON: Oxford University Press, 2002), 1–16.
6. Paul Martin, 'A Global Answer to Global Problems,' *Foreign Affairs* 84, no. 3 (May/June 2005), 2–6.

8

MANAGING CANADA–US RELATIONS IN THE POST-9/11 ERA: DO WE NEED A BIG IDEA?[1]

Don Barry

The remarkable growth of Canadian–US economic integration, combined with the security implications of the September 11, 2001, terrorist attacks on the United States, have brought the management of Canada–US relations into sharp focus. The biggest challenge facing Canadian decision-makers is how to respond to the new security environment while ensuring the uninterrupted flow of people and commerce across the 8,893-kilometre border. The dimensions of the challenge became apparent in the aftermath of 9/11, when the United States virtually closed its borders in reaction to the attacks. Quick action by the Canadian government led to the 'Smart Border Declaration' in December 2001, to secure the border while facilitating the flow of low-risk travellers and goods. Building on the declaration in November 2004, Ottawa and Washington launched a 'New Partnership in North America' with an agenda to promote security, prosperity, and quality of life. In March 2005, Canada, the US, and Mexico announced a 'Security and Prosperity Partnership of North America', a broad plan to strengthen security and economic relations based upon the earlier initiatives.

Some observers have argued that bolder action is required to deal with US security concerns and to protect Canada's access to the US market. The theme running through their proposals is that security and trade are closely linked and that explicit trade-offs can be made between them.[2] This so-called 'big idea' approach is not new. It extends and formalizes the partnership paradigm that provided the framework for the management of Canada–US relations during the early years of the Cold War. This essay outlines the history of the concept and assesses its applicability in contemporary Canada–US relations. It argues that the erosion of international conditions sustaining the approach, the proliferation of issues and actors in Canada–US relations, and institutional changes on both sides of the border limit the application of the concept, and that focused cooperation in areas where interests converge provides a more workable basis for the management of the relationship.

THE PARTNERSHIP PARADIGM

The partnership paradigm informed the conduct of Canada–US relations during the first two decades after World War II. Created by the Soviet threat, the partnership was managed in a quiet, pragmatic way by government elites who held compatible worldviews, were in firm control of their governmental processes, and were in a position to sustain trade-offs that were crucial to the stability of the relationship. The United States gave Canada favourable economic treatment in return for Canada's willingness to maintain an open investment climate and to contribute to continental and North Atlantic defence.[3] This regime was supported at the official level by a common 'diplomatic culture' that 'placed great emphasis on consultation, exchange of information, personal friendship, informal communication, and easy access to points of decision'.[4]

However, the partnership approach masked a growing Canadian dependence on the United States that became evident as the Cold War conditions sustaining the paradigm began to erode. In the late 1960s the Canadian government responded to domestic pressures by protecting key economic and cultural sectors, although when Washington took steps to address chronic balance of payments problems Ottawa sought and received exemptions that were not granted to other allies. Concerns that Canada had become too dependent on the United States were matched by US concerns that the United States had been too generous with its friends and that it needed to take a more self-centred approach. As both countries adopted more nationalistic policies it became more difficult, or perhaps it no longer seemed necessary, to continue the trade-offs that were central to the partnership approach

COMME LES AUTRES

In 1972, President Richard Nixon and Prime Minister Pierre Trudeau formalized the new approaches. Nixon gave notice that the United States no longer considered it necessary to give special concessions to Canada.[5] Trudeau would seek to reduce Canada's 'vulnerability' to the United States through the 'Third Option', consisting of internal measures to strengthen the Canadian economy and culture, and diversification of external economic relations.[6]

Yet, interdependence between the two countries continued to grow, bringing more issues and interests into play and further complicating the management of the domestic politics of their interaction. Canadian provinces and especially the US Congress, both highly responsive to their constituencies, became more visible players. Provincial governments showed a new determination to exercise their constitutional responsibilities to the full. Dominance of US foreign policy by the executive, with the support of key congressional leaders, gave way to a more decentralized system in which a democratized Congress became an increasingly important player. The tradition of close bureaucratic cooperation between Ottawa and Washington was also affected by these developments.

Relations improved in the mid-1970s under Trudeau and presidents Gerald Ford and Jimmy Carter. But new strains emerged during the Trudeau–Ronald Reagan years. The worldviews of Ottawa and Washington had seldom been more different. Reagan sought to bolster US strength in the face of unsettled global economic conditions and deteriorating relations with the Soviet Union by reducing government intervention at home and increasing American power abroad. Trudeau tried to focus attention on the North–South dialogue while limiting Canada's dependence on the United States by increasing Canadian control over the economy and expanding ties with Mexico and other oil-producing and newly industrializing countries.

Trudeau's government antagonized the Americans by introducing the National Energy Program

(NEP), to increase Canadian ownership of the US-dominated energy industry, and strengthened the existing Foreign Investment Review Agency (FIRA), which regulated foreign investment. Canada had concerns about US policies, including the handling of the East Coast fisheries treaty, acid rain, and budget deficits. On the international front, Ottawa and Washington were frequently at odds over East–West relations. Early tensions yielded to more cooperative relations as both governments, alarmed by the deterioration, determined to manage relations more effectively.[7] After abandoning its nationalistic economic policy in the wake of the global recession of the early 1980s, Ottawa sought sectoral free trade negotiations with Washington, which responded favourably. The discussions failed, but they drew attention to the possibility of concluding a more comprehensive agreement.

REVIVING THE PARTNERSHIP PARADIGM

Prime Minister Brian Mulroney, who took power in September 1984, saw closer trade and investment relations with the United States as the key to Canada's prosperity. He attempted to revive the partnership paradigm, offering the United States foreign policy and defence support and more liberal investment laws with the expectation that the Reagan administration would give Canada a sympathetic hearing on economic issues.[8] A dramatic improvement in East–West relations made it relatively easy for Mulroney to support Reagan's policies. Ottawa temporarily boosted its defence spending and, when it mattered, Mulroney endorsed or did not oppose US actions to protect important interests. Mulroney's government also dismantled the NEP and replaced FIRA with the more liberal Investment Canada. But Reagan, although a strong president, could not provide the favourable economic treatment Mulroney sought. Accordingly, maintaining the partnership facade, Ottawa sought to exploit Canada's interdependence with the United States while subjecting US power to legal constraint.

Reagan welcomed Mulroney's proposal for free trade negotiations, which furthered his long-held goal of closer North American co-operation.[9] But in order to secure fast-track authority from Congress to negotiate the agreement, he agreed to act on US lumber interests' complaints about Canadian softwood lumber exports that occupied an increasing share of the US market.[10] The Canada–US Free Trade Agreement (CUSFTA), which came into effect in 1989, and its successor, the North American Free Trade Agreement (NAFTA) among Canada, the United States, and Mexico, launched in 1994, improved Canada's access to the US market and established dispute settlement arrangements to constrain the application of US trade remedy laws.

However, Washington's unwillingness to agree to uniform trade laws because of pressure from special interests and their congressional allies led to disputes over such issues as softwood lumber and agricultural products that would become a continuing source of friction. The tendency of the special interests to look to their congressmen and senators for redress in response to what the special interests charged were unfair Canadian trade practices, and the willingness of the legislators to respond, escalated the political significance of the disputes. As a result, they became politicized at the official level as well. When Canada successfully challenged unfavourable US trade decisions, the special interests often persuaded their legislative supporters to change US laws or renew pressure on Canada. As a result, Ottawa and affected Canadian interests, fearing the costs of drawn-out battles, often were forced into negotiating 'a series of strategic retreats'.[11]

BUSINESS-LIKE RELATIONS

Prime Minister Jean Chrétien came to office in November 1993 promising to take a business-like approach. Chrétien and President Bill Clinton had a good relationship, made easier by the fact that their governments shared 'a fundamental compatibility' in their foreign and domestic policy outlooks.[12] However, ongoing trade disputes over such issues as softwood lumber continued to be difficult to manage.

In response to growing pressures of trade and travel, Ottawa and Washington undertook measures to improve the management of the border, including a 'Canada–US Partnership Forum' to foster dialogue among governments, border communities, and other stakeholders.[13] But the task was complicated by an emerging US tendency that began with NAFTA, to view Canada–US relations in trilateral terms. This could be seen in congressional efforts to deal with certain issues by taking a common approach to Canada and Mexico despite major differences between the United States' southern and northern borders.[14] In 1996, Congress passed the Illegal Immigration Reform and Immigrant Responsibility Act, requiring all foreigners to register when entering or leaving the United States. Although it was aimed at Mexico, Canada was included reportedly because legislators feared protests from Hispanic-Americans if stronger action were taken against Mexico than against Canada.[15] Concerned that the measure would produce gridlock at the Canada–US border, US businesses, border state legislators and Canadian authorities mounted a sustained lobbying effort to overturn it. Matters became complicated when US customs officers arrested Ahmed Ressam, an Algerian living illegally in Canada, in December 1999, when he tried to enter the United States from British Columbia with bomb-making materials in his car. The lobbying effort succeeded, but the incident put Canada's refugee policy under scrutiny.

George W. Bush, the new US president, appeared to have his own North American agenda, which seemed to some Canadians to emphasize Mexico at Canada's expense. But Bush's focus on Mexico was not surprising. As former state governors, Bush and Mexico's president, Vicente Fox, were well-acquainted and recognized that there were pressing problems such as immigration that needed to be addressed. Bush also knew that 35 million Spanish-speaking Americans (20 million of whom are of Mexican descent) had become a significant factor in US electoral politics. The two leaders wanted to work with Canada 'to consolidate a North American economic community' that would include a common approach to energy resources—a matter of special interest to Bush's administration.[16]

In April 2001, Bush, Fox, and Chrétien established a North American Energy Working Group to explore ways of facilitating North American energy trade, although in Canada's view NAFTA made a continental policy unnecessary.[17] Paul Cellucci, the US ambassador to Canada, suggested that the countries expand their ties in a 'NAFTA-plus' arrangement with harmonized border controls, immigration, law enforcement, energy, and environmental policies. The goal would be to create a security perimeter resulting in more open borders. Foreign affairs minister John Manley reacted cautiously, saying that Ottawa preferred to approach border issues on a bilateral basis by means of administrative changes.[18]

AFTERMATH OF 11 SEPTEMBER 2001

The al-Qaeda terrorist attacks on New York and Washington on 11 September 2001, elevated security to the top of the US policy agenda. Washington briefly shut down its airports and seaports.

Detailed customs inspections at land borders resulted in long traffic delays, forcing some Canadian companies temporarily to close. Chrétien created an Ad Hoc Cabinet Committee on Public Security and Anti-Terrorism, headed by Manley, to map out Canada's policy.[19] However, the government's response was complicated by widespread criticism of Canadian security policies by US media outlets and politicians, fuelled by false reports that the terrorists had entered the United States via Canada. Attorney General John Ashcroft, citing the Ressam case, called the border a 'transit point' for terrorists and announced plans to strengthen security.[20]

The Canadian business community called for a continental security perimeter. 'We have to make North America secure from the outside,' said the president of Canadian Pacific Ltd. 'We're going to lose increasingly our sovereignty, but necessarily so.'[21] The Coalition for Secure and Trade-Efficient Borders, consisting of forty business groups from the manufacturing, transportation, and resource sectors, supported the idea, as did the Canadian Chamber of Commerce.[22] Significantly, US businesses, not wanting to be out of step with Washington's security priorities, were silent.[23]

Manley preferred to deal with 'specific areas of concern' saying, 'Perimeter implies NAFTA. . . . I think it makes the problems, whatever they are, much more complex if you try and do two borders at once.'[24] Bush seemed to agree, telling Chrétien, 'You pass your laws; we'll pass our laws.'[25] The goal, as Michael Kergin, Canada's ambassador to the United States, put it, would be to create a 'zone of confidence' with the two governments adopting parallel measures that met each other's concerns.[26] Border relations with Mexico would be approached in a similar way.

Manley was the point man in discussions with US Homeland Security Adviser Tom Ridge. As Ridge had not yet assembled a team of advisers, an experienced Privy Council Office Borders Task Force, operating under Manley's cabinet committee, drafted an action plan, which became the basis of the Smart Border Declaration in December 2001.[27] The aim was to ensure the security of the border and to expedite the movement of low-risk shipments and travellers. The declaration was accompanied by a 30-point Action Plan, which included the development of common biometric identifiers for permanent resident cards and travel documents, expedited clearance for pre-approved travellers, visa policy coordination, a safe third country agreement for refugee claimants, pre-screening of air passengers, compatible immigration databases, border infrastructure improvements, complementary commercial processing systems, joint posting of customs officers at seaports, integrated border and maritime enforcement, intelligence sharing, and exchange of fingerprint data.[28] Ottawa allocated $7.7 billion over five years to improve border infrastructure and enforcement, and $1.2 billion to boost the country's military, which had been weakened by earlier budget cuts. Washington committed US $10.7 billion to improve security along the US–Canada and US–Mexico borders.[29] In March 2002, US and Mexican authorities signed a 'Border Partnership Agreement', modelled on the Smart Border Declaration.[30]

The Canadian government made good on its commitment to the war on terrorism, deploying a naval task force to the Persian Gulf as part of US-led operations against Al Qaeda terrorists and the Taliban government in Afghanistan that sheltered them. Ottawa dispatched a special forces unit and a battle group that operated alongside US forces for six months. Overall, Canada contributed the fourth-largest military contingent to the initial campaign. In August 2003, it assigned troops to the International Security Assistance Force (ISAF) protecting the new government of Afghanistan, taking command for a six-month period in February 2004.[31]

Although the Smart Border Declaration established an agenda for border management, negotiations were affected by the determination of the administration and Congress to forge ahead with US security priorities. In May 2002, Congress passed the Enhanced Border Security and Visa Entry Reform Act to record the entry and exit of all foreign visitors.[32] But there were signs that the step-by-step approach set out in the Smart Border Declaration was gaining currency.[33] Manley and Ridge noted advances in intercepting high-risk travellers, the deployment of fast-track programs for low-risk travelers (NEXUS) and commercial shipments (FAST), intelligence sharing, and the establishment of joint customs teams at Canadian and US ports. They initialled a 'Safe Third Country Agreement' to prevent asylum shopping by requiring refugee seekers to make their claims in whichever of the two countries they entered first.[34] Progress was sufficiently encouraging that when the Global Business Forum called for closer North American integration measures, Ambassador Cellucci offered no support, saying, 'those are big questions that involve sovereign issues and I do not want the progress we are making on a smart, secure border to get held up because of this'.[35]

In December 2002, the Smart Border Declaration was expanded to include the sharing of airline passenger lists and other forms of intelligence, exchange of criminal files by the RCMP and the FBI, and joint Canada–US customs facilities and databases.[36] Canadian and US defence authorities established a Bi-national Planning Group charged with improving military, security and public emergency response planning. Canadian and US forces would be allowed to cross the border to respond to emergency situations with the permission of the host government.[37]

Relations deteriorated when Chrétien declared in March 2003 that Canada would not join the US-led invasion of Iraq without the backing of the United Nations. Ottawa was skeptical of Washington's claims that Saddam Hussein's regime had weapons of mass destruction and ties to al-Qaeda. The public was solidly behind the government. However, business interests feared the action and anti-American outbursts from some members of the governing Liberal Party would damage relations with Washington.[38] Their fears appeared to be confirmed when Ambassador Cellucci, on instructions from the White House, publicly criticized Canada for not supporting the war and Bush cancelled a planned visit to Ottawa.[39]

A group of Canada's top business leaders travelled to Washington to mend fences. But it quickly became apparent that the economies of the two countries were so closely intertwined that reprisals would be very difficult. One participant blamed 'overheated rhetoric' for exaggerating the consequences of Chrétien's decision.[40] Underscoring the fact that relations between the two countries were operating effectively despite the chill at the top, Cellucci revealed that Canadian citizens would be exempted from the planned US entry-exit registration system—a long-sought Canadian objective. And returning to a central theme in the Bush administration's policy, he reasserted Washington's interest in establishing a North American energy market.[41]

But public opposition to Bush's policies was growing. An opinion poll released in July reported that although Canadians viewed the United States positively, most reacted unfavourably to Bush. Contributing factors were continuing instability in Iraq, and the failure to find banned weapons or to establish a connection between Saddam Hussein and al-Qaeda. More that 70 per cent of Canadians polled thought Chrétien had been right in opposing the war and that Bush had knowingly used unreliable intelligence to justify the invasion. A polling firm spokesman observed that the findings went beyond Iraq 'to the credibility of the US administration', and would make it difficult for Bush 'to get Canadian support for any platform'.[42]

MARTIN AND BUSH

Paul Martin, who succeeded Jean Chrétien as prime minister in December 2003, sought to establish 'a more sophisticated relationship' with the United States, which was welcomed by the Bush administration.[43] Shortly after taking office, Martin created a cabinet committee to improve the co-ordination of Canadian policy and a Department of Public Safety and Emergency Preparedness to take charge of intelligence, border security, public health and disaster response. But with the public uneasy about Bush's policies and a general election in the offing, Martin's officials warned the White House to 'expect some mixed signals' from the prime minister 'even if his overall intention remains to improve bilateral ties'.[44]

Pointing to Canada's commitment to provide $300 million in reconstruction aid to Iraq, Martin criticized the administration's decision to bar countries that had not participated in the war from bidding on primary contracts funded by Washington. He also condemned US authorities' treatment of Mahar Arar, a citizen of Canada and Syria, who had been arrested as a suspected terrorist in New York in September 2002 while en route to Canada. American officials sent Arar to Syria where he was imprisoned and tortured for several months before Ottawa secured his release.[45] A Canadian commission of inquiry subsequently cleared Arar of any wrongdoing, but Washington still refuses to allow him to enter the United States.

In January 2004, Martin and Bush held their first meeting during a summit of Western Hemisphere leaders.[46] Martin promised closer security cooperation; Bush confirmed that Canadian firms would be eligible to compete in a second round of US-sponsored contracts in Iraq. They approved a non-binding protocol by which each government would inform the other of any planned deportation of its citizens and consult at the other's request. Bush also said the United States would work with Canada to reopen the border, which had been closed to live Canadian cattle and certain beef products following the discovery of a case of bovine spongiform encephalopathy, or mad cow disease, in Alberta in May 2003. Both sides agreed that the relationship was off to a good start.[47]

Martin's officials developed a plan to expand security and economic collaboration with the United States through administrative and regulatory change based on the Smart Border model.[48] Measures included harmonization of government regulations; review of rules of origin requirements; common standards for electronic commerce; energy and environmental cooperation; and business mobility; and would be open to participation by Mexico. Designed to circumvent congressional involvement at a time when protectionist pressures in the US were on the rise, and to avoid intensifying anti-Bush sentiment in Canada, the plan fell short of the grand bargain favoured by big idea enthusiasts. The emphasis, as one commentator put it, was on making 'tangible progress in areas where a lack of cross-border co-ordination has a substantial impact'.[49]

With Martin scheduled to visit Bush in Washington in April, Ottawa announced new defence and security initiatives, including a $7 billion increase in military spending, a move the Bush administration welcomed. Some $690 million would be allocated to upgrade maritime security, government computer networks, passports, security agency staffing, and intelligence assessment. As well, a new advocacy secretariat was opened at Canada's embassy in Washington to manage contacts with Congress and to support the lobbying efforts of Canadian legislators and provinces.[50] At the meeting, Martin touted Canada's contributions to North American defence and security, and pledged assistance in helping to rebuild failed states. Bush praised Canada's role in the ISAF in Afghanistan and the UN stabilization mission in Haiti. He also wanted the US border opened to Canadian cattle 'as quickly as possible'.[51]

A NEW PARTNERSHIP IN NORTH AMERICA

Martin and Bush met again in Ottawa in November 2004. The principal outcome was a statement on 'A New Partnership in North America', which committed the two governments to 'deepening' their cooperation, working 'bilaterally to address Canada–US priorities' and 'with Mexico on issues of trilateral concern'. Described by Martin as 'an agenda in which our two nations will co-operate in a practical way towards common goals', of security, prosperity and quality of life, the statement set out a series of priorities, including improved intelligence sharing, law enforcement, security infrastructure, passports, maritime surveillance and defence, NORAD renewal, regulatory reform, reduction of rules of origin costs, energy efficiency, environmental and public health coordination, advancement of democracy, response to humanitarian crises, enhancement of multilateral institutions, and completion of the Doha Round of WTO trade negotiations and free trade in the Americas.[52] Designated Canadian and US cabinet ministers would devise proposals by June 2005.

There was movement on the mad cow issue in December 2004 when the US Department of Agriculture proclaimed new rules to reopen the border to live cattle under 30 months of age. But the discovery of two new cases in Washington State and Alberta, both involving Canadian cattle, gave American ranching opponents ammunition. Although American officials were satisfied with Canadian control measures, in March 2005

a district judge in Montana granted an injunction putting the plan on indefinite hold. It was overturned by a US federal appeals court in July 2005, but the governor of Montana ordered inspections of Canadian cattle destined for his state.[53] (The border was finally opened to most Canadian cattle in November 2007.) Challenges to wheat sales, the ongoing softwood lumber dispute, and the refusal of Congress to comply with a World Trade Organization (WTO) ruling to repeal the Continued Dumping and Subsidy Offset Act of 2000 (Byrd Amendment) intensified Canadian dissatisfaction with US policies.[54]

Meanwhile, participation in Bush's missile defence program, which had been an important part of Martin's plan to improve relations with Washington, came to naught in February 2005 when Martin announced that Canada would not join. Martin's government had been reduced to minority status in the June 2004 election. Public opposition, the uncertain prospect of approval by Parliament where the NDP and Bloc Quebecois opposition parties and many of Martin's own Liberal members were against involvement and the once-supportive Conservatives were non-committal, together with Bush's untimely intervention in the debate during his visit to Canada, prompted the prime minister to withhold support. Although Ottawa tried to appease Washington by boosting defence spending by $12.8 billion, Secretary of State Condoleezza Rice postponed a planned visit to Canada, and the president delayed returning Martin's phone call to discuss a North American leaders' meeting in Waco, Texas, the following month.[55] The Bush administration was puzzled by the missile defence decision but the Canadian public was not. Two-thirds of those surveyed in an opinion poll endorsed the action. A polling firm representative observed that opposition had more to do with Bush's foreign policy, especially the war in Iraq and US trade protectionism, than with missile defence.[56]

WACO SUMMIT EXTENDS PARTNERSHIP TO MEXICO

The Waco summit was intended to bring Mexico into North American cooperation arrangements. Although business interests pressed for a 'major initiative', American, Canadian and Mexican authorities had a more limited goal in mind. As a US official put it, 'The intention will be to focus on things that can be done without legislation in any of the three states'.[57] Seeking to influence the outcome, the co-chairs of the Independent Task Force on the Future of North America, sponsored by the Canadian Council of Chief Executives, the US Council on Foreign Relations, and the Mexican Council on Foreign Relations, called for the creation of a North American community with a continental security perimeter and a common external tariff within five years. The group's Canadian chair, John Manley, who as a member of Jean Chrétien's government had supported a pragmatic approach, urged the three leaders to 'think big'.[58] However, the Canadian and US governments continued to play down the likelihood of far-reaching change.[59]

Bush, Martin, and Fox established a 'Security and Prosperity Partnership of North America' (SPP) to advance common economic and security goals. It was 'trilateral in concept', but any two countries could take the lead on an issue with the third joining later. The agreement contained commitments to advance common security and prosperity goals, including border security and bioprotection strategies, strengthened infrastructure and facilitation of cargo and travellers, improvements to maritime and aviation security, regulatory reform, cooperation in energy, transportation, financial services and technology, and environmental and food safety collaboration. But it stopped short of committing the governments to a North American security perimeter, a common external tariff, or improved trade dispute resolution. A team of three cabinet ministers from each country would develop work plans with 'specific, measurable, and achievable goals' and 'implementation dates'. The initial report would be due within 90 days, with others to follow on a semi-annual basis.[60] Success would depend upon committed leadership, a manageable agenda and the accessibility of the negotiations to interested groups.

The leaders went out of their way to differentiate their approach from that of grand bargain proponents. 'We're not talking about a big bang, we're talking about big progress,' said Martin. 'We are three sovereign nations—jealous of our sovereignty—but we recognize that sovereignty is stronger if North America is competitive and compatible.'[61] A senior US State Department official was even more emphatic. 'The "Security and Prosperity Partnership" is not an effort to launch a new "big idea" in North America,' the official observed. 'NAFTA was and remains the "big idea". Indeed, the Security and Prosperity Partnership recognizes that one of the foundations of NAFTA's success has been integrating our trade and our markets while maintaining our distinct sovereignties and national identities.'[62]

In June, the team Canadian, US, and Mexican ministers issued their first report on initiatives underway or planned. The agenda consisted of 300 items assigned to 20 working groups of officials, under the direction of representatives from the three countries at the assistant secretary or equivalent level. Progress had been made in facilitating electronic commerce, liberalizing rules of origin, public health and safety protection, labelling of textiles and apparel, entry of temporary workers, migratory bird protection, harmonizing approaches to mad cow disease, aviation navigation safety, prosecution of smugglers, border infrastructure, science and technology cooperation, and port and cargo security. Plans included the establishment of a single North American Trusted Traveler Program for frequent travellers, common standards for screening visitors, a trilateral Regulatory Cooperation Framework to streamline regulations, a North American Steel Strategy to enhance steel industry competitiveness, an Automotive Partnership Council of North America to make recommendations on developing an integrated auto sector, and a sustainable North American energy economy to promote the long-term supply and use of energy.[63]

THE BILATERAL AGENDA

The SPP negotiations had little impact on the day-to-day conduct of Canada–US relations, which were dominated by border security and trade issues. In April 2005, pursuant to the Intelligence Reform and Terrorism Prevention Act of 2004, the Homeland Security and State departments had proposed the Western Hemisphere Travel Initiative (WHTI), requiring passports or other secure documents for anyone entering the United States from Canada, Mexico, Bermuda, the Caribbean, and Panama after December 31, 2005. With only 23 per cent of Americans and 40 per cent of Canadians holding passports, the proposal created alarm in both countries.

Pressured by the administration and Congress, the departments proposed that the scheme be implemented in two stages: January 1, 2007, for air and sea travellers, and January 1, 2008, for land crossings. Air traffic, which accounted for only 15 per cent of Canada–US travel, was not a significant issue. Travel by land was a different matter. A Conference Board of Canada study predicted that US tourist visits to Canada by would drop by 7.7 million, with a loss of $1.8 billion, by the end of 2008, and that Canadian visits to the United States would decline by 3.5 million, costing the American economy $785 million.[64] The revised deadlines brought some breathing room. But another hitch arose when the Department of Homeland Security

announced plans to require Canadian airlines to provide passenger lists for up to 3000 domestic flights passing through US air space each week. Concerned that this would amount to 'ceding to the American government authority to determine who could fly in Canada', Ottawa decided to adopt its own no-fly list.[65]

Meanwhile, Washington's willingness to meet its trade obligations was called into question when the Bush administration refused to comply with a NAFTA Extraordinary Challenge Committee that ruled US penalties on Canadian softwood lumber imports were illegal under American law and ordered repayment of US $5 billion in duties. Brandishing a parallel WTO decision that the duties complied with international trade law, the administration called for negotiations. Martin's government went on the offensive. It would not negotiate until Washington acknowledged the authority of NAFTA and enlisted the support of US business interests and consumers. It also threatened to seek redress in US courts, unveiled a strategy to diversify lumber exports, and hinted that the United States could jeopardize access to secure Canadian energy by undermining NAFTA.[66]

On a visit to Ottawa in October Condoleezza Rice downplayed the controversy. Claiming that 'the word of the United States has been as good as gold in its international dealings and in its agreements', she urged the government to abandon its 'apocalyptic language', adding '[i]t is an important issue, but it is a trade dispute'.[67] As Jeffrey Simpson explained, 'apart from a flinty-eyed view of international agreements, the Bush administration doesn't really wish to settle the softwood file because to do so would require the expenditure of considerable political capital for a cause it does not believe merits the effort'. A rules-based solution would not serve the US lumber producers' interests. 'Not wishing to upset these groups, whose political supporters the Bush administration needs, neither the President nor anyone else in his administration will do anything but insist that the negotiations resume.'[68]

Although it kept up its pressure in public, Martin's government realized that a legal victory would not end the dispute. There was nothing to prevent the American lumber interests from launching a new challenge if they lost, necessitating a negotiated settlement. Ottawa quietly floated a proposal that would see Washington refund some 75 per cent of the duties in return for Quebec and Ontario export quotas and higher stumpage fees in British Columbia. But it was shelved when the government fell in a parliamentary vote in November, out of concern that it would damage the Liberals' prospects in key ridings in British Columbia.[69]

HARPER COMES TO POWER

During the election, which brought Harper's minority Conservative government to power in February 2006, Martin went out of his way to criticize American policies and to link Harper to the unpopular Bush administration. Harper tried not to seem supportive of Bush, stressing differences over issues like Arctic sovereignty. However, his party's platform, which called for a more robust military to bolster Canada's international presence and expressed skepticism about the Kyoto Protocol approach to climate change, was consistent with the Bush administration's policies, although it was justified in 'Canada First' terms.[70]

Although Canadians still reacted negatively to Bush, polling executive Darryl Bricker observed, 'You can get into all the atmospherics about too close or not close enough but ultimately what it all comes down to is whether we can get some solutions to the problems that are dogging the relationship'.[71] Attempting to link Canada's international contributions to the resolution of bilateral issues, Harper highlighted Canada's mission in Afghanistan, where Canadian forces had redeployed from Kabul to the volatile Kandahar region, while emphasizing the need to settle the softwood lumber dispute, which had created 'serious stresses'. He also expressed concern about the impact of the pending WHTI passport regulation on cross-border trade and tourism.[72] Bush acknowledged there was 'skepticism about the United States' arising out of 'some of the decisions I made' but would work to 'convince the people of Canada we genuinely care'. He wanted to settle the softwood lumber dispute and was optimistic that a solution to the passport issue could be found.[73]

In contrast, the SPP process appeared to be 'paralyzed by its scope and lack of stakeholder input'. When Bush, Harper, and Fox met in March, they found that progress had been limited to items taken up before the SPP got under way. They established a North American Competitiveness Council (NACC), composed of business representatives from each country, to provide advice to the SPP working groups. The NACC would bring much needed focus to the discussions, but the exclusion of other groups would erode public confidence.[74]

Intent on showing he could do business with Bush, Harper began pursuing a deal to end the softwood lumber dispute. In July, the two governments reached a seven-year agreement creating free trade in lumber as long as prices remained above existing levels, and imposing a mixed export quota sliding export tax if they dropped. The United States would return US $4 billion to Canada. American lumber producers would receive $500 million, with $450 million earmarked for 'meritorious initiatives', and $50 million for a bilateral industry council 'to strengthen and further integrate the North American lumber industry'. In a telling admission that the NAFTA and WTO dispute settlement processes had failed in this case, the agreement made the London Court of Arbitration the final arbiter of disputes.[75]

Border security was a more daunting challenge. A State Department report claiming that 'liberal Canadian immigration and asylum policies' had made Canada a 'safe haven' for suspect groups to 'raise funds, arrange logistical support and plan terrorist attacks', gained credibility when Canadian Security and Intelligence Service officials admitted that applicants from Afghanistan and Pakistan were not adequately screened owing to limited resources.[76] Although Condoleezza Rice praised the arrest of 18 Canadians for plotting terrorist attacks on Toronto and Ottawa in June as an example of bilateral security cooperation, Washington put US border officials on high alert. A senior Homeland Security official said the episode compelled stricter security measures and a collaborative approach to documenting cross-border travel.[77]

Harper, whose government had recently announced that it would spend an additional $1.4 billion to improve national security and equip future passports with biometric technology, defended Canada's immigration laws and dispatched security experts to Washington to allay legislators' concerns.[78] Meanwhile, Ottawa continued its strategy of aligning with Washington on international security, joining the Bush administration in renewing the NORAD agreement indefinitely and adding maritime surveillance to its mandate, boosting defence spending by a further $17 billion dollars, and extending Canada's mission in Afghanistan until 2009.

Border security figured prominently in Harper's meeting with Bush in Washington in July. Urging the administration to delay implementing the passport requirement, Harper argued that if 'the US becomes more closed to its friends, then the terrorists have won'. Bush acknowledged Harper's 'deep concerns' and pledged that depending on what Congress decided, he would 'work with the Canadian government to extend deadlines [or] to make the law work'.[79]

US efforts to tighten border security persisted. Seeing Canada as a 'potential conduit for bioterrorism', the Department of Agriculture announced plans to increase border inspections, the costs to be borne by travellers and commercial shippers. Congressional Republicans introduced a bill authorizing the construction of a fence on the border with Mexico and a study of a similar barrier on the boundary with Canada. Congress rejected the northern fence study but approved funds for a Department of Homeland Security-sponsored 'Secure Border Initiative' in the form of a 'virtual fence' to complement recently introduced surveillance by aircraft and unmanned drones.[80] Harper, who had announced the government would arm its border guards and hire additional officers, declined to join Mexico's president-elect Filipe Calderon in opposing the southern border fence, limiting himself to a call to avoid 'unnecessary barriers'.[81] He set his sights on the WHTI, telling a New York business audience that 'this initiative threatens to divide us at exactly the time we should be collaborating closely on global economic and security challenges'. He urged Washington 'to take the time to get it right'.[82]

Warning of the possible Mexicanization of the Canada–US border, Allan Gotlieb called for the creation of a North American community of law. Harper had fashioned a sensible strategy by building good rapport with Bush and strengthening lobbying efforts on Capitol Hill, which had begun to produce results at home in terms of the public's improved view of the United States. However, the strategy had reached the limits of its effectiveness and it was time 'to look to binding legal rules and effective bi-national institutions to constrain arbitrary political action'.[83] But the Bush administration, weakened by controversies over the war in Iraq, its response to Hurricane Katrina, and the loss of Republican majorities in the Senate and House Representatives in the recent mid-term elections, was in no position to respond.

A breakthrough on the WHTI came in mid-2007 when the Department of Homeland Security extended the passport deadline until at least the summer of 2008 in response to pressure from US legislators who had been deluged with complaints about the State Department's inability to keep up with the demand. It also accepted a proposal from the State of Washington, which had collaborated with British Columbia on a high-tech driver's licence containing proof of citizenship and other information that could be scanned by border officials.[84]

However, progress on another front stalled when Washington abandoned a pilot project to expedite cross-border traffic that would have seen Canadian and US customs officers co-located on the Canadian side of the Peace Bridge linking Fort Erie, Ontario, and Buffalo, New York. The Americans demanded the right to fingerprint persons who refused to cross the border in violation of Canada's Charter of Rights. US officials would not accept Canadian assurances to investigate suspicious people.[85]

Cross-border trade, some 40 per cent of which involved integrated supply chains, was especially affected by post 9/11 border security requirements. The Ontario Chamber of Commerce estimated that that processing times had grown by 300 per cent at an annual cost of $14 billion to the Canadian and US economies. The Conference Board of Canada reported that some exporters had been forced to abandon just-in-time delivery and return to the earlier practice of warehousing goods, thereby eroding some of the advantages achieved under the Canada–US and North American free trade agreements.[86]

SPP WOES

Meanwhile, the SPP was under attack from critics in the United States who charged that it would merge US sovereignty into a European-style North American community, and those in Canada who claimed it was a vehicle for imposing a US agenda on Canada. But as Andrew Potter observed, 'The big risk we face now is not that North American integration is happening too quickly, but that it has ground to a halt'.[87] This could be seen in the communiqué issued by Canadian, US, and Mexican ministers at the end of their review meeting in February 2007, which charged officials with 'revitalizing and streamlining their work plans to ensure that initiatives are more focused and results-oriented'.[88] But by the time of the next North American summit in August, none of the leaders was willing 'to make the SPP a central focus'. They agreed on a North American Plan for Avian and Pandemic Influenza in public health emergencies but made little headway in addressing the critics' concerns or advancing the SPP agenda.[89]

BORDER CONCERNS

Border security continued to dominate Canada–US relations. In September, a report by the US Government Accountability Office, whose investigators had crossed the border with simulated radioactive material undetected by American Border Patrol officers, prompted certain legislators to revive complaints about Canadian security. Harper noted that although the exercise was intended to test US security, 'obviously we have to be concerned'. He would 'work hand and glove with American authorities dealing with any kinds of threats or potential threats'.[90] But US concerns were reinforced when Canada's auditor general reported that Ottawa lacked an effective system for assessing threats at the border despite the upgrades.[91]

Ottawa expressed its reservations about US policy after Canadian firemen rushing to a blaze in upstate New York were detained and an ambulance carrying a critically ill patient for emergency surgery in Detroit was stopped for a secondary inspection.[92] A US Customs and Border Protection spokesperson would only say that while the agency recognized 'the necessity of processing emergency crews as quickly as possible [it] has a primary mission of protecting and securing our borders'. Homeland Security secretary Michael Chertoff contended that more than a dozen persons with suspected terrorist ties had been arrested attempting to cross the border, and that he was more worried about Canada's security than Mexico's. Still, Congress approved legislation directing the Department of Homeland Security to postpone the WHTI passport requirement until June 2009. Meanwhile, the department would require those entering the United States to provide proof of citizenship and identity rather than an oral declaration as had been the case previously.[93]

With the Bush era drawing to a close, Harper began to distance his government from the administration. Claiming he had been concerned 'for some time' about the direction in US policy, Harper was 'looking for an opportunity for a fresh start with a new administration'. He pointed to 'an increasing thickening of the border . . . sometimes disguising protectionist sentiment'. And although he had once dismissed the Kyoto protocol as a 'socialist scheme', Harper asserted that Ottawa's participation in international climate change negotiations had been 'undermined by an energy partner that doesn't have targets and hasn't seen it as a priority'.[94]

Some observers argued that the prospect of a new Democratic administration provided an opportunity to engage Washington with a big idea. Claiming that Canadian governments had reacted 'defensively and anxiously to American security concerns', Michael Hart argued it was time to 'work with' Washington 'to build a much-better functioning, more open, and more integrated North America'.[95] But Senator Barack Obama, the leading contender for the party's presidential nomination, showed no interest. In a close contest with Senator Hillary Clinton in primaries in Ohio and Pennsylvania, where NAFTA was blamed for major job losses, he said an Obama administration would withdraw from the agreement if Canada and Mexico refused to incorporate enforceable labour and environmental standards.[96]

In April, Bush, Harper, and Calderon held their final meeting. They warned that reopening NAFTA would cost jobs and investment. But they made no progress in advancing the SPP agenda.[97] According to Derek Burney, the SPP morass showed that efforts to 'triangulate' Canada–US relations had 'produced little of substance and allowed attention to be diverted from more pressing bilateral concerns'.[98] But as Edward Alden observed, the actions 'Washington is taking to harden its border have little to do with what Canada has or has not done to shore up its defences against terrorists. Canada is facing a tamer version of the same thinking that is leading the United States to build hundreds of miles of steel barriers on its Mexican border. It is the quest for perfect security.'[99]

HARPER AND OBAMA

With elections approaching in both countries, attention shifted to domestic politics. In October, Harper returned to power with a strengthened minority government. Shortly thereafter, Obama won a decisive victory in an election that also saw the Democrats increase their majorities in the Senate and House of Representatives. There was no shortage of advice on how to approach the new administration. A group of prominent academics and former diplomats involved in Carleton University's Canada–US Project urged Ottawa to exercise 'bold and inspired leadership' by adopting a comprehensive approach to 'the bilateral and broader global issues at the heart of the relationship'.[100] Although the relationship was a priority for Canadians, it was only one of many issues confronting the new administration, which came to office with an ambitious agenda including health care reform and climate change, an inherited economic crisis, and wars in Iraq and Afghanistan.

Obama softened his stand on renegotiating NAFTA. But his climate change goal of cutting greenhouse gas emissions by means of a cap-and-trade system to 80 per cent below the 1990 level by 2050, contrasted sharply with Canada's modest objective of lowering emissions by 50 per cent from the 2006 level by 2050, using intensity-based targets. Obama's pledge to end US reliance on 'dirty, dwindling and dangerously expensive' energy alarmed Canada's oil sands producers, most of whose production was destined for the American market. Harper's government, which had viewed Canada's role as the largest supplier of energy to the United States as an important bargaining chip in any reassessment of NAFTA, would be forced to alter its approach.[101]

If Harper's government needed to accommodate the new direction in US policy, Obama's overwhelming popularity among Canadians provided the opportunity. Calling Obama's election 'a tremendous and truly inspiring moment', Harper described Canada as the United States' 'most important reliable ally and its best friend and partner in the world'. He welcomed Obama's commitment to Afghanistan 'as positive and consistent with Canadian policy', and proposed a bilateral climate change agreement to capitalize on US concern about energy security while shielding oil sands exports from punitive measures. But the most pressing issues were protectionist tendencies within the Democratic majority in Congress that could affect the administration's response to the deepening economic crisis, and the ongoing problem of border security.[102]

Ottawa and Washington cooperated in supporting failing North American auto makers and introduced stimulus packages to revive their ailing economies. However, Congress inserted a 'Buy American' requirement into the US program. Under pressure from Canada and other countries the final legislation specified that it should be 'applied in a manner consistent with United States' obligations under international agreements'. But much of the package was intended for state and local projects that were exempt from such measures. Canada was vulnerable on that score because unlike other countries it had not negotiated an agreement with the United States providing reciprocal access to sub-national markets.[103]

Border security also remained an irritant. Homeland Security Secretary Janet Napolitano ordered a review of 'northern border security' to develop strategies for dealing with vulnerabilities and remaining risks. Leslie Campbell suggested that Napolitano's record as the former governor of Arizona gave 'some confidence that a new border plan won't be punitive', but warned that 'most of those calling for increased attention to the northern border are hardly friendly to Canada and not likely to advocate freer border movement'.[104]

Canadians remained overwhelmingly supportive of Obama despite concerns about his policies. Many agreed with the *Globe and Mail* that the president's decision to make Ottawa his first foreign trip confirmed the importance he attached to 'restoring strong relations with Canada as a top foreign-policy priority'.[105] Obama met with Harper during a whirlwind visit in February. To foreign affairs minister Lawrence Cannon they were 'two pragmatic leaders who wanted results'. Obama stressed that the United States wanted to rebuild its international relationships and would do 'everything that I can' to strengthen Canada–US ties. Harper said collaboration would 'demonstrate exactly how that model can operate'. Harper welcomed Obama's assurance that Washington would respect its trade obligations, and would look at ways to incorporate environmental and labour standards into NAFTA. But he expressed concern about 'the thickening of the border', using the occasion to send a message that Canada took security 'as seriously as our American friends'. Obama agreed 'that it is possible for us to balance our security concerns with an open border', adding 'we have no doubt about Canada's commitment to security in the United States as well as Canada'. The leaders finessed the climate change issue, establishing a Clean Energy Dialogue involving technological collaboration to reduce greenhouse gas emissions.[106]

A FRESH START?

Harper's government launched a diplomatic offensive to engage the administration and Congress, with little effect. Secretary Napolitano disputed Harper's characterization of the border, saying she was 'very cognizant of the balance' that had to be struck between security trade and transit.[107] Differences in how the two countries assessed risks, screened people and goods, and dealt with immigration and visa issues were 'a security concern' for the United States. She also had to take into account 'the very real feeling among the southern border states . . . that if things are being done on the Mexican border, they should also be done on the Canadian border'.[108]

Napolitano agreed that the Canadian and Mexican borders were not identical but maintained that 'suspected or known terrorists', including the 9/11 attackers who had entered the United States had done so from Canada. She later acknowledged the al-Qaeda operatives were not among them but others, including Ahmed Ressam, were.[109] Secretary of State Hillary Clinton dispelled any doubt that Washington would relax its approach, saying it had to 'harden' the border with Canada, which was

still 'too porous'. Napolitano did agree to involve Canadian authorities in assessing security risks. But even as Ottawa was announcing that it would phase in new rules requiring biometric data for all foreign visitors, Washington was dispatching more agents to the border.[110]

Added to Canada's border anxieties were US economic policies, including new country-of-origin labelling requirements for imported meats that imposed additional costs on Canadian exporters. American producers pushed back against Ottawa's attempts to secure an exemption, forcing the government to take its case to the WTO. US legislators also extended Buy American provisions in the stimulus program to other legislation, including highway construction and energy bills. With manufacturers pressing for an easing of the restrictions and some municipalities threatening to exclude US bidders from contacts, Harper asked the provinces to support a plan to negotiate a subnational procurement pact liberalizing access to local markets in both countries.[111] Meanwhile, the Canadian and US Chambers of Commerce warned that border delays, which had eased as a result of the recession, would accelerate when the economies recovered unless progress were made in easing low-risk trade and travel.[112]

Before long, observers were calling Canada the missing link in Obama's engagement strategy. 'With hindsight', said Leslie Campbell, 'it's clear that we should have read the signs, but the too-good-to-be-true Canadian press coverage of Obama's trip masked the fact that there was no evidence of new thinking toward Canada emanating from Washington'. Allan Gotlieb agreed. Canada had 'to think strategically and long term in its relations with the United States', with the goal of achieving 'a single economic space and a common security perimeter'. But columnist James Travers warned, 'There's a Canadian price to be paid for easy US access. It involves accepting the reduced sovereignty that comes with a common North American trade, security and immigration perimeter managed by Washington rules'.[113]

WHETHER TRILATERALISM?

Although Obama's other preoccupations had 'cast a shadow over the Western Hemisphere alliance', the president recognized the value of trilateral summitry. The next meeting in August 2009 would differ in tone and substance from its predecessors. Gone from the agenda would be the SPP, which had been in 'hibernation' since the beginning of Obama's presidency. Reflecting the president's 'results oriented' approach, discussion would focus on 'specific shared priorities', with the US, Canadian, and Mexican publics being kept abreast of what 'their governments are attempting to do'. Obama's national security advisor, James Jones, called the meeting 'a step in the continuing dialogue from which agreements will undoubtedly come'.[114]

But frayed bilateral relations among the three countries complicated deliberations. Harper was in damage control mode with Calderon in the wake of Ottawa's surprise decision to impose visa requirements on Mexican visitors due to a dramatic rise in refugee claims. Harper claimed this was necessary to give the government time to revamp its ineffective refugee law. He attempted to mollify Calderon by assigning $400,000 from a recently budgeted $15 million Anti-Crime Capacity Building Program to help train Mexican police involved in an escalating war against the country's drug traffickers.[115]

Washington and Mexico City were at odds over issues of drug violence, immigration, and protectionism. Obama admitted that the American demand for drugs had contributed to Mexico's drug war, which had crossed the border into the United States and Canada, and promised to review the recent withholding of funds to help battle drug cartels because of concerns about human rights abuses committed by the Mexican army. He would press for a revamped immigration law, including a path for illegal immigrants to acquire citizenship. He would also revisit the administration's decision, in violation of NAFTA, to cancel a pilot project allowing Mexican trucks to cross into the United States.[116]

Harper pressed Obama on the Buy American issue. The president asked Canadians to keep it 'in perspective', claiming that it 'in no way has endangered the billions of dollars of trade taking place between our two countries'. But he hinted 'there may be mechanisms whereby states and local jurisdictions can work with the provinces to allow for cross-border procurement practices that expand the trading relationship'.[117]

Harper had another meeting with Obama in Washington in September, with trade dominating the agenda. Obama, who noted that Harper had raised the Buy American issue 'every single time we've met', said the administration was attempting 'to make sure that these sources of tension diminish'. But he continued to downplay the issue, asserting that 'There is no prospect of any budding trade wars between our two countries'. Harper agreed that problems 'are relatively small compared to the overall scale of Canadian-American trade', but they 'are important irritants; they are having some real impacts'.[118]

BIG IDEA PROPOSALS

Critics contend that it will take a big idea to satisfy US security concerns and protect Canada's access to the US market. They argue that border management requires a stronger basis than administrative changes, which are vulnerable to the uncertainties of politics and unforeseen crises.[119] Wendy Dobson claims that '[s]mall ideas or temporizing will get lost in the highly diffused (and highly focused)

US political system. Staying with the status quo will see our sovereignty eroded when we are forced to react to, rather than shape, our assertive neighbor's initiatives.'[120] 'For any initiative to succeed', says Allan Gotlieb, 'it must be bold, it must come from Canada and be espoused at the highest level. It must be comprehensive so as to allow trade-offs and broad constituencies to come into play. It must address the US agenda as well as ours'.[121] Given its stake in the outcome, Thomas d'Aquino asserts, the business community must take the lead in building support for a new paradigm as it did when it campaigned for the Canada–US and North American free trade accords.[122]

Although grand bargain proposals differ in some respects, they are all based on the assumption that only an integrated approach to economic and physical safety can provide a durable basis for managing Canada–US relations. Dobson's big idea would see Canada improve border security, tighten immigration policy, accelerate energy and resources development, and increase contributions to continental defence in exchange for expanded access to the US market in the form of a customs union or common market. This would be managed by 'functional co-operative mechanisms'. Increased cooperation would not undermine Canada's distinctiveness because the two countries would be equal partners. 'Harmonization may be proposed, but the other partner has a say in whether the proposal is accepted'.[123]

Gotlieb's North American community of law would subject political power to the rule of law in Canada–US relations. It would include a common external tariff, abolition of trade remedy laws, binding rules for the free movement of people, goods and investment, mutual recognition of standards, immigration rules, a common security perimeter, and increased defence cooperation. The community of law would not require overarching political architecture, although 'in a few areas, joint institutions might help the smooth functioning of the common space'.[124]

The North American Security and Prosperity Initiative, championed by the Canadian Council of Chief Executives, would see Ottawa adopt 'a comprehensive strategy for strengthening its economic and security partnership with the United States', with Mexico joining in when it was in a position to do so. The strategy would require negotiations on a range of issues, resulting in 'a single overarching agreement', or 'a series of interlocking and mutually supporting agreements'. Key elements would be a common external tariff or customs union, suspension of trade remedy measures, an improved dispute settlement process, regulatory convergence, full labour mobility, a comprehensive resource security pact containing a common energy strategy, improved border management with expanded infrastructure, common procedures for processing immigrants and refugees, joint watch lists and visa requirements, and enhanced defence cooperation. Joint commissions, modelled on the International Joint Commission (IJC), would facilitate policy coordination and resolve problems.[125]

The Independent Task Force on the Future of North America envisages a continental security perimeter with an expanded NORAD assuming responsibility for land and naval defence, a North American border pass with biometric identifiers, a joint border action plan with harmonized visa and asylum regulations, additional customs facilities, infrastructure, and information sharing. The plan includes a common external tariff, a permanent tribunal for adjudicating trade and investment disputes, a unified approach to unfair trade practices, review of sectors excluded from NAFTA, a North American Competition Commission, a continental regulatory plan and resource strategy, full labour mobility, an economic development plan for Mexico, and increased educational exchanges. Annual North American summit meetings would oversee implementation. A North American Advisory Council of eminent persons would offer ideas, while a North American Interparliamentary Group would provide legislative input.[126]

The Carleton University Canada–US Project recommends a 'new blueprint' for managing relations, the centrepiece of which would be a reinvigorated partnership in which Ottawa would collaborate closely with Washington to advance shared global goals, with the expectation that Americans would give greater attention to more immediate concerns. They would adopt a perimeter security system by means of expanded defence cooperation, and improved handling of cross-border commercial traffic, crime and terrorist threats, updated infrastructure, and integrated regulatory regimes. The agenda would also include a joint energy and environmental agreement, and collaboration on such pressing issues as Arctic sovereignty. Regular meetings between the prime minister, the president, and cabinet ministers would 'provide the necessary goad for productive preparatory effort at the working level and a basis for national decisions that are in harmony with the interests of both countries'. A reinvigorated Canada–US Partnership Forum could offer advice on how to broaden NAFTA cooperation. Both sides could also make use of the relationship's 'hidden wiring' in the form of contacts at the state/provincial, legislative, and private sector levels. The approach would be bilateral rather than trilateral because 'there is much more common ground between Canada and the United States—i.e., 'Upper North America'—than there is between Mexico and either of its northern partners'.[127]

ASSESSING THE BIG IDEA

It is highly unlikely that a grand bargain could be achieved or that it would serve Canada's interests. The Conference Board of Canada observes that the sheer size and complexity of the Canada–US relationship 'would make one sweeping "grand bargain" extremely difficult to negotiate'. Big negotiations, moreover, 'often do not favour the weaker party'.[128] Richard Falkenrath, a former US Homeland Security official and member of the Independent Task Force on the Future of North America, has argued that because the United States has a greater interest in security than in economic collaboration, it should press Canada to cooperate 'across an even broader range of national and homeland security issues' than the group recommended, 'including nuclear and ballistic missile threats', as a condition for closer trade ties.[129] Even so, it is far from certain what steps Ottawa could take that would cause Washington to forgo its own security measures. As Kathleen Macmillan points out, 'The big worry about big ideas is that we will end up capitulating in areas where we pay a price in terms of our policy sovereignty only to find out that, down the road, the US remains unsatisfied'.[130] In practice, negotiations would have to be disaggregated into manageable parts, and the deals struck would reflect the bargaining strengths of the two countries. Also, it is doubtful that Ottawa and Washington would agree to hand over control of politically sensitive issues to International Joint Commission-like institutions. The two sides have used the IJC to make recommendations and decisions on technical issues, but they have not been prepared to extend this to political matters.[131]

In addition, as Prime Minister Mulroney discovered when he attempted to revive the partnership paradigm in the 1980s, US presidents continue to play an indispensable role in the management of the relationship, but they no longer have the necessary leverage vis-à-vis Congress to implement the trade-offs that are central to the approach. Matters such as trade remedy laws that were not resolved in the Canada–US and North American free trade agreements, when circumstances were relatively favourable, would be even harder to settle in today's difficult trade environment. Moreover, 'on specific issues', Bill Merkin, a former US trade negotiator, observes, 'if it makes domestic political sense any administration is usually willing to temporarily set aside its free-trade principles'.[132] The Bush administration's response to the NAFTA Extraordinary Challenge Committee's ruling on softwood lumber in 2005 shows that Washington will do so even at the expense of its international obligations. Nor is there any evidence that Congress would be more willing to compromise if the agenda were broadened to include border security and transit. As Geoffrey Hale points out, 'the pursuit of a North American security perimeter . . . fundamentally ignores US domestic political debates and vastly misjudges the willingness of either party in Congress to weaken sovereign control over national borders'.[133]

Although Obama's popularity in Canada has made it easier for Harper's minority government to engage Washington, the administration, preoccupied with its own issues 'has little time or energy to spare for a benign northern neighbour'.[134] In any case, it would be politically difficult for the United States to deepen ties with Canada without involving Mexico. Greg Anderson observes that Canada's tendency to view Mexico as a barrier to progress on Canadian–American issues 'fails to recognize the degree to which Mexico City figures in US policy-making and in American politics generally'. He adds, 'Washington invested heavily in political and economic reform in Mexico City when it supported NAFTA and a new administration is not going to allow this to be eroded through a return to bilateral relations.' Besides, issues of 'development and drug violence and are not simply bilateral'. They 'should concern Canada because they seriously complicate Washington's ability to move trilaterally on border security and immigration reform'. They can also affect Canada directly, as the Harper government discovered when it imposed

visa requirements on Mexican travellers as a result of rising refugee claims while it revamped outdated regulations. Tightening the system will please the United States, but Canada needs to join the United States and Mexico in addressing the issues that created the refugee problem in the first place. For example, Ottawa has yet to participate in the governance structure of or contribute to the capital fund of the North American Development Bank, established by Washington and Mexico City in 1994 to assist with Mexico's development and environmental issues, although it has begun to help the Mexican government in its efforts to curb the country's drug trade.[135]

Anderson agrees that 'the paralysis generated by the security-economics nexus' has dimmed prospects for major integration initiatives. He predicts that 'the dynamics emanating from the national capitals will likely continue, but momentum toward shared governance is going to be increasingly driven more by regional and local participants than from Ottawa, Washington or Mexico City'.[136] Regional initiatives, though, can be a double-edged sword. Acceptance of the Washington State–British Columbia initiative to substitute enhanced drivers' licences for passports at land crossings shows that state–provincial cooperation can make a positive contribution to border management. However, the attempts by US cattle producers to use the US court system and the inspections imposed by the Montana government to stymie Washington's efforts to open the border to Canadian beef following the discovery of mad cow disease in Alberta show that influence is not always benign.[137]

The SPP process, too, has failed to resolve outstanding issues. Christopher Sands points out that it deepened relations among the three governments, including working-level public servants, and facilitated coordinated responses to a salmonella outbreak in Mexican tomatoes and peppers, and the spread of the H1N1 virus.[138] But the overall goal of reconciling security, trade, and transit imperatives was defeated by weak leadership, an unwieldy agenda, and a lack of transparency, which fuelled suspicions that the project would erode national sovereignty.

Still, Harper and Obama share a managerial approach emphasizing practical results over grand designs that offers opportunities for cooperation on shared priorities. But Ottawa needs to bring workable solutions to the table.[139] Its views are heeded on such matters as international financial regulation, because its strict banking rules enabled the country to withstand the economic crisis better than most, and Afghanistan, because of its long military involvement, although its impact will diminish as the mission comes to an end.[140] But

Ottawa must deepen its involvement in such issues as climate change and relations with Mexico, which are important not only to the United States but also to Canada. On the bilateral front, Senator Colin Kenny, pointing to the imbalance of attention and resources the two countries give to border security, suggests that Canada boost its efforts in order to get the United States to take its concerns more seriously. This could serve as a prelude to a negotiated 'results-based agreement', in which they would commit to 'providing the personnel, infrastructure and systems' to ensure the timely flow of cross-border trade and travel.[141] Similarly, a comprehensive sub-national procurement agreement with the United States opening up access to local markets on a reciprocal basis would insulate Canada from Buy American provisions in US legislation.[142]

Key Terms

Big Idea
Border Security

Buy American
Partnership Paradigm

Notes

1. This chapter is an expanded version of a paper, 'Managing Canada–U.S. Relations in the Post-9/11 Era: Do We Need a Big Idea?' CSIS *Policy Papers on the Americas*, XIV, Study 11 (November 2003), © 2003 by the Center for Strategic and International Studies, Washington, D.C. All rights reserved. I would like to thank Chris Sands for his comments on an earlier draft.

2. See Wendy Dobson, 'Shaping the Future of the North American Economic Space: A Framework for Action,' *C.D. Howe Institute Commentary*, no. 16 Allan Gotlieb, 'A North American Community of Law,' *Ideas That Matter* 2, no. 4 (2003), pp. 25–30.2 (April 2002); Thomas d'Aquino, 'Security and Prosperity: The Dynamics of a New Canada–United States Partnership in North America,'presentation to the annual general meeting of the Canadian Council of Chief Executives, January 14, 2003, www.ceocouncil.ca; *Building a North American Community: Report of the Independent Task Force on the Future of North America.*, May, 2005 (The task force was chaired by Pedro Aspe, former secretary of the treasury of Mexico in the Salinas

government; John Manley, former foreign minister, minister of finance and deputy minister of Canada in the Chrétien government; and William Weld, former governor of Massachusetts. It was sponsored by the Council on Foreign Relations in association with the Canadian Council of Chief Executives and the Consejo Mexicano de Asuntos Internacionales), www.cfr.org/pub8102/independenttask forcereport/buildinganorthamericancommunity.php; and 'From Correct to Inspired: A Blueprint for Canada–US Engagement,' Carleton University, Canada–US Project,' January 19, 2009.

3. To be sure, explicit linkages across issue areas were rare, with President Lyndon Johnson's support for the Auto Pact Agreement in 1965, reportedly in return for the Pearson government's role in establishing a UN peacekeeping force in Cyprus being one of the few examples cited. Rather, the trade-offs generally took the form of contextual linkages wherein each side attempted to accommodate the other's priorities when it was in a position to do so in the interest of maintaining the

partnership. See Robert Bothwell, *Canada and the United States: The Politics of Partnership* (Toronto: University of Toronto Press, 1992), p. 93; and Charles F. Doran, *Forgotten Partnership: U.S.–Canada Relations Today* (Baltimore: The Johns Hopkins University Press, 1984), pp. 20–25, 36–41.

4.   Kal J. Holsti and Thomas Allen Levy, 'Bilateral Institutions and Transgovernmental Relations Between Canada and the United States,' in *Canada and the United States: Transnational and Transgovernmental Relations*, Annette Baker Fox and Joseph S. Nye, eds. (New York: Columbia University Press, 1971), p. 291.

5.   Roger F. Swanson, ed., *Canadian–American Summit Diplomacy, 1923–1973: Selected Speeches and Documents* (Toronto: McClelland and Stewart, 1975), p. 298.

6.   Hon. Mitchell Sharp, 'Canada–U.S. Relations: Options for the Future', *International Perspectives* (Autumn 1972).

7.   See Joseph T. Jockel, 'The Canada–United States Relationship after the Third Round: The Emergence of Semi-Institutionalized Management,' *International Journal* XL, no. 4 (Autumn 1985), p. 689–715.

8.   Confidential source. See also L. Ian MacDonald, *Mulroney: The Making of the Prime Minister* (Toronto: McClelland and Stewart, 1984), pp. 304–306.

9.   See Donald Barry, 'The Road to NAFTA,' in *Toward a North American Community? Canada, the United States, and Mexico*, ed. Donald Barry (Boulder, Colo.: Westview Press, 1995), pp. 3–14.

10. G. Bruce Doern and Brian W. Tomlin, *Faith and Fear: The Free Trade Story* (Toronto: Stoddart, 1991), pp. 35–39.

11. Jeffrey Simpson, 'When it comes to trade, the Americans just never give in or give up,' *Globe and Mail*, February 16, 1996; confidential source.

12. John Kirton, 'Promoting Plurilateral Partnership: Managing United States–Canadian Relations in the Post–Cold War Period,' *American Review of Canadian Studies* 24, no. 4 (Winter 1994), p. 464.

13. George Haynal, 'Interdependence, Globalization and North American Borders,' *Policy Options* 23, no. 6 (September 2002), p. 21.

14. Christopher Sands, 'Fading Power or Rising Power: 11 September and Lessons from the Section 110 Experience,' in *Canada Among Nations 2002: A Fading Power*, ed. Norman Hillmer and Maureen Appel Molot (Toronto: Oxford University Press, 2002), pp. 49–73.

15. Drew Fagan, 'Canada: stand on guard,' *Globe and Mail*, December 4, 2001.

16. The White House, Office of the Press Secretary, 'Joint Statement by President George Bush and President Vicente Fox Towards a Partnership for Prosperity,' February 16, 2001, www.whitehouse.gov/news/releases/2001/02 (11/18/2003).

17. Steven Chase, 'New pact on energy not needed, Ottawa says,' *Globe and Mail*, August 6, 2001. CUSFTA and NAFTA established free trade in energy between Canada and the United States. Canada received easy access to the U.S. market for oil and gas in return for which it agreed not to impose higher limits on exports than those in force in Canada.

18. Mike Trickey, 'U.S. ambassador favours closer links with Canada,' *Calgary Herald*, June 30, 2001; Alan Toulin and James Baxter, 'Border divides Liberal ranks,' *National Post*, August 3, 2001.

19. Shawn McCarthy and Campbell Clark, 'Canada will make its own laws, PM vows,' *Globe and Mail*, September 20, 2001.

20. John Ibbitson and Campbell Clark, 'Canada and U.S. tighten borders,' *Globe and Mail*, September 26, 2001. Ashcroft later admitted that Canadian officials had provided information leading to Ressam's arrest. See Daniel Leblanc, 'Canada praised for tip to U.S. on Ressam,' *Globe and Mail*, December 4, 2001.

21. Murray Campbell and Lily Nguyen, 'Security perimeter backed,' *Globe and Mail*, September 15, 2001.

22. Nancy Hughes Anthony, 'Resolving U.S. border-fears vital for Canadian business,' *Calgary Herald*, October 15, 2001; Heather Scoffield, 'Business coalition pushes for common border rules,' *Globe and Mail*, December 3, 2001.

23. Confidential source.

24. Paul Wells, 'We don't pull our weight: Manley,' *National Post*, October 5, 2001.

25. Steven Frank and Stephen Handelman, 'Drawing a Line,' *Time* (Canadian edition), October 8, 2001, p. 45.

26. Shawn McCarthy, 'Manley doubts perimeter idea,' *Globe and Mail*, October 5, 2001.

27. Canada, House of Commons, Standing Committee on Foreign Affairs and International Trade, *Partners in North America: Advancing Canada's Relations with the United States and Mexico* (Ottawa: House of Commons, December 2002), pp. 167–168.

28. Government of Canada, 'Canada and the United States Sign Smart Border Declaration,' *News Release*, no. 162, December 12, 2001.

29. House of Commons, Standing Committee on Foreign Affairs, *Partners in North America*, p. 168.

30. The White House, 'U.S.–Mexico Border Partnership Agreement,' March 22, 2002, www.whitehouse.gov/infocus/usmxborder/22points.html (11/18/2003).

31. Department of Foreign Affairs and International Trade, 'Canada's Actions against Terrorism Since September 11th —Backgrounder,' October 10, 2002, www.dfait-maeci.gc.ca/can-am/menuen.asp?act=v&mid=1&cat=1&did=1250 (1/9/2003); Daniel Leblanc, 'Canada takes Afghan mission,' *Globe and Mail*, February 13, 2003.

32. Lisa M. Seghetti, 'Border Security: U.S.–Canada Border Issues,' Congressional Research Service Report for Congress, July 8, 2002, www.usembassycanada.gov/content/can_usa/border_crs_070802.pdf (11/18/2003).

33. Perhaps the most notable example was the introduction of the US. National Security Entry-Exit Registration System (NSEERS), which required citizens of Canada and other countries or dual nationals born in Iran, Iraq, Libya, Sudan, and Syria to be photographed, fingerprinted, and interviewed when entering the United States. The zealous application of the law by U.S. immigration inspectors drew charges of racial profiling and prompted Ottawa to issue a travel advisory to affected Canadians. Washington subsequently modified the policy so that place of birth would no longer automatically trigger a special interrogation. Elizabeth Thompson, 'Racial profiling by U.S. denounced,' Calgary Herald, October 31, 2002; Mike Trickey, 'U.S. backs down on security plan,' Calgary Herald, November 1, 2002.

34. Campbell Clark, Estanislao Oziewicz, and Tu Thanh Ha, 'Canada–U.S. agree to "safe third country" refugee pact,' Globe and Mail, June 29, 2002.

35. Angelo Persichilli, 'Cellucci says Canada–U.S. relationship "a role model for the world,"' Hill Times, October 7, 2002.

36. Department of Foreign Affairs and International Trade, 'Governor Ridge and Deputy Prime Minister Manley Issue One-Year Status Report on the Smart Border Action Plan,' December 6, 2002, www.dfait-maeci.gc.ca/can-am/menu-en.asp?act=v&mid=1&cat=10&did=1671 (12/17/2002).

37. Canada, Department of National Defence, 'Enhanced Canada–U.S. Security Cooperation, News Release BG-02.041, December 9, 2002.

38. Eric Reguly, 'Iraq stance will burn Canada,' Globe and Mail, March 20, 2003. For a discussion of Canadian and U.S. policies toward the war see my 'Chrétien, Bush, and the War in Iraq,' The American Review of Canadian Studies 35, 2 (Summer 2005), 215–245.

39. Paul Cellucci, 'Speech by U.S. ambassador to Canada to the Economic Club of Toronto,' Toronto, March 25, 2003; Canadian Press, 'Envoy links Bush snub to war policy,' Toronto Star, April 17, 2003.

40. Quoted in Sinclair Stewart, 'Rift over Iraq expected to heal,' Globe and Mail, April 7, 2003.

41. Shawn McCarthy, 'U.S. plans border exemption for Canada,' Globe and Mail, April 17, 2003; Shawn McCarthy, 'Forgive, forget; it's good for business,' Globe and Mail, April 18, 2003.

42. Shawn McCarthy, 'Canadians vote Bush least liked president,' Globe and Mail, July 12, 2003; Wallace Immen, 'Canadian public skeptical of war in Iraq, poll shows,' Globe and Mail, July 19, 2003.

43. Bruce Cheadle, '"Grits" criticism of GOP hurting Martin, MP says,' Globe and Mail, September 7, 2004; Stephen Handelman, 'Agenda for Canada,' Time (Canadian edition) November 17, 2003, p. 31.

44. Drew Fagan, 'On the balance beam,' Globe and Mail, January 7, 2004.

45. Jeff Sallot and Paul Koring, 'Martin wades into spat over U.S. contracts,' Globe and Mail, December 11, 2003; Jeff Sallot, 'Martin reminds Washington to respect Canadians' rights,' Globe and Mail, November 26, 2003; DeNeen L. Brown and Dana Priest, 'Chrétien Protests Deportation of Canadian,' Washington Post, November 6, 2003.

46. Drew Fagan, 'Canada, U.S. seal Arar deal,' Globe and Mail, January 13, 2004.

47. Susan Delacourt, 'Vibes were very, very good,' Toronto Star, January 14, 2004.

48. See Graham Fraser, 'Plan would give U.S. a say in our energy,' Toronto Star, January 9, 2003; Drew Fagan, 'Is it time for a summit?' Globe and Mail, January 14, 2003; Steven Chase and Greg Keenan, 'Canada, U.S. consider one steel market,' Globe and Mail, February 1, 2003; Drew Fagan, 'PM looks at closer relations with U.S., Globe and Mail, February 24, 2003.

49. Drew Fagan, 'Brison maps out proposals for closer U.S. ties,' Globe and Mail, April 1, 2004.

50. Jeff Sallot, 'Ottawa unveils security plan to beef up defences,' Globe and Mail, April 28, 2004.

51. Susan Delacourt, 'Bush, Martin promise closer ties,' Toronto Star, May 1, 2004; Sheldon Alberts, 'Historic meeting strikes a balance,' Calgary Herald, May 1, 2004.

52. The White House, Office of the Press Secretary, 'Remarks by President George W. Bush and Prime Minister Paul Martin in a Joint Press Availability,' November 30, 2004, www.usembassycanada...on2=&document=bush_visit 2004_joint press, (12/1/2004); Office of the Prime Minister, 'Joint statement by Canada and the United States on common security, common prosperity: A new partnership in North America,' November 30, 2004.

53. Gina Teel and Jim Gransbery, 'U.S. court blocks cattle,' Calgary Herald, March 3, 2005; Dawn Walton and Barrie McKenna, 'U.S. Senate backs border ban on Canadian beef,' Globe and Mail, March 4, 2005; Dave Ebner, 'U.S. ruling raises hope for end to cattle ban,' Globe and Mail, July 15, 2005; Grant Robertson, 'Montana orders extra red tape,' Calgary Herald, July 23, 2005.

54. The Byrd Amendment allowed Washington to give domestic companies duties from foreign firms deemed to be trading unfairly with the United States, thereby complicating the resolution of Canada–U.S. trade disputes. Congress finally repealed the measure in 2006, but it was not phased out until 2007.

55. Sean Gordon and Bruce Campion-Smith, 'It's no to missile plan,' Toronto Star, February 25, 2005; Brian Laghi and Jane Taber, 'It was not an easy decision to make,' Globe and Mail, February 25, 2005; Susan Delacourt,

'Bush phone call surprises Martin, *Toronto Star*, March 6, 2005.

56. Alexander Panetta, 'PM gets thumbs-up on missile defence,' *Chronicle-Herald*, March 23, 2005.

57. Alan Freeman, 'NAFTA partners mull summit,' *Globe and Mail*, January 19, 2005.

58. Tim Harper, '"Fortress America" sparks new fears,' *Toronto Star*, March 15, 2005. See also *Chairman's Statement, Independent Task Force on the Future of North America, 'Creating a North American Community.'*

59. Canada, Office of the Prime Minister, 'Prime Minister to attend meeting of North American leaders,' *News Release*, March 21, 2005, www.pm.gc.ca/eng/news.asp?id=441 (3/21/2005).

60. Office of the Prime Minister, 'Security and Prosperity Partnership of North America Established,' March 23, 2005, www.pm.gc.ca/eng/news.asp?id=443 (6/10/2005).

61. John Ivison, 'Relationship nowhere near consummation,' *National Post*, March 24, 2005.

62. Linda Jewell, deputy assistant secretary of state, 'The Current State and Future Prospects for U.S. Studies in Canada: Towards a National Strategy Perspectives on the United States – The View of the U.S. Government,' Remarks to the U.S. Studies Conference, Montréal, 06 May 2005, www.usembassycanada.gov/content/textonly.asp?section=can_... (5/13/2005).

63. *Security and Prosperity Partnership of North America*, Report to Leaders, June 2005, www.fac-aec.gc.ca/spp/spp-menu-en.asp (6/28/2005); Greg Anderson and Christopher Sands, 'Negotiating North America: The Security and Prosperity Partnership,' Hudson Institute, Updated Edition, September 7, 2008, pp. 15–16.

64. Lara Jordan, 'US border passport plan a "damaging change",' *Telegram* (St John's), June 14, 2005; Simon Doyle, 'Passport rules may coat $1.8B to tourism,' *Calgary Herald*, September 3, 2005.

65. John Ibbitson, 'More than U.S. charm needed,' *Globe and Mail*, September 27, 2005; Shawna Richer and Simon Tuck, 'No-fly list in the works, Transport Minister says,' *Globe and Mail*, August 6, 2005.

66. Steven Chase, 'U.S. brushes off Canada's NAFTA softwood victory,' *Globe and Mail*, August 11, 2005; Rob Portman, 'Washington speaks: Good neighbours must talk,' *Globe and Mail*, September 3, 2005; Michael den Tandt, 'Ottawa warns U.S. of risk to NAFTA,'*Globe and Mail*, September 28, 2005; Shawn McCarthy, 'PM links softwood to energy,' *Globe and Mail*, October 7, 2005; Susan Delacourt, 'Martin warns Bush on trade disagreement,' *Toronto Star*, October15, 2005.

67. Jeff Sallot, 'Cool rhetoric, Rice urges Canada,' *Globe and Mail*, October 26, 2005.

68. Jeffrey Simpson, 'Softwood lumber now and forever,' *Globe and Mail*, October 26, 2005.

69. Lawrence Herman, 'Here's the path to a deal on softwood,' *Globe and Mail*, November 3, 2005; James Travers, 'Did Emerson block deal?' *Toronto Star*, February 9, 2006.

70. For an account of the campaign see Lisa Young, 'Electoral Instability in Canada: Implications for the Canada–U.S. Relationship,' *American Review of Canadian Studies* 37, no 1 (Spring 2007), 7–21.

71. Brian Laghi, 'Canadians turning more sour on U.S.' *Globe and Mail*, March 29, 2006; Allan Woods, 'Harper to walk fine line with Bush,' *National Post*, March 30, 2006.

72. Susan Delacourt, 'Harper has hope for lumber solution,' *Toronto Star*, March 29, 2006.

73. Sheldon Alberts and Peter Morton, 'Bush to Canada: "we care",' *National Post*, March 26, 2006; Susan Delacourt, 'PM, Bush mend fences,' *Toronto Star*, March 31, 2006.

74. Anderson and Sands, 'Negotiating North America,' pp. 21, 21–24.

75. United States Trade Representative, 'U.S., Canada Reach Final Agreement on Lumber Dispute,' News *Release*, July 1, 2006. http://ottawa.usembassy.gov/content/textonly.asp?section=can_usa&s... (7/11/2006); (Although the softwood lumber deal has been portrayed as a vindication of Harper's more cooperative approach, former Department of Commerce undersecretary for international trade Grant Aldonas claims that the Bush administration was 'desperate' to get a deal. American lumber producers refused to admit that they could not compete with their Canadian counterparts. 'It was much easier to put a Canadian face on the problem,' Aldonas said. He predicted that the complex agreement would lead to frequent legal challenges. Paul March, 'Softwood pact clock ticks,' *National Post*, April 12, 2007).

76. Paul Koring, 'Citing 'liberal' immigration laws, U.S. berates Canada on terrorism,' *Globe and Mail*, April 29, 2006. James Gordon, 'CSIS admits security shortcoming,' *National Post*, May 30, 2006.

77. Sheldon Alberts, 'Canada "on the job," Rice declares,' *National Post*, June 5, 2006; Sheldon Alberts, 'Congressman renews call for fence along our border,' *National Post*, June 6, 2006; Grahan Fraser, 'U.S. tightens border after arrests,' *Toronto Star*, June 6, 2006; Lauren Mansen, 'U.S. Western Hemisphere Travel Initiative Seeks to Boost Security System,' June 8, 2006, U.S. Embassy, Ottawa, Information Resource Center, Washington File, www.usembassycanada.gov/outreach/ca0614c.htm, (6/15/2006).

78. Dawn Walton, 'Security forces can confront terror threat head on, PM says,' *Globe and Mail*, June 8, 2006; Beth Gorham, 'Canada seeks to soothe U.S.,' *Chronicle Herald* (Halifax), June 16, 2006; Susan Delacourt, 'Ottawa takes "big step" to biometric ID,' *Toronto Star*, June 30, 2006.

79. U.S. Embassy, Ottawa, 'President Bush Participates in Press Availability with Canadian Prime Minister Stephen Harper, 06 July, 2006.

80. Steven Chase, 'U.S. plans tougher inspections at border,' *Globe and Mail*, September 1, 2006; Tim Harper, 'Canada–U.S. fence idea "boneheaded"', *Toronto Star*, September 21, 2006; Sheldon Alberts, ' "Virtual fence" "one step closer"', *National Post*, September 22, 2006; Kerry Williamson, 'Black Hawks patrolling Alberta-U.S. border,' *Calgary Herald*, October 17, 2008.

81. Allan Woods, "Mexico's next leader deplores America's own 'Berlin wall',", *Calgary Herald*, October 27, 2006; Petti Fong, 'Armed guards hit border in 2007,' *Globe and Mail*, September 1, 2006.

82. Rt. Hon. Stephen Harper, 'Speech to the Economic Club of New York,' 20 September 2006.

83. Allan Gotlieb, 'A new phase of diplomacy awaits,' *Globe and Mail*, December 18, 2006; Brian Laghi, 'Canada, U.S. have growing rapport, poll finds,' *Globe and Mail*, October 5, 2006; Lori McLeod, 'Harper seen as healer of Canada–U.S. tensions,' *National Post*, October 30, 2006.

84. Andrew Taylor, 'House Delays Rules Requiring Passports,' *Washington Post*, June 15, 2007; Spencer S. Hsu and William Branigan, 'New U.S. Passport Rules Postponed for at Least Six Months,' *Washington Post*, June 21, 2007; Patrick Brethour, 'BC, Washington plan similar high-tech licences,' *Globe and Mail*, August 17, 2007; Governor Chris Gregoire and Premier Gordon Campbell, 'The British Columbia/Washington State Partnership on Enhanced Driver's Licences,' *Canadian Parliamentary Review* 31, no. 1 (Spring 2008), pp. 2–5.

85. Beth Gorham, 'U.S. ditches plans to pre-clear travelers,' *Calgary Herald*, April 27, 2007.

86. Steven Chase, 'Border security chills trade relations,' *Globe and Mail*, December 17, 2007; Canadian Chamber of Commerce, 'SPP Priorities,' May 25, 2007; Danielle Goldfarb, 'Reaching a Tipping Point? Effects of Post 9/11 Border Security on Canada's Trade and Investment,' The Conference Board of Canada (June 2007).

87. Andrew Potter, 'Whatever happened to the new American continent,' *MacLean's*, January 29, 2007; Kelly Patterson, 'Continental Divide,' *Ottawa Citizen*, August 18, 2007.

88. Roland Paris, 'A trilateral mismatch,' *Globe and Mail*, February 26, 2007.

89. Anderson and Sands, 'Negotiating North America,' 25; James Travers, 'Communication breakdown, but no conspiracy,' *Toronto Star*, August 22, 2007.

90. United States Government Accountability Office, Testimony before the Committee on Finance, U.S. Senate, 'Border Security: Security Vulnerabilities at Unmanned and Unmonitored U.S. Border Locations,' September 27, 2007, GAO-07-884T; Beth Gorham, 'U.S. senators want border security boost,' *Toronto Star*, September 27, 2007.

91. Andrew Mayeda, 'Border agency failing to halt security risks,' *National Post*, October 31, 2007.

92. Editorial, 'Backed up at the border,' *Globe and Mail*, November 19, 2007.

93. Caroline Alphonso, 'Day urges U.S. to reconsider border policies,' *Globe and Mail*, November 20, 2007; Ian Macleod, 'Terrorists tried to enter via Canada: U.S.,' *National Post*, February 13, 2008; 'U.S. border passport law hits roadblock,' *National Post*, December 21, 2009.

94. L. Ian MacDonald, 'A conversation with the Prime Minister,' *Policy Options* (February 2008), p. 11; Harper's letter dismisses Kyoto as a 'socialist scheme,' *CBC News*, January 30, 2007, www.cbc.ca/canada/story/2007/01/30/harper-kyoto-html?ref=rss (1/22/2009).

95. Jacqueline Thorpe, 'Time to repair trade relations,' *National Post*, February 11, 2008; Michael Hart, 'Canada blew it,' *National Post*, February 12, 2008.

96. Tim Harper, 'Obama, Clinton would rip up NAFTA,' *Toronto Star*, February 27, 2008. Harper got off on the wrong foot with Obama after an official in the Prime Minister's Office apparently leaked to a Republican Party source a memo of a follow-up conversation between Canada's consul general in Chicago and Obama economic advisor Austan Goolsbee. Republican candidate Senator John McCain was a strong supporter of NAFTA. Goolsbee reportedly described Obama's remarks as 'political positioning.' Obama campaign officials accused Harper of meddling in U.S. politics. See: Brian Laghi, 'Harper meddling in U.S. primaries, Democrats say,' *Globe and Mail*, March 3, 2008; Jennifer Parker, Teddy Davis, and Kate Snow, 'Obama Campaign Denies Duplicity on Trade,' *ABC News*, March 3, 2008, http://abcnews.go.com/print?id=4380122 (3/4/2008); Neil MacDonald, 'Anatomy of a leak: What we know about NAFTA-gate,' *CBC News*, March 10, 2008, www.cbc.ca/news/reportsfromabroad/macdonald/20080310.html (3/10/2008); and James Travers, 'Signs Point to PMO in NAFTA leak,' *Toronto Star*, May 27, 2008.

97. Brian Laghi, 'Bush voices NAFTA support amid Democratic criticism,' *Globe and Mail*, April 22, 2008; Norma Greenway, 'PM Plays Energy Card,' *National Post*, April 23, 2008.

98. Derek Burney, 'Our free trade priorities needn't include Mexico,' *Globe and Mail*, April 7, 2008.

99. Edward Alden, 'The great wall of the United States,' *Globe and Mail*, October 4, 2008. For an expanded version of Alden's argument see his *The Closing of the American Border: Terrorism, Immigration, and Security Since 9/11* (New York: Harper Collins, 2008).

100. Carleton University, Canada–US Project, 'From Correct to Inspired,' January 19, 2009, p. I, 1.

101. Sheldon Alberts, 'Obama's fight against "dirty oil" could hurt oil sands,' *National Post*, June 24, 2008; Norma Greenway, 'PM plays energy card,' *National Post*, April 23, 2008.

102. Mike Blanchfield, 'Harper foresees common climate change plan with U.S.,' Canwest News Service, November 6, 2008: Siri Agreil, 'The world picks Obama for president-4 to 1,' Globe and Mail, October 22, 2008; Jeffrey Simpson, 'What's a Canadian to do when there's no Bush to beat around,' Globe and Mail, October 28, 2008.

103. Sheldon Alberts, 'U.S. Senate compromise a "great step",' Calgary Herald, February 6, 2009.

104. Leslie Campbell, 'Congress up to old tricks at Canada's expense,' Embassy, January 28, 2009.

105. Editorial, 'Well-placed priority,' Globe and Mail, January 13, 2009; 'Canadians feel the love for Obama, but they are lukewarm to his plans,' CBC News, January 19, 2009, www.cbc.ca/canada/story/2009/01/18/obama-poll.html (1/19/2009).

106. Mitch Potter and Bruce Campion-Smith, 'Obama and Harper forge common front,' Toronto Star, February 20, 2009; The White House, Office of the Press Secretary, 'Press Availability by President Obama and Prime Minister Harper of Canada,' February 19, 2009, www.whitehouse.gov/the_press_office?Press-Avaliability-by-President-Obama-and...(11/25/2009); Donald Barry, 'Clean Energy Dialogue: A Bridge Too Far?' Embassy, March 4, 2009.

107. Andrew Mayeda, 'Homeland security chief says Canada–U.S. border "misconstrued",' National Post, February 27, 2009; Paul Koring, 'Canada's safety minister skirts "no-fly"blacklist issue,' Globe and Mail, March 19, 2009.

108. Janet Napolitano, Brookings Briefing, March 25, 2009.

109. 'Canada more lax than U.S. about whom it lets in, Napolitano says,' CBC News, April 21, 2009, www.cbc.ca/canada/story/2009/04/21/napolitano-border-canada021.html (11/27/2009).

110. Sheldon Alberts, 'U.S. must "harden" border with Canada: Clinton,' National Post, May 19, 2009; Bill Curry, 'U.S. to include Canada in assessing terror risks,' Globe and Mail, May 28, 2009; Bill Curry, 'Ottawa to seek biometric data on all visitors,' Globe and Mail, June 10, 2009; Ian MacLeod, 'U.S. boosts Canada border patrolling,' Calgary Herald, June 12, 2009.

111. Campbell Clark and Rhéal Séguin, 'Ottawa pushes for new chapter in free trade with U.S.,' Globe and Mail, June 4, 2009; Barrie McKenna, 'Despite assurances Buy American lives,' Globe and Mail, March 11, 2009.

112. Sheldon Alberts, 'Long border delays loom as recession eases; report,' Calgary Herald, July 22, 2009.

113. Leslie Campbell, 'Where did Obama's love for Canada go?' Embassy, May 6, 2009; Allan Gotlieb, 'Proximity, reality, strategy, destiny,' Globe and Mail, June 27, 2009 (Gotlieb added that Canada should expand its trade with 'the giant economies of the Far East,' in order to reduce its

vulnerability 'to protectionist and other restrictive measures from the south'); James Travers, 'Border myths hurt both sides,' Toronto Star, April 23, 2009.

114. 'Obama, Calderon Meet at Mexico Summit,' CBS/AP, August 9, 2009, www.cbsnews.com/stories/2009/08/09/world/main5228536.shtml (11/26/2009); Jeff Davis, 'Obama's arrival sets North American integration adrift,' Embassy, August 5, 2009: Christopher Sands and Greg Anderson, 'The Summit Pandemic,' Edmonton Journal, August 8, 2009; Ginger Thompson and Marc Lacey, 'Obama Arrives in Mexico for Start of Summit,' New York Times, August 10, 2009; The White House, Office of the Press Secretary, 'U.S.–Mexico Announce Bilateral Framework Agreement on Clean Energy and Climate Change,' April 16, 2009, www.whitehouse.gov/the_press_office/U.S.-Mexico-Announce-Bilateral-Framework... (12/1/2009).

115. Steven Chase, 'Harper blames Canada for visa furor,' Globe and Mail, August 10, 2009.

116. 'Obama, Calderon Meet at Mexico Summit,' CBS/AP, August 9, 2009.

117. Les Whittington, 'Obama: deal on protectionism possible,' Toronto Star, August 10, 2009.

118. The White House, Office of the Press Secretary, 'Remarks by President Obama and Canadian Prime Minister Harper During Joint Press Availability,' September 16, 2009.

119. Canadian Council of Chief Executives, 'The North American Security and Prosperity Initiative: Background, Questions and Answers,' March 2003, p. 8, http://www.ceocouncil.ca/English/Publications/reports/apr3-03.pdf (11/18/2003).

120. Wendy Dobson, 'Trade can Brush in a new border,' Globe and Mail, January 21, 2003.

121. Allan Gotlieb, 'A grand bargain with the U.S.,' National Post, March 5, 2003.

122. Canadian Council of Chief Executives, 'Security and Prosperity: Toward a New Canada–United States Partnership in North America,' January 2003, pp. 1–2, http://www.ceocouncil.ca/English/Publications/reports/jan-2003.pdf (01/30/2003).

123. Dobson, 'Shaping the Future of the North American Economic Space,' p. 29.

124. Gotlieb, 'A North American Community of Law,' p. 30.

125. 'New Frontiers: Building a 21st Century Canada–United States Partnership in North America,' A Discussion Paper of the Canadian Council of Chief Executives, April 2004, p.26, www.ceocouncil.ca/en/view/?document_id=312&area_id=1; Thomas d'Aquino, 'Security and Prosperity'; Thomas d'Aquino 'Beyond Free Trade – A Canada–United States Partnership for Security and Prosperity,' Notes for remarks in Dallas, Tucson, Phoenix, Cleveland and Buffalo, February 24-March 3, 2005, www.ceocouncil.ca/en/view/?area_id=1&document_id=393 (4/30/2005).

126. *Building a North American Community, Report of the Independent Task Force on the Future of North America*, www.cfr.org.

127. Carleton University, Canada–US Project, 'From Correct to Inspired,' 1, 15, 4, V.

128. David MacDuff, *Course Correction: Advice on Canada's Future Foreign Policy* (Ottawa: The Conference Board of Canada, 2003), p. 6.

129. Richard A. Falkenrath in *Building a North American Community*, p.37.

130. Proceedings of the Standing Senate Committee on Foreign Affairs, Issue 2: Evidence, February 3, 2003, www.parl.gc.ca/37/2/parlbus/commbus/senate/com-e/FORE-E/02eva-e.htm? Language=E&Parl=37&Ses=2&comm_id=8 (11/20/2003).

131. Doran, *Forgotten Partnership*, pp. 12–13.

132. Barrie McKenna, 'Looming U.S. vote poses trade dilemma for Canada,' *Globe and Mail*, May 10, 2004.

133. Geoffrey E. Hale, 'Western Hemisphere Travel Initiative: Now for the Hard Part,' *Fraser Forum* (December 2006/January 2007), p. 14.

134. James Travers, 'Continental divide will overshadow summit,' *Toronto Star*, August 8, 2009.

135. Greg Anderson, 'Border Security and Economic Policy for the Obama Administration,' SPP *Briefing Papers*, School of Public Policy, University of Calgary 2/4 (September 2009), p. 1, 11, 12. See also Jeremy Kinsman, 'The Three Amigos—A Work in Progress,' *Policy Options* (October 2009), pp. 57–62.

136. Anderson, 'Border Security and Economic Policy for the Obama Administration,' 4.

137. The msf cow case also shows what can happen when trade agreements lead to the creation of a single market but offer no corresponding means of dealing with issues that arise from this. Ashley Proceviat, 'Canada–US Relations During BSE,' unpublished honours essay, Department of Political Science, University of Calgary, April 2008.

138. Christopher Sands, 'A Vote for Change and U.S. Strategy for North American Integration,' *PNA North American Policy Brief*, no. 1 (October 2008); Christopher Sands and Greg Anderson, 'The Summit Pandemic,' *Edmonton Journal*, August 8, 2009.

139. David Dyment, 'Doing the continental the right way,' *Embassy*, September 9, 2009; Christopher Sands and Greg Anderson, 'The summit pandemic,' *Edmonton Journal*, August 8, 2009.

140. Jeffrey Simpson, 'Harper can command. Obama can cajole – but Canada has little to say,' *Globe and Mail*, September 16, 2009.

141. Colin Kenny, 'The Canada–US border: Time to smarten up,' *Embassy*, October 21, 2009.

142. In February 2010, the Canadian and U.S. governments reached a deal exempting Canadian businesses from the Buy American provisions of the U.S. economic stimulus program. In return, Canadian provinces allowed American businesses to compete for provincial procurement contracts. Ottawa and Washington also agreed to begin discussions leading to a permanent sub-national procurement agreement.

9

CANADA AS A G8 AND G20 PRINCIPAL POWER

John J. Kirton

INTRODUCTION

A key test of whether Canada is becoming, or has become, a principal power in a rapidly changing world comes from its behaviour in the Group of Eight (G8) and Group of Twenty (G20). The mere fact of Canada's membership in these exclusive clubs, containing the most powerful leaders of the most powerful countries in the world, strongly suggests that Canada has asserted its position and acquired an acknowledged status as a principal power. But to be a principal power, Canada must use its position to take initiatives according to its national interests and distinctive national values, align with any coalition of countries within these clubs to secure its desired outcomes, and have the G8 and G20 shape world order as a result.

Canadian prime ministers have suggested that this happens. In his definitive doctrine on Canadian foreign policy in February 1995, Jean Chrétien proclaimed: 'Canada can further its global interests better than any other country through its active membership in key international groupings, for example, hosting the G7 Summit this year'

(Canada, Department of Foreign Affairs and International Trade 1995). In 2004, Paul Martin (2008) proposed that the more systemically significant G20 countries, which had been meeting at the finance ministers' level since 1999, should assemble at the leaders' level, which they started to do in 2008. On the way to his first G8 summit, in Russia in July 2006, Stephen Harper spoke of Canada as an emerging energy superpower, devoted to providing global leadership abroad.

The debate

Such far-reaching claims contradict the views of the first group of scholars who see Canada as being constrained by an American-dominated, neoliberal G8 that constantly diverts Canada's attention, investments, and policy positions away from the United Nations-based multilateral institutions so loved by liberal internationalism (LI) (Helleiner 1995; Lovbraek 1990; Keating 1993, 2002). They argue that America uses the G8 and G20 to entice Canada to adopt policies of free market fundamentalism, or neo-liberal corporate globalization, instead of its humane middle power international-ism of old.

A second school sees Canada as a 'sensational-ist', using the summits as a 'global hot tub party' with Canada merely 'being there' to bask in the reflected glory of the great (Keating 1993; Wood 1988). This school suggests that 'the summits pro-vided a sensation of power without its reality' while Canadian attempts to influence the agenda 'resulted in little, if any, success' (Keating 1993, 196).

A third school of declinists portrays an initially deserving Canada as no longer important enough economically by the 1990s to be worthy of mem-bership. Robert Bothwell (2006: 516) writes that in the 1970s 'Canada qualified to be a member of the Group of Seven industrialized nations' forum because it had, in fact, the world's sixth or seventh largest economy. By the mid-1990s that was no longer the case.'

A fourth school portrays Canada as an ineffect-ive activist (David and Roussel 1998). Andrew F. Cooper, Richard Higgott, and Kim Nossal (1993) conclude that Pierre Trudeau 'did get North-South issues onto the agenda' at his 1981 Montebello Summit, that Canada was able to 'take advantage of the manoeuvrability that its economic capabil-ities allowed' on agricultural subsidies, and that 'the willingness of the Canadian government to move out well in front of its G7 partners was designed to move these states into adopting a more coercive policy towards South Africa.' But these Canadian actions failed to influence summit out-comes or world order.

A fifth school sees Canada showing some movement in the G8 on development issues related to Africa. Accordingly, it calls on Canada to be a bridge between Africa and the donors to set the needed new rules of the game (Culpeper, Emel-ifeonwu, and Scarpa de Masellis 2003).

A sixth school presents the G8 as an institution increasing influence for Canada. Offered largely by Canadian G8 practitioners, it sees a significant Canadian role in, and successes from, the G8 (Got-lieb 1987; Artis and Ostry 1988; Ostry 1986, 1990; Summit Reform Study Group 1991; Dobson 1991a, 1991b; Macmillan and Delvoie 1999; Fowler 2003; Axworthy 2003; Haynal 2005; Bartleman 2005; Burney 2005; Mulroney 2007; Chrétien 2007; Mar-tin 2008).

A seventh school claims Canada exercises selective leadership at the G8 on specific issues such as African development, finance, land-mines, nuclear disarmament, and HIV/AIDS, and at specific summits, notably as host of Halifax in 1995 and Kananaskis in 2002 (Gordon 2005; Rioux 2006; Tomlin, Hillmer, and Hampson 2008; Press 2008). David Black (2005,[1]) argues that Canada's approach 'has been on balance, "good enough"' to sustain Canadian leadership claims, at least in relation to other rich countries, but it has fallen short of genuine leadership in relation to the real needs of African countries and people'. Duncan Wood (2006) credits Canada with several forms of leadership in finance, persevering with innovations based on Canadian values and preferences, to some success in the end.

CANADA'S DIPLOMACY OF CONCERT

The evidence, however, supports an eighth argu-ment highlighting Canada's effective G8 global leadership. The G8 and even now the G20 are emerging as effective centres of global governance, enabling a principal power to Canadianize the global order according to its national interests and distinctive national values (Dewitt and Kirton 1983; Kirton 2007a, 2007b, 413–430). Since the G8's 1975 origins, with France, the United States, Britain, Germany, Japan, and Italy as the initial attendees, it has moved Canada from the old, UN-centred diplomacy of constraint to the new,

G8-focused diplomacy of concert (Stairs 1974; Kirton 1994). Canada no longer concentrates on using likeminded middle power coalitions in the multilateral UN to constrain a much more powerful America from pursuing its preferred unilateral, military path. Instead, Canada increasingly creates issue- and interest-specific groupings of principal powers in a flexible, leaders-driven G8 concert and reinforcing G20 companion in order to infuse Canadian interests and values into the global order, even without an initially supportive United States. Canada expands the summit's agenda, creates innovative principles and agreements on key issues, complies with G8 commitments and induces its G8 colleagues to do likewise, and helps develop the G8 system for global governance as a whole. This behaviour arose early, strengthened over time, and pushed Canada over the principal power threshold at Harper's first G8 summit in St Petersburg in 2006. It has now reached a new stage, with Canada chosen to co-chair the first institutionalized G20 summit with the Republic of Korea, in tandem with Canada's fifth G8 summit in Muskoka in June 2010.

Canada's successful diplomacy of concert arises primarily because the G8-G20 system is now a centre of global governance, reinforcing and replacing the order long provided by the older UN and North Atlantic institutions, and changing how its members and outsiders behave. The G8 as a democratic concert, and the G20 as a systemic club, offer the concerted power, common principles, political control, and controlled participation needed to address the systemic and state-specific shocks brought by the new vulnerability, at a time when the old multilateral organizations and America alone can no longer cope among the major powers. Canada enjoys a relatively invulnerable position, especially on the key new security threats of energy, terrorism, finance, the environment, and health. Its major power presence is thus reinforced,

allowing it to reap domestic acclaim and advance national interests, distinctive values, and preferences. It can forge fluid partnerships and secure its preferred policy agenda, principles, and positions, catalyze international compliance and develop supportive global governance. Backed by a domestic public united on the values of globalism, international institutionalism, openness, anti-militarism, multiculturalism, and environmentalism, Canada increasingly leads in shaping and securing the G8- and G20-centred global order it prefers.

AN OVERVIEW OF CANADA'S G8 AND G20 PERFORMANCE

Canada's successful diplomacy of concert is evident in Canada's performance since it first arrived physically at the then G7 summit in 1976. First, Canada has been an increasingly successful host. Canadian-hosted summits have earned a B-minus grade, on average. The B+ rankings for Halifax in 1995 and Kananaskis in 2002 are the third highest grades up to that time and the highest since the Cold War ended in 1989 (Bayne 2005).

Second, the number of specific, actionable, future-oriented collective commitments produced by each summit confirms Canada's success as host (Kokotsis 1999). Montebello in 1981 produced 40 such commitments, and Toronto in 1988 only 27. But Halifax generated 76 and Kananaskis produced 188, the highest ever to that time.

Third, Canada, which has long complied highly with its summit commitments, has increasingly induced its more powerful G8 partners to do so. From 1975 to 1989, Canada ranked second in compliance (von Furstenberg and Daniels 1991). From 1988 to 1995, its compliance with the commitments on sustainable development, debt relief for the poorest, and Russian assistance rose, as did that of the G8's most powerful member, the United States (Kokotsis 1999). From 1996 to 2008, Canada again ranked first, while most of the other members continued to comply quite well.

Fourth, Canada has also contributed to developing the G8 as an institutionalized centre of global governance. In helping to create G8 ministerial institutions in 1995 for terrorism, where no UN body existed, and in 2002 for health security and development, where the World Health Organization (WHO) and International Labour Organization (ILO) had long operated, ⌈Canada was reinforcing and even replacing the UN as the effective governance centre.⌋

More expansively, since 1999 Canada has done much to found, chair, and shape the G8-incubated G20 forum of finance ministers and central banker governors. Paul Martin led in creating the club, in response to the Asian-turned-global financial crisis of 1997–99 (Kirton 2001; Summers 2008, Kirton 2010). It hosted the second meeting in Montreal in 2000. It also hosted the third in Ottawa in November 2001, when the September 11 terrorist attacks meant that the designated host, the United States, no longer could (Kirton 2005). It was the successful performance of the G20 finance forum that led George W. Bush to choose it to be elevated to the 'leaders' level in November 2008, to respond to the American-turned-global financial crisis of 2008–09 (Price 2009, Alexandroff and Kirton 2010).

CANADA'S SUMMIT LEADERSHIP, 1995–2001

Since post–Cold War globalization assumed full force, Canada has increasingly acted as a G8 leader and delivered results that have shaped the G8 system and global order as a whole.

At its Halifax summit in 1995, Canada succeeded in encouraging Russia's participation, in advancing the principles of sustainable development, in curtailing development assistance to recipients with excessive military expenditures, and in fostering a report on the implementation of G7 commitments (Bartleman 2005; Bayne 2000; Smith 1996; Boehm 1996). Canada also staved off an ill-prepared American initiative to launch a neoliberal 'Open Markets 2000' round of trade liberalization immediately after the Uruguay round had successfully come to an end. In December, as its hosting ended, Canada presciently helped create a G7 forum for ministers responsible for counterterrorism.

At Lyon in 1996, Canada was eager to show that, as the only other francophone G7 power, it was a full partner of host France. Both were enthusiastic about the summit's priorities of development, debt relief for the poorest, development assistance, and Africa. Canada also helped the summit to support the democratic forces in Russia in securing their electoral victory and to reassure Ukraine, and the many Canadians who could trace their origins there, that they would not be forgotten. It also helped show that the nuclear plant at Chernobyl would be closed, that nuclear proliferation would be stopped, and that Canada's CANDU program was safe. Canada worked with France and Russia to host a special Political Eight (P8) nuclear safety summit in Moscow prior to Lyon, and to strengthen Canada's distinctive national values of opposing nuclear weapons and supporting environmentalism as a result (Bartleman 2005). Canada also helped a newly vulnerable America, just hit by a new deadly attack from terrorists in the Middle East in Saudi Arabia, by extending the new G8 counterterrorism ministerial forum into the Lyon Group.

At Cologne in 1999, Canada joined with the German host, with its 'red-green' coalition government, to produce a new 'Cologne consensus' on socially sustainable globalization. (Kirton, Daniels, and Freytag 2001). Along with Britain and France, Canada advanced debt relief for the poorest. With Britain it pushed to inject ground forces for combat into Kosovo, leading the Yugoslav forces to withdraw voluntarily and prevent the emerging genocide there. At Cologne and afterward, Canada joined with Germany and Italy to mount a major G8 conflict prevention program (Kirton and Stefanova 2004).

At Okinawa in 2000, Canada supported host Japan's desire to focus on information technology for development across the growing digital divide, rather than just for economic liberalization in the rich North (Kirton and von Furstenberg 2001). Canada helped the G8 adopt the principle of cultural diversity, infusing Canada's distinctive national value of multiculturalism into the twenty-first century world order. Canada also helped move the G8 foreign ministers' agreement in principle on conflict prevention into five specific items, mostly in areas that Canada's human security initiative had pioneered (Kirton and Takase 2002; Lamy 2002). However, Canada failed to get much on debt relief for the poorest or on a food safety regime that respected Canada's use of genetically modified organisms.

For the 2001 Genoa Summit, Canada and host Italy collaborated on a strategy that would extend into Canada's hosting the next year. Canada sought to have the summit focus on reducing poverty, providing debt relief, controlling infectious disease, closing the digital divide, linking trade and development, and preventing conflict. It succeeded in having the summit focus on Africa, establish the Global Fund to Fight AIDS, Tuberculosis and Malaria, and recognize that multilateral trade liberalization should support development. It also saw the summit appoint special African personal representatives (APRs), with Canada's in the chair from the start, to help develop an action plan for Africa for the Canadian-hosted summit the following year.

At Genoa Canada, Italy, and Germany also broadened the G8's conflict prevention program into the environmental and gender domains.

Canada agreed with Japan and Russia that all three would ratify the Kyoto protocol, renounced by America's Bush, and thus bring the protocol into international legal force. Yet the innovative Canadian-supported Renewable Energies Task Force and the Digital Opportunities Task Force (DOT Force), created at Okinawa, but disliked by Bush, did not have their mandates renewed (Stephens 2006; Hart 2005).

CANADA'S LEADERSHIP, 2001–8

Al Qaeda was thwarted in its plans to kill the G8 leaders assembled at the Palazzo Ducale in Genoa during the summit on July 20–22, 2001, by crashing a hijacked civilian aircraft into the building. Seven weeks later, on 11 September 2001, it succeeded in striking the Pentagon in Washington DC and the World Trade Center in New York City in the same way.

Canada's immediate reaction was to mobilize the G8 to deliver a compelling collective response. Canada's finance officials drafted a statement saying that the G8 had faith in the world's financial system, and it was immediately issued in Italy, the G8 host (Gray 2003, 214–15). Martin's finance department also mobilized the G7/8 members to fight terrorist financing, building on the work of the 1989 Financial Action Task Force on Money Laundering (FATL), where implementation had been slow (Scherrer 2006). Jean Chrétien brushed aside the suggestion made by Alberta's premier Ralph Klein that Canada's G8 summit in Alberta 2002 be cancelled or moved.

G7 finance ministers met in Washington soon after the September 11th attacks, even though most multilateral organizations stayed closed. In November in Ottawa, Martin hosted the G20 ministerial, which would otherwise have been cancelled, as well as the International Monetary Fund's

(IMF's) International Monetary and Financial Committee (IMFC) and the IMF–World Bank's Development Committee (Kirton 2001b). The G20 meeting produced a strong consensus on combating terrorist finance, which was endorsed by the IMF and World Bank. It also endorsed Canada's preferred themes for the Kananaskis G8 of global growth and poverty reduction.

As Canada's 2002 Kananaskis Summit approached, Chrétien remained determined that the September 11 terrorists would not hijack the G8 summit agenda agreed to at Genoa, and that the summit would unfold the way he had long planned (Kirton 2002b; Smith 2001–02). At the final sherpa meeting of the Italian presidency in December 2001, Canada proposed an agenda for Kananaskis that focused tightly on terrorism, growth, and Africa. Canada sought to deliver a new paradigm for development in which recipient governments, the private sector, and civil society were full partners. It also sought to strengthen global growth prospects through structural reforms that enhanced productivity and were tailored to local circumstances, and to have existing commitments against terrorism fully implemented, made comprehensive, and reinforced by new capabilities.

To help realize its first objective of African development Canada added $1 billion in official development assistance (ODA) in its December 2001 budget, and created the Canada Fund for Africa with another $500 million to be disbursed over three years. This down payment helped catalyze major new pledges from the US, Europe, and Japan at the 2002 UN Conference on Financing for Development in Monterey. Canada also looked for a compromise between the Americans' desire for the International Development Association (IDA) to give money as grants rather than concessional loans and the Europeans' concern that such a shift would soon deplete the IDA's resources unless new money was added. Canada continued

its campaign for greater private sector participation in responding to financial crises, securing greater support after Argentina produced one of the world's largest defaults to that time in 2001.

On sustaining global growth, Canada emphasized greater productivity as key to overcoming the costs of terrorism being priced into G7 economies, and to resolving the debate between an America preferring fiscal stimulus and a Europe favouring fiscal restraint. Canada saw the recent launch of Doha Development Agenda by the World Trade Organization (WTO) as helping generate productivity-led global growth.

Kananaskis turned out to be the most successful summit to that time (Fowler 2003; Langdon 2003; Kirton and Kokotsis 2003). It produced a historically high 188 commitments. It also mobilized close to $50 billion in new monies for global public goods—$20 billion for the Global Partnership against Weapons and Materials of Mass Destruction, up to $6 billion for African development, $1 billion to top up the trust fund for heavily indebted poor countries (HIPCs), and $28 billion for the 13th replenishment of IDA funds. Only in the finance field were there few results.

At Kananaskis, four leaders from Africa's leading democratic middle powers participated as equals in the final summit session. The G8 further agreed that Russia would host the summit for the first time, in 2006. It did much to make the G8 a permanent body by defining the hosting order for the next eight years. Kananaskis thus successfully shaped global order, in the development, disarmament, and democratization domains.

THE SUBSEQUENT SUMMITS

The French-hosted Evian Summit in June 2003 took place amidst severe transatlantic tension between France and the United States over the US-led invasion of Iraq in March. Canada's objectives were to preserve the Kananaskis legacy and ensure its commitments were implemented (Kirton 2005a). Canada succeeded, both in the substance of the 206 commitments made at Evian and in the participation of the African leaders once again. Canada also strongly supported a European initiative, resisted by Japan, to tighten rules on maritime tanker safety, and saw this initiative carry the day. Canada's environmental values were further advanced by the Evian commitments on water and on science and technology for sustainable development. Evian for the first time welcomed the leaders of India, China, Brazil, Mexico, and other emerging economies, a step supporting Canadian's values of international institutionalism and globalism. Their session with G8 leaders, judged productive by all, provided a precedent that Canada's next prime minister—Paul Martin—could use as he sought to realize his vision of having the G8 summit broadened into a G20 one (Martin 2005).

The Sea Island Summit, hosted by the US in June 2004, was the first for Paul Martin as prime minister. Canada succeeded in extending the Kananaskis legacy with further action on the transport security component of counterterrorism, and the launch of the Secure and Facilitated International Travel Initiative (SAFTI). On the non-proliferation of weapons of mass destruction (WMD), Canada pushed to add a newly converted Libya and still conflict-ridden Iraq to the list of eligible recipients of support. And Canada sought and secured, over US reluctance, money for Africa as well as participation from that country.

Canada also helped lead the substantial summit accomplishments on controlling polio and HIV/AIDS. Using the UN report written by Paul Martin and former Mexican president Ernesto Zedillo, Martin also led on private sector–led development (Commission on the Private Sector and Development 2003). A multicultural Canada concerned about national unity had the G8

spontaneously include Haiti in its discussions of security issues on the summit's second night. Most broadly, a globalist Canada succeeded in having a skeptical George Bush produce a full-strength, highly successful summit with a very broad range of subjects, including African development, that reflected the priorities of both America as host and its G8 partners (Kirton 2005a; Bayne 2005). Martin's performance earned him a badly needed bounce in his sagging popularity back home amidst the general election in which he was campaigning.

At the British-hosted Gleneagles Summit in July 2005, Canada again advanced its interests and values, without much initiative or effort from a prime minister constrained by both a minority government and a national unity-related scandal at home. The two British priority themes of African development and climate change were tailor-made for a Canada committed to environmentalism. Early on, Canada helped stop some ill-conceived British initiatives to have all G8 leaders commit to giving 0.7 percent of gross domestic product (GDP) to ODA and to creating a massive international finance facility. Paul Martin worked successfully with host Tony Blair to eliminate the debt of the poorest, double ODA, and involve America and others, outside the Kyoto protocol's cutback commitments, in a new inclusive dialogue with the major emerging powers on climate change.

STEPHEN HARPER'S SUMMITS

The 2006 St Petersburg Summit marked the first outing on the full world stage for Stephen Harper, who had been elected as prime minister with a minority government on January 23. It was the second time in G8 history that Canada was represented at a summit focused on energy security by a young Albertan with little previous interest or involvement in international affairs, no ministerial experience, and at the helm of a new Conservative party, a minority government, and a cabinet with virtually no foreign policy experience at all.

Harper held several bilateral summit meetings on the way to the summit. At St Petersburg, he met with host Vladimir Putin and held a Canada–European Union summit. By the time he sat down at the G8 table, he had already met six of his fellow leaders. Harper participated substantially, speaking French half the time. He intervened on several issues, helping the summit set new market-friendly and environmentally sensitive directions on energy security.

Harper's major contribution came over the Middle East. When Hamas and Hezbollah attacked Israel just before the summit, Canada ensured that the G8's recently forged consensus on Iran's nuclear program extended to the war against terrorists in Lebanon as well. The Russians, as host, had drafted a four-paragraph statement on the Middle East that reflected their standard approach. Canada, despite summit protocol, immediately circulated an alternative, longer draft. It infuriated the Russians but secured the support of the Americans. Harper emphasized that the G8 had to consider how this crisis had started, namely with the attacks on Israel. The leaders decided on the three outstanding details, in the way the Russian host wanted, and then largely accepted the Canadian draft. In the outreach session the following day, UN secretary general Kofi Annan said he would ask for a UN resolution based on the G8 text. The balance and substance of the G8 statement were well reflected in UNSC Resolution 1701 that August. Due to the presence at St Petersburg of Annan, as well as the P5 veto power of China and the presence of the other members of the G8's Plus Five, the G8 directions and decisions were directly accepted by the much broader UN in the days that followed the summit. Due to Harper's leadership, they were also accepted by the Francophone Summit in the fall.

On energy, Canada's stress on the core principle of open markets, shared by the US and Britain, prevailed. On education, Canada's effort to reframe the priority as human capital and innovation was supported by a US focused on the knowledge economy. Canada was successful in avoiding separatist resistance in Quebec even if areas of provincial jurisdiction remained in the G8 text. On the Middle East and Lebanon, Harper's initiative and the Canadian draft flowed from his own commitment to democracy and anti-terrorism. Canada also worked closely with Nicholas Burns, the US undersecretary of state for political affairs, in producing the successful statement.

At Heiligendamm in 2007, Harper dealt with several sensitive issues. On climate change, the Germans were pushing for a hard target and timetable in the communiqué. With America's failure to ratify the Kyoto Protocol still in mind, Canada was reluctant to sign on. After several sherpa meetings and a phone call with Chancellor Angela Merkel, however, Harper relented. By May 31, Canada agreed that it would accept the proposed reduction target of 50 per cent by 2050. On June 4, at a Canada–EU summit, Canada confirmed its support for tackling greenhouse gas emissions and committed to building an effective post-Kyoto framework. For Canada, this meant getting both the Americans and emerging economies—particularly China and India—on board. The Germans and Europeans were very pleased with Canada's shift. Canada thus became the mediator between the hesitant United States and the aggressive Europeans. In the lead-up to the G8 environment ministerial, environment minister John Baird announced that Canada was working hard to include the United States and the emerging economies in the climate change discussions. By the end of the summit, Harper had brought America's Bush, along with China's Hu Jintao and India's Manmohan Singh, into a converging consensus on climate change.

On G8 expansion, Heiligendamm was the fourth summit to which the Group of Five (G5, also known as the Outreach Five and Plus Five) of China, India, Brazil, Mexico, and South Africa, had been invited since 2003. Whether they should be included more substantially was up for G8 discussion. The Japanese, Canadians, Germans, and Russians were reluctant to expand the G8. Harper understood the importance of having these emerging powers included in discussions on climate change and the economy. But the democratic values on which the G8 was founded and that Harper was keen to promote, were not shared with all, most importantly China. In the end, Harper and the others compromised when the G8 established the Heiligendamm Process of an officials-level, two-year dialogue on designated topics among the G8 and G5 members as equals (Kirton 2008). The process would give the G5 a more concrete, but still partial, role in the club, allowing the reluctant G8 members time to test the waters and see what full expansion might entail in the future.

Within the G8, many leaders, including Harper, were concerned about Russia's democratic deficit. The summit gave Harper a chance to express his concerns directly to Putin and allowed the G8 to reaffirm democratic principles throughout their communiqués.

On development, Canada was reluctant to commit more money at Heiligendamm. Instead, it emphasized the need to strengthen aid effectiveness. As a result, celebrity activist Bono called Canada a 'laggard' on African aid and accused it of blocking G8 progress in the area (Canadian Broadcasting Corporation 2007). Harper continued to lead on Afghanistan. Canada pledged $200 million for reconstruction efforts and continued to encourage fellow members to help promote democracy in the region by sending troops.

At the Hokkaido-Toyako Summit in July 2008, leaders convened just as the world economy was about to enter its biggest downturn since the Great Depression. However, despite skyrocketing oil prices and warnings from the Bank for International Settlements that things were about to get much worse, G8 leaders continued to declare that their economies were strong. They stated 'We remain positive about the long-term resilience of our economies and future global economic growth' (G8 2008).

On climate change, the summit's biggest achievement was the agreement between the G8 and their major outreach partners on a central architecture for a climate control regime to replace the flawed Kyoto approach. All leaders agreed that they must and would control their carbon emissions. They endorsed a sectoral, bottom-up approach that enabled everyone to contribute to carbon control right away, and to improve their performance as knowledge, technology and competitive pressures expanded. They also accepted the relevance of carbon sinks, starting with avoiding deforestation. This would allow the biodiversity powers of Brazil, Indonesia, the US, Canada, and Russia to make an enhanced contribution that was finally counted. Together these new principles of 'all in', 'bottom up', and 'sinks count' formed the foundation for a 'beyond Kyoto' regime that promised to cope effectively with the urgent and existential problem of climate change. All leaders agreed to cut their carbon emissions by at least 50 per cent by 2050. They also agreed on the importance of setting medium-term targets and timetables, which would build on the considerable commonality created to that point. These agreements represented a striking acceptance of Harper's core approach.

On food, the G8 endorsed a strategic grains reserve. Here the countries promised to stockpile in a coordinated manner grains that would be released into the market when scarcity arose. This was meant to lower food prices, inflation, and stagflation in the G8 and stop starvation, malnutrition, and social unrest in the developing world. As one of the world's great grain-producing powers, Canada, along with the US and Russia, contributed substantially to the reserve. Canada also urged the G8 to invest in innovative agriculture technologies for Africa, to help improve food production there.

On Zimbabwe, in response to the failure of Robert Mugabe to hold a free and fair election just before the summit, the G8 stated that his regime was illegitimate. At the summit Harper intervened strongly, stating that this regime could not be tolerated and that there was need for fundamental change in the country. He hoped for the restoration of the rule of law and a renewed commitment to democratic processes and respect for human rights. While other members were less willing to question the undemocratic government, Canada pushed for immediate sanctions.

Canada and the G8 also pushed for a more democratic and transparent regime in Myanmar. The population, devastated by a recent cyclone, desperately needed aid. The G8 was willing to provide it, but the Myanmar government was denying it entry. On Afghanistan, which remained a Canadian priority, the G8 foreign ministers issued a standalone statement that highlighted continued support for Afghanistan's national development strategy. At the summit, the G8 leaders reiterated their support. They recognized that there was still much work to do in regard to coordination on the ground.

There was no further move to expand the G5's role in the G8 process. As host and the most reluctant member, Japan did not place the issue on their agenda. The interim report on the Heiligendamm Process, delivered at the summit, received a warm welcome.

Harper used the summit to reinforce Canada's bilateral relationship with Japan. As Canada owed Japan a bilateral visit, Harper met with Prime Minister Yasuo Fukuda in Tokyo on the day after the summit. The two discussed the Japanese abduction issue and intervention in Burma. They also continued the discussions that had taken place at the G8.

The 2009 L'Aquila Summit was more flexible and fluid than many previous summits. It involved a very large number of participants and a wide range of topics. On G8 architecture, the G8 strengthened its internal operations and external credibility by starting the first serious process of accountability. Led by Canada, Britain, and the US—the G8's leading compliers with their commitments—it centred on identifying the meaning of the many commitments the G8 leaders collectively made at L'Aquila and previous summits, as well as compliance measures for G8 members.

Harper also led on aid to Africa. Canada was the first member to keep its 2005 commitment to double aid to Africa—doing so one year ahead of time, in the spring of 2009. Canada was also an early contributor to and supporter of Barack Obama's initiative on food security. Harper, personally moved by the devastation of the earthquake in L'Aquila, had Canada donate to the rebuilding effort there.

The G8 and G5 extended the Heiligendamm Process by two years and renamed it the Heiligendamm L'Aquila Process (HAP). They broadened its mandate to include any subject and allow other countries to join on a case-by-case basis. They agreed that this increased inclusiveness would take place at 'all levels'.

The many widespread references to the G20 in the communiqués issued by the G8 and others at L'Aquila showed that leaders wanted the G20 to reinforce rather than rival the G8, and that the G8 would continue to be the source of leadership within and for the wider G20. Above all, the G8, alone as well as with the G5, repeatedly agreed in their communiqués that the G8 summit would take place in France in 2011—the usual time and place for a new cycle of G8 summitry to begin.

G20 SUMMITRY

As Canada looked forward to its G8 summit in Huntsville in June 2010, it did so knowing that a key question was how to coordinate the summit with the new G20 summit process that had been catalyzed by the American-turned-global financial and economic crisis erupting with full force with the failure of Lehman Brothers in September 2008. A decade earlier, the Asian-turned-global financial crisis had led Paul Martin as finance minister to create the G20 club where the finance ministers and central bankers of systemically significant countries could gather every autumn to consider and come to consensus on ways to strengthen financial stability and make globalization work for all (Kirton 2001b). During the following decade, the G20 had proved its worth (Kirton 2005b; Kirton and Koch 2008). It was thus rational for Bush, who had earlier resisted Martin's pleas to elevate it to the leaders' level, to do just that when the new financial crisis struck (Price 2009).

After Lehman collapsed, Canada helped bridge the differences between Bush and France's Nicolas Sarkozy, who had very different views on where the summit would take place, who would be invited, and who would host. While Bush won on these issues, Canada successfully supported France's desire to invite its fellow Europeans, Spain and the Netherlands. To prepare the first G20 summit, held in Washington on November 14–15, 2008, Harper gave the lead to his personal representative for the G8 to facilitate coordination between the two clubs.

At Washington, Canada sought an agreement on coordinated fiscal and monetary stimulus. Harper spoke out strongly, to the Americans' approval, on the need to design exit strategies from the start. Harper, along with Korean president Lee Myung-bak, also wanted the leaders to take a strong anti-protectionist pledge in order to foster open trade. On these priorities Canada succeeded, even if the first was implemented more reliably than the second. Harper also went along with Sarkozy's crusade to crack down on tax havens, although at the IMF Canada represented some Commonwealth Caribbean countries whose status as offshore financial centres was important as their economies had been badly hit. Canada strongly supported implementing the principles on domestic financial regulation with a firm deadline, through work done by the G20 finance ministers and the FSF.

Canada continued to promote these priorities at the second G20 summit, held in London, England, on 1–2 April, 2009 (Kirton and Koch 2009a). On trade, Canada's credibility was enhanced by the unilateral tariff reductions Canada had introduced in its budget of January 29, 2009. Canada succeeded in securing a stronger version of the anti-protectionist pledge, with a commitment to redress protectionist measures taken in the recent past. As this was the first G20 summit attended by the new US president, Barack Obama, whose preferences and instincts on trade were uncertain, it was important to have Obama accept this pledge. It was also important to have him buy into the value of such summitry, which he did. Canada also supported the summit's signature accomplishment of raising $1.1 trillion in new money to support global stimulus and development. As its contribution, Canada gave the International Monetary Fund another $10 billion, in accordance with its relative weight there.

At the third G20 summit, held in Pittsburgh on 24–25 September, 2009, Canada again succeeded in advancing these priorities. Moreover, it played a key part in institutionalizing the summit in the desired way as a permanent global governance forum (Kirton and Koch 2009c). Canada secured a strong summit commitment to stay the course on stimulus until recovery was assured, and to start designing the smart strategies that would be needed when the stimulus could be taken off. To support the stimulus message, Canada maintained its Bank of Canada program that offered $1.25 million in mortgage support. On financial regulation, ahead of the summit Harper said Canada would accept whatever consensus emerged on banking capital, although it had experienced no problems with its regulatory system at home. On trade, just before the summit, Canada reinforced its open markets message by again unilaterally cutting tariffs on imported machinery and equipment. And as the summit opened, Canada unilaterally announced that it would offer $2.6 billion in callable capital to the African Development Bank to support development on the continent, adding to its status as the first G8 country to meet its Gleneagles commitment to double aid to Africa by 2010.

Canada's greatest success came with the institutionalization of G20 summitry. Knowing that the Republic of Korea would chair the G20 finance ministers' forum in 2010, when Canada served as G8 host, Canada started at an early stage to discuss with Korea how best to coordinate the two events. Harper sent his sherpa to Seoul and spoke with Lee Myung-bak directly at the G8 L'Aquila Summit. While the Koreans had hoped to host the next G20 summit in Korea in April 2010, the encounter had to be deferred when Obama scheduled his nuclear summit, strongly supported by an anti-militarist Canada, in Washington in late March. Harper and Lee then agreed that they would co-chair the next G20 summit and hold it in June in tandem with the G8 summit Harper would host that month in Canada. Korea would host a stand-alone G20 summit in Korea in November, the traditional time when the annual G20 finance ministers' meeting was held. All G20 leaders agreed to institutionalize the G20 as the primary forum for international economic governance.

Thus all agreed to start permanent, premier G20 summitry in Canada, with Canada as co-chair, and as a coordinated addition to the G8 summit that Canada would host. This result was especially favourable for Canada.

The addition of the G20 fit well with the priorities and agenda Canada had constructed for its G8 Muskoka Summit. Harper had strategically announced Muskoka themes, along with the location, in the summer of 2008, signalling that open markets, global warming, democracy, and the rule of the law would form the foundation of his approach. In July 2009 he expanded his agenda into the four pillars of economic management, climate change through clean energy technology and the Major Economies Forum, development, and democracy (Kirton and Koch 2009a). The economic pillar has grown beyond trade to focus on exit strategies and employment, and the assumption of these topics by the tandem G20 summit has given the G8 and its invited partners more time to focus on the remaining pillars. The big winner was development, which was added to the 2008 trilogy and given greater definition with the choice of ODA, infectious disease, health, education, and maternal and childhood well-being.

On the road to both the G8 summit in Huntsville and the G20 summit in Toronto, Canada's influence was increasingly clear. All G8 partners endorsed Canada's agenda of making children's and maternal health the top priority, and featuring food security, Haitian reconstruction, nuclear security, vulnerable states, and Afghanistan-Pakistan. Most agreed to make accountability and effectiveness the defining feature of both summits. And in the G20 preparatory process, Canada was able to lead a coalition of Japan and most non-G8 members of the G20, to beat back a domestically-driven proposal for a new bank tax from fiscally beleaguered Britain, France, and the United States.

CAUSES OF CANADA'S SUMMIT SUCCESS

External determinants

Canada's increasingly energetic and effective leadership was driven at the systemic level by a post–Cold War, rapidly globalizing, post–September 11 world that increased America's new non-state vulnerability and reinforced it with a succession of ever stronger shocks.

American vulnerability to state and then non-state forces soared, in energy after 1973, in civilian nuclear power after 1979, in terrorism after 1979, and in finance after 1998. In each case, a relatively invulnerable Canada stood out among the G8 partners with the relevant specialized capabilities to help.

In energy, amidst the oil shocks of 1973 and 1979, American dependence on imported oil rose from 35 per cent of its national requirement in the late 1970s to more than 50 per cent by 2004. During this time energy-rich Canada became America's secure, terrorist free Saudi Arabia right next door, while energy-superpower Russia joined the G8 club. The solution to America's growing energy security vulnerability lay largely within the G8 and with the two otherwise weakest members of the club.

In civilian nuclear power, the shocks of America's Three Mile Island explosion in 1979, Chernobyl in the USSR in 1986, and the nuclear accident at Japan's Tokaimura plant in 1999 reduced the easy availability of the first alternative energy source for first-ranked America and second-ranked Japan (Donnelly 2002). Canada remained an accident-free, civilian nuclear power.

In terrorism, the threat soon spread from a Palestinian skyjacking in Germany in 1977 to the US, starting with Iran in 1979, then Lebanon in 1983, the Persian Gulf in 1996, Africa in the late 1990s, and America itself in 1993, 2001, and again in almost deadly form in 2009 and 2010. Canada remained the only G8 member without an international terrorist death on or over its own soil since 1975.

In finance, the 1998 collapse of American hedge fund Long-Term Capital Management during the 1997–99 financial crisis transformed America from a producer to a consumer of financial security. Even though Canada had a smaller, more open economy, it escaped unscathed. Its growing fiscal surplus allowed it to provide financial support to afflicted countries around the world, even when America could not. This difference was magnified in 2008 when the American-turned-global financial crisis did much to constrain America's economic capability, while a financially unscarred Canada led the G8 in having the lowest projected government debt as a share of GDP from 2009 to 2014.

In the environment, the 2005 devastation of New Orleans by Hurricane Katrina dramatically showed America its vulnerability to sea-level rise from climate change, especially as its political capital, economic capital, and most of its major cities lie on coastlines. The April 2010 oil rig accident in the Gulf of Mexico reinforced the shock. Despite the potential problems of a melting Arctic, Canada, with few of its major cities on the sea coast, was the G8 country least vulnerable to uncontrolled climate change.

In social cohesion, where America had been vulnerable to civil strife since the riots of 1964, the twenty-first century brought a more pervasive threat. The 2005 hurricane damage to New Orleans exposed the entrenched racial divisions there. Elsewhere, the home-grown terrorist attacks in London in 2005, the riots around Paris, and racially motivated murders in Russia highlighted a threat throughout the G8. Yet Canada, once the October

1995 Quebec referendum on separatism was won, stood apart, with its strong social cohesion reinforced by its relatively high multicultural capability rank (Culpeper, Emelifeonwu, and Scarpa de Masellis 2003).

Furthermore, the G8 institutionally thickened as an informal, leaders-driven concert, where the smallest number of democratically committed major powers could efficiently and cohesively decide how best to combine the maximum amount of predominant capability to provide global governance and global public goods. The addition of only democratic powers—the EU in 1977 and Russia in 1998—and the expansion of the EU to include 25 countries by 2004, helped maintain its small size, expanded its combined capabilities, and reduced the number of its rivals outside the club. At the same time, only democratic polities were allowed in. In its 2003 rankings, Freedom House gave its highest grade of 1 on a 1–7 scale to Canada, France, Germany, Italy, the US, and Britain, 1.5 to Japan, and 5.0 to Russia, for an average score of 1.6. The G8 also became more of a leaders-driven body after 1998, when the finance and foreign ministers stopped joining their leaders at the summit itself.

The arrival of the supplementary G20 summit in 2008 continued this pattern of controlled participation on overwhelmingly democratic foundation, especially as the democratic Netherlands and Spain were added to the initial summits, offsetting the G20's Chinese and Saudi Arabian authoritarian regimes. The arrival of the G20 summit alongside the G8 again showed the deep failure of the old multilateral organizations, born at San Francisco in 1945 and Bretton Woods in 1944.

Societal determinants

At the societal level, the Canadian public consistently supported the G8 summit as an institution as well as the particular priorities that Canada brought there. This consensus survived the delegitimizing violence of the 2001 Genoa Summit and the distraction of the September 11 terrorist attacks. Most Canadians consistently recognized that the G8 bestowed principal power status on their country, helped it preserve its national unity and security, and allowed it effectively to advance its distinctive national values in the world. Even as the G8 and G20 took up deeply domestic subjects, such as education and securities regulation respectively, Canada's provincial governments were decreasingly able to inhibit the federal government's diplomacy in the summit clubs. Moreover, Canadian interest groups became increasingly involved directly in G8 governance, through the many civil-society G8 institutions that arose from 2000 on.

Governmental determinants

At the top level of the federal government, Canada usually sent highly experienced leaders to the summit, notably Trudeau from 1976 to 1984 (save for 1979), Mulroney from 1984 to 1992, Chrétien from 1994 to 2003, Martin in 2004 and 2005, and Harper from 2006 on. Moreover, Chrétien had been involved in the G7 as Trudeau's finance minister, and Martin had nine years of G7/8 experience as Chrétien's minister of finance.

At the official level, Canada's G8 and G20 participation was usually led by the prime minister's group or the foreign affairs deputy minister, who simultaneously served as the prime minister's personal representative, or 'sherpa'. That individual was supported by a permanent, well-resourced office within the Department of Foreign Affairs and International Trade (Kokotsis 1999). In 2008 he was given the responsibility for preparing the G20 summits too, helping ensure coordination between the two clubs.

CONCLUSION

In order to behave as a principal power, Canada must have a continuing, comprehensive effectiveness in shaping world order in its own image, in terms of the ideas and institutions that dominate global governance as a whole. Through, and due to, the G8 and G20 summits, Canada has accomplished this. Since the 1975 start of the G8 summit-centred system, Canada secured a first-tier place as an equal in all its institutions. It used its position to advance its interests, values, and preferences; to assemble partners that supported them; to prevail in summit outcomes; and to have all ranking members comply with them to a high degree. Canada helped the G8 and G20 develop as effective institutionalized centres of global governance, with summits that together innovatively integrate all of the world's economic, social, and political security priorities, and with a ministerial and official-level system that operates continuously in support. Canadian leadership has helped the G8 to develop as the effective ideational centre of global governance. Through its war in Kosovo in 1999, the G8 produced the practice and precedent of the international responsibility to protect that the UN was to accept in principle in 2005.

In 1975, Canada began to emerge as a principal power when America—affected by its defeat in Vietnam, its energy vulnerability in the 1973 oil shock, and the collapse of its old multilateral regimes for nuclear non-proliferation, finance, trade, and democratization—reached out to Canada and to its other ranking allies to create the G8. Through the early years of G8 summitry, Canada emerged as a principal power, sometimes aligning itself with the Unites States, but often taking the lead among lesser G8 powers, including Italy, Germany, and Japan. Canada began to shape the G8 agenda, bringing development, open trade and debt relief to the table. Through the early years of the twenty-first century, Canada's role as a G8 leader was cemented during the Asian-turned-global financial crisis, the September 11, 2001, terrorist attacks, and the most recent American-bred financial crisis. By 2008, now far more vulnerable to new, often non-state threats in Iraq and Afghanistan, and from now globalized terrorism, WMD, and concerns about energy, the environment, health, and finance, a declining America reached out to create a summit of the G20 that Canada had promoted, in order to defend America and shape global order as a whole. As a result, Canada finally attained the position of a principal power in a much-changed world guided by co-operating G8 and G20 clubs with Canada leading from inside.

Key Terms

Diplomacy of Concert
Heiligendamm Process

Sherpa
Summit

Notes

1. Canada had been included in the G7 in 1976 not primarily because the US wanted or needed another North American neighbour to balance the Europeans, or because former Michigan congressman Gerald Ford liked his Canadian neighbours. It was included because Henry Kissinger knew from the start that an oil- and resource-dependent America needed the first-tier capabilities of a foremost nation—Canada—within the new concert governance club (von Reikhoff 1974).

References

Alexandroff, Alan, and John Kirton. (2010). 'The "Great Recession" and the Emergence of the G-20 Leaders' Summit.' In Alan Alexandroff and Andrew Fenton Cooper, eds., *Rising States, Rising Institutions: Can the World be Governed?* (Brookings Press).

Artis, Michael, and Sylvia Ostry. (1988). 'Summitry: The Medium and the Message.' Bissell Paper No. 3 (Toronto: University of Toronto, Centre for International Studies).

Axworthy, Lloyd (2003). *Navigating a New World: Canada's Global Future* (Toronto: Knopf).

Bartleman, James. (2005). *Rollercoaster: My Hectic Years as Jean Chretien's Diplomatic Advisor, 1994–1998* (Toronto: McClelland and Stewart).

Bayne, Nicholas. (2000). *Hanging In There: The G7 and G8 Summit in Maturity and Renewal* (Ashgate: Aldershot).

Bayne, Nicholas (2003). 'Impressions of the Kananaskis Summit, 26–27 June 2002.' In Michele Fratianni, Paolo Savona, and John Kirton, eds., *Sustaining Global Growth and Development: G7 and IMF Governance* (Aldershot: Ashgate).

Bayne, Nicholas. (2005). *Staying Together: The G8 Summit Confronts to 21st Century* (Aldershot: Ashgate).

Black, David. (2005). 'From Kananaskis to Gleneagles: Assessing Canadian "leadership" on Africa.' *Behind the Headlines* 62 (May): 1–16.

Boehm, Peter. (1996). 'There Was a Summit in Halifax.' *Bout de Papier* 13 (Spring): 5–7.

Bothwell, Robert. (1993). 'Canada and G7: The Adventures of a Marginal Power at the Summits.' In Fabrizio Ghilardi, ed., *Canada and Italy in the World: Current Opportunities, Future Possibilities*, pp. 95–103 (Pisa: Edizioni ETS).

Burney, Derek. (2005). *Getting It Done: A Memoir* (Montreal and Kingston: McGill-Queen's University Press).

Canada. Department of Foreign Affairs and International Trade. (1995). *Canada in the World: Canadian Foreign Policy Review.* www.international.gc.ca/foreign_policy/cnd-world/menu-en.asp (October 2009).

Canadian Broadcasting Corporation. (2007). 'Bono, Geldof Slam Canada as a "Laggard" on African Aid.' June 9. www.cbc.ca/world/story/2007/06/08/harper-g8.html (October 2009).

Chrétien, Jean. (2007). *My Years as Prime Minister* (Toronto: Knopf).

Cohn, Theodore. (2002). *Governing Global Trade: International Institutions in Conflict and Convergence* (Aldershot: Ashgate).

Commission on the Private Sector and Development. (2003). *Unleashing Entrepreneurship: Making Business Work for the Poor.* United Nations Development Programme, New York. www.undp.org/cpsd/report (October 2009).

Cooper, Andrew F., Richard Higgott, and Kim Nossal. (1993). *Relocating Middle Powers: Australia and Canada in a Changing World Order* (Vancouver: University of British Columbia Press).

Culpeper, Roy, David Emelifeonwu, and Luigi Scarpa de Masellis. (2003). 'Architecture Without Blueprints.' *International Journal* 58 (autumn): 667–700.

Dam, Kenneth. (2001). 'Hunting Down Dirty Cash.' *Financial Times* (December 12): 17.

David, Charles-Philippe, and Stéphane Roussel. (1998). 'Middle Power Blues: Canadian International Security after the Cold War.' *American Review of Canadian Studies* (Spring/Summer): 131–56.

Dewitt, David, and John Kirton. (1983). *Canada as a Principal Power* (Toronto: John Wiley).

Dobson, Wendy. (1991a). *Economic Policy Coordination: Requiem or Prologue?* (Washington DC: Institute for International Economics).

Dobson, Wendy. (1991b). 'Rethinking the G7: A New World Coordination Process.' *International Economic Insights* 2 (March/April): 34–35.

Dobson, Wendy. (1995). 'Summitry and the International Monetary System: The Past as Prologue.' *Canadian Foreign Policy* 3(1): 5–15.

Donnelly, Michael. (2002). 'Nuclear Safety and Criticality at Tokaimura: A Failure of Governance.' In John Kirton and Junichi Takase, eds., *New Directions in Global Political Governance: The G8 and International Order in the Twenty-First Century* (Aldershot: Ashgate).

Eayrs, James. (1974). 'Defining a New Place for Canada in the Hierarchy of World Powers.' *International Perspectives* (May/June): 15–24.

Fowler, Robert. (2003). 'Canadian Leadership and the Kananaskis G8 Summit: Toward a Less Self-Centred Policy.' In David Carment, Fen Osler Hampson, and Norman Hillmer, eds., *Canada Among Nations 2003: Coping with the American Colossus*, pp. 219–241 (Toronto: Oxford University Press).

Fréchette, Louise. (1995). 'The Halifax Summit: A Canadian Perspective.' *North American Outlook* 3 (June): 7–13.

G8. (2008). 'World Economy.' July 8, Toyako, Hokkaido. www.g8.utoronto.ca/summit/2008hokkaido/2008-economy.html (October 2009).

G8 Research Group. (1996–). Annual compliance reports. www.g8.utoronto.ca/compliance (October 2009).

Gordon, Nancy. (2005). 'Humanitarian Challenges and Canadian Responses.' In David Carment, Fen Osler Hampson, and Norman Hillmer, eds., *Canada Among Nations 2004: Setting Priorities Straight*, pp. 93–100 (Montreal and Kingston: McGill-Queen's University Press).

Gotlieb, Allan. (1987). *Canada and Economic Summits: Power and Responsibility.* Bissell Paper No. 1 (Toronto: University of Toronto, Centre for International Studies).

Gray, John. (2003). *Paul Martin: The Politics of Ambition* (Toronto: Key Porter).

Hajnal, Peter. (1999). *The G7/G8 System: Evolution, Role, and Documentation* (Aldershot: Ashgate).

Haynal, George. (2005). 'Summitry and Governance: The Case for a G-xx.' In David Carment, Fen Osler Hampson, and Norman Hillmer, eds., *Canada Among Nations 2004: Setting Priorities Straight*, pp. 261–274 (Montreal and Kingston: McGill-Queen's University Press).

Hart, Jeffrey. (2005). 'The G8 and the Governance of Cyberspace,' in Michele Fratianni, John Kirton, Alan Rugman, and Paolo Savona, eds., *New Perspectives on the Global Governance: Why America Needs the G8* (Aldershot: Ashgate).

Heinbecker, Paul, and Rob McRae. (2001). 'Case Study: The Kosovo Air Campaign.' In Rob McRae and Don Hubert, eds., *Human Security and the New Diplomacy* (Montreal and Kingston: McGill-Queen's University Press).

Helleiner, Gerald. (1995). 'Testimony on "Agenda for the G7 Summit in Halifax"' Canada, House of Commons, Standing Committee on Foreign Affairs and International Trade, Minutes of Proceedings and Evidence, Issue 16, February 21.

Keating, Tom. (1993). *Canada and World Order: The Multilateralist Tradition in Canadian Foreign Policy* (Toronto: McClelland and Stewart).

Keating, Tom. (2002). *Canada and World Order: The Multilateralist Tradition in Canadian Foreign Policy*, 2nd ed. (Toronto: Oxford University Press).

Kirton, John. (1995). 'The Diplomacy of Concert: Canada, the G7, and the Halifax Summit.' *Canadian Foreign Policy* 3 (Spring): 63–80.

Kirton, John. (1998). 'Towards Trans-Pacific Partnership: Canada and Japan in the G7, 1975–1995.' In Michael Fry, John Kirton, and Mitsuru Kurosawa, eds., *The North Pacific Triangle: United States, Japan, and Canada at the End of the Century*, pp. 292–313 (Toronto: University of Toronto Press).

Kirton, John. (1999). 'Canada as a Principal Financial Power: G7 and IMF Diplomacy in the Crisis of 1997–99.' *International Journal* 54 (Autumn): 603–624.

Kirton, John. (2000a). 'The Dynamics of G7 Leadership in Crisis Response and System Reconstruction.' In Karl Kaiser, John Kirton, and Joseph Daniels, eds., *Shaping a New International Financial System: Challenges of Governance in a Globalizing World* (Aldershot: Ashgate).

Kirton, John. (2000b). 'The G8, the United Nations, and Global Peace and Security Governance.' In Winrich Kuhne with Jochen Prantly, eds., *The Security Council and the G8 in the New Millennium: Who Is in Charge of International Peace and Security?* (Berlin: Stiftung Wissenschaft und Politik).

Kirton, John. (2001). 'The G20: Representativeness, Effectiveness and Leadership in Global Governance.' In John Kirton, Joseph Daniels, and Andreas Freytag, eds., *Guiding Global Order: G8 Governance in the Twenty-First Century*, pp.143–173 (Aldershot: Ashgate).

Kirton, John. (2002). 'Canada's Kananaskis G8 Summit: What Can and Should be Done?' *Canadian Foreign Policy* 9 (June).

Kirton, John. (2005a). 'America at the G8: From Vulnerability to Victory at the Sea Island Summit.' In Michele Fratianni, John Kirton, Alan Rugman, and Paolo Savona, eds., *New Perspectives on Global Governance: Why America Needs the G8*, pp. 31–50. (Aldershot: Ashgate).

Kirton, John. (2005b). 'Towards Multilateral Reform: The G20's Contribution.' In John English, Ramesh Thakur, and Andrew F. Cooper, eds., *Reforming from the Top: A Leaders' 20 Summit*, pp. 141–168 (Tokyo: United Nations University).

Kirton, John. (2007a). 'Canada as a G8 Principal Power.' In Duane Bratt and Christopher Kukucha, eds., *Readings in Canadian Foreign Policy: Classic Debates and New Ideas* (Toronto: Oxford University Press), pp. 298–315.

Kirton, John. (2007b). *Canadian Foreign Policy in a Changing World* (Toronto: Thomson).

Kirton, John. (2008). 'From G8 2003 to G13 2010? The Heiligendamm Process's Past, Present, and Future.' In Andrew F. Cooper and Agata Antkiewicz, eds., *Emerging Powers in Global Governance: Lessons from the Heiligendamm Process* (Waterloo ON: Wilfrid Laurier University Press).

Kirton, John. (2008/9). 'Consequences of the 2008 US Elections for America's Climate Change Policy, Canada, and the World,' *International Journal* 64(1): 153–162.

Kirton, John. (2010). 'The G20 Finance's Global Governance Network.' In Alan Alexandroff and Andrew Fenton Cooper, eds., *Rising States, Rising Institutions: Can the World be Governed?* (Brookings Press).

Kirton, John, Joseph Daniels, and Andreas Freytag, eds. (2001). *Guiding Global Order: G8 Governance in the Twenty-First Century* (Ashgate: Aldershot).

Kirton, John, and Jenilee Guebert. (2009). 'Canada's G8 Global Health Diplomacy: Lessons for 2010.' *Canadian Foreign Policy* 15(3).

Kirton, John, and Madeline Koch. (2008). *Growth, Innovation, Inclusion: The G20 at Ten* (London: Newsdesk).

Kirton, John, and Madeline Koch. (2009a). *G8 2009: From La Maddalena to L'Aquila* (London: Newsdesk).

Kirton, John, and Madeline Koch. (2009b). *The G20 London Summit: Growth, Jobs, Stability* (London: Newsdesk).

Kirton, John, and Madeline Koch. (2009c). *The G20 Pittsburgh Summit 2009* (London: Newsdesk).

Kirton, John, and Ella Kokotsis. (2003). 'The G7/8 Contribution at Kananaskis and Beyond.' In Michele Fratianni, Paolo Savona, and John Kirton, eds., *Sustaining Global Growth and Development: G7 and IMF Governance* (Aldershot: Ashgate).

Kirton, John, Marina Larionova, and Paolo Savona. (in press). *Making Economic Global Governance Effective: Hard and Soft Law Institutions in a Crowded World* (Farnham UK: Ashgate).

Kirton, John, and Radoslava Stefanova, eds. (2004). *The G8, The United Nations, and Conflict Prevention* (Aldershot: Ashgate).

Kirton, John, and Junichi Takase, eds. (2002). *New Directions in Global Political Governance: The G8 and International Order in the Twenty-First Century* (Aldershot: Ashgate).

Kirton, John, and George von Furstenberg, eds. (2001). *New Directions in Global Economic Governance: Managing Globalisation in the Twenty-First Century* (Ashgate: Aldershot).

Kissinger, Henry. (1979). *White House Years* (Boston: Little, Brown).

Kokotsis, Eleanore. (1999). *Keeping International Commitments: Compliance, Credibility, and the G7, 1988–1995* (New York: Garland).

Lamy, Stephen. (2002). 'The G8 and the Human Security Agenda.' In John Kirton and Junichi Takase, eds., *New Directions in Global Political Governance: The G8 and International Order in the Twenty-First Century* (Aldershot: Ashgate).

Langdon, Steven. (2003). 'NEPAD and the Renaissance of Africa.' In *Canada Among Nations 2003: Coping with the American Colossus*, pp. 242–255 (Toronto: Oxford University Press).

Lovbraek, A. (1990). 'International Reform and the Like-Minded Countries in the North-South Dialogue 1975–1985.' In Cranford Pratt, ed., *Middle Power Internationalism: The North-South Dimension* (Montreal and Kingston: McGill-Queen's University Press).

Maclean's. (2001). 'Maclean's Year-End Poll: Since September 11,' *Maclean's* 114, no. 53 (31 December).

Martin, Paul. (2005). 'A Global Answer to Global Problems: The Case for a New Leaders' Forum, *Foreign Affairs* 84 (May–June): 206.

Martin, Paul. (2008). *Hell or High Water: My Life In and Out of Politics* (Toronto: McClelland and Stewart).

MacMillan, Charles, and Louis Delvoie. (1999). 'Taming the South Asian Nuclear Tiger: Causes, Consequences and Canadian Responses.' In Fen Osler Hampson, Michael Hart, and Martin Rudner, eds., *Canada Among Nations 1999: A Big League Player?* (Toronto: Oxford University Press).

Mulroney, Brian. (2007). *Memoirs: 1939–1993* (Toronto: McClelland and Stewart).

Ostry, Sylvia. (1986). 'International Economic Policy Coordination.' *Chatham House Papers*, Vol. 30. (London and New York: Routledge & Kegan Paul).

Ostry, Sylvia. (1990). 'Canada, Europe, and the Economic Summits.' Paper presented at the All-European Canadian Studies Conference, The Hague, October 24–27.

Press, Kate. (2008). 'International Assistance to Secure Access to Essential Medicines.' In Brian Tomlin, Norman Hillmer, and Fen Osler Hampson, eds., *Canada's International Policies: Agendas, Alternatives, and Policies*, pp. 349–360 (Toronto: Oxford University Press).

Price, Daniel. (2009). 'Recovery and Reform.' In John Kirton and Madeline Koch, eds., *G8 2009: From La Maddalena to L'Aquila* (London: Newsdesk).

Rioux, Jean-Sébastien. (2006). 'Canadian Official Development Assistance Policy: Juggling the National Interest and Humanitarian Impulses.' In Patrick James, Nelson Michaud, and Marc O'Reilly, eds., *Handbook of Canadian Foreign Policy*, pp. 209–234 (Lanham MA: Lexington Books).

Scherrer, Amandine. (2006). 'Explaining Compliance with International Commitments to Combat Financial Crime, the G8, and FATF.' Paper presented at the 2006 annual meeting of the International Studies Association, San Diego, March 22–25. www.g8.utoronto.ca/scholar/scherrer.pdf (October 2009).

Smith, Gordon. (1996). 'Canada and the Halifax Summit.' In Fen Osler Hampson and Maureen Appel Molot, eds., *Big Enough to Be Heard: Canada Among Nations 1996*, pp. 83–94 (Ottawa: Carleton University Press).

Smith, Gordon. (2001–02), 'It's a Long Way from Halifax to Kananaskis.' *International Journal* 57 (Winter): 123–127.

Stairs, Denis (1974). *The Diplomacy of Constraint: Canada, the Korean War, and the United States* (Toronto: University of Toronto Press).

Stephens, Gina. (2006). 'G8 Institutionalization as a Cause of Compliance: The DOT Force Case.' Paper presented at the annual meeting of the International Studies Association, San Diego, March 22–25. www.g8.utoronto.ca/scholar/stephens_060326.pdf (October 2009).

Summers, Lawrence. (2008). 'The Birth of the G20.' In John Kirton and Madeline Koch, eds., *Growth, Innovation, Inclusion: The G20 at Ten* (London: Newsdesk).

Summit Reform Study Group. (1991). *The Summit Process and Collective Security: Future Responsibility Sharing* (Washington DC: Group of Thirty).

Tomlin, Brian, Norman Hillmer, and Fen Osler Hampson. (2008). *Canada's International Policies: Agendas, Alternatives, and Policies* (Toronto: Oxford University Press).

Von Furstenberg, George, and Joseph Daniels. (1991). 'Policy Undertakings by the Seven "Summit" Countries: Ascertaining the Degree of Compliance.' *Carnegie-Rochester Conference Series of Public Policy* 35: 267–308.

Von Reikhoff, Harald. (1974). 'The Natural Resource Element in Global Power Relationships.' *International Perspectives* (September–October): 18–22.

Wood, Bernard. (1988). 'Critical Choices.' In John Holmes and John Kirton, eds., *Canada and the New Internationalism* (Toronto: Canadian Institute of International Affairs).

Wood, Duncan. (2006). 'Canada and International Financial Policy: Non-hegemonic Leadership and Systemic Stability.' In Patrick James, Nelson Michaud, and Marc O'Reilly, eds., *Handbook of Canadian Foreign Policy*, pp. 265–286 (Lanham MA: Lexington Books).

10

THE ACHILLES' HEEL OF CANADIAN GOOD INTERNATIONAL CITIZENSHIP: INDIGENOUS DIPLOMACIES AND STATE RESPONSE

Andrew F. Cooper and P. Whitney Lackenbauer

Since the Second World War, First Nations leaders have regularly sought the support of international bodies and agencies in the struggle to have human rights respected by Canada. The international presence is driven by the failure of Canadian governments and courts to sensitively address First Nations concerns. Given that Canada prides itself on its international human rights commitments, raising issues at the international level has been an important way for us to gain attention for our grievances. (Ovide Mercredi quoted in Mercredi and Turpell 1993: 187–88)

At the core of Canada's identity as a diplomatic actor is the image of good international citizenship. Vigorous debates have ensued about the form, intensity, and targeting of this role in the world. What can be termed the 'maximalist approach' focuses on an upgraded position in which Canada elevates itself to the position of global model country (Welsh 2004). The traditional position, however, is cautious about Canada over-stretching its commitments, but is eager to locate particular areas where Canada can make a difference on an issue-specific basis. Functional areas—or niches—are sought where Canada can run with well-defined campaigns (Cooper 1997). As revealed by the differences between the Chrétien–Axworthy push on landmines and the International Criminal Court, Paul Martin's enthusiasm for a Leaders' 20, and Mulroney's departure from the Thatcher/Reagan consensus on South Africa, the 'what, where, and why' behind this type of initiative diplomacy may differ, but the 'how' keeps to a well rehearsed script which prioritizes the value of global governance.

Some attention has been devoted to areas that reveal Canada's negative side as an international player. Canada's tendency to seek status has become a common theme. So has the tendency for Canada to backslide on some of its international promises in the areas of human rights and the environment. Words and deeds have been mismatched across a wide spectrum of issues. Above all, the gap between Canada's self-image as a good international citizen and the flaws in its own record is highlighted by Indigenous issues. Unlike the situational aspects of targeting specific governments for their human rights records, the Indigenous question is in many respects an embedded structural predicament, juxtaposing the mainstream identity of Canada as a country with a colonial past and the identity among the Aboriginal peoples of Canada as territorial occupants. The full extent of this predicament—what we term the 'Achilles heel' of Canada's international image—needs to be more fully appreciated in any account of the workings of Canadian foreign policy.

Without the emergence of a hybrid form of Indigenous diplomacy, however, this structural condition would have been a moot point. What makes Canada exceptional in this arena is the blend of a particular form of agency to a highly distinctive embedded structure. Canada's state responses to Indigenous diplomacy reveal the high stakes attached to this domain. The seriousness—even heavy-handedness—with which Canadian diplomats have dealt with Indigenous challenges, is striking. The political dimension of the Canadian government's approach was paramount, as issues of Indigenous rights in the Indigenous arena became wrapped up with core issues of self-determination and national unity in the context of Quebec. Canadian diplomats, however, set off the tone of this response, defending a narrow and rigid position that rejected any need to address the legacy of colonialism or the effects of 'past injustices' (Barsh 1995: 109).

Although the diversity of Indigenous voices and experiences precludes any definitive statement of Aboriginal positions on how best to use international bodies to overcome domestic abuses by states (see Niezen 2003; Beier 2005), most Indigenous diplomats have sought recognition of their inherent right to self-determination. In a few cases, such as the Six Nations/Haudenosaunee, this is interpreted as parallelism, in the sense of separate statehood (or, in the case of the Cree, the right to not be forcibly included in a sovereign Quebec). Most Canadian Indigenous groups, however,

promote this language as an assertion of equal participation, rather than a congruent status. More generally, Aboriginal groups seek redress for the myriad legacies of colonialism, from forced assimilation (cultural genocide) to the dispossession of traditional homelands in violation of Indigenous land and resource rights.

Indigenous leaders have articulated a common message ' . . . that they have the right to maintain their distinctiveness and to collectively determine their future development' (Niezen 2000: 130). Indigenous actors exploit Canada's Achilles heel through a combination of passion and professionalism. Although Aboriginal peoples are often cast as helpless, noble victims of progress struggling to maintain their cultures and spiritual relationship to the land and resources in the modern world (see Tennant 1994), their representatives have borrowed some of the most Canadian habits of diplomacy. Similarly, they have provided a healthy dose of blame-and-shame tactics designed to take advantage of Canada's discomfort with having its most basic structural flaws revealed for the entire diplomatic world to see. Sanders (0985: 302) observes that Aboriginal peoples' supranational strategies can be construed as political theatre in which international fora serve as stages upon which to embarrass the nation-state, but that they are more complex than they appear at first glance. 'The tactic of international accusations serves both the short-term goal of applying pressure on the nation-state', he explains, 'and the long-term goal of developing international standards' (See also Niezen 2000: 122).

This article offers a general exploration into how Aboriginal peoples and groups in Canada have used international relationships and global governance fora to challenge the legitimacy of the Canadian state, scaling up their own skill set and tactical repertoire in the process. Using historical and contemporary case studies, we unpack and analyze evolving strategies to assert and constrain Indigenous rights and forces on the international stage.

BACKGROUND

Rick Ponting (1990: 86) has astutely commented '. . . Indians would be quick to assert that the internationalization of aboriginal affairs in Canada is nothing new'. Indeed, scholars have acknowledged that groups like the Six Nations engaged in complex diplomacy before also the various contributions to this special issue. Aboriginal peoples forged intimate economic and cultural networks with the newcomers, served as military allies during the struggles for continental supremacy in the eighteenth and nineteenth centuries, and entered into formal treaties which they believed would solidify relationships on a nation-to-nation basis. The Royal Proclamation of 1763 recognized Indian territorial and political rights, and pledged to protect them from fraud and abuse by local settlers. By the mid-nineteenth century, however, Canada's Indian policy was fixed on the goals of 'protection, civilization and assimilation' (Tobias 1976), and colonialism rather than accommodation prevailed. Reports of mistreatment of Aboriginal peoples in North America did attract criticisms from groups like the Aborigines' Protection Society (formed in England in 1837), a Protestant anti-slavery coalition that challenged segregationist policies and promoted assimilation of Aboriginal peoples into colonial British society. In retrospect, however, the imposition of official wardship status through the *Indian Act*, the introduction of modern and elected, rather than traditional and local, governance systems, and other legislative tools such as enfranchisement did not eradicate distinct Aboriginal political identities as they were designed to do. Historians have established that Aboriginal peoples did not become passive victims of federal policy, but continued to be creative, active agents resisting the imposition and exercise of state control. At times, this resistance included international diplomacy.

Treaty relationships with the British monarch led quite naturally to Aboriginal appeals within imperial structures. In the first decade of the twentieth century, British Columbia Indian delegations went to London to secure political assurances from King Edward that existing royal promises guaranteeing their rights and lands would be honoured. Keith Carlson concludes that the 1906 delegation met with deceit and insincerity on the part of Canadian and British officials, who politely told them to return home and deal with federal officials. Nevertheless, BC chiefs believed the signed portraits received from His Majesty represented '. . . the honour of the British Crown and the justness of British law, as well as a new local authority for themselves derived directly from London' (Carlson 2005: 29). Policy-makers did not derive the same message, and oral traditions surrounding Royal promises had little traction in domestic political discourse. Although attempts to seek redress through imperial authorities failed, Indians continued to assert a special relationship with the Crown and clung to the possibility of positive monarchical intervention (Sanders 1985: 295–297).

As Canada became more active in global governance structures, Aboriginal peoples recognized that supranational fora offered the possibility to draw international scrutiny to the state's treatment of them. In the interwar years, the Canadian government's participation in the League of Nations reflected more a superficial desire to take a symbolic seat at the table as an autonomous member of the Empire than any practical commitment to Wilsonian ideals. An international presence could also be a double-edged sword. Sanders (1992: 486) has observed that no minority rights provisions were written into the Covenant of the League of Nations, but it was a potential forum for activism, particularly when Aboriginal groups had support from the Geneva-based Bureau International pour la Défense des Indigènes. The Six Nations of the Grand River maintained adamantly that they were allies of the Crown with distinct status, not Canadians, tracing their arguments back to the original treaties reached with the British. The well-known story of Deskaheh's representations to the League in 1923–1924, recounted by Yale Belanger in this issue (see also Veatch 1975; Tidey 1986; Niezen 2003: 31–36), sought recognition for the Six Nations Confederacy as an internationally recognized state. The states that formed the United Nations after the Second World War did not envision space for Indigenous peoples as official international actors. From the onset, however, Aboriginal groups appealed to the body for representation and support. The Six Nations, for example,' . . . appeaJ[ed] to the conscience of the democratic nations' whose delegates met at the San Francisco Conference (which created the United Nations) on 13 April 1945, asking for support to repossess or get compensation for Haldimand Treaty lands that had been alienated over the previous centuries.] They asserted that they had . . . fought as allies of the British Crown during the American revolutionary war, [and] accepted the grant of lands described in the Haldirnand Treaty and came to Canada from the United States to settle on these lands in the spirit and in the understanding that we were doing so as a sovereign people' (quoted in *Logan v. Styres* 1959). This lobbying was unsuccessful. Other Aboriginal groups petitioned the United Nations annually, but their efforts were never publicly acknowledged. Indeed, when the North American Indian Brotherhood sent three BC Indians and a non-Indian lawyer to lobby the United Nations in New York in 1953, John Humphrey (the Canadian who headed the Human Rights Division) told them to return to Ottawa and deal with the Canadian government directly (Sanders 1980; 1992: 487).]

Canadians had a growing awareness of their commitments to human rights principles after the Second World War, and pressured governments at all levels to live up to international commitments in this regard (Walker 1997; Bangarth 2003; Lambertson 2003). This self-perception was central to Canada's evolving activism as a committed middle power in the international system. Although Aboriginal peoples did not factor directly in any foreign policy decision making, apart from bilateral stipulations to protect Inuit from American personnel sent north to construct and man radar lines (for example, the DEW Line Treaty signed in 1955), Canada's evolving international role could also be used to embarrass the government for the plight of Aboriginal peoples at home. In the late 1950s, after the establishment of the Primrose Lake Air Weapons Range occupied a large expanse of the Cold Lake Chipewyan band's homeland and disrupted their traditional hunting, trapping, fishing, logging, and berry-picking activities, they demanded a ' . . . livelihood for a livelihood'. A band resolution lamented, ' . . . Whereas we lost everything for the common good and Defence of Canada', the federal government was 'generous with moneys when helping the Poor Countries of Asia (Colombo Plan) [and] when helping Hungarian Refugees' but provided the band with very little for their plight. 'Charity should begin at home', they pleaded, 'and Justice should never be forgotten' (quoted in Lackenbauer 2007: 160). When Prime Minister John Diefenbaker opposed South Africa's continued membership in the Commonwealth because of its segregationist policies, representatives from that republic retaliated with the observation that Indians lacked political representation in Canadian Parliament. Stung by this criticism, Diefenbaker justified granting the franchise to Indians in 1960 on the grounds that it would ' . . . remove in the eyes of the world any suggestion that in Canada colour or race places any citizen in an inferior category to other citizens of the country' (quoted in Sanders 1992: 488) .

In the last third of the twentieth century, the internationalization of Aboriginal issues took hold in a very distinctive manner via the United Nations. The UN system first formally addressed Indigenous issues in 1949 when the General Assembly invited the Sub-Commission to study the cultural and material welfare of Indigenous Americans. Eight years later, the International Labour Organization (ILO) adopted Convention No. 107 related to the 'protection and integration' of Indigenous peoples so that they would share in ' . . . the progress of the national community of which they form a part' (Barsh 1986: 370). The United Nations first began to really consider Indigenous issues as a special category in the context of its work on racial discrimination. In 1970, the Sub-Commission on the Prevention of Discrimination and Protection of Minorities recommended a comprehensive study on discrimination against Indigenous peoples and appointed Jose Martinez Cobo as Special Rapporteur to recommend national and international measures to eliminate this discrimination (Martinez Cobo 1986: 7).

The emerging concept of the Fourth World articulated the desire for Canadian Native groups to connect with other Indigenous peoples around the world who shared in the struggle against colonialism. When George Manuel, the President of the National Indian Brotherhood, (NIB) participated in a Canadian delegation to Australia and New Zealand to compare native policies in 1971, he was struck by the common experience of Maori and Australian Aborigines and their shared values with Canadian Indians. The following year, he announced the need for a world conference of Indigenous peoples (Manuel and Posluns 1974). After this point, Aboriginal groups began to actively cultivate UN bodies as allies, beginning with Manuel's 1972 trip to the UN Conference on the Human Environment. The federal government did not object to the NIBs application for NGO status by the UN Economic and Social Council, which was granted in May 1974 (Ponting 1990: 87). The creation of the World Council of Indigenous People in 1975, funded largely by church groups and the International Working Group for Indigenous Affairs (CIWGIA), provided a forum both for the collective Indigenous voice and a site for the assertion of Canadian leadership.

The force of international activism by Canadian Aboriginal groups became politically salient in the collective opposition to constitutional initiatives in the late 1970s and early 1980s. When the federal government devised a constitutional package without consulting Aboriginal groups, Native representatives appealed to the Queen, to the British parliament, and to the British courts in an effort to stymie Canadian patriation efforts until Aboriginal issues had been discussed substantively. In October 1980, the NIB established a London office to lobby British MPs and, ironically, as Pal and Campbell (1991: 314) observe, ' . . . there was much more attention paid to the aboriginal question in the British Commons debates on the constitution than in the Canadian ones'. Coupled with the Charter of Rights and vexatious federal–provincial tensions, both of which also had potential champions amongst British backbenchers and could lead to endless amendments in Westminster, the Aboriginal rights lobby compelled the Canadian government to send a constitutional team to London (Granatstein and Bothwell 1990: 356). When an amendment to recognize and affirm Aboriginal rights was dropped to secure provincial consent to the Charter in November 1981, Native groups launched court cases in Britain asserting that unilateral patriation was illegal without their consent. In January 1982, Lord Denning upheld the Canadian government's right to patriation but his ruling offered several comments sympathetic to the Aboriginal cause (Woodward and George 1983).

Sanders (1983: 301) describes the Indian lobby as ' . . . the least expected and most exotic part' of the political story to patriate the constitution. While politicians dismissed the 'complex and expensive' Aboriginal strategy 'as naive and quixotic', antagonizing the federal and provincial governments, the experience encouraged Aboriginal groups to try to coordinate their efforts. Above all, it reflected an awareness of the value of forming transnational networks along the lines analyzed by Keck and Sikkink (1998). Although this approach still contained important limitations, the transition showed that Canada's Aboriginal peoples were willing and able to locate their activities in a complex two-level game with a heightened international and domestic face visible across a wide spectrum of institutional sites and issue areas.

THE HUMAN RIGHTS COMMITTEE AND CANADIAN ABORIGINAL COMPLAINTS

Robinson (2004) explains that Canada's promotion of international human rights is highly dependent upon its credibility as an upholder of the six major UN human rights treaties. The question remains as to how Canada applies these rights standards within its own borders. Using the treaty-based human rights system, Canadian Aboriginal people (as individuals) have repeatedly invoked complaint mechanisms to seek redress for alleged government violations of their rights since the 1970s.

Article 27 of the International Covenant on Civil and Political Rights (ICCPR) guarantees minority cultural rights.[1] The UN Human Rights Committee (HRC), which monitors state compliance with the ICCPR, was asked to apply this provision to the case of Sandra Lovelace, a status Indian born and raised on the Tobique reserve in New Brunswick who had married (and later divorced) a non-Indian man and, therefore, had lost her status under Section 12(1)(b) of the Indian Act. A status Indian man would not have lost his rights and identity, thus exposing gender discrimination in the domestic legislation. Lovelace asserted that her right to live on her home reserve depended on her Indian status, and without this, neither she nor her children could practise their Maliseet language and culture (Mercredi and Turpel 1993: 188). After the Supreme Court of Canada rejected her appeals, she complained to the HRC in December 1977, asserting that Canada had violated Article 27 of the ICCPR by denying her the right to live on a reserve. In its decision, the HRC held that ' . . . the continuing effect of the Indian Act' breached her right to enjoy her own culture in her home community (OHCHR 1977; Bayefsky 1982).

If Canada responded with ambivalence to some Human Rights Committee opinions, Nolan (1988: 109) has observed ' . . . most frequently Canadian governments have responded to committee criticism by admitting shortcomings and introducing legislative or administrative remedies'. Although the issue of sexual discrimination in the Indian Act was not new (Whyte 1974), the HRC's decision that the legislation violated human rights made the issue more politically salient. The federal government responded in 1983 that it was ' . . . anxious to amend the Indian Act so as to render itself in fuller compliance with its international obligations pursuant to Article 27 of the International Covenant on Civil and Political Rights', and that Canada was committed to remove discriminatory provisions that offend human rights (Sandra Lovelace v. Canada 1983). In response, the federal government amended the Indian Act to comply with the decision. Bill C-31 (1985) eliminated sexual discrimination in determining Indian status, including the right to live on reserve. This has had profound impacts on Aboriginal demographics, particularly because thousands of Aboriginal women and their descendents have been reinstated or registered as status Indians (McGoldrick 1991: 246).

International concerns were also reflected in government policy reports and court decisions. The Penner Report of 1983 cast its recommendations for self-government in the context of international law, citing the UN International Covenant on Economic, Social and Cultural Rights and suggesting that Canada could become ' . . . an international leader in governmental relations with indigenous peoples' (Canada 1983: 136). The Supreme Court of Canada deliberated on the international law character of Indian treaties, concluding by 1990 that British authorities had regarded the Indians as 'independent nations' and had related to them on a 'nation-to-nation' basis (quoted in Sanders 1992: 491). In 1985, the Coolican report on comprehensive land claims observed that the international community was increasingly recognizing ' . . . the responsibility of nation states to ensure the survival of their indigenous peoples', and that Canada had been called to account for its treatment at the United Nations. 'If it is to have credibility in promoting the observance of human rights by other countries', the report noted, 'Canada will have to demonstrate its willingness to respect the rights of its most vulnerable peoples' (quoted in Sanders 1992: 490).

The South Africa case during the Mulroney era signalled the degree to which Aboriginal issues could represent the Achilles heel of Canada's self-designation as an unimpeachable advocate of human rights. South African representatives had long pointed to Canada's Indian policies to counteract criticisms of apartheid. This counterattack continued through the 1980s when the Canadian government took a leadership role in pushing Britain and the Commonwealth to impose sanctions against South Africa, earning the comment from one South African journalist that Canada's anti-apartheid action made it ' . . . the conscience of the major Western governments' (Freeman 1997: 5). When Mulroney criticized South African policy during a visit to the African continent, however, Chief Louis Stevenson of the Peguis First Nation invited Glenn Gabb, the South African ambassador to Canada, to visit the largest Manitoba reserve and requested $99 million in foreign aid. 'Before criticizing the actions of other countries, Canada should clean up its own back yard', Stevenson told the press, adding ' . . . Canada's treatment of its aboriginal people is hypocritical and makes a mockery of the image it portrays to the rest of the world' (Smith 1987; York 1987). His tactics, explicitly designed to attract international attention to the plight of Canadian Indians, provoked national controversy—and were disavowed by most Indian leaders across the country (*Globe and Mail* 1987a). South African newspapers widely publicized Gabb's visit and that of four Saskatchewan Indians to South Africa in August, during which they presented Foreign Minister Roelof (Pik) Botha with a red-and-white feathered headdress, explaining that its colours symbolized that it could have been ' . . . dipped in the blood of our ancestors'. Likening the headdress to an Indian national flag, they purported to adopt the South African foreign minister as their own. In response, Botha pledged to investigate whether South Africa could sign a goodwill treaty with Canadian Indians, adding ' . . . I know how your history has been distorted' (*Globe and Mail* 1987b). The visits of other international figures to Canada to experience Indian conditions directly—such as Britain's Lord Michael Killanin's visit arranged by Joe Miskokomon and Billy Diamond, and Archbishop Desmond Tutu's 1990 visit to the Osnaburgh reserve in Ontario (MacGregor 1989: 190–192; Ponting 1990: 88)—demonstrate the high potential for embarrassment in a country that often prides itself on serving as the world's human rights conscience.

INDIGENOUS DIPLOMACIES AND MILITARIZATION

Aboriginal groups raised similar criticisms that the Canadian state was violating basic human rights when they opposed the effects of militarization on their homelands. During the late 1980s and 1990s, their definitions of security stretched beyond the traditional, state-centric boundaries to include the protection of Aboriginal rights. As we have explained elsewhere (Cooper 1997: 126; Lackenbauer 2007), the national interest basis upon which the military had traditionally secured rights to land for military training and testing activities no longer seemed inviolable in the face of unofficial Aboriginal peoples' definitions of human and environmental security. The Inuit Circumpolar Conference (ICC), for example, worked to reshape the Arctic security discourse in the 1980s, promoting the link between peace, human rights, development, and the Inuit homeland. Toward this end, ICC President Mary Simon 0989: 32) highlighted the need to measure security according to all of these aspects. 'The ICC is working towards reversing the trend to militarize the North . . . 'she explained at a March 1989 inquiry. 'We are committed to promoting peaceful and safe uses of the Arctic. We strive for initiatives that benefit not only those of us whose home is in the North, but all of humankind'. As long as states excluded Inuit and other Aboriginal peoples from policy- and decision-making, their perception of 'lasting peace and real security' could not be achieved. 'For thousands of years, Inuit have used and continue to use the lands, waters, and sea ice in circumpolar regions', Simon continued. 'As aboriginal people, we are the Arctic's legitimate spokespersons'. The ICC stressed this message repeatedly at the UN Working Group on Indigenous Populations (WGIP).

The military faced increasingly complex pressures from Aboriginal groups who built new international alliances to leverage their power, and reined a new discourse that suggested Aboriginal and military activities were irreconcilable. The foremost debate was over low-level flying in Labrador and northeastern Quebec in the late 1980s. In the public presentation of issues and events, scholars Peter Armitage and John Kennedy (1989) explain how the Innu manipulated ethnic symbols and rhetorical devices to forward their agenda, while proponents of military expansion tried to undermine the factual basis of the Innu arguments and their claims to traditional activities and rights that would be inherently prejudiced by low-level flying. In this 'David versus Goliath' competition for legitimacy (Ashini 1990), the Innu 'ethnodrama' mobilized polarized oppositions with non-Aboriginal interests to depict that the primary existential threat to their survival came not from the Soviets but from Western flight training. Nationally and internationally, Aboriginal peoples affected by low-level flying found willing allies and established networks to assist them in their politics of dissent. Even the European Parliament passed a resolution on 14 April 1989 in support of the Aboriginal position, making reference to ' . . . the violation of the territory of the Innu Indians by low-altitude flights' (quoted in Ponting 1990: 89). No longer did the military hold a sacrosanct position in international political discourse.[2]

The 1990 confrontation at Oka proved even more destabilizing, exposing the fragility of Aboriginal-government relations and suggesting that Aboriginal communities were volatile powder kegs that might erupt into open violence over deep-seated historical grievances. The story of the 74-day standoff between the Mohawks and their allies, who set up blockades at Kanesatake and Kahnawake, and the Quebec provincial police and, later, the Canadian Forces, is well known and need not be repeated here (see York and Pindera 1991; Goodleaf 1995; Pertusati 1997). At its core, sociologist Radha Jhappan (1990: 35) has observed, the Oka Crisis was a battle of symbols and rhetorical strategies designed to de-legitimate the opposing side. Aboriginal leaders worked concertedly to assert that the crisis was the product of government coercion. On 20 July 1990, about 150 chiefs from across Canada appealed to the United Nations and to the international community to impose sanctions on Canada similar to those levelled against South Africa (*Globe and Mail* 1990: At). Native spokespersons framed their discourse as 'sovereign nations' and the national and international media took note. In response, the federal government sent an envoy to the UN WGIP in Geneva to try to explain the situation from a government standpoint. On 8 August, the Quebec government requested Canadian Forces intervention at the blockades, and the WGIP asked Canada to explain both its treatment of the Mohawks and the Quebec government's ultimatum to the Mohawks to bring down the barricades. Four days later, a federal-provincial-Mohawk agreement called on twenty-four international observers from the Paris-based International Federation of Human Rights to monitor events. This represented a symbolic victory for the Mohawks, implying their equality in status with the Canadian state (Pal and Campbell 1991: 286). The observers' activities were severely constrained by military security and they left in frustration. International concern did not end there, however. In January 1991, a committee of European Parliamentarians came to Canada on a fact-finding mission. Although diplomatic conventions necessitated that the visitors deny they represented parliament or that they would pass judgement on Canadian actions, their purpose was clear and represented an innovation in international investigative work with the potential to influence Canadian political opinion (Ponting 1990: 86; Sanders 1992: 499–500).

FIRST NATIONS AND THE UN WGIP: THE POLITICS OF EMBARRASSMENT

The UN Economic and Social Council established the Working Group on Indigenous Populations (WGIP) in 1982 as a pre-session working group of the UN Sub-Commission on Prevention of Discrimination and Protection of Minorities. Each year, week-long WGIP meetings give representatives from Indigenous groups around the world a chance to make contact with one another, give speeches, and register their grievances at the United Nations (Sanders 1994; OHCHR 2006, leaflet 2). In declaratory terms, at least, the Canadian government was an enthusiastic proponent of the extension of UN mechanisms into this domain, having regarded the establishment of the WGIP in 1982, for example, as a constructive way forward. The Canadian government also worked hard throughout the 1980s for the entry of Indigenous representatives into the wider operational machinery of the United Nations, most notably through the drafting of international legal standards in the WGIP and through the drafting group of its parent body, the Sub-Commission on Prevention of Discrimination and Protection of Minorities. It also supported its commitment by delivery, making a contribution through the UN Voluntary Fund for Indigenous Populations to enhance the capabilities of the Indigenous groups to work within the system (Barsh 1995). Furthermore, Canadian diplomats mounted a vigorous defence of Canada's historical treatment of its Indigenous population in comparative terms, as well as its efforts to correct matters, and became far more responsive in drawing selected Indigenous representatives into the work of the United Nations.

Concurrently, Canadian diplomacy became increasingly defensive as Indigenous groups became more autonomously and deeply embedded in the

UN system, and tried to control the agenda and restrict any extension of the institutional apparatus. The Canadian government resisted the WGIP's push for a comprehensive legal study of treaties signed with Indigenous peoples. Canada also tried to confound and restrict the parameters of the initiative for an International Year of Indigenous Peoples in 1992. In terms of process, Canadian diplomats were portrayed as using muscling tactics, such as threats to curtail the WGIP's activities if it targeted Canada. By the mid-1990s, Barsh (1995: 107) concluded, Canada had lost its reputation as '. . . the principal champion of indigenous peoples at the UN [and had become] more commonly aligned with countries such as Brazil and India in advising caution and delay'. Indeed, Canada drew closer to countries that it deemed troublemakers in other aspects of the human rights agenda, such as China and Bangladesh, to incorporate the inviolability of the UN Charter in terms of sovereignty and territorial defence of states and to stymie the treaty study. Ted Moses (1994), the Cree ambassador to the United Nations, charged that Canada '. . . sought and established alliances on indigenous issues at the United Nations with states that are notorious for their lack of respect for human rights and their ill-treatment of indigenous peoples and whose interests are inimical to Canada and to the indigenous peoples of Canada'.

The level of controversy on Indigenous rights reached the point where the two sides became thoroughly estranged from one another. Instead of employing the positive attributes of the traditional diplomatic culture, with special reference to mediation, diplomatic engagement produced heightened tensions and alienation. Rather than adopting skilled and sensitive techniques of diplomacy, obstruction, delay, and deflection were the characteristic responses of Canadian statecraft.

What was striking, however, was the determination with which Canadian diplomats defended not only what was judged to be the national or sovereign interest but also their own professional standing. The outward-directed campaign of the Indigenous peoples constituted a fundamental challenge to the activities of professional diplomats as well as existing constitutional arrangements. In some ways, the diplomatic defence may be interpreted as the instinctive response of the established machinery to outside forces determined to do things differently. After all, Indigenous diplomacy was performed very differently on the world stage. It showed little of the self-imposed constraint characterized by official diplomatic practice. Through the 1980s and 1990s, Indigenous representatives went beyond the usually accepted boundaries of activity. They were willing to join with countries of the Global South, and at the same time they were prepared to work with representatives of countries such Cuba – which the United States, a principal Canadian ally, condemned for human rights violations and which it attempted to isolate at the United Nations (Barsh 1995: 114, 116). They also tended to deploy any tactics that were necessary to achieve results, including concerted efforts to shame the Canadian diplomats away from what was considered recalcitrant statecraft.

This process of estrangement was exacerbated by the Indigenous peoples' appropriation of some of the traditional techniques of Canadian diplomacy. Through the WGIP and other components of the UN machinery, Aboriginal representatives moved appreciably from having an outsider to an insider status and adopted certain forms of technical and entrepreneurial diplomacy. Although they continued to protest about colonialism and unlawful occupation, and used traditional regalia and garb to accentuate their differences, groups such as the Cree of Quebec, the Lubicon of Alberta, the Mi'kmaq, and the Mohawks (assisted by a number of legal advisors) also became immersed in the minutiae of UN conventions and proceedings. They frequently referred to Article 1 of the International Covenant on Civil and Political Rights and other international human-rights treaties, as well as to Section 35 of the *Constitution Act, 1982* and other Canadian legal decisions and precedents. They made skilful use of opportunities to widen the scope of UN conventions, particularly in the revision of the International Labour Organization (ILO), the treaty study, and the campaign for an Indigenous Year (Barsh 1995).

The ability of Indigenous groups to build multi-layered forms of support showed that they could provide entrepreneurial leadership. One layer of coalition building consisted of enhanced ties of solidarity with other Indigenous groups on a transnational basis (such as the World Council of Indigenous Peoples, Indigenous Survival International, and the Indigenous Initiative for Peace). Tighter networks of activity with key individuals within the UN human rights system—such as the Greek legalist Erica-Irene Daes; the Chair of the WGIP, Halima Warzazi of Morocco; and the Cuban legal expert Miguel Alfonso Martinez—represented another layer. Furthermore, Indigenous peoples built up a solid working relationship with a classic set of Canada's like-minded allies such as Australia (particularly in the years that the Labour Party was in power), Norway, Denmark, the Netherlands, and Austria. Although all shared an interest in extending Indigenous rights, there was no common point of application amongst these countries. Australia was trying to work out a new comprehensive deal with its own Indigenous peoples, while European countries got involved in Indigenous affairs on a more selective basis. The Dutch were especially interested in the effect of NATO low-level flights on the Indigenous way of life in Labrador, the Danes focused on the extension of Indigenous rights and the ILO, and the Austrians ran with the issue of the term 'Indigenous peoples'.

UN CONFERENCES

The hard edge in Canada's diplomacy was revealed most clearly during the high-profile UN World Conferences.[3] At the 1992 Vienna conference on human rights this tone was exhibited during negotiations on the acceptability of using the term Indigenous 'peoples' rather than 'people' or 'populations'. From the perspective of the Canadian government, the question of the 's' reflected the high stakes invested in the Indigenous dossier. According to some strands of international law, and especially Article 1 of the Covenant, the word 'peoples' opened up the prospect of unqualified acceptance of self-determination. This potential scenario was regarded as problematic in terms of its specific application to Indigenous groups. It also raised the possibility that Quebec sovereignty might implicitly be defensible. As the head of the Canadian delegation working on drafting the declaration on Indigenous rights during the Vienna process claimed, ' . . . We would not be serving the people of Canada as a whole if we did not ask for a rider (a legal definition of self-determination). . . . We would not be serving Canadians if we allowed anything that would imply the splitting up of Canada' (Ross Haynes quoted in Platiel 1993).

The Indigenous representatives dismissed this official stance as what Krasner (1999) terms 'organized hypocrisy'. At the domestic level, the Canadian government was not averse to the word 'peoples', including its use in the Canadian constitution. It was only externally that a more rigid line was drawn. Although the term 'peoples' would have considerable instrumental value for Aboriginal representatives, its value was largely tactical. Few, if any, considered secession from Canada to be a realistic option; indeed, some explicitly denied that independence was the objective. Rosemary Kuptana, the President of the Inuit Tapirisat of Canada, accused Ottawa of 'scaremongering tactics' by making the connection (quoted in Platiel 1993). Mary Simon (1994), member of the board of the Inuit Tapirisat, declared,

> We wish to emphasize again that the Inuit agenda for the exercise of our right to self-determination is not to secede or separate from Canada but rather that we wish to share a common citizenship with other Canadians while maintaining our identity as a people, which means maintaining our identity as Inuit.

If the threat of secession was to be used at all as a bargaining tool, this card was more likely to be played against the physical integrity of Quebec than Canada. Recognizing this possibility, the Canadian government became sensitive to the potential spill-over effect of conceding the legitimacy of the principle of self-determination, or at least of creating gaps and ambiguities that could be exploited in the context of national unity. At a news conference well into the Vienna conference, Canadian diplomats specifically warned that groups such as the Cree of Northern Quebec could potentially use their recognition as peoples to declare their sovereignty.

The full extent of the evasiveness of Canadian diplomacy and its estrangement from the Indigenous peoples peaked in the midst of the most crucial phase of the Vienna process. Preconference negotiations raised Indigenous groups' expectations about their ability to win out on the 'peoples' issue. The WGIP's Chair, Mme Daes, had downplayed the breadth of the practical implications of moving forward on this principle, focusing on the need to work out new formulae for political arrangements and representation within the existing state structure rather than on the potential demand for Indigenous independence. She argued that the emphasis should be on bargaining in good faith about power devolution, not on maintaining

barriers to secession. However, these expectations received a serious setback when the latest version of the UN's draft document, issued just one day before the conference was to start, reverted to the term 'people' not 'peoples'. Indigenous representatives interpreted this setback as further evidence of official Canadian recalcitrance to the question of the 's' and as a sign of the divergence between declaratory and operational policy with respect to a new form of inclusive diplomacy. Canadian diplomats may have been fully prepared to open up in an exploratory direction on many routine procedural matters, but on issues with substantive meaning they were accused of working to consolidate the logic of a traditional state-centric world. Perceiving the Indigenous challenge as a threat, they warded it off with power-based tactics. The Indigenous-oriented media quickly assembled evidence to support this interpretation, which portrayed this episode as a backroom betrayal of Indigenous interests. Not wanting to be seen as the obstacle in public, they claimed, the Canadian government had mounted its opposition safe from the scrutiny of non-state actors. As the *Windspeaker* summarized: 'They went into the meeting in Geneva, the fourth preparatory committee, with the "s" there. That was scheduled to be a two-week meeting that was later stretched to three weeks. The third week, during secret sessions that were closed the "s" went out' (Smith 1993).

With growing confidence in their international standing, Indigenous groups spent little time on repair work with Canadian diplomats. Instead, the Indigenous representatives raised their offensive on the 's' question another notch. Employing the skill-set they had assembled, they concentrated on closer networking with their list of allies. By extending the coalition-building exercise, they could count on an impressive cluster of like-minded countries on the 'peoples' issue, ranging from Australia and New Zealand, as well as Norway and Denmark, to a number of Latin American countries. The Austrian foreign minister, Alois Mock, added impetus to this mobilization process with his expression of support for reopening the Indigenous 'peoples' issue. As chair of the conference, Mock intended to ask the final plenary to amend the drafting committee's language to re-insert the 's' (*Toronto Star* 1993) for which Indigenous groups circulated a letter of gratitude. As this campaign built momentum, the Canadian government was backed into an increasingly isolated corner. Non-Indigenous sympathizers such as Max Yalden and Stephen Lewis, taking their cue from the Indigenous groups, vociferously played the shame card. Arguing that such obstructionist behaviour was detrimental to Canada's reputation as a good international citizen, they expressed regret that this fight had been pursued. The question was not about semantics and possible worst-case scenarios; the question was about right and wrong. As Stephen Lewis put it: 'If you have a large indigenous population and you don't say yes to this kind of initiative it is clear where your instincts are' (quoted in Platiel 1993).

Canadian officials were not willing to sever the connection between self-determination and the preservation of the territorial integrity of Canada. While Indigenous representatives might challenge the authority of the state to operate according to this organizing notion, their ability to cut into the state's capacity in a still primarily state-centred context was limited. Facing an awkward position, Canadian diplomats resorted to procedural imperatives and hardening coalitions of the unlike. They reminded Mock *inter alia* that, in terms of process, no language could be reopened in the plenary and emphasized the political risks of such a move. Raising the 'peoples' question would precipitate an acrimonious fight, pitting the supporters of the 's' against hard-line countries such as Brazil, China, Bangladesh, and Malaysia, which would in turn immobilize a variety of other human rights issues.

These tactics thoroughly alienated even those Indigenous representatives who had been willing to work with the Canadian government. Rosemary Kuptana, the President of the Inuit Tapirisat, became frustrated that Canada had not embraced the World Conference as an ' . . . opportunity to reach a consensus on some substantial and practical measures'. Expressing her disappointment with the Canadian government's performance, she remarked at one meeting: 'To be perfectly frank, there is no true dialogue between indigenous peoples and Canada on these issues despite our efforts to do so' (Kuptana 1993). The refusal of the Canadian government to accede on the 's' issue, however, precipitated an open and complete break. Going public with her view that Canada's position on Indigenous issues had become an 'adversarial' one, Kuptana told the Canadian media: ' . . . Canada's done a very good job of trampling on our rights at this conference' (quoted in Platiel 1993).

The Canadian strategy at the World Conference against Racism (WCAR) held in Durban, South Africa in August and September 2001 was to take a . . . leadership role [via] forward-looking recommendations to combat racism and discrimination, [to] share the Canadian experience of diversity, [to] influence world progress on fighting racism and related intolerance, [and to] advance Canada's domestic agenda to combat racism'. As the public document outlining Canada's participation at Durban put it, ' . . . Civil Society participation at the World Conference against Racism is an international priority for Canada'. In the preparations for the WCAR, Aboriginal peoples' unique status in Canada was given privileged attention. Canadian Heritage was careful to highlight the ' . . . specific challenges related to racism and intolerance' that this constituency faced. In considering solutions, emphasis was placed on the need for a ' . . . parallel consultations process established by Aboriginal peoples themselves [in order to] respond to their

needs and respect their traditions, cultures, customs, and languages' (Canadian Heritage 2002).

Despite these efforts to find symmetry between
their interests, Durban exacerbated rather than
tempered the relations between Indigenous groups
and the Canadian state. No internal dynamic of
serious negotiations was launched through the
Durban process; nor was there any new meeting of
the minds on policy direction or delivery apparatus. This rift was reflected in a public display of
bad temper and discordant views even before the
conference officially started. Before leaving for
Durban, Matthew Coon Come, the newly elected
Grand Chief of the Assembly of First Nations
(AFN), expressed concern that Canada would 'not
tell the truth about racism, and even the ongoing
use of state violence against indigenous peoples'
(*Globe and Mail, 2001*). At the NGO Forum, Coon
Come pursued this theme by comparing the Canadian ' . . . racist and colonial syndrome of dispossession and discrimination' with the experience of
South Africa under the apartheid system (quoted
in Schuler 2001). Leaders from the federal government replied that such language was unhelpful and
would have the effect of freezing the AFN leader out
of any future talks on an agenda of reform. Prime
Minister Jean Chrétien added that ' . . . for Matthew
Coon Come to be [at Durban] dumping on Canada' was 'not very useful' (quoted in *Toronto Star
2001*).

From the perspective of the Canadian state,
these tactics of embarrassment indicated just how
far Indigenous groups were prepared to go to
shame Ottawa before an international audience.
Rather than attempting to embrace a form of constructive engagement with the government on the
basis of an anti-racism agenda, the AFN seemed
to be trying to undermine Canada's reputation
as a good international citizen. Fuelling this official backlash further was a frustration with what
was seen as the Indigenous groups' ingratitude.

Gestures of generosity by the federal government
(including providing funds for the six-member
delegation from the AFN) were not reciprocated by
good diplomatic behaviour. From the perspective
of the Indigenous groups, the true test for sovereignty rested not just on the willingness of the Canadian state to release policy determinism in favour
of a bargaining process and subsidiary processes,
but on whether it was ready to embrace forms of
segmented territoriality. As long as the state clung
onto this fundamental expression of inequality of
status, manifested above all by Ottawa's claim to
territorial supremacy, the basic questions of sovereignty remained open and hotly contested.

Having previously lost ground on the use of the
term 'Indigenous peoples', the federal government
was now seen to be pushing for the inclusion in the
Government Declaration of paragraph 27, which
negated these gains, affirming that the term
'Indigenous peoples' in the Declaration and Programme of Action ' . . . cannot be construed as having any implications as to rights under international
law'. Ted Moses, the former ambassador to the
United Nations and now the Grand Chief of the
Grand Council of the Cree, complained that, by
this logic, the concepts at the heart of the conference's agenda did not apply to Indigenous groups
(Moses 2002). Their rights would not be inherent
within inalienable and universal principles but
would be determined by state actors in the context
of ongoing multilateral negotiations.[4]

CONCLUSION

Ronald Niezen (2000: 122) observes that some
Aboriginal leaders have proven, ' . . . despite their
limited power and resources, [to be] among the
most effective political strategists in the contemporary national and international scenes'. Their ability
to navigate complex international fora to go around
and/or to confront their own state officials needs to

be recognized for what it is—an impressive form of hybrid diplomacy with both an inside and outside component. The former contains a strong technical skill-set, and the latter showcases the embedded style associated with naming and shaming.

The advances by Indigenous diplomats in the international arena are intimately connected with domestic politics. This is especially so *vis-à-vis* the United Nations, as this is the site of Indigenous diplomacy that is most visible and sensitive. Consistent with the approach taken by Keck and Sikkink (1998), the boomerang effect of this outward-looking strategy has facilitated change at the domestic level by putting pressure on Canada through activities directed at international fora. Bureaucratically, the agency of the Indigenous transnational movement has been translated into tangible results at both the international and domestic levels. Within the UN system, a major sign of success has been the creation of the Permanent Forum, allowing an entrenched site for Indigenous diplomats. In Canada, a parallel move came with the establishment of an 'Indigenous desk' within DFAIT.

If the Indigenous transnational movement has to be privileged as a major change-agent, so have the bending of the structural conditions under which they work. In an increasingly globalized world, in which the normative power of the Westphalian system is no longer sacrosanct (as witnessed by the push for the doctrine of the Responsibility to Protect and the heightened attention given to minorities), Indigenous peoples—and their diplomats—have advantages now that they have not been offered before (Nairn 2003). Yet, amidst all of these positive signs, the influence of structural conditions still weighs heavily. As Neizen (2003: 23) soberly notes,

> . . . It is tempting to romanticize the efforts of indigenous leaders at the United Nations and to overestimate their impact on world affairs. The language of participants in the process of human rights standard setting provides us with a reality check and a reminder that significant obstacles remain to be overcome before a new order of relations between indigenous peoples and the state can be said to have truly arrived.

Indeed, the capacity of political power to reverse the normative claims of Indigenous peoples is never too far from the surface. The UN Human Rights Council's support for a Declaration on the Rights of Indigenous Peoples in June 2006, and the new Conservative government's decision to reject it on the grounds that provisions in the draft declaration respecting land, resources, and territories were incompatible with Canadian laws, prompted National Chief of the AFN Phil Fontaine to call the decision a ' . . . stain on Canada's reputation as a leader in human rights'.[5] The contradiction between Canada's image of good international citizenship and its relationship—through its legacy as a settler state—to Indigenous peoples will continue to hit raw nerves to the detriment of Canadian diplomacy.

Key Terms

Indigenous Diplomacy
1992 Vienna Conference on Human Rights
UN Permanent Forum

Notes

1. The Article reads, 'In those States in which ethnic, religious or linguistic minorities exist, persons belonging to such minorities shall not be denied the right, in community with other members of their group, to enjoy their own culture, to prove and practise their own religion, or to use their own language.'

2. The Working Group on Indigenous Populations authored a report on the 'Utilization of Indigenous Peoples' Lands by non-indigenous Authorities, Groups or Individuals for Military Purposes' in June 2006.

3. For more comprehensive analysis of the roles and positions adopted by Canadian and Aboriginal diplomats at UN world conferences, see Cooper (2004: 122–51, 242–44).

4. The continuing attempt to impose stricter parameters on the question of sovereignty by the Canadian state and like-minded countries promoted a vigorous response from the NGO community as well. Paragraph 142 of the NGO Forum explicitly called for a breaking of state-centric notions of territorial-based sovereignty: 'Indigenous Peoples have the inherent right to possession of all their traditional and ancestral lands and territories.' Furthermore, the resistance of states with respect to withdrawing paragraph 27 led to a decision to abandon the conference on the part of the Indigenous People's Caucus of the NGO Forum in general and the AFN in particular.

5. Adeba (2006). For the official rationale, see Mayer (2006).

References

Adeba, Brian. (2006). 'Aboriginal Rights Treaty Should Have Been Signed.' *Embassy*, 4 October. www.embassymag.ca/html/index.php?display-story&fultpath-/2006/october/4/treaty/ (20 March 2007).

Armitage, Peter, and John C. Kennedy. (1989). 'Redbaiting and Racism on our Frontier: Military Expansion in Labrador and Quebec.' *Canadian Review of Sociology and Anthropology* 26 (5): 798–817.

Ashini, Daniel. (1990). 'David Confronts Goliath: The Innu of Ungava versus the NATO Alliance.' In Boyce Richardson, ed. *Drumbeat: Anger and Renewal in Indian Country*. Toronto: Summerhill Press.

Bangarth, Stephanie D. (2003). '"We Are Not Asking You to Open Wide the Gates for Chinese Immigration": The Committee for the Repeal of the Chinese Immigration Act and Early Human Rights Activism in Canada.' *Canadian Historical Review* 84(3): 395–422.

Barsh, Russel Lawrence. (1995). 'The Aboriginal Issue in Canadian Foreign Policy, 1984–1994'. *International Journal of Canadian Studies* (Fall) 12: 107–134.

Barsh, Russel Lawrence. (1986). 'Indigenous Peoples: An Emerging Object of International Law.' The *American Journal of International Law* 80(2): 369–385.

Bayefsky, A.F. (1982). 'The Human Rights Committee and the Case of Sandra Lovelace.' *Canadian Yearbook of International Law* 20: 244–265.

Beier, J. Marshall. (2005). *International Relations in Uncommon Places: Indigeneity, Cosmology, and the Limits of International Theory*. New York: Palgrave Macmillan.

Canada. (1983). *Report of the Special Committee on Indian Self-Government in Canada*. House of Commons. Ottawa: Supply and Services.

Canadian Heritage. (2002). www.canadianheritage.gc.ca/wn-qdn/wear-cmer/wear.htrnl[el]

Carlson, Keith Thor. (2005). 'Rethinking Dialogue and History: The King's Promise and the 1906 Aboriginal Delegation to London.' *Native Studies Review* 16(2): 1–38.

Cooper, Andrew F. (2004). *Tests of Global Governance: Canadian Diplomacy and United Nations World Conferences*. Tokyo: United Nations University Press.

Cooper, Andrew F. (1997). *Niche Diplomacy: Middle Powers After the Cold War*. New York: St Martin's Press.

Fenton, William N. (1998). *The Great Law and the Longhouse: A Political History of the Iroquois Confederacy*. Norman: University of Oklahoma Press.

Freeman, Unda. (1997). The *Ambiguous Champion: Canada and South Africa in the Trudeau and Mulroney Years*. Toronto: University of Toronto Press.

Globe and Mail. (2001). 'Coon Come's Contention'. 28 August: A14.

Globe and Mail. (1990). 'Chiefs Urge Swift Recall of Parliament'. 21 July: AI.

Globe and Mail. (1987a). 'Aboriginal Rights'. Editorial, 12 March: A6.

Globe and Mail. (1987b). 'Indians Present Botha with Headdress'. 19 August: A8.

Goodleaf, Donna. (1995). *Entering the War Zone: A Mohawk Perspective on Resisting Invasions*. Penticton: Theytus Books.

Granatstein, J.L. and Robert Bothwell. (1990). *Pirouette: Pierre Trudeau and Canadian Foreign Policy*. Toronto: University of Toronto Press.

Jennings, Francis, ed. (1985). The *History and Culture of Iroquois Diplomacy: An Interdisciplinary Guide to the Treaties of the Six Nations and their League.* Syracuse: Syracuse University Press.

Jhappan, C. Radha. (1990). 'Indian Symbolic Politics: The Double-Edged Sword of Publicity'. *Canadian Ethnic Studies* 22(3): 19–39.

Keck, Margaret E. and Kathryn Sikkink. (1998). *Activists Beyond Borders: Advocacy Networks in International Politics.* Ithaca: Cornell University Press.

Krasner, Stephen D. (1999). *Sovereignty: Organized Hypocrisy.* Princeton: Princeton University Press.

Kuptana, Rosemarie. (1993). Speaking Notes for the North American Region Indigenous Nations UN Satellite Meeting, 7 April.

Lackenbauer, P. Whitney. (2007). *Battle Grounds:* The *Canadian Military and Aboriginal Lands.* Vancouver: UBC Press.

Lambertson, Ross. (2005). *Repression and Resistance: Canadian Human Rights Activists, 1930–1960.* Toronto: University of Toronto Press.

Logan v. Styres. (1959). 20 D.L.R. (2d) 416: 422–24.

MacGregor, Roy. (1989). *Chief:* The *Fearless Vision of Billy Diamond.* Markham: Viking.

Manuel, George and Michael Posluns. (1974). The *Fourth World: An Indian Reality.* Toronto: Collier.

Martinez Cobo, Jose R. (1986). *Study of the Problem of Discrimination Against Indigenous Populations.* UN document E/CN.4/Sub.2/1986/7 and Add. 1–4.

McGoldrick, Dominic. (1991). The *Human Rights Committee: Its Role in the Development of the International Covenant on Civil and Political Rights.* Clarendon: Oxford University Press.

Mercredi, Ovide and Mary Ellen Turpel. (1993). *In the Rapids: Navigating the Future of First Nations.* Toronto: Viking.

Meyer, Paul. (2006). Ambassador Paul Meyer's address to the Working Group on the Draft Declaration on the Rights of Indigenous Peoples. 29 June. www.dfait-maeci.gc.ca/canada_un/geneva/HRC_June29_06-en.asp (20 March 2007).

Moses, Ted. (2002). 'Antiracist Except for Us.' *Globe and Mail,* 29 August.

Moses, Ted. (1994). 'Testimony before the Special Joint Committee of the Senate and the House of Commons on Reviewing Canadian Foreign Policy.' *Minutes of Proceedings and Evidence,* 36: 25, 9 June.

Naim, Moises. (2003). 'An Indigenous World: How Native People Can Turn Globalization to Their Advantage'. *Foreign Policy* 139: 95–96.

Niezen, Ronald. (2003). The *Origins of Indigenism: Human Rights and the Politics of Identity.* Berkeley: University of California Press.

Niezen, Ronald. (2000). 'Recognizing Indigenism: Canadian Unity and the International Movement of Indigenous Peoples'. *Comparative Studies in Society and History* 42(1): 119–148.

Nolan, Cathal J. (1988). 'The Human Rights Committee'. In Robert O. Matthews and Cranford Pratt, eds., *Human Rights in Canadian Foreign Policy.* Kingston and Montreal and Kingston: McGill-Queen's University Press.

OHCHR. (2006). *United Nations Guide for Indigenous Peoples.* Leaflets 1–12. New York: Office of the United Nations High Commissioner for Human Rights. www.ohchr.orgienglishlissues/indigenous/guide.htm (20 March 2007).

OHCHR. (1977). Sandra Lovelace v. Canada, Communication No. 24/1977: Canada, CCPC, 13th Sess. Geneva: Office of the United Nations High Commissioner for Human Rights. www.unhchr.ch/tbs/doc.nsf/0/cc245da4e1c73a55c1256al6003b21a8?Opendocument (20 March 2007).

Pal, Leslie and Robert Malcolm Campbell. (1991). The *Real Worlds of Canadian Politics,* 2nd ed. Peterborough: Broadview Press.

Pertusati, Linda. (1997). *In Defense of Mohawk Land: Ethnopolitical Conflict in Native North America.* Albany: State University of New York Press.

Platiel, Rudy. (1993). 'Ottawa out to Sabotage Native Rights, Leaders Say.' *Globe and Mail,* 23 June.

Ponting, Rick. (1990). 'Internationalization: Perspectives on an Emerging Direction in Aboriginal Affairs.' *Canadian Ethnic Studies* 22(3): 85–109.

Robinson, Andrew M. (2004). 'Multi-level Governance, Federalism, and International Human Rights Regimes: Assessing the Impact on Canadian Sovereignty.' Paper presented at the annual conference of the Canadian Political Science Association, 3–5 June, Winnipeg.

Sanders, Douglas. (1994). 'Developing a Modem International Law on the Rights of Indigenous Peoples'. www.ubcic.bc.ca/files/PDF/Developing.pdf (20 March 2007).

Sanders, Douglas. (1992). 'Remembering Deskeheh: Indigenous Peoples and International Law'. In Irwin Colter and F. Pearl Eliadis, eds., *International Human Rights Law: 'Theory and Practice.* Montreal and Kingston: The Canadian Human Rights Foundation.

Sanders, Douglas. (1985). 'Aboriginal Rights: The Search for Recognition in International Law.' In Menno Boldt and J. Anthony Long, eds., *'The Quest for Justice: Aboriginal Peoples and Aboriginal Rights.* Toronto: University of Toronto Press.

Sanders, Douglas. (1983). 'The Indian Lobby.' In Keith Banting and Richard Simeon, eds., *And No One Cheered: Federalism, Democracy and the Constitution Act.* Toronto: Methuen.

Sanders, Douglas. (1980). 'The Formation of the World Council of Indigenous Peoples.' Lethbridge: WCIP-Secretariat.

Sandra Lovelace v. Canada. (1983). Communication No. 24/1977, UN Document Supp. No. 40 *(Al38/40).* wwI.

umn.edulhumanrts/undocs/session38/24-1977.htm   (20 March 2007).

Schuler, Corinna. (2001). 'Canadian Apartheid Grabs Local Headlines.' *National Post,* 31 August.

Simon, Mary. (1994). 'Testimony before the Special Joint Committee of the Senate and the House of Commons on Reviewing Canadian Foreign Policy.' *Minutes of Proceedings and Evidence.* 36: 30, 9 June.

Simon, Mary. (1989). 'Security, Peace and the Native Peoples of the Arctic.' In Thomas Berger et al., eds., The *Arctic: Choices for Peace* & *Security.* West Vancouver: Gordon Soules.

Slaughter, Anne-Marie. (1997). 'The Real New World Order.' *Foreign Affairs* 76(5): 183–197.

Smith, Donald B.. (1993). 'Missing's' a Threat to Rights.' *Windspeaker* 11(7): 1.

Smith, Doug. (1987). 'An Awkward Visit.' *Maclean's,* 23 March.

Tennant, Chris. (1994). 'Indigenous Peoples, International Institutions, and the International Legal Literature from 1945–1993.' *Human Rights Quarterly* 16(1): 1–57.

Titley, E. Brian. (1986). *A Narrow Vision: Duncan Campbell Scott and the Administration of Indian Affairs in Canada.* Vancouver: UBC Press.

Tobias, John. (1976). 'Protection, Civilization, Assimilation: An Outline of Canada's Indian Policy.' '*The Western CanadianJournal of Anthropology* 6(2): 13–30.

Toronto Star. (2001). 'Minister Demands Native Leader Apologize.' 7 September: AI.

Toronto Star. (1993). 'Austria Opposes Canada to Back Indigenous Peoples.' 24 June: A24.

UN. (June 2006). 'Utilization of Indigenous Peoples' Lands by Non-Indigenous Authorities, Groups or Individuals for Military Purposes.' Report authored by The United Nations Working Group on Indigenous Populations.

Veatch, Richard. (1975). *Canada and the League of Nations.* Toronto: University of Toronto Press

Walker, James W. St G. (1997). '*Race', Rights and the Law in the Supreme Court of Canada: Historical Case Studies.* Toronto: The Osgoode Society for Canadian Legal History and Wilfrid Laurier University Press.

Welsh, Jennifer. (2004). *At Home in the World: Canada's Global Vision for the 21st Century.* Toronto: HarperCollins.

Whyte, John D. (1974). 'The Lavell Case and Equality in Canada.' *Queen's Quarterly* 81: 28–42.

Woodward, Michael and Bruce George. (1983). 'The Canadian Indian Lobby of Westminster *1979–1982'. Journal of Canadian Studies* 18(3): 119–143.

York, Geoffrey. (1987). 'Indian Blanket, Aid Request Greet Babb at Peguis Reserve.' *Globe and Mail,* 11 March.

York, Geoffrey and Loreen Pindera. (1991). *People of the Pines: The Warriors and the Legacy of Oka.* Toronto: Little, Brown.

11

NATO IN CANADIAN FOREIGN POLICY: FROM 'ATLANTICIST' FEAR AND HOPE TO A FUTURE OF ENVIRONMENTAL CRISIS AND 'CIVILIZATIONAL RALLYING'?

Douglas Alan Ross

NATO's diamond anniversary was 4 April 2009. The moment passed with modest public attention, occurring as it did during a worldwide economic recession triggered by American financial industry venality and lack of effective regulatory discipline. In North America few were in the mood for celebration, not knowing whether the free fall in global equity markets could be halted and the 'Great Recession' managed. Neither was there much enthusiasm for the political running sore known as the 'Afghan mission' that had been pressed upon NATO allies by the Bush Administration after 2003 as an alternative to military support in Iraq. The Afghan intervention was to be NATO's first great test of 'out-of-area' military engagement; such operations had been promoted for almost a decade by American policy-makers. Six years later the collaborative, NATO-anchored ISAF 'mission' was in serious disarray. From a low-level counter-terrorism (CT) operation it escalated sharply into a major counter-insurgency (CI) war. In late summer 2008, British, French, and American military analysts had suggested that the Taliban insurgency was on the verge of winning the war.

For Ottawa, Afghan policymaking about was *de facto* policy about NATO. Defeat in Afghanistan with recriminations on both sides of the Atlantic might well end NATO—where, rather unexpectedly, the disappearance of the Cold War Soviet threat in the early 1990s could not. As a matter of international security *strategy,* the Canadian national political elite and foreign policy-attentive public need to think hard about Ottawa's security interests in managing a tolerable Afghan outcome, thus maintaining the political cohesion of the alliance, while furthering Canada's 'grand strategy' of cooperative security promotion.[1] A decade of overly celebratory, blinkered optimism following the NATO expansion debate of the mid-1990s has come to an end. History did not end; war and scarcity did not disappear; nor did politics degenerate into a simple game of dividing up the spoils of accelerating technical prowess and globalization's economies of scale. A more realistic collective Canadian assessment of the trend line of world affairs is in order.[2]

Containing and neutralizing radical Islamist terrorism is important, but so too is the international nuclear non-proliferation effort that has tried to rein in and reverse the spread of Weapons of Mass Destruction (WMDs) of all types. The decades-long non-proliferation effort that began in the years following the terrifying Cuban missile crisis has been a pillar of subsequent Canadian international security relations.[3] After 2002, a myopic fixation on the Afghan war, pleasing the US managers of the 'war on terrorism', and keeping cross-border trade flowing deflected Canadian attention from working toward this larger objective. But since early 2007 significant forces in the American policy community,[4] and since January 2009 a new American government, have been trying to reinvigorate the nuclear disarmament process. Now a broader-based international movement has arisen to support this effort.[5] Canadian input is likely to enter this debate most usefully via the NATO policy forum. The NORAD alliance link (the bilateral North American Aerospace Defence relationship) has never provided any real opportunity for Ottawa's deliberative input into American nuclear strategy and arms control goals—just the courtesy of advanced briefings on American aerospace policy changes and latterly a venue for private discussion of 'homeland security' issues.

Growing fear of nuclear terrorism on US soil, combined with a recognition that Bush Administration policies of nuclear primacy (i.e., global nuclear, disarming, first-strike superiority over all potential 'peer competitors', namely Russia and China) and counter-proliferation coercive

diplomacy, or preventive war, towards 'rogue' regimes (in Iraq, Libya, North Korea, and Iran) had met with limited success, called for a revised approach.[6] Strategic unilateralism simply did not work quickly enough and had provoked considerable mistrust and 'balancing against' American foreign policy in foreign governments. A renewed multilateralism in arms control and disarmament is now thought to be essential by Obama Administration officials in their effort to reshape American international security relations.

Looming just over the policy horizon is an additional grave threat, one that Americans in particular (prior to Obama) have been loath to recognize: the prospect of compounded environmental/economic crises. The threat of 'coming anarchy'[7] in the warmest parts of the planet is growing as the climate heats up, pollution worsens, ocean fisheries collapse, deserts spread, monsoon rains fail, water tables fall, and crops shrivel. Fears that scores of millions will try to flee eco-catastrophes and the possible death of nations are growing more intense. Israel may not be involved in the world's first bilateral nuclear exchange. That horrific event may be more likely to occur as an 'environmentally' driven scenario between India and Pakistan—as the monsoon rains falter, and the Himalayan snowpack and summer run-off shrinks, triggering a war over Indus river water allocation.[8] Casualty estimates for such a conflict have ranged from 100 million to 400 million dead, depending on assumptions of nuclear arsenal size.[9] Renewed Sino-Indian border tensions that have been driven in part by concerns over access to water (damming of the upper reaches of the Brahmaputra, diversion of India-destined river waters out of Nepal to China) have also been added to the list of potential eco-scarcity/conflict scenarios.

A world without NATO would not likely be a better or safer place as the ecological stability of the planet continues to erode and entire countries slide towards chaos. Without a healthy NATO community it is doubtful that any global WMD disarmament campaign can be brought to a successful conclusion. Staying on as an active member of NATO would not be an easy process in the era of trans-Atlantic feuding that may be in the offing. But Canadian international security interests arguably are more likely to be promoted via sustained 'Atlanticist' unity for as long as is practicable—General Rick Hillier's negative views notwithstanding.[10] The myth of Europe-as-strategic-counterweight in Canadian foreign policy may have expired, as some analysts have argued.[11] But the value of a broader multilateral security community in which Canadians can advance and promote useful reforms is increasing steadily as the spectre of severe planetary disorder edges nearer.

The conflict in Afghanistan has been examined in detail in other chapters. Nonetheless, a few comments on the stakes at issue for NATO are in order, followed by a brief historical review of the major phases of Canada's engagement with NATO, along with some of the 'lessons learned' from each period. In the final portion of the chapter, Canada's grand strategy options will be assessed in light of how the existence, or absence, of an effective and cooperatively consultative NATO would affect them.

For Canada, the conflict in Afghanistan is now more a moral obligation than a strategic vital interest. For governments in Ottawa it was an 'unexpected war'.[12] From the outset Canadian authorities intended to be 'early in and early out'.[13] The expectation was simply wrong. From 2002 to 2009 it was the 'other war' for the Pentagon. Only with the Obama Administration's troop surge after September 2009 did Washington commit to an effort to 'win' the counter-insurgency war that had dragged on indecisively for eight years. For the Bush Administration Iraq had been the priority. Hoping that Iraq is now on the road to stability

through 'Iraqization' of the fighting, the Obama team has tried to replicate progress in Iraq via 'Afghanization' of the fighting in Afghanistan. But allied NATO governments are weary of a fight that few of them ever embraced wholeheartedly. Canada, the Netherlands, and Denmark are committed to imminent exits from the war. Britain may soon join them given the UK's developing fiscal calamity.[14] With over 140 combat deaths by early 2010, Ottawa is unlikely to reverse a parliamentary decision to withdraw all military forces by the end of 2011. Despite the US deployment surge, there simply are too few ISAF troops and trainers (for the Afghan military and national police) to defeat an insurgency that has been gaining steadily in strength since 2007. The government in Kabul is corrupt, incompetent, and ethnically unrepresentative. The porous Pakistani border permits the insurgents to import weapons, ammunition, and personnel. And the economy cannot shake its dependence on the sale of narcotics. With a mostly illiterate and grindingly poor population 'sitting on the fence' politically because of Taliban intimidation, the prospect of an early victory by the end of 2011 is next to nil. Regardless of who succeeds President Hamid Karzai, any future use of Afghan territory for terrorist training can still be dealt with through aerial strikes and Special Forces raiding. 'Containment' is therefore a feasible alternative approach.

The probability of al Qaeda wanting to return to Afghanistan, or of a new Taliban government being willing to invite them back, is almost certainly minimal—as retired General Lewis Mackenzie has bluntly noted.[15] The Canadian decade in Afghanistan was the product of three prime ministers attempting to mollify the US government after Ottawa had refused to endorse either the US intervention in Iraq or the quarter century-long American drive to develop a global system of Anti-Ballistic Missile (ABM) defences. Afghanistan is not a strategic interest of Canada's; but it has become a morally painful burden caused by giving false hope of self-determination to millions of Afghans who sooner or later are likely to fall under Taliban rule and an extremist version of Sharia law.[16]

The future of Pakistan, on the other hand, is a vital concern. Pakistan has over six times the population of Afghanistan, and a rapidly growing nuclear and ballistic missile arsenal. It has a large, literate, modern middle class. Because of its WMD-possessing status,[17] Pakistan must be saved from the extremists lest some of its 80- to 100-plus atomic bombs fall directly into terrorist hands. In 2007 and 2008, three separate attacks by Islamist extremists occurred at nuclear facilities in Pakistan.[18] In October 2009, Islamic extremists attacked the Army's headquarters near Islamabad, taking 42 people hostage at one point. Pakistani nuclear (and other WMD) vulnerabilities have become a powerful argument for retrenching the international effort in Afghanistan and redirecting US and alliance resources to Islamabad's campaign in the 'tribal areas' along Pakistan's western border. Arguably, Pakistan is pivotal, while Afghanistan is but a costly distraction.

A failure by NATO in Afghanistan would be serious, but it need not be a terminal threat to the alliance. Heading off the threat of Pakistani state collapse, and the looming risk of compounded crises of environmental deterioration, uncontrolled human migration, and possible accompanying acts of mass violence, may be a more appropriate path for the Trans-Atlantic alliance over the next thirty years. If the great democratic alliance of 'the West' is the last best hope for human survival, its rescue mission for planet Earth may have to begin not in the mountains of Afghanistan but rather in an effort to stabilize Pakistan and forestall the threat of an Indo-Pakistani nuclear war.[19]

CANADA IN NATO: LESSONS FROM THE CLASSICAL COLD WAR PERIOD IN THE DIPLOMACY OF CONSTRAINT

In 1945 the Canadian Armed Forces were the fourth most powerful in the world with nearly 750,000 soldiers in arms. Only armies in the US, the USSR, and Britain were larger. In the ensuing decade they shrank to one-tenth this size, and then grew quickly again, fielding a capable expeditionary force in France and West Germany while Western Europe rearmed slowly. The RCAF was expanded to handle both a serious military role in Europe and the challenge of helping to protect American Strategic Air Command (SAC) nuclear bombers in North America against surprise attack during the era of bomber-based nuclear deterrence that lasted until the early 1960s. At sea, the RCN operated jet fighters and ASW patrol aircraft from shore bases and from two aircraft carriers in the North Atlantic. Later, three Oberon submarines helped keep the North Atlantic Sea Lane of Communication (SLOC) open in the event of a long conventional war in Europe.

This expensive effort was willingly undertaken during the dark years of the 'first' Cold War (1948 to 1972). Canada was not merely 'also present at the Creation'[20] of NATO; Canadians actually started the process that culminated in the Washington Treaty and the successful multilateral containment of Soviet communism. In August 1947 Escott Reid, one of Canada's foremost scholar diplomats, was the very first government official in any Atlantic country to give a public speech laying out the case for a North Atlantic collective defence treaty.[21] The campaign began with Canadian and British initiatives to try to persuade key American officials that such an alliance was the best way to ensure Western European security in the face of Soviet subversion and communist seizures of power throughout Eastern Europe in the 1945–48 period. American isolationism in the 1930s had made it possible for Hitler's Wehrmacht to conquer Western Europe; for Canada's geostrategic thinkers, any repetition of that scenario by the Red Army had to be prevented if at all possible. Communist 'salami tactics' of subverting and then conquering one country at a time, while less dramatic in the late 1940s than Hitler's blitzkrieg, were no less ruthless.

At least cost to all its members (the main reason for alliance formation generally), NATO would deter overt aggression, and, through hope and moral leadership, it would discourage repetition of 'the blasphemy that a Third World War is inevitable', as Mackenzie King's Foreign Minister Louis St Laurent put it.[22] For St Laurent, both as Foreign Minister and then as King's successor as Prime Minister, it was critical that a 'preponderance of material and moral strength on the side of peace' be established, and that the values and institutions of 'our democratic Christian civilization' be promoted to keep the 'atheistic communist world' at bay. The message of St Laurent's 'crusade' for NATO was based on a rejection of totalitarian repression of individual human rights, and a belief that in time even Russian communists might one day undergo a 'spiritual transformation'.[23] St Laurent's views reflected a certain empathy for the enemy that was sorely lacking among American leaders of the day. From the beginning, the Canadian campaign was based on an impulse to deter and contain Soviet expansionism—not defeat it on the field of battle. In the atomic age, war risked mutual suicide. Canadian efforts to sell the NATO concept were based on the immediate goals of reassurance of Western European publics, deterrence of any possible military attack by the Soviets (although only the Norwegian and the Danes felt in imminent danger),[24] and a complete halt to the communist bloc's subversion-driven *political* momentum.

To American officials, Canadian diplomats like Hume Wrong shrewdly stressed that NATO would help resolve Canadian doubts about greatly heightened military cooperation with the US in North America. With NATO in play, 'the defence of North America fell into place as part of a larger whole and would diminish difficulties arising from fears of invasion of Canadian sovereignty by the US'. The Canadian approach was also based on the calculation that, without such an organization, sooner or later the USSR and the communist governments would be driven out of the UN. To save the UN as a symbol of global community and a place for world dialogue, John Holmes noted, NATO had to be created rather than driving Moscow out of an increasingly partisan UN.[26] Canadian officials never intended NATO to replace the UN, but rather to supplement it by providing the practical security cooperation that the UN could not. The Canadian article, Article 2 of the NATO charter, that called for economic cooperation among members was central to the government's 'crusade' to make NATO 'more than an alliance of the old kind'.[27] Prime Ministers King and St Laurent believed deeply in its importance based on their *practically idealist* views.[28] In the case of Article 2, however, their hopes for a strong social, economic, and cultural dimension to NATO membership were not realized. Nonetheless, they did succeed in having the article included despite strong American objections. John Holmes, his realism and pragmatism notwithstanding, could still speak very idealistically in the middle of the alliance's second decade about NATO's broader purpose:

The Atlantic community is a spiritual idea, but it has a function. That function is to use its enormous wealth and power to protect the weak and stimulate prosperity. Its function is initiative, to save the world, and not itself alone. It can be the breeder of racial isolationism or a new internationalism. Its primary duty is to promote its mission, not its unity.[29]

The central lesson for Canadians from the formative years of NATO was this: Smaller states can have an important impact on patterns of great power behaviour and issues of war and peace, if they can advance proposals that sensibly mesh the national interests of a broader community of nations sharing similar values. Universal collective security organizations cannot perform this function.

NATO DURING THE COLD WAR AND CANADA'S NUCLEAR WEAPONS CHALLENGE

Ottawa played an important military role from 1951 to 1956 by providing the Canadian First Air Division in Europe with nearly 200 front-line, all-weather/day-night fighter interceptors in 12 squadrons in France, and an armoured brigade in West Germany. The interceptors arrived at a time when the US Air Force was still relatively thin on the ground in Europe because of the priority of deployment in the 'hot' war in Korea. The Canadian deployment amounted to only about one-third of the 20,000 troops and 600 aircraft that NATO had requested from Ottawa.[30] But that request was to be part of a grossly unrealistic alliance force plan of some 90 divisions that had been conceived in Lisbon in 1952. After 1958, Canadian forces in Europe were equipped with nuclear weapons that were much less expensive than armoured divisions and were thought to be psychologically far more effective in deterring aggression. For Western Europeans, the last thing they wanted to do was tempt Soviet war planners into the idea that a major conventional war might be fought in Europe that might stay non-nuclear. The European preference for relying on a nuclear

'crutch' is now familiar: since the early 1990s both Russia and Pakistan have adopted nuclear first-use postures intended to deter neighbours armed with superior conventional forces.

For the next two decades NATO was at the heart of both Canadian defence and foreign policy. Lester Pearson, a strategic thinker *par excellence*, took pride in helping found the alliance and as prime minister made sure that Canada's nuclear obligations to the alliance were fulfilled. His diplomatic manoeuvres in establishing international peacekeeping forces to resolve the 1956 Suez and 1965 Cyprus crises were aimed at saving NATO as much as they were at snuffing out brushfire wars that carried with them the risk of superpower intervention and nuclear escalation. Pearson understood that Western Europe was seen in Washington as the most strategically vital part of the Eurasian continent that had to be preserved from Soviet expansionism.[31] Thus to the extent that official Ottawa wished to practise what Denis Stairs called the diplomacy of constraint,[32] maintaining a healthy Euro-American relationship was very important for Canadian vital security interests. Constructive Canadian preferences since 1949 for containment and deterrence, not anti-communist rollback via limited or preventive wars, were promoted by joining with other like-minded Europeans.

John Diefenbaker constantly tried to link NORAD to NATO's broader collective defence mission—bearing out Hume Wrong's forecast a decade earlier. While Diefenbaker reversed course on accepting nuclear-armed roles for the Canadian forces during his last years as prime minister, he nonetheless was a strong supporter of NATO and the containment of Soviet imperialism. Diefenbaker's growing misgivings about the Soviet-American nuclear arms race, his interest in stimulating good-faith nuclear disarmament negotiations, and his mistrust of American nuclear adventurism, were—with the advantage of historical hindsight—wholly justified. His political tactics, however, were inept and his badly divided Cabinet lacked strategic competence.

The Cuban missile crisis of 1962, just prior to Diefenbaker's electoral defeat, was a watershed in Canadian–American relations. It marked a realization by Canadian politicians that the NORAD relationship established in 1958 would *in no way* provide a guarantee of meaningful consultation on issues that could lead to central nuclear war. From Ottawa's perspective, the US violated NORAD's fundamental guarantee to Canadians in the weeks leading up to the Cuban crisis. That crisis starkly demonstrated that nuclear war might arise elsewhere than in central Europe, and that it could occur over issues and American strategies that Ottawa might not approve but could not influence. A classic small-power dilemma of potential 'entrapment' in an allied great power's strategic initiatives had become all too clear. The sense of entrapment was all the more galling when the RCAF put itself on alert without Cabinet authorization, while the RCN defied civilian control and engaged in joint military operations with US forces to bring maximum pressure on Soviet naval forces during the crisis, and for weeks after the public had been told the crisis was over. This clear breach of civilian control of the military during the most dangerous crisis of the entire Cold War would lead to the rapid unification of the Canadian Armed Forces and their subjection to permanent micromanagement by a large civilian bureaucracy.[33]

Following the Liberals' electoral victory in 1963, the RCAF contributed a theatre-wide nuclear strike capability to the alliance via CF-104 'Starfighters' armed with variable-yield (up to 1.45 megatons each[34]) thermonuclear bombs, as well as low-yield, short-range, nuclear-armed, surface-to-surface missiles (the temperamental, slow-to-fire 'Honest John' rockets). The RCAF and the Canadian army were happy to have such roles in the alliance,

but all was not well in terms of the strategic concept of operations. Early Cold War Canadian officialdom was thoroughly and autonomously conversant with core nuclear deterrence concepts.[35] With Britain and France acquiring independent nuclear deterrent forces by the late 1950s and mid-1960s respectively, and with the European economies mostly recovered, doubts arose in Ottawa as to the appropriateness of expensive deployments overseas and the desirability of contributing to the further proliferation of nuclear weapons capability through 'two key' nuclear sharing within NATO itself.

For a decade, involvement in shared nuclear strike planning on NATO's central front kept Ottawa 'in the game' even as its percentage contribution to the alliance's conventional forces fell to a militarily inconsequential level. When the nuclear strike role, with its potentially megaton-range payloads and deep-strike capacity, was eliminated for the three squadrons of CF-104s and the low-yield Honest John short-range rockets in 1972 and 1970 respectively,[36] symbolic participation was all that was left so far as European perceptions were concerned.

In the conventional tale, analysts refer to Canada's disengagement from nuclear deterrence as causing a radically diminished status. Canada then became the 'odd man out' in the alliance.[37] Canadian politicians agreed with the Europeans that NATO was, and should remain, a purely defensive, containment-oriented alliance. Both Conservatives and Liberals opposed those American hawks who wanted to 'roll back' the Iron Curtain wherever opportunities might exist.[38] From the late 1970s to February 1992, when Canadian Forces were ordered to close their bases in Germany, some new tanks and fighter interceptors were added but not in sufficient numbers to impress the Europeans. After the 1972 termination of Canadian sharing of the nuclear strike burden, the Europeans were apparently disillusioned with Ottawa's military contribution. They rarely, if ever, acknowledged that Ottawa had to attend to continental security in NORAD (especially after the Cuban missile crisis) nor that such work contributed indirectly to their own security. Neither did they note that maintaining a significant 'blue-water' navy able to conduct Anti-Submarine Warfare (ASW) work in the North Atlantic was further reason to reduce the Canadian role on the central front in Germany to symbolic dimensions. From the perspective of London, Bonn and Paris, the Canadians had shown they no longer identified with European military preferences and no longer appeared willing to shoulder a fair part of the collective deterrent burden.[39]

Of course, the criticism was partly valid. The Canadians, like the Americans, wanted a robust *conventional warfighting* capability for NATO; they did not want to stake everything on threats to use nuclear weapons early on in any major NATO–Warsaw Treaty conflict. In this aspect of alliance policy, Canadian and American strategic preferences were convergent. The Cuban Missile Crisis had demonstrated clearly that Canadians needed to think through what their strategic nuclear doctrinal commitments should be. When they did, they realized that they liked nuclear weapons far less than the Europeans did. Geography matters. The Trudeau government's rationale for CF-104 termination was the intrinsically *destabilizing* character of the deployment. As Trudeau and his foreign policy adviser, Ivan Head, noted retrospectively:

> . . . in the eye of the Soviets, they [the Starfighters] could only be regarded as a first-strike or at least a first-use system. They flew from soft target airbases, and they could not expect to escape incoming, pretargeted ballistic missiles or bombs from attacking aircraft in surprise circumstances.[40]

The nuclear-armed CF-104 aircraft were thus a standing temptation for pre-emptive destruction, and thus were an incentive for the Soviets to escalate suddenly, without warning, in some future crisis. Far better that NATO's deterrent forces should be deployed on survivable weapon platforms such as submarines armed with ballistic or cruise missiles. Trudeau and Head had left office before they could take up that challenge. The Mulroney government actually may have liked the decapitation threats implicit in American INF deployments during the early to mid-1980s (464 Ground Launched Cruise Missiles and 108 rapid-strike Pershing II ballistic missiles), or it may have feared American displeasure if Ottawa objected to an emerging American first-strike, counter-leadership deployment. But by the end of his career in the early 1980s, Prime Minister Trudeau had completely reversed course and come to appreciate the importance of the alliance as a politico-strategic stabilizer and as an institutional amplifier of Canadian political and diplomatic thinking. Without a continued Canadian role in NATO there would have been no opportunity for his 'peace mission' among the nuclear powers in the autumn of the nuclear crisis year of 1983.[41] Brian Mulroney developed plans for a greater role in the alliance, culminating in a White Paper in 1987 that envisioned a far more active, militarily meaningful presence that included a dozen nuclear-powered hunter-killer submarines. These would have given Canada a 'three ocean navy' and its first ability to project power into the Arctic ocean—even at the risk of alienating the US Navy, which had indicated that it would do all it could to block Canadian purchase of British Trafalgar-class submarines. But the Cold War began to disintegrate a year later and the grand plans of the White Paper were shelved. In February 1992 Mulroney's government ordered the complete withdrawal of Canadian forces from their last two bases in Germany; by 1994 the last Canadian troops in Germany were gone.

Following his electoral victory of 1993, Prime Minister Jean Chrétien enthusiastically endorsed alliance expansion to the hilt, hoping to transform the strategic landscape of Europe and create new export markets in the process—especially, it was hoped, for Canadian nuclear reactors. Peacekeeping in Bosnia and later 'peace enforcement' over the Kosovo crisis saw significant Canadian roles. In Brussels the Canadians pushed hard for the transformation of the alliance along co-operative security lines. NATO continued as a foundational element of Canadian international security planning for the post-Cold War period.

In hindsight, the commitment to the alliance through the Cold War and after was well worth it. The North Atlantic community has been a force for stability, prosperity, democracy, and human rights. As an institution it made security policy-making in Europe predictable and reliable. It fostered European defence forces that were 'interoperable' and aimed at collective defence, rather than narrow national interest that might tempt thoughts of national offensive capability. By entangling the US, Britain, and Canada in the security affairs of Europe, NATO helped promote an ever greater political unity and common process of political decision-making among the peoples of Europe. West Germany was reintegrated into the community of nations—without it becoming a nuclear weapon state (as more than a few American hawks and 'offensive realist' international relations scholars had hoped). NATO and the EU together made war among Europeans unthinkable—and after 100,000 Canadian dead in two major wars in Europe that must be seen as a major geopolitical accomplishment. Arguably NATO's defensive character helped to make the peaceful disintegration of the Soviet state possible. And even the politically and strategically ill-advised expansion of NATO after 1995 produced only a partial backlash in the form of Russian strategic nuclear force renewal and arms control rejectionism.

NATO'S COLD WAR POLICIES IN STRATEGIC PERSPECTIVE

As a set of relationships, the Atlantic community helped to dampen and moderate excessive or extreme behaviour on both sides of the Atlantic, notably: American nuclear adventurism (1954– 55, 1962, 1973, 1983); Anglo– French imperialism over Suez (1956); Gaullist nuclear nationalism from the 1960s to the 1980s; Reagan's nuclear warfighting doctrinal recidivism of the early 1980s; and most recently President George W. Bush's campaign of 'counterproliferation' preventive war against the 'axis of evil'. In each instance dangerous policies were initiated and actions taken—but *far worse actions* were inhibited or prevented altogether. Intra-community deterrence of potentially catastrophic international security policies 'worked', however imperfectly.

Henry Kissinger was wrong: over the decades the alliance *has* acted as an inhibiting drag on successive generations of American 'hawks'. NATO's moderating impact on American behaviour was stimulated by European and Canadian fears of American nuclear adventurism. NATO European members were so defensively minded that they were clearly incapable of threatening their neighbours with anything more serious than prosperity and seduction. While Vladimir Putin may now rail against NATO troops or ABM launchers on Russian borders, the complaints seem more theatrical than credible, since Europe is the key source of Russian prosperity. For Canadian purposes, it is vital to appreciate that the peoples of the Atlantic security community, in their size- and defence-dominant, containment-preferring approach to regional security, have acted very much like a sheet anchor in the stormy weather of global security crises both during and after the Cold War.

Since World War II, when American geopolitical planners were determined to deny the 'rimlands of Eurasia' to any expansionary would-be regional hegemony,[42] all the way up to twenty-first century efforts to establish an American nuclear primacy and a preponderance of power throughout the world,[43] the Europeans have been a disproportionately important part of 'world opinion' so far as Washington policymakers were concerned. A large part of NATO's value to Canadians has been its role as an inhibitor of American strategic excess and as an institutional means for promoting nuclear arms control, détente with the USSR, and a strong global non-proliferation regime.

Preventive war on China did not occur—though many American hawks favoured it prior to 1968. Tactical nuclear weapons were not used during the Korean conflict, during the Chinese offshore islands crises of 1954–5 and 1958, or during the Vietnam war—though senior American military leaders like Admiral Arthur Radford, Generals Curtis LeMay and Lyman Lemnitzer, and presidential candidate Barry Goldwater, all were known to favour their use as 'just another weapon'. Soviet– American relations, except for the early 1960s and early 1980s, were characterized by a heavily armed, grudging, but still peaceful commitment to mutual tolerance of the superpowers' respective spheres of influence.[44] Because of NATO, moderate American leaders could be attentive to Western European thinking, implicit criticism, or plain common sense in a way that they never could have been to Canadian opinion or strategic preferences, given Ottawa's 'free riding' reputation and marginal military assets.[45]

Canadian motivation in building a North Atlantic security community was decidedly less abstract than American geopolitical or realist strategic calculations. It grew out of distinctly Canadian liberal idealist sentiments that valued Western European 'Christian civilization' in its own right as a partner in world security affairs, as a geographically linked set of national communities whose history and destiny were inextricably interwoven with that of the peoples of northern North America, and as a vital resource in the building of global security and democracy. This pragmatically idealist understanding of the basis of the North Atlantic community still constitutes the basis for the Alliance's continued popularity in all parts of Canada. In this respect the Canadian adherence to NATO through its first half century reflected an almost Huntingtonian commitment to a belief in 'the West'—specifically its political culture and social values.[46] Thus, taking actions that might risk the demise and dissolution of NATO—such as precipitately disengaging from the Afghan stabilization effort—is not a course of action to be undertaken lightly. The consequent near-extinction of a meaningful Canadian voice on international security issues would be unwise in a time of impending global shortages and environmental crises.

NATO evolved over its sixty years to become what Samuel Huntington called 'the premier Western institution'.[47] If present challenges are dealt with responsibly and amicably through intra-alliance dialogue, it will remain so. But for now the Afghan conflict, the effort to foster a stable denouement for US intervention in Iraq, and the challenge of containing seemingly perennial American preferences for nuclear primacy, remain serious pressing security issues for which no obvious consensus yet exists.

For Canadian officials and security-minded academics, NATO's longevity for two decades beyond the end of the Cold War has been a pleasant surprise. Despite the forecast of eminent American realist scholars such as Kenneth Waltz and John Mearsheimer,[48] the alliance found useful things to do. The great conventional armies were dismantled; the extraordinarily dangerous array of tactical and theatre nuclear weapons were mostly retired and dismantled. Peacekeeping operations were mounted extensively to help the members of the Commonwealth of Independent States. Eastern European states were aided in improving democratic governance that would qualify them for eventual alliance membership. Germany and Ukraine did *not* acquire nuclear arsenals. The rule of law, democracy, and respect for human rights were strengthened across Eastern Europe. European unity continued to progress. Membership in NATO was seen as the anteroom for membership in the EU, so the alliance grew. Poland, Hungary, and the Czech Republic entered in 1995; Estonia, Latvia, Lithuania, Bulgaria, Romania, Slovakia, and Slovenia all joined in 2004; Albania and Croatia joined in April 2009. The founding 12 had become an unpredictable crowd of 28—with an aggregate population of nearly 1 billion of the richest, best educated people on the planet.

The pleasant surprise for Ottawa was that much of the new NATO agenda and activity grew out of policies and principles that can best be described by the summary label of co-operative security. Collective defence was still the essence of the treaty relationship, but something more had been added that was highly pleasing to Canadian officials and most non-governmental observers. Peacekeeping and economic stabilization were now central aspects of the life of the alliance. Article 2 now lived. David Haglund's optimistic assessment penned in the year prior to 9/11, was that 'in the absence of an enemy', and 'in an era of no (great power) threat', the transformation of NATO toward the adoption of the techniques of cooperative security had created what would be for Canadians 'the alliance of their dreams'.[49] The phrase 'co-operative security' (CS) was first used during Joe Clark's tenure as Foreign Minister and described an effort by Ottawa to promote a wider security

community in the Asia-Pacific region. CS entailed, as Haglund notes, 'a more sustainable, because realistic and interest-based appeal to co-operation'. The co-operative/human security doctrinal construct emphasized protecting the safety and human rights of individuals, the preventive use of international peacekeeping and peacebuilding efforts, greater attention to environmental and economic drivers of conflict, and finally collaborative institution-building with a view to enhancing measures for conflict prevention, not just conflict resolution. All were all part of the CS paradigm.

Nearly a decade after Haglund's monograph, it must be said that his apprehended international context of 'no great power threat' to the countries of NATO was sadly premature. The aftermath of 9/11 shelved the alliance of Canadian dreams for the duration of the Bush years. In early 2000 the Bush-Cheney 'revolution' in American international security policy was not yet visible, nor were the deeply provocative and destabilizing foreign policy ventures on which Washington would embark, such as overturning the ABM Treaty of 1972 by the summer of 2002 and setting the stage for preventive counterproliferation warfare in 2003.

The unilateral repudiation of the ABM treaty by the Bush Administration opened the floodgates to visions of multiple layers of ABM defences (ground-, sea-, and space-based) and American weaponization of space. In 2002 US military spending was more than that of the rest of the world's defence budgets combined. American neo-conservative hawks revealed themselves to be not realists but crusading neo-Wilsonian interventionists bent on turning 'rogue states' into functioning democracies—no matter how many people had to be sacrificed in the process.[50] Neo-conservative hawks about Bush brought with them their commitment to a new double 'primacy' for the US: first, nuclear over all potential adversaries;[51] and second, a grand strategy primacy enunciated in the National

Security Strategy of 2002 that called for building American pre-eminence in all aspects of military capability to a degree that would dissuade all potential peer competitors from even trying to compete with the US militarily.[52]

NATO'S NUCLEAR STRATEGIES FROM BUSH TO OBAMA

Canada refused to condone the former Bush Administration's strategically dubious plans for unilaterally controlled global missile defence on the grounds that additional Russian and Chinese nuclear arms were sure to follow. This rejection ultimately diminished Ottawa's standing in Washington. NORAD's 'new' status after 2006 as a treaty relationship was more a reflection of US efforts to strengthen the air–naval dimensions of the 'Great Wall of America' than any belief that Ottawa would be a 'strong state' player in shoring up US defences against long-range, bomber/cruise missile attack or terrorist infiltration.

Canadian fears were borne out. For the Russians, new investments in refurbished intercontinental-range bombers and a new generation of faster, longer range, stealthier Air-Launched Cruise Missiles (ALCMs) began. A new Submarine-Launched Ballistic Missile (SLBM) for a new class of missile-launching submarines was begun. With higher oil export revenues mostly earned from the NATO members of the EU, Putin's Russia accelerated construction of additional Topol-M land-mobile ICBMs. In 2008 new short-range, nuclear-capable 'Iskander' MRBM rockets were announced to be set for deployment into Kaliningrad should the Bush Administration move forward with the deployment of new Ground-Based Interceptors (GBIs) in Poland and an ABM tracking radar in the Czech Republic.[53] After a long moratorium on such activity, Russian long-range bombers resumed nuclear attack training flights towards North America in

2007.[54] Such probing missions into the Western hemisphere have also included recent 'test flights' by the Russian Air Force's supersonic Tu-160 out of a Venezuelan air base over the Caribbean.[55] Moscow defence planners, not to mention Prime Minister Vladimir Putin and President Medvedev, no doubt saw strategic 'encirclement' as very much part of American ABM deployments in Eastern Europe. For Moscow, fledgling ballistic missile programmes in Iran and North Korea are merely a US excuse to deepen American nuclear warfighting superiority over Russia and China.

For the Russians the prospect of Ukraine and Georgia joining NATO was completely unacceptable. The entire process of expanded membership since March 1999 (when Poland, Hungary, and the Czech Republic joined) was often denounced as a violation of the assurances that Mikhail Gorbachev claimed he had been given by NATO foreign ministers that the accession of East German territory to NATO status in 1990 would not see 'a centimetre' of any other eastern European territory added thereafter to NATO—or the establishment of NATO military bases anywhere near Russian borders.[56] Partly to try to deter Georgian membership, Russian military actions in early 2008 in support of the 'breakaway' Georgian territories of South Ossetia and Abkhazia culminated in a brief 'war' in August that led to NATO suspending relations with Moscow until March 2009. Given these developing problems, the Bucharest NATO summit in April 2008 saw Germany and France veto any early decision on Ukrainian and Georgian admission, against Bush Administration preferences. Once more the sheet anchor or braking function of the European members of the alliance came into play.

Chinese leaders were even more distressed than the Russians by the American nuclear challenge, fearing that American ABM and enhanced offensive global strike plans were intended to eliminate China's modest retaliatory capacity.[57] In a bid to restore such retaliatory credibility, they accelerated new missile-launching submarine deployment at a giant, partially subterranean submarine base on the southern tip of Hainan Island, on the east side of the Gulf of Tonkin. The Chinese land-based nuclear force was exceptionally slow to modernize with solid-fuel rockets (liquid-fuelled missiles require lengthy preparation for launch) after an exceedingly long period of extreme vulnerability to an American first strike with either nuclear weapons or simply conventional ones.[58]

China is the largest source of American imports and the largest holder of American Treasury notes. Russia is critical to meeting the EU's energy needs. But in the military–strategic dimension they are at risk of becoming serious nuclear-armed adversaries once more because of unilateral Bush-era defence policy decisions. The US drive for missile defence technology deployment was never a collective alliance decision or strategy. The American drive for ABM dominance was, as John Holmes noted, an example of 'brutal unilateralism' in which there was 'no opportunity for Canadian influence at the formative stage'.[59] Reagan's Strategic Defense Initiative began this surge toward nuclear primacy in 1983, and George W. Bush's Nuclear Posture Review of 2002 called for completing the task.

The problem with that approach was that it alienated governments and public opinion throughout the NATO community, not just in Beijing and Moscow. As Stephen Walt first explained in 1987, the US enjoyed a permanent imbalance of power in its favour throughout the Cold War because its allies in NATO rallied toward the US— the most powerful country in the world. We live in a world dominated by calculations of 'balance of threat', not 'balance of power'. For the duration of the Cold War and for a decade after it, countries continued to augment US power and security. NATO grew and economic co-operation was enhanced. The most powerful state in the world was the US, but countries were eager to enlist its security protection. And thus American power continued to grow for a decade into the post-Cold War world. The Soviet state in its last decade had enormous military capabilities but was far less powerful than the US. For Western Europeans, and for the Chinese and Japanese too, the dominant threat to their well-being and independence was the menace of Soviet imperialism and more specifically Soviet offensive conventional and nuclear strike capability. NATO's lesser states did not balance against Soviet 'power' (because it was not the most powerful state in the system) but against the specific Soviet threat to their independence and security. In the abstract, balance-of-power theorists expect states to balance against dominant, ascendant great powers. Walt realized that this is simply not true: states balance against the most dangerous threat in their international environment, and that might or might not be the most powerful state.[60]

American assertions of a will to strategic preponderance under George W. Bush have been roundly condemned within the American political–strategic debate for very good reason.[61] Bush-era strategic unilateralism seriously damaged the highly favourable 'imbalance of power' in the international system that supported the US throughout the Cold War. With Russian abilities now a shadow of the demographic, military, and economic capability of the old Soviet Union, even an unhappy re-arming Russia will not be enough to sustain NATO alliance cohesion if American leadership falters and degenerates into aggressive unilateralism. With the perceived external threat to NATO Europe posed by Russia dramatically lessened, deference to the US as leader of the alliance has shrunk considerably. Outright political and diplomatic opposition by France, Germany, Belgium, and Canada to the American invasion and occupation of Iraq without UN approval exemplified what has been termed 'soft balancing' against any US international security policy built on 'unipolar', unilateralist force projection.[62]

Bush Administration efforts to sell the 'war on terrorism' as the focal point of NATO's security planning and operations in a new 'long war' (some neo-conservatives have likened it to a World War IV, World War III being the successful anti-Soviet Cold War) were not convincing to most Europeans—hence the waning enthusiasm for staying the course in Afghanistan. Neither were Europeans or most Canadians attracted by the American declaration of a goal of permanent US nuclear primacy. The obvious provocation to Moscow and Beijing threatens the peaceable mutually beneficial economic relations that have been built up over the last two decades—not to mention the risk that helps to justify the retention of centralized autocratic power in both countries.

NATO'S NUCLEAR AND GRAND STRATEGY FUTURE

While many Europeans over the past decade have warmed to the idea of a missile defence against IRBMs coming from the Middle East, Iran, or North Africa, they still recoil from the thought of starting a new Russo-American or Sino-American nuclear arms race. So, too, do most Canadians. Multilateralizing any layered ABM defences so that they involve both Russia and China, and capping national deployments of ABM systems so that crisis instabilities can be precluded, should be a high priority for disarmament advocates. For Canada, participation in an alliance-wide system of capped, perhaps treaty-defined, ABM deployments should now be investigated. The Obama administration's clear commitment to serious nuclear disarmament, as reflected in its 2010 Nuclear Posture Review and the recent conclusion of the 'New START' strategic nuclear arms agreement with Russia, has opened the door to a broad range of stability-enhancing arms control and disarmament measures. The September 2009 decision to cancel the original planned ABM deployments in Poland and the Czech Republic convinced Moscow that the US was serious about 'resetting' the bilateral strategic relationship in a more cooperative way. Central strategic systems will now be reduced by some 25 percent over the next seven years below the targets set in 2002 by the SORT agreement. The next steps toward 'a nuclear-free world' will be more difficult though.

The issue of cooperative missile defences should be viewed from the perspective that ABM systems may ultimately be necessary as insurance for the nuclear-armed states to enable them to move to very low numbers of 'minimum deterrent' nuclear forces. Without them, fears of surprise attacks on their leadership might pose insuperable obstacles to progress toward a 'global zero' end state.

Current American thinking is based on the idea that the US's 'extended deterrent' nuclear guarantees to allies will have to be sustained through enhanced short- and medium-range ABM deployments (to nullify 'rogue' state regional missile threats) coupled with steadily enhanced, very long-range, precision strike non-nuclear forces (to destroy them).[63] Such new capabilities are intended to replace extensive American nuclear counterforce targeting capacity that will now be shrinking as a result of 'New START'. European NATO governments, especially in France, Germany, and the UK, are eager to develop a Euro–NATO-wide ABM architecture. Romania, with Russia's approval, has offered to accept alternative American ABM systems built around the SM-3 Navy mid-course interceptor and associated radars.[64] Poland has accepted advanced Patriot ABM systems for deployment near Kaliningrad in the wake of the GBI deployment cancellation. But the issue of US tactical nuclear weapons (TNWs) 'shared' with Belgium, Nether- lands, Germany, Italy, and Turkey may prove to be very politically awkward since they are all 'Non- Nuclear Weapons States' under the NPT—yet they have military personnel trained and able (with American concurrence) to deliver high-yield nuclear bombs to Russian targets.

As recently as January 2007, the US was thought to have some 480 nuclear gravity bombs deployed in Europe, with 180 of them slated for distribution to the national air forces of Belgium, the Nether- lands, Germany, Italy, and Turkey—all of whom are non-nuclear weapon state signatories of the Nuclear Non-Proliferation Treaty.[65] As of July 2007 the American military appears to have withdrawn over 100 weapons, lowering the total inventory to some 350 B-61 bombs.[66]

Ten years ago Canada pressed for the early elimination of this long-standing practice of 'nuclear sharing'. Only the Italians and Germans expressed interest. Presently Germany, Belgium, the Netherlands, Norway, and Luxembourg are pressing for complete withdrawal of all such tac- tical nuclear weapons (TNWs). Turkey and eastern European NATO members strongly oppose the pro- posal, seeing TNWs as a vitally needed deterrent against future Russian aggression. Washington is resisting because it wishes to negotiate a radical reduction in Russian TNWs (estimated to be some ten times the US deployment in Europe) This greatly improved the security for these weapons in a few centralized, highly secure locations.[67] The price for attracting American support for full with- drawal may be a parallel effort to forge a renewed 'coalition of the willing' inside the alliance to deal effectively with the Afghan problem and, in real terms, to absorb a far greater share of the costs of 'Afghanization' of the conflict (perhaps covering most of the estimated $10 billion per year cost of sustained expansion of the Afghan army and

national police). Ottawa clearly should consider committing 600 training staff to Afghanistan once the Canadian combat role is ended in July 2011.[68] The prospect of victory may be dim, but with a stronger Afghan military a future government in Kabul may be able to negotiate a less regressive armistice with Taliban moderates.

At the level of alliance strategy, leaders in Ottawa need to decide what broad strategic orien- tation is most appropriate to carry Canada and its allies forward safely over the next two to three dec- ades. If Canadians wish to support a TNW-free NATO, will it necessitate greater spending on con- ventional forces to create a replacement deterrent? If so, how will Canadians play a role? Secondly, should Ottawa be pressing for an ever-expanding NATO ('from Vancouver to Vladivostok' in some formulations)—or is it time to halt the process of growth? Thirdly, should Ottawa be pressing for the adoption of minimum deterrent forces by the P-5 states and a formal repudiation of counterforce and 'decapitation' capabilities by all the nuclear weapon states? Will a nuclear-free world be sus- tainable in terms of verification and enforcement capacity in the event that cheating occurs? Or would the maintenance of perhaps six or seven minimum deterrent forces that are 'well managed' and 'survivable' be a safer bet for the long term— free of the risk of 'rearmament races'?

At the level of grand strategy, Canadian leaders need to consider whether our post-Cold War world really does require indefinite involvement in the NATO collective defence endeavour. Will a NATO of 28 or 30 members still be able to act as a moderat- ing force on the US? Will North Americans be able to play the same role with respect to bouts of immoderate European behaviour? Is the concept of 'civilizational rallying' little more than an excuse for meddling in other peoples' affairs? Are Can- ada's immediate national defence and security needs likely to be sufficiently demanding that

Ottawa should be exploring an explicitly continentalist approach to security, with an emphasis on naval, air and aerospace investments focused on Canadian territory—particularly the northern approaches—rather than on the ability to project army battalions for years at a time to remote parts of the planet? Should the age of liberal internationalism and co-operative security be brought to a close in the face of the qualitatively new threats of mass casualty warfare and terrorist attack that have become evident over the past twenty years?

A world of worsening nuclear and bio-weapon proliferation is likely to have a most unhappy ending. Barack Obama's Prague speech of April 2009 and his UN Security Council summit call of September 2009 for progress toward a world without nuclear weapons was criticized as 'amateurishness wrapped in naiveté inside credulity' by one notable American right-wing critic.[69] But both speeches drew on disarmament proposals developed by a bipartisan group of 'wise men' with impeccable American security credentials.[70] Nuclear terrorism, they argued, is the central threat facing the US and the world today. Only by containing all fissile materials completely and stopping the further accumulation of weapons-grade material can the threat to American cities be neutralized. The Harper government has endorsed the 'locking down' of all insecure fissile nuclear materials, but it has not yet decided on whether a commitment toward a nuclear-free world is desirable. Historically it is only the Liberals and NDP who have pushed strongly for concrete action in nuclear disarmament.

The current US-led disarmament initiative is a potentially historic turning point in the nuclear weapons era. Deep cuts in the current levels of Russian and American arsenals might be able to begin to wind down the nuclear weapons era towards a happy ending—a true ending to the still 'unfinished twentieth century' as Jonathan Schell has called it.[71] Canadian nuclear disarmament policy entrepreneurs and tactically shrewd Canadian diplomatic initiatives are, alas, nowhere to be found at the moment. And just as in the period from 1945 to 1948, the need for vision, common sense, moral conviction, shrewd judgement, and tactical diplomatic ingenuity has never been greater.

Key Terms

Atlanticist Unity
Cooperative Security
NATO Transformation

Notes

1. Strategy, following Carl von Clausewitz, is most simply the art and skill of applying military means to the ends of governmental policy. A cooperative security (CS) strategy may be defined by its goals: building an overlapping regime framework of collective security and collective defence organizations and capabilities to deter war and promote arms control and disarmament; promoting conflict prevention and management via law-like norms and doctrines of cooperative behaviour among states, such as the responsibility to protect (R2P); and working towards a

Weapon of Mass Destruction (WMD)-free global order backed up by capable verification and enforcement commitments from the major powers in an enhanced treaty-defined context. For American (but not Canadian) CS advocates, support for preventive war to suppress covert WMD development violations might also be added to the mix. For a review of five grand strategy options for the US and thus indirectly for Canada, see Douglas Alan Ross, 'Nuclear Weapons and American Grand Strategy: essential pillar or terminal liability?' *International Journal*, v. 63

n. 4 (Autumn 2008), 847–73. Other grand strategy options which Canada might support include neo-isolationism, balance-of-power selective engagement, unipolar primacy or overt liberal imperialism.

2. For earlier counsel in the same vein, see Douglas Alan Ross, 'Canada and the world at risk: depression, war, and isolationism for the 21st century?' *International Journal*, v. 52 (Winter 1996–7), 1–24.

3. For an overview of Cold War arms control approaches by Canada, see Douglas A. Ross, 'Arms Control and Disarmament and the Canadian Approach to Global Order', in David B. Dewitt and David Leyton-Brown, eds., *Canada's International Security Policy* (Scarborough: Prentice-Hall, 1995), 251–86

4. George Shultz, William Perry, Henry Kissinger, Sam Nunn, 'A World Free of Nuclear Weapons,' *Wall Street Journal*, 4 January 2007; George Shultz, William Perry, Henry Kissinger, Sam Nunn, 'Toward a Nuclear Free World', *Wall Street Journal*, 15 January 2008.

5. See nuclear disarmament information and proposals at www.globalzero.org; also the analyses and approach of the Middle Powers Initiative at www.gsinstitute.org/mpi/index.html.

6. On American perceptions of the threat of nuclear terrorism, see Richard Betts, 'The New Threat of Mass Destruction,' *Foreign Affairs*, v. 77 n. 1 (Jan/Feb 1998): 26–41; Graham Allison, *Nuclear Terrorism: the Ultimate Preventable Catastrophe* (New York: Times/Henry Holt, 2004); Peter Zimmerman, Jeffrey Lewis, 'The Bomb in the Backyard', *Foreign Policy*, (Nov–Dec 2006): 33–39; Ashton Carter, Michael May, and William Perry, 'The Day After: Action Following a Nuclear Blast in a US City', *Washington Quarterly*, v. 30 n. 4 (Autumn 2007): 19–32; and Roger Molander, 'Perspectives on the Threat of Nuclear Terrorism', RAND Report CT–304 (April 2008). For a skeptical Canadian perspective, see Robin M. Frost, 'Nuclear Terrorism After 9/11', *Adelphi Paper No. 378* (London, New York: International Institute of Strategic Studies/Routledge, 2005).

7. A phrase coined by Robert Kaplan. See his original essay that forecast a 'reprimitivized man' in the 21st century, the end of the Westphalian state era, 'unprecedented resource scarcity and planetary overcrowding', and the collapse of India, Pakistan, China, and most of Africa into deep disorder or criminality: 'The Coming Anarchy', Atlantic Monthly, February 1994. On a future of attempted mass migrations from the collapsing global south to what Thomas Homer-Dixon has called 'the stretch-limo' societies of the affluent 'north', see Matthew Connelly and Paul Kennedy, 'Must It Be the West against the Rest?' Atlantic Monthly, December 1994.

8. See Gwynne Dyer, *Climate Wars* (n.p.: Random House Canada, 2008).

9. Richard Burt advised then presidential candidate George W. Bush in the autumn of 2000 that a 'limited' nuclear exchange might kill 100 million on both sides. Dyer's scenario for a hypothetical 'water war' in 2036 with larger nuclear arsenals forecast 400–500 million deaths and a Pakistani seizure of all of Jammu/Kashmir. See Dyer, Climate Wars, pp. 113–23.

10. Hillier's views on NATO have been quite disparaging since his retirement as chief of the defence staff. In his recent autobiography he wrote: 'Afghanistan has revealed that NATO has reached the stage where it is a corpse decomposing and somebody's going to have to perform a Frankenstein-like life-giving act by breathing some life-saving air through those rotten lips into those putrescent lungs or the Alliance will be done. Any major setback in Afghanistan will see it off to the cleaners, and unless the alliance can snatch victory out of its feeble efforts, it's not going to be long in existence in its present form.' See Gen. Rick Hillier, *A Soldier First: Bullets, Bureaucrats and the Politics of War.* (Toronto: HarperCollins, 2009), p. 477. Notwithstanding his lurid diagnosis he also asserted that, 'I cast a lot of rocks at NATO and I think deservedly so. Out of all the countries in NATO, Canada needs it most. We need it as a bit of a balance across the Atlantic with that superpower to the south. . . .' (Mike Blanchfield, 'I was sometimes at war with Ottawa: Hillier,' *National Post*, 27 October 2009).

11. David G. Haglund, and Tudor Onea, 'Sympathy for the devil: myths of neoclassical realism in Canadian foreign policy,' *Canadian Foreign Policy*, v.14 n.2 (Spring 2008), 53–66.

12. For a review of the incremental, 'non-rational' Canadian decision making that led to an ongoing military role in Afghanistan, see Janice Gross Stein and Eugene Lang, *The Unexpected War: Canada in Kandahar.* (Toronto: Penguin, 2007).

13. Stein and Lang, *The Unexpected War*, 2–3, 15, 61.

14. British governmental deficit as a percentage of GDP for 2010 is estimated at 13.3 compared with 9.8 for Greece, 5.4 for Italy, 8.5 for Spain, 7.6 for Portugal, and 12.2 for Ireland. David Pett, 'UK at Fiscal Crossroads', *National Post*, 6 May 2010.

15. Rejecting the conventional arguments, Maj.-Gen MacKenzie (ret'd.) noted that the Taliban are very parochial, and that al-Qaeda operatives are more interested in internet recruitment and 'training'—not physical bases in remote areas of the world. The only compelling argument for staying the course is to try to head off Indian intervention to prevent the emergence of a radical Islamist government in its region. Indian intervention, in turn, might trigger Chinese, Russian, and Iranian intervention or an Indo-Pakistani nuclear-armed crisis. See his 'NATO's objective: If the Taliban win, there goes the neighbourhood,' *Globe and Mail*, 16 October 2009.

16. While it is true that 'Taliban ideology is rejected by the vast majority of Afghans', this fact does not change the deteriorating political-military situation on the ground. Quote from Lauryn Oates, 'Tyranny is not peace', *National Post*, 6 May 2010.

17. In addition to its nuclear weapons capability, Pakistan, like India, has long been thought to possess a capacity to weaponize biological pathogens, despite its early accession to the Biological and Toxin Weapons Convention of 1972. Delivery could be by ballistic or cruise missiles, by aircraft or individual agents.

18. See Thom Shankar and David E. Sanger, 'Pakistan is Rapidly Adding Nuclear Arms, US Says', *New York Times*, 17 May 2009. In 2002 the Federation of American Scientists estimated that Pakistan had fewer than 55 atomic bombs—90 per cent of them based on Highly Enriched Uranium (HEU). In recent months Pakistanis have created an extensive tunnel network to enable them to store and transport warheads covertly—free from the risk of possible American or Russian efforts to seize their arsenal. See Seymour Hersh, 'Defending the Arsenal: In an unstable Pakistan can nuclear warheads be kept safe?' *The New Yorker*, 16 November 2009.

19. See MacKenzie, 'NATO's objective', note 15.

20. Dean Acheson's immodestly titled memoir, 'Present at the Creation', led John Holmes to note with gentle humour but perhaps too diffidently that Canadians were 'also present'.

21. Both Lester Pearson, then the senior official in DEA, and the then foreign minister Louis St Laurent concurred in approving Reid's speech at the Lake Couchiching conference of the Canadian Institute of Public Affairs. See Reid's definitive account of the origins of NATO, *Time of Fear and Hope: The Making of the North Atlantic Treaty, 1947–1949*. (Toronto: McClelland and Stewart, 1977), p. 31.

22. From 'Canada and Collective Security', 11 June 1948, in R.A. Mackay, ed., *Canadian Foreign Policy, 1945–1954*. (Toronto: McClelland and Stewart, 1971), p. 185.

23. Ibid.

24. Reid, *Time of Fear and Hope*, pp. 70, 76.

25. Ibid., 108–09.

26. At the time, some were advocating expulsion of the USSR because of its excessive use of its Security Council veto. See 'Odd man out in the Atlantic Community', in John W. Holmes, *Canada: A Middle-Aged Power*. (Toronto: McClelland and Stewart, 1976), p. 127.

27. A phrase used by both the then secretary of state for external affairs, Louis St Laurent, and prime minister Mackenzie King in describing what they hoped to create in March and April 1948. See 'The Brussels Treaty', in R.A. Mackay, ed., *Canadian Foreign Policy, 1945–1954* (Toronto: McClelland and Stewart, 1971), p. 182–3.

28. For a discussion of the 'practical idealist' notion first coined by James Eayrs, and a further discussion of the traits of 'liberal realists', see Kim Richard Nossal, 'Right and Wrong in Foreign Policy 40 Years On', *International Journal*, v. 62 n. 2 (Spring 2007).

29. John W. Holmes, *The Better Part of Valour: Essays on Canadian Diplomacy*. (Toronto: McClelland and Stewart, 1970), 131.

30. Tom Keating, 'Canada and World Order: The Multilateralist Tradition' in *Canadian Foreign Policy*, 2nd edition. (Don Mills: Oxford University Press, 2002), p. 86.

31. See John Lewis Gaddis, *Strategies of Containment*, revised edition. (Oxford, New York: Oxford University Press, 2005), chapters 2, 3 esp. 29–30.

32. Denis Stairs, *The Diplomacy of Constraint: Canada, the Korean War and the United States* (Toronto: Univ. of Toronto Press, 1974). In the same vein, with respect to Canadian goals in Ottawa's Vietnam War diplomacy, see Douglas A. Ross, *In the Interests of Peace: Canada and Vietnam* (Toronto: Univ. of Toronto Press, 1984). The American intervention in Korea was fought while the European infrastructure was first being built. Some 27,000 Canadians saw military service in Korea, serving alongside 63,000 British and nearly 1.8 million American service personnel. During the American intervention in Indochina neither the UK nor Canada contributed military forces to the fighting. In both of these 'limited wars' Canadian and British officials were intent on discouraging any American thought of use of tactical nuclear weapons.

33. Such was the opinion of Gen. Lewis McKenzie. For a defence of the initiatives taken and the 'greater objectivity' shown by the Canadian military, see Cmdr Peter T. Haydon (retd), *The 1962 Cuban Missile Crisis: Canadian Involvement Reconsidered* (Toronto: Canadian Institute of Strategic Studies, 1993). Haydon concurs with McKenzie that the crisis caused the end of the elitist semi-autonomous capacity by the three services via unification and strict civilian control.

34. See remarks by former minister of national defence, Paul Hellyer, and author's data on the variable yields of the Starfighter in its theatre nuclear strike role in John Clearwater, *Canadian Nuclear Weapons: The Untold Story of Canada's Cold War Arsenal* (Toronto, Oxford: Dundurn Press, 1998), pp. 91–4. Hellyer had little or no idea of the exceptionally destructive capacity of the Canadian strike force—just as NATO allies really had no idea of the truly genocidal level of destruction planned for by SAC across the entire communist bloc. See David Alan Rosenberg, 'The Origins of Overkill: Nuclear Weapons and American Strategy, 1945–1960', *International Security*, v. 7 n. 4 (Spring 1983), 3–71.

35. For unassailable evidence on this point, see Andrew Richter, *Avoiding Armageddon: Canadian Military Strategy and Nuclear Weapons, 1950–63* (Vancouver, Toronto: UBC Press, 2002).

36. On the poorly understood history of Canadian nuclear weapons capability, see Don Munton, 'Going fission: tales and truths about Canada's nuclear weapons,' *International Journal*, v. 51 n. 3 (Summer 1996), 506–28. For full, final details on weapons characteristics, see John Clearwater, *Canadian Nuclear Weapons: The Untold Story of Canada's Cold War Arsenal* (Toronto, Oxford: Dundurn Press, 1998).

37. Joseph T. Jockel and Joel Sokolsky, *Canada and Collective Security: Odd Man Out* (New York: Praeger, 1986).

38. Paul Buteux, 'NATO and the Evolution of Canadian Foreign and Defence Policy,' in David B. Dewitt and David Leyton-Brown, eds., *Canada's International Security Policy* (Scarborough: Prentice-Hall, 1995), p. 158.

39. Ibid., p. 163.

40. Ivan Head and Pierre Trudeau, *The Canadian Way: Shaping Canada's Foreign Policy, 1968–1984* (Toronto: McClelland and Stewart, 1995), p. 91

41. Trudeau appealed to leaders in India, China, and the Soviet Union to halt what he correctly saw as the drift towards East–West war. But his final appeal to President Ronald Reagan, whom Trudeau privately regarded as 'a fool', may have been significant in persuading the president to end his 'evil Empire' anti-Soviet rhetoric and thus ease Soviet paranoia about an impending American nuclear attack. For a brief discussion of Trudeau's use of his NATO voice in the alliance's nuclear debate of 1983, see Robert Bothwell, *Alliance and Illusion: Canada and the World, 1945–1984* (Vancouver, Toronto: UBC Press, 2007), pp. 383–86.

42. Protecting the autonomy of Eurasia's 'rimlands' from central strategic control was declared to be a core geopolitical goal of US foreign policy from World War II according to American geopolitician Nicolas Spykman's application of Halford Mackinder's thesis to US security. See one of the most widely used textbooks in the US on American foreign policy that stressed this policy axiom to generations of American students: John W. Spanier, *American Foreign Policy Since World War II*, 3rd rev. ed. (New York: Praeger, 1965), 3–4.

43. Preponderance is highlighted as George W. Bush's main but quite inappropriate goal by American realist analyst Stephen M. Walt. See his *Taming American Power: The Global Response to American Primacy* (New York, London: Norton, 2005), 29–61.

44. On American elite Cold War hawkishness in Asia, see Franz Schurmann, *The Logic of World Power* (New York: Random House/Pantheon, 1974), parts II and III. See also details of alleged military plans for fabricating pretexts for an invasion of Cuba in James Bamford, *Body of Secrets* (New York: Random House/Anchor, 2002), 82–91.

45. For an insightful explanatory review of the logic of the 'free rider' aspect of the Canadian-American security relationship, see Donald Barry and Duane Bratt, 'Defense

Against Help: Explaining Canada–US Security Relations,' *American Review of Canadian Studies*, v. 38 issue 1 (Spring 2008), esp. 64–68. For a persuasive summation of recent Canadian intra-NATO thinking, see Joseph T. Jockel and Joel J. Sokolsky, 'Canada and NATO: Keeping Ottawa in, expenses down, criticism out . . . and the country secure,' *International Journal*, v. 64 n. 2 (Spring 2009), 315–36.

46. For his argument on Western civilization being under severe threat of internal cultural rot and external challenge from China and an emerging Islamic civilization, see Samuel P. Huntington, *The Clash of Civilizations and the Remaking of World Order* (New York: Simon and Schuster, 1996), chapters 4, 5 and 12.

47. Ibid., 307. The late Samuel Huntington argued NATO was the most important institutional vehicle for the survival of Western civilization. The expansion of the alliance in the mid-1990s based on candidate country acceptance of principles of common defence, 'shared belief in the rule of law and parliamentary democracy', 'liberal capitalism and free trade', and the cultural legacy of classical Greece, Rome and the European Renaissance (Malcolm Rifkind's list) reflected the fact that what had been just a military alliance had evolved into something much more significant.

48. Kenneth N. Waltz, 'The Emerging Structure of International Politics', *International Security*, v. 18 n. 2 (Fall, 1993), 44–79, esp. pp. 75–6. Waltz declared, 'Without the shared perception of a severe Soviet threat, NATO would never have been born. The Soviet Union created NATO, and the demise of the Soviet threat 'freed' Europe, West as well as East. . . . NATO's days are not numbered, but its years are.' Mearsheimer, like Waltz, foresaw an increasingly divided future for the NATO community as well as a very high probability and desirability of nuclear proliferation to Germany, Japan, and even Ukraine—to be accomplished with Washington's support as American power ebbed and its nuclear 'umbrella' was gradually withdrawn. See John J. Mearsheimer, 'Back to the Future: Instability in Europe After the Cold War,' *International Security*, v. 15 n. 1 (summer 1990); and 'The Case for a Ukrainian Nuclear Deterrent', *Foreign Affairs*, v. 73 n. 2 (Summer 1993), 50–66. For Mearsheimer, 'the best formula for maintaining stability in post-Cold War Europe is for all the great powers—including Germany and Ukraine—to have secure nuclear deterrents and for all the minor powers to be nonnuclear' (p. 51).

49. David G. Haglund, 'The North Atlantic Triangle Revisited: Canadian Grand Strategy at Century's End', in *Contemporary Affairs*, n. 4 (Toronto: CIIA/Irwin Publishing, 2000), pp. 86–7, 90.

50. A careful dissection of the anti-realist, neo-Wilsonian character of George W. Bush's interventionary foreign

wars can be found in John J. Mearsheimer, 'Hans Morgenthau and the Iraq war: Realism Versus Neo-conservatism', 19 May 2005: see www.opendemocracy.net/democracy-americanpower/morgenthau_2522.jsp, accessed 15 September 2009.

51. A controversial but persuasive case for declaring the de facto arrival of American nuclear weapons primacy was made by Keir A. Lieber and Daryl G. Press, 'The End of MAD? The nuclear dimension of US primacy', *International Security* v. 30 n. 4 (Spring 2006): 7–44.

52. The National Security Strategy called for taking into account the vital interests of all the great powers, who would then, it was assumed, tolerate a 'benign American hegemony' over the international security environment.

53. John M. Doyle and Amy Butler, 'Missile Messages', *Aviation Week and Space Technology*, 16 February 2009.

54. Steven Chase, 'Ottawa rebukes Russia for military flights in Arctic', *Globe and Mail*, 28 February 2009. The aircraft did not enter Canadian airspace or even NORAD's formal airspace identification zone. Their closest approach was 190 km northeast of Tuktoyaktuk in international airspace.

55. Peter Goodspeed, 'Russia Manoeuvres Into US Backyard', *National Post*, 17 September 2008.

56. See 'Gorbachev Blasts NATO Eastward Expansion', RIA Novosti, 2 April 2009; http://en.rian.ru/russia/20090402/120879153.html; accessed 15 October 2009. Former Secretary of State James Baker denied that any such assurance had been given. See Lucian Kim, 'Baker says Gorbachev got no promises . . .', at www.bloomberg.com/apps/news?pid=newsarchive&sid=aN0Q_J9CA6GU; accessed 12 October 2009. German diplomatic records suggest otherwise. See Uwe Klussmann, Matthias Schepp, and Klaus Wiegrefe, 'NATO's Eastward Expansion: Did the West Break Its Promise to Moscow?', translated from Der Spiegel, 26 November 2009 as at www.globalresearch.ca/index.php?context=va&aid=16289; accessed 6 May 2010.

57. It did not help to have Steve Forbes, presidential candidate for the Republican nomination, call for an anti-China ABM defence that would guarantee China's strategic nuclear subordination. On Bush's enhanced conventional and nuclear offensive strike see David McDonough, 'The New Triad, Bunker Busters and "Counterproliferation Wars": Nuclear Primacy and Its Implications for Canadian Security Policy', in David S. McDonough and Douglas A. Ross, eds., *The Dilemmas of American Strategic Primacy* (Toronto: Royal Canadian Military Institute, 2005), pp. 89–123.

58. See 'vulnerability' comment in Hans M. Kristensen and Robert S. Norris, *Chinese Nuclear Forces and US Nuclear War Planning* (New York, Washington: Federation of American Scientists and The Natural Resources Defense Council, Nov. 2006), p. 69.

59. John W. Holmes, 'Collective Engagement', in John W. Holmes, Malcolm N. Bow, and John G. H. Halstead, *Canada, NATO and Arms Control in Issue Brief No. 6*, (Ottawa: Canadian Centre for Arms Control and Disarmament, March 1987), p. 8.

60. Steven M. Walt, *The Origins of Alliances* (Ithaca, London: Cornell Univ. Press, 1987).

61. See Walt, *Taming American Power*, (op. cit.); and Andrew J. Bacevich, *The Limits of Power: The End of American Exceptionalism* (New York: Henry Holt/Metropolitan, 2009). Also relevant is the attack on the permanently expansive ambitions of American liberal internationalism made by Christopher Layne in *The Peace of Illusions; American Grand Strategy from 1940 to the Present* (Ithaca, London: Cornell Univ. Press, 2006).

62. T.V. Paul, 'Soft Balancing in the Age of US Primacy', *International Security*, v.30 n. 1 (Summer 2005), 46–71.

63. For details on non-nuclear ICBM, SLBM deployments that may soon be available to the newly established Global Strike Command, see David E. Sanger and Thom Shanker, 'US Faces Choice on New Weapons for Fast Strikes,' *New York Times*, 23 April 2010; Paul Koring, 'Obama resurrects controversial first-strike weapons,' *Globe and Mail*, 14 April 2010; and Guy Norris, 'Strategic Stress,' *Aviation Week and Space Technology*, 1 February 2010.

64. Nicholas Kulish and Ellen Barry, 'Romanians Accept Plan For Basing of Missiles,' *New York Times*, 5 February 2010.

65. See the Nuclear Information Project, 'US Nuclear Weapons in Europe,' as at: www.nukestrat.com/us/afn/nato.htm; accessed 11 October 2009. Several score are allocated for use by British and American forces in the UK, which is a Nuclear Weapon State under the NPT.

66. Hans M. Kristensen, 'United States Removes Nuclear Weapons from German Base, Documents Indicate', in FAS Strategic Security Blog as at: www.fas.org/blog/ssp/2007/07/united_states_removes_nuclear.php; accessed 11 October 2009.

67. Mark Landler, 'US Resists Push by Allies for Tactical Nuclear Cuts,' *New York Times*, 23 April 2010.

68. David Bercuson, 'The US plea is a Harper saver,' *Globe and Mail*, 26 March 2010. NATO agreed in 2009 to provide some 2500 of the 5000 trainers thought to be needed to expand the Afghan military and police forces.

69. Charles Krauthammer, 'Obama's Foreign Policy: Apologize, Stumble, Retreat', *National Post*, 19 October 2009.

70. See their more detailed second proposal in 'Toward a nuclear-free world', *Wall Street Journal* 15 January 2008. See also Henry A. Kissinger, 'Our Nuclear Nightmare', 16 February 2009

71. See Schell, 'The Unfinished Century', *Harper's Magazine*, (January 2000).

SELECTED BIBLIOGRAPHY

Blanchard, James J. *Behind the Embassy Door: Canada, Clinton, and Quebec.* Toronto: McClelland and Stewart, 1998.

Bothwell, Robert. *Alliance and Illusion: Canada and the World, 1945–1984.* Vancouver: University of British Columbia, 2007.

Bow, Brian. *The Politics of Linkage: Power, Interdependence, and Ideas in Canada–US Relations.* Vancouver: UBC Press, 2009.

———. 1992. *Canada and the United States.* Toronto: University of Toronto Press.

Cellucci, Paul. *Unquiet Diplomacy.* Toronto: Key Porter Books, 2005.

Chapnick, Andrew. *The Middle Power Project: Canada and the Founding of the United Nations.* Vancouver: UBC Press, 2005.

Cooper, Andrew F. *Tests of Global Governance: Canadian Diplomacy and United Nations World Conferences.* Tokyo: United Nations University Press, 2004.

Doran, Charles. *Forgotten Partnership: US–Canada Relations Today.* Baltimore: Johns Hopkins University Press, 1984.

Gattinger, Monica, and Geoffrey Hale. *Borders and Bridges: Canada's Policy Relations in North America.* Don Mills, ON: Oxford University Press, 2010.

Granatstein, J.L., and Norman Hillmer. *From Empire to Umpire: Canada and the World to the 1990s.* Toronto: Copp Clark Longman, 1994.

———. *For Better or for Worse: Canada and the United States to the 1990s.* Toronto: Copp Clark Longman, 1992.

Haglund, David G. *The North Atlantic Triangle Revisited: Canadian Grand Strategy at Century's End.* Toronto: Irwin, 2000.

Holmes, John W. *Life with Uncle: The Canadian–American Relationship.* Toronto: University of Toronto Press, 1981.

Jockel, Joseph T. *Canada in NORAD, 1957–2007: A History.* Montreal and Kingston: McGill-Queen's University Press, 2007.

Keating, Tom, and Larry Pratt. *Canada, NATO and the Bomb: The Western Alliance in Crisis.* Edmonton: Hurtig Publishers, 1988.

Kirton, John. 2001. 'Guess Who is Coming to Kananaskis? Civil Society and the G8 in Canada's Year as Host', *International Journal* 57, 1 (Winter): 101–22.

Lennox, Patrick. *At Home and Abroad: The Canada–US Relationship and Canada's Place in the World.* Vancouver: UBC Press, 2009.

MacMillan, Margaret O., and David S. Sorenson, eds. *Canada and NATO: Uneasy Past, Uncertain Future.* Waterloo, ON: University of Waterloo Press, 1990.

Mahant, Edelgard and Graeme S. Mount. *Invisible and Inaudible in Washington: American Policies toward Canada.* Vancouver: UBC Press, 1999.

McKenna, Peter. *Canada and the OAS: From Dilettante to Full Partner.* Ottawa: Carleton University Press, 1995.

Potter, Evan H. *Transatlantic Partners: Canadian Approaches to the European Union.* Ottawa: Carleton University Press, 1999.

Rochlin, James. *Discovering the Americas: The Evolution of Canadian Foreign Policy Towards Latin America.* Vancouver: UBC Press, 1994.

Simpson, Erika. *NATO and the Bomb: Canadian Defenders Confront Critics.* Montreal and Kingston: McGill-Queen's University Press, 2001.

Smith, Gordon and Daniel Wolfish, eds. *Who Is Afraid of the State? Canada in a World of Multiple Centres of Power.* Toronto: University of Toronto Press, 2001.

Stairs, Denis. 'Global Governance as a Policy Tool: The Canadian Experience', pp. 67–85 in *Globalization and Global Governance*, Raimo Väyrynen, ed. Lanham, MD: Rowman and Littlefield, 1999.

Stairs, Denis. *Diplomacy of Constraint: Canada, The Korean War and the United States.* Toronto: University of Toronto Press, 1974.

Stevenson, Brian J.R. *Canada, Latin America, and the New Internationalism: A Foreign Policy.* Montreal and Kingston: McGill-Queen's University Press, 2000.

Taylor, Rupert, ed. *Canada in Action: Canada and the G7.* Waterloo, ON: Taylor Publishing, 1995.

Thompson, John Herd, and Stephen J. Randall. *Canada and the United States, Ambivalent Allies.* Montreal and Kingston: McGill-Queen's University Press, 2000.

PART III

DOMESTIC FACTORS AND CANADIAN FOREIGN POLICY

Part 3 examines the relevance of domestic influences on Canada's international relations. Studies of foreign policy are often problematic given the separate realms these issues occupy. The term 'foreign' implies a context in which theories of international relations or global political economy might apply. The 'policy' aspect, however, draws attention to public administration or public policy frameworks. In the first edition, the goal was to highlight these divergent trends by focusing on Kim Richard Nossal's and Cranford Pratt's dialogue in the Winter 1983–4 edition of *International Journal*. In this 'classic' exchange Nossal proposed a 'modified statist' approach, which acknowledged that societal pressures had some impact on Canadian foreign policy.[1] Pratt's response, however, stressed the influence of a dominant class in Canada that was consistent with the objectives of élites in other states. Therefore, a counter-consensus was required to challenge these entrenched values.[2] As noted in the first edition, the importance of Pratt's work should not be underestimated. His discussion of dominant-class theory includes a wide range of variables related the construction of knowledge, class, ideology, and political culture. The absence of ethical and normative considerations in Canadian foreign policy is also highlighted. The influence of Pratt on future scholars, such as Mark Neufeld (Chapter 7), is both important and obvious.

In contrast, the second edition focuses primarily on specific domestic issues in the formulation of Canadian foreign policy. Paul Gecelovsky, for example, argues that the prime minister has decisive control in the formulation of Canada's international relations, although this influence is dependent on the economic and political significance of specific issues. John English also evaluates the relevance of Parliament (from the first edition), with an update by the editors on the different partisan dynamics of minority governments. Patrice Dutil, on the other hand, examines the relevance of the bureaucracy in matters of foreign policy, with an emphasis on institutional structures from a historical perspective. Chris Kukucha, who questions whether current federal and provincial initiatives contribute to the 'dismembering of Canada', also addresses the international activity of Canadian provinces. Finally, Stéphane Roussel and Jean-Christophe Boucher question whether the historical record supports the idea that Québécois are, in fact, 'pacifists'.

Despite the thoroughness of these chapters, some important domestic considerations were not included. The Winter 2008–2009 edition of *International Journal*, for example, highlighted the need to better understand the role of political parties in the formulation of Canadian foreign policy. Articles focusing on trade, climate change, and defence policy suggested that parties in Canada had considerable flexibility in this policy area due to the low priority given to these issues by Canadian voters.[3] This resulted in foreign relations that are often ad hoc, personality-driven, focused on tactical coalition-building, and in many cases shaped by US preferences.[4] Although Quebec's legislative review of international treaties is documented in Chapter 15, there is also no in-depth discussion of treaty-making and Canadian provinces. Article 27 of the 1969 Vienna Convention on the Law of Treaties, for example, states that signatories must not use domestic law as justification for violating international treaty obligations. Article XXIV:12 of the General Agreement on Tariffs and Trade (GATT), which was later incorporated into the World Trade Organization (WTO), and Article 105 of the North American Free Trade Agreement (NAFTA) also outlines the compliance of local and regional governments. These realities create additional constraints for Ottawa in the negotiation and implementation of international treaties. Finally, an additional weakness of Part 3 is its failure to include further critical analysis as well as its exclusion of a wide range of scholarship on the democratization of Canadian foreign policy. Having said that, other domestic issues are addressed, using both traditional and critical approaches, elsewhere in this volume. As noted, Mark Neufeld adopts a Gramscian perspective to assess the democratization of Canadian foreign policy (Chapter 7) and Andrew F. Cooper and P. Whitney Lackenbauer evaluate the impact of aboriginal groups (Chapter 10).

Notes

1. Kim Richard Nossal, 'Analyzing Domestic Sources of Canadian Foreign Policy,' *International Journal* 39, 1 (Winter 1983–4): 1–22.

2. Cranford Pratt, 'Dominant Class Theory and Canadian Foreign Policy: The Case of the Counter-Consensus,' *International Journal* 39, 1 (Winter 1983–4): 235–258.

3. Paul Gecelovsky and Christopher Kukucha, 'Much Ado about Parties: Conservative and Liberal Approaches to Canada's Trade Policy with the United States,' *International Journal* 64, 1 (Winter 2008–09): 29–46; Heather

A. Smith, 'Political Parties and Canadian Climate Change Policy,' *International Journal* 64, 1 (Winter 2008–09): 47–66; and Brian Bow, 'Parties and Partisanship in Canadian Defence Policy,' *International Journal* 64, 1 (Winter 2008–09): 67–88.

4. See also, Kim Richard Nossal, 'Opening Up the Policy Process: Does Party Make a Difference?' in Nelson Michaud and Kim Richard Nossal, eds., *Diplomatic Departures: The Conservative Era in Canadian Foreign Policy, 1984–93* (Vancouver: UBC Press, 2001), pp. 276–289.

12

OF LEGACIES AND LIGHTNING BOLTS REVISITED: ANOTHER LOOK AT THE PRIME MINISTER AND CANADIAN FOREIGN POLICY

Paul Gecelovsky

INTRODUCTION

The purpose of this chapter is to examine the role played by the prime minister in the formulation of Canada's foreign policy. Other contributors to this volume have looked at various domestic factors which influence Canada's foreign policy, including parliament (English), the provinces (Kukucha), and the bureaucracy (Dutil). What these contributors have overlooked, for the most part, is that the prime minister is the key person in deciding both the direction and the content of Canada's foreign policy, and that the prime minister when so choosing may override the interests of these other actors and have Canada pursue a foreign policy of his/her liking. The prime minister, in the making of Canada's foreign policy, is *primus* without *pares*, to borrow from Donald J. Savoie.[1] To demonstrate that the prime minister has no equal in setting the content and course of Canada's foreign policy, this paper is divided into two parts. The first part examines the powers possessed by the prime minister, while the second looks at the constraints within which the prime minister operates. It will be shown that the former outweigh the latter significantly and that, furthermore, the constraints are only constraints if the prime minister allows them to stop him/her from acting. In short, the powers possessed by the prime minister are decisive.

POWERS OF THE PRIME MINISTER

The prime minister possesses a vast range of powers. The chapter focuses on only those powers possessed by the prime minister that are relevant to the formulation of Canada's foreign policy. The powers discussed in the chapter are divided between those possessed by the office of the prime minister, which is referred to as the role or positional variable, and the extent or degree to which a prime minister seeks to distinguish the international behaviour of his/her government from other administrations, which is often referred to as the idiosyncratic variable.[2]

In examining the role or positional variable, four main constitutional powers need to be addressed. The first power of office to be discussed concerns the power of appointment. The prime minister has the authority to name persons to various positions within the state including, inter alia, ministers, deputy ministers, ambassadors, and high commissioners. Who ultimately sits in the foreign minister's chair and for how long that person occupies that chair is, in large part, determined solely by the prime minister. While the department charged with maintaining Canada's foreign relations was created in 1909, it was not until 1946 that the prime minister relinquished the position of Secretary of State for External Affairs (SSEA) to another minister.[3] Louis St Laurent was coaxed out of retirement by then Prime Minister William Lyon Mackenzie King to become the first person who was not also the prime minister to hold the external affairs portfolio. It needs to be noted that King believed that in giving up the position of SSEA to St Laurent, he was jettisoning the mundane chores of departmental administration and management while freeing up time to deal with the more important foreign policy concerns of the state; St Laurent was to do the housekeeping while King focussed on diplomacy. Since the naming of St Laurent in 1946, successive prime ministers have appointed others to be responsible for the foreign affairs portfolio.

Appointing others to be responsible for Canada's international behaviour, however, does not mean that those holding the office of prime minister were not interested or influential in setting both the tone and course of Canada's foreign policy. It is the prime minister who establishes the parameters within which the foreign minister operates, and determines what leeway the occupant of the foreign minister's chair is given. This setting of the boundaries is accomplished through various means including the prime minister actively involving him/herself in any departmental matter of his/her choosing.

The prime minister may also discharge what Don Johnston, a former minister in the Trudeau government, has referred to as 'lightning bolts'.[4] That is, the prime minister is able to change the content and direction of Canada's policy at his/her discretion without consultation with a minister, Cabinet, or departmental officials: what the prime minister says is policy. A lightning bolt was fired in late 1997 by then Prime Minster Chrétien when he decided that Canada would commit forces to help protect those attempting to escape the violence in the Great Lakes region of Africa. Andrew Cooper has argued that Canadian involvement in the region came as a result of Mr Chrétien's wife, Aline, watching television news coverage of the atrocities while she and her husband were on a weekend getaway at their cottage in Québec. Also influencing the prime minister's decision to intervene was information obtained from his nephew, Raymond Chrétien, who had served as a United Nations Special Envoy to the Great Lakes region in 1996 and as Canada's Ambassador to Zaire (with joint accreditation to Rwanda, Burundi, and the Congo) in the late 1970s.[5] The actions of Jean Chrétien demonstrate that it is the prime minister who ultimately decides which issues or crises are important for Canada and how Canada will respond to those issues or crises.

It is not only through direct involvement in foreign policy matters that a prime minister establishes the boundaries for a foreign minister. Another way in which the prime minister can set the parameters for a foreign minister is through the appointment of more senior ministers to the foreign affairs troika. Since 1982, responsibility for Canada's foreign affairs has fallen to a triumvirate of ministers, including the minister of foreign affairs, the minister of international trade and the minister of international co-operation.[6] Within this triad of ministers, the minister of foreign affairs is usually the most senior, and lead, minister, followed by the minister of international trade and, finally, the minister of international co-operation, who is the most junior. There have been occasions, however, when the prime minister has appointed a more junior parliamentarian to the foreign minister portfolio. This occurred in 1989 when then Prime Minister Brian Mulroney was dissatisfied with the overly cautious approach to foreign policy exhibited by then Secretary of State for External Affairs Joe Clark. Mulroney replaced Clark with the more junior Barbara McDougall. Concurrent with this move, Mulroney moved Michael Wilson from finance to replace John Crosbie as Minister for International Trade. Monique Landry maintained her position as the minister responsible for the Canadian International Development Agency, the third member of the triad. With these moves, Wilson rather than McDougall assumed the position of lead minister in the foreign affairs troika.[7] The main effects of this cabinet shuffle were that for the remainder of Mulroney's term in office, trade issues came to dominate Canada's foreign relations and control over Canada's foreign policy effectively shifted to the prime minister and the Prime Minister's Office (PMO), with the foreign minister lacking any real freedom of action.

A third way in which the prime minister outlines the parameters of permissibility for foreign ministers is through the issuing of mandate letters. Mandate letters are given to all ministers upon their being sworn into cabinet and also to those who have been assigned to a new portfolio as a result of a cabinet shuffle. A mandate letter will outline those issues and areas of importance on which the minister is to focus. The letters most often span only two or three pages and are prepared by officials in the Privy Council Office after they have consulted with relevant members of the PMO and the Deputy Minister(s) affected by the change. As Savoie has noted, there are two basic types of mandate letters. The first is the 'Don't call us, we'll call you' letter which, in effect, tells a minister to do nothing but maintain the status quo and stay out of trouble. The second type of mandate letter outlines the major challenges and the specific objectives with which the minister is to concern him/herself during his/her tenure.[8] The mandate letters effectively set the terms on which the minister is to serve in the appointed position.

A fourth manner in which the prime minister sets the boundaries for the foreign minister is through the appointment of senior civil servants. Since the coming to office of Pierre Trudeau in 1968, prime ministers and their staffs have increasingly involved themselves in the appointment of senior civil servants at the rank of deputy minister. All deputy minister appointments are vetted by the prime minister and the PMO as to the applicant's suitability for the position. All deputy ministers are also given mandate letters upon their appointment. This is done, in part, to ensure that the minister and the deputy minister are both working from the same set of priorities and expectations, as determined by the prime minister.

A second constitutional power of the office possessed by the prime minister, in addition to the power of appointment and of relevance to our discussion, concerns the design of the administrative structures of government. The prime minister is the architect of government, as he/she has the authority to create, redesign, amalgamate, and/or eliminate departments. This power has been used most recently by Prime Minister Stephen Harper, in February 2006, when he reconsolidated the Department of Foreign Affairs and International Trade. Two years earlier, in January 2004, then Prime Minister Paul Martin had separated the Department of Foreign Affairs and International Trade into Foreign Affairs Canada (FAC) and International Trade Canada (ITCAN). This move by Martin undid the previous 'consolidation and re-organization' initiatives of the Trudeau government in the 1980–83 period when Trudeau integrated sections of the Departments of Industry, Trade and Commerce, and Employment and Immigration with the Department of External Affairs.[9]

While not of the same degree of importance as structural changes to administrative departments, the prime minister also has the authority to change the names of government departments. This power was exercised, in June 1989, by Prime Minister Mulroney when he changed the name of the Department of External Affairs, as it had been known since its creation 1909, to External Affairs and International Trade Canada. Prime Minister Chrétien wasted little time in changing the name of the department when he renamed it the Department of Foreign Affairs and International Trade on 5 November 1993, only one day after assuming office. As noted above, Prime Minister Martin changed the name in 2004 to FAC and ITCAN only to have it changed back to the Department of Foreign Affairs and International Trade by Prime Minister Harper in 2006. Concurrent with the changes in the name of the department is a change in the title of the minister's position—from secretary of state for external affairs from 1909 to 1993, to minister of foreign affairs after that time.

In addition to the constitutional powers of appointment and the design of administrative structures, the prime minister has the constitutional authority to mould the processes of decision-making within his/her own administration. This power is demonstrated clearly by a comparison of the decision-making processes instituted by Prime Ministers Trudeau and Mulroney. While a full rendering of these contrasting decision-making styles is beyond the scope of this chapter, it is necessary to highlight some of the key characteristics of each prime minister's approach. When he assumed the prime ministership in 1968, Trudeau

wanted to inject a greater degree of discipline and rationality into the decision-making system of government. He was critical of what he regarded as the 'partisanship' and the 'incremental drift' of the Pearson era.[10] To overcome these problems, Trudeau implemented a series of changes to the committee system in an effort to introduce more discipline into the decision-making process. Decisions were to be channelled through a number of committees at various levels of government in order that they be the result of debate and deliberation by numerous persons throughout government. The objective of implementing a more structured and formalised decision-making process was to have decisions made on a more rational basis than had been done previously. Decisions were to flow from the application of reason to the problem at hand to come up with the best possible course of action for Canada under the prevailing conditions. Decisions would not be quick and immediate but rather slow and deliberate.

Conversely, the primary concern for Brian Mulroney was for a 'policy and a process that succeeds', and was 'popular with the Canadian public'.[11] Replacing a concern for rationality was a focus on whether or not a decision had 'political appeal'.[12] Mulroney's philosophy of political leadership stressed the 'accommodation of interests' over Trudeau's concern for an 'interplay of ideas'.[13] Further, Mulroney's background as a labour negotiator meant that he was more comfortable working out solutions to problems on a one-to-one basis with ministers and other heads of state.

While there are notable differences among prime ministers regarding their decision-making styles, one discernible trend in decision-making processes has been a move to centralise foreign policy-making in the PMO. While there was some movement in this direction under Trudeau, it was during Mulroney's tenure in office that this shift was more discernible, especially after the 1989 cabinet shuffle in which Barbara McDougall replaced Joe Clark as secretary of state for external affairs. This trend has accelerated further with the current Harper government which has sought to control fully within the PMO not only decision-making but also communicating the results of those decisions to the Canadian public. Major policy decisions of the Harper government are taken by the prime minister and the PMO and, then, announced by the prime minister, leaving the various ministers to play a much diminished role in the government. This desire to control information—including infrequent press conferences, the use of media lists whereby reporters are required to sign up prior to a press conference if they want to pose questions to the prime minister, and, most recently, not allowing photographers access to the prime minister while providing staged pictures of Harper to the media—is evidence of what Jeffrey Simpson has referred to as the Harper government's 'obsessive control of information'.[14] This intense control over policy substance and communication by the prime minister and the PMO is the Harper style of foreign policy making.

The final role variable to be addressed concerns the plenipotentiary power possessed by the prime minister. The prime minister has the authority to negotiate and sign international agreements, a power first put to use in 1923 with the negotiating and signing of the Halibut Treaty with the United States. This bilateral treaty established that fishing for Pacific halibut would not occur during the winter spawning months (November to February) to help preserve the fish stock. More recently, the authority of the prime minister to negotiate, sign, and ratify treaties that concern those classes of subjects that are within the ambit of provincial authority has been called into question. Decisions of the Supreme Court of Canada have not fully or clearly articulated the extent of the prime minister's authority to act as an agent of the provinces in

the international realm.[15] The current state of affairs is that the prime minister may negotiate, sign, and ratify international treaties but he/she cannot force provinces to implement those agreements, or to be bound by the provisions of the ratified agreements. What the prime minister may do, however, is focus the public's attention on an issue and put that issue on the agenda of the provinces. A recent example of this concerns Canada's negotiating, signing, and ratifying of the Kyoto Protocol. Facing pressure from the provinces, industry, and even from within his party, then Prime Minister Chrétien moved forward with the ratification of the Protocol. Chrétien went so far as staking the continuation of his government on the ratification of the legislation in the House of Commons by declaring Kyoto a motion of confidence. The Kyoto Protocol was ratified by Parliament in December 2002, providing what Kathryn Harrison has called a 'triumph' for the prime minister.[16] The ratification of Kyoto was a clear demonstration of the prime minister's plenipotentiary power.

Having looked at the four constitutional powers of the office of the prime minister of relevance to our discussion regarding foreign policy making (i.e., power of appointment, design of administrative structures, design of decision-making processes, and plenipotentiary authority), the chapter now moves to analyse the idiosyncratic component of prime ministerial authority. In particular, this section of the chapter focuses on the prime minister's own predilections, that is the set of objectives that the prime minister seeks to fulfill during his/her time in power. All prime ministers have a sense of what is to be accomplished during the term in office. They want to leave a legacy for future generations; they want to make a difference. A prime minister, however, cannot do everything that he/she wants to do and so needs to choose a few main policy objectives on which to focus the resources of the state. This 'strategic prime ministership', as it has been termed by Thomas Axworthy, the former principal secretary to Pierre Trudeau, aids both the prime minister and the PMO in staying on track and in 'saying no to hundreds of other requests' not related to the prime minister's strategic policy agenda.[17] While the prime minister's strategic policy agenda will be primarily shaped by domestic issues, prime ministers usually have a couple of policy priorities that they seek to have met in the area of Canada's foreign policy.

The continuation of the policy of apartheid in South Africa was just such a priority concern for Prime Minister Mulroney. Although the issue of apartheid played an insignificant role in the 1984 election campaign, wherein Mulroney and the Progressive Conservative Party captured a majority of seats in the House of Commons to become the government, the increasing violence within South Africa in the fall of 1984 brought the issue to Mulroney's attention. The newly elected prime minister, as Kim Richard Nossal has averred, 'demonstrated a visceral and intensely personal anger at the institutionalized racism of apartheid'.[18] This palpable anger was evident in public statements, speeches, and interviews given by Mulroney during this period. The anger was also demonstrated in the use of increasingly punitive measures adopted by the Canadian government, including the possibility of breaking diplomatic relations with South Africa. Mulroney attempted to lead both the Commonwealth and the Group of Seven (G7) in adopting a stronger position towards South Africa. Canadian resources were employed to move the leaders of member states of these organisations to adopt a stricter stance towards South Africa. Mulroney even used his position as chair of the Commonwealth Heads of Government Meeting in Vancouver in 1987 and as host of the G7 Summit in Toronto in 1988 to press these organisations to assume a more censorious position regarding

apartheid. The prime minister, however, was 'rebuffed' in his efforts. Fearful of becoming a 'lightweight' and losing 'all capacity for exercising influence in other areas of interest to Canada'[19], Mulroney retreated from his 'gut commitment to fight for stronger measures'[20] to be imposed on South Africa. The end result of Mulroney's efforts is that the policies of his government towards South Africa are believed by many to have worked to bring about an end to the system of apartheid. While contestable, a significant portion of the foreign policy legacy of the Mulroney government is the role that its policies and actions played in ending the apartheid system in South Africa.[21]

For those persons who have had the opportunity to plan their retirement from the prime minister's chair, the ability to focus the resources of the state on a few priority issues has allowed them to better plan their legacies. Prior to his retirement in December 2003, Prime Minister Chrétien used his position as host of the G8 Summit in 2002 'to ensure that African concerns would have their full place' in the discussions.[22] Chrétien's focus on Africa meant that discussions at the Kananaskis Summit would not be overtaken by discussions regarding the terrorist attacks on the United States on September 11, 2001 and the debates concerning the proper response to the acts of terrorism and how to quell the terrorist threat. Steven Langdon has noted that it was 'Canadian leadership' that moved the G8 to adopt an Action Plan for Africa at Kananaskis and that Canada's commitments to Africa were 'particularly specific and enthusiastic'.[23] This action by Canada, moreover, was the result of Chrétien's 'deep sense of personal engagement and a strong sense of identification with issues of poverty in Africa'.[24] Knowing that the G8 Summit in Kananaskis was to be his last as host, Chrétien used this occasion to help build a legacy of compassion for his prime ministership.

CONSTRAINTS ON A PRIME MINISTER

While the prime minister does possess an array of powers that enable him/her to dominate the policy-making process, there are a number of constraints which may act to inhibit a prime minister from getting his/her way.

The first, and most important, constraint on a prime minister is time. The prime minister's schedule at the best of times is hectic, what with having to attend to Cabinet business, Parliament, the legislative calendar, party caucus, party fundraising and other functions, and to government and patronage appointments. Added to this list is the amount of time taken up with consultations and meetings with personal staff, the principal secretary, the clerk of the Privy Council Office and individual ministers, as well as provincial premiers, foreign heads of state, and business leaders. On top of this already crowded schedule, the prime minister must make time for constituency matters and for maintaining contact with members of the riding association. A prime minister, then, must be careful with his/her time as there are always issues and people who seek to have 'just a few minutes of time'. If a prime minister does not prioritise, he/she will soon fall victim to 'political overload', that is 'a pervasive sense of urgency and an accompanying feeling of being overwhelmed both by events and the number of matters needing attention'.[25] To avoid overload, a prime minister needs to be selective with his/her time and focus only on those issues on his/her strategic policy agenda.

In addition to time, there are a number of issues with which all prime ministers have had to be concerned and which operate as constraints on the freedom of manoeuvrability. Donald Smiley has referred to these as the 'enduring axes' of Canadian politics. They are: French–English relations, regionalism, and Canada–US relations. The first two are of importance because they deal with national unity, always a primary concern for any prime minister. The first, moreover, is a foreign policy concern as Quebec has since the mid-1960s pushed for recognition abroad as an independent actor in foreign affairs.[26] In relations with other states of importance to Quebec, especially other French-speaking states, the prime minister will be cognisant of the position of Quebec on the issue(s) at hand—a position most likely at variance with that of the federal government—and the ramifications of the Canadian position on Quebec and on politics within that province.

In terms of Canada–US relations, the bilateral relationship affects all of Canada's international behaviour. This is not to argue that Canada's relationship with the US determines Canada's foreign policy but rather that the bilateral relationship is an important factor in decision-making. For example, John Holmes argued that it was 'the fact of American policy' that hampered Canada's recognition of the People's Republic of China as the government of China,[27] a position that Canada had favoured since 1949 when Mao Zedong and the Chinese Communist Party first came to power. The 'fact' to which Holmes was referring, and which prevented Canada from moving forward on recognition until 1970, was that communist states were seeking to expand their influence and needed to be 'contained' in both their geographic boundaries and international influence. A similar 'fact of American policy' is operative today, namely the 'fact' that terrorism is perceived by American policymakers as a serious threat to the American homeland, a threat from which the US needs to protect itself—and the protection of the US begins outside of its borders. To this end, Canada has instituted a number of measures including legislation dealing with terrorism, a new Smart border agreement with the US, and a restructuring of the civil service to create a Department of Public Safety and Emergency Preparedness.[28] The point is that the prime minister needs to be aware that any action Canada takes that might be construed as not being in line with the security concerns of both the American government and the prime minister will need to be weighed in terms of its costs and benefits to the bilateral relationship.

The media is another constraint on the prime minister's freedom of action in foreign affairs because it helps to set the public's agenda. By focusing attention on certain events or issues, the media imparts a sense of importance to those events or issues for Canadians. What is often referred to as the 'CNN effect' is a result of the power of that television network's 'all day, every day' coverage of news events to shape the public's agenda. Media coverage of events work as a constraint on a prime minister's power when the public, as a result of media coverage of an event or issue, presses for its prime minister to take action when he/she may not necessarily want to do so. In short, problems arise when the public's agenda differs from the prime minister's strategic agenda.

That events happening in far-off places would strike a chord with a significant portion of the Canadian populace, who would then press their government for action, was demonstrated by the Ethiopian famine crisis of 1984 and 1985. In this case, it was the television coverage of the famine and the images of children starving on the evening news that moved Canadians to become active in grassroots campaigns and to push their government to respond to the catastrophe.[29] In other words, media coverage of the famine moved the issue first onto the public agenda and then onto the prime minister's agenda.

The ability of the public to move the government to respond to a particular issue or event is heightened if either a large or well organised domestic group or industry is involved. An example of the former is Canada's response to the Tiananmen Square massacre on June 4, 1989. In May 1989, Chinese students and workers began holding demonstrations in Tiananmen Square to press their government for changes. After six weeks, the Chinese government ordered lethal force to be used to clear the Square. During this period, demonstrations were held in all major Canadian cities in support of the Chinese students and workers. A number of pro-democracy groups were formed in larger Canadian cities with a sizable Chinese population (e.g., Vancouver and Toronto). These groups were very vocal and active in pushing the Canadian government to support the demonstrators and to adopt stern measures in response to the Chinese government's decision to use violence to quell the demonstrations. The Mulroney government's response was a series of measures that were more strict than the response of most Western nations, including the United States. Part of the reason for this reaction has to do with the size and organization of the Chinese-Canadian community.[30]

An example of the latter is Canada's involvement in the creation of the Kimberley Process, a certification scheme to ensure that diamonds from areas of conflict, so-called 'blood diamonds', are excluded from the legitimate diamond market. In 2008, Canada was the fifth-ranked producer of diamonds in terms of carat volume and ranked third in terms of production export value.[31] In early 2000, a series of reports were released by civil society organizations around the globe on the impact of blood diamonds on the conflicts in Africa. One report was of particular importance for our discussion as it was produced by a Canadian civil society organization—Partnership Africa Canada—and it brought the issue of blood diamonds to the attention of many Canadians.[32] The combination of pressure from both the Canadian diamond industry and from Canadian civil society organizations ultimately put the issue on the agenda of the Chrétien government.

[Moving attention away from the media and public opinion, there are three additional constraints on a prime minister's power. Each of these remaining constraints derives from the workings of the Canadian system of parliamentary government: they are institutional factors. The first institutional constraint concerns whether or not the prime minister commands a majority in the House of Commons. The issue of support from the House is only problematic should the prime minister not command a majority in that body. Then, the prime minister needs to be cognizant of the level of support within the House for his/her initiatives, in both domestic and foreign policy. In the case of a minority government, the prime minister's freedom of action may be somewhat circumscribed by the composition of the House. That being the case, the prime minister is not without some power over the House as no party leader would want the Government to fall over a matter of little importance to the Canadian public, and much of Canada's foreign policy falls within the ambit of minimal importance to Canadians. It is rare for a foreign policy issue to dominate Canadian politics and even more rare for a foreign policy issue to be more than a peripheral factor in a General Election. For example, the 1988 General Election is often cited as an example of an election in which a foreign policy issue—whether or not Canada should sign a bilateral free trade agreement with the US—played a key role in determining the outcome. The major political parties were divided on the issue, with the Progressive Conservatives in favour of an agreement and both the Liberals and NDP opposed to one. In their analysis of the election, Clarke et al. found that only 15.6 per cent of Progressive Conservative voters, 9.8 per cent of Liberal voters, and 6.5 per cent of NDP voters cast their ballot on the basis of their party's position on free trade.[33] For the overwhelming majority of voters, then, free trade was not the most important issue in the election and people did not cast their ballots on the basis of their party's support for, or opposition to, a Canada–US free trade agreement.

There are instances when a foreign policy issue is of importance to a particular riding, or even a few ridings within a region, but seldom does an issue go beyond being of regional significance to affect a national campaign. For example, a new border crossing connecting Windsor, Ontario with Detroit, Michigan would help to speed up the movement of trucks between Canada and the US and, thereby, to increase the attractiveness of cross-border commercial relations. In addition, the increase in the movement of trucks would help to reduce air pollution in Windsor caused by trucks idling on city roads. The issue of a new border crossing has little electoral salience beyond Windsor's border, however, although the Windsor–Detroit link is the major commercial thoroughfare for Canadian exports to the US and, as such, is theoretically an issue of importance to all Canadians.

A second institutional constraint on the prime minister derives from the role of opposition parties in the House of Commons. The main role of Opposition parties is to find fault with the Government and to provide an alternative choice for Canadians come the next General Election. To this end, the Opposition parties use Question Period and other occasions to demonstrate the weaknesses of the current regime, and especially of the prime minister. Each Opposition party puts forward an alternative agenda, including a different foreign policy platform, to be implemented should one of them win the next General Election and form the Government. Other than putting forward an alternative to the present Government and attempting to uncover ministerial misdeeds or departmental indiscretions, there is little that the Opposition parties can do to effect change in Canada's foreign policy.

A final institutional constraint on the prime minister comes from the need to involve the provinces in decision-making. The workings of federalism and the need for federal–provincial co-operation in a range of foreign policy-related issues limits the range of possible choices for a prime minister. As this material is covered in a more detailed and nuanced manner by Kukucha herein, there is no need to repeat that discussion here.

CONCLUSION

In examining the various constraints under which a prime minister operates it must be noted that none of them is decisive, with the exception of the last constraint concerning the provinces. There are areas of constitutional responsibility accorded to the provinces in the Constitutional Act of 1982 and through decisions of the courts on which a prime minister, however desirous, may not tread. Given this, none of the other constraints discussed presents an insurmountable challenge to the authority of the prime minister. All of the obstacles presented herein may be overcome by a prime minister who has the determination and desire to do so: it is a question of political will. A prime minister can use the powers of office to discharge lightning bolts to deal with unplanned events or crises and plan his/her legacy by focusing on a few key issues. In short, if a prime minister has the will, he/she can have his/her way.

Key Terms

Idiosyncratic Variable
Mandate Letters
Role or Positional Variable

Notes

1. Donald J. Savoie, *Governing from the Centre: The Concentration of Power in Canadian Politics.* (Toronto: University of Toronto Press, 1999).

2. James N. Rosenau, 'Pre-theories and Theories of Foreign Policy,' in R.B. Farrell, ed. *Approaches to Comparative and International Politics* (Evanston: Northwestern University Press, 1966), 43.

3. From 1909 to 1993, the minister was known as the secretary of state for external affairs and, after 1993, the minister became the minister of foreign affairs.

4. As cited in Savoie, 319.

5. Andrew Cooper, 'Between Will and Capabilities: Canada and the Zaire/Great Lakes Initiative,' in Andrew F. Cooper and Geoffrey Hayes, eds., *Worthwhile Initiatives: Canadian Mission-Oriented Diplomacy.* (Toronto: CIIA Irwin, 2000), 64–78.

6. While the names of the various ministerial positions within the troika have all changed over the years, the troika has consistently comprised ministers responsible for foreign relations (i.e., political, security, and consular issues), international trade, and international development (i.e., the Canadian International Development Agency).

7. Charlotte Gray, 'New Faces in Old Places: The Making of Canadian Foreign Policy,' in Fen Osler Hampson and Christopher J. Maule, eds., *Canada Among Nations 1992–93: A New World Order?* (Ottawa: Carleton University Press, 1992), 15–28.

8. Savoie, 137.

9. Kim Richard Nossal, *The Politics of Canadian Foreign Policy, 3rd ed.* (Scarborough: Prentice Hall, 1997), 245–7.

10. Peter Aucoin, 'Organizational Change in the Machinery of Canadian Government: From Rational Management to Brokerage Politics,' *Canadian Journal of Political Science* 19: 1 (March 1986), 3–27.

11. John Kirton, 'Managing Global Conflict: Canada and International Summitry,' in Maureen Appel Molot and Brian W. Tomlin, eds., *Canada Among Nations 1987: A World of Conflict.* (Toronto: James Lorimer, 1988), 23.

12. Andrew F. Cooper, *In Between Countries: Australia, Canada, and the Search for Order in Agricultural Trade*. (Montreal and Kingston: McGill-Queen's University Press, 1997), 188.

13. Aucoin (1986), 17.

14. Jeffrey Simpson, 'Why do the Conservatives use these tactics? They think they work' *Globe and Mail*, November 24, 2009, A23.

15. For a cogent discussion of this issue, see Chris Kukucha, 'From Kyoto to WTO: Evaluating the Constitutional Legitimacy of the Provinces in Canadian Foreign Trade and Environmental Policy,' *Canadian Journal of Political Science*, 38:1 (March 2005), 129–52.

16. As cited in Kukucha, 148.

17. Thomas S. Axworthy, 'Of Secretaries to Princes,' *Canadian Public Administration* 31, 2 (Summer 1988), 247–64.

18. Kim Richard Nossal, *Rain Dancing: Sanctions in Canadian and Australian Foreign Policy*. (Toronto: University of Toronto Press, 1994), 106.

19. Nossal, *Rain Dancing*, 250.

20. Linda Freeman, *The Ambiguous Champion: Canada and South Africa in the Trudeau and Mulroney Years*. (Toronto: University of Toronto Press, 1997), 286.

21. See Freeman, *The Ambiguous Champion*; and Nossal, *Rain Dancing*.

22. Robert Fowler, 'Canadian Leadership and the Kananaskis G-8 Summit: Towards a Less Self-Centred Foreign Policy,' in David Carment, Fen Osler Hampson, and Norman Hillmer, eds., *Canada Among Nations 2003: Coping with the American Colossus*. (Toronto: Oxford University Press, 2003), 219.

23. Steven Langdon, 'NEPAD and the Renaissance of Africa,' in Carment, Hampson, and Hillmer, 249–50.

24. Ibid., 251.

25. Donald J. Savoie, 'The Federal Government: Revisiting Court Government in Canada,' in Luc Bernier, Keith Brownsey, and Michael Howlett, eds., *Executive Styles in Canada: Cabinet Structures and Leadership Practices in Canadian Government* (Toronto: University of Toronto Press, 2005), 26.

26. See Louis Belanger, 'The Changing World Order and Quebec's International Relations: An Analysis of Two Salient Environments,' in Michael J. Tucker, Raymond B. Blake, and P.E. Bryden, eds., *Canada and the New World Order: Facing the New Millennium* (Toronto: Irwin, 2000), 163–84.

27. John Holmes, *The Better Part of Valour: Essays on Canadian Diplomacy* (Toronto: McClelland and Stewart, 1970), 215.

28. Paul Gecelovsky, 'Northern Enigma: American Images of Canada,' *American Review of Canadian Studies* 37, 4 (Winter 2007), 517–35.

29. Andrew F. Cooper, Richard A. Higgott, and Kim Richard Nossal, *Relocating Middle Powers: Australia and Canada in a Changing World Order*. (Vancouver, UBC Press, 1994), 23.

30. See Paul Gecelovsky, 'The Canadian Response to the Tiananmen Square Massacre,' *Canadian Foreign Policy* 8, 3 (Spring 2001), 75–98.

31. See Annual Global Summary: 2008 Production, Imports, Exports, KPC Counts. Available at https://mmsd.mms.nrcan.gc.ca/kimberleystats/public_tables/Annual%20Summary%20Table%202008.pdf.

32. Ian Smillie, L. Gberie and R. Hazleton, *The Heart of the Matter: Sierra Leone, Diamonds, and Human Security* (Ottawa: Partnership Africa Canada, 2000).

33. Harold D. Clarke, Lawrence LeDuc, Jane Jenson, and Jon H. Pammett, *Absent Mandate: Interpreting Change in Canadian Elections, 2nd ed* (Toronto: Gage, 1991), 145–8. Thanks to Harold Jansen for bringing this to my attention. The Reform Party ran candidates in the 1988 general election; however, none was elected. The Bloc Québécois was not formed until 1990.

13

THE MEMBER OF PARLIAMENT AND FOREIGN POLICY

John English

For most of Canadian history, Canada's House of Commons had no committee on foreign affairs. When Paul Martin arrived in Ottawa in 1935, fresh from studying international affairs in Geneva and international law at Harvard, he discovered there was little that a government backbencher interested in foreign affairs could do to express that interest. He quickly made friends with some members of the bureaucracy who shared his foreign policy interests. One of them, Norman Robertson, encouraged him to ask a question in the House on Japanese politics. He did so and discovered quickly, in his own words, 'from the expression' on Mackenzie King's face 'that [he] had pulled a boner'. Mackenzie King, Martin later recalled, 'did not encourage private members to speak out on international relations'. The Foreign Affairs portfolio remained within the Prime Minister's Office until 1946; no separate committee on foreign affairs would be established until 1949, when King left office (Martin, 1983: 181).

Things are better now for private members. There is a Committee on Foreign Affairs and International Trade, and the Liberal Party Red Book of 1993 called for a participatory foreign policy in which members of Parliament played a central role. 'A Liberal government', the Red Book declared, 'will also expand the rights of Parliament to debate major Canadian foreign policy initiatives, such as the deployment of peace-keeping forces, and the rights of Canadians to regular and serious consultation on foreign policy issues' (Liberal Party of Canada, 1993: 109). Following another Red Book undertaking, the Liberal government, after the 1993 election, established a Special Joint Committee of the Senate and the House of Commons to Review Canadian Foreign Policy. The government responded specifically to the recommendations of the report and accepted many of them. The parliamentary committee has also produced significant reports on a range of matters, from circumpolar co-operation to child labour and government assistance to small business exporters, and, in this Parliament, the Multilateral Agreement on Investment. The Red Book commitment to consult Parliament before significant foreign policy decisions are made was initially met through House of Commons debates on each commitment, but, lately, the committee has held the debates and has received expert testimony from Foreign Affairs officials and others. The device has worked well and seems to command non-partisan support.

Until the mid-1980s, committees could study specific questions only when a minister authorized them to do so. This practice sometimes had embarrassing consequences. One committee chair noted for his controversial views waited for over a year for a minister's authorization. One day the phone call from the minister finally came. The minister asked that the committee undertake hearings on a highly significant topic. The chair quickly called together the committee. Just as the committee was assembling, the party whips rushed in and announced, 'The House has been dissolved.' The minister laughed last and no doubt heartily. In 1983 and 1985, however, committees gained the authority to meet year-round and determine their own agenda. Committees now have great freedom to choose topics and to study them with vigour and appropriate assistance. When one considers that Mackenzie King would not even allow a committee on foreign affairs to exist, one realizes that such independence is important for the MP interested in foreign policy questions.

There are other apparent improvements. When Paul Martin reflected on his colleagues in 1935 and those elected in Trudeau's first government in 1968, he claimed that the latter group was far more interested in broader questions and international aspects of Canadian politics than the members in 1935. The concern of the first Trudeau class was no longer the local post office or the appointment of a customs inspector. Today, the class of 1968 seems parochial when compared with members elected in 1993. In 1970, in a Parliament of 263 members, 16 were born outside of Canada, 26 had studied outside of Canada, and 17 had worked outside of Canada. In 1994, in a Parliament of 295 members, 29 were born outside of Canada, 50 studied outside of Canada, and

22 had worked outside of Canada. Canada now enjoys a Parliament with many members with international experience, a committee structure that permits considerable freedom, and assistance far beyond the wildest imaginings of Paul Martin in 1935. Why, then, do so many members of Parliament echo his frustration of those earlier times?

The statistics mask many differences as well as the major limits that face the Canadian Member of Parliament, especially when compared with his/her counterparts in the United States and Great Britain. He/she faces such limits because of the character of the Canadian Parliament, the type of background MPs possess, the nature of constituency politics, the diversity of the Canadian population, and the committee system of Parliament.

Canada's Parliament meets approximately 60 per cent of the year, except in election years when the number of days in session drops considerably. The majority of members do not live in Ottawa but rather commute weekly to their homes, often many hours distant. The availability of virtually unlimited air passes makes this vagabond life possible, but it also makes sustained focus on particular issues most difficult. When one member of Parliament read Jack Pickersgill's memoir, *Seeing Canada Whole*, published in 1994, he remarked on how much more interaction there was among members in Pickersgill's day when committees were not interrupted by votes in the House and, most significantly, when members lived too far from home to permit them to fly home on weekends or, more accurately, on Thursday afternoon to return on Tuesday morning.

Members now have passes allowing them to fly anywhere in Canada with or without spouse or children, but they have neither budget nor 'points' that would permit them to travel outside of Canada. In Parliament itself, the multi-party system and, in this Parliament, the narrow majority means that much time is occupied with voting, procedural matters, and other time-consuming parliamentary tasks. Moreover, party discipline prevents the kind of initiatives available to American congressmen and senators. Bill Richardson's active personal diplomacy as a congressman, which led to his appointment as the American UN ambassador, would not have been possible for a parliamentarian in Canada. One finds Richardson's counterparts in Britain, Germany, and especially Scandinavia, where less stringent rules on legislators' activities make personal diplomacy possible and where legislative tenure has tended to be much longer. Indeed, some Scandinavian legislators are absent for months at a time on international work.

Recent academic research supports this argument. David Docherty's *Mr Smith Goes to Ottawa* concludes that 'Parliament acts to push members away from the capital and to pull them towards their local ridings'. The result is they spend more time in their constituencies 'at the expense of their more parliamentary-based responsibilities'. This tendency is particularly marked by recently elected members and is less prevalent among senior members, of whom there have been few recently (Docherty, 1997: 203).

Canadian MPs today have considerable interest in foreign policy, but when compared with their counterparts of 25 years ago they have, on the whole, less international background in terms of their education or work experience, limiting their understanding of the contemporary international system. Certainly, more have been born outside the country and in countries not represented in previous Parliaments. In 1970, seven of the 16 non-Canadian births were from Britain and five from the United States. In 1994, six of the 29 were born in Britain but only two in the United States. There were five from Asia and five from Italy alone. Members can speak of the Punjab, Croatia, Hungary, Armenia, and other countries with personal experience lacking in previous decades. The partisan nature of this experience tends to make government and opposition leaders nervous.

In the Parliament elected in 1993, the Official Opposition was a party dedicated to Quebec separation. The practice of earlier times, even in the days of Mackenzie King, of taking opposition members to international conferences became difficult, if not impossible, to follow. In the Parliament of 1949, several private members from the Liberals, the Conservatives, and the CCF attended the UN in the fall for six weeks. The technique was cleverly used by Lester Pearson to create non-partisan support for his foreign policy initiatives, even with John Diefenbaker in the early 1950s (English, 1993: 213–14). That practice rarely occurs now. In part, the explanation lies in the character of recent Parliaments. Bloc Québécois members, it was feared, might use the occasion of international gatherings or activities to promote the cause of separation. In the Parliament elected in 1997, the Official Opposition, the Reform Party, is wary not only of foreign travel by Members of Parliament but also of the cost of Canadian internationalism. The Reform Party refuses to 'pair', a practice whereby a member of the governing party and of the opposition agree to be absent for parliamentary votes, that allowed some independent initiatives by members. In some senses, the Reform Party reflects the isolationist tendencies found among neo-conservatives in the United States, who regard international institutions and commitments with deep suspicion. This mood and attitude have been largely absent from the Canadian House of Commons since the 1930s.

In the case of the Liberal Party, one finds many members with extensive international experience and interests. However, most of those members find their place in the cabinet or as parliamentary secretaries. Although Prime Ministers Mulroney and Chrétien both reduced the size of the cabinet, the current cabinet is only slightly smaller than in the early Mulroney days. When over 35 members of the Liberal parliamentary group are part of the ministry, it means that nearly all of the Liberals with strong foreign affairs background are part of the government. About 25 of the remainder are parliamentary secretaries, whose workload and other activities prevent them from working in a sustained way on foreign policy issues. Parliamentary secretaries, for example, are forbidden to accept payment for travel to attend conferences outside of Canada and have no independent budgets to carry out such work.

These constraints are worth noting, but they are probably less important than constituency demands. Because of improvements in transportation and communication, the Member of Parliament is now closer to his/her constituency than ever before. Indeed, it is astonishing to think that most constituencies had no members' offices until the 1970s. Members shared a secretary in Ottawa, and that secretary apparently could deal with most of their correspondence. The private member now has an office in the constituency, a personal office in Ottawa, and a staff of four or five employees. Free long distance telephone and fax are available, as well as electronic mail. In Parkinsonian fashion, the work has expanded to meet the staff available. Docherty's surveys of recent members revealed that members spend over two-fifths of their working time on constituency affairs (Docherty, 1997: 178). Today, the average MP in an urban constituency in Toronto, Vancouver, Calgary, and many other smaller cities receives approximately 100 calls per day. According to Toronto MP Dennis Mills, over three-quarters of his calls deal with immigration. In this sense, there is involvement with aspects of Canada's relations with other countries, but that involvement is very specific. In many cases, the presence of significant ethnic communities profoundly influences not only the interests but also the origins of MPs. Although Canada has always had members who have spoken for the interests of other nations such as Israel and

Ireland, recent Parliaments have seen an explosion of the 'special interest' politician.

At the first meeting of candidates on foreign policy that I attended as a candidate just before the 1988 election, we began to talk about 'issues' when one of the senior members blurted out: 'The only Canadian foreign policy issue which matters in my constituency is an independent Punjab.' The candidates were not as startled as one might expect, for many had fought nomination battles where the support of the Sikh community was a valuable commodity. Indeed, Liberal membership lists before the 1988 and 1993 elections and the 1990 leadership convention bore testimony to the involvement in the party of Canadians from various areas who, unlike most Canadians, did have strong views on foreign policy issues in their area of origin. At my own nomination battle in 1987, the Kitchener Liberal Association had about 3,000 members, of whom about 800 were of Greek or Cypriot origin and about 600 of Sikh background. Their willingness to come out to vote on a cold December night was much more pronounced than was the case for other association members.

The diversity of the Canadian population has had several effects on the Member of Parliament's interest in foreign policy. On the one hand, it has created the special interest MPs described above and particular focus on issues such as locating a Canadian consulate in Amritsar. On the other hand, it has provided new resources that draw Canadian attention to areas previously ignored and give Canada a capacity it earlier lacked when members were overwhelmingly French or British in origin. There are now lively debates about Greek and Turkish issues in which members of Greek origin and others with considerable Turkish populations in their ridings take their respective sides. On the whole, these debates probably have little impact on policy, but they are not ignored. Numerous international parliamentary associations now reflect these interests. The Reform Party generally refuses to participate in their activities, and many others regard their activities with a skeptical eye. For many years, overseas trips have been the method for purchasing loyalty for both government and opposition since party whips decide who participates. Whatever their political purpose, these associations are the principal contact that private members have with international fora.

The major associations receive parliamentary funding, although these funds have been much reduced since 1993. No longer can members take spouses and fly business class, and rarely is there a full delegation. Indeed, Canadian delegations to such parliamentary groups as the North Atlantic Assembly or the Parliamentary Assembly of the Organization for Co-operation and Security in Europe are smaller than those from countries of much less international weight. Moreover, there are problems of balance: there is a funded Canada–Israel Parliamentary Association but no Arab counterpart. Even more troubling are other associations, usually termed 'friendship groups', which have neither parliamentary funding nor sanction. The Canada–Taiwan Friendship Group creates obvious problems, if not for the members who take their spouses on first-class flights to first-class hotels in Taipei. The televised sight of Canadian MPs cavorting in the streets at a presidential rally during the last election in Taiwan no doubt horrified the Asia-Pacific desk at Foreign Affairs.

Some members devote much of their time to parliamentary association work and find it extremely rewarding. Senior members, often with earlier ministerial experience and less concern about re-election, tend to become chairs of these groups. Charles Caccia, for example, has given strong leadership to the Canada–Europe group. His extensive network of connections with European parliamentarians provided valuable assistance to the government during the 'Turbot War' with Spain.

Similarly, another former minister, Sheila Finestone, prodded the Inter-Parliamentary Union to consider the land mine ban in 1997. Members of Parliament, however, share places with senators who have more freedom and, in recent times, more funds to participate in these associations. Although senators and MPs tend to work well together, the tendency of non-Canadians to treat the senators as the 'senior' delegate members irks those from the Commons. Other difficulties arise from the time constraints on Canadian members, especially when parliamentary majorities are narrow or non-existent. The Council of Europe, at which Canada gained observer status, has 60 days of meetings each year. One Danish parliamentarian told me that she spent about 80 days per year on parliamentary association business. Such a commitment would be unacceptable in Canada to one's caucus, one's colleagues, and, almost certainly, one's constituency. For Canadians, the substance of parliamentary association business does not merit the time of such commitments even though Europeans believe that in their case it does.

It could be argued that Canada does have a direct interest, similar to that of European parliamentarians, in creating links with the United States Congress. The Canada–United States parliamentary group, established, surprisingly enough, by John Diefenbaker, meets regularly for approximately three days to discuss bilateral issues. Discussions have been lively, but the group is less active than it was in the 1980s and certainly cannot be said to be an important component of the bilateral relationship. In the 1980s Peter Dobell, the founder of the Parliamentary Centre, which provides assistance to many groups, called for more exchanges and closer contact because of the growing importance of Congress. Legislators, he argued, have an 'instinctive' respect for each other, which could be useful in Washington where legislators traditionally have distrusted diplomats (Dobell, 1992: 131). His argument was cogent but had little effect. Canadian and American legislators meet rarely and accomplish little of substance together. North American integration may parallel Europe in some respects but not at the legislative level.

For most MPs, foreign policy in the sense one encounters in academic circles is of little concern or interest. There have been major debates on foreign policy issues in the 1990s. One thinks immediately of the Gulf War debate, when many members gave eloquent speeches and revealed serious study of the issue. There have also been good debates on peacekeeping commitments since the Liberals were elected in 1993, and many private members have spoken passionately and well on human rights issues. Reform MP Keith Martin's focus on land mines has been rightly lauded, and Liberal MP Paddy Torsney's interest in women's issues on the international level is well known. But in the hundreds of pages of Hansard, these moments are relatively rare.

The most significant focus on foreign policy occurs in the Committee on Foreign Affairs and International Trade. That committee, chaired by Bill Graham, a distinguished international lawyer, has had two subcommittees in recent times. One deals with trade matters, the other with human rights concerns. According to the Liberal whip, more Liberal members ask to be members of the Foreign Affairs Committee than any other committee. Since 1994, after the Special Joint Review Committee reported, the Foreign Affairs Committee has carried out numerous special studies, most of which have been well received by the media. Some have enjoyed unanimous support, a rare quality for committee reports in recent years and an indication that normal partisan spirits abate in foreign affairs discussions. According to Peter Dobell, the Foreign Affairs Committee has been highly innovative and, in many ways, has created new possibilities for parliamentary committees (1997).

Nevertheless, there are many difficulties with the committee's operation. Some are specific to it;

others are common to the Canadian committee system. Specifically, the Foreign Affairs and International Trade Committee has a vast territory to survey but little time to contemplate the details. Three ministers—Foreign Affairs, International Trade, and International Cooperation—report before the committee, as do two secretaries of state (Asia-Pacific and Africa and Latin America). Ministerial appearances are brief and offer little time for detailed questioning. Moreover, departmental business plans and estimates are complex and vague. The most determined parliamentary efforts to find out what, for example, Canada is doing in and about southern Africa are exercises in fact-finding futility. Because of the range of issues, the committee is often required to 'fight fires' and respond to immediate demands. Although the committee under Graham's able leadership has carried out some important and valuable studies, long-range thinking and analysis about Canada's foreign policy priorities have given way to the urgent though not necessarily most prescient issues. A high turnover of committee membership means that final consideration of studies occurs after many of the committee members who heard witness testimony have left.

Graham's frustrations are expressed in a broader sense in a report of the Liaison Committee of Committee Chairs of the 35th Parliament, which he chaired. In this report, the chairs of committees reviewed the current effectiveness of committees in carrying out their functions. The review made several interesting observations. Reports, it claimed, had little impact on policy. Indeed, the situation may have been better before 1985 when committees could not set their own agendas. In those days, 'Ministers who had proposed orders of reference, usually paid close attention to the committee's report because they and their advisers had selected areas of policy where the government was undecided on how best to proceed and was looking for advice.' Moreover, committee members of all parties proceeded on the assumption that their work would be taken seriously by the government since the government commissioned it (Liaison Committee, 1997: 9).

Even more troubling is the claim that the new power to select subjects of inquiry has meant that the committees pay less attention to the estimates than they did before 1985. A separate report by the Standing Committee on Procedure and House Affairs came to the same conclusion and issued an even more strongly worded recommendation that departmental estimates be given more than perfunctory attention. In the 35th Parliament, several members of the Foreign Affairs Committee tried to discover a way to examine CIDA estimates effectively. After taking advice from independent experts on development assistance, they considered focusing on one country and examining CIDA assistance in detail, but the task was beyond the capacity of a committee whose budget is meagre and whose members' time is limited. In assessing the reasons for the lack of 'conscientious scrutiny of proposed expenditures', the subcommittee on procedure and house affairs pointed to problems with 'rules and structures' (House of Commons, 1996: 81).

The Liaison Committee report, however, suggested the problems are not merely technical. Here some comparisons were made. According to the report:

> Compared to many other legislatures, where committee members have greater security of tenure, this practice of substantial change in committee membership mid-way through a Parliament inevitably means that Canadian members lack the acquired background and the institutional memory that contribute greatly to the quality of committee work. (1997: 11)

The Canadian House has other unique problems. There are only 12 committee rooms to serve 19 committees, and the need for interpretation (translation) is absent in other parliaments. Although the multiparty system was not mentioned, the need to deal with five parties rather than two or three, as is the case in the United States and Britain, obviously complicates committee work. There are not only more parties but also more interest groups, and the demand to hear witnesses exceeds the time available to members. Those who appear before committees often find audiences that are a fraction of the full committee. There is, very simply, neither world enough nor time for adequate committee work (Liaison Committee, 1997: 11).

The private member in Canada has a shorter political life expectancy than his/her British counterparts and therefore less ability to undertake separate initiatives. In comparison with American congressmen, the Canadian MP lacks the staff, budget, and independence to carry out foreign policy initiatives or even sustained study of a foreign policy issue. Rewards in the constituency for foreign policy interest, with the notable exception of highly ethnic ridings, are rare. Moreover, in the view of the private member, the Canadian bureaucracy is unsympathetic to such initiatives and considerably stronger than its American counterpart. Whether true or not, the comment of a first-term Liberal member—'If the bureaucrats don't buy it, it's dead'—is a widely held opinion among private members on both sides of the House (Docherty, 1997: 234).

The rise of non-governmental organizations allows the bureaucracy to argue that there is an alternative to Parliament in gauging and understanding popular opinion. At the first National Forum on Canadian Foreign Policy, MPs were initially not invited despite the clear statement in the Red Book that the Forum would include 'representation from Parliament and non-governmental organizations, and members of the general public who have an interest or involvement in world affairs' (Liberal Party of Canada, 1993: 109).

The chair of the Foreign Policy Review, Jean Robert Gauthier, complained loudly. Nevertheless, at some sessions at the 1994 forum, members of Parliament were not permitted to speak. At one session, the MPs took seats at the back of the room while others gathered around the central table. Someone asked the chair: 'Who are those people at the back?' She replied rather sternly: 'They are members of Parliament. They may stay but cannot speak.' Although NGO representatives and academics were vocal, Canada's elected representatives were stifled. The ambiguity of public representation was clear.

In summary, the Canadian MP is tied tightly to his/her constituency, and most have few incentives to pursue an interest in foreign policy issues unless there is a distinct constituency connection. Nevertheless, foreign affairs debates bring out the best in parliamentarians, and the Foreign Affairs Committee is prestigious for members. This contradiction probably signals that the present does not predict the future, just as it does not reflect the past. The upheavals of the Canadian party system in the past decade are mirrored in Parliament, a Parliament that is clearly in transition. For now, the fragmented Parliament brings a fragmented focus when Canadian parliamentarians look beyond their boundaries.

References

Canadian Parliamentary Guide. 1970, 1993, 1994.

Dobell, Peter. 1992. 'Negotiating with the United States', in J.L. Granatstein, ed., *Towards a New World: Readings in the History of Canadian Foreign Policy*. Toronto: Copp Clark Pittman.

Dobell, Peter, and Lynda Chapin. 1997. 'Renewal at the House of Commons', Parliamentary Government (November).

Docherty, David. 1997. *Mr Smith Goes to Ottawa: Life in the House of Commons*. Vancouver: UBC Press.

English, John. 1993. *The Worldly Years: The Life of Lester Pearson 1949–1972*. Toronto: Knopf.

Liaison Committee of Committee Chairs. 1997. 'Report of the Liaison Committee on Committee Effectiveness'. Parliamentary Government (September).

Liberal Party of Canada. 1996. *A Record of Achievement: A Report on the Liberal Government's 36 Months in Office*. Ottawa.

———. 1993. *Creating Opportunities: The Liberal Plan for Canada*. Ottawa.

Martin, Paul. 1983. *A Very Public Life: Volume 1. Far From Home*. Ottawa: Deneau.

Pickersgill, J.W. 1994. *Seeing Canada Whole: A Memoir*. Toronto: Fitzhenry and Whiteside.

Standing Committee on Procedure and House Affairs. 1996. 'The Business of Supply: Completing the Circle of Control'. Ottawa.

THE ROLE OF PARLIAMENT IN A MINORITY GOVERNMENT

UPDATE

Duane Bratt and Christopher J. Kukucha

Studies on the role of Parliament in Canadian Foreign Policy often do not distinguish between majority and minority governments. This makes sense because the governing party, whether in a majority or minority situation, still controls the apparatus of government. For example, even through Parliament was not in session, the minority government of Stephen Harper was still able to dispatch the military and emergency humanitarian assistance to Haiti following its horrific January 2010 earthquake.

Nevertheless, there are critical differences between majority and minority governments. The need to assess the changing role of Parliament in a minority government setting is also important because it appears that Canada is going through a period of permanent minority government rule. Overall, minority governments are characterized by their short duration (usually between one and two years), constant election speculation and preparation, and hyper-partisanship. Since the government is out numbered in the House of Commons, including its committees, the government does not have complete control of the legislative agenda. These differences have an obvious impact on domestic politics, but they also affect the making of Canadian foreign policy.

This brief update to John English's preceding chapter focuses on three ways in which Parliament's role in Canadian foreign policy is changed in a minority government situation. First, it has exacerbated the growing trend of the frequent shuffling of Foreign Affairs Ministers. Since Paul Martin's election victory in June 2004, there have been five Foreign Affairs Ministers in less than six years (Pierre Pettigrew, Peter MacKay, Maxime Bernier, David Emerson, and Lawrence Cannon). Compare that to the tenure of previous ministers like Lester Pearson (nine years), Paul Martin Sr (five years), Mitchell Sharp (six years), and Joe Clark (seven years). Ministers are changing more rapidly because minority governments last less than half as long as majority governments. Even if a government is re-elected, the prime minister has a new team to choose from due to election defeats, retirements, and the arrival of freshly elected MPs. This may explain the shuffling of ministers, but it does have consequences. There are often delays as the new minister tries to get up to speed with his/her new portfolio and precious time is spent going through briefing books and meeting new officials. New ministers, especially in a high-profile post like Foreign Affairs, often want to make a mark by shifting policy, reorganizing the department (structural changes or adding, deleting, reassigning senior staff), and developing pet projects. Frequently replacing Foreign Ministers is rare in most of the world, especially among Canada's key allies, because the position is usually the most senior cabinet post. This means that the Canadian minister's interpersonal relations with his/her counterparts are hindered, which can create uncertainties in policy.

A second feature of minority governments is the enhanced use of Parliamentary motions to guide foreign policy. In the past, there have been take-note debates and resolutions on important decisions such as Canadian participation in the Gulf War (1991) and Kosovo War (1999), but the Parliamentary process was closely controlled by the government. In a minority situation, the governing party has to work with at least some of the opposition parties to ensure passage of resolutions, especially those that are a matter of confidence. During Stephen Harper's first minority government (January 2006–October 2008), there were two significant Parliamentary resolutions on Canada's military deployment to Afghanistan. Since both the NDP and Bloc Québécois opposed the military mission and would vote against any government resolution, the Conservatives had to work with the Liberals (or at least some of them) to ensure passage. In May 2006, a resolution was passed extending Canada's participation in the International Security

Assistance Force, which was due to expire in February 2007, until 2009. This resolution was a free vote and saw several prominent Liberals, including interim leader Bill Graham (who was also a former Foreign Affairs and Defence Minister) and future leader Michael Ignatieff, support the government. A second resolution, co-written with the Liberals, was passed in March 2008 that has Canada withdrawing its soldiers by December 2011.

In Parliament there are also committees in both the Senate and House of Commons dedicated to Canada's international affairs. In the lower chamber, the first and second sessions of the 40th Parliament divided the study of Canada's foreign relations into two committees: the Standing Committee on Foreign Affairs and International Development (FAAE) and the Standing Committee on International Trade (CIIT). The potential for partisan politics in the parliamentary committee system was most evident with FAAE. Although the committee studied and reported on a wide range of issues, including the oil and gas sector, Canada–US relations, the Baha'i community in Iran, and corporate social responsibility, it was the committee's work on Afghanistan that highlighted its politicization. In late 2009, the committee heard testimony suggesting that Afghan detainees were tortured after being handed over to local authorities by Canadian troops. In one attempt to de-rail the committee, Conservative MPs boycotted meetings required for scheduling future hearings and witnesses. Laurie Hawn, the parliamentary secretary for the Defence Minister, justified this act by accusing opposition members of seeking to 'satisfy their political bloodlust'.[1] Stephen Harper's controversial decision to prorogue Parliament for the first three months of 2010 was also critically viewed as an attempt to stop the committee's ongoing work on Afghanistan.

In the 40th Parliament, CIIT also studied numerous issues, including proposed trade agreements between Canada and Jordan, and Peru, and economic relations with the United States and South America. The committee's report on NAFTA Chapter 11, however, adopted on March 31, 2009, focused exclusively on a challenge launched in 2005 by Dow Agroscience. In its claim, the American company argued that Quebec's ban on the sale of lawn pesticides containing the active ingredient 2, 4-D limited investment opportunities in Canada. Not surprisingly, the committee 'vigorously defended' Quebec's right to enact legislation in the public interest. Some observers, however, questioned why the committee failed to address any of the other fourteen recently launched challenges under Chapter 11, several of which had implications for several Canadian provinces. In fact, this proliferation of new Chapter 11 cases has re-focused attention on NAFTA's investment provisions and the potential impact these commitments have on Canadian sovereignty. Surprisingly, these additional cases were not highlighted in the committee's report.

The CIIT's examination of the World Trade Organization (WTO) and supply management also focused on a politically important issue in Quebec. The title of the report, *Defending Supply Management at the WTO*, clearly articulated the committee's approval of Quebec's protectionist agricultural practices. Although supply management is a highly controversial issue in ongoing WTO negotiations, the report called on the Government of Canada to 'affirm its unequivocal support of, and commitment to defend, Canada's supply management system'.[2] While this is a politically important topic in Quebec, critics have long noted the lack of a pan-Canadian consensus on supply management. In fact, other provinces seeking greater market access for competitive agricultural goods reject these practices. The CITT's membership is dominated by Conservative Members of Parliament, and the party has adopted a wide range of strategies to appeal to voters in the province of Quebec. Two members of the Bloc Québécois also served on the CITT, one as vice-chair of the committee. Once again, there was no attempt to engage any other highly controversial issues being negotiated within the Doha framework, including services and procurement.

In the Senate, the Standing Committee on Foreign Affairs and International Trade (SCFAIT) reviews Canada's international relations. During recent minority governments, however, SCFAIT has largely avoided rigid partisan politics. The committee also examines a much smaller range of issues than FAAE and CITT. During the 40th Session of Parliament, for example, SCFAIT reviewed Canada–US border issues and Canadian trade agreements with Peru and the European Free Trade Association (Iceland, Liechtenstein, Norway, and Switzerland). The committee's most significant work, however, focused on the increasing influence of China, Russia, and India, in the global political economy, and a review of Export Development Canada (EDC). The study of emergi ng economic powers did not result in the publication of a formal Senate report. SCFAIT did publish its findings regarding EDC, but the committee simply reinforced Canada's commitment to trade promotion.

Despite the apolitical nature of these developments, it is important to consider two important facts when considering the partisanship of this Senate committee. First, in the Canadian parliamentary system, the upper chamber lacks the legitimacy to defeat or challenge government policy. Although the Senate delayed previous legislation, most notably the Canada–US Free Trade Agreement (CUFTA), there is no evidence to suggest that this chamber will highlight and politicize matters of foreign policy in a minority setting. Second, SCFAIT avoids partisan issues due to its membership. Unlike FAAE and CITT, appointees represent a relatively equal number of Liberals and Conservatives. Although future appointments can alter these relations, the Senate does not currently alter Canadian foreign policy in any significant manner.

Key Terms

Committee on Foreign Affairs and International Trade
Standing Committee on Foreign Affairs and International Development
Standing Committee on International Trade

Notes

1. Steven Chase, 'Tory Boycott Halts Hearings on Transfer of Afghan Detainees,' *Globe and Mail*, 16 December 2009, A4.
2. House of Commons Standing Committee on International Trade, Defending Supply Management at the WTO, November 2009, 40th Parliament, 2nd Session, www2.parl.gc.ca/HousePublications/Publication.aspx?DocId=4206172&Language=E&Mode=1&Parl=40&Ses=2&File=18 (26 January, 2010).

14

THE INSTITUTIONALIZATION OF FOREIGN AFFAIRS (1909–2009)

Patrice Dutil[1]

I am in the midst of an argument with the Department at home. What a jealous old hippopotamus the Department is, whose service is perfect submission and who never forgets even if she sometimes has to forgive.

—Charles Ritchie, Canadian Ambassador
to the United States, 1962[2]

Does bureaucratic structure matter? A number of people in the Prime Minister of Canada's office thought so in 2004 when the Paul Martin minority government tabled two bills in the House of Commons (C-31 and C-32) to sever the Department of Foreign Affairs and International Trade (DFAIT) into two ministries. The approach was inspired by the concern that the two missions of the department were at odds, specifically that 'trade' pursuits were undermined by concerns for diplomatic issues and a human rights agenda. The proposal, which had been announced on the first day of the Martin government in 2003, was never well received. Many in the opposition (and quietly, among a substantial portion of Liberal MPs) pronounced it half-baked at best and irresponsible at worst: suddenly, the structure of a bureaucracy had

become a hot political potato debated in the House of Commons, newscasts, and editorial pages of Canada's newspapers. It mattered because the institutional shape of the department said something about its mission and about its expectations. There was, at a subconscious level, a consensus that the structure that had been adopted in 1982 was effective, though far from perfect. Ultimately, the critics won out: the bills were defeated in the winter of 2005.

Much as in this episode, many people over the past century nurtured a love/hate relationship with the Department of External Affairs (DEA). Prime ministers, for one thing, relied on it, but had trouble trusting it. While the department found its footing in its early years, Prime Minister Borden repatriated a young outsider, Loring Christie, a Canadian working in the United States government, to provide him directly with advice on foreign policy.[3] His successor, Mackenzie King, encouraged a sophistication of the department but was often suspicious of the bureaucracy. John Diefenbaker never fully overcame his doubts about it. Even Diefenbaker's successor, Lester Pearson, who had practically spent his entire career at External either as an employee or as its Minister, often had doubts about its advice. This had a lingering impact on even the youngest recruits. 'Nobody, not even the undersecretary, was able to say if Canada had an overriding goal or goals in its foreign policy', remembered James Bartleman about his budding career in 1966.[4] For all its structural innovations, the DEA often seemed to play a complementary role to the prime minister in executing foreign policy, but rarely shaped it.

Then it got worse. When Pierre Trudeau came to power in 1968, he openly said to department officials that their ideas were as outdated as their methods and, like Borden many years before, hired a personal advisor (Ivan Head) to help him steer foreign affairs.[5] His Liberal successor, Jean Chrétien, was never comfortable with the organization and recruited his own diplomatic advisors, including James Bartleman. It seems that only Louis St-Laurent, Lester Pearson, and, to a great extent, Brian Mulroney, found a way to work effectively with the department.[6] The St-Laurent years were described as a golden period and the Mulroney period was febrile with activity around the globe.

Even the staff complained about the department. It was a mixed blessing that while the department has continuously attracted brilliant minds, it also recruited writerly candidates. Many of them (vastly more of them than any other department) have written books and scholarly articles about their experiences, and the External Affairs bureaucracy hardly ever comes off in a good light, even with the benefit of nostalgia. Allan Gotlieb's ambassadorial diaries of the 1980s often display frustration with the department's apparent inertia.[7] John Kneale and James Bartleman described the department in the 1990s as suffering 'a deep malaise'[8] and as 'demoralized'.[9]

Prime ministerial and staff suspicions aside, 'External' developed an enviable reputation that endures in large part because of the way it was structured. Like any department, people who study it and its role in defining Canada's international relations inevitably ponder why some decisions are made, are delayed, or indeed never made. In part, the answer lies in the philosophical predispositions of the political leadership that dominates a state. Answers are also found in particular circumstances. For instance, crises provoked abroad necessarily focus thinking and prompt decision-makers to take positions they would not normally rush into. Thirdly, decision-making depends on a level of comfort and confidence that prime ministers and ministers have in the advice they receive from fellow politicians, parliament, the media, and their constituents. It also depends critically on the advice they receive from the public service, and in Canada the staff in the Department of External Affairs and then the Department of Foreign Affairs and International Trade have played a key role in advising and in executing the foreign policy of Canadian governments.

This chapter examines the structural evolution of this department since its incarnation in 1909. The purpose is to identify the key points of expansion and contraction of 100 years of evolution and to demonstrate how the department 'institutionalized' the government's priorities by translating key objectives into bureaucratic responsibilities. In this sense, the shape of the department took on the features required of it in response to what was expected from it by the prime minister, his cabinet, and the minister responsible. As government required more advice, it expanded certain divisions. As Canadians travelled further and more often for both business and pleasure, the department extended its presence and ability to provide service. At other times, it needed better intelligence and penetration of foreign places, so it developed or added other branches. These changes reflected changing priorities, different sensitivities, and different preoccupations.

BUILDING CAPACITY: 1909–41

In terms of structure, Canada's external relations were nothing more than a concern of the prime minister and a handful of officials from the first summer of confederation until the turn of the twentieth century. There were relatively few decisions to make, and those were often determined in London, where the British government spoke on behalf of the Commonwealth. With the 1900s, however, particularly over issues of trade and boundaries, the Laurier government felt the need for more rigour and better policy-making in dealing with other countries. It created a Department of External Affairs in 1909 that would be headed by Charles Murphy, a cabinet minister who would be designated as Secretary of State for External Affairs (SSEA). (Interestingly, the whole 'department' was housed above a barber shop on Sparks Street). The undersecretary (or senior public servant for the department) was Joseph Pope, a man who had served first Sir John A. Macdonald as personal secretary and then Sir Wilfrid Laurier as a senior official. Pope had long argued that Canada's external affairs needed continuous attention: 'The present state of our external affairs can only be described by the one word "chaotic"', he wrote in his diary in the fall of 1908.[10]

In 1912, Prime Minister Robert Borden assumed the role of Secretary of State for External Affairs and the undersecretary was made to report directly to the prime minister, a practice that would be sustained by the following four prime ministers (Borden, King, Meighen, Bennett) until 1946 and, briefly, by John Diefenbaker in 1957. Pope would continue to manage the small department, but in a manner that increasingly seemed out of step with the policy demands of a government emerging from the searing experience of the First World War. He left his functions in 1924 after decades of selfless service, but the department he left behind had 'not the shadow of a system, and things . . . [were] in a continual muddle'.[11]

The first thirty years of the Department of External Affairs were marked by a very personal, informal and indeed idiosyncratic style of administration. It depended almost exclusively on the personality of the undersecretary, and for most of those years that was Joseph Pope, followed by Oscar D. Skelton, a Queen's University economist who was invited by Mackenzie King in 1925 to

Table 14.1: Undersecretaries of State for External Affairs/Deputy Ministers Foreign Affairs

Sir Joseph Pope (1909–1925)	A. Edgar Ritchie (1970–1974)
Oscar Douglas Skelton (1925–1941)	H. Basil Robinson (1974–1977)
Norman A. Robertson (1941–1946, 1958–1964)	Allan E. Gotlieb (1977–1981)
Lester B. Pearson (1946–1948)	Gordon F. Osbaldeston (1982)
Escott M. Reid (1948–1949)	Marcel Massé (1982–1985)
Arnold D.P. Heeney (1949–1952)	James H. Taylor (1985–1989)
L. Dana Wilgress (1952–1953)	de Montigny Marchand (1989–1991)
H. Hume Wrong (1953–1954)	J. Reid Morden (1991–1994)
Robert A. MacKay (1954)	Gordon S. Smith (1994–1997)
Jules Léger (1954–1958)	Donald W. Campbell (1997–2000)
Marcel Cadieux (1964–1970)	Gaetan Lavertu (2000–2003)
Leonard J. Edwards (2007–)	Peter Harder (2003–2007)

succeed the retiring Pope. Skelton, who was focused on building the department's capacity to investigate foreign policy issues and advise the government on the best options for Canada, instituted a competitive recruitment system for foreign service officers that included country-wide exams and interviews. Skelton personally recruited, in the 1920s and 1930s, some of the most highly-regarded public servants of the twentieth century. While the department developed an unparalleled reputation for its intelligent advice and energetic approach to files and issues, it was also known to be very poorly administered. This inevitably led to frustration, compounded by the fact that the department consistently had to manoeuvre in order to secure the attention of its busy minister, the Prime Minister of Canada himself, who insisted that most decisions be cleared with him first.

Canada's foreign policy in the 1930s was often confused, and was especially confusing for the public servants who had to help define it and act on it. Mackenzie King was a careful politician who did not like to act unless he had no choice. As an individual, King trusted few people, and certainly did not always trust the diplomats he had agreed to hire. Though the department's senior executives worked tirelessly long hours, morale was reported as low. It was, as one employee put it, 'a small, ramshackle Department where eccentricity was tolerated and where everyone was a generalist who flew by the seat of his pants'.[12] One diplomat complained in the late 1930s that the department was in a 'woeful state' as it was unable to be decisive in recruiting new people and overly conservative in its approach to a host of issues.[13] O.D. Skelton—a brilliant thinker and strategist—could not administer the department beyond a 'normal haphazard way'.[14] Lester Pearson, who joined the department in 1928, described the office in the 1930s as 'a hive of unorganized activity—the senior men are so busy that they haven't time . . . to delegate work to

juniors who are, in consequence, not busy enough. I find, however, that very real and sincere attempt is being made to reorganize the Department. . . . I am not sanguine, however, that this scheme will achieve the decentralization essential for the speedy and effective conduct of departmental work'.[15] This would be a recurring theme. 'Lord, how I would like to be given the job of pulling External Affairs and the Foreign Service apart and putting it together again, with a few pieces left out', wrote Lester Pearson in 1935, during a posting in London.[16]

WAGING WAR AND MANAGING PEACE: 1941–51

O.D. Skelton died in harness in 1941 and was replaced by another imaginative policy advisor, Norman Robertson, who had joined the department in 1927. Upon Skelton's death, Escott Reid, who joined the department in 1938, wrote a long memorandum arguing for 'a new conception' of DEA: 'We must become a planning, thinking, creative body and not be content merely to solve day-to-day problems as they arise.'[17] That opinion was widely shared, especially as Canada waged war on an unprecedented scale. Robertson launched a reorganization of the department to put it on a more professional footing that would respond to wartime demands. At a time when Canada's external relations and the autonomy King so cherished were tested by the shifting alliances brought about by global war, Robertson felt ill-suited to manage a large department. He often asked the prime minister to reassign him to a job that suited him better, but nevertheless oversaw a frenetic expansion and reorganization of DEA.

Robertson assumed leadership of a department that, in 1940, had 44 officers and 328 support staff. Within three years 14 new foreign missions were opened. By 1944, the department had 72 Foreign Service officers, 474 employees, and administered

20 foreign delegations. It also acted as the principal liaison to the twenty embassies that were now installed in Ottawa (there had been five before the war). The department's structure was formalized in 1941 (see figure 14.1) with a clear hierarchy. Four assistant undersecretaries reported to the Under-secretary of State for External Affairs. Each of their divisions, in turn, brought together ten sections.

But Robertson was not satisfied with the structure. As wartime demands intensified, he continued to expand its functions. Within a few years (see Figure 14.2) the department was headed by an undersecretary and an associate undersecretary. Reporting directly to the undersecretary were five divisions: Diplomatic, Economic, Legal, a Special Affairs Division, and Administration.

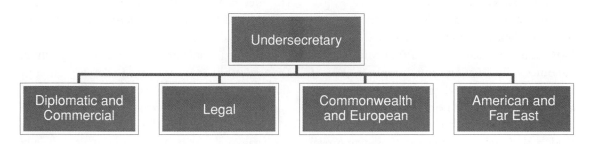

Figure 14.1 Secretariat of State for External Relations, 1941

Source: John Hilliker, *Canada's Department of External Affairs*, Vol 1: *The Early Years, 1909–1946* (McGill-Queen's University Press and the Institute of Public Administration of Canada, 1990), p. 243.

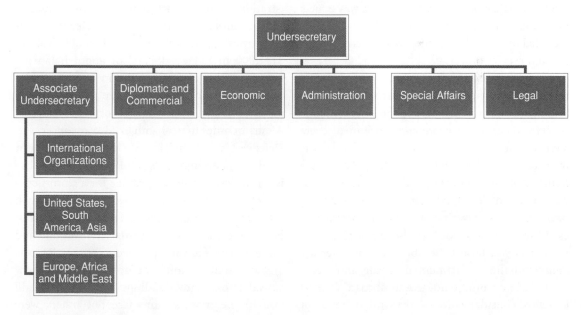

Figure 14.2 Department of External Relations, 1945

Source: JL Granatstein, *A Man of Influence*, p. 195. Reprinted with permission from JL Granatstein.

Three political divisions—one responsible for international organizations, a second for European, African and Middle Eastern affairs, and a third for the United States, South America, and Asia)—reported first to the associate undersecretary. Robertson also instituted a rudimentary training program for new recruits and appointed a full-time personnel officer to manage human resource issues.

That structure would be inherited by Lester Pearson when he became undersecretary late in 1946 (almost coinciding with Prime Minister King handing off External Affairs to a minister, Louis St-Laurent). Pearson was determined to improve the organization of the department by hiring more employees at a time when, according to Escott Reid, 'a revolution took place in Canadian foreign Policy' as Canada broke out of its traditional isolationism and asserted itself in the postwar world of the United Nations and the beginnings of the Cold War.[18] In 1948, Pearson's last full year as the top public servant, the first annual report was issued, outlining the progress of the department. It reported that it had 1213 employees, including 216 Foreign Service officers.

As Canada joined the United Nations and its associated agencies and later confronted the Cold War through its membership in the North Atlantic Treaty Organization, more and more men (there were very few women) were hired by the department to follow files, investigate issues, and prepare policy proposals. The rest of the 1940s and 1950s were years of 'consolidation and strengthening both of the organization at home and of existing establishments abroad'.[19] It also emphasized the co-management of issues between the Department and the Department of Trade and Commerce, again both at home and abroad. Canada launched consular offices in the United States, for instance, and the trade work previously carried on by the Department of Trade and Commerce in

Chicago and San Francisco was assumed by the Consulates General, which reported to the SSEA. In countries where Canada had no established diplomatic missions, the consular functions of the Department of External Affairs were carried on by the Trade Commissioners. To facilitate the process, a Committee, on which both departments were represented, was established to 'regularly to consider common problems relating to foreign service, and to ensure the close coordination of effort abroad'.[20]

In comparison with O.D. Skelton's long tenure, the leadership at DEA changed relatively often in the late 1940s. Pearson moved into politics in 1949 and immediately was named to cabinet by Prime Minister St-Laurent as the Secretary of State for External Affairs. His deputy, Escott Reid, briefly assumed the mantle until Arnold Heeney was named to the post of undersecretary in March 1949 with the expectation that he would bring to the post the 'emphasis on organization and administration in the Department which his predecessors at times tended to overlook'.[21] Heeney, it was worth noting, earned a salary of $15,000 (about $121,000 in today's dollars, or about half what current deputy ministers earn in Ottawa).[22] The money was well spent, as Heeney pushed forward on even greater expansion to organize External Affairs in order to deal with Cold War concerns. A Defence Liaison Division was created to monitor Cold War developments. In 1950, a finance division was established to provide for a closer scrutiny of expenditures. Sections dealing with international conferences and supplies and properties were also set up, while the Archives unit and the Library were incorporated in a new Reports and Research section. The department was now spread across many buildings: the East Block still housed the most senior staff, but others were posted in the Langevin Block and other buildings in downtown Ottawa.

COLD WAR DEPARTMENT: 1951–68

Working with an ambitious Secretary of State for External Affairs—Lester Pearson—and a prime minister who wished Canada to be active on the world stage, Heeney built a larger bureaucracy (see figure 14.3). As the undersecretary, he created more hierarchy to funnel decision-making. He maintained the role of deputy undersecretary and added three assistant undersecretaries. Escott Reid, as deputy undersecretary, was responsible for the United Nations, as well as the American and Far Eastern Division. The department's budget became a concern, and within a year, the department felt that it could report that '[a]fter a full year's operation of the reorganized Finance division, a further improvement in the financial operations of the Department can be reported. Uniformity in accounting methods and a speeding up of submission of revenue and expenditure statements from posts abroad have made it possible to reflect these transactions in the Departmental account more promptly. This has resulted in better control which will result in closer estimating. The Department is, at present, financing a few of its posts abroad with local funds received from countries repaying their military relief accounts or with funds received in payment of war reparations, which represents a temporary conservation of Canadian dollars.'[23]

An office of Historical Research and Reports was created, as well as a secretariat for 'special studies', and made to report to Reid directly. Charles Ritchie, as Assistant Undersecretary, was responsible for Defence Liaisons, 'Information' and the European Division. Jules Leger, the first French-Canadian to attain this level of seniority in the department (he would be named Undersecretary in 1954), looked after the functional divisions: 'America and Latin America'; the Commonwealth, as well as diplomatic concerns such as the 'consular division'; the 'protocol division'; and the 'supplies and properties division' that reflected Canada's

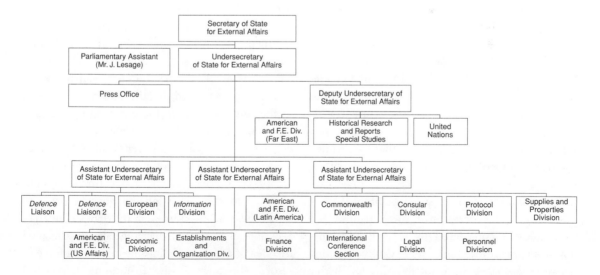

Figure 14.3 Department of External Affairs, April 1952

Source: Annual Report of the Department of External Affairs, 1953.

growing external presence. In 1953, Canada staffed 21 embassies, nine legations, six high commissioners' offices and eight consulates or consulates general. As the Cold War raged through the last half of the 1950s, Canada added fourteen more embassies, four legations, nine high commissioners' offices, and thirteen consular offices in Asia, Latin America, and Eastern Europe. According to Escott Reid, there were 276 heads of missions and Foreign Service officers by the end of that decade (and no fewer than 37 of them would have written books by 1989).[24]

An interesting feature in the breakdown of responsibilities was the general policy 'area' of the United States. It was shared in a way that left no doubt as to what side Canada favoured in the proxy wars of the Cold War, but its organizational structure was confused. Indeed, the Far Eastern and Latin American divisions both included 'American' concerns. H.O. Moran, for example, looked after his own 'American and Far East Division' policy areas as well as an Economic Division and an Establishment and Organization Division. In addition, he was responsible for administrative divisions such as Finance, International Conference management, Legal, and Personnel.

The senior management structure that featured a deputy undersecretary and assistant undersecretaries reporting to the Undersecretary of State was maintained through these years, concentrating responsibility in a remarkably small group of men who had worked alongside each other for decades. The leadership of DEA was drawn from within, never from outside.

It did not matter if the structure of the department sometimes occasioned some redundancy. Its employees considered their work a 'calling', not a bureaucratic function.[25] Conceding that his work absorbed him 'totally', Charles Ritchie observed that 'there is an underlying assumption that anyone who is not overworked, underpaid,

eye-strained, joy-starved—in fact, not a civil servant—is frivolous or materialistic, that these are the hallmarks of a higher calling, the stigmata of the faithful. [. . .] That a man should so mismanage his life as to be totally immersed in office work is lamentable, unless he loves it. If he loves it, he is doing what he wants.'[26]

Earl Drake joined the department in 1953 and left an insightful account of his first impressions. 'My first boss in External Affairs', he remembered, 'was an Ontario Anglophone, stern, pedantic, bitter, and without a discernible spark of humour or humanity. He seemed to take a sadistic pleasure in criticizing everything I wrote and in rejecting every idea I put forward I was terribly discouraged and ready to resign after the first six months.' He then worked for Marcel Cadieux, a future undersecretary: 'working for [him] was very satisfying but I feared that he was an exception, not the norm'.[27]

External Affairs was evidently a place that demanded rigour, but frowned on freewheeling discussions, particularly among younger recruits. 'When I see the tired, aging men who are my friends and who work in the Department I think it as well that I don't have to face that ordeal [of 'buttoning up their nature']. There is something wrong here but it is the same thing that it has always been—overwork, the panic desire [sic] to escape before they get too old, and the fascination of being in the centre of things, these pulling in opposite directions. I know that dilemma and I have no desire to go through it all over again.'[28] Nevertheless, the department kept a steady course through the 1950s as Arnold Heeney's structure seemed to respond to the needs of the government and growth was steady, if uneven. In 1956, as Canada's Secretary of State for External Affairs spearheaded the idea of a United Nations peacekeeping force to resolve the Suez Crisis, 'Communications' and 'Middle East' Divisions were created in the Department in order to support his efforts.

If Louis St-Laurent gave External Affairs its 'golden years', the department had reason to be despondent with his successor. John Diefenbaker was troubled by the External Affairs bureaucracy. He saw in it the lifelong friends of the man he faced in the House of Commons on most days, Liberal leader Lester Pearson. For a time, Diefenbaker hesitated in even naming a Secretary of State, assuming the job himself for a few months like the prime ministers before 1947 had done. Diefenbaker asked that a 'financial adviser' and an 'Inspection Service' be added to the bureaucratic structure in 1958, signalling that he wanted the government to keep closer oversight on how the department managed its funds. In 1960, a new division was created to monitor 'Africa and the Middle East', a reflection of the prime minister's hostility to the Apartheid regime in South Africa and his growing interest in the area. In 1963, a special branch was created to deal with Congo affairs only. In 1963, another division was created to cater exclusively to issues related to the United States.

The department also added personnel to respond to the demand for services. In 1961, for instance, it welcomed 66 new people and in 1962 the 'Passport' division was formally added to the structure, showing that the processing of personal data had become an increasingly important activity as Canadians began to travel in unprecedented numbers.

The changes to the 'Heeney' structure grew more dramatic following the release, in April 1963, of the report of the Royal Commission on Government Organization (the 'Glassco' Commission). The Commission focused one of its studies (Report 21) on the Department of External Affairs, examining both its headquarters in Ottawa and its missions abroad. The commission made a number of recommendations that were well received by External: 'Some of the steps recommended in this and other reports had, in fact, been taken before the

report was published; others have been taken since; still others have far-reaching implications both for this Department and other departments and agencies of government, which required detailed examination and consultation. This process, begun immediately after publication of the report, continued throughout the rest of the year and will go on in concert with departments and agencies concerned and, in particular, the Bureau of Government organization.'[29]

A number of steps were taken to improve the department's performance. A revised and broadened training program for foreign service officers, which was conceived towards the end of 1962, was in full operation within a year. This included advanced training in the French language for certain Foreign Service officers, at Laval University. Steps were also taken to improve existing departmental machinery to promote and facilitate the use of either the English or French language in departmental correspondence at the option of the author. In addition, a training unit was established in the Personnel Division to provide training for administrative staff proceeding abroad. The purpose of this training is to equip staff, particularly at smaller posts, to perform a wide variety of duties during which they normally do not come in contact in Ottawa. For the department's veterans, the changes were far-reaching and sometimes intimidating. 'The Department of External Affairs is becoming more and more a branch office of a huge expanding bureaucracy', bemoaned Charles Ritchie in 1962.[30] But for new recruits, the pace of change was glacial. James Bartleman joined the ranks of External in the summer of 1966 and paints a memorable picture of a department that was only slowly experiencing change. 'The senior ranks . . . received the new recruits in their cluttered offices, desks overflowing with neglected papers marked with tags appealing for urgent attention, security cabinets bulging with files, and every available space adorned with enough kitsch from faraway places to do any garage sale proud. They would hitch up their suspenders, and take one last puff on the pipe every self-respecting officer seemed to possess in those days. To us they would, of course, provide their views on Canadian foreign policy. Each in his own way would describe his specific duties and Canada's place in the world as seen from the perspective of his division or bureau.'[31]

The sum of these parts did not, however, a whole make. Bartleman also vividly described the process of acculturation: 'Consciously or not, they [the senior officers] were describing their transitions from junior officers in small posts having the time of their lives to senior diplomats in major missions putting into practice decades of apprenticeship. For in those days, that is how officers learned their trade. Formal training did not exist as it does today; new officers were expected to pick up the art of diplomacy largely through a process of osmosis. And these sessions with experienced colleagues constituted the best training anyone could have for the profession of foreign-service officer—and perhaps for life in general.'[32]

An Administrative Improvement Unit was established and better management techniques were adopted. Human resource planning strategies were installed. Studies were launched of the existing and future needs of the department for specialist staff. The department also assumed more authority in deciding how it would allocate its resources, although this was done in close consultation with the staff of the Treasury Board.

The reforms developed even faster after the Pearson government took office in 1963 and the economy recovered. Cold war détente made it possible to open new missions in Eastern Europe, while decolonization in Africa, the Caribbean and Asia demanded an appropriate response (and new missions) from Ottawa. The number of countries with which Canada maintained diplomatic relations

had increased from 41 to 84. During this period, the number of Canadian diplomatic and consular posts abroad had risen from 53 to 77. Of these, 44 were embassies, 12 were high commissioners' offices, six were permanent missions to international organizations and 15 were consulates or consulates general'.[33]

In 1964, the department's recruiting was intensified for almost all classes. The number of officers recruited was almost double that in 1963. In the administrative-staff classes, the number recruited rose from 116 to 214 at the end of 1964. During 1965, for instance, the Administrative Improvement Unit focused hiring in the administrative divisions such as 'Supplies and Properties', 'Personnel', 'Administrative Services', 'Registry', and 'Organization and Methods', with over 50 new recruits.[34] Increasingly, the bulging department was spread across Ottawa: the East Block still housed the most senior staff, but others were posted in the Langevin Block and other buildings in downtown Ottawa.

As the number of personnel grew, the department pursued an aggressive programme of acquiring real estate assets abroad to house embassies, consulates and key personnel. In 1963 alone, it was engaged with the Department of Public Works in 16 projects concerned with the planning, construction or alteration of chanceries, official residences or staff quarters. In addition, the department pursued 47 furnishing schemes for accommodation either owned by the Canadian government or held by it on long leases.

Perhaps the most important improvement in the department's organization was in the registry's records management. Progress in the field of paperwork and records management was most noticeable during the year in the registry field. Last but not least, the department adopted a new filing system, designed to provide headquarters and personnel abroad with a uniform records-classification system.[35]

Derek Burney, who joined in the summer of 1963, remembered the process of absorbing intelligence and his recollection of the department in those days was indicative of where priorities lay and how knowledge was organized. 'External Affairs still thrived on reporting', he wrote. 'Dispatches of greater and less moment poured in daily from all parts of the globe to be analyzed, summarized, and, for the most part, filed by the responsible desk or division. Reports from major embassies got broader and more significant distribution in Ottawa and to her embassies. Instructions flowed from headquarters; replies and reports came from the embassies.'[36] His first years in the External Affairs were not promising. 'Early days at External were anything but inspirational', he remembered. 'There were many moments when I seriously wondered whether I had made a sensible choice of career. In time, I discovered that "moaning and

groaning" was an External mantra, the not surprising consequence of so many reportedly bright people in search of something more to do with less. But the department did very little to develop or inspire its new recruits. Assignments were *ad hoc* and the selection of postings was random at best. All were expected, presumably to learn "on the job", but the lessons were often as varied as the mentors. The hard reality is that many of the tasks are mundane, if not routine. Many of the posts are dull. Some are indeed arduous, even hazardous, but the opportunities for real influence and achievement were the exception, not the rule.'[37]

Not least, the department launched a new attempt to improve its accounting by installing mechanisms to ensure better reporting of how money was spent, but progress was slow. In 1966, the Department appointed an experienced officer as Financial Management Advisor to develop a

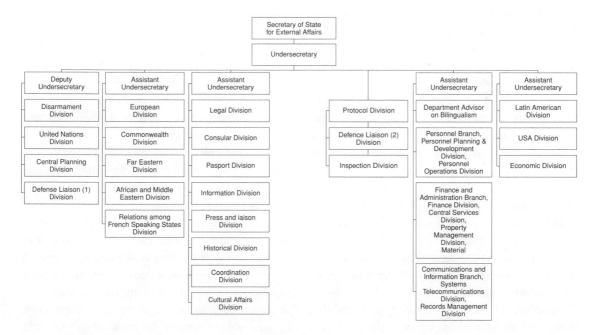

Figure 14.4 Department of External Affairs, 1968

Source: Hilliker and Barry, p. 415.

more sophisticated financial management program and efforts were made to tie funding deliberately to individual programs so as to improve accountability and improve 'long-term planning, budgetary reporting and control accounting systems'.[38] An Organization and Methods Unit was established to 'improve the department's management and operating procedures',[39] the Supplies and Properties Division was strengthened, and the Personnel Division was divided into a Personnel Operations Division and a Personnel Services Division. The Personnel Operations Division was to be 'responsible for recruitment, establishment, training, research, and employee services, and the Personnel Services Division, with promotions, postings, and career planning'. The administrative divisions of the department were re-grouped under a single Assistant Undersecretary for Administration. Perhaps the most important new measure was the introduction of a more efficient and simplified accounting procedures were put into use at all missions abroad in 1964.[40] In 1967, an expert in computer techniques was lent to External by Treasury Board to ascertain ways in which computer services might be employed by the Department; the possibility was explored of '"computerizing" such routine work as the keeping of cumulative records of expenditures and the maintenance of detailed inventory listing of furnishings and equipment at headquarters and posts'.[41]

By the time Lester Pearson ended his tenure as prime minister in April 1968, over 700 officers worked at External Affairs working on a structure that was vastly expanded in terms of scope. There were four assistant undersecretaries in addition to the deputy undersecretary. Two of them worked on recognizably 'country files' while the two others focused on administrative issues and processes such as information, passport, personnel, and communications. Of interest here was the rise of a 'cultural affairs' division, a reflection of the fact that Canada, in preparation for the *Man and His World* (Expo '67) had recognized that Canada's culture could be an instrument of diplomacy and useful in supporting Canada's image around the world. In terms of country files, the files on Latin America and the United States were brought into closer proximity, reporting to one assistant undersecretary. Indicative of its links with the Americas file, the 'economic division' also reported to the same assistant undersecretary, while the rest of the globe was the purview of another The Deputy Undersecretary focused on more strategically pivotal files such as 'central planning', defence liaison, the United Nations and Disarmament.

NEW PRIORITIES: 1968–82

Even before he assumed the prime ministership, Pierre Trudeau was known to have been critical of External Affairs, but his arrival did not halt the modernization efforts of the department. Indeed, there would be a major expansion of the department in the 1970s as Trudeau's search for a 'Third Option' to develop relations with the world beyond the superpowers was operationalized.

Two new sections were created in 1969 to help the department strategize. A Manpower Planning and Forecasting Section assumed the responsibility for advising senior management on the qualitative and quantitative requirements for human resources.[42] The second new section was Information Systems Division. Its Communications and Information Systems Branch consisted of three divisions —telecommunications, records management, and information systems. Typical of all bureaucracies in the 1970s, the department added dramatically more support staff and systems to improve its machinery of policy analysts and diplomats. Perhaps more importantly, the department assumed its own audit and accounting functions as a result of amendments to the *Financial Administration Act* in 1969, which assumed all the more importance when it was called to cut its budget in 1970.[43]

But there were other structural changes that reflected Canada's concern with the USSR and with its relations with its allies: 'arms control' was added to the 'disarmament' division in 1970, and a new division was created to concentrate on 'North American Defence and NATO'. Finally, division was created to focus on the emerging movement to bring francophone nations into some sort of international alliance and a new division was shaped to facilitate international policy on 'scientific relations and environmental problems'.

A Central Services Division was created to integrate a variety of common support services and to ensure adequate office space, furnishings, and equipment at headquarters, including general building alterations and maintenance. Another priority was knowledge management: as the department continued to grow, a Communications and Information Systems Branch was created, bringing the existing Records Management Division and Telecommunications Division under common direction.[44]

A departmental Training and Development Committee was formed early in 1970 to review and advise the Senior Committee on training and development policy, needs, priorities, budgets, and content of programs. The most welcome news, however was that the government had approved the building of a new headquarters for External Affairs, and in 1973 the department moved into the Pearson Building on Sussex drive, away from its historically proximate location near the prime minister's office. John G. Kneale, who started work in the summer of 1973, wrote that the Pearson building 'was a perfect physical expression of the idea that foreign policy is arcane, secret and not for public consumption. There is no fresh air in the place, either intellectually or atmospherically. It is inbred. Those who work in the building must also

eat in the building with one another, since the nearest restaurant or fast food place is a fifteen-minute walk away, and this too fosters an inward-looking, monastery-like environment.'[45]

The explosion in branches in the Pearson building was even more dramatic the following year as new portfolios were unveiled to monitor issues and advise the government on issues as varied as 'transport communications and energy', 'commercial policy', 'academic relations service', 'security and intelligence liaison', 'foreign travel and removal service', 'material management', 'property management', and 'telecommunications'. In 1971, a fifth Assistant Undersecretary was created, followed by a sixth in 1974 and a seventh in 1977, to help manage the rapidly growing department. The creation of a Consular Affairs Bureau reflected the new priority of managing these files in a consistent manner. The creation of a NATO and NORAD Division, which married two existing divisions, reflected the desire to integrate the two files.

In 1978, the senior ranks were transformed. Reporting to the Undersecretary of State for External Affairs were now five deputy undersecretaries and four assistant undersecretaries as well as the chief air inspector and the inspector general. Reporting to this cadre were 26 branches that contained anywhere between one and six bureaus. The largest of this was the Passport Office.

The expansion of the department did not equate to better foreign policy advice, as far as the government was concerned, largely because most departments were not establishing their own international affairs departments. The task of maintaining liaisons with departments to ensure consistent advice had always been a key— and exhausting—function of the department of external affairs. In the past, key relationships were particularly nurtured with the Departments of Finance, Trade and Commerce, and Defence. As the department grew in numbers and size to respond to a growing international agenda, they also recognized that their concerns had international dimensions, making the task of ensuring consistent and knowledgeable advice all the more demanding.

The Trudeau government wanted a better co-ordination of policies affecting foreign relations and a better integration of the management, programming, and resource allocation processes for foreign operations. It also wanted to stem the tide of other departments setting up their own 'external' activities and wished to see External play a better role in co-ordinating the Canadian government's activities abroad. To this end, Trudeau named Allan Gotlieb to the position of Under-secretary of State for External Affairs on the understanding that the department would assert its role as a sort of central agency that would co-ordinate the government's actions abroad. A Committee of Deputy Ministers on Foreign and Defence Policy was established in 1980 to replace the Interdepartmental Committee on External Relations (ICER). The new committee of deputies, chaired by Gotlieb to demonstrate its elevated importance, had a mandate to review major policy and expenditures issues referred to it by Cabinet committee, or prepared by departments for Cabinet committee.[46]

International Relations in the 1970s changed dramatically with the introduction of regular summits among leaders. The ease of air travel, and just as importantly, the sophistication of television broadcasts, made summitry politically advantageous for leaders around the world. Prime Minister Trudeau travelled the globe regularly, as did many of the ministers. The Commonwealth became more active, and the Group of Seven nations began regular meetings in 1975, with Canada joining the following year. Summitry greatly reinforced the prime minister's role in foreign policy and made him, rather than the secretary of state for external affairs, the most important actor.

THE INTEGRATION OF TRADE AND DIPLOMACY: 1982–93

The department boasted over 5,000 employees (1,450 positions at headquarters, 1,250 employees in the field and another 2,375 locally hired people) and a budget of almost $400 million when the Trudeau Liberals were returned to government in 1980 and embarked on a revamping of the department.[47] In what turned out to be the most dramatic reorganization, the Trudeau government amplified DEA's mandate in 1982 by entrusting it with the 'trade' responsibility of the Department of Industry, Trade and Commerce (which simply became Industry Canada). The Department of External Affairs now had responsibility for trade policy and trade promotion along with the traditional areas of foreign policy and functions related to immigration. The new trade policy units of the department were mandated to work closely with the regional offices of the Ministry of State for Economic and Regional Development and the Department of Industry Trade and Commerce/Regional Economic Expansion. As a result of this reorganization, all foreign service officers from the Canadian International Development Agency, trade commissioners, and Canadian Government Office of Tourism employees would be fully integrated into the Department of External Affairs, along with the trade policy and trade promotion sections of the former Department of Industry, Trade and Commerce.

The 1982 reorganization announced a departure for the government of Canada's foreign policy. While the Cold War waged in the form of arms races between the United States and the Soviet Union and various proxy wars in Asia, Africa, and South America, the government openly tied its foreign policy focus to trade. In the words of the department itself, the intention was to 'give greater weight to economic factors in the design of foreign

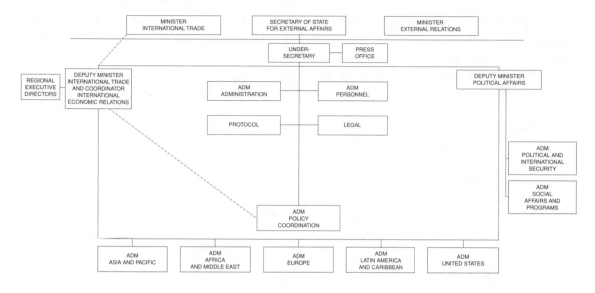

Figure 14.5 Department of External Affairs, 1984.

Source: Department of External Affairs, Annual Report, 1985.

policy, to ensure that the conduct of foreign relations served Canadian trade objectives, to improve the service offered exporters in an increasingly competitive international marketplace and to ensure policy and program coherence in the conduct of Canada's whole range of relations outside of the world'.[48]

Within months, the bare bones of a new structure were in place, but it would take years to fill out the department. External Affairs and Trade would be headed by the Undersecretary, as before. Reporting to him were deputy ministers: a Deputy Minister for International Trade to manage trade and economic matters and a Deputy Minister (Political Affairs) to oversee all other matters regarding Canadian policies and programs in the regions. The responsibility for all geographically formed policies and programs was invested in five new geographic branches, each headed by an assistant deputy minister (Africa and Middle East, Asia and Pacific, the United States, Europe,

and Latin America and Caribbean). These ADMs, in turn, were also responsible for the management both of the posts in their regions abroad and their branch at headquarters. The purpose of creating these five geographic branches was to provide clear accountability for regional and bilateral policies and operations, and to improve the development of coherent policies and programs across the full range of departmental activities.[49]

Changes continued in the department as the Mulroney government was installed in 1984. That year, the Policy Development Secretariat, headed by a sixth ADM, was renamed the Policy Development Bureau and reorganized to include three divisions: Political and Strategic Analysis, Economic and Trade Analysis, and Cabinet Liaison and Co-ordination. Its purpose was to lead a foreign policy review, but also to monitor international economic and political developments and relevant long-term trends. It would play a critical role in co-ordinating policy responses and drafting speeches.

The Cabinet Liaison Division was mandated to manage cabinet submissions emerging from the department and to respond to cabinet submissions made by other departments. A year later, this Division was moved into the Corporate Management Bureau.[50] By 1987, there were 13 assistant deputy ministers. Eight of them were responsible for a wide range of integrated portfolios: Economic and Trade Policy; International Trade Development; Legal, Consular and Immigration Affairs; an Ambassador for Disarmament; Political and International Security Affairs; Personnel; Finance and Administration; and finally Communications and Culture. Five more were responsible for the traditional geographic portfolios.

DEA changed with the times. As the cold war subsided and then disappeared in the early 1990s, new challenges emerged. The Mulroney government negotiated a free trade agreement with the United States calling in no small part on the resources of the department. Derek Burney was hired out of the department to assume the role of principal secretary to the prime minister, and Allan Gotlieb, a former undersecretary of state for external relations, played a key role as Canada's ambassador to the United States (he would continue to serve as Ambassador under the Mulroney government). Its role was diminished in this case, as the negotiations were led by a specially designed team of mostly former Department of Finance officials. In 1990, Canada declared war on Iraq (for the second time in history—the declaration of war on Hitler's Germany was the first time) and was involved in the Balkan conflict that ultimately led to the demise of Yugoslavia. In both those cases, it was the Department of National Defence that assumed the lead response, as it would again in the invasion of Afghanistan following the attack on a NATO partner on 11 September 2001.

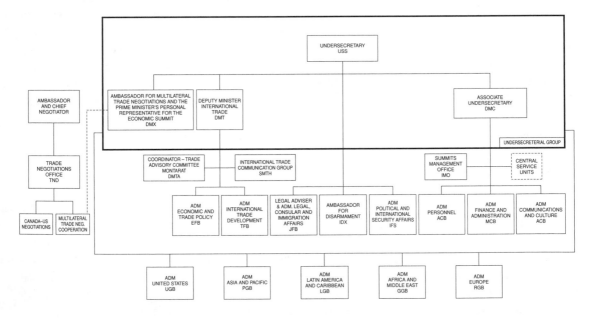

Figure 14.6 Department of External Affairs, 1988

Source: Department of External Affairs, Annual Report, 1989.

GLOBALISATION AND RETRENCHMENT, 1993–

As part of a major reorganization of departments in 1993, DEA was renamed the Department of Foreign Affairs and International Trade (DFAIT). But with the mid-1990s also came a serious challenge to the budget of the department. The 1995 Statement Canada and the World announced that the Department would create two new bureaus to deal with 'global' change. Another a key aspect of the foreign policy of the 1990s was Canada's support for the campaign in favour of a larger 'human security' agenda hat. This included campaigns to end the enlistment of children in militias, removing anti-personnel landmines, and the establishment of an International Criminal Court. That policy issue relied on Canada's 'soft power' to convince key stakeholders to sign on and highlighted their importance. In this regard, DFAIT played a somewhat reluctantly supportive role to a minister who invested himself heavily in ensuring that the agreement, known as the 'Ottawa Accords' was ratified.[51] The other marked conflict pitted Canada and the European Union, particularly Spain, over the Atlantic fisheries. DFAIT played an assistive role on this issue again, as the lead was assumed by Fisheries and Oceans, egged on by an energetic and motivated minister.

The austerity measures imposed on all aspects of government by the 1995 budget hit the department particularly hard. The DFAIT budget was slashed by fifteen per cent in 1995–6 and similar reductions were imposed in the following two years. Programs were rationalized and hundreds of employees took up early retirement or were persuaded to leave government.[52] The grand structure of the late 1980s can only be dimly perceived. The executive structure has been expanded considerably and now features six assistant deputy ministers (Afghanistan Task Force; Europe, Middle East,

Mahgreb and Chief Political Economic Officer; Global Issues; International Security Branch and Political Director; Latin America and Caribbean; and North America). High ranking officials also direct the Strategic Policy and Planning Departments as well as International Business Development, Investment and Innovation Division. The Office of the Chief Trade Negotiator is housed in the department. Passport operations were spun off as a quasi-agency of the government, allowing Passport Canada to develop more freely its citizen-centred service culture.

Perhaps most telling of the structure of DFAIT is the appearance of a 'Transformation Office'. This office was created to lead the discussions over the shape that the department is to assume in order to manage the issues of the future. The clear-cut structure of the past no longer respond to the fluid and complex issues of the twenty-first century, in which traditional trade issues now mix with environmental, human rights, and broad political concerns on a wide plane. Canada belongs to many international groups and consequently places heavy 'summitry' demands on the prime minister and cabinet that must be managed by the department, in concert with the Office of the Prime Minister and the Privy Council Office. 'Global' issues require sophisticated communications practices and innovative approaches.

CONCLUSION

There has been a consistency in the structure of the Department of External Affairs over its hundred year history. It has been mostly headed by career foreign service officers—though there have been exceptions, particularly in the 1980s. With the exception of the 1982 integration of 'trade', the growth of the bureaucracy was organic, particularly after the Robertson reforms of the 1940s and the Heeney consolidations of the early 1950s.

While it has always reflected its policy pursuits along geographical lines, a greater concern has been the integration of knowledge and operations over the century. First relying on exceptional minds that could scope the complexity of a handful of issues virtually at a glance, it has evolved into a sophisticated machine that now relies on information systems to digest the vast amounts of information now available.

The department has also been consistent in its mission: to advise the prime minister as well as the Secretary of State for External Affairs on what courses to take to advance Canada's position in foreign lands—whether they be peaceful, aggressive, or in need of peacekeeping; to co-ordinate foreign policy among many departments; to manage the representation of Canada abroad for political and trade purposes; and finally to serve as the focus of foreign embassies in Ottawa. This has created a need for specialization of sorts among policy analysts, but more importantly has challenged the organization to develop systems that will allow the

integration of information to happen and to be acted upon. This is undoubtedly the greatest challenge faced by the department and in this it shares its burden with all bureaucracies, whether they are in the public or private sector.

The current incarnation of the DFAIT is the product of a slow and steady bureaucratic evolution. Starting with a handful of men one hundred years ago who were mostly concerned with Canada's relationship to Great Britain and the United States, it now employs over 13,000 people deployed to all parts of the world as well as in Ottawa. In 2009, it spent over $2.5 billion on a daily menu of activities that range from thinking about the loftiest questions of international politics, including war and peace, to routine matters of communications with Canadians at home and abroad, to managing real estate. The DFAIT machine thus continues to be the subject of constant tinkering, even if it has been a topic of hot controversy. How well its leaders manage to finesse its ability to do the right thing at the right time will determine the pace and stability

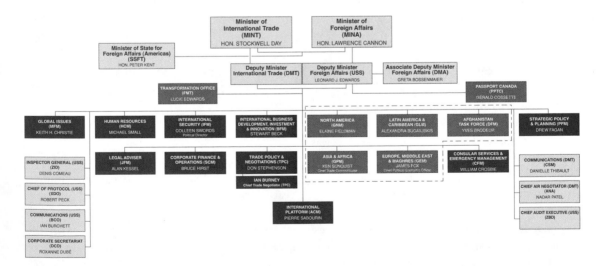

Figure 14.7

Source: DFAIT 2008 (www.international.gc.ca/about-a_propos/assets/pdfs/DFAIT_062009.pdf.

of its evolution. The pursuit of better intelligence compels it to maintain relations with all the departments in Ottawa as they all pursue a variety of international activities, and as their efforts to understand the complexity of their portfolios move them to cooperate with foreign counterparts.

Key Terms

Capacity
The Golden Age of Canadian Foreign Policy
Undersecretary of State

Notes

1. The author thanks Greg Donaghy, head of the historical section of the Department of Foreign Affairs and International Trade, and David MacKenzie, professor of history at Ryerson University, for their insightful comments and suggestions on an earlier draft of this text. Mathew Horvatin was a great help in research.
2. Charles Ritchie, *Storm Signals: More Undiplomatic Diaries, 1962–1971* (MacMillan, 1983), 37.
3. On Christie, see Robert Bothwell, *Loring Christie: The Failure of Bureaucratic Imperialism* (New York: Garland Publishers, 1988). Margaret MacMillan, 'Sir Robert Borden: Laying the Foundation' in Greg Donaghy and Kim Richard Nossal (eds.) *Architects and Innovators: Building the Department of Foreign Affairs and International Trade, 1909–2009* (Montreal and Kingston: McGill-Queens University Press, 2009). On Ivan Head, see John English, 'Two Heads are Better than One: Ivan Head, Pierre Trudeau and Foreign Policy' in the same book, 240–52. See also Head's own book, *Shaping Canada's Foreign Policy, 1968–1984: The Canadian Way* (Toronto: McClelland & Stewart, 1995).
4. James Bartleman, *On Six Continents: A Life in Canada's Foreign Service, 1966–2002* (Toronto: McClelland and Stewart, 2004), 11–12.
5. Flora Macdonald, the secretary of state for External Relations under the short-lived Clark Government (1979–80) accused the department of 'entrapping' her.
6. See Mulroney's memoirs, as well Nelson Michaud and Kim Richard Nossal (eds.), *Diplomatic Departures: the Conservative Era in Canadian Foreign Policy, 1984–93* (Vancouver: UBC Press, 2001). Mulroney reaffirmed this view in the Ottawa Citizen, 17 February 2010.
7. Allan Gotlieb, *The Washington Diaries, 1981–1989* (McClelland and Stewart, 2006).
8. John G. Kneale, *Foreign Service* (Toronto: Captus Press, 1993), 2.
9. James Bartleman, *Rollercoaster: My Hectic Years as Jean Chrétien's Diplomatic Advisor, 1994–1998* (McClelland and Stewart, 2005), 27.
10. Maurice Pope (ed.) *Public Servant: The Memoirs of Sir Joseph Pope* (Toronto: University of Toronto Press, 1960), 212.
11. John Stevenson to J.W. Dafoe, 31 August 1922, quoted in Carman Miller, 'Sir Joseph Pope: A Pragmatic Tory' in Greg Donaghy and Kim Richard Nossal (eds.) *Architects and Innovators: Building the Department of Foreign Affairs and International Trade, 1909–2009* (Montreal and Kingston: McGill-Queens University Press, 2009), 25.
12. Charles Ritchie, *Storm Signals: More Undiplomatic Diaries, 1962–1971* (MacMillan, 1983), 19.
13. Hume Wrong to R. Finlayson, 18 October 1935, cited in John English, *Shadow of Heaven: The Life of Lester Pearson, Volume 1: 1897–1948* (Toronto: Lester & Orpen Dennys, 1989), 189.
14. See J.L. Granatstein. *'A Man of Influence': Norman A. Robertson and Canadian Statecraft, 1928–1968* (Ottawa: Deneau Publishers, 1981), 184.
15. Ibid., 186.
16. John English, *Shadow of Heaven: The Life of Lester Pearson, Volume 1: 1897–1948* (Toronto: Lester & Orpen Dennys, 1989), 189. On Skelton, see Norman Hillmer, 'O.D. Skelton: Innovating for Independence' in Donaghy and Nossal, op. cit., 59–73.
17. Quoted in Denis Smith, *Diplomacy of Fear: Canada and the Cold War, 1941–8* (University of Toronto, 1988).
18. Escott Reid, *Radical Mandarin: The Memoirs of Escott Reid* (Toronto: University of Toronto Press, 1989), 241.
19. 1949 report, 81.
20. Ibid.
21. Letter from Pearson to Norman Robertson cited in John English, *The Worldly Years: The Life of Lester Pearson, 1949–1972* (Toronto: Alfred Knopf Canada, 1992), 21. On Heeney, see Francine McKenzie, 'A.D.P. Heeney: The Orderly Undersecretary' in Greg Donaghy and Kim Richard Nossal (eds.) op. cit., pp 151–68.
22. Reid, *Radical Mandarin*, 241.
23. 1951 report, 45.

24. Escott Reid, *Radical Mandarin*, 242.

25. See Greg Donaghy article in Bothwell and Daudelin.

26. Charles Ritchie, *Diplomatic Passport: More Undiplomatic Diaries, 1944–1962* (Toronto: MacMillan Paperback, 1981), 46. Sadly, Ritchie's published diaries reveal nothing about his professional functions.

27. Earl Drake, *A Stubble-jumper in Striped Pants: Memoirs of a Prairie Diplomat* (Toronto: University of Toronto Press, 1999), 17–18. On Cadieux, see Robert Bothwell, 'Marcel Cadieux: The Ultimate Professional' in Greg Donaghy and Kim Richard Nossal (eds.) op. cit., 207–22.

28. Charles Ritchie, 26 June 1958 entry, 148.

29. Ibid.

30. Charles Ritchie, *Storm Signals: More Undiplomatic Diaries 1962–1971* (MacMillan, 1983), 19.

31. Bartleman, 12.

32. Ibid. On the world of Canadian diplomats, see David Reece, *Ambassador Assignments: Canadian Diplomats Reflect on our Place in the World* (Toronto: Fitzhenry and Whiteside, 2007); Robert Wolfe (ed.), *Diplomatic Missions: The Ambassador in Canadian Foreign Policy* (Kingston: School of Policy Studies, Queen's University, 1998). An interesting portrait of female diplomats can be found in Margaret K. Weiers, *Envoys Extraordinary: Women of the Canadian Foreign Service* (Toronto: Dundurn Press, 1995).

33. 1963 report, Paul Martin-Secretary of State for External Affairs, January 1964, 49.

34. 1965 report, 55.

35. p. 57.

36. Derek Burney, *Getting It Done: A Memoir* (Montreal and Kingston: McGill-Queens University Press, 2005), 10.

37. Burney, 11.

38. 1966 report, dated 3 Jan 1967.

39. 1964, 55.

40. 1964 report, 53.

41. 1967 report, 66.

42. 1969 report, 78.

43. 1970 report, 92–93.

44. 1968 report, 64.

45. John G. Kneale, *Foreign Service* (Toronto: Captus Press, 1993), 2.

46. 1980 report, 83. See Kim Richard Nossal, 'Allan Gotlieb and the Politics of the Real World' in Greg Donaghy and Kim Richard Nossal (eds.), op. cit., 272–88.

47. 1980 report, 82.

48. 1983–85 report, vii.

49. Ibid.

50. 1984–85 report, 53.

51. The combination of budget cuts and expanding 'human security agenda' provoked grave concerns inside the Department. In part, this was a regret that Canada was pursuing an unfocused foreign policy agenda. It also betrayed a resentment that Axworthy seemed more comfortable with the advice he received from the Canadian Centre for Foreign Policy Development. The account of the tensions between the minister and the department is described by Daryl Copeland, an employee of DFAIT, in 'The Axworthy Years: Canadian Foreign Policy in the Era of Diminished Capacity' in Fen Osler Hampson, Norman Hillmer, Maureen Appel Molot (eds.), *Canada Among Nations, 2001: The Axworthy Legacy* (Toronto: Oxford University Press, 2002), 152–72. See also Lloyd Axworthy's account of his years as minister, *Navigating a New World: Canada's Global Future* (Toronto: Vintage Canada, 2004), hardly mentions DFAIT.

52. See Evan Potter, 'Redesigning Canadian Diplomacy in an Age of Fiscal Austerity' in Fen Osler Hampson and Maureen Appel Molot (eds.), *Canada Among Nations 1996: Big Enough to be Heard* (Ottawa: Carleton University Press, 1996).

15

DISMEMBERING CANADA? STEPHEN HARPER AND THE FOREIGN RELATIONS OF CANADIAN PROVINCES

Christopher J. Kukucha

Stephen Harper has pursued an admittedly decentralist agenda since becoming Prime Minister in 2006. Specifically, Harper has pledged to limit Ottawa's use of the federal spending power and reduce new social programs in areas of provincial jurisdiction. As leader of a minority Conservative government, Harper also declared Québec a 'nation,' and promised to revisit existing fiscal transfers to the provinces. One of the most controversial issues, however, was Harper's decision to grant Québec a formalized role in Canada's delegation at the United Nations' Educational, Scientific, and Cultural Organization (UNESCO). Québec's proposed bilateral labour mobility agreement with France, and Ottawa's support for the international economic autonomy for all provinces, also drew significant criticism. Some observers, such as Andrew Coyne, have suggested that granting provinces greater foreign autonomy contributes to the 'dismembering of Canada' and 'blurs our national identity'. However, Paul Heinbecker, Canada's former ambassador to the

United Nations has suggested that this is simply 'the same old bullshit'.[1]

This chapter will explore Harper's decentralist agenda in relation to the foreign activity of Canadian provinces. It will argue that the Prime Minister's use of the term 'autonomy' requires clearer analytical parameters to allow for an extended evaluation of sub-federal international engagement. In examining the historic role of Québec, trade promotion, foreign offices, trade policy, cross-border functional relations, development assistance, and the environment, it becomes clear that Canadian provinces have exercised both partial and significant autonomy in these policy areas long before the arrival of Harper and the Conservatives. There is a tendency to think that autonomy is simply granted to provinces by specific prime ministers but in this policy area it more accurately reflects the increasing intrusiveness of international trade agreements into areas of provincial jurisdiction, federalism's response to these pressures, and the ongoing decentralization of federal–provincial relations in Canada. There is also the fact that provincial governments are increasingly influencing both Canadian foreign policy and, in some cases, the evolution of international norms and standards.

DEFINING TERMS

A number of terms must be clarified to evaluate Harper's position regarding provincial international activity. First, a distinction must be made between foreign policy and sub-federal international relations. Foreign policy focuses on the specific international goals of officials, and the values and mechanisms used to pursue these objectives.[2] In contrast, 'foreign relations' is a much broader term, and refers to functional issues and other non-controversial international activities.[3] There are also important distinctions between trade and economic policy. Economic policy engages matters of economic growth and fiscal and monetary issues. Trade policy, however, focuses on the exchange of goods and services and the negotiation and implementation of international (and domestic) trade commitments. It also includes policies of protectionism and liberalization, which can be transparent (tariffs and quotas), or more difficult to identify (subsidies and non-tariff barriers). Trade promotion, on the other hand, is the expansion of export markets for domestic goods, and in some cases the pursuit of investment. There are also important distinctions between the term 'autonomy', and the related concepts of independence and sovereignty. Independence is the 'ability to be free from the control of others' whereas sovereignty encompasses the 'juridical recognition' of modern states to control territory and exercise authority over citizens.[4] Autonomy, on the other hand, is the ability to achieve specific preferences. Although all political communities pursue these goals, none is able to consistently

exercise complete autonomy due to internal and external demands and constraints. Autonomy is also a concept of degree, varying among minimal, partial, and significant. This discussion will argue that Canadian provinces have exercised partial and significant autonomy in terms of foreign policy and a wide range of foreign relations for several decades.

Although there is considerable literature focusing on the foreign relations of sub-federal governments, few directly reference the autonomy question, especially in a Canadian context. On a broad level, Ivo Duchacek, Hans Michelmann, and Panayotis Soldatos introduced the concepts of 'paradiplomacy' and 'perforated sovereignty' to evaluate the international activity of a wide range of federal states.[5] In a recent update, Francisco Aldecoa and Michael Keating stressed the need to move paradiplomacy beyond domestic institutional variables to include sectoral issues, institution-building, and civil society.[6] In a similar fashion, Brian Hocking has focused on the interaction of state and non-governmental actors in the formulation of international and domestic trade policy.[7]

A number of American scholars have also reviewed the foreign relations of US states. Earl Fry has examined sub-federal trade and investment promotion, foreign offices, export financing, and Canada–US cross border regional associations.[8] Michelle Sager has highlighted a similar range of topics in her study of federalism and international trade in the United States.[9] In his studies of American federalism, John Kincaid has published numerous articles focusing on the foreign affairs of American states.[10] In contrast, Robert Stumberg has specifically highlighted provisions of international trade agreements with implications for the autonomy of US states.[11]

In terms of the Canadian literature, Douglas Brown, Grace Skogstad, and Bruce Doern and Brian Tomlin have all reflected on the roles of provincial actors, questions of centralization and decentralization, and the institutional frameworks that exist in this policy area.[12] Stephen de Boer has explored the potential for a greater provincial role in North American integration.[13] A number of economic studies have also reviewed provincial trade patterns, especially in terms of North American regional economies and the global exports of the provinces.[14] In addition, several authors have examined Supreme Court of Canada rulings that extend a level of constitutional legitimacy to the international activity of Canadian provinces, especially in terms of foreign trade and environmental policy.[15] The international relations of Québec is well documented, covering France and la Francophonie, provincial representation within Canadian federalism, and the province's foreign trade policy, especially in the context of the United States.[16] In contrast, little or no attention has been directed at the foreign trade relations of other provincial governments, with the possible exception of Ontario during the negotiation of the North American Free Trade Agreement (NAFTA).[17] Analysis directly engaging the question of sub-federal autonomy, however, is limited. On one hand, Ian Robinson has suggested that neo-liberal agreements expose the vulnerability of provinces in terms of regional development programs, worker rights, environmental programs, and health regulations.[18] This author reached a different conclusion in the context of the provinces and Canadian foreign trade policy.[19]

QUÉBEC

Québec has the most active foreign policy agenda compared to other provinces. From the outset, these initiatives were designed to highlight the province's cultural and linguistic differences and focused, for the most part, on other Francophone countries.[20] Initially, Québec's efforts were limited to a series of foreign offices. In 1882, the province appointed an agent-general in Paris, and in 1911 Québec opened a 'commercial' office in Britain, followed by a provincial posting in Brussels in 1915. Although these offices were subsequently closed, the provincial government re-established its presence in Paris by the 1960s. In 1965, Québec also negotiated an educational exchange with France, its first formal international agreement. Provincial objectives were further clarified in the 1965 Gérin-Lajoie doctrine, which argued that Québec had the right to pursue international objectives consistent with its cultural identity or in constitutionally defined areas of jurisdiction. In February 1968, Gabon, with the encouragement of the French government, directly extended an invitation to Québec for an international education conference. The following year, Canada was represented by a joint-delegation at a Francophone conference in Congo due to a cooperative agreement between Ottawa and Jean-Jacques Bertrand's provincial government. A similar framework was used to allow a federal-provincial delegation to attend a subsequent meeting in Niger.[21]

In the 1970s, however, René Lévesque's Parti Québécois (PQ) separatist government used foreign policy as a means of generating support for a proposed referendum on Québec independence. Specifically, the PQ sought diplomatic immunity for its foreign representatives, made statements on human rights issues, such as South African apartheid, and considered an independent defence policy for a sovereign Québec, including its potential withdrawal from both the North Atlantic Treaty Organization (NATO) and the North American Aerospace Command (NORAD).[22] During the following decade, Québec's foreign ambitions began to fade, primarily due to the PQ's defeat in the 1980 separatist referendum and a loss of support from the French government. The arrival of Brian Mulroney as Prime Minister in September

1984, the resignation of Lévesque in October 1985, and the PQ's subsequent defeat in provincial elections the following month, also created a shift in federal-provincial relations. Instead of independence, Québec returned to the priorities of Gérin-Lajoie, which was reflected in an agreement between Mulroney and the new Liberal government of Robert Bourassa that granted both Québec and New Brunswick formal representation at the first la Francophonie summit in Paris.

The election of a PQ government in Québec in 1994 ensured a return to the province's previous approach to international relations. Jacques Parizeau fought proposed la Francophonie reforms that had the potential to weaken Québec's status in the organization prior to the Marrakech Ministerial Conference in 1996. The province also expanded its standing in la Francophonie at the 1999 summit in Moncton, New Brunswick, to include all ministerial meetings. Support for Québec separatism and the province's foreign policy agenda was further bolstered by the success of the Bloc Québécois (BQ) in the 1993 federal election. In fact, in an address to the United Nations in March 1994, Lucien Bouchard, the leader of the BQ, made it clear that separatism was once again at the forefront of Québec's political agenda. Bouchard continued to embrace issues of sovereignty and international legitimacy after he became Premier of Québec in 1996. Under the current Liberal government of Jean Charest, however, Québec has returned to its historic Gérin-Lajoie agenda. In terms of international institutions, Québec has called for direct provincial participation in WTO negotiations, and in 2006 was granted a formal role in the United Nations Educational, Scientific, and Cultural Organization (UNESCO). In October 2008, the province also negotiated a bilateral labour mobility agreement with France regarding the recognition of professional credentials from both countries.

Although the UNESCO announcement and the bilateral labour deal are unprecedented developments, they need to be kept in context. Critics of the UNESCO decision, for example, note that Québec's role is limited to shaping Canada's overall UNESCO policies, and does not extend to the province an independent seat, vote, or presence in the organization. This raises the question of whether Québec's standing in UNESCO will diverge significantly from the province's other established participation in la Francophonie. Other observers have pointed out that Paul Martin made a similar UNESCO commitment to Québec in 2004, before withdrawing the offer. The labour-mobility agreement also hinges on the successful negotiation of future bilateral Mutual Recognition Agreements (MRAs) encompassing over one hundred professions and trades. Although improved movement of professionals between Québec and France will need to be negotiated under numerous MRAs, recognition agreements are now in place for several professions, including doctors, lawyers, and some construction trades. Ongoing progress, however, will be limited to those professions where both governments suffer from a shortage of qualified workers.[23]

Finally, Québec's Legislative Assembly was granted the right to 'review' all federal treaties focusing on relevant areas of sub-federal jurisdiction in the *Act to Amend the Act Respecting the Ministère des Relations Internationales*. As Stéphane Paquin has noted, elected legislators now have an obligation to approve a treaty before its adoption, especially when the implementation of these commitments impact existing laws or regulatory practices.[24] Peter Hogg, on the other hand, has made it clear that the 'ratification' of treaties is the prerogative of the Crown and/or the federal executive, and there is no formal role for any elected legislatures in this process, unlike the United States Congress. Although parliamentary approval for significant agreements has occurred in the past, Hogg also points out that in recent years it has become increasingly less common to require formal ratification for international commitments.[25] Therefore, it is important to emphasize that Québec's right of review is not the equivalent of ratifying international treaties. The province's new legislation is not insignificant, as it provides a mechanism to examine foreign commitments in areas of provincial jurisdiction. It does not, however, create a constitutional crisis on the question of ratification. As in other cases involving Québec, this autonomy pre-dates the current Harper government.

TRADE PROMOTION & PROVINCIAL FOREIGN OFFICES

Most provinces engage in trade promotion at the international level. In some cases, these efforts are part of federal initiatives, such as Jean Chrétien's Team Canada program. Other provinces, however, organize independent trade missions. In the 1990s, Alberta targeted the Pacific Rim with the goal of diversifying its trade relations. Ontario also completed a trade mission to Asia in 2005, its first in two decades, and pursued markets in India, the Middle East, Japan and Western Europe.[26] New Brunswick has also focused its trade promotion efforts in China, Germany, Japan, Mexico, Eastern Europe, and members of la Francophonie. In addition to trade missions, the province also organizes training for both exporting companies and members of the provincial bureaucracy.[27]

Despite the significance of provincial trade missions, it is important to keep these efforts in perspective. During Ontario's 2005 Asian tour Premier Dalton McGuinty attempted to lower expectations by stressing that the mission was not focused on 'announce-ables' (actual contracts) but on educating the Chinese about the province's economic potential. The Alberta government has also recently acknowledged that numerous barriers exist in its attempts to diversify trade relations in Asia. These include a lack of railway infrastructure to transport exports through British Columbia and capacity problems in coastal ports. Therefore, Alberta relies on other methods of advancing provincial trade interests, including the protection of oil and gas exports in international trade agreements, reductions in tariffs in the agricultural sector, and an ongoing commitment to foreign trade offices.[28]

In fact, most provincial governments use foreign offices as a primary means of pursuing international trade and investment. As already noted, Québec was the first province to establish a series of foreign provincial offices in the early 1900s. During this period, Ontario was the only other province with an international office in London, established in 1918. For the most part, these offices were designed to supplement expanding federal representation abroad. In 1868, Canada's Dominion Agency for Emigration was opened in London and several other immigration offices were established throughout Europe. By 1907 twelve trade commissions were located in such diverse locations as Yokohama, Sydney, Cape Town, and Mexico City. As Kim Nossal has noted, however, these federal and provincial officials were 'not diplomats in anything but the most superficial sense. They were not accorded diplomatic status; nor, notably, were they representatives of a government with an independent international personality, capable of conducting an independent foreign policy'.[29]

Most provincial offices were closed by the 1930s but provinces began to revisit the idea of foreign delegations following the Second World War. In 1945 Ontario reopened its London office and established a presence in Chicago (1953), New York (1956), and Los Angeles and Cleveland (1967). The province also opened offices in Europe and Asia, including Milan (1963), Stockholm (1968), Brussels, Vienna and Tokyo (1969), Frankfurt (1970), and Mexico City (1973). Québec, on the other hand, posted a delegation to New York in 1941 and added several offices in subsequent years, including Brussels (1972), Tokyo (1973), Mexico City (1980), and Buenos Aires (1998). For the most part, however, other provincial governments did not follow a similar pattern. Alberta limited its offices to London (1948), Los Angeles (1964) and Tokyo (1970). Remaining provinces either had no interest or an 'idiosyncratic' approach to overseas representation. New Brunswick opened a London office in 1970, and subsequently established a presence in Hamburg and Boston, all of which were closed by the 1990s.[30] Manitoba posted representatives in Minneapolis in 1975 and Saskatchewan opened and closed a series of offices in the late 1980s, including London, Zurich, Hong Kong, Minneapolis and New York.[31] Nova Scotia also recalled its delegation from London, but maintained a trade and investment presence in Boston until 2002.[32] In addition, British Columbia had various contacts in the Pacific Northwest and California. Regardless, by the 1990s the majority of these offices, including those from Ontario and Québec, had become targets for provincial budget cuts.

In 2001, however, Mike Harris and the Conservatives announced plans to open Ontario missions in New York, Shanghai, Tokyo, Munich, and London. The province also opened, and closed, offices in several American cities, including Boston and Atlanta. The McGuinty government continued this trend, establishing the London and Tokyo delegations first announced by Harris and opening offices in Los Angeles, New York, Paris, Mexico City, Munich, New Delhi, Shanghai, and Beijing.[33] Alberta is another province with an expanding list of foreign representation, with offices in Beijing, Hong Kong, Tokyo, Seoul, Taipei, Mexico City, and European postings in London and Munich. The United States, however, is the key focus of Alberta's trade promotion efforts. At the institutional level,

this is best reflected with the opening of its mission in Washington, DC in March 2005. The decision to establish an office in Washington, connected to the Canadian embassy, was explicitly designed to protect the province's energy and agricultural interests. During the Smithsonian's Folklife Festival in 2006 the Premier and ten cabinet ministers visited Washington and participated in several conferences. Meetings were also held with Vice President Dick Cheney and other prominent members of Congress. For two weeks, a large truck from the oil sands was parked in front of the Smithsonian, as a friendly reminder to Americans of their dependence on Alberta oil and natural gas.

Not surprisingly, Québec has also maintained its international presence with twenty-five offices in seventeen countries. These include general delegations in Brussels, London, Mexico City, New York, Paris, and Tokyo. A less comprehensive range of services is available in Buenos Aires, Boston, Chicago, and Los Angeles. Government bureaus, on the other hand, are in Barcelona, Beijing, Damascus (Immigration Office), Hong Kong (Immigration Office), Miami, Munich, Shanghai, Vienna (Immigration Office), and Washington (Tourism Office). Finally, Québec has trade branches in Atlanta, Berlin, Rome, Santiago, Seoul, and Taipei, including additional business agents in Lima, Milan, and Hanoi.[34] Québec's presence in Washington, DC, was officially established as a tourism office in 1978. Since its inception, however, it was reluctantly accepted, but not approved by the federal government, that Québec would use its office to develop working relationships with members of Congress and the executive branch to protect provincial interests. In recent years, Québec has also worked to develop ties with Washington universities, think tanks, and non-governmental organizations, in the pursuit of these objectives. In an attempt to discourage other provinces from establishing offices in the US capital, and to monitor ongoing efforts by

Québec and Alberta, Paul Martin established an 'Advocacy Secretariat' in the Canadian embassy in Washington. The Harper government has renamed this position, the 'Minister (Legislative/Sub-National/Public Affairs) and Head, Washington Advocacy Secretariat'.[35]

TRADE POLICY

Unlike trade promotion, 'trade policy' is a distinctly separate matter, related to the negotiation and implementation of international commitments. At the international level, foreign trade agreements now include areas of sub-federal jurisdiction, such as services, agriculture, alcohol, government procurement, national health and safety standards, energy, and environment and labour issues. In response, Ottawa has attempted to institutionalize provincial consultation within existing institutions of Canadian federalism. During the Tokyo Round of the General Agreement on Tariffs and Trade (GATT), for example, the federal government adopted traditional practices of 'executive federalism' to engage provinces on matters of trade policy.[36] At this point, the only formal mechanism for provincial input was the Canadian Trade and Tariffs Committee (CTTC), which was responsible for gathering briefs from business, unions, consumer groups, the provinces, and other interested parties. An ad hoc federal-provincial committee of deputy ministers was established in 1975, which was then replaced by a Canadian Coordinator for Trade Negotiations (CCTN) in 1977. Following the implementation of the Canada–US Free Trade Agreement (CUFTA), the CCTN became the Committee for the Free Trade Agreement (CFTA) on which each province had one official representative. Ottawa also set up a series of consultative committees with various provincial departments to address sectoral concerns and ongoing trade irritants. During negotiations for the NAFTA, the CFTA remained in place but Ottawa and the provinces also agreed to create the Committee for North American Free Trade Negotiations (CNAFTN).

Ultimately, the CNAFTN process evolved into the CTRADE committee system for international trade. CTRADE currently involves a series of meetings between Ottawa and the provinces that occur four times annually. Initially, some provinces expressed concerns with the content and quality of information available through CTRADE. More recently, however, the federal government has attempted to improve access to information and the agenda-setting process. Canadian provinces have also enjoyed an expanded level of engagement in ongoing trade negotiations between Canada and the European Union (EU). In the early phase of talks, approximately 12 negotiating groups were established, with provinces actively involved in six, and often seven, of these forums. Provincial officials, however, are quick to point out that these developments do not represent a change in the 'culture' of federal–provincial engagement in matters of trade policy. In fact, EU demands for an expanded sub-federal role, due to concerns over provincial compliance, do not include direct participation in all areas of negotiations. In some cases, EU negotiating positions have also contributed to an increase in federal–provincial tensions when Ottawa's administrative procedures are not consistent with those of the provinces.[37]

In addition to consultation, Canadian provinces have also aggressively protected specific provincial sectoral interests. For example, pressure from Québec contributed to Canada's contradictory approach to agriculture during both the Uruguay Round of GATT and NAFTA negotiations. Specifically, Ottawa promoted the liberalization of grains and red meats, due to the market advantage enjoyed by Western provinces, but protected dairy and poultry, which are vital to the economy of Québec. Alberta, in response to the NEP, also ensured that energy provisions in NAFTA guaranteed its exports of oil to the United States.

These trends are also evident in relation to services, softwood lumber, and procurement. In terms of services, pressure from Canadian provinces was directly reflected in Annex I and Annex II of NAFTA. Annex I excluded all provincial health measures, as defined in Article 1206, that existed prior to January 1, 1994 relating to national treatment, Most-Favoured Nation (MFN) status, and local presence requirements. As Mark Crawford has noted, this reservation immediately excluded most health services as the 'basic nature of provincial schemes have not changed since 1994'. Less clear, however, was whether emerging privately funded healthcare services would be exempt. The Supreme Court of Canada's decision to strike down Québec's prohibition of private health insurance in *Chaoulli v. Québec (Attorney General)*, rendered 9 June 2005, further reinforced the possibility that these services could be exposed to the NAFTA dispute settlement process. The Annex II 'Social Service Reservation' clause, on the other hand, excluded provincial social services 'established or maintained for a public purpose'. As a result, Canadian officials have argued that Annex II includes 'private-delivery' of 'publicly-funded' services. Ultimately, BC pushed for a clear definition of social services in Annex II, which resulted in 'public education, public training, health, and child care' being included in provisions, related to cross-border services and investment.[39]

BC also argued for a broader exemption related to Article 1.3 of the World Trade Organization (WTO) General Agreement on Trade in Services (GATS). These provisions excluded services provided by regional and local governments 'supplied neither on a commercial basis, nor in competition with one or more service suppliers'. As Crawford points out, BC was the only province to dispute what it believed was the narrow definition of the

exemption. Other federal and provincial officials argued that the existing language of Article 1.3 could be 'interpreted broadly' and suggested the recognition of the 'right to regulate' and 'due respect for national policy objectives' in the GATS preamble protected sub-federal interests.[40] Although Article 1.3(c) states that all competition should be 'economically rational as well as legally and practically possible,' Anthony VanDuzer has also argued that health and education services are likely 'within the exclusion'.[41] Regardless, in the case of GATS, the BC government had an impact on Canada's negotiating position but did not alter the language of the WTO agreement.

In the current Doha Round a wide range of services are again open to negotiation. In the decade following the GATS, however, most provincial officials have reviewed existing legislation and now make a distinction between 'defensive' and 'offensive' interests. Defensive considerations require ongoing support for government regulatory capacity, especially in the area of health and education. Offensive interests, on the other hand, are service-based issues potentially benefiting from a reduction of market barriers, such as GATS Mode IV, or business travel. For example, in Ontario there is sensitivity to defensive concerns, but the province also supports greater Mode IV liberalization, especially in relation to professional services, such as architecture, engineering, management, and accounting.[42] Regardless, it is important to remember that WTO rulings related to GATS are limited. In fact, only twelve of 332 complaints dating back to 1995 are in direct reference to services. Only three of these targeted Canada: *Certain Measures Affecting the Automotive Industry*, *Certain Measures Concerning Periodicals*, and *Measures Affecting Film Distribution Services*.

It is also clear that in some cases, provincial interests are considered so important that separate international agreements are negotiated. The automobile industry in Ontario, for example, motivated Ottawa to negotiate the Canada–United States Auto Pact in 1965. Another example is the 1986 Canada–United States Memorandum of Understanding (MOU) on softwood lumber. In this case, however, the MOU was only a partial victory for Canadian provinces. The agreement placed a 15 per cent export tax on all lumber shipments to the United States, which the provinces could decrease by increasing stumpage fees. In BC the export tax was eventually eliminated and in Quebec it was reduced in various stages before stabilizing at 3.1 per cent. The problem, however, was that higher stumpage fees raised timber costs to all markets, not just those in the United States. Not surprisingly, it was pressure from the provinces and industry that contributed to Canada's decision to terminate the MOU after its five-year term expired in 1991.[43]

In contrast, some observers viewed the 2006 Canada–US Softwood Lumber Agreement (SLA) as a direct challenge to provincial interests. In April 2005, Ottawa forwarded a US proposal to Canadian producers that included export taxes, ongoing quotas, and a commitment to return some, but not all, of the approximately $5 billion in duties already collected by Washington. Within hours, Ontario had rejected the proposal with BC and Quebec expressing similar reservations. For British Columbia the proposal was especially difficult to accept given that approximately half of the duties paid to the United States came from provincial producers. Despite this pressure, a 'terms sheet' outlining the parameters of a final agreement was signed by both Canada and the United States on 27 April 2006. Opposition from British Columbia was immediate, but divisions within industry appeared as Canfor, Weyerhaeuser, and Abitibi-Consolidated, publicly endorsed the tentative settlement. After initial concerns, Ontario and Quebec also decided to support the Softwood Lumber Agreement, which was formally signed on July 1, 2006.

Although BC initially refused to endorse the SLA, the province was able to negotiate several changes to the agreement, including acceptance of the province's market-based pricing system and a review of the commercial viability of proposed 'running rules'. A 'standstill clause' was also included, prohibiting any US trade remedy cases for a one-year period.[44] The province also demonstrated its autonomy with the publication of its Forestry Revitalization Plan (FRP) in March 2003. The FRP included significant provincial reforms including a 20 per cent tenure reallocation of logging rights to allow greater access for First Nations, new entrepreneurs, and re-manufacturers. The FRP also maintained export restrictions, ensuring that timber cut in BC remained in the province for processing. Finally, the FRP protected long-standing government–industry alliances with extensive compensation for companies losing licenses, which could then re-bid for access.[45]

Canadian provinces were also successful in defending sub-federal procurement practices in both the NAFTA and Uruguay Round negotiations. In NAFTA, for example, provincial priorities were protected with exemptions related to research and development, health and social services, utilities, communications, education and training, and financial services.[46] Although Article 1024 of NAFTA committed all three signatories to pursue further liberalization in procurement, at all levels of government, these negotiations have not occurred. Canada's commitment to the WTO's Agreement on Government Procurement (GPA) also exempted Canadian provinces. Unlike other signatories, Canada did not grant foreign parties equal status with domestic suppliers and specifically excluded provincial, municipal, and regional governments from the GPA. Thus, Canada is not able to bid on government contracts in the jurisdictions of other signatories. Canadian provinces, however, can gain access to procurement contracts by negotiating specific agreements with individual US states.[47]

Provincial autonomy in this sector, however, resulted in unforeseen economic consequences due to a 'Buy American' clause in the 2009 economic stimulus legislation in the United States, the *American Recovery and Reinvestment Act* (ARRA). Much of this federal funding was designed to give preferred access to US iron, steel, and related materials for construction projects. For the most part, however, state and municipal governments directly controlled the contracts for these projects. Therefore, Canadian bidders were excluded unless specific local governments waived Buy American provisions. Interestingly, other governments, including Britain, France, Germany, Australia, Chile, Mexico, Chile, Peru, and Singapore, did not face similar exemptions due to separate agreements ensuring reciprocal sub-federal procurement rights with the United States.[48] Canada also had no means of challenging Buy American provisions using NAFTA or WTO dispute mechanisms due to already noted exclusions.

Therefore, Canada's only option was to pursue a negotiated settlement offering greater US access to Canadian provincial and municipal contracts. Initially, a successful outcome was considered unlikely, as the American procurement market is significantly larger than Canada's. As a senior provincial trade official noted at the time, the 'US is operating within existing agreements', which means that Ottawa is essentially 'asking for a favour'.[49] Despite these challenges, a bilateral agreement on procurement was successfully negotiated in February 2010. Under the terms of the deal, Canada was granted permanent access to the procurement markets of the 37 US states compliant with the WTO's GPA. Temporary admittance, until September 2011, was also permitted for specific projects funded by the ARRA. In return, permanent access was granted to US suppliers in provincial procurement markets. Temporary entry to provincial and municipal construction contracts not covered by the GPA was also granted until September 2011. Almost immediately, however, critics pointed out that the majority of ARRA funding was already committed prior to the new agreement. Annexes 2, 4, and 5 of the deal also outlined numerous exemptions for Canadian provinces, especially in terms of services and construction procurement.

CROSS-BORDER FUNCTIONAL RELATIONS

Provinces engage in a wide range of cross-border activity, including issues related to the environment, transportation corridors, water management, security, road maintenance, and fire-fighting. This interaction takes place in a number of formal and informal settings. At the executive level, the oldest ties exist in Atlantic Canada. The Conference of New England Governors and Eastern Canadian Premiers (NEGECP) was formalized following an initial meeting focusing on energy issues in 1973. A wide range of issues are addressed in the NEGECP, including energy, tourism, trade irritants, transportation, and economic development. New Brunswick, however, has also developed linkages with the Eastern Regional Conference of the Council of State Governments and signed agreements with Maine related to highway and bridge maintenance and management of the St Croix Waterway.[50] For the most part, other provinces in Atlantic Canada have not pursued additional regional linkages due to the absence of a land border with the United States. Competing economic interests, including lobsters, blueberries, and potatoes, also limit the incentive for stronger sub-federal cooperation.[51]

In evaluating cross-border functional relationships in central Canada it is important to make a distinction between Ontario and Québec. Both provinces are associate members of the Council of Great Lakes Governors (CGLG), but Québec's ties to Atlantic Canada, and the importance of hydro-electricity, are such that its cross-border relations are more extensive. In fact, Ontario's sub-national activity is limited to a narrow range of water management issues within the CGLG, specific trade disputes, assorted functional agreements, and direct ties with US state representatives. Dalton McGuinty's Liberal government, however, has prioritized closer sub-federal linkages with US states. For the most part, this has occurred at the executive and official level, including a bilateral meeting with the governor of Georgia in 2005. The assistant deputy minister and other officials in the Ministry of Economic Development and Trade (MEDT) have also developed contacts in several American states, especially New York and Pennsylvania. For the most part, however, Ontario's cross-border relations are driven by issue-specific concerns.[52]

Québec, on the other hand, has a number of well-developed sub-federal relations, which are the result of the provincial energy interests and its participation in the NEGECP. Therefore, the province has a historic commitment to cross-border linkages that does not exist in Ontario. In fact, much of the motivation to participate in the NEGECP was to secure a stable market for Québec's energy exports. Although energy remains a crucial issue for Québec, this forum also expanded its focus following 11 September 2001. For example, at the 2002 NEGECP meetings in Québec City trade, security, and environmental issues were on the agenda. At the same time, however, there are Québec officials that view the Conference of Governors and Premiers as a forum driven by American interests. Although Québec is currently a member of the conference's sub-committee on trade and globalization, provincial officials cite minimal interest from US representatives unless it focuses on cross-border infrastructure projects.[53] Therefore, Québec has pursued other institutionalized linkages in the region, including annual bilateral 'summits' with New York, which date back to 1983.

The provinces of Manitoba and Saskatchewan also have cross-border linkages with US states. Saskatchewan is an associate member of the Midwestern Legislative Conference (MLC), a regional forum linked to the Council of State Governments Midwest. For the most part, the MLC focuses on functional issues, such as economic development, the environment, education, health and human services, and natural resources and energy. However, the MLC also has a Mid-West Canada Relations Committee, which was first created in 1991.[54] Although Manitoba recently joined the MLC, the province has historically emphasized cross border linkages within the Western Governors Association (WGA). Manitoba is not a formal member of the WGA but former Premier Garry Doer emphasized this forum for trade promotion and functional agreements, such as the Memorandum of Understanding on Drought and Wildland Fires signed in September 2003. In addition, Manitoba has negotiated bilateral MOUs with several US states and municipalities. The province, for example, recently completed a series of agreements with Minnesota related to economic development, trade, tourism, water issues, and education. In addition, the province signed a MOU with Texas on trade and economic development, and engaged in preliminary discussions with California on clean energy strategies. Manitoba also signed a recent MOU on bioscience technology with the city of Atlanta.[55]

Among the Western provinces, Alberta has the most prolific agenda related to cross-border functional issues. In fact, the province is associated with the WGA, the Council of State Governments West (CSG-West), the Pacific Northwest Economic Region (PNWER), the Rocky Mountain Trade Corridor, the Montana–Alberta Bilateral Advisory Council (MABAC), and the CanAm Border Trade Alliance. In terms of the WGA, Alberta has also entered into agreements on cross-border technical issues, such as the protocol 'Governing the Siting and Permitting of Interstate Electric Transmission Lines in the Western United States,' signed in June 2002.[56] An addendum to the initial protocol was also negotiated by Alberta in April 2004. Another example of Alberta's cross-border regional agenda is its involvement in PNWER. Although Alberta's primary interest in PNWER is the development of export markets, it has also used the forum to address other issues, such as CANAMEX, a proposed trade corridor through Alaska, the Yukon, BC, Alberta, Montana, Idaho, Utah, and Nevada to the Mexican border. Following 11 September 2001, PNWER also focused on issues aimed at preventing the disruption or slowdown of cross-border shipping and business travel.[57]

BC's interest in cross-border functional issues has also increased in recent years. The province is now associated with the WGA, CSG-West, PNWER, and the International Mobility and Trade Corridor (IMTC). Not surprisingly, BC's influence is often linked directly to the mandate and membership of these organizations. In the WGA, BC has articulated provincial concerns related to the Canada–US softwood lumber dispute. In addition, BC has also signed bilateral agreements with other WGA members, most notably Idaho and Montana, on environmental protection and conservation. Unlike the WGA, BC has official standing within the CSG-West. BC became an 'associate' member in 2000 but its influence remains limited in this forum. BC's membership in PNWER is also driven by matters of international trade. A dispute between Oregon, BC, and Alberta regarding horticultural producers and provincial phytosanitary restrictions, for example, was addressed within PNWER.[58] Whistler, BC also hosted the first PNWER meeting outside of the United States in July 2001. Finally, issues of cross-border access for BC are primarily addressed in the IMTC or as part of the Peace Arch Crossing Entry (PACE) and CANPASS programs.[59]

INTERNATIONAL DEVELOPMENT ASSISTANCE

In recent years, Québec has placed considerable emphasis on international development initiatives. Specifically, the province has developed an *International Solidarity Program* that targets social issues in Francophone developing countries in Africa, the Caribbean, and Latin America. In most cases the province's Ministère des Relations Internationales (MRI) works with provincial private sector organizations and non-governmental groups that are members of the Association Québécoise des Organismes de Coopération Internationale (AQOCI). One solidarity initiative is *Québec Without Borders*, which was created in 1995 to sponsor the participation of Québec citizens, between the ages of 18 and 39, in international development projects. The province's *Public Awareness Program on Development and International Solidarity Issues* also promotes dialogue and citizen engagement on a wide range of international issues. The *Québec International Development Program* (PQDI), however, works more specifically with international cooperation agencies, such as la Francophonie and UNESCO, and focuses on issues of education, food safety, health, the environment, and human rights. For the most part, funding for these projects comes from the Canadian International Development Agency (CIDA) or international organizations, although one percent of Lotto Québec net profits are targeted for these programs.[60] A specific example of Québec's interest in development was the November 2007 Tripartite Agreement between the governments of Canada, Québec, and Haiti. This Agreement, which focused on the reform of Haiti's public service, pledged $5 million in federal funding, with an additional $1.5 million from the Québec government in the form of 'salaries of the government department and agency employees' engaged in related governance initiatives.[61]

Alberta is another province with an established program of international development. Alberta's decision to establish an International Governance Office (IGO), however, was driven by economic and development concerns. On one hand, Alberta has demonstrated a commitment to governance issues, such as the province's extension of its twinning agreement with Mpumalanga, South Africa. The fact that recent exchanges have focused on social issues, gender equality, civic participation, and the delivery of services for poor and disenfranchised citizens in Malawi, China, South Africa, and Vietnam, further reinforces this point. At the same time, however, it is important not to overstate Alberta's international development efforts. First, it is clear that Alberta has no long-term agenda related to international culture or development and, unlike Québec, is not seeking formal status in institutions such as UNESCO. Further, any efforts by Alberta are also tied directly to CIDA or private sector funding. The exception to this would be Alberta's International Financial Institutions (IFI) branch, but these initiatives focus on economic development and not governance or development issues. Therefore, IGO initiatives in Alberta tend to be ad hoc and limited to study tours and exchanges of government officials and other professionals.[62]

THE ENVIRONMENT

In an environmental context, the international impact of the provinces is most evident with the NAFTA Side Deal on the Environment and international negotiations on climate change. For example, Annex 41 of the North American Agreement on Environmental Cooperation (NAAEC) outlines compliance provisions for Canadian provinces. There are no similar sections dedicated to US or Mexican states. As a result, Ottawa implemented the Canadian Intergovernmental Agreement (CIA),

which came into force in 1995 when Alberta became the first province to ratify the framework. To date, only Québec and Manitoba have joined Alberta in ratifying the NAAEC CIA. Despite this fact, a number of provinces, including non-signatories to the CIA, have been targeted under Articles 14 and 15 of the NAAEC's citizen submission complaint process. At this point, however, these cases have not posed significant problems for Canadian provinces. In *BC Logging*, the final factual record refused to rule on several complaints dealing with publicly owned land.[63] The *BC Mining* case also excluded the Tulsequah Chief and Mount Washington mining projects due to pending legal actions.[64] In other decisions, panels explicitly noted an unwillingness to contradict existing domestic judicial precedent. Finally, and perhaps most importantly, NAAEC citizen submission cases are not binding on Canadian provinces, signatories or non-signatories, in any tangible way.[65]

Provincial autonomy was also evident with the Kyoto Protocol, which the Chrétien government signed in 1997 and ratified in 2002. From the very start of negotiations, Alberta opposed the agreement and promoted a 'made in Alberta' solution. Alberta's opposition was further reinforced when the United States announced its intention to not sign Kyoto in 2001. The current Alberta government under Premier Ed Stelmach has extended this 'industry-friendly' path by promoting intensity-based emissions. In March 2007, in anticipation of new federal measures, the provincial government announced standards for slowing the growth of greenhouse gas emissions. Under the regulations, large-scale industries would be asked to lower the amount of energy used per unit of output. The effect would be to reduce the rate of emissions growth, rather than the actual amount of greenhouse gases being emitted. The provincial policy was taken both to establish its jurisdictional credentials in case of potential constitutional challenges, but also to send a strong signal to the federal government of the province's main priorities.

In the end, the 'call to arms' was unnecessary, as the province's approach was closely mirrored in the federal plan released at the end of April 2007. In putting forward intensity-based reductions, Ottawa imposed no ceiling on greenhouse gas emissions and protected Alberta's lucrative oil sands producers from having to undertake actual reductions in greenhouse gas emissions for the foreseeable future. The provincial and federal plans were so close that there was little room for either the province or the private sector to raise objections. The federal policy was even more favourable to provincial commercial interests, as it excluded oil sands from the new regime of regulations that were brought into place. It also left open a three-year window in which new investments were to be protected from meeting standards.[66]

BC, Ontario, Manitoba, and Québec, have also pursued autonomous positions on international environmental policy. All four provinces, along with Arizona, California, Montana, New Mexico, Oregon, Utah, and Washington State, are members of the Western Climate Initiative (WCI), which was formed in February 2007 to address regional solutions to climate change in North America. Saskatchewan, and six states in both the US and Mexico have observer status in the WCI. The origin of the WCI can be traced back to the West Coast Governors' Global Warming Initiative in 2004, when Washington State, Oregon, and California, agreed to cooperate on issues related to global warming. The WCI, however, has focused on sub-federal legislation targeting greenhouse gas emissions and the development of a cross-border Climate Registry and regional cap and trade systems. All of these programs exceed the environmental programs and initiatives of federal governments in the US and Canada. Unlike Alberta, however, the WCI cap and trade system will set overall limits on total emissions, and then lower these caps over time to reduce overall levels of pollutants.[67] To date, however, a comprehensive cap and trade system has not been established.

DISMEMBERING CANADA? EVALUATING THE HARPER AGENDA

Any suggestion that Harper's Conservatives represent a new era of international autonomy for Canadian provinces is disingenuous. In fact, evidence suggests that sub-federal governments in Canada have enjoyed partial or substantial levels of autonomy for extended periods. Historically, Québec was the first province to open foreign offices, establish linkages with international organizations, such as la Francophonie, and articulate a clear foreign policy agenda under Gérin-Lajoie. Under PQ governments, the province also adopted international positions with sovereignty objectives, including the possibility of diplomatic status for Québec officials abroad and the potential removal of an independent Québec from existing western security alliances. Although Québec's recent international initiatives have received considerable attention in the media, they do not represent a significant departure from previous activity. The province's formalized role in UNESCO does not grant Québec a seat or vote in the organization and the bilateral labour-mobility agreement with France requires the uncertain completion of numerous MRAs. As noted earlier, Québec's legislative initiatives are also limited in their overall impact.

Trade missions and the establishment of other provincial offices also demonstrate a significant level of long-term provincial autonomy. During the past several decades, most provinces have participated in federal or provincial foreign trade missions to Asia, Europe, and the Middle East. In addition, almost all provinces have maintained international offices in the pursuit of investment and expanded export markets. Québec and Alberta also have established an unprecedented presence in Washington, DC, but in both cases these offices were opened prior to the arrival of the current Conservative government. Perhaps the clearest indication of partial and significant provincial autonomy is in the area of trade policy. In fact, there are several examples of provinces influencing not only Canadian foreign policy but also the development of international norms and standards. Canada's contradictory positions on agriculture, for example, reflect protectionist pressures from dairy and poultry farmers in Québec, and demands from Western red meat and grain producers for greater liberalization. NAFTA's energy provisions were a direct result of pressure from Alberta in the aftermath of the NEP, while provincial interests tied to softwood lumber and the automotive sector were evident in the Auto Pact and previous lumber agreements in 1986, 1996, and 2006. Similar provincial interests were protected in Article 2.2 of the SCM and NAFTA's Annex I and II provisions dealing with services. Federal and provincial consultation on matters of trade policy has also become an established part of executive federalism dating back to the 1970s.

Levels of partial to significant autonomy are also evident when reviewing sub-federal cross-border functional relations. In Atlantic Canada and Québec, these ties date back several decades in established forums such as the NEGECP. In Ontario, linkages are not as entrenched, but the province is an active participant in the CGLG and has a presence related to cross-border disputes and other functional issues. On the prairies, Manitoba and Saskatchewan have signed a number of bilateral MOUs and have standing in forums such as the WGA and MLC. Alberta, on the other hand, is actively involved in the WGA, CSG-West, PNWER, and MABAC. BC has a similar range of relations with the WGA, CSG-West, and PNWER, as well as the IMTC. In contrast,

a relatively new area of provincial international activity is development assistance. In Québec, the province has established programs such as *Québec Without Borders* and the *Québec International Development Program*. The province has also participated in a joint federal-provincial initiative in Haiti. In addition, Alberta has established an International Governance Office and participated in study tours and professional exchanges with South Africa, China, Malawi, and Vietnam. The majority of these initiatives, however, are directly tied to funding provided by CIDA and other NGOs.

Finally, Canadian provinces have demonstrated long-term autonomy in relation to international environmental issues. One of the first examples was the standing granted to Canadian provinces in the NAAEC, which was not extended to Mexican and US states. Provinces then had the opportunity to ratify these provisions, which the majority of provincial governments rejected. Although the citizen complaint process of the NAAEC has targeted Canadian provinces, including those governments not bound by the agreement, factual records to date have not directly challenged existing domestic judicial precedent or sub-federal policy capacity. Similar patterns are evident in terms of the Kyoto Protocol, where Ottawa was significantly influenced by Alberta's intensity-based framework. Finally, the involvement of several provinces in the WCI demonstrates that sub-federal commitments to a Climate Registry and regional cap and trade systems exceed those of the federal government.

Based on this discussion, it is clear that Harper was not a primary catalyst for greater provincial international autonomy. Instead, this decentralization, which occurred over several decades, was due to a number of factors. The first is the increasing intrusiveness of foreign trade agreements into areas of domestic policy space. As these commitments included areas of provincial jurisdiction, provinces began developing expertise and bureaucratic resources in these issue areas. The institutions of Canadian federalism were able to respond to these sub-federal pressures by incorporating provincial governments into existing frameworks of inter-governmental relations, especially those related to federal-provincial consultation.

Greater provincial autonomy was also consistent with the ongoing decentralization of Canadian federalism in general. As Donald Savoie has suggested, 'it became much more fashionable to talk about autonomy' for Canadian provinces in the 1980s, especially with Joe Clark's 'community of communities' approach to federal-provincial relations. Brian Mulroney's cancellation of the NEP, and the Meech Lake Accord, further reinforced this agenda. Subsequent Liberal governments under Chrétien and Martin also embraced devolution of powers, primarily to appease Québec.[68] It is interesting to note that before Coyne complained about the 'dismembering of Canada,' Michael Bliss critiqued Martin's willingness to give Québec greater international autonomy as legitimizing an 'independent country within the hollow shell of something called Canada'.[69] Finally, there is the fact that new prime ministers rarely lead

to significant change in this policy area. Most sub-federal international issues in Canada are handled at the desk officer or middle management levels of Foreign Affairs and International Trade and/or other line departments, which typically guarantees considerable continuity on these files.

A cynic might wonder why Harper would claim credit for the apparent expansion of provincial international autonomy. One of the oldest rules of politics is to 'grab the low-hanging fruit' and it is easy for elected officials to seek thanks for developments that already exist. There are also obvious political benefits to be gained by appealing to Québec voters, who may not support independence in this current political climate, but certainly endorse greater provincial autonomy. In that regard, it is also interesting to note that few provinces desire significant autonomy in sub-federal foreign affairs due to limited budgets and bureaucratic resources. In fact, it can be argued that Alberta is the only other province seeking similar levels of control in this policy area. Once again, this provides political benefits for the Prime Minister as he seeks to secure political support in his home province.

Key Terms

Autonomy

Economic Policy

Foreign Policy

Foreign Relations

Trade Policy

Trade Promotion

Notes

1. Andrew Coyne, 'Dismembering Canada,' *Ottawa Citizen*, 30 May 2006, A14.
2. Eugene R. Wittkopf, Charles W. Kegley Jr, and James M. Scott, *American Foreign Policy: Pattern and Process*, 6th ed. (Belmont CA: Thomson Wadsworth, 2003), 14.
3. Earl H. Fry, 'The United States of America' in *Foreign Relations in Federal Countries: A Global Dialogue on Federalism, vol. 5*, ed., Hans J. Michelmann (Montreal and Kingston: McGill-Queen's University Press, 2008).
4. Kim Richard Nossal, *The Patterns of World Politics* (Scarborough ON: Prentice-Hall Allyn and Bacon Canada, 1997), 279.
5. The first consolidated efforts to deal with the international activity of sub-federal units occurred in, Ivo Duchacek, ed., 'Federated States and International Relations,' *Publius* 14, no. 4 (Fall 1984). For a review of perforated sovereignty and paradiplomacy, see Ivo Duchacek, Daniel Latouche and Garth Stevenson, eds., *Perforated*

Sovereignties and International Relations: Trans-Sovereign Contacts of Subnational Governments (New York: Greenwood Press, 1988); and Hans J. Michelmann and Panayotis Soldatos, eds., *Federalism and International Relations: The Role of Subnational Units* (Oxford: Clarendon Press, 1990).

6. Francisco Aldecoa and Michael Keating, eds., *Paradiplomacy in Action: The Foreign Relations of Subnational Governments* (London: Frank Cass, 1999).

7. Brian Hocking, *Localizing Foreign Policy: Non-Central Governments and Multilayered Diplomacy* (New York: St Martin's Press, 1993); and Brian Hocking, ed., *Foreign Relations and Federal States* (London: Leicester University Press, 1993).

8. Earl H. Fry, *The Expanding Role of State and Local Governments in US Foreign Affairs* (New York: Council of Foreign Relations Press, 1998).

9. Michelle Sager, *One Voice or Many? Federalism and International Trade* (New York: LFB Scholarly Publishing, 2002).

10. John Kincaid, 'Globalization and Federalism in the United States: Continuity in Adaptation' in *The Impact of Global and Regional Integration on Federal Systems: A Comparative Analysis,* eds., Harvey Lazar, Hamish Telford, and Ronald L. Watts (Montreal and Kingston: McGill-Queen's University Press, 2003). See also John M. Kline, 'Continuing Controversies over State and Local Foreign Policy Sanctions in the United States,' *Publius* 29, no. 2 (Spring 1999), 111–134.

11. Robert Stumberg and Matthew C. Porterfield, 'Who Preempted the Massachusetts Burma Law? Federalism and Political Accountability Under Global Trade Rules,' *Publius* 31, no. 3 (Summer 2001): 181–182.

12. Douglas M. Brown and Earl H. Fry, eds., *States and Provinces in the International Economy* (Berkeley: Institute of Governmental Studies Press, University of California, 1993); Grace Skogstad, 'International Trade Policy and Canadian Federalism: A Constructive Tension?' in *Canadian Federalism: Performance, Effectiveness, and Legitimacy,* eds., Herman Bakvis and Grace Skogstad (Toronto: Oxford University Press, 2002); G. Bruce Doern and Brian W. Tomlin, *Faith and Fear: The Free Trade Story* (Toronto: Stoddart Publishing, 1991).

13. Stephen de Boer, 'Canadian Provinces, US States and North American Integration: Bench Warmers or Key Players?' in *Choices: Canada's Options in North America* 8, no. 4 (2002), 2–24.

14. John F. Helliwell, *How Much Do National Borders Matter?* (Washington, DC: Brookings Institution Press, 1998); and Michael A. Anderson and Stephen L.S. Smith, 'Canadian Provinces in World Trade: Engagement and Detachment,' *Canadian Journal of Economics* 32, no. 1 (1999), 22–38.

15. Robert G. Richards, 'The Canadian Constitution and International Economic Relations' in Douglas M. Brown and Murray G. Smith, eds., *Canadian Federalism: Meeting Global Economic Challenges?* (Kingston: Institute of Intergovernmental Relations, Queen's University, 1991); Gerald Baier, 'Judicial Review and Canadian Federalism' in *Canadian Federalism: Performance, Effectiveness, and Legitimacy*; and Christopher J. Kukucha, 'From Kyoto to the WTO: Evaluating the Constitutional Legitimacy of the Provinces in Canadian Foreign Trade and Environmental Policy,' *Canadian Journal of Political Science* 38, no. 1 (2005), 129–52.

16. Nelson Michaud, 'Canada and Québec on the World Stage: Defining New Rules?' in Andrew F. Cooper and Dane Rowlands, eds., *Canada Among Nations 2006: Minorities and Priorities* (Montreal and Kingston: McGill-Queen's University Press, 2006); Louis Balthazar, Louis Bélanger, Gordon Mace, et al., *Trente ans de Politique Extérieure du Québec, 1960–1990* (Québec/Sillery: Septentrion and CQRI, 1993); and Luc Bernier, 'Mulroney's International "Beau Risque": The Golden Age of Quebec's Foreign Policy,' in *Diplomatic Departures: The Conservative Era in Canadian Foreign Policy, 1984–93,* eds., Nelson Michaud and Kim Richard Nossal (Vancouver: UBC Press, 2001).

17. Donald E. Abelson and Michael Lusztig, 'The Consistency of Inconsistency: Tracing Ontario's Opposition to the North American Free Trade Agreement,' *Canadian Journal of Political Science* 29, no. 4 (1996), 681–98.

18. Ian Robinson, 'Neo-Liberal Trade Policy and Canadian Federalism Revisited,' in *New Trends in Canadian Federalism,* 2nd ed., François Rocher and Miriam Smith eds. (Peterborough: Broadview Press, 2003).

19. Christopher J. Kukucha, *The Provinces and Canadian Foreign Trade Policy* (Vancouver: UBC Press, 2008).

20. Kim Richard Nossal, *The Politics of Canadian Foreign Policy* (Scarborough: Prentice-Hall Canada, 1985), 199–200.

21. Kim Richard Nossal, *The Politics of Canadian Foreign Policy*, 3rd ed. (Scarborough: Prentice Hall Canada, 1997), 326.

22. Stéphane Roussel and Charles-Alexandre Théorêt, 'A "Distinct Strategy"? The Use of Canadian Strategic Culture by the Sovereigntist Movement in Québec, 1968–1996,' *International Journal* 59, no. 3 (2004), 557–78.

23. Gouvernement du Québec, Ministère des Internationales, Labour Mobility: France and Québec Sign Historic Agreement, www.mri.gouv.qc.ca/en/_scripts/Actualites/ViewNew.asp?NewID=5898&lang=en (17 October 2008).

24. Stéphane Paquin, 'Quelle Place pour les Provinces Canadiennes dans les Organisations et les Négociations Internationales du Canada à la Lumiére des Pratiques au Sein d'Autres Fédérations?' *Canadian Public Administration* 48, no. 4 (2005): 477–505.

25. Peter W. Hogg, *Constitutional Law of Canada*, vol. 1 (Toronto: Thomson Carswell, 1997), 11:3 –11:18.

26. Sarah McGregor, 'McGuinty's Trip to China set on Making Business Contacts, not Announcements,' *Embassy: Canada's Foreign Policy Newsweekly*, 21 September 2005, 9.

27. Brian Abeda, 'New Brunswick Looking Beyond US Relationship: Maritime Province Eyes New Markets in France and China,' *Embassy: Canada's Foreign Policy Newsweekly*, 21 September 2005, 12.

28. Christina Leadlay, 'Alberta-Asia Trade Will Need Infrastructure Improvements,' *Embassy: Canada's Foreign Policy Newsweekly*, 21 September 2005.

29. Nossal, *The Politics of Canadian Foreign Policy*, 236.

30. Personal interview, 2 June 2003. The federal, provincial, and industry officials interviewed for this study spoke on the condition of anonymity with the understanding there would be no direct quotations without permission. Future references will cite only the dates of these meetings. Locations are excluded given the small number of officials working in this policy area (to best ensure confidentiality).

31. Personal interview, 28 May 2003.

32. Personal interview, 29 May 2003.

33. Ontario, Ministry of Economic Development, Ontario Opens Marketing Centre in Paris: McGuinty Government Promoting Ontario's Economy In France, www.ontariocanada.com/ontcan/page.do?page=6143&lang=en (10 July 2008).

34. Gouvernement du Québec, Ministère des Internationales, Québec Offices Abroad, www.mri.gouv.qc.ca/en/ministere/bureaux_etranger/bureaux_etranger.asp (10 July 2008).

35. Jane Taber, 'The Empty Spot on the Prime Minister's Wall,' *Globe and Mail*, 23 December 2006), A5.

36. Donald V. Smiley, *The Federal Condition in Canada* (Toronto: McGraw-Hill Ryerson, 1987).

37. Personal interview, 12 November 2009.

38. Mark Crawford, 'Truth or Consequences? The Law and Politics of the GATS Health Care Debate,' *Canadian Foreign Policy* 12, no. 2 (2005), 108.

39. Personal interview, 2 August 2004.

40. Crawford, 'Truth or Consequences?' 104–5.

41. J. Anthony VanDuzer, 'Health, Education, and Social Services in Canada: The Impact of the GATS,' www.dfait-maeci.gc.ca/tna-nac/documents/health-edu-ss-gats-en.pdf (11 June 2005), 78.

42. Personal interview, 30 May 2002.

43. T.M. Apsey and J.C. Thomas, 'The Lessons of the Softwood Lumber Dispute: Politics, Protectionism and the Panel Process,' www.acah.org/aspey.htm (13 August 2006), 12–19.

44. Wendy Leung, 'BC OK's Amended Softwood Agreement,' *Vancouver Sun*, 17 August 2006, A1.

45. British Columbia, *Ministry of Forests, BC Heartlands Economic Strategy—Forests: The Forestry Revitalization Plan* (Victoria: Ministry of Forests, 2003), 10–20.

46. Denis Lemieux and Ana Stuhec, *Review of Administrative Action Under NAFTA* (Scarborough: Carswell, 1999), 65–66.

47. International Trade Canada, Consultations on FTAA and WTO Negotiations: Sectoral Consultations—Government Procurement, www.dfait-maeci.gc.ca/tna-nac/discussion/govproc-en.asp (17 May 2005).

48. 'Buy American: NAFTA did its Best to Help,' *Globe and Mail*, 10 June 2009, A14.

49. Personal interview, 12 November 2009.

50. Personal interview, 2 June 2003.

51. Personal interview, 28 May 2003; Personal interview, 29 May 2003.

52. Personal interview, 31 August 2005.

53. Personal interview, 4 June 2003.

54. Personal interview, 31 May 2004.

55. Personal interview, 2 June 2004.

56. Western Governors Association et al., 'Protocol Among the Members of the Western Governors Association Governing the Siting and Permitting of Interstate Electrical Transmission Lines in the Western United States,' www.fs.fed.us/specialuses/documents/interagency_wga_elec_trans_Protocol.pdf (23 June 2002).

57. Alberta, International and Intergovernmental Affairs, US Pacific Northwest–Alberta Relations (Edmonton: Government of Alberta, 2004); and Alberta, International and Intergovernmental Affairs, Montana–Alberta Relations (Edmonton: Government of Alberta, 2004).

58. Personal interview, 19 December 2002.

59. Theodore H. Cohn, 'Transportation and Competitiveness in North America: The Cascadian and San Diego-Tijuana Border Regions,' in *Holding the Line: Borders in a Global World*, eds., Heather N. Nicol and Ian Townsend-Gault (Vancouver: UBC Press, 2005), 205–08.

60. Gouvernement du Québec, Ministère des Internationales, 'MRI's Role in International Solidarity,' www.mri.gouv.qc.ca/en/solidarite_internationale/index.asp (30 September 2008).

61. Gouvernement du Québec, Ministère des Internationales, 'Support for Governance in the Republic of Haiti – Signing of Tripartite Agreement Between the Governments of Canada, Québec and Haiti,' www.mri.gouv.qc.ca/en/informer/salle_de_presse/communiques/textes/2007/2007_11_07.asp (30 September 2008).

62. Personal interview, 29 August 2008.

63. Secretariat, Commission for Environmental Cooperation, Factual Record: BC Logging Submission (SEM-00-004), www.cec.org/files/pdf/sem/00-4-FFR_en.pdf (27 June 2003).

64. Secretariat, Commission for Environmental Cooperation, Factual Record: BC Mining Submission (SEM 98–004), www.cec.org/files/pdf/sem/98-4-FFR_en.pdf (27 June 2003).

65. Jeremy Wilson, 'The Commission for Environmental Cooperation and North American Migratory Bird Conservation: The Potential of the NAAEC Citizen Submission Procedure,' *Journal of International Wildlife Law and Policy* 6, no. 3 (2003), 205–31.

66. Christopher J. Kukucha and Tom Keating, 'Of "Bad Boys" and "Spoiled Brats": Alberta in Canadian Foreign Policy' in *Canada Among Nations 2007: What Room for Manoeuvre?* eds., Jean Daudelin and Daniel Schwanen (Montreal and Kingston: McGill-Queens University Press, 2007), 108–27.

67. BC Climate Action Secretariat, Western Climate Initiative, www.climateactionsecretariat.gov.bc.ca/clas/mediaroom/fact/initiative.html (15 September 2008).

68. Les Perreaux, 'Four Degrees of Centralization: The Recent History of Provincial Autonomy in Canada can be Divided into Four Distinct Eras,' *Globe and Mail*, 30 July 2008, A7.

69. Michael Bliss, 'A Country Going to Pieces,' *National Post*, 22 October 2004, A18.

16

THE MYTH OF THE PACIFIC SOCIETY: QUÉBEC'S CONTEMPORARY STRATEGIC CULTURE

Stéphane Roussel and Jean-Christophe Boucher[1]

INTRODUCTION

One of the most enshrined notions in Canadian foreign policy is that the French-speaking Québécois have a different attitude toward many issues than other Canadians, resulting in a national division that has come to be known as 'the two solitudes'. This attitudinal difference is said to be particularly striking on defence and security policy issues. Historian J. L. Granatstein calls the phenomenon 'the pacifist Québec'[2]—a phenomenon labelled by Jean-Sébastien Rioux as 'conventional wisdom'. According to this view, Rioux claims,

'English and French-Canadians hold differing views on security and defence issues, with French-Canadians being more dovish, isolationist, and antimilitary than their Anglophone counterparts. This world-view allegedly causes Québécois to oppose increases in defence spending, to be against military interventions overseas, and to favour using the Canadian Forces (CF) only in humanitarian or peacekeeping roles'.[3] In short, Québécois are more pacifist, isolationist, and/or antimilitary than their compatriots. Two sets of evidence are generally used in the literature to support that claim. The first is a list of historical events, usually centered on the two world wars, which are used to describe the defiance and the hostility of French-Canadians toward military institutions, and their reluctance to serve in the armed forces. The second is public opinion polls that allegedly show, one after the other, a considerable difference on foreign and defence matters between the two linguistic groups (or, more precisely, between Québec and other Canadian provinces).

Quite aside from any political instrumentalization that one can make of such claims (from outright accusations that the Québécois are cowards and anti-Canadian, to a proclamation of the distinctiveness of Québec's society), this difference in attitude is believed to be a major factor in Canada's foreign policy decision-making. According to J.L. Granatstein, Québécois are given a disproportionate influence in this process and are thus 'deforming' Canada's foreign policy. This phenomenon is supposed to be at work in such events as the decision of the Chrétien government not to participate in the 'coalition of the willing' against Iraq in March 2003 and Paul Martin's failure to support the US program on missile defence.[4] The thesis that Québec's stance affects Canada's foreign policy is part of the 'conventional wisdom' since the latter tends to perceive the opposition to the two above-named US initiatives as an extension of Québec's hostility to the creation of a Canadian Navy at the beginning of the twentieth century or to the conscription measures during the two world wars.

This chapter offers a different interpretation of the nature of Québécois' views on military issues and questions whether the historical record supports the idea that Québécois are, in fact, 'pacifists'. In other words, is it true that Québécois are generally more distrustful or critical than other Canadians toward the use of the armed forces as an instrument of national and international policy? Has this attitude changed over time? Is the conventional wisdom regarding Québec still useful in

explaining contemporary trends in public opinion? Is the critical stance observed in 2003 on the Iraq issue the same as the one observed in 1910, 1917, or 1942? We will try to show that neither of the two main sets of data used to support the claim of the 'pacifist Québec' thesis are as convincing as they seem. If French-Canadians could be labelled as antimilitary or isolationist (but certainly not 'pacifist') until the mid-twentieth century, things have changed since then. Indeed, we will argue that French-Canadians have expressed an 'internationalist' attitude toward defence and security matters.

One of the key problems in defining a society's attitude toward a given issue is the definition of the concepts. Notions such as 'pacifism,'[5] 'antiwar,'[6] 'antimilitarism,'[7] 'anti-imperialism,' 'isolationism,'[8] and 'neutralism'[9] are generally left undefined and vague by authors. As a result, these central concepts are treated as if they were 'naturally' linked to each other. In some cases, they are considered synonymous. Worse yet, they are generally associated (as a cause and/or a consequence) with other political attitudes, such as 'anti-Americanism'[10] or, more commonly, 'nationalism'. Not surprisingly, this confusion obscures any attempt to understand the origin or the nature of Québécois' stance toward defence issues. In fact, it allows commentators to explain any critical attitudes toward war or defence by the same vague clichés, as if public opinion in Québec has been (and remains) homogeneous and unanimous over the last 250 years, no matter the context.

For our purposes, the term 'pacifism' is defined as an opposition on moral, legal, emotional, and/or ideological grounds to the use of force (war in particular) to settle political differences.[11] 'Antimilitarism' is defined as a rejection of or reluctance toward military institutions, ethos, and values. While historically associated with the labour movement of the early twentieth century, this concept, as we define it, includes those who are opposed to military institutions without necessarily rejecting violence as a political instrument (i.e., insurrection against a tyrannical government). 'Isolationism' is defined as an opposition to military commitments abroad in general, while 'anti-imperialism' is defined as an opposition to military commitments that serve first and foremost the interests of a great power. However, it must be noted that neither 'isolationism' nor 'anti-imperialism' precludes military preparedness (including high defence spending) or involvement in a conflict if it serves the defence of the national territory or any other clear national interest. 'Anti-Americanism' is a critical attitude toward what is perceived as US values, ethos, culture, and politics. In its moderate version, it represents a critical attitude toward *some* of these ideas, or toward *some* American leaders or even some decisions made by the US government.[12] In the latter case, however the adequacy of the concept itself remains debatable, since it encompasses situational attitudes.

Finally, the notion of 'internationalism,' which is central in this chapter, is frequently defined as the opposite of isolationism. However, the chief aim of internationalism is to contribute to the peace and stability of the global system through policies premised upon functional and institutionalist principles. It calls for a reinforcement of international institutions (including international law) and organizations, and rests on the belief that international problems must be addressed by an active policy. In Canada, this set of ideas is strongly associated, sometimes wrongly, with the figure of Lester B. Pearson, who was minister of foreign affairs from 1948 to 1957 and prime minister from 1963 to 1968).[13]

Another concept that brings confusion is the word 'Québécois'. For the vast majority of authors addressing the 'pacifist Québec' question, the word designates, implicitly or explicitly, the French-speaking population living in the territory of the province of Québec. This definition makes sense, in that the linguistic divide in that province is the most visible manifestation of a cultural and historical distinctiveness that might explain differences in the attitude toward war and defence. Nevertheless, this definition falls short on two counts. First, it omits two other important groups—out-of-Québec Francophones and English-speaking Québécois. To what extent do Anglo-Québécois (as well as non-Francophone Québec immigrants of the first generation) share the same views as their Francophone neighbours? Similarly, to what extent do Francophone communities of New Brunswick or Ontario share the same views on issues relevant to a study such as this one? Unfortunately, it is difficult to answer these questions since there is little data that tracks the opinions of these specific groups. Therefore, they will not be included in this study.

The second problem with the common definition of 'Québécois' is that a fair number of authors assume the existence of a straight connection between the attitudes displayed by pre-1960s French-Canadians and post-1960s Québécois. Such assumptions are commonsensical on the surface, since identity and culture (including strategic culture) extend some of their roots into history. Nevertheless, this connection must be verified on an issue-by-issue basis. Again, however, a lack of comparative data makes this verification difficult, especially for the pre-1945 period, during which polls were almost non-existent. Moreover, the context after the *révolution tranquille* is different enough to raises doubts. Thus, in this article, we are not making that assumption regarding attitudinal continuity in Québec; we will consider various historical periods separately. We will *not* assume, for example, that the critical attitude displayed by French-Canadians toward conscription in 1917–18 is an expression of the same phenomenon as the demonstration against the invasion of Iraq by the US-led coalition forces some 85 years later. On the contrary, our main hypothesis, as expressed below, will question directly this assumption. This approach will allow us to provide alternative and separate interpretations for behaviours that could otherwise be viewed as similar in essence.

Heuristic considerations aside, we recognize, as do most commentators, that the Québécois hold a different attitude than other Canadians toward military issues and the use of force. *However*, the intensity and motivation explaining this viewpoint have evolved over time, such that the nature of this stance has changed since the 'Quiet Revolution', if not since the end of the Second World War. Nowadays, if Québécois are still hesitant about the use of force, they have lost their isolationist and antimilitarist reflexes. In short, their strategic culture has changed.[14] Although they openly support military operations to re-establish the rule of law or to assist endangered populations, they remain reluctant to use force as a means to resolve conflicts or solve other social and political problems, especially if an intervention seems designed to serve the interests of a greater power. In sum, this chapter questions the usual clichés and attempts to formulate a more nuanced understanding of what Québec wants in terms of defence and foreign policy.

LESSONS FROM THE PAST: ISOLATIONISM AND ANTIMILITARISM (1760–1945)

The image of Québécois as pacifists, isolationists, and antimilitarists comes primarily from an interpretation of history; therefore, we must look at the past to understand the origins of today's perception. In this historical overview of Québec's relationship with military issues, we first try to show that, for about two hundred years—the span from 1760 to 1945—Québécois society (or 'French-Canadian society,' as it called itself before the 1960s) generally saw military force in a critical light. It was

during this period that the foundations of the 'pacifist Québec' were established. Then, because some indicators suggest that since the end of the 1960s, Québécois have come to see military force from a different perspective, we argue that although attitudes may seem similar, Québécois' position on military issues has evolved. From an antimilitarist and isolationist stance, Québec's society has become more internationalist, and nowadays regards the use of force as legitimate, albeit only under specific conditions. Finally, we propose a hypothesis to explain this gradual transformation, which took place between the 1970s and 1990s.

Rejecting the Army and the Empire?

At first glance, the history of Québec seems to support (and justify) the idea that this society is pacifist, antimilitarist, and isolationist. Although it is rarely mentioned today, the Conquest of 1758–1760, in which Nouvelle-France was defeated by British troops, was a violent and traumatizing experience that left deep scars.[15] Humiliated by the Conquest, French-Canadians turned their backs on military affairs and transformed their defeat into an 'antimilitarist tradition'.[16] In a relatively short period of time, the French-speaking population forgot the years when Nouvelle-France was a 'vast military camp perpetually at war'[17] and adopted an attitude of indifference to British–US bickering over territory or commercial issues. Even though the Catholic Church, which saw its status confirmed by the Québec Act of 1774, encouraged collaboration with the new political and economic masters of Québec and was critical of any idea of an annexation by the United States, French-Canadians showed a reluctance to defend the colony in the name of the English king or of London's merchants. The disappearance of the French military elite following the 1760 defeat further weakened the interest of French-Canadians in military institutions. According to historian Roch Legault, this phenomenon would have an effect on subsequent generations of Québécois.[18]

The attitude of French-Canadians toward the military events of the late nineteenth century and first half of the twentieth century is often used to explain the origins of their antimilitarism.[19] For the most part, French-Canadians refused to participate in British efforts to defend the colony from American invasions in 1775 and 1812, notwithstanding the romantic image of Canadian Charles Michel de Salaberry and his men in the Châteauguay skirmishes of 1813. Likewise, in 1899, Henri Bourassa and Canadian nationalists opposed Canadian participation in the Boer War, arguing that they were Canadians and not members of the British Empire.[20] Ten years later, they contested with the same passion the creation of a Canadian navy destined essentially to reinforce the British Royal Navy.

Probably one of the most cited events in the making of the pacifist myth occurred in 1917–18. Because the battles of the First World War were devouring men at an alarming rate, Robert Borden's Unionist government decided in May 1917 to introduce conscription measures in Canada. The opposition to such a policy was fierce in Québec, mainly from the nationalist and union elites, but also among the people generally. Riots broke out in Montreal and Québec City, and on Easter Monday, 1918 troops fired into the crowd, killing four and wounding scores of protestors.[21] Anti-conscription movements did not necessarily overlap with antiwar positions, however. Henri Bourassa, for example, initially supported participation in the First World War, but strongly opposed conscription measures. It is important to note that the trigger for these uprisings were the conscription measures, not the participation in the war effort.

This gloomy scenario seemed to repeat itself a generation later when, in 1942, Prime Minister William Lyon Mackenzie King asked the population to allow him to repudiate his promise not to implement conscription—a promise made to help Québec's Liberals defeat Maurice Duplessis's Union Nationale in the 1939 provincial elections. The 1942 plebiscite illustrated once again the schism separating the two 'solitudes' of Canada. While 80 per cent of English-speaking Canadians agreed to the federal government request, 85 per cent of French-speaking Canadians did not.[22] It was not until 1944 that Mackenzie King implemented conscription, forced to enact that drastic policy in an attempt to compensate for the losses in the battle of Normandy. However, the crisis of the Second World War was very different than the one of 1917–1918. While Borden bluntly imposed his decision on French-Canadians, Mackenzie King proceeded much more carefully, and this second conscription crisis did not leave the same acrimonious historical legacy as the first.[23]

Surely, many factors explain the uneasiness or indifference of French-Canadians toward military issues, and the persistent mistrust of the use of force. On the one hand, through the Cold War, the regular army in Canada remained fundamentally a British institution, one in which career opportunities for French-Canadians were few unless at the price of assimilation. There were many Francophone militia regiments in Québec but, like their English counterparts, they were essentially social clubs in which military values were not strong. In 1914, Francophones constituted only 4 per cent of the first contingent formed to fight in Europe. It must be pointed out, however, that Anglophones of Canadian origin were not doing significantly better, since 70 per cent of the volunteers were born outside the country. Similarly, fewer than 4 per cent of the Royal Military College graduates were Francophones.[24] The creation in September 1914 of French-speaking battalions, including the one which would soon be raised to regiment status—the Royal 22e Régiment—improved the situation, if only marginally.

In light of these facts, defiance toward a military institution perceived as 'foreign' in nature is the first argument explaining the French-Canadian attitude. In this context, labelling French-Canadians as 'antimilitaristic' (that is, as rejecting military institutions of the time) appears clearly more appropriate than the usual 'pacifist' epithet, because their antimilitarism was not dictated by ideological or moral principles (although some unions were close to their European counterparts when they denounced participation in a 'capitalist war' prior to 1914[25]). 'Identity' seems a more convincing motivation here, especially where French-Canadian resentment was fuelled by issues that were perceived as attacks against their identity such as the schools' linguistic legislation in Ontario (embodied in 1912 in the infamous Bill 17, which limited French instruction).

The motivation to fight on foreign battlefields was also weak. The defence of the British Empire was hardly a compelling notion for a population that had lived for generations in North America. The Canadian territory was not threatened, and, if it were to be, it would be from the south, following a clash between Britain and the United States. Furthermore, if this threat were to materialize, there would not be much that Canada could do to counteract it. This was the central argument that the nationalists, rallying behind Henri Bourassa, made against the dual allegiance (British and Canadian) espoused by the imperialists, for whom, more often than not, the former—i.e., British— was more important than the latter. Thus, French-Canadian negative perception of military institutions was not counterbalanced by a feeling of insecurity from an external threat that would justify the existence of such institutions.

Consequently, it seems more fitting to use the terms 'isolationism' or 'anti-imperialism' to qualify the French-Canadian attitude toward war during the 1760–1945 period. Québec's political and religious elites essentially tried to discourage the Canadian government from participating in imperial wars and to prevent French-Canadians from joining foreign military ventures. In general, this position stemmed from the ability to make a distinction between Canadian and imperial interests, which by and large was lacking in the English-Canadian community.[26] Those Anglo-Canadians who had this ability, such as Oscar D. Skelton, under-secretary of state for external affairs in the Mackenzie King government, were more inclined to accept isolationistic logic.[27] In French Canada, this isolationism was mostly the manifestation of a desire to protect Canadian society from negative external influences. However, it is conceivable that for many French-Canadians, the perception that a war was an *imperial* one seemed the most important variable in determining the legitimacy of Canadian participation in armed conflicts. Unfortunately, it is very difficult to establish a clear difference between isolationism (an opposition to military expedition abroad *in general)* and anti-imperialism (an opposition to war fought to defend the interests of the British Empire), since the two are closely related during the time period under review.

It must be noted that while isolationism/anti-imperialism and antimilitarism have common roots (both being a rejection of British institutions), they do not necessarily go hand in hand. For example, Henri Bourassa and some high representatives of the Catholic Church were not against the creation of military institutions or the Canadian participation in the Boer Wars or the First World War, but against the imperialist dimension that they represented. For French-Canadian nationalists, a Canadian armed force organized to protect the Canadian territory was perfectly acceptable.

The Military Record of a 'Pacifist' Nation

Arguing that French-Canadians have, since the Conquest, adopted a pacifist attitude and that pacifism still dominates the society is factually and ideologically flawed. As a brief historical overview of Québec's military history will show, the foundation of Québécois' attitude cannot be pacifism.

During the nineteenth century, French-Canadians participated in numerous armed conflicts. In November 1837, the Patriots of Lower Canada, under the leadership of Louis-Joseph Papineau and Dr. Jean-Olivier Chénier, took up arms in hopes of getting out of the constitutional quagmire in which the two provinces (Upper and Lower Canada) had been sinking for more than twenty years. In 1838, a series of violent incidents took place which were promptly put down by British troops. Hundreds of Patriots were killed or injured; twelve were hanged in February 1839; and the villages where the insurgents had gathered—namely, St-Charles, St-Denis, St-Eustache, and St-Benoit—were plundered and burned.

Similarly, during the American Civil War (1860–1865), thousands of French-Canadians (including Americans of French-Canadian origin) joined the Union army. For many years it was believed that their numbers may have been as high as 40,000,[28] but recent research by the historian Jean Lamarre established that the actual figures were from 10,000 to 15,000. According to Lamarre, most of these French-Canadians were following a more economic than ideological call, and their participation should be put in the larger context of the massive French-Canadian emigration to the United States during the nineteenth century.[29]

In 1868, 498 French-Canadian volunteers enrolled in the Papal Zouave corps, hoping to defend the papal territory from the nationalist forces of Giuseppe Garibaldi during the Third Italian War of Independence. Members of this small group were treated like heroes by the Catholic Church and Québec's population. Ultimately, only 300 of them crossed the Atlantic Ocean to Italy, where their sole combat experience was the ragtag defence of Rome in September 1870.[30] Although this adventure appears quite quixotic, it nonetheless reveals a willingness on the part of the Québécois to participate in wars on foreign territories if the cause was upheld by the Catholic Church. In contrast, French drafters trying to recruit volunteers to defend the Napoleon III Empire were not nearly as successful.[31]

In 1869, and most of all in 1885, the Northwest Métis (in what became Manitoba and Saskatchewan) did not hesitate to follow Louis Riel and take up arms in defence of his provisional provincial government. At the same time, some French-Canadians joined the *voyageurs* group formed to assist the expeditionary force sent to Sudan in the hope of rescuing the troops of the British General Charles Gordon, trapped inside Khartoum. This force was composed of Francophones, Anglophones, and Amerindians from the Montreal area. While the disaster of Khartoum stirred commotion in the imperialist Canadian elite,[32] in Québec it was the hanging of Louis Riel in November that attracted attention.

Finally, we must remember the enrolment of 63 French-Canadians in the International Brigades that fought during the Spanish Civil War (1936–9). Half of those individuals served in the Mackenzie-Papineau Battalion (the 'Mac-Pap'). Most were members of the Canadian communist party.[33]

From this brief, and obviously non-exhaustive, historical survey, three things should be inferred. First, French-Canadians have participated in numerous armed conflicts—sometimes in small numbers, as in Spain, and sometimes constituting a significant force, as in the American Civil War. The conscription crisis surrounding the two world wars often masks the fact that many Francophones voluntarily enlisted and fought on European battle-fields. There is no doubt that French-Canadians have had an essentially negative historical experi-ence with the use of force and military institutions, and it is possible that this experience has to some extent conditioned their attitude toward military expeditions. However, it did not lead to a well thought out, structured discourse on the origins of war and on the condemnation of the use of force on moral, legal, or ideological grounds. Their reaction remained more visceral than rational, limiting an alternative discourse, such as a fundamentally paci-fist one, to provide the basis for a coherent decision-making. More than that, on occasion—in 1837–8, for example, as in 1885—the use of violence seemed like a viable and acceptable solution to most French-Canadians. Thus, it is inappropriate to speak of them as being fundamentally 'pacifist'.

Second, religious institutions played an import-ant role, influencing the French-Canadian outlook on military matters. These institutions helped establish the legitimacy, or lack thereof, of military endeavours, with legitimacy dependent on the atti-tude of the protagonists toward the Catholic Church. Thus, the clergy encouraged the constitu-tion of Papal Zouave units in 1868, but stayed mute on the invasion of Ethiopia in May 1936 by Fascist Italy, which had recovered some legitimacy in Catholic eyes following the Lateran Agreement of 1929. This religious influence was felt, at least for a brief period, during the Cold War as well. If French-Canadians finally accepted extraordinary measures such as the creation of the North Atlantic Alliance (1949) or the Korean intervention (1950), it was partly because the Church brandished the threat of communism—perceived as a direct men-ace to conservative values upheld in Québec.

However, Québec was not completely a priest-driven society during this period. There were limits to Catholicism's influence. For example, in spite of sermons arguing to the contrary, the Church was unable to stop the flow of Canadian volunteers joining the Union army during the American Civil War in the hope of improving their own and their families' lives. In contrast, the Church's tepid sup-port for the Métis repression or for the conscrip-tion measures during the two world wars—mainly from a small group of churchmen who wanted to remain in the good graces of the federal govern-ment—was insufficient to calm the people's anger. As for the creation of the Papal Zouave corps, which we might call a success compared to the numbers enrolled in the International Brigades during the Spanish Civil War 70 years later, fewer than 500 vol-unteers is quite a small figure for a population so allegedly attuned to Catholic values.

THE TRANSFORMATION OF QUÉBÉCOIS' ATTITUDE TOWARD MILITARY ISSUES (1945–2006)

A Deceptive Sense of Continuity

The attitude of the Québécois in the debates follow-ing the Second World War has tended to reinforce the myth of a pacifist, isolationist, and antimilitar-ist people. During the Cold War, the Québécois—as they would soon call themselves—showed a greater distrust than their English-Canadian com-patriots toward foreign military commitments. Thus, in 1949, Prime Minister Louis St Laurent launched a 'crusade' to convince the Canadian population, mainly in Québec, to support Can-ada's membership in the Atlantic Alliance.[34] The skepticism against which St Laurent's crusade was directed can be seen in Québec's attitude toward all of Canada's foreign military commitments, such as involvement in Korea, mandatory military service, the acquisition of nuclear weapons by the Can-adian Forces, military cooperation with the United

Kingdom and the Commonwealth, and peaceful coexistence with the USSR. Furthermore, the Québécois were more inclined to be pessimistic during this period than English-Canadians.[35]

After the Cold War, this inclination seemed to endure. For example, in the first moments of the Gulf War in 1990, public opinion among Québécois was significantly less supportive than the opinion expressed by English-Canadians toward the Mulroney government's decision to contribute to the coalition to thwart Iraq's invasion and then to liberate Kuwait.[36] In mid-February 2003, 150,000 Montrealers took to the streets to demonstrate their opposition to possible Canadian participation in the Iraq War.[37] On a lesser scale, in the summer of 2006, many rallies were organized to protest against the Israeli bombardment of Lebanon and Prime Minister Stephen Harper's support for this operation. In early August, one such demonstration, attended by representatives of Québec's political elite as well as by some Hezbollah sympathizers, led to a short but heated debate in Canada. Some English-Canadian columnists saw participation in this event by political leaders as an endorsement of terrorism on the part of Québec, a criticism that triggered a strong response from French editorialists.[38] Finally, one of the key issues championed by the Bloc Québécois in 2003–6 was its opposition to Canadian participation in the ballistic missile defence program proposed by Washington.

Many authors studying this phenomenon see an element of continuity between the Québécois' attitude toward war in the nineteenth century and public sentiment of the early twenty-first century. However, this perceived continuity between the attitudes of French-Canadians before 1960 and those of Québécois after the Quiet Revolution is probably only an illusion. As shown, the historical record does not support the central claim of the 'pacifist society' perspective. Moreover, the argument

behind the Québécois' critical attitude toward the use of force and military institutions changed over time, even if some traces of the traditional concept of isolationism and antimilitarism remain.

There is no doubt that Québec's society has changed since the Quiet Revolution of the 1960s. If this change is particularly striking in the political, social, and economic spheres, what effect has this revolution had on the public's attitude toward defence and security issues? There are many indications that Québec has evolved from a conservative and isolationist society to a more progressive and internationalist one where the use of force is considered acceptable under specific conditions. In his study of Québécois' attitudes between 1945 and 1960, James I. Gow already saw a tendency toward internationalist ideas.[39] During the period of the Quiet Revolution (1960s), this tendency grew, and probably continues to grow today. Two indicators allow us to observe this trend: the political programs of sovereigntist parties aimed mainly at Francophones in Québec, and public opinion polls conducted after the Cold War. Since we have already covered the political program elsewhere,[40] we will focus our attention on the polls.

Québec's Public Opinion Regarding Defence and Security Issues Since 1990

Overall, public opinion polls demonstrate a shift toward internationalist values from an earlier isolationist position. Since the beginning of the 1990s, the publication of more than 60 public opinion polls representing Québécois' views on defence and security issues makes it possible to trace the development of Québec's attitudes on these matters. Although enlightening, Canadian public opinion polls should always be used with great caution, especially if they pertain to foreign policy issues. There are several reasons for this:

- First, there is no systematic examination of public attitudes toward international issues in Canada. Public opinion polls are sparse, and rarely does a pollster ask repetitively the same question on the same issues over a prolonged time span. Hence, comparing the 'evolution' of public opinion over time is a dubious undertaking.

- Second, data on public attitudes regarding Canadian military deployments have not been collected for *all* military missions in the last 30 years. For example, we lack data on most Canadian participation in UN peacekeeping missions across the 1970s and the 1980s.

- Third, methodological considerations have changed over time. Many pre-1980 polls do not publish results by provinces; some acknowledge the linguistic divide between French and English respondents without the province of affiliation. Many polls present significant margins of error, which make comparative analyses troublesome (since we must add the margins of error for the two compared data sets).

- Fourth, polls ask questions, but do not require the respondents to elaborate – to tell *why* he or she feels a certain way. Thus polling results may not always reflect public *knowledge* of an issue. However, as Page and Shapiro demonstrated, even when survey figures signals how ignorant the public are of the complexities of an issue, they still reproduce stable and rational responses to polls.[41]

Hence, we are quite limited by the data provided by pollsters, meaning that any conclusions derived from these results should be made carefully.

The generally consensus, which conforms to the 'pacifist society' thesis, is that the majority of Québécois are opposed to foreign military interventions and that this opposition is much more pronounced than in English-Canadian circles. The dominant image is one of a massive schism between the two communities, recalling the polarized society of the 1942 plebiscite on conscription.[42] This image of the 'two solitudes' is strengthened by episodic bursts of 'inflamed expression' (especially at the beginning of a conflict), when Québécois tend to react vigorously to international events, notably by street demonstrations or other means.

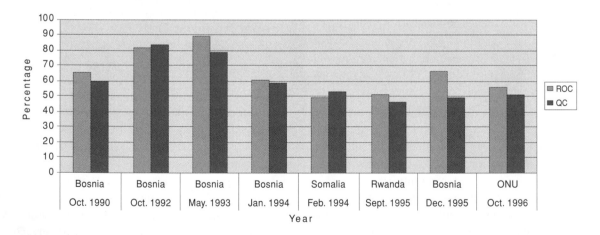

Figure 16.1 Evolution of ROC and QC Public Opinion Regarding Canadian Participation in UN Missions (1990–96)

However, if we analyze the trend over a longer period, another image appears.[43]

The 'pacifist society' label rests on the premise that the majority of French-speaking Québécois are opposed to international Canadian military commitments, and that when Québécois do support such missions, it is generally with great reluctance. However, as shown in Figure 1, a quick overview of public opinion polls reveals that Québécois are generally in favor (i.e., by more than 50 per cent) of missions conducted under the auspices of the United Nations (UN).[44] This support tends to shrink slightly when these missions are led by other organizations or by ad hoc coalitions, as shown in Figure 16.2.

One of the most surprising findings revealed by these polls is a phenomenon of 'strategic convergence' between the French- and the English-Canadian communities. Far from corresponding to the figures of the 1942 plebiscite, polls conducted after 1990 show that the margin separating the two communities is rarely over 10 per cent, regardless of the issue. As illustrated by Figure 2, between 1990 and 2006 there were only four cases where the

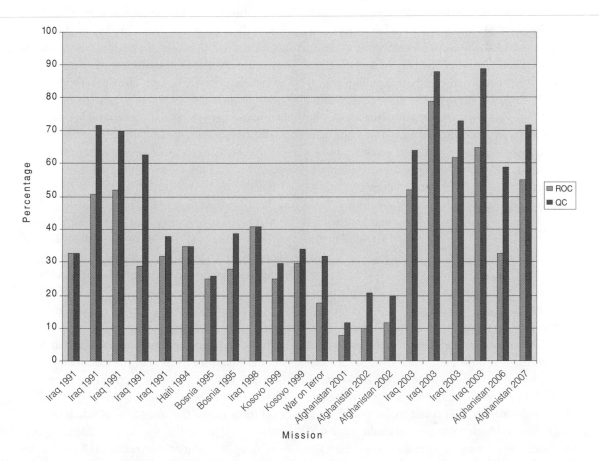

Figure 16.2 Evolution of ROC and QC Public Opinion Opposed to Canadian Participation in Non-UN Missions (1991–2007)

difference between the Québécois and rest of Canada exceeded 10 per cent: the Gulf War of 1991, the War on Terror following September 11th, the participation of Canada in a possible Iraq War in 2003, and the involvement of Canadian troops in southern Afghanistan. For all other cases, even Kosovo—a war which was not UN-sanctioned—the average margin between the two linguistic groups is less than 6 per cent, with the margin of error accounted for.

Another dimension of the 'strategic convergence' between Québec and the rest of Canada is that both groups tend to move in the same direction, reacting similarly to the same events, even if sometimes we observe a temporal lag in reaction. Therefore, when we observe a favourable opinion on a certain mission on the part of French-Canadians, we generally find a corresponding movement in English public opinion—and vice-versa. In brief, not only are the opinions expressed by the Québécois and English-Canadians more comparable than conventional wisdom would have us believe, but also both opinion curves follow the same pattern in time. In light of these results, we can say only that the Québécois are simply more vocal in their opposition to Canadian endeavours abroad; we cannot claim that they are fundamentally different from other Canadians on defence and security issues.[45]

The clear 'Pearsonian' element in the phenomenon of 'strategic convergence' between Québec and rest of Canada— that Prime Minister Pearson's 'liberal internationalism' prevails throughout the country—should help qualify the traditional perception that there is a great divide between the two Canadian communities on defence and security issues. However, that is not to say that there is no difference. On the contrary, we could argue that the Québécois are more internationalist than the Canadian federal government.

So how can we explain the difference—though minimal—that persists between these groups, despite strategic convergence? We could interpret it as an echo of the isolationist and antimilitarist attitude that manifested itself in Québec before 1945, with a very important nuance: until the creation of the United Nations and the invention of peacekeeping missions, it was barely conceivable that Canada would be involved in an overseas military mission that did not somehow serve the interests of the British Empire. (The Papal Zouave expedition, which was not sponsored by the government, is possibly the sole exception.) As noted earlier, during this period, it was very difficult to make a distinction between anti-imperialism and isolationism. Because nowadays multilateral institutions offer the possibility of contributing to missions that are not clearly serving great power interests, it is possible now to make the distinction between isolationism and anti-imperialism. Hence, as Figure 2 indicates, the largest differences between Québec and other provinces occur on conflicts where American interests are at stake (Iraq 1991; Iraq 2003; the War on Terror in 2001 and Afghanistan from 2006–9), while they disappear on conflicts where these interests are less apparent (Haiti, Bosnia, Kosovo). Even if the hypothesis remains fragile, it is tempting to identify at least one element of historical continuity: until 1945, the principal legitimizing factor for military interventions abroad from a French-Canadian perspective was that those interests were serving Canadian rather than British interests; since the end of the Cold War (if not since the 1960s), a similar trend is taking place, but this time in relation to the United States. This conclusion raises the question, which is no less controversial than the Québécois' alleged 'pacifism,' of an 'anti-American' reflex in Québec public opinion.[46]

CULTURE SHIFT: SOCIAL AND CULTURAL TRANSFORMATIONS IN CONTEMPORARY QUÉBEC

The effect of the Quiet Revolution and other societal changes

How can we explain the shift from an isolationist attitude to an internationalist one? On the one hand, it is possible to state that, in fact, Québécois' attitude *did not significantly change*—the old anti-imperialist reflex remains alive, but it is now directed against the United States as a 'successor' of the British Empire. On the other hand, by taking an internationalist stand through the (non-imperialist) UN, Québécois are simply exercising an option that had not existed before the Cold War era. Unfortunately, this second hypothesis is impossible to verify. However, it is possible to gather evidence indicating that a change has occurred in Québec society since the mid-twentieth century, and this change could provide an explanation for the shift from an isolationist attitude to an internationalist one.

Our explanation, which agrees in part with *both* options presented in the preceding paragraph— deals with the concept of 'strategic culture,' by which we mean a set of ideas (concepts, metaphors, images, symbols, etc.) shared by a given community, forming a coherent and persistent whole and helping to shape the group's attitude toward the use of force and the role of military institutions.[47] Because a strategic culture is formed primarily by historical experience, it tends to remain stable over time. However, 'stable' does not mean 'immutable'; strategic culture can change. Sometimes this happens brutally, following a collective trauma (such as the attacks on Pearl Harbor or the World Trade Center), sometimes quite gradually, as socio-political evolution brings about new experiences and influences the reinterpretation of old lessons.[48]

Québec society has not been subjected to a brutal, traumatic shock during the past several decades, but the socio-political context has radically changed since the 1960s. The most prominent socio-political transformations took place during the Quiet Revolution: changes in Québec nationalism, religious practices, attitudes toward military institutions, and the level of education within the population. We examine each in turn.

French-Canadian nationalism (which would become Québécois nationalism) has certainly reinforced the idea that Francophones should refrain from fighting on foreign battlefields to defend foreign—that is, 'English'—interests (meaning British, American, or even English-Canadian interests). However, this nationalism has changed, especially during the 1960s and 1970s, moving from a conservative framework of *survival* to a more *reformist* context—sometimes liberal, sometimes more critical and social democratic.

Traditional Québec nationalism was clerical, rural, and anti-liberal. In the twentieth century, it was personified by Maurice Duplessis, who ruled the province from 1936 to 1939 and from 1944 to his death in 1959. It was concerned first and foremost with the survival of the French-Canadian community and the control of its institutions—in particular, the Catholic Church and the provincial government. However, it did not seek to take Québec out of Confederation. With regard to relations with the rest of the world, Québec's conservative nationalism was rooted in isolationism and a resistance to any commitment (including military commitments) that symbolized or accentuated the perceived oppressed status of French-Canadians or that did not correspond to a narrow definition of Catholic values. This attitude, often interpreted as being pacifist, masks nationalistic values that have very little to do with a judgment on the legitimacy of the use of force to resolve political problems.

Québec's traditional nationalism was called into question after the Second World War because of its inability to meet the needs of a society that was becoming increasingly urbanized, industrialized, prosperous, and educated. According to historian Michael Behiels,[49] this reappraisal was led by two groups. The first group, identified as *Citélibristes* (named after *Cité libre*, the movement's main publication), whose most popular figure was a future prime minister, Pierre E. Trudeau, was driven by the conviction of the universal value of liberalism. Rejecting any project that would encourage the drawing of boundaries and thus the erection of obstacles to the movement of people and the exchange of ideas, the *Citélibristes* saw Québec as a rightful member of the Canadian federation, to which she might contribute and in the midst of which she would benefit through a process of political modernization.

The second group, usually identified as 'neo-nationalists', also wished to modernize Québec's state and society, but following a more social-democratic program. This group grew out of the *Bloc populaire* and the ideas published in *Le Devoir* and *L'Action nationale*. More open to radical social change, they espoused a nationalism that attracted the labour movements, left-wing intellectuals, artists, and the leaders of populist movements.[50] Since the affiliation to Canada was alleged by this group to have caused Québec's backwardness and servility, the combination of their nationalism and reformism brought the movement toward an independentist project, contrary to the *Citélibristes* agenda. The inspiration of left-wing ideas is especially clear in the defence section of the first edition of the Parti Québécois' (PQ) political program, disseminated in 1968.

One of the main differences between traditional nationalism and neo-nationalism is in the groups' understanding of relations with the world. The earlier 'survival nationalism', essentially founded on a relation of otherness with English Canada, resulted in an attitude of inwardness that translated, in the realm of international security, into an isolationist position. Its counterpart, neo-nationalism gradually evolved into a more endogenous vision: it was not enough for Québec to protect and distinguish itself from English Canada anymore. Rather, there was a need to promote an identity and interests considered exclusive to Québec. This logic brought about a desire for affirmation on the international scene and, consequently, the adoption of a more open attitude toward the world, for two reasons. First, both modernization and independence required close ties with other societies and foreign governments. Second, the modernization process, which we have been calling the Quiet Revolution, accelerated this movement of openness by increasing the level of education (hence, of the basic knowledge of the world) and by increasing the number of non-European immigrants. Québec's diminished reluctance regarding international military commitments can be seen as a result of this phenomenon.

Moreover, Québec's nationalism is original in the sense that it is not marked by a glorification of a military past, as it is for many other societies. As Roch Legault said: 'The close relationship between nationalism, nationality, and patriotism on the one hand, and armed forces on the other hand, as can be observed in most Western countries, is almost nonexistent'.[51] Neither is the growth of Québec nationalism a response to a sense of physical insecurity, as is often the case elsewhere. On the contrary, it grew in a context of rejection of, and then a sense of caution in, the use of force. This identity shift might well explain, at least in part, the movement of the Québécois from an isolationist attitude to an internationalist vision, which became a tenet of the PQ's official discourse.

Neo-nationalism's internationalist dimension fed upon the growing openness to the world that swept the province in the second half of the 1960s. From the 1967 World's Fair to the 1976 Olympic Games, international events burgeoned in Québec, while the provincial government began to develop relations with other Francophone governments, especially in Europe and Africa.

Another socio-political phenomenon that transformed the context in which Québécois public opinion has developed was the drastic diminution of the Catholic Church's influence on civil society in the 1960s. This was a remarkable phenomenon, since 'from a society with staunch Catholic roots [. . .] Québec has evolved into the most post-modern region of this continent'.[52] The principal consequence of interest for us here is the fading importance of religious factors as a criterion of the legitimacy of foreign missions. The Church cannot encourage or condemn the people's attitude in favour of a mission anymore.[53]

The third factor worth mentioning is the apparent reconciliation of the Québécois with the Canadian Forces (CF). In the last 60 years, the institution lost its 'British' character to become a Canadian, rather than an imperial, entity. The Canadian Forces also lost the reputation of being an 'English' institution and now is seen as being more open to Francophones. Finally, and more significantly, the CF are not considered an instrument of repression anymore, despite the role played by Canadian troops in the so-called October Crisis of 1970 (involving the kidnapping of a public official by separatists and the enactment of the draconian War Measures Act by the federal government, albeit at the request of the provincial government). This gradual change has probably been influenced by events in which the CF have played (or could have played) a useful role. The conflict in Bosnia (1991–95), the Rwandan genocide (1994), and the Kosovo crisis (1999)—all extensively covered by the media in Québec—have certainly demonstrated the importance of armed forces as an instrument

of peacekeeping and peacemaking. (Note that peacekeeping operations are conducted predominantly by land elements, and it is in this service that a majority of Québécois enlist.) Similarly, local events such as the Oka crisis (1990), involving a property dispute between the First Nations and a Québec municipality, the Saguenay flood (1996), and the North American ice storm (1998) are all positive experiences of military intervention. Images from these experiences have replaced, in Québec's collective memory, the images of repression associated with the conscription crises.

A higher level of scholarship is most certainly another important factor. One of the most tangible signs of the strategic culture shift in Québec's society (though it is difficult to know whether this is a cause or an effect) is the emergence, since the mid-1990s, of a Québec military history. For a long time, Québec maintained a distant relationship with its military past. Academic works on the subject were rare prior to the mid-1990s, and commemorations were ignored by the people and the political elite. The contrast with the current situation is salient – the public celebration in Québec City to support the Valcartier-based contingent to be deployed in Afghanistan for example—as many authors contends.[54]

In short, the Québec society that emerged after the 1960s looked less and less like the French-Canadian society that had been struggling to survive in North America since the Conquest. This transformation is felt in the way the Québécois now view military issues.

The case of Canada's participation to the international mission in Kandahar, Afghanistan (2006–09)

The Canadian government's decision to take part in the international effort in Kandahar, Afghanistan, offers a good, albeit anecdotal, case study to examine further Québec's specificity in regards to defence and security issues in the post-9/11 world. By itself, the Canadian presence in southern Afghanistan since 2006 offers all the essential elements necessary to study Québec's hypothesized pacifism: overseas intervention, no obvious and direct Canadian national interests, combat operations using ground forces (the first time since the Korean war in 1950) and significant military fatalities. Taken collectively, these factors would theoretically point toward a strong Québec's opposition and an explosive political situation that would

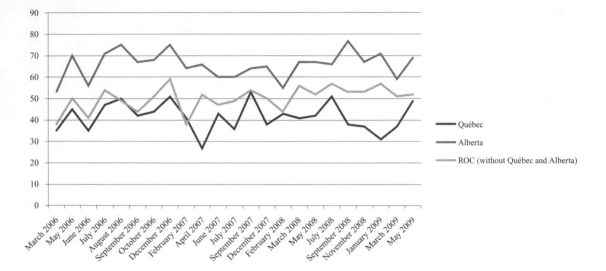

Figure 16.3 Québec, Alberta, and ROC public opinion opposed to Canada's involvement in Afghanistan (2006–2009)[I]

[I] These data were collected from polls conducted by Angus-Reid strategies and Strategic counsel. Specifically: *Angus Reid Strategies*. 2007. Canadians assess Afghan mission: It's about war, not peace (data collected from February 20 to February 21, 2007); *Angus Reid Strategies*. 2007. Canada in Afghanistan: Canadians grow impatient with Afghan mission (data collected from April 19 to April 20, 2007); *Angus Reid Strategies*. 2007. Afghanistan: Canadians still unhappy with Afghan mission (data collected from May 25 to May 28, 2007); *Angus Reid Strategies*. 2007. Afghanistan: Gender gap grows over Afghan mission (data collected from July 9 to July 10, 2007); *Angus Reid Strategies*. 2007. Afghanistan: Canadians think Afghans are benefiting but troops should come home soon (data collected from September 11 to September 12, 2007); *Angus Reid Strategies*. 2007. Afghanistan Mission: Canadians see benefits for Afghan people but a majority still calls for an early end to mission (data collected from December 19 to December 20, 2007); *Angus Reid Strategies*. 2008. Afghanistan Mission: Canadians agree with key points in Manley Report on Afghan mission (data collected from January 31 to February 1, 2008); *Angus Reid Strategies*. 2008. Afghanistan Mission: Canadians disagree with extending mission in Afghanistan until 2011 (data collected from March 17 to March 18, 2008); *Angus Reid Strategies*. 2008. Mission in Afghanistan: Canadians still oppose Afghan mission extension; Reject talks with Taliban (data collected from May 7 to May 8, 2008); *Angus Reid Strategies*. 2008. Mission in Afghanistan: Support for Afghan mission and talks with Taliban dwindles in Canada (data collected from July 2 to July 3, 2008); *Angus Reid Strategies*. 2008. Mission in Afghanistan: Only a third of Canadians agree with Afghanistan mission extension (data collected from September 9 to September 10, 2008); *Angus Reid Strategies*. 2008. Mission in Afghanistan: Canadian majority wants troops out of Afghanistan before 2011 (data collected from November 11 to November 12, 2008); *Angus Reid Strategies*. 2009. Mission in Afghanistan: Canadians question Afghanistan mission, but Alberta bucks the trend (data collected from December 11 to December 12, 2008); *Angus Reid Strategies*. 2009. Mission in Afghanistan: Almost half of Canadians would end Afghanistan mission before 2011 (data collected from February 27 to February 28, 2009); *Angus Reid Strategies*. 2009. Mission in Afghanistan: Half of Canadians adamant about ending Afghan mission before 2011 (data collected from April 30 to May 1, 2009).

potentially strain Canadian national unity. Indeed, the image of 'pacifist Québec' was still alive in the minds of many observers in the summer and fall of 2008. On the eve of the deployment of soldiers from the Royal 22e Régiment, commentators from both from French and English Canada foresaw a harsh reaction when the first soldier bearing a French name was killed in action.[55] However, as we shall argue, public reaction to the Kandahar experience is not characteristic of a pacifist Québec and, instead, exemplifies Québec's contemporary strategic culture.

The opinion polls published between March 2006 and May 2009 examining the fluctuation of attitudes in Québec, Alberta and other provinces (ROC without Québec and Alberta) toward Canada's operation in southern Afghanistan reveal that Québécois remained robustly opposed to Canada's presence in Kandahar. As illustrated by Figure 16.3, an average of 65.7 per cent[56] of Québec's population disagreed with Canada's mission in Afghanistan and would have preferred an early withdrawal. Compared with the rest of Canada, Québécois appear to be more critical than other Canadians on an average of 15 per cent. However, we must note that rest of Canada attitudes remained quite ambiguous in their support to the Afghan intervention, maintaining an average of 50 per cent opposing the mission. Alberta, for its part, stayed generally supportive across the time period with an average of 36.5 per cent opposing Canada's deployment in Kandahar. Nevertheless, the image of a fundamental split between the Francophone and Anglophone communities does not appear to materialize. In truth, Canadian public opinion seems to move along a continuum ranging from Québec to Alberta and indicating a regional divide more than a linguistic one.[57] Accordingly, the rest of Canada looks as if to be caught between two hard places—dovish Québec and hawkish Alberta.

Yet despite Québec's strong objection regarding Canadian involvement in southern Afghanistan, this perception has not translated into an activist and militant movement that could have forced the federal government to reconsider its policy. In hindsight, Québécois opposition remained passive with little or no political consequences for Ottawa and remained a non-factor in the two federal elections of January 2006 and October 2008. This missed opportunity for the 'pacifist' Québec thesis tends to reveal that the province's relationship with defence and military issues is complex and is more than what is conventionally assumed. In our mind, two main factors associated with Québec shifted strategic culture account for this passive opposition.

First, Québec's political and public opinion elites have remained largely sympathetic to the Canadian mission in Kandahar, Afghanistan. Most adopted an internationalist stance toward the Afghanistan mission, wishing for a better equilibrium between combat and humanitarian objectives, but still supporting Canada's presence in Central Asia. Politically, Conservative, Liberal, and even Bloc Québécois leaders in Québec advocated for a military participation in Afghanistan. On this, the Bloc Québécois' position is extremely telling. Although it always demanded that Ottawa refocus its actions toward diplomatic, reconstruction and foreign aid, it still maintained that security was an essential aspect of any endeavour in Afghanistan and that Canada's international responsibilities required its participation in the international effort.[58] On many occasions the Bloc Québécois asserted this position through its comments and votes in the House of Commons. For example, when the NDP proposed a motion for the withdrawal of Canadian troops on 24 April 2007, the Bloc Québécois voted against the motion, insisting that the mission in Kandahar mostly needed a 'rebalancing' to address the causes of terrorism such as poverty. Again in March 2008, during the debate leading to the parliamentary resolution to extend the Canadian mission in southern Afghanistan, where ultimately the Bloc Québécois voted against the extension, Gilles Duceppe legitimized his party's rejection of the motion on the ground that it would be 'irresponsible' to prolonged the mission until 2011 when the government had not specified how much such an extension would cost.[59] Likewise, most print[60] and electronic media have been supportive or nuanced in their coverage of the Canadian military engagement in southern Afghanistan. Following this general consensus from Québec's elites, pacifist movements in Québec have lacked the political clout to convert their position into official policy. Consequently, although Québécois remain circumspect toward *how* the Kandahar mission is handled (opinion unambiguously asserted by Figure 16.3), this attitude is dormant and has not become politically contentious.

Second, since 2006 more and more Québécois have looked favourably upon the province's military personnel rotating in and out of Kandahar. Unlike military adventures of the past where the Canadian Forces seemed estranged from the French-speaking community and where Québécois had a hard time relating to its British tradition, Québec's own Valcartier-based (the province's main military base near Québec City) regiments—most notably the Royal 22e Régiment and the 12e Régiment blindé du Canada—symbolize Québécois ideals and acceptance of a certain (albeit recent) military history. This 'connection' with Canadian military institutions is juxtaposed with a sense of ambivalence where Québécois still oppose the Kandahar mission but support its military personnel deployed abroad. This 'love-hate' relationship toward Canada's participation in the mission in Kandahar is splendidly epitomized by the personal experience of one of Québec's main pacifist advocate, Francis

Dupuis-Déri. A professor of political science at Université du Québec à Montréal (UQAM), he is well known in the province's pacifist circles and media. Throughout the Kandahar deployment, he has been an active participant in public demonstrations and a critic in the media. At the same time he also has a sister holding a Captain's commission in the Canadian Forces. In June 2007, he published an opinion letter in *Le Devoir* titled 'Lettre à ma soeur militaire qui part en Afghanistan' ('Letter to my military sister leaving for Afghanistan')[61] where he condemns and denounces Canada's presence in Central Asia while wishing the best for his family member. In this letter, all the ambiguity and the ambivalence of Québec's public opinion toward the Kandahar operation is symbolized; the objections are based on philosophical grounds without being transferred to the institution and the members of the Canadian Forces. One could argue that this nationalistic, even emotional, connection with Francophone regiments of the Canadian Forces has moderated Québec's hostile manifestation toward the overall Afghan policy.

Contrary to what was expected, even in the midst of mounting military losses, public opinion in Québec has remained unsympathetic but stable towards Canada's participation in the international effort in Afghanistan. Surprisingly, Québécois attitude seemed to have crystallized within the first weeks of the Kandahar deployment in 2006 and no issues, either negative or positive, have resulted in any significant changes in the years following. It seems clear that, in light of this, nothing will change Québec's attitude until Canada's withdrawal from southern Afghanistan in 2011. Nevertheless, it is not at all clear that a different Canadian involvement in Afghanistan after 2011, one that would focus on reconstruction and less on military operations, would be met with the same opposition in Québec. Québécois appear to oppose *what* the Canadian Forces are doing in Afghanistan, not necessarily *why*.

CONCLUSION

The conventional wisdom about Québec's attitude toward the use of force and the role of military institutions must be seriously nuanced. It is a historical fact that the Québécois experienced a very different relationship to the use of force than did English-Canadians, and this experience probably explains lingering attitudinal differences between the two linguistic groups. Remnants of the old isolationist attitude may still be observed among Québécois from time to time. Nevertheless, the remaining differences between the 'two solitudes' are certainly much less apparent and much less important than the majority of Canadians (including the Québécois themselves) would like to think.

Contemporary Québécois are, from a certain perspective, more attached to the classical 'Pearsonian model' in Canadian foreign policy (usually called 'liberal internationalism') than are many English-Canadians. The key features of Québec's 'strategic culture' are: (1) a central role in UN undertakings; (2) the use of military force for peacekeeping operations rather than for combat missions; and (3) the primacy of Canadian interests. This is largely congruent with the image that Canadians as a whole have of their own foreign policy.

The upending of conventional wisdom regarding Québec's attitude toward the use of military force—an upending for which we argue in this article—has important policy implications. First, it reveals as an exaggeration the claim that Québec is hijacking Canadian foreign policy. If the Québécois are not so different from other Canadians, there is no point in accusing them of pursuing their own foreign policy agenda. Moreover, focusing on Québec's opposition to a given mission ignores other pockets of opposition in Canada. Second, emphasizing the differences between Québec and the rest of Canada tends to result in ignoring other potential differences within the various regions of Canada. Furthermore, it tends to place the responsibility for those differences on Québec, seeking (for example) an explanation in Québec's alleged pacifism rather than in other regions' 'war-proneness'. Finally, the claim for a different attitude can also be used by sovereigntist political leaders to support the rationale for independence, as Bernard Landry, then head of the PQ, did during the debate on the possible Canadian contribution to the American-led alliance against Iraq in 2003.[62]

The Québécois have started to revisit their military past through different lenses than their parents and grandparents did. Their recent contribution to the strategic debate is likely to grow, and, as guardians of Pearsonian orthodoxy, they could force a debate on alternatives to liberal internationalism, such as continentalism, in Canadian foreign policy.

Key Terms

Internationalism

Isolationism

Pacifist Quebec

Québécois

Quiet Revolution

Strategic Culture

Notes

1. The authors thank the two anonymous evaluators from the *American Review of Canadian Studies* who reviewed this manuscript for their invaluable insights. We also greatly benefited of David Rudd's helpful comments (strategic analyst, Department of National Defence).

2. J. L. Granatstein, *Whose War Is It? How Canada Can Survive in the Post-9/11 World* (Toronto: HarperCollins, 2007), chapter 6.

3. Jean-Sébastien Rioux, *Two Solitudes: Québecers' Attitudes Regarding Canadian Security and Defence Policy* (Calgary: CDFAI, 2005), 1. See also Antoine Robitaille, 'Québecers: A Pacifist People?' *Inroads* 14 (2003): 62–75; Serge Mongeau, 'La tradition antimilitariste au Québec,' in *Pour un pays sans armée*, ed. Mongeau (Montreal: Écosociété, 1993), 81–9.

4. J. L. Granatstein, 'Québecers Are at the Helm,' *The Ottawa Citizen* (November 1, 2005): A-15. See also his *Who Killed the Canadian Military?* (Toronto: HarperCollins, 2004, 193–4) and his 'Multiculturalism and Canadian Foreign Policy' in David Carment and David Bercuson, eds., *The World In Canada: Diasporas, Demography, and Domestic Policy* (Montreal and Kingston: McGill-Queen's University Press, 2008), 87–8; Janice Gross Stein and Eugene Lang, *The Unexpected War: Canada in Kandahar* (Toronto: Viking Canada, 2007), 73 and 170. Another example of such a perception is the one expressed by Ted Morton, an Alberta member of the provincial legislation, in 'A New Québec Alberta Alliance?' *National Post*, May 20, 2003; also available at www.tedmorton.ca. For an opposite view, see Pierre Martin, 'All Québec's Fault, Again? Québec Public Opinion and Canada's Rejection of Missile Defence,' *Policy Option* 26, no. 4 (2005): 41–44.

5. Granatstein (2007); Robitaille (2003).

6. David Carment and David Bercuson, 'Conclusion: Putting Canada's Diversity into Canadian Foreign Policy,' in Carment and Bercuson, eds., 211.

7. Serge Mongeau; J. L. Granatstein, 'Multiculturalism and Canadian Foreign Policy,' in Carment and Bercuson, eds., 87.

8. Robert Comeau, 'L'opposition à la conscription au Québec,' in *La Première Guerre mondiale et le Canada*, ed., Roch Legault and Jean Lamarre (Montreal: Méridien, 1999), 109; P.B. Waite, 'French-Canadian Isolationism and English Canada: An Elliptical Foreign Policy, 1935–1939,' *Journal of Canadian Studies* 18, no. 2 (1983): 132–148.

9. Granatstein (2007), 141.

10. David G. Haglund, 'Québec's "America Problem": Differential Threat Perception in the North American Security Community,' *American Review of Canadian Studies* 36, no. 4 (2006): 552–567; David G. Haglund, 'The Parizeau-

Chrétien Version: Ethnicity and Canadian Grand Strategy,' in Carment and Bercuson, eds., 92–108.

11. Definition inspired by Marcel Merle, 'Pacifisme,' in Thierry de Montbrial and Jean Klein, eds., *Dictionnaire de stratégie* (Paris: Presses universitaires de France, 2000), 396–403. Of course, this definition does not capture all the distinctions between different forms of pacifism, from a general condemnation of the use of force in all circumstance to a specific condemnation, motivated by opposition to a particular a war (as the war in Vietnam) or a particular weapon system (for example, nuclear weapons). Nevertheless, in the context of this article, this nuance is unnecessary.

12. Jocelyn Coulon, 'Le nouvel antiaméricanisme,' *Argument* 7, no. 2 (2005): 49.

13. Kim Richard Nossal, *The Politics of Canadian Foreign Policy* (Scarborough: Prentice-Hall, 1997), 154–5.

14. Stéphane Roussel and Charles-Alexandre Théorêt, 'A "Distinct Strategy"? The Use of Canadian Strategic Culture by the Sovereignist Movement in Québec, 1968–1996,' *International Journal* 59, no. 3 (2004): 557–577; Stéphane Roussel, 'Une culture stratégique en evolution,' in *Histoire des relations internationales du Québec*, ed. Stéphane Paquin, with Louise Beaudoin (Montreal: VLB, 2006), 278–287.

15. See Guy Frégault, *La Guerre de la Conquête* (Montreal: Fides, 1955).

16. Béatrice Richard, *La mémoire de Dieppe: Radioscopie d'un mythe* (Montreal: VLB, 2002), 34.

17. Ibid.

18. Roch Legault, *Une élite en déroute: Les militaires canadiens après la Conquête* (Montreal: Athéna, 2002), 161–7.

19. Serge Mongeau, 81–9. This view can also be found in Robitaille, 'Québecers: A Pacifist People?' and in his 'Le pacifisme, maladie ou vertu québécoise?' *Le Devoir* (September 23, 2006): A-1 and A-10.

20. Carman Miller, *Painting the Map in Red: Canada and the South African War, 1899–1902* (Montreal and Kingston: McGill-Queen's University Press, 1993), 27–30.

21. Gérard Filteau, *Le Québec, le Canada et la guerre 1914–1918* (Montreal: Éd. de l'Aurore, 1977), 158–163; see also Robert Comeau.

22. Paul-André Linteau, René Durocher, Jean-Claude Robert, and François Ricard, *Histoire du Québec contemporain: Le Québec depuis 1930* (Montreal: Boréal, 1986), 138. For Canada, the total of 'yes' votes would be 2,943,514 against 1,643,006. In contrast, the Québec vote would be 993,663 'no' against 376,188 'yes'. These figures come from C.P. Stanley, *Armes, hommes et gouvernements: Les politiques de guerre du Canada, 1939–1945* (Ottawa: Department of National Defence, 1970), 441.

23. Marc-André Cyr, 'De l'engagement à la révolte: Les Canadiens français et les guerres mondiales,' *Arguments* 10, no. 2 (forthcoming 2008).

24. Serge Bernier, *Le Royal 22ᵉ régiment, 1914–1999* (Montreal: Art Global, 1999), 15–16 and 18. See also Granatstein (2004), 102–03.

25. Robert Comeau, 100. See also Jean-Yves Gravel, ed., *Le Québec et la guerre* (Montreal: Les Éditions du Boréal Express, 1974).

26. Of course, even in English-Canadian circles, the relationship between nationalism and imperialism took many forms and should not be considered a clear dichotomy. See, for example, the excellent study by Carl Berger on Canadian imperialism between 1867–1914. Carl Berger, *The Sense of Power* (Toronto: University of Toronto Press, 1970).

27. P.B. Waite, 'French-Canadian Isolationism and English Canada: An Elliptical Foreign Policy, 1935–1939,' *Journal of Canadian Studies* 18, no. 2 (1983): 132–148.

28. Robin W. Winks, *Canada and the United States: The Civil War Years* (Montreal and Kingston: McGill-Queen's University Press, 1998), 178–184.

29. Jean Lamarre, *Les Canadiens français et la Guerre de Sécession* (Montreal: VLB, 2006), 25, 45–51.

30. Antoine Robitaille, 'Pacifisme des Québécois—Vous avez oublié les zouaves!' *Le Devoir* (September 25, 2006).

31. Stéphane Paquin, 'Les relations internationales du Québec avant la Révolution tranquille,' in Paquin, ed., 14.

32. C.P. Stanley, *Canada and the Age of Conflict: A History of Canadian External Policies,* vol. 1: *1867–1921* (Toronto: Macmillan Canada, 1977).

33. See Jean-François Gazaille, 'Les Canadiens français dans la guerre d'Espagne: Des héros très discrets,' in *Dix ans d'histoire militaire en français au Québec: Actes du 10ᵉ colloque en histoire militaire* (Montreal: Chaire Hector-Fabre, 2005), 77–83. See also Caroline Désy, *Si loin, si proche: La Guerre civile espagnole et le Québec des années trente* (Québec: Les Presses de l'Université Laval, 2003).

34. C.P. Stanley, *Canada and the Age of Conflict,* vol. 2: *1921–1948, The Mackenzie King Era* (Toronto: University of Toronto Press, 1981), 416–17.

35. James Ian Gow, 'Les Québécois, la guerre et la paix, 1945–1960,' *Canadian Journal of Political Science* 3, no. 1 (1970): 104–111.

36. Jocelyn Coulon, *La dernière croisade: La guerre du Golfe et le rôle caché du Canada* (Montreal: Méridien, 1992), 108.

37. Claire-Andrée Cauchy, 'La plus grosse manifestation de l'histoire du Québec,' *Le Devoir* (February 17, 2004): A-1.

38. Don MacPherson, 'It's Safe to Support Terrorists Again,' *The Gazette* (August 8, 2006): A-19; Barbara Kay, 'The Rise of Québecistan,' *National Post* (August 9, 2006): A-18; André Pratte, 'The Myth of Québecistan: Counterpoint,' *National Post* (August 16, 2006): A-14; Yves Boisvert, 'Writer's Québecistan Label a Cheap Shot,' *The Toronto Star* (August 20, 2006): A-17. On this episode, see Jean-Christophe Boucher and Stéphane Roussel, 'From Afghanistan to "Québecistan": Québec as the Pharmakon of Canadian Foreign and Defence Policy', in Jean Daudelin and Daniel Schwanen, ed., *Canada Among Nations 2007. What Room for Manœuvre?* (Montreal and Kingston, McGill-Queen's University Press, 2008): 131–2.

39. J.I. Gow. See also Gérard Bergeron, 'Le Canada français; du provincialisme à l'internationalisme,' in *The Growth of Canadian Policies in External Affairs*, ed. John S. Gillespie (Durham, NC: Duke University Press, 1960), 99–130.

40. See Roussel and Théôret (2004). The shift in the PQ's attitude is described in Stéphane Roussel (with Chantal Robichaud), 'L'élargissement virtuel: Un Québec souverain face à l'OTAN (1968–1995),' *Les cahiers d'histoire* 20, no. 2 (Winter 2001): 147–193; Stéphane Roussel and Charles-Alexandre Théôret, 'Defence Policy Distorted by the Sovereignist Prism? The Bloc Québécois on Security and Defence Issues (1990–2005),' in Carment and Bercuson, eds., 169–188.

41. B.I. Page and R.Y. Shapiro, *The Rational Public: Fifty Years of Trends in Americans' Policy Preferences.* (Chicago, Il: Chicago University Press, 1992).

42. Guy Lachapelle, 'La guerre de 1939–1945 dans l'opinion publique: Une comparaison entre les attitudes des Canadiens français et des Canadiens anglais,' *Bulletin d'histoire politique* 3, no. 3/4 (1995): 201–226.

43. Data supporting these arguments were presented by the authors on two occasions: 'Les Québécois face au maintien de la paix, 1956–2006,' Conference *50+ Years Canada and Peacekeeping: History, Evolutions and Perceptions*, Organization for the History of Canada (OHC), Ottawa, May 11–14, 2005; 'From Anti-Militarism to Internationalism? The Evolution of Québec's Public Opinion Regarding the Use of Military Force,' biannual meeting of the Middle Atlantic and New England Council for Canadian Studies (MANECCS), Montreal, September 21–24, 2006.

44. No major polls were conducted by principal Canadian pollsters after 1996. This 'blind spot' in our data is concordant with the fact that Canada has not made a major contribution to UN peacekeeping operations in the last 10 years.

45. These figures were published by the following polls: Gallup, *The Gallup Report: 58% Agree with NATO Offensive in Bosnia* (September 1995, poll conducted September 6–11, 1995); Gallup, *The Gallup Report: Mulroney Applauded for Persian Gulf War Performance* (June 1991, poll conducted March 6–9, 1991); Gallup, *The Gallup Report: Majority Favor Canadian Participation in Persian Gulf War* (February 1991, poll conducted February 6–9, 1991); Gallup, *The Gallup Report: Majority of Canadians Remain Opposed to War Against Iraq* (January 1991, poll conducted January

2–5, 1991); Gallup, *The Gallup Report: Majority of Canadians Opposed to War Against Iraq* (December 1990, poll conducted December 5–8, 1990); Gallup, *The Gallup Report: Canadians Approve of Sending Forces to Persian Gulf* (October 1990, poll conducted September 12–15, 1990); Gallup, *The Gallup Report: Canadians Assess Country's Role in Haiti* (November 1994, poll conducted October 3–8, 1994); Gallup, *The Gallup Poll: 80% Consider Iraq a Threat to World Peace, Majority Would Favour Canada Joining Military Offensive* (March 1998, poll conducted February 18–24, 1998); Gallup, *The Gallup Poll: Majority of Canadians Approve of NATO's Actions in Kosovo* (April 1999, poll conducted April 12–18, 1999); Gallup, *The Gallup Poll: Canadians Approval of NATO's Actions in Kosovo Declines* (June 1999, poll conducted May 14–23, 1999); Gallup, *The Gallup Poll: Majority Sees Enough Canadian Participation in Military Actions in Afghanistan* (November 2001, poll conducted October 17–23, 2001); Gallup, *The Gallup Poll: Opinion Polarizing on Military in Afghanistan, but Majority Still Sees Right Amount of Canadian Participation* (February 2002, poll conducted January 15–20, 2002); Gallup, *The Gallup Poll: Few Canadians See Not Enough Military Participation in Afghanistan* (March 2002, poll conducted February 11–16, 2002); Decima Research, *Canadians Solidly Behind the War Against Terrorism* (September 2001, poll conducted September 18–22, 2001); Decima Research, *Les Canadiens divisés sur l'Afghanistan* (April 2006, poll conducted March 31–April 4, 2006).

46. David G. Haglund, (2006 and 2008); Jean-Frédéric Légaré-Tremblay, 'Le soleil à l'ombre de Gulliver,' *Argument* 7, no. 2 (2005): 40–7.

47. Stéphane Roussel and David Morin, 'Les multiples incarnations de la culture stratégique et les débats qu'elles suscitent,' in *Culture stratégique et politique de défense: L'expérience canadienne*, ed. Stéphane Roussel (Montreal: Athéna, 2007), 17–42.

48. 'Conclusion,' in *Neorealism Versus Strategic Culture: A Debate*, ed. John Glenn, Darryl Howlett, and Stuart Poore (London: Ashgate, 2004), 224–5.

49. Michael Behiels, *Prelude to Québec's Quiet Revolution: Liberalism Versus Neo-Nationalism, 1945–1960* (Montreal and Kingston: McGill-Queen's University Press, 1985).

50. A group that Vera Murray calls 'participationist,' as opposed to the 'technocrats' that make up the second militant pillar of the Parti québécois in its formative years.

Vera Murray, *Le Parti québécois: De la fondation à la prise du pouvoir* (Montreal: Hurtubise, 1976).

51. Roch Legault, 163.

52. Michael Adams, *Fire and Ice: The United States, Canada and the Myth of Converging Values* (Toronto: Penguin Canada, 2003), 82.

53. At the end of the 1960s, some authors were already arguing that the diminishing religious fervor, the increase in the average income, and of the level of education would affect Québec's public opinion toward war and peace issues. See J. I. Gow, 90–1.

54. Béatrice Richard, 34–42. Jean-Pierre Gagnon, 'Dix ans de recherche, dix ans de travail en histoire militaire: Que peut-on dire de ces dix ans?' in *Dix ans d'histoire militaire*, 7–20; Yves Tremblay, 'Entre l'arbre et l'écorce: Douze ans d'histoire militaire officielle au Québec,' *Bulletin d'histoire politique* 15, no. 3 (2007): 63–80.

55. Bruce Campion-Smith, 'NATO fails to round up new troops; Delay could endanger soldiers on front line Deployment from Québec may erode support further', *The Toronto Star*, September, 14, 2006: A10. For a similar argument, but in a Francophone newspaper, see also, Vincent Marissal, 'Réaction prévisible, problème tenace', *La Presse*, August, 22, 2007: A11.

56. Standard deviation of this result is 6.34 per cent. Considering a margin of error of approximately 6 per cent for Québec's figures, this fluctuation is not important and we can argue that Québec's public opinion remains quite constant across the time period.

57. We have made the same argument in Boucher and Roussel, 'From Afghanistan to "Québecistan"' (2008).

58. Bloc Québécois, 'Le Canada en Afghanistan', Position paper available online at www.blocquebecois.org/dossiers/mission_afghanistan/accueil.asp.

59. This was the official Bloc Québécois' spin in Québec's newspapers to explain their position to the motion. Joëlle-Denis Bellavance, 'Les troupes seront maintenues à Kandahar jusqu'en 2011', *La Presse*, 14 March 2008. Alec Castonguay, 'La mission en Afghanistan est prolongée jusqu'en 2011', *Le Devoir*, 14 March 2008.

60. One notable exception is *Le Devoir*, who has kept an anti-Afghanistan stance.

61. Francis Dupuis-Déri, 'Lettre à ma soeur qui part en Afghanistan', *Le Devoir*, 15 June 2007.

62. Antoine Robitaille (2003), 62.

SELECTED BIBLIOGRAPHY

Balthazar, Louis, and Louis Bélanger, Gordon Mace, et al., 1993. *Trent Ans de Politique Extérieure du Québec 1960–1990*. Québec/Sillery: Septentrion and CQRI.

Bélanger, Louis. 1997. 'The United States and the Formative Years of an Independent Quebec's Foreign Policy', *American Review of Canadian Studies* 27, no. 1: 11–25.

Brown, Douglas and Murray Smith, eds. 1991. *Canadian Federalism: Meeting Global Challenges?* Kingston, ON: Queen's University Institute of Intergovernmental Relations.

Burney, Derek. 2005. *Getting it Done: A Memoir*. Montreal and Kingston: McGill-Queen's University Press.

Burton, B.E., W.C. Soderlund, and T.A. Keenleyside. 1995. 'The Press and Canadian Foreign Policy: A Re-examination Ten Years On', *Canadian Foreign Policy* 3 (Fall): 51–69.

Copeland, Daryl. 2009. *Guerrilla Diplomacy: Rethinking International Relations*. Boulder, CO: Lynne Rienner.

De Boer, Stephen. 2002. 'Canadian Provinces, US States and North American Integration: Bench Warmers or Key Players?' *Choices: Canada's Options in North America* 8 (November): 1–24.

Donaghy, Greg and Kim Richard Nossal, eds. 2009. *Architects and Innovators: Building the Department of Foreign Affairs and International Trade, 1909–2009*. Montreal and Kingston: McGill-Queen's University Press.

Drake, Earl. 1999. *A Stubble-Jumper in Striped Pants: Memoirs of a Prairie Diplomat*. Toronto: University of Toronto Press.

English, John. 1992. *The Worldly Years: The Life of Lester Pearson. Vol II: 1949–1972*. New York: Knopf.

Gotlieb, Allan. 2007. *The Washington Diaries: 1981–1989*. Toronto: McClelland and Stewart.

———. 1991. *'I'll be With You in a Minute, Mr Ambassador': The Education of a Canadian Diplomat in Washington*. Toronto: University of Toronto Press.

Granatstein, J.L., and Robert Bothwell. 1990. *Pirouette: Pierre Trudeau and Canadian Foreign Policy*. Toronto: University of Toronto Press.

Halton, Dan. 2001. 'International News in the North American Media', *International Journal* 56, 3 (Summer): 499–515.

Head, Ivan, and Pierre Trudeau. 1995. *The Canadian Way: Shaping Canada's Foreign Policy, 1968–1984*. Toronto: McClelland and Stewart.

Hilliker, John. 1990. *Canada's Department of External Affairs, Vol. 1: The Early Years, 1909–1946*. Montreal and Kingston: McGill-Queen's University Press.

Hilliker, John and Donald Barry. 1995. *Canada's Department of External Affairs, Vol. 2: Coming of Age, 1946–1968*. Montreal and Kingston: McGill-Queen's University Press.

———. 1994. 'The PM and the SSEA in Canada's Foreign Policy: Sharing the Territory, 1946–1968', *International Journal* 50, 1 (Winter): 162–88.

Jensen, Kurt F. 2008. *Cautious Beginnings: Canadian Foreign Intelligence, 1939–51*. Vancouver: UBC Press.

Kirton, John. 1978. 'Foreign Policy Decision-Making in the Trudeau Government: Promise and Performance', *International Journal* 33, 2 (Spring): 287–311.

Kukucha, Christopher J. 2008. *The Provinces and Canadian Foreign Trade Policy*. Vancouver: UBC Press.

Lackenbauer, P. Whitney, ed. 2002. *An Inside Look at External Affairs During the Trudeau Years: The Memoirs of Mark MacGuigan*. Calgary: University of Calgary Press.

Lortie, Marc, and Sylvie Bedard. 2002. 'Citizen Involvement in Canadian Foreign Policy: The Summit of the Americas Experience 2001', *International Journal* 57, 3 (Summer): 323–40.

McNiven, James D., and Dianna Cann. 1993. 'Canadian Provincial Trade Offices in the United States', pp. 167–84 in Douglas M. Brown and Earl H. Fry, eds., *States and Provinces in the International Economy*. Berkeley: University of California Press; Kingston, ON: Institute of Governmental Studies Press and Institute of Intergovernmental Relations.

McRae, Rob. 2001. 'Human Security, Connectivity, and the New Global Civil Society', pp. 236–49 in Rob McRae and Don Hubert, eds., *Human Security and the New Diplomacy: Protecting People, Promoting Peace*. Montreal and Kingston: McGill-Queen's University Press.

MacDonald, Laura C. 2002. 'Governance and State-Society Relations: The Challenges', pp. 187–223 in George C. Hoberg, ed., *Capacity of Choice: Canada in a New North America*. Toronto: University of Toronto Press.

Mace, Gordon, Louis Bélanger, and Ivan Bernier. 1995. 'Canadian Foreign Policy and Quebec', pp. 119–44 in Maxwell A. Cameron and Maureen Appel Molot, eds., *Canada Among Nations 1995: Democracy and Foreign Policy*. Ottawa: Carleton University Press.

Matthews, Robert. 1983. 'The Churches and Foreign Policy', *International Perspectives* January/February: 18–21.

Michaud, Nelson. 2002. 'Bureaucratic Politics and the Shaping of Policies: Can We Measure Pulling and Hauling Games?' *Canadian Journal of Political Science* 35, 2 (June): 269–300.

Munton, Don, and Tom Keating. 2001. 'Internationalism and the Canadian Public', *Canadian Journal of Political Science* 34, 3 (September): 517–49.

Nossal, Kim Richard. 1996. 'Anything But Provincial: The Provinces and Foreign Affairs', pp. 503–18 in Christopher Dunn, ed., *Provinces: Canadian Provincial Politics*. Peterborough: Broadview Press.

———. 1995. 'The Democratization of Canadian Foreign Policy: The Elusive Ideal', pp. 29–43 in Maxwell A. Cameron and Maureen Appel Molot, eds., *Canada Among Nations 1995: Democracy and Foreign Policy*. Ottawa: Carleton University Press.

———. 1994. 'The PM and the SSEA in Canada's Foreign Policy: Dividing the Territory, 1968–1993', *International Journal* 50, 1 (Winter): 189–208.

———. 1984. 'Bureaucratic Politics and the Westminster Model', pp. 120–7 in Robert Mathews et al., eds., *International Conflict and Conflict Management: Readings in World Politics*. Scarborough: Prentice-Hall.

———. 1983–84. 'Analyzing Domestic Sources of Canadian Foreign Policy', *International Journal* 39, 1 (Winter): 1–22.

Pearson, Geoffrey A.H. 1994. *Seize the Day: Lester B. Pearson and Crisis Diplomacy*. Ottawa: Carleton University Press.

Pratt, Cranford. 1983–4. 'Dominant Class Theory and Canadian Foreign Policy: The Case of the Counter-Consensus', *International Journal* 39, 1 (Winter): 99–135.

Reece, David Chalmer. 2007. *Ambassador Assignments: Canadian Diplomats Reflect on Our Place in the World*. Markham, ON: Fitzhenry and Whiteside.

———. ed. 1996. *Special Trust and Confidence: Envoy Essays in Canadian Diplomacy*. Ottawa: Carleton University Press.

Rempel, Roy. 2002. *The Chatter Box: An Insider's Account of the Irrelevance of Parliament in the Making of Canadian Foreign and Defence Policy*. Toronto: Dundurn.

Riddell-Dixon, Elizabeth. 1985. *The Domestic Mosaic: Domestic Groups and Canadian Foreign Policy*. Toronto: Canadian Institute of International Affairs.

Skogstad, Grace. 2002. 'International Trade Policy and Canadian Federalism: A Constructive Tension', pp. 159–77 in Herman Bakvis and Grace Skogstad, eds., *Canadian Federalism: Performance, Effectiveness, and Legitimacy*. Don Mills, ON: Oxford University Press.

Stairs, Denis. 2001. 'The Changing Office and the Changing Environment of the Minister of Foreign Affairs in the Axworthy Era', pp. 19–38 in Fen Osler Hampson, Norman Hillmer, and Maureen Appel Molot, eds., *Canada Among Nations 2001: The Axworthy Legacy*. Don Mills, ON: Oxford University Press.

Taras, David, ed. 1985. *Parliament in Canadian Foreign Policy*. Toronto: Canadian Institute of International Affairs.

Thordarson, Bruce. 1972. *Trudeau and Foreign Policy: A Study in Decision-Making*. Don Mills, ON: Oxford University Press.

Wolfe, Robert, ed. 1998. *Diplomatic Missions: The Ambassador in Canadian Foreign Policy*. Kingston, ON: Queen's University School of Policy Studies.

PART IV SECURITY

Adam Smith famously wrote that government has three main responsibilities: 1) enforcing rules of conduct within society, 2) settling disputes between its members, and 3) protecting society from external attack. The primary purpose of a country's foreign policy, then, is Smith's last responsibility—the protection of its citizens. Canada is in an unusual circumstance. It has only the United States as a close neighbour and war between the two countries is inconceivable. In many respects Canada remains, in the words of Liberal Senator Raoul Dandurand at the League of Nations in 1924, 'a fire-proof house, far from inflammable materials'. Due to its favourable geographic situation, Canada has also felt an obligation to help build a more secure world. This section of *Readings in Canadian Foreign Policy* examines how Canada's foreign and defence policies are used to protect its territorial integrity and political independence (Canada–US border security and Arctic Security), as well as to contribute to international peace and security (e.g., Canada's deployment to Afghanistan).

The first chapter in this section, by Kim Nossal, sets the table by providing a nice historical overview of Canadian defence policy. Nossal uses the concept of 'defending the realm', to show how Canada has constantly redefined its military commitments beyond the Canadian territory. Two examples should suffice here. From 1867–1918, the realm included the British Empire, highlighted by Canadians fighting in the Boer War and World War I. During the Cold War era, 1945–1991, the realm was the 'West' and led to the peacetime deployment of Canadian forces in Europe.

Afghanistan has been one of Canada's major foreign policy priorities for almost a decade. Involvement consists of a multi-faceted approach that contains defence, development, and diplomatic aspects. Ottawa calls it a 'whole of government' strategy. This is why several chapters in this volume touch on Canada's role in Afghanistan. In Chapter 6, Claire Sjolander and Kathryn Trevenen conduct a content analysis of Canadian government speeches on Afghanistan in 2006 and 2007 to show how the government's narrative was used to 'frame' the mission. In Chapter 11, Doug Ross shows the effect that the Afghanistan mission has had on Canada's relations with its NATO partners. In Chapter 16, Stéphane Roussel and Jean-Christophe Boucher discuss the Afghanistan mission as part of a larger study on the attitudes of Quebecers on peace and security matters. Chapter 17, by Kim Nossal, places the Afghanistan mission into context by showing how it fits into the history of Canadian defence policy.

This section's contribution, Chapter 18 by Duane Bratt, focuses exclusively on the military mission. Canadian forces have now been deployed in Afghanistan longer than in either World War and have suffered the highest causalities since the Korean War. While some commentators continue to use the word 'peacekeeping', the fact is that Canada is at war. Bratt explains why Canada initially deployed to Afghanistan in the fall of 2001, and why it has stayed (and in fact heightened its role through its activities in Kandahar since 2006), and assesses the future of the military mission in light of a Parliamentary resolution calling for the end of the mission by December 2011. Bratt's analysis emphasizes the ideological convictions of Prime Minister Stephen Harper and the institutional interests of former Chief of Defence Staff General Rick Hillier.

The 1990s saw the gradual weakening of borders among many developed states. The EU has only minimal restrictions on individuals going from one member country to the next and NAFTA has opened up the Canadian–American and American–Mexican borders for the freer flow of goods. In fact, much of the North American discussion in the late 1990s was about making cross-border traffic even easier.[1] This debate ended suddenly on 11 September 2001 when, in response to the terrorist attacks on the United States, the Americans closed their borders. Since 9/11 the United States has taken significant steps to tighten border security, including along what used to be proclaimed as the 'longest undefended border'. Peter Andreas has referred to this as the 'Mexicanization of US–Canada border politics'.[2] The essential question of border security is straightforward: how to prevent terrorists and criminals from crossing the border, while simultaneously ensuring minimal restrictions on legitimate traffic? In Chapter 19, Monica Gattinger and Geoffrey Hale assess Canada's post-9/11 efforts to maintain secure access to the American market for Canadian goods and services in light of significant American security concerns about the border that it shares with Canada. These go beyond the securitization of the physical border to issues of the virtual border (US trade protectionism, efforts at bilateral policy harmonization, etc.). In this way, Gattinger and Hale provide a companion piece to Don Barry's Chapter 8.

Gattinger and Hale discuss Canada's southern neighbour and border, but what about our northern neighbours and border? Canada's Arctic region was securitized during the Cold War because the territory was the shortest distance between the United States and the Soviet Union. This led to the building of radar stations, the deployment of the Canadian Air Force, the creation of the Arctic Rangers, and strengthened defence co-operation with the United States in the region. Despite the end of the Cold War, the Arctic has taken on greater importance in Canadian foreign and defence policy, and this will continue to increase. This is because climate change has made travel through the Arctic, especially the contested Northwest Passage, easier due to melting ice. Not only will international shipping be enhanced due to climate change, but so will resource development, especially the exploration and production of oil and gas. In order to protect their national interests, other northern states (Russia, United States, Norway, Denmark) have mobilized their diplomats, international lawyers, and militaries. In Chapter 20, Rob Huebert, one of the foremost experts on the Arctic, outlines a strategy for Canada to respond to these challenges.

Notes

1. See Fen Osler Hampson and Maureen Appel Molot, eds., *Canada Among Nations 2000: Vanishing Borders* (Don Mills, ON: Oxford University Press, 2000).
2. Peter Andreas, 'A Tale of Two Borders: The US–Canada and US–Mexico Lines after 9/11', in Andreas and Thomas J. Biersteker, eds., *The Rebordering of North America: Integration and Exclusion in a New Security Context* (New York: Routledge, 2003), 9.

17

UNDERSTANDING CANADIAN DEFENCE POLICY

Kim Richard Nossal

For many in the international system, security is about efforts to protect the political community against the possibility of predations by others—in other words, it seeks the maintenance of the community's territorial integrity and the protection and advancement of the interests of citizens. In most cases, the focus of national defence is relentlessly fixed on the state and its citizens alone. Indeed, most understandings of defence employ the elementary binary 'inside/outside' division that underwrites most understandings of the contemporary world politics (Walker, 1990). In this view, those 'inside' the state are the proper focus of efforts to provide citizens with security and well-being. By contrast, those 'outside' the state are unambiguously defined as the 'Other' and thus beyond the definition of altruism, to be assisted and defended only if it is in the state's interests to do so. Of course, this relentless pursuit of self-interest, defined purely in terms of the state and its citizens, is a core assumption of most theorizing about international relations, particularly realism and its many strands.

In the Canadian context, however, defence policy actually makes little sense if it is examined using such standard assumptions. It is not that Canadians have been any less self-centred, selfish and ungenerous towards outsiders in world politics. Rather, Canadian defence policy can only be understood when it is conceived as a policy designed to defend something more than just Canadian territorial integrity and the security and well-being of Canadians.

But to be able to frame an analysis of Canadian defence, we need an ideational construct that goes beyond the restrictive definition of the sovereign state that is imposed on us by most strands of contemporary international relations theorizing. Instead, we need a concept that more closely reflects the way in which Canadians and their governors have conceptualized what—and who—is to be defended and made secure. I suggest that Canadians have conceived of defence policy as seeking to defend a broader definition of political community than just 'Canada'; they have sought traditionally to defend a broader 'realm', and it is only when Canadian security policy is seen as having been framed within this broader definition that it makes sense.

To be sure, 'realm' is a word that long ago passed from common usage, perhaps not surprisingly given its intimate connection to a form of governance that has long been discarded in most places in the world. For the commonest meaning of realm is the jurisdiction of a monarch, reflecting its etymological origins from the Old French *réaume*, derived from the Latin *regimen*, rule. While it has evolved a related meaning—a sphere or domain—it is still most commonly used in reference to the monarchy, sometimes with a hint of irony.

However, my choice of a term that is deeply rooted in nineteenth century government is purposeful. While recognizing the word's linkage to a monarchical past, I use realm with an eye to both its meanings: a realm connotes a sphere or domain that is both a political space and an ideational construct of political identity and community that goes beyond the state as it is usually defined in international relations. In particular, as the term is used here, the 'realm' refers to a political space defined by Canadians as including more than 'Canada'—in other words, places and peoples that were (or are) defined as being 'Inside' rather than 'Outside'.

My purpose is to provide a broad survey of the way in which Canadians have defined the 'realm' to be defended since 1867. Mirroring what have been termed 'dominant ideas' in Canada's international policies (Nossal, Roussel and Paquin, 2011: 117–53), I suggest that the definition of 'realm' has shifted over the years. From 1867 to 1918, the 'realm' for many (but not all) Canadians was expansive, including not only Canada but the broader British Empire of which Canada was a part—even though this expansive definition was deeply contested within Canada, with English-speaking Canadians and French-speaking Canadians having radically different perspectives on how the realm should be most appropriately defined.

From 1919 to 1939, the definition of 'realm' was in transition, as Canadians responded to the grand shift in global politics occurring in the interwar period—in particular the rise of the United States and the emergence of the Axis challenge to the order established in 1919 that culminated in the Canadian decision to enter the war that broke out on 1 September 1939.

With the emergence of the Cold War (1945–1991), the definition of 'realm' reflected the rivalry between the United States and the Soviet Union and the threat that Soviet forces posed to both Western Europe and North America: in Canada's embrace of the North Atlantic Treaty of 1949 and the continentalization of air defence in 1957, the realm included both the countries of western Europe and the United States.

In the post-Cold War era (1991–2001), the definition was again in transition; during this period the Canadian government experimented with alternative conceptions of security, expanding the definition of the Canadian 'realm' to what some have suggested are 'post-modern' limits. But in the era of world politics that began on 11 September 2001, it can be argued that the definition of the realm has once again been narrowing. In the post-9/11 era Canadians are no longer enthusiastic about expansive definitions of what should be defended, exemplified by the persistently tepid support for the struggle against global jihadism and the widespread opposition to Canadian participation in the US Ballistic Missile Defense System (BMDS).

CANADA AND THE IMPERIAL REALM: 1867–1918

Whatever definition of security embraced by Canadian policy-makers in the first decades of Canada's existence had to be framed within the context of the legal position of Canada as a self-governing dominion in the British Empire. As a polity created by an act of the British Parliament—the British North America Act of 1867—Canada was to be self-governing in matters of domestic policy, but matters of foreign and defence policy were to be left to the authority of the imperial government in London. The legal regime established in 1867 bound Canada and Canadians tightly to the structures of Empire.

However, for many—though not all—Canadians, the connection to the British Empire was not just simply a matter of formal allegiance to a legal order. More importantly, the connection was an emotional attachment to the *patria*, the land of

their (or their parents') birth—even though English-speaking Canadians at the time tended to use the more maternal appellation, 'Mother Country'. But the love for Britain demonstrated by many English-speaking Canadians in the late nineteenth century was not simply patriotism. Nor was it nationalism: most English-speaking Canadians, while they might have had a love for 'Canada' as a nascent nation, did not embrace the core nationalist goal of establishing a separate and sovereign government to protect and nurture the nation (Berger, 1970: 259–65; Holmes, 1970: 28–31). Rather, imperialism was a hybrid identity that incorporated a simultaneous attachment to 'Canada', 'Empire', and *patria*. However, this identity did not always have a clear political articulation. As H. Blair Neatby (1969: 2) put it, most English-speaking Canadians were 'bound to the old country by less clearly formulated sentiments [of] a natural affection for their Motherland'.

As Canadian decision-makers in the last quarter of the nineteenth century sought to formulate a security strategy for the new dominion, the idea of Empire and its defence framed much of their decision-making. To be sure, Canadian 'defence' in the late 1800s was still fixed on the United States, despite the Treaty of Washington of 1871 that had cleared away some of the irritants that had beset Anglo-American relations. But Canadian defence policy also focused on the defence of the British Empire.

The impetus to contribute to the defence of the Empire can best be seen in Canadian responses to the outbreak of the Boer War in October 1899. This was a conflict that involved the defence of the interests of British subjects; but the interests of Canada or Canadians were by no means affected by the outcome of the Imperial government's quarrel with the Transvaal. But this is not how public opinion in English-speaking Canada saw it. Rather, public opinion in English Canada was affected by what John W. Holmes (1970: 30) called the 'hallucinations of Jubilee imperialism', with young men flocking to recruiting centres to volunteer their services for the British cause. As Carman Miller (1993) has demonstrated so clearly, public support for a Canadian contribution of troops to fight in South Africa had been whipped up by an organized and coordinated campaign by the English-language press. As the editor of *The Globe*, a Liberal newspaper, said to Liberal prime minister Sir Wilfrid Laurier: 'either send troops or go out of office' (Stacey, 1977: 59–60). When a Liberal government Member of Parliament, Henri Bourassa, criticized the Imperial government for its war policies in South Africa in the House to Commons, he was hissed at by his fellow MPs, and called a traitor in the press (Levitt, 1970: 35–43). But Bourassa was reflecting the strong opposition among French-speaking Canadians to sending Canadian troops to fight in South Africa. Despite this opposition, however, Laurier bent to pressure from English Canada and authorized the dispatch of troops to South Africa in response to an implicit request for military support from the imperial government in London.

The South African war demonstrated the degree to which the imperialist sentiments of English Canadians were basically incompatible with the dualistic nature of the Canadian polity. While Canadians of British extraction had no difficulty with the idea of loyalty to Canada and loyalty to Britain, such imperialist sentiment found little favour amongst French Canadians. As Bourassa put it in 1917: 'French-Canadians are loyal to Great Britain and friendly to France; but they do not acknowledge to either country what, in every land, is considered the most exclusively national duty: the obligations to bear arms and fight. The only trouble with the French-Canadians is that they remain the only true 'unhyphenated' Canadians. . . . Canadians of British origin have become quite unsettled as to their allegiance. The French-Canadians have remained,

and want to remain, exclusively Canadian' (Levitt, 1970: 174). However, as long as the Empire—and therefore Canada—was at peace, this incompatibility could remain largely latent. It was when the Empire was at war that the contradictions broke into the open.

The degree to which English Canadians identified with the British Empire as the 'realm' to which sacrifices of blood and treasure could and should be made is reflected in the willingness with which many Canadians went to war in August 1914. The declaration of war on Germany may have been issued by the King on the advice of his ministers in London, but for the vast majority of English Canadians, such legalities were quite irrelevant. The result would have been the same—willing participation on the side of the 'Mother Country'. Indeed, when the prime minister, Sir Robert Borden, asserted that 'the 'national' interests of Canada and the 'imperial' interests of Canada during the Great War were demonstrably the same' (quoted in Brown, 1992: 44), he would have been speaking for many English-speaking Canadians. (For French-speaking Canadians, in contrast, there was no such automatic identification of their interests with the European war.)

SHRINKING THE REALM: 1919–1939

The actual process of fighting the Great War fully exposed the internal contradictions within the Empire—and within Canada. For the massive human and material costs posed a serious problem for all the dominions of the Empire: the Imperial government in London expected the empire to contribute young men and wealth for the successful prosecution of the war, but the various parts of the Empire were given no say over the conduct of the war. The enthusiasm that had been so evident in 1914 waned. By the end of 1916, volunteers for overseas duty had dramatically declined. The Conservative prime minister, Sir Robert Borden, had to decide whether to introduce conscription. For French-speaking Canadians, who shared little of the emotional commitment to the war that had spurred voluntary recruitments in English Canada, the prospect of being forced to fight what many in Québec regarded as an 'English' war posed a major threat to their interests, and they voted against Borden's Conservative-led coalition Unionist government in the elections of December 1917. For many English Canadians, the reaction of French-speaking Canadians to conscription was merely more evidence of Québec's abandonment of the 'Mother Country' in its hour of need. There were violent clashes over the Easter weekend of 1918, as both sides gave vent to these divergent interests.

Involvement in the war diminished the enthusiasm for imperialism among many English-speaking Canadians and gave rise to a desire to control *all* elements of policy, domestic and external. It was a logical outgrowth of the autonomy in domestic policy achieved with Confederation in 1867, and was manifested in Borden's insistence on separate representation for Canada at the peace conference in Paris; and separate Canadian membership in the new international organization, the League of Nations, that had been created at Versailles. And it did lead directly to the Statute of Westminster, 1931, which granted sovereignty to all the self-governing Dominions, thus bringing a formal end to the Empire.

The achievement of formal independence in 1931 did not suddenly extinguish those imperialist sentiments that had fuelled the enthusiasm for war in 1914. Imperial sentiment would linger throughout the interwar period. However, its political impact was more limited. For example, the Liberal government of Mackenzie King had no difficulty in turning down a request from the Imperial government in London for military assistance to be

sent to the Gallipoli peninsula in September 1922, arguing that the Canadian Parliament would need to authorize any despatch of troops abroad (Stacey, 1981: 17–31). The Chanak affair demonstrated the degree to which definitions of the 'realm'—among English-speaking Canadians in particular—had shifted as a result of four years of war fighting.

In the interwar period, Canadians adopted an isolationism that was in many respects comparable to the traditional isolationism of American politics and foreign policy (Haglund, 2002–3). In the aftermath of a war that had cost over 60,000 Canadian lives, Canadians began to express that basic tenet of American isolationism: a deep resentment of European politics. The major concern was that the collective security provisions of the new League of Nations in Geneva would drag Canadians into another European war. More than one speaker in the debate on the Versailles treaty sounded the theme raised by MP Lucien Cannon: 'I am not in favour of England ruling this country, but I would rather be ruled by England than by Geneva' (quoted in Veatch, 1975: 29). For many Canadians, there was an additional impetus: the emotional remoteness from France inclined French-speaking Canadians to define themselves as a North American people rather than a European people (Waite, 1983: 141).

Another major Canadian concern with collective security was that the arrangement seemed entirely one-sided. In North America, Canadians had no fear of the need to invoke the help of the League. The classic position was put by Raoul Dandurand, the Liberal leader in the Senate, at the League Assembly in 1924: 'in this association of Mutual Assistance against fire, the risks assumed by the different States are not equal. We live in a fire-proof house, far from inflammable materials' (Riddell, 1962: 462–65; Paquin, 2009: 41–55). Such sentiments were reflected in King's isolationist policies during the 1920s and 1930s. While Canada relished its separate seat as a member of the League, the government tried as hard as possible to avoid any involvement in international commitments. The reason was simple: King was always concerned to avoid the fate of Borden's Conservatives after the conscription crisis of 1917. King feared that Canada would be dragged into another European war, exposing the deep fractures between English- and French-speaking Canadians, and running the possibility that the Liberal party would be consigned to the electoral wilderness in Québec, just as the Conservatives had been after 1917. From this concern, isolationism—and a feeble security policy (Eayrs, 1964)—came naturally. In particular, the 'realm' shrank as imperialist sentiment diminished and more and more English-speaking Canadians embraced the more limited definition of security common among French-speaking Canadians.

To be sure, sentiments of attachment to Britain were still clearly evident in the late 1930s, the legal and constitutional freedoms won in the Statute of Westminster notwithstanding. Supporting Britain in the Second World War was never in question for the majority of Canadians. As J.L. Granatstein and Robert Bothwell (1986: 125) put it, 'support for Britain was first a moral duty, and a political duty, if it was at all, a long way after'. They quote Stephen Leacock, who in the summer of 1939 summed up English-Canadian attitudes about the impending war in Europe this way: 'If you were to ask any Canadian, "Do you have to go to war if England does?" he'd answer at once, 'Oh, no'. If you then asked, "Would you go to war if England does?" he'd answer "Oh, yes". And if you asked "Why? " he would say, reflectively, "Well, you see, we'd have to."' (Leacock, 1939).

However, while many Canadians may have been isolationist and may have had a more restricted vision of the 'realm' to be defended, there were fewer and fewer Canadians who viewed the rise of Adolf Hitler and Nazi Germany with indifference.

When the Canadian government declared war on Germany on 10 September 1939, the country went into the Second World War relatively united.

THE REALM IN THE COLD WAR: 1945–1991

The Second World War radically transformed Canadian definitions of the 'realm'. After 1945, that realm was greatly expanded from the constricted definition of the isolationist interwar period. Instead, those who inherited the responsibility for defining Canadian foreign and defence policy in the mid-1940s had a markedly different calculation about Canadian defence and security than those of the interwar years.

First, the Liberal government of Prime Minister Louis St Laurent did not share Mackenzie King's almost pathological fear that international commitments would involve Canada in war, expose the contradictions between English- and French-speaking Canadians, and spell electoral disaster for the Liberals. On the contrary: St Laurent and many of his officials took the view that the primary 'lesson of the 1930s' was that countries should be actively engaged in global politics in order to work for the maintenance of an international order that would prevent the recurrence of the events of the 1930s that led to the Second World War. This was the essence of Canada's postwar internationalism: a deep commitment to international institutions and to active involvement in international affairs (Keating, 2002).

This activism manifested itself in a number of ways, including strong support for international institutions and a willingness to contribute Canadian resources to the creation and maintenance of international order. But it also involved a willingness to embrace an expansion of the de facto alliance that Canadians had entered into with the United States at the outset of the Second World

War. After 1945, and the re-emergence of the enmity between the Soviet Union and Western countries that had lingered throughout the inter-war period following the armed intervention by the United States and other Western states, Canada included, in the Russian civil war, [Canadians⤢ expanded the definition of 'realm' to include all the countries of Western Europe who joined in the North Atlantic alliance of 1949 (Reid, 1977; Eayrs, 1980; Holmes, 1982: 98–122).]

The North Atlantic Treaty and the Organiza-tion that grew out of it represented one way in which Canada's definition of the defence 'realm' expanded after 1945. For the alliance committed Canadians to a defence of Western Europe com-parable to the defence of Britain and France in 1939–40. It also reflected a willingness on the part of Canadians to identify themselves clearly as being part of the 'West' in what was emerging as a global confrontation led by the two new superpowers. And while the negotiation of this alliance commit-ment was a governmental initiative, implemented by state officials, there can be little doubt that Can-adians strongly supported the new alliance. The willingness to commit resources to NATO—not only the stationing of significant Canadian forces in Europe, but, more metaphysically, the readiness to fight a third European war in as many genera-tions—suggests that the process of fighting the Second World War produced as radical a shift in Canadian sentiment as the process of fighting the First World War had.

The second expansion of the realm also grew out of the strategic shifts that had occurred with the 'revolution of 1940'—the agreement between Canada and the United States establishing a joint mechanism for the mutual defence of North Amer-ica (Haglund, 1999)—and the subsequent emer-gence of a threat to the United States from Soviet intercontinental bombers. The decision of the Can-adian government in the 1950s to continentalize

air defence by entering into the North American Air Defence (NORAD) command was not only a pragmatic response to the defence requirements of the United States, but also a manifestation of the willingness of Canadians to draw their security perimeter and their definition of what was 'inside' more widely than simply Canadian borders.

To be sure, the concrete Canadian commit-ments to NATO diminished over the long years of the Cold War (Nossal, 2001). In the early 1960s, the Progressive Conservative government of John Dief-enbaker was undecided on the wisdom of arming Canadian forces in Europe with nuclear weapons, raising broader questions about Canada's commit-ment to the alliance. The Liberal government of Pierre Elliott Trudeau came to office in 1968 want-ing to withdraw Canadian forces from Europe, but, faced with both domestic and external opposition, opted in 1969 to dramatically reduce the number of forces stationed in Europe. Trudeau's desire for withdrawal was based on strategic calculations: a belief that stationing large numbers of Canadian troops in Europe was unnecessary for Canadian interests given the changes in the relationship between the United States and the Soviet Union in the late 1960s. The Progressive Conservative gov-ernment of Brian Mulroney (1984–1993) also sought to reduce the Canadian presence in Europe, but eventually backed away when faced with stiff opposition from other allies. Indeed, it was not until the Cold War was over that the Mulroney gov-ernment finally closed Canada's bases in Europe.

But if Canadian governments exhibited dimin-ishing levels of concrete support for NATO and NORAD in the last two decades of the Cold War, it can be argued that public support for the *idea* of a wider definition of the Canadian 'realm' persisted throughout the 1970s and 1980s. While a vocal opposition to Canada's strategic alignments in world politics emerged in the late 1950s and remained active through to the end of the 1980s, the majority of Canadians continued to embrace the idea that Canada should contribute to the defence of the West.

EXPANDING AND SHRINKING THE REALM: 1991–2001

The end of the Cold War between 1989 and 1991 ushered in an era in Canadian foreign and defence policy markedly different from earlier eras. The dismantling of the Soviet Union had a dramatically disruptive effect on the thinking of some Canadians about security policy, since so much of the grand strategy of the Cold War era was structured around the existence of the Soviet Union as the enemy.

With the benefit of hindsight, we can now see that Canadian strategic thinking in the ten years after 1991 was marked by a certain confusion. First, despite the end of the conflict that gave rise to the institutional arrangements of Cold War security policy, these institutions lingered long after the Cold War itself was over. The North Atlantic Treaty was designed to protect the states of Western Europe against an attack by the Soviet Union. However, with the disappearance of that threat, NATO did not simply fold its tent, its job done; rather, the alliance reinvented itself throughout the 1990s, expanding eastwards, embracing new members, and assuming new tasks that were more and more 'out of area'. Likewise, freed of the need to protect against an air-breathing threat from the USSR, NORAD did not wrap up its operations, but adapted to new tasks, including the interdiction of drugs being smuggled from Latin America and the Caribbean. The efforts to transform these two institutions to reflect the new realities of the post-Cold War environment received strong support from the governments of both Brian Mulroney and Jean Chrétien.

Second, with the disappearance of the Soviet Union and the sharp east/west divide that had marked the Cold War years, Canadian definitions

of the 'realm' were radically altered. To be sure, the Canadian government experimented with different conceptions of security during this period. For example, Lloyd Axworthy, Canada's foreign affairs minister from 1996 to 2000, welcomed the constant expansion of NATO, arguing that he could conceive of one day admitting Russia to NATO, forming a giant alliance that would stretch from Vancouver to Vladivostok. Likewise, Axworthy championed the idea of 'human security' (Paris, 2001), the notion that Canadians should be concerned about not only about the security of states, but the security of all human beings, and that the Canadian state should occupy itself with improving the security of human beings under threat (Hillmer and Chapnick, 2001; Nossal, 2010).

But these attempts to redefine the 'realm' appeared to have limited resonance among the Canadian public. The alliance formalized in 1949 was very easy to understand: the Soviet Union posed a threat to the countries of Western Europe, and the alliance was a means to deter a Soviet attack and to defend the countries of Western Europe should deterrence fail. After the Soviet Union ceased to be a threat, NATO transmogrified into an eminently post-modern construction: an alliance that existed without a clearly identifiable external threat to defend against. While Canadian public opinion polls demonstrate that NATO continues to command support, there is little evidence that Canadians expanded their definition of the 'realm' along with NATO's eastward expansion. In the early 1950s Canadians might have been willing to devote blood and treasure to defend Belgians and Dutch against potential predations from the Soviet Union; in the 1990s, it was unlikely that Canadians would apply that same logic to the new members of the alliance.

Likewise, Axworthy's effort to expand the realm of Canadian security to include human security had little resonance at a concrete level. It is true that during the 1990s the Canadian government used the Canadian Armed Forces (CF) for a number of expeditionary missions designed to bring an end to intrastate conflicts in a variety of countries, including Yugoslavia, Somalia, Haiti, Rwanda, Sierra Leone and East Timor. The CF was also involved in one war during this period—the 78-day bombing of the Federal Republic of Yugoslavia in 1999—that was justified by the Canadian government as necessary to protect the human security of Kosovar Albanians. But while Canadians might have approved of the deployment of the armed forces for such missions, and while the rhetorical embrace of human security by their government appears to have generated some approval, there was little evidence that Canadians actually conceived of Kosovar Albanians, or Timorese, or Bosnian Muslims as being on the 'inside', part of the 'realm' of Canadian concern.

Thus the period from the end of the Cold War to the attacks of 9/11 reveals a paradoxical trend: while the formal and rhetorical Canadian definitions of the 'realm' were expanding as a consequence of the enthusiasms of government officials—the expansion of NATO to include new members, the expansion of the 'human security agenda'—the real and concrete definition of the 'realm' actually shrank during the 1990s, with Canadians inclined to narrow their perimeter of concern. This narrowing can readily be seen in the response of Canadians to the activities of their government over the course of the 1990s: the absolute lack of concern expressed by Canadians as the Chrétien government dramatically reduced Canada's actual operations internationally (Nossal, 1998–9; Cohen, 2003); and the overwhelming silence of Canadians when they were confronted with unambiguous evidence of genocide in Rwanda, brutalities in Sierra Leone, violence in Chechnya, or human rights violations in a variety of other countries.

THE POST-9/11 ERA: THE NARROWING OF THE REALM

In the years after the attacks against the United States on 11 September 2001, we have seen another paradoxical trend emerge. On the one hand, the Liberal government of Jean Chrétien responded to NATO's invocation of Article 5 of the North Atlantic Treaty—deeming that the attack on the United States had been an attack on all NATO members—by contributing to the United States-led invasion of Afghanistan.

Canada's contribution to what was widely called the 'global war on terror' could be seen as yet another example of an expansive definition of what was to be defended that we have seen in conflicts from the Boer War in 1899 to the war in Kosovo in 1999: in the 'global war on terror', the defence of Canada was conflated with a defence of the United States and, more broadly, the West. The mission in Afghanistan extended through the decade, with three distinct phases: Canada's contribution to the multilateral campaign in 2001–2 that led to the overthrow of the Taliban regime; the deployment to Kabul from 2003 to 2005 with the International Security Assistance Force (ISAF) that had been deployed to support the new post-Taliban government of Hamid Karzai; and the deployment of a battle group to Kandahar province from 2006. From 2001 until 2010, thousands of Canadians served with the armed forces in Afghanistan; more than 140 Canadians lost their lives while on duty there, most killed by improvised explosive devices; over 400 were wounded. In 2009, the official calculation of the overall cost of the mission was $11.2 billion. Certainly the commitment of Canadian blood and treasure to a ten-year war in a country physically remote from Canada that did not directly affect the interests of Canadians seemed to be a continuation of the same dynamic that led earlier generations of Canadians to embrace an expansive conception of defence; indeed Pigott (2007: 9–10) draws an explicit comparison between the Boer War and the Afghanistan mission.

On the other hand, a closer look at attitudes towards defence in the decade after 2001 suggests that Canadians' definition of what is to be defended actually continued to narrow. First, as I have argued elsewhere (Nossal, 2003), a more careful reading of the immediate Canadian response to 9/11 reveals that the initial support for a military contribution to the emerging American-led 'global war on terror' was actually quite short-lived. While Canadians generally supported the initial deployment of forces to the US-led war in Afghanistan aimed at removing the Taliban regime, there was also general support for the return of the forces in 2002, particularly after four soldiers were killed by 'friendly fire' from an American jet fighter in April.

Second, there was little willingness in Canada to identify with all elements of the American strategy, such as the attempt by the administration of George W. Bush to entwine Iraq in the global war on terror. As the impending invasion of Iraq loomed in the winter of 2002–03, opposition in Canada mounted. Simply put, most Canadians did not buy the arguments being advanced by Bush in the United States and Prime Minister Tony Blair in Britain that the overthrow of Saddam Hussein's regime was an integral part of the anti-jihadist struggle (Barry, 2005; Richter, 2005).

Third, the way in which Canada 'returned' to Afghanistan after 2002—to Kabul with ISAF in 2003 and Kandahar in 2006—also suggests that factors other than a broad desire to include Afghanistan in the 'realm' of Canadian defence were at work. The deployment to Kabul was driven in large part by the desire of Canada's allies, notably the United States, to have Canada fill a gap to allow the redeployment of American forces to the coming invasion of Iraq.

And this certainly suited the Chrétien government, which had little desire in joining the 'coalition of the willing' in Iraq, for the deployment to Kabul could be used to argue that Canada did not have sufficient forces to join the American operation in Iraq (Granatstein, 2007: 91n; Stein and Lang, 2007: 44–70). Likewise, the Martin government decided in early 2005 to despatch a battle group to Kandahar under Operation Enduring Freedom in order to soothe American annoyance not only over Canada's refusal to support Operation Iraqi Freedom but also Martin's decision not to participate in the Ballistic Missile Defense System, discussed further below. In short, Canada's mission in Afghanistan was driven by alliance politics rather than defence considerations.

Canadian public opinion on the Afghanistan mission persistently reflected the ambiguities underlying the mission. Polls after 2006 revealed that support for the mission was less than 50 per cent, with a strong degree of opposition to the mission (Boucher and Roussel, 2008; Fletcher et al., 2009; Nossal, 2010). Moreover, these polling numbers remained remarkably consistent, even when the Kandahar mission produced large numbers of Canadian casualties (Nossal, 2008; Boucher, 2010). Importantly, none of the explanations put forward by the Harper government altered this scepticism. The Harper government, which had come to office in 2006 strongly supportive of the Canadian mission in Afghanistan, tried to articulate different justifications for the mission, but without success. As Fletcher et al. (2009: 931) put it: 'The government's message was received; the public, however, was not persuaded. Something was missing'. Eventually, Harper simply bent to the polls. Seeking to transform its minority status into a majority, the Conservative government cooperated with the Liberal opposition to secure approval for a parliamentary resolution withdrawing from

Afghanistan in 2011 (Nossal, 2009). This had the desired effect of removing Afghanistan as an issue in the 2008 elections. However, when the Conservatives were returned with another minority, Harper gave up trying to convince Canadians of the rightness of the Afghanistan mission. It was clear that the government was waiting for the clock to run out on the mission, recognizing that Canadians were simply not buying the idea that Canadian blood and treasure should be expended making Afghanistan secure.

We can also see a shrinking conception of the 'realm' in the post-9/11 era in the Canadian attitude to ballistic missile defence. While Canadians had been comfortable during the early Cold War with the continentalization of air defence against the Soviet bomber threat, this sentiment began to slowly evaporate, beginning in the 1970s. By the early 1980s, when the administration of Ronald Reagan outlined the Strategic Defense Initiative—a space-based missile defence system designed to thwart a nuclear attack by the Soviet Union—and invited Canada to participate, there was so much opposition to SDI in Canada that the Progressive Conservative government of Brian Mulroney decided in 1985 not to participate. By the post-Cold War era, when the United States was still experimenting with more limited ballistic missile programs—National Missile Defense and Theatre Missile Defense—to defend itself and its allies from possible ballistic missile attacks from 'rogue' states, the evanescence was complete. There was considerable public support for the Chrétien government's lack of enthusiasm for ballistic missile defence in the 1990s.

That lack of enthusiasm gelled into strong Canadian opposition in the post-9/11 era. The strength of that opposition can best be seen by looking at the policies of Paul Martin and Stephen Harper towards ballistic missile defence. Before they assumed the prime ministership, both Martin and Harper had publicly expressed their support for BMDS and had promised to accept the US invitation to join if they won power. Once in office, however, both Martin and Harper changed their minds. Martin announced in February 2005 that Canada would not participate (Fergusson, 2005); when he came to power in February 2006, Harper did not move to revisit Martin's decision (Nossal, 2007).

The cases of the 'global war on terror' and ballistic missile defence suggests that Canadian conceptions of the realm continue to shift, and narrow. Indeed, if present trends persist, Canadians will be in a situation where the defence 'realm' will have shrunk to the borders of Canada itself—for the first time in Canadian history.

CONCLUSION

Making sense of Canadian defence policy requires an understanding of the fact that over the years Canadians have tended to define who and what is to be made secure in terms broader than the Canadian state. I have suggested that the term 'realm' is a useful way to capture this dynamic, particularly because its etymological origins are apposite for an analysis of the Canadian experience in the nineteenth and early twentieth centuries, when Canadian sovereignty was still located with the government in London.

Now it is true that those who make Canadian foreign and defence policy do not use the term now, and did not in the past. Even the most cursory examination of the historical record reveals that Canadian policy-makers have always framed their discourse in concrete terms—'Canada', or 'the Empire', or 'the West'. But given the restrictive vocabulary of traditional IR theorizing that tends to limit discussions of strategic culture to the state, we need an ideational construct that permits an analysis that more accurately reflects the reality of identity as it has been manifested in the Canadian historical experience.

Originally published as 'Defending the "Realm": Canadian Strategic Culture Revisited', *International Journal* 59:3 (Summer 2004): 503–520; updated for this volume

Key Terms

Inside/Outside
Isolationism
Realm

References

Barry, Donald. 2005. 'Chrétien, Bush, and the War in Iraq', *American Review of Canadian Studies* 35, 2: 215–45.

Berger, Carl. 1970. *The Sense of Power: Studies in the Ideas of Canadian Imperialism, 1867–1914.* Toronto: University of Toronto Press.

Brown, Robert Craig. 1992. 'Sir Robert Borden, the Great War, and Anglo-Canadian Relations', in J.L. Granatstein, ed., *Towards a New World: Readings in the History of Canadian Foreign Policy.* Toronto: Copp Clark, 28–46.

Boucher, Jean-Christophe. 2010. 'Evaluating the 'Trenton effect': Canadian public opinion and military casualties in Afghanistan (2006–2009)'. *American Review of Canadian Studies* 40, 2: 237–58.

Boucher, Jean-Christophe, and Stéphane Roussel. 2008. 'From Afghanistan to 'Quebecistan': Quebec as the Pharmakon of Canadian Foreign and Defence Policy', in Jean Daudelin and Daniel Schwanen, eds., *Canada Among Nations 2008: What Room for Manoeuvre?* Montreal and Kingston: McGill-Queen's University Press, 128–56.

Eayrs, James. 1964. *In Defence of Canada*, vol. 1: *From the Great War to the Great Depression.* Toronto: University of Toronto Press.

———. 1980. *In Defence of Canada*, vol. 4: *Growing Up Allied.* Toronto: University of Toronto.

Fergusson, James. 2005. 'Shall We Dance? The Missile Defence Decision, NORAD Renewal, and the Future of Canada–US Defence Relations', *Canadian Military Journal* 6, 2: 13–22.

Fletcher, Joseph F., Heather Bastedo, and Jennifer Hove. 2009. 'Losing Heart: Declining Support and the Political Marketing of the Afghanistan Mission,' *Canadian Journal of Political Science* 42, 4: 911–37.

Granatstein, J.L. 2007. *Whose War Is It? How Canada Can Survive in the Post-9/11 World.* Toronto: HarperCollins.

Granatstein, J.L., and Robert Bothwell. 1986. '"A Self-evident National Duty": Canadian Foreign Policy, 1935–1939', in J.L. Granatstein, ed., *Canadian Foreign Policy: Historical Readings.* Toronto: Copp Clark Pitman, 125–44.

Haglund, David G. 1999. 'The North Atlantic Triangle Revisited: (Geo)political Metaphor and the Logic of Canadian Foreign Policy', *American Review of Canadian Studies* 29, 2: 211–35.

———. 2002–3. 'Are *We* the Isolationists?' *International Journal* 58, 1: 1–23.

Hillmer, Norman, and Adam Chapnick, 'The Axworthy Revolution', in Fen Osler Hampson, Norman Hillmer, and Maureen Appel Molot, eds., *Canada Among Nations 2001: The Axworthy Legacy.* Toronto: Oxford University Press, 67–88.

Holmes, John W. 1970. *The Better Part of Valour: Essays on Canadian Diplomacy.* Toronto: McClelland & Stewart.

———. 1982. *The Shaping of Peace: Canada and the Search for World Order, 1943–1957*, vol. 2. Toronto: University of Toronto Press.

Keating, Tom. 2002. *Canada and World Order: The Multilateralist Tradition in Canadian Foreign Policy*, 2nd edition. Toronto: Oxford University Press.

Leacock, Stephen. 1939. 'Canada and the Monarchy', *The Atlantic*, June, 735–44.

Levitt, Joseph, ed. 1970. *Henri Bourassa on Imperialism and Biculturalism, 1900–1918.* Toronto: Copp Clark.

Miller, Carman. 1993. *Painting the Map Red: Canada and the South African War, 1899–1902.* Montreal and Kingston: McGill-Queen's University Press.

Neatby, H. Blair. 1969. 'Laurier and imperialism', in Carl Berger, et al., *Imperial Relations in the Age of Laurier.* Toronto: University of Toronto Press.

Nossal, Kim Richard. 1998–9. 'Pinchpenny Diplomacy: The Decline of "Good International Citizenship" in Canadian Foreign Policy', *International Journal* 54, 1: 88–105.

———. 2001. 'The Decline of the Atlanticist Tradition in Canadian Foreign Policy', in George A. MacLean, ed., *Between*

Actor and Presence: The European Union and the Future of the Transatlantic Relationship. Ottawa: University of Ottawa Press, 223–34.

———. 2003. 'Canadian Foreign Policy after 9/11: Realignment, Reorientation or Reinforcement?' in Lenard Cohen, Brian Job, and Alexander Moens, eds., *Foreign Policy Realignment in the Age of Terror.* Toronto: Canadian Institute of Strategic Studies, 20–34.

———. 2007. 'Defense Policy and the Atmospherics of Canada–US Relations: The Case of the Harper Conservatives', *American Review of Canadian Studies* 37, 1: 23–34.

———. 2008. 'The Unavoidable Shadow of Past Wars: Obsequies for Casualties of the Afghanistan Mission in Australia and Canada', *Australasian Canadian Studies* 26, 1: 91–124.

———. 2009. 'No Exit: Canada and the "War without End" in Afghanistan', in Hans-Georg Ehrhart and Charles C. Pentland, eds., *The Afghanistan Challenge: Hard Realities and Strategic Choices.* Montreal and Kingston: McGill-Queen's University Press, 157–73.

———. 2010. 'Rethinking the Security Imaginary: Canada and the Case of Afghanistan', in Bruno Charbonneau and Wayne S. Cox, eds., *Locating Global Order: American Power and Canadian Security after 9/11.* Vancouver: UBC Press.

Nossal, Kim Richard, Stéphane Roussel, and Stéphane Paquin. 2011. *International Policy and Politics in Canada.* Toronto: Pearson Canada.

Paquin, Stéphane. 2009. 'Raoul Dandurand: Porte-Parole de la Conscience Universelle', in Greg Donaghy and Kim Richard Nossal, eds., *Architects and Innovators: Building the Department of Foreign Affairs and International Trade,*

1909–2009. Montreal and Kingston: McGill-Queen's University Press, 41–55.

Paris, Roland. 2001. 'Human Security: Paradigm Shift or Hot Air?' *International Security* 26, 2: 87–102.

Pigott, Peter. 2007. *Canada in Afghanistan: The War So Far.* Toronto: Dundurn Press.

Reid, Escott. 1977. *Time of Fear and Hope: The Making of the North Atlantic Treaty, 1947–1949.* Toronto: McClelland & Stewart.

Richter, Andrew. 2005. 'From Trusted Ally to Suspicious Neighbor: Canada–US Relations in a Changing Global Environment', *American Review of Canadian Studies* 35, 3: 471–502.

Riddell, Walter A., ed. 1962. *Documents on Canadian Foreign Policy, 1917–1939.* Toronto: Oxford University Press.

Stacey, C.P. 1977. *Canada and the Age of Conflict: A History of Canadian External Policies,* vol. 1: *1867–1921.* Toronto: Macmillan Canada.

———. 1981. *Canada and the Age of Conflict: A History of Canadian External Policies,* vol. 2: *1921–1948: The Mackenzie King Era.* Toronto: University of Toronto Press.

Stein, Janice Gross, and Eugene Lang. 2007. *The Unexpected War: Canada in Kandahar.* Toronto: Viking Canada.

Veatch, Richard. 1975. *Canada and the League of Nations.* Toronto: University of Toronto Press.

Waite, P.B. 1983. 'French-Canadian Isolationism and English Canada: An Elliptical Foreign Policy, 1935–1939', *Journal of Canadian Studies* 18, 2: 132–48.

Walker, R.B.J. 1990. 'Security, Sovereignty, and the Challenge of World Politics', *Alternatives* 15, 1: 3–27.

18

AFGHANISTAN: WHY DID WE GO?
WHY DID WE STAY? WILL WE LEAVE?

Duane Bratt

Afghanistan is Canada's number one foreign policy commitment with billions of dollars being spent, the establishment of a permanent diplomatic presence in the country, and over a hundred and fifty Canadian lives being lost. How did a small, geographically remote, economically insignificant country in Central Asia become the focus of Canadian foreign policy? What does this say about the foreign policy priorities of successive governments in Ottawa? What is the future of Canadian–Afghan relations? These are the questions that this chapter will explore, in three sections. The first part explains why Canada initially deployed to Afghanistan in 2001. The second part explains why Canada remained in the country and committed to an ambitious project that involved defence, development, and diplomatic roles. Finally, it contemplates the future of Canada's engagement in Afghanistan beyond the promised military pull-out date of 2011.

WHY DID WE GO?

Prior to 11 September 2001, Afghanistan was one of the few places in the world that lacked any sort of Canadian connection. It was not until 1968 that Canada established diplomatic relations with Afghanistan, and these were severed in 1979 as a result of the Soviet invasion. Canada is both a country of immigrants and a trading nation, but there were few immigrants from Afghanistan and even less bilateral trade. Even foreign aid to a country stricken by almost continuous warfare was less than $10 million a year. As Ken Calder, then assistant deputy minister of policy in the Department of National Defence (DND), commented, '[w]e don't know anything about this country'.[1] It was not until planes starting crashing into the World Trade Center that Afghanistan appeared on Ottawa's radar.

Canada became engaged with Afghanistan for two reasons. First, the 9/11 terror attacks were seen as an attack not just on the United States, but on the Western world (Canada included) as a whole. Over 30 Canadians died that day in the World Trade Center. In the week after 9/11, Chrétien defended war as an instrument to 'destroy the evil of terrorism'.[2] While it was seen as undiplomatic, there was a lot of truth in former Defence Minister

Gordon O'Connor remarks that Canada went to Afghanistan in 'retribution' for the 9/11 attacks.[3]

A second reason was that the invasion of Afghanistan was supported by Canada's most important ally, the United States. It was also supported by two critical international institutions: the United Nations (UN) and the North Atlantic Treaty Organization (NATO). When the 9/11 attacks began, early that morning, the United States immediately went into a defensive posture, clearing its airspace and shutting down its borders. However, once the initial shock of the attacks started to reside, Washington began to prepare for an offensive attack aimed at the Al-Qaeda bases in Afghanistan and their Taliban hosts. US action was given official authorization by both the UN and NATO. The United Nations Security Council passed Resolution 1368 which classified the terrorist attacks as a threat to international peace and security and recognized the 'inherent right of individual or collective self-defence'.[4] Meanwhile, NATO, for the very first time in its existence, invoked Article V of the North Atlantic Treaty which calls for collective self-defence.[5] This obliged all member countries, including Canada, to assist the United States by all means necessary.

For these reasons, Canadians overwhelmingly demanded that Ottawa join with the Americans and its other allies in responding, including using military force, to the 9/11 attacks. This began almost immediately: for instance, in the days after the terrorist attacks, Canadian recruiting centres were swamped by applicants.[6] 100, 000 Canadians also showed up at Parliament Hill in a major pro-US rally. In the weeks after 9/11, polls showed that almost three-quarters of Canadians supported joining the United States in its war on terror.[7] 9/11 also created the conditions for an increase in military spending after years of downsizing. The Chrétien government passed anti-terror legislation, put money into border security, added a couple

of billion dollars to the budget of the Canadian Forces (CF), and announced plans for increasing its strength. Both the Martin and Harper governments followed up on all these measures.

The Chrétien government, in October 2001, deployed its special forces unit, the JTF-2, and 750 ground troops from the Princess Patricia's Canadian Light Infantry (PPCLI) to assist US efforts in killing and capturing Al-Qaeda and Taliban members. This was not a peacekeeping mission like Cyprus or the Golan Heights. It was not even a more robust second-generation peacekeeping mission like Bosnia or Somalia. This was a war and, as such, was the first time since the Korean War of the early 1950s that Canadian troops had been deployed into explicit ground combat. While these were the only Canadian Forces (CF) in Afghanistan, there were additional naval and air surveillance assets stationed in the Arabian Sea. In total, Canada deployed almost three thousand soldiers in response to the 9/11 attacks.

WHY DID WE STAY?

Following Chretien's initial decision in the fall of 2001 to deploy to Afghanistan, successive governments took further actions that brought Canada deeper into the conflict. The second decision occurred in February 2003 when the Chrétien government sent 1,700 ground troops to Kabul as part of NATO's International Stabilization Assistance Force (ISAF). Canada also supplied General Rick Hillier as the ISAF Commander. ISAF's mandate was to provide security assistance to the interim Afghan government and help the country prepare for its presidential and parliamentary elections. The decision to deploy troops to Kabul in February 2003 was made partly to avoid making a military commitment to the coming US war in Iraq. According to then Defence Minister John McCallum, US Defence Secretary Donald Rumsfeld was 'fully cognizant of the fact that this mission limits the deployment of Canadian land forces to other parts of the world for well over a year'.[8]

The third decision occurred in May 2005 when the Paul Martin government announced the withdrawal of its forces from Kabul and their redeployment in Kandahar in February 2006. The CF would form one of the provincial reconstruction teams that would be assigned to different NATO countries and would be spread out across Afghanistan. Since Kandahar was the most dangerous province, the CF was also given significantly enhanced combat responsibilities to help root out remaining Taliban/Al-Qaeda elements. As with the earlier decision to go to Kabul, the deployment to Kandahar was also partially connected to Iraq. Michael Kergin, Canada's Ambassador to the United States, said that the 2005 decision to deploy Canadian troops to Kandahar was aimed at placating the Americans after refusing to support them in Iraq and on the Ballistic Missile Defence initiative. 'There was this sense that we had let the side down,' he said, '. . . and then there was the sense that we could be more helpful, militarily, by taking on a role in Afghanistan. . . .We could make a contribution in a place like Kandahar.'[9]

The fourth decision, made in the midst of heavy fighting in Kandahar, occurred when Prime Minister Stephen Harper both extended and expanded Canada's mandate in Afghanistan. On 17 May 2006, Harper pushed a motion through the House of Commons to extend Canada's participation in ISAF, which was due to expire in February 2007, until 2009. A second resolution, in March 2008, would extend the mission until 2011. In response to the sustained fighting, the Harper government also increased its military commitment in September 2006, thereby i) increasing the size and strength of the CF to 2,500; ii) adding an additional infantry company (250 soldiers); iii) deploying a Leopard tank squadron; iv) adding a counter-mortar capability; and v) including military engineers (and an armoured engineering vehicle) to enhance the Provincial Reconstruction Team's (PRT's) capability to manage quick impact reconstruction and development projects.[10]

The 9/11 attacks explain why Canada initially went to Afghanistan, but they do not explain the subsequent decisions to stay in the country for a decade. According to Ottawa, 'Canada is in Afghanistan to help Afghans rebuild their country as a stable, democratic and self-sufficient society. We are there with over 60 other nations and international organizations, at the request of the democratically-elected Afghan government and as part of a UN-mandated, NATO-led mission'.[11] This was broadened into three intertwined goals:

- Help the government of Afghanistan and its people to build a stable, peaceful and self-sustaining democratic country;
- Provide the people of Afghanistan with the hope for a brighter future by establishing the security necessary to promote development;
- Defend Canadian interests at home and abroad by preventing Afghanistan from relapsing into a failed state that provides a safe haven for terrorists and terrorist organizations.[12]

These may be the stated goals of the mission, but they do not really explain why Canada remains in Afghanistan. Nor do they explain the extent of Canada's unprecedented military commitment. Afghanistan was being used to advance two additional foreign policy goals: 1) supporting the Canada–US relationship; and 2) rebuilding the Canadian military. These two objectives were promoted by Prime Minister Stephen Harper and former Chief of Defence Staff General Rick Hillier.

Stephen Harper's Motivations

After remaining silent about Afghanistan throughout the 2005–06 election campaign, Harper made his feelings known on the day after the election. 'We will continue to help defend our values and democratic ideals around the world—as so courageously demonstrated by those young Canadian soldiers who are serving and who have sacrificed in Afghanistan'.[13] The focus on Afghanistan by the new Harper government was intensified with his surprise visit in March 2006. The destination for a new prime minister's first international visit is important, as it highlights the key priority for Canada's foreign policy. Most prime ministers select New York and Washington to show the importance of Canada–US bilateral relations. However, Harper went to Afghanistan. The symbolic value of this trip cannot be overstated. Moreover, when a prime minister travels, he brings along the national media—not the few foreign correspondents that the Canadian media still utilize, but the much larger parliamentary press gallery as well as some special feature reporters. Harper's visit provided an opportunity to educate a Canadian media which, in general, was inexperienced in and uninformed about war coverage. This ultimately magnified and broadened Canada's media coverage of the Afghan mission.

In his speech to Canadian troops during his March 2006 visit, Harper stated quite clearly that 'it's never easy for the men and women on the front lines. And there may be some who want to cut and run. But cutting and running is not your way. It's not my way. And it's not the Canadian way. We don't make a commitment and then run away at the first sign of trouble. We don't and we won't'.[14] Since that time, Harper has often repeated these types of phrases. For example, during the May 2006 debate on expanding Canada's operation in Afghanistan to February 2009, Harper warned that 'Canada is not immune to such [terror] attacks. And we will never be immune as long as we are a society that defends freedom, democracy, and human rights. Not surprisingly, Al-Qaeda has singled out Canada along with a number of other nations for attack—the same Al-Qaeda that, together with the Taliban, took an undemocratic Afghanistan and made it a safe haven from which to plan terrorist attacks worldwide. . . . [W]e just cannot let the Taliban, backed by Al-Qaeda, or similar extremist elements, return to power in Afghanistan.'[15] In September 2006, during an address to the United Nations General Assembly, Harper maintained that 'if we fail the Afghan people, we will be failing ourselves. For this is the United Nations' strongest mission and, therefore, our greatest test. Our collective will and credibility are being judged. We cannot afford to fail. We will succeed.'[16]

Harper also tried to link the Afghanistan operation with Canadian values. While in Afghanistan, Harper made it clear that 'serving in a UN-mandated, Canadian-led security operation . . . is in the very best of the Canadian tradition.' Harper went on to assert that 'reconstruction is reducing poverty; millions of people are now able to vote; women are enjoying greater rights and economic opportunities that could not have been imagined under the Taliban regime; and of Afghan children who are now in school studying the same things Canadian kids are learning back home.' Harper concluded that these tasks demonstrated that this involved 'standing up for . . . core Canadian values'.[17]

Paradoxically, the promotion of Canadian values is not a Conservative idea, but was initiated by the Liberals. Jean Chrétien's 1995 foreign policy review and Paul Martin's 2005 International Policy Statement both stated that Canadian foreign policy was based on three pillars: physical security, economic prosperity, and the promotion of Canadian values.[18]

Stephen Harper had very little international experience, or even interest, before becoming prime minister. In his previous political jobs within the Reform Party, National Citizens Coalition, and Canadian Alliance, his focus was on reforming Canadian federalism, reducing the size of government, cutting taxes, and eliminating the government's deficit and debt.[19] This lack of interest in foreign affairs extended to much of his caucus. Beyond Gordon O'Connor (who had been a Brigadier General in the Canadian Forces), and David Emerson (a former Liberal Industry Minister who had worked on the softwood lumber file), there were few Conservatives who had had any international responsibilities prior to forming the government.[20] Therefore it was not a surprise that there were no international dimensions to his famous five campaign priorities (accountability, lower taxes, crime, child care, and health care). What, then, explains his decision to make Afghanistan the centrepiece of his foreign policy?

The party platforms of the Reform Party, Canadian Alliance, and the merged Conservative Party, were weak on foreign policy. Nevertheless, starting with the formation of the Reform Party in 1987, its members were clear on two key foreign policy principles: better relations with the United States and a stronger Canadian military. These two themes cropped up over and over again in their attacks on the Liberals. An example of the intertwining of these two issues was a major speech delivered soon after Harper became leader of the Canadian Alliance. Harper argued that 'for nine years the government has systematically neglected the Canadian forces and undermined our ability to contribute to peace enforcement and even peacekeeping operations, including recently our premature withdrawal from Afghanistan. Most recently we have been inclined to offer knee-jerk resistance to the United States on national missile defence despite the fact that Canada is confronted by the same threats from rogue nations equipped with ballistic missiles and weapons of mass destruction as is the United States.'[21]

As director of policy for the Reform Party, Harper had been very critical of the domestic policies of the Mulroney government (Meech Lake and Charlottetown, deficit/debt), but he praised Mulroney's foreign policy, in particular his ability to manage Canada–US relations. Mulroney's role in achieving the Canada–US free trade agreement was an obvious reference point, but Harper also wanted to show that Mulroney (and implicitly, Harper himself) could also stand up to the Americans. Therefore, he would frequently invoke Mulroney's leadership (later acknowledged by Nelson Mandela) in the global fight against South African apartheid. Harper would make it clear that Mulroney was capable of 'disagreeing with the United States without being disagreeable, without in any way jeopardizing our bilateral relationship'.[22] This was in direct contrast to some insulting statements by the Liberal government towards the Bush administration during the debate over participation in the Iraq War. What Harper was saying was that a Conservative government would follow the practice of the Mulroney government in its handling of Canada–US relations. Mulroney, according to Harper 'understood a fundamental truth. He understood that mature and intelligent Canadian leaders must share the following perspective: the United States is our closest neighbour, our best ally, our biggest customer, and our most consistent friend.'[23]

Harper's foreign policy ideas started to crystallize during the debate about Canadian participation in the US–Iraq War. Many of his comments on Iraq would foreshadow his actions in Afghanistan. Harper devoted his maiden speech as leader of the Canadian Alliance in October 2002 to discussing the build-up to war in Iraq. 'The time has come for Canada to pledge support to the developing coalition of nations, including Britain,

Australia, and the United States, determined to send a clear signal to Saddam Hussein that failure to comply with an unconditional program of inspection, as spelled out in either new or existing UN resolutions, would justify action to ensure the safety of millions of people in the region from Iraq's suspected weapons of mass destruction.' Harper went on to add that if the Liberal government did not support military action against Iraq it would be undermining 'Canada's reputation with its allies and [would be doing] nothing to uphold the credibility of the United Nations by not joining in sending a clear message to Hussein that failure to comply will bring consequences'.[24] A few months later, when war was looking more and more imminent, Harper reminded the House of Commons of Canada's previous participation in wars and criticized the Liberals for making decisions on war and peace via public opinion polls and focus groups. In contrast, a Harper government would 'take our position the way real leaders and great nations make decisions at such moments in history'.[25] Finally, in a speech on 25 April 2003, one month after the start of the US-led war against Iraq, Harper stated that the

emerging debates on foreign affairs should be fought on moral grounds. Current challenges in dealing with terrorism and its sponsors, as well as the emerging debate on the foals of the United States as the sole superpower, will be well served by conservative insights on preserving historic values and moral insights on right and wrong. . . . Conservatives must take the moral stand, with our allies, in favour of the fundamental values of society, including democracy, free enterprise, and individual freedom. This moral stand should not just give us the right to stand with our allies, but the duty to do so and the responsibility to put 'hard power' behind our international commitments.[26]

In his speeches on Iraq, Harper touched on a number of themes that would become important with respect to Afghanistan. First, Canada should support its allies. Canada went to Afghanistan in support of the United States, the United Nations, and NATO—its most important bilateral partner and its most important multilateral alliances. A second theme was the need for Canada to be a world leader. During his trip to Afghanistan, Harper would assert that he wanted 'an international leadership role for our country. Not carping from the sidelines, but taking a stand on the big issues that matter.'[27] A third theme was the promotion of Canadian values like democracy and freedom. In Harper's election night victory address, he stated that 'we will continue to help defend our values and democratic ideals around the world—as so courageously demonstrated by those young Canadian soldiers who are serving and who have sacrificed in Afghanistan'.[28] The final theme was the need for hard power, like military force, to achieve foreign policy objectives. Harper would frequently argue that the Taliban remained a security challenge in Afghanistan and that was 'threatening the well-being and economic development and social development of the people of Afghanistan'.[29]

When the Harper government was elected it took concrete steps to rebuild the Canadian military after decades of neglect. The 2006 and 2007 budgets allocated an increase of $1.1 billion a year in core funding for the military.[30] The government also addressed procurement, with purchases worth $17.1 billion on strategic and tactical airlift planes and helicopters, supply ships, and transport trucks.[31] This was followed up in April 2007 with the purchase of up to 100 Leopard 2 tanks from the Netherlands and the rental of 20 Leopard 2A6 tanks from Germany.[32] By 2009, the CF's budget was $19.1 billion.[33]

The emphasis on the military also extended to ways of protecting Canada's Arctic sovereignty.

During the 2006 election campaign, Harper promised to purchase new icebreakers to patrol the Arctic waters and got into a war of words with the US Ambassador over jurisdiction of the Northwest Passage.[34] Once in power, the Canadian Forces initiated regular military patrols of the Arctic.[35]

Harper also hoped to use participation in Afghanistan to re-engage Canada on the world stage. Many foreign policy observers have noticed a precipitous drop in Canada's global influence.[36] While in Afghanistan, Harper asserted that the operation was 'about more than just defending Canada's interests. It's also about demonstrating an international leadership role for our country.'[37] A couple of weeks later, the Harper government pledged in its first throne speech to 'a more robust diplomatic role for Canada, a stronger military and a more effective use of Canadian dollars'.[38] This type of rhetoric was quite common coming from Canadian governments. The difference is that the Harper government put its money where its mouth was. As was mentioned earlier, the 2006 and 2007 federal budgets increased military spending. On the foreign aid side, the previous Liberal government had made Afghanistan the number one recipient of Canadian foreign aid. Once taking office, the Harper government increased the level of funding. The May 2006 budget brought the total Canadian commitment to $1.2 billion in the 2001–11 period. The 2007 budget found an additional $200 million in new money for reconstruction and development activities.[39]

A final motivating factor for Harper's interest in Afghanistan is as a partisan wedge issue to demonstrate his leadership abilities to the Canadian public and to divide the Liberal party. Harper wanted to portray himself as a decisive leader, in contrast to the dithering of Paul Martin, and Afghanistan was an excellent opportunity to show leadership. Parliament was used for a significant take-note debate on Afghanistan in March 2006 and again in May 2006 when the House voted to extend the mission until 2009. At the time of these Parliamentary manoeuvres, the Liberals were undergoing a leadership race. Afghanistan was a source of division between the leadership contenders with the frontrunner Michael Ignatieff in strong support of the mission, but with everybody else, including the eventual winner, Stéphane Dion, in various degrees of opposition. There were also some senior Liberals in the House, who had been part of the decision-making process under the Chrétien and Martin governments and who, like Interim Leader Bill Graham, were also in support of the operation. Harper hoped to use the debate/vote on Afghanistan to highlight the divisions and contradictions within the Liberal Party and to show Canadians that the Conservatives were the best choice on issues of international peace and security.

Rick Hillier's Motivation

For most of Canada's post–World War II history, the Chief of Defence Staff (CDS) was a largely invisible figure, a manager rather than a shaper of Canadian foreign and defence policy. This would change with Rick Hillier. Hillier's appointment as CDS 'would fundamentally change the philosophy, the strategy, the organization, and the culture of the Canadian Forces. He would become the most important and influential CDS in living memory.'[40] Hillier believed that the CF had become 'backwards-looking, bureaucratic, cumbersome and risk-averse'.[41] Therefore, his preoccupation when he became CDS was to transform and rebuild the Canadian military. There were two specific ways that Hillier wanted to do this. First, there needed to be an improved status that showcased the CF's combat capabilities. Second, there had to be sustained funding increases.

The Canadian military wanted to end the view that it was to be used for everything but fighting wars. Prior to Afghanistan, the CF was deployed primarily for UN peacekeeping operations and humanitarian relief operations. It was also used domestically to support civilian authorities in fire-fighting, snow removal, and flood relief. These are all worthwhile missions, but many members of the Canadian military believe that they are ancillary to their primary function of war fighting.

Coming in for particular scorn was the image of Canada as peacekeepers. Public opinion polls have consistently shown over the decades that Canadians are in love with peacekeeping.[42] Former Foreign Affairs Minister Bill Graham declared that 'for many Canadians, and in the eyes of the world, peace-keeping is fundamental to who we are as a nation'.[43] Peacekeeping, as historian Norman Hillmer has pointed out, fit 'the government's international objectives and appeal[ed] to a public anxious to believe that Canada could be the world's conscience, untainted by power politics and considerations of narrow or selfish interests'.[44] Peacekeeping is cele-brated in many ways: with a special monument on Parliament Hill, with a Heritage Minutes television segment, and with an image on the Loonie.

Peacekeeping may be loved by Canadian civil-ians, but it is not by the Canadian military. As Major Edward Denbeigh asserted, 'I have laboured under the incessant tyranny of the peacekeeping myth. The professional military in Canada has suf-fered denigration and neglect since the mid-1960s as successive governments and an apathetic public have viewed the profession as an embarrassment, and sought to hide us like poor cousins that no wanted to talk about'.[45] Hillier believed that 'for so many years our political landscape had been dom-inated by a select group in Canadian society, self-proclaimed opinion leaders who I prefer to think of as snake-oil salesmen, who had been allowed to create the impression that Canadian were very sensitive, would advocate only "soft power" and would support their military only in the role of

peacekeepers'.[46] Previous CDSs were reluctant to speak out in public, but Hillier eagerly grabbed the bully pulpit to signal to Canadians that the CF was, first and foremost, a fighting force. In the summer of 2005, Hillier maintained that the military were 'not the public service of Canada, we're not just another department. We are the Canadian Forces, and our job is to be able to kill people.' The targets of CF activity, Taliban and Al Qaeda forces, were described as 'detestable murderers and scumbags'.[47]

In the immediate aftermath of 9/11, there was a debate over the precise military role of the Can-adian Forces. There were elements in DFAIT that wanted Canada to play a 'traditional' peacekeeping role, but the CF wanted 'to get into the fight'.[48] Eventually, the CF, in combination with the civil-ians in the DND, got what they wanted when the Chrétien government deployed the 3 PPCLI to Afghanistan in October 2001. That initial deploy-ment did much for the morale of the CF. The Com-mander of Canadian ground troops in Afghanistan would later brag that Canadian participation in the war 'established our credibility in the coalition. Canada had been tainted with an image of being blue-hatted peacekeepers, and I think . . . the aggressiveness and tenacity that the troops showed . . . dispelled the myth. . . . [W]e were like a pack of rabid pit bulls in satisfying the coalition's end state.'[49]

After the initial deployment, the CF, especially under Hillier, would consistently lobby for greater combat responsibilities in Afghanistan.[50] Kirton has identified a wing of the Canadian military that had trained with the Americans and wanted 'to do some real war fighting'.[51] They were led by Hillier, who had served as the first Canadian Deputy Com-manding General of III Corps, US Army in Fort Hood, Texas from 1998 to 2000. The CF saw Afghanistan as an opportunity to establish its cre-dentials as a credible fighting force among its NATO peers. Interviews with Canadian soldiers revealed a distinct preference for NATO-led operations as opposed to UN operations. In too many UN operations, Canadians are forced to work with, and compensate for, poorly trained and equipped troops from Jordan, Kenya, or Nepal, but they prefer to work with professionally trained and equipped troops from the United States and Britain.[52] While the Canadian soldiers greatly respected the Americans and British, that respect was not always reciprocated. For example, when ISAF was formed in 2002, the Europeans did not want a Canadian contingent. According to Hillier,

> Canada was not being invited because the Brits believed we had lost our ability to be a war-fighting nation. . . . As far as they were concerned, Canada could not be relied upon to do the tough stuff and was therefore or no use. The British command structure remembered the years in the former Yugoslavia when 'Can'tbat'—Canada's contribution to the UN, and later to NATO, forces—needed days or even weeks to get approval from Ottawa before we would take on an operation, assuming we were even allowed to do so.[53]

When Hillier accepted the CDS job he made his section objective clear: he wanted the government 'to commit to financial support in future federal budgets'.[54] As was shown above, the Harper government, building on the modest increases of the Martin government, pumped billions in core funding and procurement into the Canadian military. This has to be seen as a success for Hillier because, as Philippe Lagassé points out, '[f]rom the perspective of the military as a bureaucratic organization, an ability to protect existing budgets and secure budget increase is the mark of a strong, politically effective leader'.[55] There is little doubt that the mission in Afghanistan was the key driver for the increased

spending. The operation on the ground—especially the growing casualties—showed the need for new equipment: strategic and tactical aircraft, light armoured vehicles, tanks, and helicopters. Although the government has tried to keep the detailed costs quiet, parliamentary budget officer Kevin Page has estimated that by 2011 the Afghan mission will have cost Canada $18.1 billion.[56]

WILL WE STAY LONGER?

On 13 March 2008, the House of Commons voted for a Conservative–Liberal negotiated resolution (opposed by the NDP and Bloc Québécois) that called for 'the government of Canada [to] notify NATO that Canada will end its presence in Kandahar as of July 2011, and, as of that date, the redeployment of Canadian Forces troops out of Kandahar and their replacement by Afghan forces [will] start as soon as possible, so that it will have been completed by December 2011'.[57] The 2011 deadline is usually viewed in political terms: a Parliamentary compromise found by a minority government. In other words, somehow, with a majority or without, the Harper government would find a way to maintain its military presence in Afghanistan. Kim Nossal, for one, has concluded that the motion of 13 March 2008 was actually 'a motion permitting the Canadian government to remain militarily committed to Afghanistan'.[58]

However, there are a number of important reasons why Canada's military role will largely be over by the end of 2011. Politically, the war is increasingly becoming unpopular. Angus Reid has shown that over the years, public support for the military operation in Afghanistan has been falling. By December 2009, 53 per cent of Canadians opposed the war, and only 42 per cent supported it.[59] The extent of Canadian causalities has contributed to this opposition. Since 2006, and the deployment to

Kandahar, over 30 Canadian lives have been lost each year. This has been magnified by sustained media coverage of the deaths, including ramp ceremonies, repatriation back to Canada, and the drive down the 'Highway of Heroes'. This is combined with a concern that Canada's efforts are too militarized and skewed away from development and diplomatic activities. Even the government has recognized this fact. For example, the resolution of 13 March 2008 emphasized that 'Canada's contribution to the reconstruction and development of Afghanistan should be revamped and increased to strike a better balance between our military efforts and our development efforts in Afghanistan'.[60]

There is a strong sense that despite Canada's blood and treasure, little progress is being made in Afghanistan. The government of President Hamid Karzai is widely seen as corrupt, and the sense that his 2009 election win was greatly tainted by fraud, if not completely stolen. The Taliban insurgency has not been defeated, and its tactics continue to evolve, as its use of more powerful improvised explosion devices (IEDs) and suicide bombers shows.

Militarily, the 2011 deadline has also become an imperative. The army is overworked; many soldiers have been on multiple tours of duty in Afghanistan and need an operational pause. As for the Air Force, the Chinook and Griffin helicopters are beat up after frequent use in a hostile climate of 40 degree-plus temperatures and sandstorms.[61] Simply put, even if the Canadian government wanted to stay in Afghanistan, there is serious doubt about whether it would have the military resources to do so.

Internationally, there is a belief that many NATO countries are not pulling their weight. Germany, Italy, Belgium, and others have made sure that their soldiers stay out of harm's way. The January 2008 Independent Panel on Canada's Future Role in Afghanistan (the John Manley Report) stated that 'too many NATO governments have failed to contribute significant numbers of troops in the regions of Afghanistan most vulnerable to insurgent attack and destabilization. Others have placed caveats on their military activities—prohibiting night fighting, for instance, or refusing to authorize helicopter flights that might expose pilots to combat.'[62] Even in comparisons with British and American soldiers, who are also doing the heavy lifting in the southern part of Afghanistan, Canadian troops have suffered casualties in disproportionate numbers.[63] Why should Canadians continue to fight and die, when its NATO allies are not? The fact that the Americans also plan on a military withdrawal by 2011 will make it easier for Canada to pull out. On 1 December 2009, United States President Barack Obama announced that the United States would 'send an additional 30,000 US troops to Afghanistan. After 18 months, our troops will begin to come home'.[64]

Given the above discussion, what will Canada's role in Afghanistan look like in 2012? First, Canada will be staying and likely re-dedicating itself to a greater role in supporting Afghan development. Canada could take over a PRT in another part of Afghanistan, far away from southern Afghanistan along the Pakistani border, and definitely not in Kandahar. However, it is quite likely that there will also be a continued military role, albeit quite smaller, for Canada in Afghanistan post-2011. For example, a small military contingent to accompany the PRT, a couple of dozen JTF2 forces, and perhaps even a headquarters battle group could remain in Afghanistan. The military role would involve a couple of hundred troops at most, in largely a defensive position (except for the JTF2). This will reduce the possibility of active fighting (and Canadian casualties), give the military a needed operational pause, and allow the CF to support development activities.

CONCLUSION

This chapter posed three questions concerning Canada's role in Afghanistan. The first question was why did we go? Canada went to Afghanistan because of the 9/11 attacks. The second question was why did we stay? After the initial 2001 deployment, Canada has remained in Afghanistan, in a significant military role, to improve relations with the United States and because the mission provided an opportunity to rebuild the Canadian military. These twin goals were promoted by Prime Minister Harper and General Hillier. It was a melding of Harper's ideological convictions with the institutional interests of the Canadian Forces as articulated by its charismatic leader.

The final question was will we leave? Explaining the past is easy, but predicting the future is hard. Nevertheless, we can anticipate a fundamental shift in Canada's Afghanistan role by the end of 2011. Canada will continue its development work in Afghanistan, and in the absence of an offensive combat role, it will get more attention from the media and the public. Its military role will not end, but will be significantly reduced, both in numbers and responsibilities. This is because of growing domestic opposition to the war combined with a weary CF that has found it difficult to sustain its presence since 2006. Finally, with Obama's decision to 'surge and withdraw', there will be a lack of American pressure to continue in southern Afghanistan.

Key Terms

Peacekeeping
Provincial Reconstruction Team

Notes

1. Quoted in Janice Gross Stein and Eugene Lang, *The Unexpected War: Canada in Kandahar* (Toronto: Viking, 2007), 21.
2. Quoted in Kent Roach, *September 11: Consequences for Canada* (Montreal and Kingston: McGill-Queen's University Press, 2003), 150.
3. 'Fighting blamed on "retribution".' *Toronto Star* (22 January 2007).
4. United Nations, Security Council Resolution 1368 (12 September 2001).
5. North Atlantic Treaty Organization, 'Statement by the North Atlantic Council (Invocation Article V—attacks on US),' Press Release 124 (12 September 2001).
6. Roach, *September 11*, 148.
7. Ipsos Reid, 'While Majority (73%) Agree that Canada Should Join the United States and Also Declare War on International Terrorism it is Conditional as Support Falls to Just Over Half (54%) if War Exposes Canadian Civilians to Attack by Terrorists,' News Release (21 September 2001). Accessed on 16 May 2007 at www.ipsosna.com.
8. Quoted in J.L. Granatstein, *Whose War Is It? How Canada Can Survive in the Post-9/11 World* (Toronto: Harper-Collins, 2007), 91–2.
9. Quoted in Granatstein, *Whose War Is It?*, 91–2.

10. Department of National Defence, 'Military Strengthens its Reconstruction and Stabilization Efforts in Afghanistan,' News Release (15 September 2006). Accessed on 16 May 2007 at www.forces.gc.ca.
11. Department of Foreign Affairs and International Trade, 'Canada's Approach in Afghanistan' (2 April 2009). Accessed on 3 January 2010 at www.afghanistan.gc.ca.
12. Canadian Forces, 'Backgrounder: Military Strengthens its Reconstruction and Stabilization Efforts in Afghanistan,' Accessed on 15 March 2007 at www.forces.gc.ca.
13. Quoted in John Kirton, 'Harper's "Made in Canada" Global Leadership,' in Andrew F. Cooper and Dane Rowlands, eds., *Canada Among Nations 2006: Minorities and Priorities* (Montreal and Kingston: McGill-Queen's University Press, 2006), 37.
14. Stephen Harper, 'Address by the Prime Minister to the Canadian Armed Forces in Afghanistan' (13 March 2006). Accessed on 10 April 2007 at www.pm.gc.ca.
15. Stephen Harper, 'Prime Minister stands by Canada's commitment to Afghanistan' (17 May 2006). Accessed on 2 May 2007 at www.pm.gc.ca.
16. Stephen Harper, 'Address by the Prime Minister to the 61st Opening Session of the United Nations General

Assembly' (21 September 2006). Accessed on 2 May 2007 at www.pm.gc.ca.

17. Harper, 'Address by the Prime Minister to the Canadian Armed Forces in Afghanistan' (13 March 2006).

18. Department of Foreign Affairs and International Trade, Canada in the World (DFAIT: Ottawa, 1995) and Canada, Canada's International Policy Statement, A Role of Pride and Influence in the World (DFAIT: Ottawa, 2005).

19. There have been two book-length biographies on Stephen Harper, and both describe Harper's lack of intellectual engagement in international relations and Canadian foreign policy. See: William Johnson, *Stephen Harper and the Future of Canada* (Toronto: McClelland & Stewart, 2005); and Lloyd Mackey, *The Pilgrimage of Stephen Harper* (Toronto: ECW Press, 2005).

20. In Harper's first cabinet, O'Connor and Emerson were made ministers of Defence and Trade respectively; the remaining international ministries would be run by international neophytes who were chosen for domestic political reasons. Peter MacKay, the former Progressive Conservative leader, was named minister of Foreign Affairs and Josée Verner, a francophone female, was named minister of International Cooperation.

21. Quoted in Johnson, *Stephen Harper and the Future of Canada*, 316.

22. Quoted in Mackey, *The Pilgrimage of Stephen Harper*, 173–174.

23. Quoted in Johnson, *Stephen Harper and the Future of Canada*, 316.

24. Canada, House of Commons, Debates, 1 October 2002.

25. Canada, House of Commons, Debates, 29 January 2003.

26. Quoted in Mackey, *The Pilgrimage of Stephen Harper*, 169–170.

27. Harper, 'Address by the Prime Minister to the Canadian Armed Forces in Afghanistan' (13 March 2006).

28. Stephen Harper, 'Canadians Choose Change and Accountability' (23 January 2006). Accessed on 2 May 2007 at www.conservative.ca.

29. CTV, 'Think tank calls for new approach in Afghanistan' (24 October 2006). Accessed on 2 May 2007 at www.ctv.ca

30. Department of National Defence, 'Budget 2006 and the Department of National Defence and the Canadian Forces.' Accessed on 11 August 2006 at www.forces.gc.ca/site/Reports/budget06/index_e.asp, Department of National Defence, 'Defence and Budget 2007: Highlights.' Accessed on 30 April 2007 at www.forces.gc.ca/site/Reports/budget_2007/index_e.asp.

31. Department of National Defence, 'Canada First Defence Procurement.' Accessed on 11 August 2006 at www.forces.gc.ca/site/Focus/first/index_e.asp.

32. Department of National Defence, 'Protection the top priority with tank acquisition,' News Release (12 April 2007).

33. 'Funding the Forces,' CBC News (22 January 2009). Accessed on 3 January 2010 at www.cbc.ca/money/story/2009/01/20/f-militarybudget.html.

34. Stephen Harper, 'Harper Stands Up for Arctic Sovereignty' (22 December 2005). Accessed on 2 May 2007 at www.conservative.ca/media/20051222-Speech-Harper-Winnipeg.pdf.

35. Department of National Defence, 'CF operation demonstrates value of interagency cooperation in Canada's Arctic' (27 April 2007). Accessed on 2 May 2007 at www.forces.gc.ca/site/newsroom/.

36. For a comprehensive examination of this fact see Andrew Cohen, *While Canada Slept: How we lost our place in the world* (Toronto: McLelland & Stewart, 2003); and Norman Hillmer and Maureen Appel Molot, eds., *Canada Among Nations 2002: A Fading Power* (Oxford: Toronto, 2002).

37. Stephen Harper, 'Address by the Prime Minister to the Canadian Armed Forces in Afghanistan' (13 March 2006).

38. Canada, Canada's New Government: Turning a New Leaf (Ottawa: Office of the Governor General, 4 April 2006).

39. Canadian International Development Agency, 'Funding: Canada's Commitment to Afghanistan.' Accessed on 30 April 2007 at www.acdi-cida.gc.ca.

40. Stein and Lang, *The Unexpected War*, 151.

41. General Rick Hillier, *A Soldier First: Bullets, Bureaucrats and the Politics of War* (Toronto: HarperCollins, 2009), 3.

42. See Pierre Martin and Michel Fortmann, 'Canadian Public Opinion and Peacekeeping in a Turbulent World'. *International Journal* 50, 2 (Spring 1995), 370–400; Pierre Martin and Michel Fortmann, 'Public Opinion: Obstacle, Partner, or Scapegoat?' *Policy Options* (January–February 2001), 66–72; and 'Half polled prefer peacekeeping-only soldiers,' CBC News (20 September 2009). Accessed on 3 January 2010 at www.cbc.ca/canada/story/2009/09/20/canada-poll-soldiers.html.

43. Foreign Affairs Minister Bill Graham, 'Notes for an Address at the Peacekeeping Medal Ceremony,' Speeches 2002/NA (Ottawa: DFAIT, 22 October 2002).

44. Norman Hillmer, 'Peacekeeping: Canadian Invention, Canadian Myth', in J.L. Granatstein and Sune Akerman, eds., *Welfare States in Trouble: Historical Perspectives on Canada and Sweden* (North York, ON: Swedish Canadian Academic Foundation, 1994), 159–70.

45. Quoted in Michael Hart, *From Pride to Influence: Towards a New Canadian Foreign Policy* (UBC Press: Vancouver, 2008), 284.

46. Hillier, *A Soldier First*, 430.

47. Quoted in Daniel Leblanc, 'JTF2 to hunt al-Qaeda,' *Globe and Mail* (15 July 2005), A1.

48. Sean M. Maloney, *Enduring the Freedom: A Rogue Historian in Afghanistan* (Washington, DC: Potomac Books, 2005), 57–58.

49. Quoted in Roach, *September 11: The Consequences for Canada*, 153.

50. While it is clear that Hillier wanted a greater combat role for Canada, there is disagreement about the geographic location. Lang and Stein argue that 'Hillier wanted a deployment that would get Canada deeper and deeper into the most troubled part of Afghanistan', i.e., Kandahar. This is disputed by Hillier, who replied that 'my suggestion for a future Canadian mission in Afghanistan had been for us to take over responsibility for Kabul International Airport'. However, '[n]obody in Ottawa was interested, so the idea died. The government had already signaled its intent to go into Kandahar province, and the Department of Foreign Affairs, CID and National Defence were well into their planning of that mission by the time I came back to work at NDHQ after my time as ISAF commander.' See Stein and Lang, *The Unexpected War*, 181, and Hillier, *A Soldier First*, 342–343.

51. Kirton, 'Harper's "Made in Canada" Global Leadership,' 51.

52. Interviews with Canadian troops, Kabul, Afghanistan, November 2004.

53. Hillier, *A Soldier First*, 242–243.

54. Hillier, *A Soldier First*, 2.

55. Philippe Lagassé, 'A mixed legacy: General Rick Hillier and Canadian defence, 2005–08,' *International Journal* LXIV/3 (Summer 2009), 607.

56. 'Funding the Forces,' CBC News.

57. Canada, House of Commons, 'Vote No. 76: Afghanistan Mission' (13 March 2008).

58. Kim Richard Nossal, 'No Exit: Canada and the "War without End" in Afghanistan,' in Hans-Georg Ehrhardt and Charles C. Pentland, eds., *The Afghanistan Challenge: Hard Realities and Strategic Choices*, Queen's School of Policy Studies (Montreal and Kingston: McGill-Queen's University Press, 2009), 158.

59. Angus Reid, 'Canadians Decline Expanded Role in Afghanistan' (4 December 2009). Accessed on 3 January 2010 at www.angus-reid.com/polls/view/canadians_decline_expanded_role_in_afghanistan/.

60. Canada, House of Commons, 'Vote No. 76: Afghanistan Mission' (13 March 2008).

61. Confidential interview with senior CF officer.

62. Independent Panel on Canada's Future Role in Afghanistan, Report (2008). Accessed on 25 March 2008 at dsp-psd.tpsgc.gc.ca/collection_2008/dfait-maeci/FR5-20-1-2008E.pdf.

63. 'Canadian forces pay higher price,' CBC News (28 October 2009). Accessed on 4 January 2010 at www.cbc.ca/world/story/2009/10/26/f-afghan-deaths.html.

64. United States, White House, 'Remarks by the President to the Nation on the way forward in Afghanistan and Pakistan' (1 December 2009).

19

BORDERS AND BRIDGES ALONG A MULTIDIMENSIONAL POLICY LANDSCAPE: CANADA'S POLICY RELATIONS IN NORTH AMERICA

Monica Gattinger and Geoffrey Hale

Public policy in Canada is often shaped by the political, economic and cultural realities of its location in North America. Although many of the country's policy relationships are broadly international in scope, Canadian policy-makers often train their sights more narrowly on North America, especially on the United States. Frequently, they must balance the realities of economic interdependence with the United States with competing domestic interests in Canada and the desire of most Canadians to maintain their own identities and capacity for policy choice.

Most notably, the pursuit and maintenance of secure, predictable access to US markets has shaped Canada's economic policy relations with its southern neighbour since the Mulroney government's free trade negotiations of the 1980s. These negotiations followed growing Congressional protectionism during and after the 1981–82 recession—a cyclical pattern that has re-emerged in the first decade of the twenty-first century. The Canada–US Free Trade Agreement (CUFTA) reduced barriers to trade and investment across many economic sectors, and was expanded into the North American Free Trade Agreement (NAFTA) in 1994. However, post-9/11 border thickening, the economic downturn of 2008–9 with continuing fallout into 2009–10 and beyond, and the prospect of major US and international policy changes on environmental and other issues transcending traditional facets of economic policy, highlight the continuing challenges of managing cross-border and international policy relations.

Canada has maintained longstanding relations in non-economic sectors with the United States, including environmental and defence agreements. These issues, including, more recently, climate change and species at risk, have become increasingly significant. The last two decades have also witnessed substantial growth in sub-national policy relations involving provincial/state, regional, and even muni-cipal governments. Overall, the growing relevance of North American and broader international policy factors in areas traditionally reserved for domestic policy-making has made many Canadian policy decisions at least partially 'intermestic'[1] in character.

Domestic politics in both Canada and the United States amplify the challenges of managing cross-border and broader international policies. These include the persistence of minority govern-ments and regional decentralization in Canada, the protectionist impulses of American governments in response to the economic downturn, minimal enthusiasm for further economic integration in North America within the American public, and the cross-cutting effects of North American and global trends that are changing patterns of domestic and international political, economic and societal interaction. These effects include the persistence of national and sub-national decision-making on major economic and regulatory issues and select-ive pressures for closer policy and regulatory inte-gration from business and other interest groups frustrated with different national approaches to particular clusters of issues, ranging from freight transportation to financial sector regulation to some aspects of climate change. Other factors are also generating greater complexity in Canada's policy relations with the United States and beyond, including the increasingly international character of public policies, the growing relevance of Mexico in North American policy relations, and the effects of exchange rates and structural price shifts on bilateral trade patterns over the past decade.

This chapter addresses these various dimen-sions of Canada's policy relations on the contin-ent, arguing that these exchanges are characterized by impulses toward both integration and differ-entiation, depending on the cluster of political, economic, and institutional factors prevailing in a given policy field. As such, any analysis of cross-border policy relations must necessarily be undertaken at the level of individual policy sectors, sub-sectors or issue areas. While formal relation-ships 'at the top'—between presidents and prime ministers, governors and premiers, and the like—set the broad tone for relations across policy fields, the policy landscape itself is multidimensional and its complexity and richness is only likely to inten-sify in the coming years. The first section of the chapter identifies several enduring features of Can-ada's policy relations in North America (including differentiation and integration) and a number of emerging characteristics of the country's cross-bor-der relations. The cumulative effect of these trends is to further amplify the complexity of policy rela-tions in North America. In this context, as explored in the second section, cross-border policy relations form a continuum that ranges substantially across policy fields from conflict-laden through to policy independence, co-ordination and harmonization.

Policy-makers and students of North American integration draw on a range of conceptual tools and techniques to manage and analyze these vari-ous exchanges. To illustrate these dynamics, the third section presents two brief case studies in the energy sector and governmental regulation of for-eign investments. The chapter concludes by dis-cussing the implications of the foregoing analysis, drawing on the concept of 'variable geometry' to describe the multifaceted arrangements compris-ing Canada's policy relations in North America.

CANADA'S POLICY RELATIONS IN NORTH AMERICA: INTEGRATION AND DIFFERENTIATION

The most prominent and enduring feature of Can-ada–US relations is asymmetry between the two countries: in population, power, relative economic importance, and degree of economic openness. The American population and economy dwarf Canada's some nine and eleven times over, respectively, and Canada's economy and many of its leading industries are heavily integrated with American counterparts and dependent upon American markets.

Much of this latter characteristic, which constitutes a second enduring feature, has been driven by economic factors, especially what we have characterized elsewhere as 'bottom-up' integration: the initiatives and responses of economic actors at the sectoral and firm levels in response to market forces, leading to greater integration and interdependence (Hale and Gattinger, 2010). Canadian policy-making is both influenced and complicated by microeconomic considerations—especially the joint production structures of individual industries and companies, complex supply chain management, and logistics—more than by the formal trade policies of governments (Blank, 2005: 2; Goldfarb, 2007). This reality is reflected in the substantial integration of energy and other commodity markets, transportation systems, financial markets, and, in many cases, standards of professional practice (Blank, 2008: 232). Canadian government policies have tended to accommodate these trends as part of a progressive shift in which most Canadian provinces now consistently conduct more trade internationally than they do with other provinces. This shift has often been controversial—as reflected in the passionate debates leading up to the 'free trade' election of 1988 and continuing concerns over the extent of North American integration expressed by civil society actors in Canada, the United States, and Mexico.

However, these economic trends have not led to greater *political* integration as feared by many groups at that time. The countries of North America have steered away from political integration and economic union (as in Europe), preferring instead to pursue the broadening and deepening of their economic linkages through trade agreements and more selective regulatory initiatives. This avoidance of closer political ties, a third long-term feature, has tended to reflect Canadian and Mexican fears that common political institutions would be dominated by the United States (Clarkson, 2002). It has also reflected American political culture's strong emphasis on popular sovereignty expressed through Congressional representatives, which underpins its historical aversion to delegating sovereignty to the supranational level (Studer, 2007). More recently, backlashes against North American integration in all three countries, but particularly in the US, militate against political integration.

Instead, a variety of transgovernmental mechanisms—formal and informal relations and processes between legislative, executive, regulatory, and judicial officials outside of formal diplomatic channels (Slaughter, 2004)—have emerged to manage and facilitate the interdependence of governmental, economic and, to a lesser extent, societal actors. These connections are the organizational backbone of policy relations in North America. In some cases, they may also involve select non-governmental actors in decision-making and related advisory processes previously dominated by state actors.

The extent and complexity of these administrative relations is staggering—although not surprising, given the institutional differences among Canada, the United States, and Mexico, which constitute the fourth enduring feature of policy relations in North America. All three countries are federations. However, Canada's fiscal and regulatory division of powers remain far more decentralized than in the other two countries, whatever the pressures for closer policy harmonization resulting from globalization and North American integration (Simeon, 2003). Moreover, the separation of powers enshrined in the US and Mexican constitutions require that significant policy changes are ultimately subject to complex negotiations and bargaining between the executive branch and Congress, with the latter retaining independent legislative powers. Both Congresses have demonstrated the capacity to act unilaterally contrary to executive policy preferences (although subject to its potential veto)—sometimes in ways that complicate relations with neighbouring countries.

The potential for divided government in both the United States and Mexico—in which opposition parties frequently control one or both houses of Congress—has forced the executive in both countries to govern in ways that accommodate domestic interests with powerful Congressional patrons or negotiate the terms under which it will be allowed to pursue international agreements. Such constraints are paralleled, to some extent, by the realities of federal minority governments in Canada since 2004 and by Canadian provinces' capacity to facilitate or obstruct Ottawa's implementation of international agreements in areas of provincial jurisdiction. They may be loosened or tightened depending on the ability of political leaders to mobilize some degree of elite consensus across partisan boundaries (Rosenau et al., 2005). They may also be relaxed or constricted by the potential for state actors or societal interests to impose effective limits on policy harmonization. Well-known examples of the former include distinctive national regulatory regimes for financial services, government procurement, international migration, and anything to which governments choose to apply the label of 'national security'. As to the latter, interest group politics have been central to longstanding disputes over softwood lumber, the persistence of agricultural subsidies (and 'supply management'), and distinctive policy regimes for Mexican energy and Canadian cultural industries.

These instances of policy differentiation amidst economic and policy integration constitute the fifth enduring feature of North American policy

relations, and an important dynamic that we treat more broadly across this chapter. As described in the next section, the management of cross-border and broader policy relations may be characterized by substantial policy independence (and sometimes divergence or conflict) through varying degrees of policy parallelism, co-ordination, collaboration, or harmonization. These distinctions—and the priority given to accommodation of varied national and sub-national interests by national governments—suggest both a continued 'capacity for choice' as suggested by Hoberg (2002), and the idea that patterns of economic integration are balanced, constrained, and shaped by multiple forces of differentiation or even 'fragmentation', as noted by Rosenau (2003) and others.

The United States, being far larger, more economically diversified, and less trade dependent than Canada or Mexico, neither needs nor is inclined to co-ordinate its broader economic or related policies with its neighbours. Even so, it may encourage a degree of policy convergence to the extent that it serves broader or particular US interests, although such matters tend to be treated either as subsets of domestic policies or as policy markers for the projection of US policy goals in broader international negotiations. It may also undertake legislative, policy, or regulatory initiatives with little regard for potential spill-overs for its neighbours, prompting Canadian or Mexican governments to bring such matters to its attention. As such, policy co-ordination and collaboration in North America take place primarily at sectoral and microeconomic levels. Policy harmonization is most likely to emerge when supported by a critical mass of comparable economic—and occasionally social—interests in each country whose activities are effectively integrated, or stand to be effectively integrated, across national borders. The greater the number of interests seeking to influence national (or federal) policies in a particular field, meanwhile, the greater the likelihood that individual governments will attempt to preserve their discretion to pursue *parallel* or *distinctive* policies, often on the basis of extending reciprocal recognition to firms based in other NAFTA countries and, sometimes, their citizens.

Emerging Features in Bilateral and North American Relations

Five more recent features are emerging in Canada's policy relations in North America alongside these long-term characteristics. The first is the broadening and deepening of economic relations. As the Canadian and American economies have become increasingly integrated, the focus of trade relations has moved from 'at the border' issues such as tariffs, import quotas, and valuation, to 'behind the border' considerations ranging from investment to health and safety standards to intellectual property rights (Doern and Tomlin, 1996). These economic considerations and related interests generate pressure for greater convergence between Canadian and American policies, particularly differing policy and regulatory approaches believed to impede trade and investment. These forces often find expression in appeals by private sector and other supporters to bring an end to the 'tyranny of small differences' between jurisdictions' policy and regulatory frameworks (Doern and Johnson, 2006: 5).

The second emerging feature is the unprecedented American focus on security since the terrorist attacks of 9/11. Security has become the prime lens through which American policy relations in North America are analyzed, under both the Bush and Obama administrations. The unfortunate adage that 'security trumps trade' has led to a 'thickening' of the border and substantial requirements for border management policy co-ordination and other security relations with the US—if not necessarily to the extent desired by US officials (Rosenzweig, 2009).

The third new characteristic is the growing breadth, depth, and frequency of sub-national cross-border relations. Provinces, states, regions, and cities are increasingly relating with their counterparts in North America through provincial–state organizations (*e.g.,* the Pacific Northwest Economic Region [PNWER] and the Conference of New England Governors and Eastern Canadian Premiers), sub-national agreements (*e.g.,* the Western Climate Initiative, which includes a number of states and provinces), and various informal arrangements and contacts. Jurisdictional divisions between federal and sub-national governments across North America necessarily engage sub-national entities in cross-border relations, although the latter's administrative and institutional capacity can vary substantially.[2] In some cases, provincial and federal interests largely align in cross-border relations with the United States (e.g., Buy American or food safety related trade barriers to Canadian agricultural exports), while in others, provincial interests may diverge from those of the federal government and there may be little convergence among provincial positions on an issue (e.g., softwood lumber or climate change). This increase in sub-national activity generates complex patterns of multi-level governance, in which various levels of government interact at the domestic and international levels on matters of policy development and implementation.

The fourth emergent feature is the growing place of Mexico in North American policy relations. The negotiation of NAFTA and greater political interest in exploring trilateral approaches to North American relations in both the US and Mexico, symbolized by the Security and Prosperity Partnership process of 2005–8, have increased pressure on Canada to expand its approach to include Mexico. However, sizeable differences in Canada–US and US–Mexico relations—whether political, policy, economic, or demographic—have contributed to the persistence of dual bilateralism:

the separate treatment of policies (US–Canada, US–Mexico) to accommodate differences in cross-border relationships and the often varied policy preferences of Canadian and Mexican governments in dealing with the United States. The convergence of interests and objectives in specific areas of Canada–US policy cooperation may be reinforced by complementary initiatives from Mexico City, but such patterns have tended to be the exception since the negotiation of NAFTA. Rather than moving towards 'grand visions' of further integration advocated by some interests—and feared by their critics—trilateral cooperation has generally been piecemeal and halting in recent years, and is likely to remain so for the foreseeable future.

The final difference in Canada's evolving policy relations in North America is the increasingly prominent role of non-economic issues—notably those relating to the environment. Bilateral and, in some cases, trilateral approaches have emerged on numerous environmental issues, including both traditional topics of boundary waters, migratory species, air and water quality, and more recent concerns such as climate change and species at risk. While addressing these issues clearly involves an economic dimension, the nature of the issues themselves—whether transboundary, regional, or global in scope, or the nature of 'science-based' policies—differs from the more traditional economic character of policy relations in North America.

All of the factors above have propelled the emergence of complex economic, political, and societal relationships as part of the broader North American reality. Some economic sectors are characterized by deep integration, sometimes involving the harmonization of framework legislation governing particular sectors, but more frequently involving the development of integrated cross-border corporate and industry structures, including the specialized functions of production and distribution networks.

Other policy fields display varying degrees of policy co-ordination but also an increasing popular assertion of societal distinctiveness in all three countries in which limited or conditional societal acceptance has contributed to a common reluctance to follow-up greater economic interdependence with closer institutional integration.

As a result, Canada's default approach to North American policy processes tends to be sector-specific, incremental, and frequently 'bottom-up'—driven by the independent initiatives of market or societal actors, and sometimes of provincial governments, to which the federal government may eventually respond. The Harper government's engagement with the Obama administration to date—a largely defensive series of initiatives responding to the latter's priorities on environmental issues (Hale, 2010) and auto industry restructuring among others—is consistent with at least the sector-specific aspects of this pattern.

CROSS-BORDER POLICY RELATIONS: CONCEPTUAL TOOLS AND TECHNIQUES

Research on cross-border policy management suggests three core concepts have become increasingly relevant to analyzing these processes. The first locates cross-border relations in particular policy fields or sub-fields on a *continuum of policy relations* that allows for comparison over time and across issue areas. The second is the distinction between relationships based on 'hard law'—international agreements with formal enforcement mechanisms, and 'soft law'—more informal approaches based on diplomacy and negotiation. The third is 'fragmegration'—James Rosenau's neologism describing the simultaneous interaction of integrating and fragmenting forces at multiple levels of political, economic, or societal activity and policy development.

The first concept, the policy continuum, allows for a more fine-grained analysis of the political dimension of cross-border policy relations by identifying the diversity of relations shaped by cross-border politics that may prevail in a particular policy field. As shown in Figure 19.1 below,[3] starting from the left, relations can be characterized by open *conflict*, where diverging interests drive major policy differences between countries. With *independence*, governments regard the policies of their counterparts as given and seek neither to influence them nor to adapt their policies in response to counterparts' policy changes. *Parallelism* refers to unilateral decisions by governments to adopt the broad outlines of initiatives taken by their counterparts while attempting to retain some discretion to respond to domestic political, economic, or socio-cultural conditions.[4] With *co-ordination,* countries mutually adapt their policy frameworks to one another: each jurisdiction recognizes the other's distinct policy and regulatory framework, but gives consideration to the implications of domestic policy and regulatory change for the other. *Collaboration*, meanwhile, connotes the exchange of data, expertise, or knowledge and countries aiming together to achieve common objectives. *Harmonization*, the rightmost end of the continuum, refers to the development of common policy or regulatory frameworks, using similar and often identical policy instruments.

The distinction between 'hard' and 'soft' law helps to discern the administrative dimension of cross-border policy relations, particularly the various tools that balance integration with domestic particularities. The hard law approach is based on legally binding obligations in both domestic and international law, often expressed in the form of treaties and formal arbitration. By contrast, the soft law approach is not entrenched in legislation. Often emerging from negotiations and practical problem-solving among specialized state (and sometimes non-state) actors, it is usually expressed in more flexible, less formal instruments (e.g., memoranda of understanding, working groups, etc.), which may be translated into the domestic hard law processes of participating countries at a later time. In sum, a variety of instruments, mechanisms, and processes underpin the administration of cross-border policy relations: agreements (e.g., treaties, protocols, memoranda of understanding) and cross-border channels and/or administrative structures (e.g., presidential–prime ministerial summits, regularly scheduled meetings of Cabinet officers with similar responsibilities, task forces, and joint commissions). As shown in Figure 19.2, these arrangements range from informal exchanges between public servants and informal instruments such as Memoranda of Understanding (MOUs), to increasingly formal mechanisms and instruments ranging from working groups or task forces (e.g., the Clean Energy Dialogue or the Permanent Joint Board on Defence), to formal agreements requiring ratification by the political executive or legislature (e.g., treaties such as CUFTA or NAFTA), to joint organizations such as North American Aerospace Defense Command (NORAD) and the International Joint Commission.[5]

Conflict————————————Independence————————————Harmonization

|–Parallelism–|–Coordination–|–Collaboration–|

Figure 19.1 The Continuum of Policy Relations

Informal
(soft law)

Formal
(hard law)

←——→

| E-mails, phone calls, meetings | Workshops, forums conferences | Working groups, taskforces, exchanges of personnel, joint training, joint programs, MOUs | PM/presidential summits, formal meetings of premiers/governors, exchanges of letters, protocols | Treaties, mutual recognition agreements, joint operations and organizations |

Figure 19.2 Administrative Arrangements for Managing Policy Relations in North America

American political scientist James Rosenau coined the term fragmegration to 'capture the simultaneous and often mutually reinforcing pressures of integration and fragmentation' (2003: 11). The former pressure refers, among other things, to processes of global economic integration spurred by trade liberalization, developments in information and communications technologies, and reductions in the costs of transportation, leading to significant growth in trade, integration of production and supply chains, and a reduction in the importance of national boundaries. The political dimension of fragmentation, meanwhile, refers to the oft-noted relocation of political authority away from the nation-state: upward to supranational institutions, downward to sub-national authorities, and outward to non-governmental actors. It can also refer to spontaneous social behaviour, behaviours emerging seemingly simultaneously in various local areas (e.g., local environmental movements). Fragmegration denotes the political, economic, and social dynamics resulting from the interaction of these seemingly opposing—but often mutually reinforcing—pressures. While many of these pressures pre-existed the current era of bilateral and regional trade agreements—notably the fragmentation of political authority inherent in the federal structure of the countries of North America—the subsequent growth of economic integration and the growing engagement of sub-national political entities in cross-border policy relations are relatively new features of Canada's policy relations in North America, and reflect fragmegration's features.

These three conceptual tools and techniques can be seen in Canadian policy-makers' approach to and management of cross-border policy relations, as illustrated in the case studies below.

CASE STUDY # 1: FOREIGN INVESTMENT / TAKEOVER POLICIES

Regulating foreign investment is a perennial political challenge in Canada. Historically, Canada has depended on both foreign direct investment (FDI) (controlling investments in individual corporations), and foreign portfolio investment (non-controlling investments in the securities of Canadian businesses and governments) to finance its economic development.

Foreign investment and national-security related regulations have traditionally evolved along separate lines. However, the globalization of investment patterns, cyclical patterns of corporate mergers and takeovers, and the emergence of sovereign wealth funds—state-controlled investment funds, often deploying hundreds of billions of dollars of capital—have brought the two issues together in recent years as Canada attempts to balance the realities of economic interdependence within and beyond North America with competing domestic interests.

This case study summarizes the evolution of Canadian rules governing foreign investments and corporate takeovers since the mid-1980s, with particular attention to the period since 2001. It demonstrates that Canadian foreign investment and takeover policies simultaneously contain elements of independence from and parallelism with US government policies and those of other industrial countries, and that North American influences continue to play a major role in Canadian policy decisions.

Major elements in foreign investment and takeover policies— Canada and the United States

Canadian approaches to market capitalism and corporate governance more closely resemble those of the United States than of Western Europe, Japan, or major developing economies, despite traditionally higher levels of corporate concentration, family ownership of major firms, and a financial sector culture based more on British than American traditions. Evolving capital markets and regulatory styles in both the United States and Canada have tended to favour 'shareholder capitalism', in which ownership and/or control of major firms outside a few 'strategic sectors' is determined by shareholders' choices, over the 'stakeholder capitalism' characteristic of Western Europe and Japan since the 1940s and 1950s, in which government officials and (often) unions play major roles in corporate governance.

However, there are four major distinctions between traditional Canadian and American models of corporate ownership and governance. First,

during most of the twentieth century, Canada was far more dependent than the United States on foreign investment—prompting the Trudeau government's introduction of the Foreign Investment Review Act in 1973 and efforts to 'Canadianize' oil and gas firms under the National Energy Program (NEP) of 1980. These measures, which triggered both domestic and cross-border political tensions, supplemented existing sectoral ownership controls in banking, telecommunications, transportation, and broadcasting and other cultural industries. In contrast, direct investment abroad has greatly exceeded FDI in the United States until recent years. US restrictions on foreign investment are defined primarily on grounds of national security, although sectoral restrictions also apply to the banking, broadcasting, and transportation sectors (Ibarra and Koncz, 2009; US Government Accountability Office, 2009).

The Mulroney government relaxed foreign investment restrictions in the mid-1980s, even before negotiating the Canada–US Free Trade Agreement—shifting to a 'net benefit' test for most such investments rather than requiring investors to prove their actions would benefit Canada. Combined with changes to financial sector regulations (paralleling British and US examples) and falling interest rates in the early 1990s, these measures prompted a boom in equity markets, growing foreign investment in Canada, and even more rapid growth of Canadian direct investment abroad (CDIA). By 1997, the total value of CDIA outstripped FDI in Canada for the first time – a trend that has continued to the present (see Table 19.1), contributing to closer parallels between Canadian and US policy environments.

Second, Canadian competition regulators have traditionally been less aggressive in promoting domestic business competition (and limiting corporate concentration) than their American counterparts in the antitrust division of the

Table 19.1 Market value of foreign direct investment, 2008

	Inward (billions of Cdn dollars)	Percentage of GDP	Outward (billions of Cdn dollars)	Percentage of GDP	Ratio of outward–inward FDI
Canada	505	32.2	637	40.6	1.26
United States	3,242	18.4	4,530	25.8	1.40

Sources: Statistics Canada, 2009; Ibarra and Koncz, 2009: 23; author's calculations.

Department of Justice. Third, while the United States has had a strong national securities regulator since the 1930s, responsibility for securities regulation in Canada (including rules governing most corporate mergers and takeovers of publicly-traded companies) is primarily a provincial responsibility.[6] Canadian securities rules are more likely than their American counterparts to require corporate directors to serve shareholder interests when considering takeover offers. Fifth, since the 1980s, national security considerations have been more prominent in American regulation of foreign ownership than in Canada—due initially to concerns about growing Japanese investment in the 1980s, and more recently about state-controlled firms from China and other authoritarian countries investing in strategic industries.

Investment Canada, CUFTA, NAFTA and the WTO: From Divergence to Selective Harmonization

Canadian foreign investment policies since the mid-1980s—and the broader competition and capital markets policies in which they are embedded—have been shaped in large measure by domestic and international factors arising from Canada's location in North America. The Mulroney government's relaxation of foreign investment rules noted earlier, and its restructuring of Canadian competition policies, recognized that

encouraging the growth of competitive Canadian multinationals in foreign markets required complementary policies for foreign-based firms operating in Canada. Similarly, federal financial sector rules allowing Canadian banks (and foreign firms) to expand into investment banking were prompted initially by independent provincial actions based on selective imitation of British and US practices.

These policies were reinforced by provisions in CUFTA, NAFTA, and the Uruguay Round of the General Agreement on Tariffs and Trade (GATT) leading to the formation of the World Trade Organization (WTO). Under the latter agreement, mergers or takeovers involving firms from WTO member countries are reviewable over a substantially higher threshold ($299 million in 2010)—except for specified strategic sectors and in cases of national security. Firms from non-WTO countries are subject to pre-1995 thresholds of $5 million when acquiring Canadian-based firms and $50 million for acquisitions of existing foreign subsidiaries. Acquisitions of the latter by WTO country firms are no longer reviewable. As a result, relatively few new investments or takeovers are subject to formal review in this market-friendly environment.

Subsequent controversies over foreign takeovers have paralleled major stock market fluctuations. Market booms in 1996–2000 and 2004–7 witnessed sharp increases in the number and scale of takeovers. Overall foreign investment in Canada grew at 9 per cent annually between 1998 and 2008.

However, Canadian investment abroad has also grown steadily, despite exchange rate fluctuations, with the value of Canadian FDI in the United States exceeding that of US FDI in Canada for the first time in 2008 (Hale, 2008a; Statistics Canada, 2009).

Despite foreign takeovers of Canada's four largest steel producers and two of its largest mining companies in 2005–7, public debate was fairly muted until early 2007. With some senior corporate executives calling for tighter controls over foreign takeovers, the Harper government appointed a Task Force of senior business executives to examine the issue in the broader context of corporate competitiveness. The Task Force report, tabled in June 2008, proposed increasing the threshold from then-current levels of $295 million to $1 billion, placing the onus on Ottawa to demonstrate that a takeover would be contrary to the national interest before disallowing it, liberalizing sectoral restrictions on foreign investment, and bringing Canadian competition laws more closely into line with 'best practices' among industrial countries (Competition Policy Review Panel, 2008). These proposals appear to have been guided partly by desires to attract large-scale foreign investment in competition with the US, to facilitate international expansion by Canadian firms, and to expand tools available to Canadian regulators, who work regularly with US and European counterparts.

The Harper government responded in its 2009 budget by phasing in the proposed investment threshold, and increasing sectoral foreign ownership thresholds for firms based in countries providing reciprocal access to Canadian firms operating abroad. It also expanded the Competition Bureau's powers to review major mergers, adapting these rules more closely to American practices. The federal Throne Speech of March 2010 promised to 'open Canada's doors further to venture capital and foreign investment in key sectors, including the satellite and telecommunications industries'

(Vieira, 2010). These measures, which suggest incremental convergence with broader trends in international (including American) investment and antitrust rules, reinforced long-term Canadian policy trends. These decisions reflect a mix of business and regulatory outlooks shaped by Canada's location in North America and its general preference for rules-based approaches to international economic relations. However, Ottawa's subsequent veto of BHP Billiton's proposed takeover of Potash Corp. may signal a retreat from this openness.

National Security: Selective Parallelism

Most major industrial countries have some form of national security restrictions on foreign investments. The Committee on Foreign Investment in the United States (CFIUS), an inter-agency process led by the Treasury Department, was initiated in 1975, with expanded mandates legislated by Congress in 1988 and 2007. Although CFIUS filings by foreign firms are voluntary, the Committee may initiate reviews of any investment on national security grounds, or may impose conditions on its approval of such transactions. However, the proposed takeover of mid-sized energy firm Unocal by the China National Overseas Oil Corporation (CNOOC) and Dubai Ports World's proposed takeover of six US container ports in 2005 prompted a sharp Congressional outcry leading to the withdrawal of both offers (Larson and Marchick, 2006; Government Accountability Office, 2009).

Although implicitly covered by their 'net benefit' provisions, Canada's foreign investment rules lacked an explicit national security dimension until 2008. Indeed, the Harper government did not formally invoke security concerns when it rejected the sale of Macdonald Dettwiler's (MDA) space technology division to American defence contractor Aliant in early 2008—fearing its potential loss of control over government-funded satellite technologies used to monitor Canada's Arctic regions. This decision was Ottawa's first use of the Investment Canada Act's veto provisions since its passage in 1985 (Borgers, 2008).

However, concerns raised by the rising international activity of state-owned businesses and sovereign wealth funds, the latter valued at an estimated $3.5 trillion before the market crash of 2008–9, call into question the capacity of smaller countries, such as Canada, to regulate such firms comparably to other market actors without running significant risks of retaliation against their own corporate citizens (Scoffield, 2008). Even so, both federal and Alberta governments have welcomed investments by Chinese and Korean state oil firms in Alberta's oil sands in 2009, with their promise of alternative markets, thereby reducing political leverage by American politicians or interest groups over Canadian exports (McCarthy, 2009).

Ottawa tabled its first guidelines for takeovers by state-controlled companies in early 2008. The key tests in the guidelines were direct or indirect control of the acquiring company by a foreign government, their 'governance and commercial orientation'—in other words, their independence from operational control by governments and tendency to be governed by conventional business principles in their business decisions, transparency, adherence to Canadian corporate governance standards, and track record in complying with 'Canadian laws and practices'. These criteria parallel principles which have guided US Treasury negotiations of similar arrangements with foreign governments (US Department of the Treasury, 2008). Other commercial criteria to be used include independent decision-making in 'where to export, where to process, the participation of Canadians in its operations in Canada and elsewhere, support of ongoing innovation, research and development; and the appropriate level of capital expenditures to

maintain the Canadian business in a globally competitive position' (Industry Canada, 2009).

National security regulations proclaimed in 2009 allow firms to submit investment proposals for voluntary review, or to be reviewed by direction of the Minister—similar to CFIUS processes noted above, as well as paralleling existing Investment Canada reviews for other investments. The government then has 45 days to review the transaction, to approve it with or without written conditions, or cancel the transaction if it fails to comply with the regulations. Although the MDA/Aliant case suggests the possibility of greater politicization of foreign investments with security implications (Bhattachargee, 2009), this case was the exception in Ottawa's approach to takeovers in recent years until the 2010 Potash veto.

In summary, Canadian policies on national security dimensions of foreign investments and takeovers appear to parallel American policies in emphasizing market criteria and the negotiation of safeguards, rather than more arbitrary or dirigiste approaches to public policies. Ottawa's rejection of the MDA/Aliant sale suggests an independent approach to decision-making—although there have been no public indications of American political pressure on this or other cases. Finally, the Harper government's decision to make the liberalization of investment rules governing strategic sectors conditional on reciprocal market access signals a potential 'marker' for future negotiations with the US or European Union—especially in allowing transnational mergers of transportation firms.

CASE STUDY # 2: CANADA–UNITED STATES ENERGY RELATIONS

Canada's energy relations with the United States reflect the bottom-up nature of North American economic integration. They are composed of multiple commercial contracts, transactions, and relationships between producers, shippers, and consumers of energy on both sides of the border. The direct role of national and sub-national governments in bilateral energy affairs has declined over the past decades as a result of progressive energy market liberalization. More recently, however, the rise of non-economic issues in bilateral energy relations, notably the ascendance of climate change on policy agendas in North America and beyond, portends renewed government intervention in the energy sector and a greater role for governments in the bilateral energy relationship.

The context: reserves, trade flows and policy convergence

Canada and the United States both possess major energy reserves. In 2008, Canada's reserves of crude oil stood at 178.6 billion barrels (United States Energy Information Administration, 2009). This figure includes Canada's oil sands, which contain 173.2 billion barrels of oil, positioning the country as second only to Saudi Arabia in its oil endowment. Canada's oil reserves are more than eight times those of the United States, which stood at 21.3 billion barrels in 2008 (ibid.). The situation differs in natural gas, however, where in 2008, the United States possessed roughly four times more natural gas than Canada, at 237.7

trillion cubic feet compared to 58.2 trillion cubic feet, respectively (ibid.). In the electricity sector, in 2006, Canada and the US possessed 122.7 and 986.2 gigawatts of generation capacity, respectively (ibid.; data are preliminary).

One enduring factor has characterized Canada–US energy relations: Canada's energy production exceeds the country's demand, US demand exceeds its supply, and the US is a net energy importer from Canada. Canada exports more than half of the oil and gas it produces and all (natural gas) or virtually all (oil) of this is destined for the United States (author's calculations based on Centre for Energy, 2010). Indeed, Canada is the largest foreign supplier of oil, natural gas, and electricity to the US and these cross-border energy flows represent significant proportions of American net energy imports and domestic consumption (Centre for Energy and Department of Foreign Affairs and International Trade, 2008). Canadian and American energy markets have become increasingly integrated and interdependent since the mid-1980s as a result of trade liberalization, deregulation, and restructuring. Table 19.2 shows the bilateral trade picture from the pre-CUFTA period to recent times. American imports of Canadian energy have grown considerably: the volume of petroleum and electricity imports have more than tripled, and natural gas imports have almost quadrupled.

Table 19.2 Canada–US energy trade, selected years, 1985–2008

	Imports to US from Canada				US exports to Canada			
	1985	1990	2000	2008	1985	1990	2000	2008
Petroleum (million barrels)	281	341	661	900	0.03	0.03	0.04	0.10
Natural gas (billion cubic feet)	926	1448	3544	3567	0.2	17	73	585
Electricity (terawatt hours)	NA	16	49	56	NA	16	13	23

Notes: Data for 2008 are preliminary. 1 terawatt hour = 10^9 kilowatt hours.
Sources: United States Energy Information Administration, 2009, 2010.

Energy policy changes have propelled and been propelled by economic integration processes. Canada and the United States have both pursued policies of energy market liberalization since the mid-1980s, resulting in substantial convergence of the broad contours of their energy policies. Liberalization of energy trade began with CUFTA, whose energy chapter essentially disallows price controls in the oil and natural gas sectors, prohibits the establishment of two-price policies for domestic and export energy prices, and puts in place proportionality provisions that constrain the Canadian federal government from reducing exports unilaterally. Canada and the US have also substantially deregulated the oil and gas sectors, and restructured electricity markets to introduce competition into the wholesale generation and, in some instances, retail power markets. NAFTA carries over the CUFTA energy provisions and also includes Mexico, although Mexico accepted only minimal energy commitments owing to the political sensitivities and constitutional limitations surrounding energy market liberalization in the country. This is in contrast to Canada and the US, where constitutional arrangements (e.g., provincial jurisdiction over energy in Canada and state powers in the energy sector in the US), do not tend to militate against energy market integration given the supply/demand profiles of the two countries and provincial interest in exporting energy resources.

Canadian and American constitutional arrangements do result in greater complexity and 'fragmegration' in bilateral energy relations, however, given the sheer number of sub-national policy and regulatory frameworks within and across the two countries. This complexity is reflected in energy policy differentiation across sub-national jurisdictions—for example, policy convergence around the broad principles of electricity market restructuring but sometimes substantially different sub-national approaches to the details of electricity regulation

both within and across North America—and all of this in the midst of deep energy market integration and interdependence.

Bilateral energy dynamics: cooperative policy relations and informal administrative structures

Canada's energy relations with the US are managed primarily through bilateral trans-governmental mechanisms at the national and sub-national levels. Such arrangements, composed of functional public service specialists, have served to facilitate information exchange, policy co-ordination, and collaboration between Canada and the US, and have been underpinned by a variety of soft law agreements and understandings. More recently, these bilateral approaches have been complemented with trilateral mechanisms and, in the electricity sector, with a joint organization.

In the post-CUFTA period, Canada–US energy policy relations tend mainly toward co-ordination, collaboration, and (implicit or explicit) harmonization given the many shared interests and considerable degree of energy interdependence between the two countries.[7] Open conflict post-CUFTA is rare, although opposition from some quarters in the US to American imports of oil from the oil sands, and to American legislative measures which could have the effect of curbing oil sands imports, have generated friction in recent years, as has the enactment of renewable portfolio standards by American governments that implicitly or explicitly discriminate against renewable electricity generated in Canada.

Outside of a limited number of formal instruments (notably the energy chapters in CUFTA and NAFTA but also a number of sub-sectoral agreements) and periodic formal meetings held within the context of broader-based events (e.g., prime ministerial-presidential meetings, meetings of premiers and governors in the Western Governors' Association and Western Premiers' Conference, etc.), informal instruments and processes tend to dominate the management of bilateral energy affairs (e.g., memoranda of understanding between lead agencies, working groups, conferences, meetings, etc.).

In the first decade of the twenty-first century, a number of trilateral transgovernmental mechanisms have also been put in place. These include the North American Energy Working Group, a trilateral forum of the national energy regulators in North America, and a trilateral group of national and sub-national governments that meets on the topic of electricity reliability. Nonetheless, differences in constitutional and policy frameworks between Canada and Mexico, the lack of energy trade between the two countries, and differences in political orientation toward energy relations with the US militate against comprehensive trilateral energy talks, and relations within these forums can trend toward dual bilateralism.

A formal mechanism that complements bilateral channels is the North American Electric Reliability Corporation (NERC), a public-private organization that has developed and managed the bilateral reliability framework for the bulk power system since its establishment in 1968, following a major power outage in Ontario and the Northeastern United States in 1965. Canadian electric utilities and system operators are members of one of eight NERC regional entities, which join contiguous electricity generators and transmission systems. Up until recently, NERC developed voluntary reliability standards to which members were expected to adhere. Following the 14 August 2003 electricity blackout—the largest blackout in North American history that left some 50 million people in Canada and the United States without power—the US Congress legislated in 2005 that electricity reliability standards be made mandatory with penalties for failure to comply. Subsequent to this legislation, NERC

became the self-regulatory organization with the power to develop and enforce electricity reliability standards. NERC, now formally a joint Canada–US organization, employs a harmonized approach to standard development and approval that integrates Canadian and American interests in the development and approval of reliability standards.

The energy-climate change challenge: a renewed role for government in bilateral energy relations?

Over the past three decades, governments have reduced the level of state intervention in the energy sector substantially through trade liberalization, oil and gas deregulation and electricity sector restructuring. While governments are still major players in their jurisdictions, establishing regulatory frameworks that condition the pace and nature of energy development, and in the electricity sector in most provinces, operating crown corporations and undertaking some level of price regulation, when it comes to energy crossing the border, market forces and the myriad relationships between energy producers and consumers are at the heart of bilateral electricity relations.

Addressing the energy-climate change challenge, in contrast, heralds a renewed role for government in both domestic and cross-border energy affairs. The establishment of carbon cap-and-trade systems, renewable portfolio standards stipulating a percentage of electricity that must be generated from renewable energy sources, low carbon fuel standards, and the like, necessarily draw on state resources and authority, and, given integrated energy markets in North America, ideally would be pursued on a bilateral—if not binational—basis. Indeed, governments are pursuing bilateral climate change approaches through such mechanisms as the Western Climate Initiative, which involves a number of American states and Canadian provinces in the development of regional emissions reduction targets and a regional cap-and-trade system; the Clean Energy Dialogue, a bilateral initiative of the Canadian and American federal governments focusing on carbon capture and storage, energy science and technology and the development of smart electricity grids; and the Western Renewable Energy Zones initiative, composed of western states and provinces, which is identifying areas in the region with high renewable energy potential.

Canadian governments at both the national and sub-national levels play a strong role in this context, ensuring that Canadian interests are represented. Nonetheless, much work remains to be done to address climate change both within and between Canada and the United States, and to the extent that American climate change policy is driven by federal legislation chugging its way through Congress, the room for harmonized bilateral approaches may be slim, leaving Canadian governments in the position of adjusting through parallelism—if not harmonization—of broad policy measures and approaches.

BORDERS, BRIDGES AND MULTIDIMENSIONAL POLICY: THE VARIABLE GEOMETRY OF CANADA'S POLICY RELATIONS IN NORTH AMERICA

The enduring and more recent features of Canada's policy relations in North America—in particular the double impulse toward integration and differentiation and progressive economic integration and interdependence—shape the politics and administration surrounding these processes. The tendency of Canadian policy-makers in most sectors has been toward *parallelism* or *co-ordination* in broad policy frameworks in order to maintain a

'capacity for choice' to deal with domestic economic, societal, institutional, and political differences (Hoberg, 2002; Hale, 2008b). It is noteworthy, though, that such processes are often characterized by distinctions between formal political and informal administrative relationships. The political relationship often takes the form of a calculated projection of independent action, co-ordination, and parallelism—depending upon the political palatability of these various approaches to domestic publics and private interests. This is frequently complemented by close administrative collaboration or operational co-ordination—as long as it can be maintained below the political radar screen.

Given the distinct political, administrative and institutional settings within and across the three countries of North America, instances of pure harmonization (whether bilateral or trilateral)—as defined in the spectrum above (identical policy objectives, instruments, and instrument settings)—are rare. Nonetheless, harmonization of broad policy contours is not uncommon and in cases where salient interests align across borders, instrument settings in policy frameworks may become so similar as to verge on *de facto* harmonization (e.g., electricity reliability standards). Policy conflicts are more likely in sectors in which domestic producers in one country are more focused on serving domestic than international markets, while producers in the other are more focused on export-driven growth (e.g., American softwood producers and Canadian supply-managed agricultural sectors, or Canadian cultural industries and American entertainment conglomerates). Conflicts can also result when the consequences of policy changes in one jurisdiction disadvantage producers in another—whether such consequences are intended or not. Given Canada's far greater export dependence, Canadian policy-makers generally seek to quarantine such conflicts in their dealings with the United States by avoiding 'linkage' between disputes in one sector and relations in another.

All the while, the economic underpinnings of North American integration—microeconomic or 'bottom-up' integration, reinforced by both cross-border and broader international supply chains—have continued to deepen in many sectors (albeit impeded in recent years in some sectors by thickening of the border post-9/11, the economic downturn, and exchange rate shifts affecting terms of trade between the two countries), driving the need for greater policy co-ordination (if not harmonization as some private interests would prefer), but also progressing alongside the maintenance of domestic policy discretion in other areas. Extending national treatment to the products, services and investments of its NAFTA partners on a reciprocal basis allowed Canadian businesses and workers to benefit from the rapid growth of the US economy between 1994 and 2008, while leaving Ottawa and provincial governments with a variety of policy tools to manage domestic policy challenges and Canada's persistent regional differences.

The result has been a series of bilateral policy initiatives in different sectors based on shared interests, and the avoidance of any broader vision of North America to allow governments the discretion to pursue their own political priorities in both domestic and international arenas. The efforts of major business groups, along with American allies such as the Council on Foreign Relations, to promote such a vision after 9/11 (e.g., Dobson, 2002; Manley, Aspe and Weld, 2005) were carefully side-tracked by successive federal governments into the bureaucratic web of the Security and Prosperity Partnership (SPP) before its quiet suspension in 2009. With the recession of 2008–9 signalling a resurgence of Congressional protectionism in Washington, and the election of Barack Obama to president in 2008, these advocates have reverted to supporting the Canadian government's now traditional emphasis on

dual bilateralism in dealings with the United States and Mexico, while still promoting a more strategic approach (Burney, 2008a; Burney, 2008b; Carleton University Canada–US Project, 2009).

In sum, rather than a series of 'one-size-fits-all' processes advocated by some enthusiasts of North American integration and stigmatized by those who reject it, Canada's North American policy relations are characterized by what scholars of European integration describe as 'variable geometry'—the willingness of some countries (or, in a North American context, interests in specific industries or policy sectors) to undertake deeper integration independently of the unwillingness of other members (or sectors) to go along. This concept both recognizes the wide diversity of institutions created by national and sub-national governments to manage particular policy issues, and the different ways in which they interact with citizens, businesses, and public sector counterparts in their own countries (Cornford, 2004; Keating, 1999). Such processes are also in evidence at the sectoral and subsectoral levels, where the extent of policy co-ordination and convergence differs between sectors, within sectors over time, and at the national and sub-national levels. At a broader level, these realities are often expressed in the phrase 'three can talk, two can deal'—and in the tendency of political and institutional differences among the three countries to be expressed through the channels of 'dual bilateralism', as noted above.

It remains to be seen how these various patterns will be affected by growing Congressional protectionism under the Obama administration, the slower economic recovery and worrisome fiscal situation of the United States compared to Canada, and the as-yet unidentified shape of any successor initiative to the Security and Prosperity Partnership beyond the more generically framed North American Leaders' Summits. The current approach, whether by default or design, relies primarily on trilateral leaders' summits and periodic bilateral presidential-prime ministerial meetings, but its relative role and effectiveness remain to be seen. Nonetheless, the dual impulse toward differentiation and integration, underpinned and propelled in part by bottom-up economic integration, are likely to remain at the heart of North American policy relations, augmenting the complexity, richness and variable geometry of Canada's policy relations on the continent.

Key Terms

Dual Bilateralism

Fragmegration

Intermestic

Multi-Level Governance

Policy Parallelism

Transgovernmental Relations

Variable Geometry

Notes

1. The term 'intermestic', which combines the words 'domestic' and 'international', was coined to capture the progressive interweaving of domestic and international factors in policy-making.

2. Provinces like Quebec, Alberta, and Ontario have considerable experience and expertise in paradiplomacy while others have limited resources to dedicate to cross-border activities.

3. This continuum first appeared in Gattinger (2005) and has been modified since its original appearance based on subsequent research and the useful comments and additions by Geoffrey Hale. As explained in Gattinger (2005), it is originally developed from Dobson (1991: 2–3).

4. Parallelism is distinct from collaboration, co-ordination, and harmonization in that it does not stem primarily from joint efforts between governments to co-operate on policy change nor does it entail strong expectations that parallel decisions will directly affect a counterpart's policies (although they may contribute to an environment conducive to co-ordination).

5. This categorization draws from Slaughter (1997) and Heynen and Higginbotham (2004: 22–24).

6. The Harper government has introduced proposals for a national securities regulator, with provincial participation. However, its current approach more closely resembles British than US practice, suggesting the potential for some regulatory divergence for firms whose shares trade only in Canadian markets.

7. This stands in contrast to the period just prior to CUFTA, which saw significant bilateral conflict between Canada and the US owing to the federal government's National Energy Program of 1980, which sought to increase Canadian ownership and exploration in the oil and gas sectors, give Canadians priority access to domestic oil and gas supplies, subsidize domestic prices, and freeze natural gas exports and curtail oil exports to the US. The NEP resulted in a virulent backlash from energy-producing provinces, particularly oil and gas rich Alberta, which viewed the program as the height of federal arrogance and interventionism in an area of provincial jurisdiction, industry, especially American energy firms operating in Canada, and the American government, which viewed the export restrictions as an affront to American energy security.

References

Blank, Stephen. 2005. 'North American Integration: Looking Ahead' (mimeo, July)

———. 2008. 'Trade corridors and North American competitiveness', *The American Review of Canadian Studies* 38:2 (Summer), 231–37.

Bhattachargee, Subrata. 2009. 'National Security with a Canadian Twist: The Investment Canada Act and the New National Security Review Test', Columbia FDI Perspectives #10 (New York: Vale Columbia Center on Sustainable International Investment, 30 July).

Borgers, Oliver J. 2008. 'Investment Canada Act: Minister of Industry Blocks acquisition of MDA by Alliant Techsystems' (Toronto: McCarthy Tetrault, 12 May); www.mccarthy.ca/article_detail.aspx?id=3996; accessed 3 October 2009.

Carleton University Canada–US Project. 2009. *From Correct to Inspired: A Blueprint for Canada–US Engagement*. Ottawa: Carleton University, January.

Centre for Energy, 2010. 'The Big Energy Picture' available online at www.centreforenergy.com/AboutEnergy/Canadian

Energy/EnergyDrivesCanada.asp?page=16; accessed 10 May 2010.

———— and Department of Foreign Affairs and International Trade. 2008. *Canada: A Secure, Reliable Source of Energy.* Available online at www.centreforenergy.com/Documents/EnergyMaps/Canada.pdf; accessed 10 May 2010.

Clarkson, Stephen. 2008. *Does North America Exist?* Toronto: University of Toronto Press.

————. 2002. *Uncle Sam and Us: Globalization, Neoconservatism, and the Canadian State.* Toronto: University of Toronto Press.

Competition Policy Review Panel. 2008. *Compete to Win:* (Ottawa: Industry Canada, June); online at: www.ic.gc.ca/eic/site/cprp-gepmc.nsf/vwapj/Compete_to_Win.pdf/$FILE/Compete_to_Win.pdf; accessed 8 December 2009.

Dobson, Wendy. 1991. *Economic Policy Coordination: Requiem or Prologue?* (Washington, D.C.: Institute for International Economics).

Doern, G. Bruce, and Robert Johnson, eds. 2006. *Rules, Rules, Rules, Rules: Multilevel Regulatory Governance in Canada.* (Toronto: University of Toronto Press).

————, and Brian Tomlin. 1996. 'Trade-Industrial Policy', in G. Bruce Doern, Leslie A. Pal, and Brian W. Tomlin, eds., *Border Crossings: The Internationalization of Canadian Public Policy.* (Toronto: Oxford University Press), 167–87.

Gattinger, Monica. 2005. 'Canada–United States Electricity Relations: Policy Coordination and Multi-level Associative Governance', in G. Bruce Doern, ed., *How Ottawa Spends 2005–2006: Managing the Minority.* (Montreal and Kingston: McGill-Queen's University Press), 143–62.

Goldfarb, Danielle. 2007. *Is Just-in-Case Replacing Just-in-Time? How Cross-Border Trading Behaviour Has Changed Since 9/11.* Ottawa: Conference Board of Canada, June; http://sso.conferenceboard.ca/e-Library/LayoutAbstract.asp?DID=2050; accessed 28 May 2008.

Hale, Geoffrey. 2010. 'Canada–U.S. Relations in the Obama Era: Warming or Greening,' in *How Ottawa Spends 2010–2011*, edited by G. Bruce Doern and Christopher Stoney (Montreal and Kingston: McGill-Queen's University Press), 48–67.

————. 2008a. 'The Dog That Hasn't Barked: The Political Economy of Contemporary Debates on Canadian Foreign Investment Policies', *Canadian Journal of Political Science* 41:3, 719–48.

————. 2008b. 'Maintaining Policy Discretion: Cross-Border Policy Making and North American Integration,' in *An Independent Foreign Policy for Canada? Challenges and Choices for the Future,* edited by Brian Bow and Patrick Lennox (Toronto: University of Toronto Press), 137–62.

———— and Monica Gattinger. 2010. 'Variable Geometry and Traffic Circles: Navigating Canada's Policy Relations in North America', in *Borders and Bridges: Canada's Policy Relations in North America* (Toronto: Oxford University Press), 362–82.

Heynen, Jeff, and John Higginbotham. 2004. *Advancing Canadian Interests in the United States: A Practical Guide for Canadian Public Officials.* CSPS Action-Research Roundtable on Managing Canada–US Relations. (Ottawa: Canada School of Public Service).

Higginbotham, John, and Jeff Heynen. 2004. 'Managing Through Networks: The State of Canada–US Relations' in David M. Carment, ed., *Canada Among Nations 2004: Setting Priorities Straight.* (Montreal and Kingston: McGill-Queen's University Press), 123–40.

Hoberg, George, ed. 2002. *Capacity for Choice: Canada in a New North America.* Toronto: University of Toronto Press.

Ibarra, Marilyn and Jennifer Koncz. 2009. 'Direct Investment Positions for 2008', *Survey of Current Business* (Washington, DC: Bureau of Economic Affairs, July), 20–34; online at: www.bea.gov/scb/pdf/2009/07%20July/0709_dip.pdf; accessed 8 December 2009.

Industry Canada. 2008. 'Investment Canada Act: Investments by state-owned enterprises – Net benefit assessment' (Ottawa); www.ic.gc.ca/epic/site/ica-lic.nsf/en/lk00064e.html#state-owned; accessed 3 October 2009.

Larson, Alan P. and David M. Marchick. 2006. *Foreign Investment and National Security: Getting the Balance Right,* Council Special Report # 18 (New York: Council on Foreign Relations, July); online at: www.ciaonet.org/pbei/cfr/0002843/f_0002843_2005.pdf.

McCarthy, Shawn. 2009. 'Ottawa guidelines to get first test', *Globe and Mail,* 1 September, B1.

Rosenau, James N. 2003. *Distant Proximities: Dynamics beyond Globalization.* (Princeton, NJ: Princeton University Press).

————, David Earnest, Yale Ferguson, and Ole R. Holsti. 2005. *The Cutting Edge of Globalization: An Inquiry into American Elites.* Boulder, CO: Rowman & Littlefield.

Rosenzweig, Paul. 2009. 'Why the US doesn't trust Canada', *Macleans,* 5 October; www2.macleans.ca/2009/10/05/why-the-u-s-doesnt-trust-canada/; accessed 8 October 2009.

Scoffield, Heather. 2008, 'A major shift in power and wealth', *Globe and Mail,* 3 May.

Simeon, Richard. 2003. 'Important? Yes. Transformative? No. North American Integration and Canadian Federalism', in Harvey Lazar, Hamish Telford, and Ronald L. Watts, eds., *The Impact of Global and Regional Integration on Federal Systems.* (Montreal and Kingston: Institute of Intergovernmental Relations, Queen's University), 123–71.

Slaughter, Anne-Marie. 1997. 'The Real New World Order', *Foreign Affairs* 76, 5: 183–97.

Statistics Canada. 2009. 'Foreign direct investment', *The Daily,* 8 April; online at: www.statcan.gc.ca/daily-quotidien/090408/dq090408a-eng.htm; accessed 8 December 2009.

Studer, Isabel. 2007. 'Obstacles to Integration: NAFTA's Institutional Weakness', in Isabel Studer and Carol Wise, eds., *Requiem or Revival? The Promise of North American Integration.* Washington: Brookings Institution Press, 53–75.

US Energy Information Administration. 2009. *Annual Energy Review 2008*. Washington: US Government Printing Office.

———. 2010. 'International Electricity Imports and Exports' online at www.eia.doe.gov/emeu/international/electricity trade.html; accessed 10 May 2010.

US Department of the Treasury. 2008. 'Treasury reaches agreement on principles for sovereign wealth fund investment with Singapore and Abu Dhabi' (Washington, DC: 20 March); online at www.treasury.gov/press/releases/hp881. htm; accessed 22 December 2009.

US Government Accountability Office. 2009. *Sovereign Wealth Funds: Laws Limiting Foreign Investment Affect Certain* US *Assets and Agencies Have Various Enforcement Processes*, Report to the Committee on Banking, Housing and Urban Affairs, US Senate, Report # D09608, (Washington, DC: May); online at: www.gao.gov/new.items/d09608. pdf; accessed 8 December 2009.

Vieira, Paul. 2010. 'Speech sets out investment priorities', *National Post*, 4 March, A1.

20

CANADIAN ARCTIC SOVEREIGNTY AND SECURITY IN A TRANSFORMING CIRCUMPOLAR WORLD

Rob Huebert

INTRODUCTION

Canadian Arctic policy is faced with some of the most intriguing, yet complex, challenges in its history. Perhaps the greatest current challenge for Canada is the worldwide realization that the Arctic is melting, and so it is more accessible than ever before. Consequently, Canada must prepare for the outside world's entry into the Arctic. With international challenges to Canadian control of the region now emerging, Canada can no longer afford to ignore its Arctic. The objective of this chapter is to achieve an understanding of Canadian Arctic sovereignty and security in the context of a fundamentally changing Arctic. First, it examines sovereignty and security. The chapter then examines the forces that are transforming the very fabric of the Arctic, specifically climate change, resource development, and geopolitical forces.

PART I: UNDERSTANDING SOVEREIGNTY AND SECURITY

Sovereignty

Sovereignty is the theoretical cornerstone of the international legal state system. There are three main elements of sovereignty: a defined territory; an existing governance system and a people within the defined territory.[1] A state must have a functioning government system that is able to make final decisions that are enforced upon the people within its geographic territory. Each of these variables may appear to be straightforward but the reality is that all three are difficult to achieve within the Arctic.

The most common problem with determining sovereignty is the existence of an accepted governance system. The sovereignty of a state is said to be threatened when parties compete to govern. In such cases, until one side is defeated, either militarily or politically, or a negotiated settlement is reached whereby the competing bodies agree to share power as a single entity, there is no one sovereign body. The process for determining sovereignty is complicated by the fact that even after the competition for power is internally settled, the international community must also recognize the new governing body.

In the Canadian Arctic there is no question about the existence of an accepted governance system. This system may be evolving as power devolves to the territories, but as long as this is done on a peaceful basis, all sovereign states have the right to allocate their powers to political sub-units within their borders. Within the borders of the Canadian Arctic, the northern Canadian population has completely accepted the government's right to govern. Thus the federal government does not diminish the sovereignty of the Canadian state by transferring powers to its three northern territories: the Northwest Territories, Nunavut, and the Yukon.

This transfer leads to the issues surrounding the second variable of sovereignty, which requires that a people are contained within the defined geography of a state. Consequently, there is no sovereignty in a case where there is no local population, such as Antarctica. But there are no limits as to how small a population can be. The Canadian Arctic contains a small number of individuals, but it contains enough to give Canada sovereignty over all of the land territory of its Arctic. The only land area in Canada where Canada's sovereignty is challenged is Hans Island, a small uninhabited island.

The third variable—defined boundaries—has the greatest relevance for the discussion of Canadian Arctic sovereignty. For a boundary to have validity, the international community needs to agree on its boundaries. The number of states that need to agree before a boundary is said to be accepted remains unclear. The growing complexity of ocean boundaries is extremely pertinent to sovereignty in the Arctic. The United Nations Convention on the Law of the Sea (UNCLOS), which was finalized in 1982 and came into force in 1996, codified existing customary international law and created several new maritime zones.[2] In general, the farther that the zone moves out from the land territory of the state, the less control the state has over the activities within the zone. Thus the first main zone—the territorial sea—gives the coastal state almost complete control over all activities within it. The one important exception is that the state cannot interfere in the innocent passage of foreign vessels in these waters. Moving closer to shore, the Exclusive Economic Zone (EEZ) extends 200 nautical miles from the coastline of the state. The coastal state has control over all living and non-living resources in this zone. Therefore, only the coastal state can fish, drill for oil or gas or grant permission to a foreign state or organization. However, in the EEZ, the coastal state has no control over international shipping that is not engaged in resource exploitation. UNCLOS created a third zone of control. A state can extend its control over the ocean soil and subsurface beyond the EEZ if it can show that it has an extended continental shelf. If a state can prove that it meets the criteria required for a continental shelf, and if this shelf extends beyond 200 nautical miles, then a state can claim control of the seabed and its resources for an additional 150 nautical miles (and in some instances even beyond that). A state with this zone has control of all activities that occur on or beneath the seabed. This control is currently understood to mean that the state has authority over activities such as oil and gas development. However, the state has no control over activities in the water column such as shipping, fishing, or even scientific research.

There are two other maritime zones that depend on geography and history. If a state has a body of water that directly joins two other international bodies of water, and if it has been used in the past by international shipping, then the joining body of water, or strait, is used for international navigation. The coastal state has the right of control of all activity within this international strait except international shipping as all foreign vessels enjoy the right of passage. This control specifically allows all vessels to travel in their normal mode of transportation. Thus submarines could remain submerged as they transit an international strait.

Internal waters are the last maritime zone of significance for the Arctic. Bodies of waters such as lakes and rivers that lie entirely within the land mass of a state normally fall into this category. The host state enjoys complete control over these waters, including foreign shipping. There may be a small number of instances where a state may designate a specific body of water that lies outside its land boundaries as internal waters. Generally

these exceptions occur where there has been historical acceptance of treating them like a lake or river: this designation was codified by UNCLOS as historical bays. Some countries such as Canada, however, have attempted to extend this designation beyond bays.

A challenge to Canadian Arctic sovereignty must involve a dispute with one of the three elements of sovereignty. There is no challenge to the Canadian governance system, and there is an identifiable population that completely accepts the authority of the Canadian government. As a result, the element of sovereignty that is challenged is the recognition of Canada's borders, specifically its Arctic maritime borders. Can Canada exercise control of its Arctic borders?

Security

The concept of security has undergone a transformation in both theoretical and practical terms since the end of the Cold War. Historically, security was framed in a context that focused on the military ability of a state to either defend itself against the military actions of other states or to enforce its will on another state. If a state was powerful enough it acted alone, or it could develop alliances with other states. The critical element of security was the ability of states to utilize their economic capabilities to build militaries that could both enforce and protect their will.[3] The use of deadly force was the ultimate means of providing for the security of the state.

The development of nuclear weapons changed the nature of security because the deterrence of nuclear war rather than the waging of war became the ultimate security objective of states during the Cold War period. It was still necessary, however, paradoxically, to avoid war by preparing for war. Security was linked to the ability to build a nuclear weapon capability sufficient enough to deter the opposing side from attacking. National security was still viewed as the core responsibility of the state which could only be achieved through military force.

As the Cold War came to an end, the consensus on the nature of security was challenged. First, the end of the Cold War ended the nuclear balance that had threatened the existence of the entire international system. With the collapse of the USSR, the core military rivalry with the United States ended and the need for military forces appeared to dramatically diminish. This led many to begin questioning whether the traditional definition of security, with its focus on the military and the state, remained valid. This led to the development of human security which expanded the conceptualization of security.[4] Human security was an attempt to move security away from state-based analysis. It was recognized that in many instances the state was the cause of insecurity of some or all of its peoples, i.e., repressive regimes such as Pinochet's military dictatorship in Chile or the Khmer Rouge in Cambodia. The movement from defensive military use to the construction of international norms and institutions, such as treaties and agreements, supported this new concept of human security and created an environment whereby the affected parties could enjoy security. Efforts were made to construct international means of bringing justice to those who suffered at the hands of the state. Substantial effort was given to create means for outlawing the use and construction of certain weapons systems, such as anti-personnel landmines.

A second and related challenge to traditional security occurred when some academics and policymakers began to look to the dangers posed by environmental degradation.[5] The physical security of an individual in Bangladesh or the Seychelles who loses their home due to rising sea levels from melting ice caps as a result of climate change was just as tenuous as that of someone in a war zone. Supporters who sought to extend the meaning of security pointed to the physical dangers that pollution and environmental degradation posed to the well-being of people both within and beyond the state. As in the case of human security, greater security did not come from military action. Instead, international co-operation was required at both the individual and state levels. Conceptual extensions of security, similar to advances made by environmental security specialists, have further extended the term 'security' to include economic security, cultural security, and so on. In all cases, there was a desire to expand the definition of security beyond a focus on the state and the military.

What conclusions can be reached prior to discussing Canadian Arctic sovereignty and security? If Canadian Arctic sovereignty is threatened, then the Canadian government does not control a specific geographic territory. Sovereignty is about controlling the actions of others within the boundaries claimed by the Canadian government. From this perspective, Canada's challenge lies in the maritime nature of its boundaries of the area in dispute. International laws pertaining to maritime sovereignty are different from those for sovereignty over a land mass. Specifically, UNCLOS clearly establishes the various degrees of control over maritime zones, the rule of thumb being that the farther away from the coastline a zone is, the less control the coastal state enjoys.

The most important question that follows from the exercise of sovereignty is why exercise it in the first place? What do states gain by pursuing and then defending national sovereignty? States defend their sovereignty for the principle reason of securing their core interests and values in a specific region. Traditionally this was done through the use of military force. But it is now recognized that some threats to a state's security, such as environmental security, cannot be addressed by military action.

The underlying point is that whatever those steps are to be, they are undertaken with the objective of protecting the security of the state's citizens.

PART II: CANADIAN CONCEPTS OF ARCTIC SOVEREIGNTY AND SECURITY

Throughout much of the Cold War, the effort to have policy reflect the terms 'Arctic sovereignty' and 'Arctic security' was frustrated by the tendency of Canadian policy makers, media, and academics to assume that the two terms were separate and distinct concepts. During the Cold War, Arctic security meant defence against the Soviet Union. Canada left the maritime dimensions of Arctic security entirely in American hands while allowing them to pay for much of it. Arctic sovereignty was associated with diplomatic disputes with the United States and with reacting to American actions that were perceived to threaten Canada's claim over the region, most notably the waterways of the north. In this manner Arctic security and Arctic sovereignty were viewed as separate policy concerns. However, sovereignty and security are interconnected and cannot and should not be separated. The Canadian government attempts to defend Canadian Arctic sovereignty for the purpose of protecting the security of its citizens as well as the security of the core values and interests of Canadians.

The issue of Canadian Arctic sovereignty is complicated by its maritime dimension. Within the international law of the sea, the right to make final decisions about what activities occur within its maritime zones is not absolute but is modified by the waterway's nature. With the exception of Denmark's assertion of ownership of Hans Island, no other actors in the international system challenge Canada's right to control its Arctic land mass. However, international challenges do emerge over Canada's claim to its Arctic maritime space. The

United States disagrees on the boundary dividing the Beaufort Sea. Likewise, Denmark disagrees on division of the Lincoln Sea (though only in two small regions). Canada may also disagree with the United States, Russia, and Denmark about its anticipated claim over its continental shelf boundaries in the Arctic Ocean. Canada's most well known Arctic sovereignty issue is over the control of international maritime traffic in the Northwest Passage. Canada claims that the waterways that comprise the Northwest Passage are internal waters, and, therefore, the Canadian government has the right to control who can enter these waters and under what conditions. The position of America and the European Union is that these waters are part of an international strait which means that it is not Canada, but the international community, in this case through the International Maritime Organization (IMO), which has the final, authoritative decision-making power over international shipping in the Northwest Passage.

Ultimately whether it is dividing the Arctic Ocean seabed, determining the boundaries of Canadian sections of the Beaufort and Lincoln Sea, or shipping in the Northwest Passage, the issue is control. What are the Arctic maritime boundaries that Canada can control and what can it do within these boundaries? This is where the issue of Arctic security connects with Arctic sovereignty. If sovereignty is being pursued for the purpose of protecting the security, safety, and well-being of Canadians then not only is it worth the effort, but it is an absolute necessity.

If Canadian Arctic sovereignty is control, then Canadian Arctic security is about responding to threats. The threats to Canadian Arctic security are nebulous, multi-dimensional, and evolving. Throughout the Cold War, Arctic security was exclusive to the threat posed by the USSR to the national survival of Canada and the United States. When the Cold War ended and concerns about traditional threats to national security receded, scientists soon discovered that the Canadian Arctic was the end location for a wide number of pollutants that originated elsewhere on the globe (including seemingly improbable sources such as India and the Philippines). The environmental migration of trans-boundary pollutants such as persistent organic pollutants, like pesticides and fertilizers, into the north contaminated the food supply and negatively impacted the health of northern Canadians.[6] It was soon realized that the environmental security of the Canadian north needed protection. Issues regarding threats to the law and order of the Canadian north are arising. Recently, foreign criminal elements have made unauthorized entries into the Canadian Arctic. In the summer of 2007, a group allegedly associated with the Norwegian Hells Angels made it as far as Cambridge Bay on a small boat.[7] Other threats in the Canadian Arctic involve economic, societal, and cultural issues. It also appears that traditional security threats are re-emerging as each Arctic nation has begun rebuilding its northern military capabilities.

Canadian policy makers need to protect Canadian Arctic sovereignty in order to provide for Canadian Arctic security. The Canadian government needs to have control over its north so that it can take action to protect against a wide number of threats that will increasingly come from beyond Canadian northern boundaries. As it is impossible to protect Canadian Arctic security without protecting its Arctic sovereignty and vice versa, the two concepts are completely interlinked.

PART III: THE CHANGING ARCTIC

The Arctic is fundamentally changing. At least three unique and extremely powerful forces are leading to this transformation: climate change, resource development, and geopolitical transformation. Any one of these factors by itself would create a serious transformation in the Arctic. The reality that three such forces are at work only underlines the magnitude of the changes that are now occurring in the Canadian Arctic.

Climate change

Climate change is warming the Arctic at a considerable rate, which has garnered the attention of the world. It was only as recently as the 1990s that few even knew of climate change, let alone understood its magnitude. Amongst the many changes taking place, the most important impact of climate change in the Arctic is the melting of sea ice, which is receding at an accelerated and unprecedented rate.

The melting sea ice means that Canadian Arctic waters will be more open and therefore more accessible. This accessibility will lead to the entry of an increasing array of interests into the region. The Canadian government's ability to control what happens in its Arctic region will be tested with this entry of newcomers who will seek to exploit and benefit from a more accessible Arctic. Thus the melting sea ice will be at the root of the challenges to Canadian Arctic sovereignty and security. Debates about the expected impact of climate change are considerable. Scientists studying the issue have been continually surprised by the rapid rate of change.[8]

Regardless of when the ice will melt, two important elements must be stressed. First, the processes that are leading to the melt are speeding up. Second, the recognition that while the processes are not fully understood, they are becoming more pronounced underlies the information that is emerging from the current studies. This suggests that the physical nature of the Arctic will be transforming even more rapidly than previously thought.

So what is happening? The Arctic Climate Impact Assessment (ACIA) study remains the definitive work on the subject, although it will soon require an update. Its 2004 report was commissioned by the Arctic Council when it became clear that processes not yet understood were redesigning the physical nature of the entire Arctic region. In 2000, the Arctic Council directed two of its working groups, the Arctic Monitoring and Assessment Programme (AMAP) and Conservation of Arctic Flora and Fauna (CAFF), along with the International Arctic Science Committee (IASC), to undertake an extensive and exhaustive study of the impact of climate change on the Arctic. This brought together the world's leading experts who produced a peer-reviewed, scientific document and a more concise summary document. Its findings, which were both troubling and overwhelming, emphasized the magnitude of the problem:

1) The Arctic climate is now warming rapidly and greater changes are projected.
2) Arctic warming and its consequences have worldwide implications.
3) Animal species' diversities, ranges and distribution will change.
4) Many coastal communities and facilities face increasing exposure to storms.
5) Reduced sea ice is very likely to increase marine transport and access to resources.
6) Thawing ground will disrupt transportation building and other infrastructure.
7) Indigenous communities are facing major economic and cultural impacts.
8) Elevated ultraviolet (UV) radiation levels will affect people, plants, and animals.
9) Multiple influences interact to cause impacts to people and ecosystems.[9]

This study had its limitations; one was its scale. The report made assessments of the entire Arctic, as opposed to assessing specific areas of the Arctic. It subsequently became apparent that the changes occurring in the Arctic vary depending on local conditions. Thus the original observation that the ice is receding has now been tempered by the recognition that it recedes at different rates throughout the Arctic. Specifically, the Russian side of the Arctic has experienced the greatest rate of ice decline, followed by the central Arctic and then the Northwest Passage.[10] The Passage's slower melting rate is due to a series of geophysical forces that include prevailing ocean currents, the location of the many islands of the Arctic archipelago, and so forth. However, while it may lag behind the other regions, it is still melting.

Historically, the extreme climate and extensive ice cover prevented the outside world from entering the Canadian Arctic. This is now changing as the Arctic is melting. With a diminishing ice cover, the Arctic is becoming more accessible which, in turn, will make it easier for the world to come. But just because accessibility is eased, there is not necessarily a reason to arrive. The outside world needs a reason to take advantage of the improved accessibility. The second major set of forces that cause change in the Arctic serve to provide the world with its reason for coming to the Arctic: resource development.

Resource development

Notwithstanding the melting, the Arctic will remain a unique and dangerous place in which to operate. Regardless of the warming climate, the Earth's tilt means that for significant periods of time, the Arctic will remain in darkness. This darkness alone complicates any activities that will take place in the region. Related to this is the reality that unless the overall temperature of the earth reaches levels in which more southern latitudes are literally baking, some ice will reform during the Arctic winters. So while the Arctic Ocean will be ice-free in the summer months, it will never be completely ice-free year-round, as is the case with the other oceans.

So if that is the case, why come north? The reason is that melting sea ice allows for greater accessibility to and exploitation of the Arctic's marine resources. In terms of oil and gas, the Arctic is estimated to contain approximately 25 per cent of the world's remaining undiscovered oil and gas deposits. The US Geological Survey estimates that 13 per cent of oil and 30 per cent of natural gas remains in the Arctic.[11] If this is correct, the Arctic is the world's last major source of oil and gas.

When discussing the development of Arctic resources in Canada in 2009, it is clear that its defining features are vast and potentially tempered by uncertainty. It is becoming increasingly apparent that the Arctic is indeed a treasure trove of resources. However until the beginning of the 2000s, the market price of most of these resources did not make their exploitation economically viable. But, at the beginning of this decade, there was both an ongoing rise in most commodity prices as well as improvements in the technology that would allow for their extraction. Exxon, British Petroleum (BP), and Shell have now all expanded their exploration for oil and gas in the Arctic.

New technologies for resource development further facilitate the changes in the Arctic. Non-Arctic states have entered into the region and assumed leadership roles in advancing new technologies for use in the Arctic. The best known example is the construction of ice-capable commercial vessels. Historically, Finnish and Russian companies were the leaders in ship design and construction of ice-capable vessels, but they are now increasingly challenged by South Korean companies that have invested heavily in building ice-capable vessels.

But it is necessary to remember that all of this currently remains speculative due to the uncertainty that surrounds almost all aspects of northern resource development. The quantity of oil and gas in the Canadian Arctic is unknown, the technology to exploit these resources is in a state of rapid development, and which resources are useable and when they will even be used is further unknown. Resource exploration and development is further complicated by sliding commodity prices which demonstrates that it is impossible to expect regularity in the market.

Where does this leave the issue of Canadian Arctic sovereignty and security? The pursuit of resources will be the incentive for outside interests to enter the Canadian Arctic. However, international law gives Canada the sovereign right to control the development of these resources. Thus the Canadian government has the right to control all shipping that comes into Canadian Arctic waters for the purposes of resources, if it chooses to do so. The challenge remains controlling vessels that want to use Canadian Arctic waters as a passageway. If Canada loses its dispute with the Americans and European as to the international legal status of the Passage, then they will not be able to unilaterally control those vessels. On the other hand, if the Canadian position that these waters are internal Canadian waters perseveres, then it will also be able to control that shipping.

As the Arctic's resources are developed, Canada needs to continue strengthening its ability to enforce its rules in the Arctic. Canada has the right to control all economic activity on its Arctic lands and in its Arctic Ocean, with the exception of Arctic shipping to a distance of 200 nautical miles from its coastline. But having the right and having the ability to do so are two separate things. In order for Canada to actually control economic activity in its Arctic, the Canadian government must act to improve both its ability to know what is happening in the north as well as its ability to control any activity that takes place there. While successive Canadian governments have recognized the necessity to protect Canadian security and sovereignty in the region, they generally have been unwilling to allocate the funds to develop the means to acquire the necessary assets.[12] In particular, there were two high-profile incidents, one in 1969 and the other in 1985, involving US travel through the Northwest Passage. Each incident created a crisis in Canadian–American Arctic relations.

Geopolitical change

As if climate change and resource development were not enough forces for change, the geopolitical forces that have re-emerged after the end of the Cold War are literally redrawing the map of the Arctic. First, new international laws allow the Arctic nations to extend their control over the Arctic seabed. It is possible that almost all of the Arctic Ocean's seabed may come under the control of one of the Arctic states. Second, at the same time, most Arctic nations are beginning to strengthen the ability of their armed forces and coast guards to operate in the north. Thirdly, non-Arctic states have begun to show interest in Arctic operations. The net effect of these factors is a growing international recognition of the importance of the Arctic, concurrent with increasing international action in the region.

The media increasingly reports about a race for resources in the Arctic, with continuous references to efforts to 'carve' up the Arctic. The reality is that there is no division of the Arctic—yet. Currently, the five Arctic states with coastlines on the Arctic Ocean are about to extend their control of the soil and subsoil of the seabeds extending from their continental shelf. At the heart of this extension is the right to the minerals, oil, and gas that may be found on and in this extension.

This extension may give Canada one of the largest new territories in the Arctic. This extension is occurring under the terms of UNCLOS. This Convention is one of the most comprehensive and complex international agreements that has received almost universal agreement. UNCLOS created new zones of control over ocean space. Prior to the Convention, international law only recognized the right of a state to extend control of its adjacent ocean space to a distance of 12 nautical miles. However, UNCLOS has created different zones of control by allowing coastal states control of resources up to a distance of 200 nautical miles in an area called the EEZ. Under the terms of Article 76, if a state also sits on an extension of the continental shelf that goes beyond 200 nautical miles, it can also claim control of the resources on the soil and subsoil to an additional distance of 150 nautical miles, and in certain instances even beyond this. Unlike the EEZ which all coastal states can claim, states must prove that they have an extended continental shelf. They have ten years to engage in the research necessary to prove this. Canada, Denmark (for Greenland), Russia, and the United States are now all engaged in research programs to determine the extent of their continental shelves. When they have completed their research, each country must submit its findings to an international body named the Commission on Limits of the Continental Shelf (CLCS). The CLCS reviews and passes judgment on the technical and scientific merits of the country's submission. If the CLCS accepts the submission, and if the state's neighbours have submitted overlapping claims, then the dispute must be resolved at that stage. The Convention provides that all such disputes must be resolved peacefully and also provides a variety of means for achieving resolution. Article 280 of Section XV of the Convention allows the state parties to a dispute to use 'any peaceful means of their own choice' to resolve a dispute caused by the Convention. The overlapping claims thus created by Article 76 will constitute such a dispute.

The parties to such a dispute can also use Article 284 of Section XV of the Convention to initiate a conciliation process established within Annex V of the Convention. If either of these processes is not acceptable, then Article 287 requires the parities to the dispute to select from four options: 1(a) the International Tribunal for the Law of the Sea; 1(b) the International Court of Justice; 1(c) an arbitral tribunal constituted in accordance with Annex VII of the Convention; or 1(d) a special arbitral tribunal constituted under Annex VIII of the Convention. If the parties are not able to agree to the specific means of settlement then the fourth means is to be employed. The five Arctic states that are making continental shelf claims, which were agreed upon in June 2008 in a meeting held in Ilulissat, Greenland, will have to resolve any differences peacefully and through the mechanisms established by the UNCLOS.[13]

However, the United States, unlike Russia, Canada, or Denmark (for Greenland), has neither signed nor ratified the treaty.[14] Successive presidents since George H.W. Bush have attempted to accede to the treaty but have been prevented by a small minority of Republican senators. The American constitutional system requires all international treaties to be passed by a two-thirds Senate majority. Since the early 1990s this minority of Republican senators has been able to consolidate over 33 senators who have refused to accede to UNCLOS. Their primary motivation is an ideologically based opposition to the United Nations. However, with the recent American election, and the defeat and retirement of some of the senators in question, the anticipation is that President Obama will eventually achieve success. The United States has recognized the importance of being party to the treaty to protect its interest in the north. In anticipation of their accession they have begun mapping their extended

continental shelf. They conducted an expedition with Canada in the Beaufort Sea in 2008 and plan to continue mapping its continental shelf in 2009.

Following its ratification of UNCLOS, Canada seriously began to map its continental shelf. The 2004 budget allocated $69 million for the mapping of both the Arctic and the Atlantic seabed, with the bulk of the funds expected to be spent in the north. The 2008 budget provided an additional $20 million. This investment has enabled Canadian scientists to carry on with a robust agenda that should be completed by 2010. This will give Canada the necessary time to prepare its submission to the CLCS.

The media has focused on the potential disputes that may develop from any overlapping claims. Until all of the states have submitted their claims, it is impossible to know whether any disputes will arise or if they do how serious they will be. Currently, Canada, the United States, Denmark, and Norway have already issued diplomatic demarches against the 2001 Russian submission. After submitting their claim in 2001, the Russians were advised by the CLCS to further develop the science behind their claim, so it is possible that a revised Russian claim may not be challenged. But this would require the Russians to reduce their claimed area. This seems unlikely.

The Russians have responded to Norway's claim of an extended continental shelf in somewhat aggressive terms. In the summer of 2008, the Russian Navy resumed surface naval patrols. Specifically, two Russian warships sailed into the region that Norway has claimed around Spitsbergen Island.[15] The Russians and the Norwegians have a longstanding dispute about the island, which is undoubtedly being intensified by Norway's claim to extend its continental shelf. Under international law, the Russians have the right to sail warships into the EEZ and over the continental shelf. So by sailing into the disputed region they did not break international law. But it is hard to avoid the conclusion

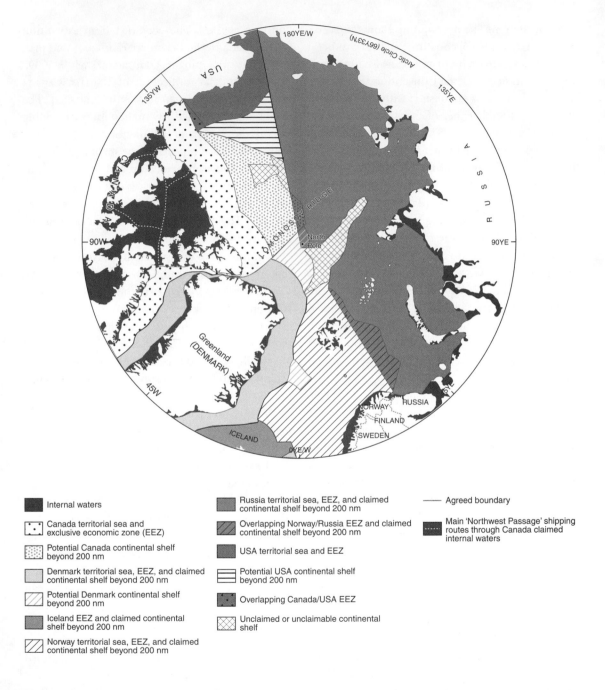

Figure 20.1 Maritime Jurisdiction and Boundaries in the Arctic Region

Source: International Boundaries Research Unit, Durham University. Accessed June 22, 2009, www.dur.ac.uk/bru/resources/arctic.

that the Russians were sending a message to the Norwegians by sailing into the disputed area.

This is not the only action that the Russians have taken to support their claim. Using a mini-submarine, they dropped the Russian flag at the North Pole in summer 2007. The other Arctic states widely dismissed this as a meaningless act. Then Canadian Minister of Foreign Affairs, Peter MacKay stated, '[t]his isn't the 15th century. You can't go around the world and just plant flags to claim territory.'[16] Yet questions remain as to why the Russians would take such potent symbolic action.

The Russians are attempting to justify their claim that the North Pole should be the delimitation point dividing their claim from Canada and Denmark (and possibly the United States). Their initial submission to the CLCS in 2001 shows that they intend to claim up to the North Pole. While such an approach appears logical on a map, it has no basis in international law. The Russian effort is based on the sector theory, which was first put forward by Canadian Senator Poirier in 1907 as a means of extending Canadian Arctic claims. Poirier suggested that each of the states on the Arctic Ocean should extend their boundaries northward until they meet at the North Pole. Such a suggestion was never supported by the Canadian government, or by international law. One of Canada's leading experts on international law in the Arctic, Donat Pharand, provided the definitive examination on the issue and came to the conclusion that such an approach is simply not valid.[17] However, the Russians are attempting to revive it. The Soviets never repudiated the principle after considering it in the 1930s. If it was accepted, this approach would benefit the Russians.

Canada and Denmark claim that the Losonomov Ridge connects to the North American/Greenland land mass. If it does, then they can make an extended claim similar to that of Russia. This means that they too can go to the North Pole. If this is the case, then Canada, Denmark and Russia can claim the entire Arctic Ocean as part of their extended continental shelf. In any other part of the globe the normal means of dividing such an overlapping claim would be to determine the equidistant point (the halfway mark) between the competing states. This point would be determined by drawing a line between the most northern Canadian, Danish, and Russian land points and then determining where the halfway mark of this line is. It is probable that this point is found somewhere on the Russian side of the North Pole. Thus the pole and its surrounding area would be either Danish or Canadian depending on the precise measuring of the ridge. The support this method gains on the Russian side can only be determined once all three states have made their submission to the CLCS.

Shortly, Canada may have to decide whether or not it will challenge Russia's claim. If it challenges this claim, this will be the first time that Canada has engaged in a territorial dispute with Russia since Russia and the United Kingdom resolved the land boundary between Alaska and the Yukon in 1825. At the meeting in Ilulissat, Greenland, the Russian government promised that all disputes arising over the Arctic continental shelf would be dealt with in a co-operative spirit and in a peaceful manner.[18] However, recent events point to an increasingly assertive (and possibly aggressive) Russia. Georgia was temporarily invaded and partially occupied by Russia over a territorial dispute. Ukraine had its gas supplies temporarily suspended as it battled with the Russians over a pricing contract. It is difficult to imagine a Canadian–Russian Arctic dispute escalating to the point of conflict, but it is easy to believe that Russia could be assertive in support of its claim. Thus Canadian officials should not shy away from challenging Russia's extended continental shelf claim, but they should be prepared for Russia to adopt 'hardball' policies.

The situation facing Canada and the United States is even more confounding. Canadian scientists have dedicated substantial effort to determine the extent of the continental shelf in the Beaufort Sea. Canada faces two problems once it submits its co-ordinates. First, Canada and the United States have a substantial boundary disagreement as to how to divide the territorial sea and the EEZ in the Beaufort Sea. The disagreement stems over the interpretation of the 1825 Treaty between Russia and the UK which provided for the drawing of land boundaries between Alaska and the Yukon, but made no reference to maritime boundaries. As a result the Canadians and the Americans dispute how to draw the boundaries for their territorial sea and the EEZ in the Beaufort. The United States contends that the border needs to be drawn at a 90-degree angle to the coastline. The Canadian position is that the maritime boundary is an extension of the land boundary. This disagreement creates a triangle-shaped disputed zone of approximately 6,250 square nautical miles, which may contain substantial oil and gas resources.

This dispute could significantly impact the determination of the Canadian continental shelf in the western Arctic. The starting point of the continental shelf will probably be determined by the tip of the top point of the farthest extent of the EEZ. The disagreement over the boundary dividing the EEZ and territorial sea may lead to a problem in dividing the extended continental shelf.

Further complicating this situation is the fact that the United States is not a party to UNCLOS. The Americans cannot formally submit a claim for their continental shelf until they accede to the Convention. As mentioned earlier, the hope is that the American Senate will pass the Convention in the American Congress. Statements by Secretary of State Hillary Clinton suggest that this will be an important priority for the new administration.[19]

Canada faces substantial uncertainty and challenges in determining the limits of its extended continental shelf. Such uncertainty makes it difficult for Canadian officials to prepare for their diplomatic campaign if there is an overlap with the other Arctic claimant states. Canadian efforts to determine its continental shelf may show that Canada's claim is limited geographically and does not extend into either the American, Russian, or Danish areas. It is also possible that Canadian efforts may result in considerable overlap with its three Arctic neighbours. It is doubtful that this issue will be resolved anytime before 2020.

Ultimately the issue is one of control. The entire purpose of Canada's effort to determine the co-ordinates of its Arctic continental shelf is to allow for its future control of the development and exploitation of any resources that may be found. This control will give Canada the right to set the rules as to how the resources are to be developed. It will also give Canada the right to decide whether it even wants to develop the resources. It may be that a future Canadian government may decide that it is simply better to leave the resources in the ground, but this will be for Canadians to decide. Consequently, the issue of control of this territory is important.

The Northwest Passage

The other issue that has perplexed Canadians in the Arctic is the Northwest Passage. This has been one of the major irritants in Canada–US relations since 1969. The Canadian position is that the passage is internal Canadian waters, which gives Canada absolute control over all activities within it. The American position is that the passage is a strait used for international navigation. If the Canadian position is correct, then Canada has the right to control all elements of shipping in the passage, including the right of controlling who can come into the passage and who cannot. If the American position is correct then Canada only has the right to control international shipping in regards to international rules and standards, and has a limited ability to stop shipping.[20]

Canadian scholars suggest that it may, or even should, be possible to work out a deal with the United States on this issue. Some writers have suggested that it should be feasible to work out a deal similar to the St Lawrence Seaway Agreement in which both states arrange for the joint management of the passage.[21] Others have suggested that as long as Canada can show that it is serious about asserting proper control and therefore maintaining the security of the region, the Americans should respond by not overly asserting its position. In other words, American agreement not to challenge Canada would be exchanged for Canadian protection of the region.

In theory this approach makes sense. However, such hopes were severely damaged in the last days of the George W. Bush administration amidst reports that the United States had been working on a national Arctic Policy since 2007. To the surprise of most observers, the Bush administration released its policy on 9 January 2009, literally less than two weeks before the 20 January Presidential Inauguration of Barack Obama. This National Security Presidential Directive reaffirmed in the strongest terms the American commitment to accede to the UNCLOS to ensure that American interests in the Arctic were protected. However, the Americans also presented one of the most direct statements of their position on the Northwest Passage:

Freedom of the seas is a top national priority. The Northwest Passage is a strait used for international navigation, and the Northern Sea Route includes straits used for international navigation; the regime of transit passage applies to passage through those straits. Preserving the rights and duties relating to navigation and overflight in the Arctic region supports our

ability to exercise these rights throughout the world, including through strategic straits.[22]

The enunciation of the American policy makes it difficult to see how any agreement can be reached unless the new Obama Administration moves to repel or replace this Directive. But any such movement seems very unlikely. The policy Directive does not state anything that is new; it only puts the American position in very stark and direct terms. The Canadian position is further complicated by a policy statement issued by the EU in December 2008. In this statement, the EU was equally clear on its position on the Northwest Passage: while acknowledging the particular environmental needs of the waterways of the Arctic, the EU also affirms that the principle of freedom of navigation through the passage must be maintained.[23]

From a Canadian position it has always been difficult to understand both the American and European positions on the Passage. There have only been three instances where vessels transiting the passage have specifically not sought the Canadian government's permission to do so: the *Manhattan* in 1969 and 1970 and the *Polar Sea* in 1985. All other transits have occurred with the explicit agreement of Canadian authorities. Thus when both the US and the EU maintain that the Northwest Passage is a strait used for international navigation, they speak of a principle and not an existing reality.

What motivates the Americans and the Europeans to oppose the Canadians on this issue? Why do they seem so intent in denying Canada the right to control shipping in what are obviously unique waterways that have not been used for international shipping? Two reasons provide the answer as to why they persist in this position regardless of the damage it may do to their relationship with Canada: the fear of setting a precedent and the anticipation of a substantially larger number of transpolar shipping transits.

The Americans are not necessarily referencing only the Northwest Passage in their discussion about freedom of navigation in their Arctic policy paper. Rather, they are worried about the Straits of Hormuz, Gibraltar, Malacca, and others that are used for international navigation worldwide. The Americans' primary concern is to ensure that the Northwest Passage does not establish a precedent which weakens the principle of free passage through international straits. The driving force behind the Americans' concern in these other straits is both strategic and economic. The Americans are determined to ensure that countries such as Iran do not acquire the right to limit or to restrict the US navy's travel through such waters. The second and related objective of the US is to ensure that commercial traffic continues to have the right of unfettered passage. It is once again feared that a country such as Iran may stop oil tankers from entering or exiting the Strait of Hormuz to load off the coast of Saudi Arabia and Kuwait.

The EU has similar interests in ensuring that its naval and commercial vessels also retain navigational freedoms through these waters. But the EU also seems to be interested in the potential future use of the Arctic as a major shipping route. The Commission of the European Communities stated in a 2008 document that:

EU Member States have the world's largest merchant fleet and many of those ships use transoceanic routes. The melting of sea ice is progressively opening opportunities to navigate on routes through Arctic waters. This could considerably shorten trips from Europe to the Pacific, save energy, reduce emissions, promote trade and diminish pressure on the main trans-continental navigation channels. It is in the EU's interest to explore and improve conditions for gradually introducing Arctic commercial navigation, while promoting stricter safety and environmental standards as well as avoiding detrimental effects. By the same token, Member States and the Community should defend the principle of freedom of navigation and the right of innocent passage in the newly opened routes and areas.[24]

This commercial interest is the basis for the European Union's interest to protect its future Arctic shipping interests.

Where does this leave Canada? Even with a melting Arctic, shipping in the region will still remain extremely challenging. The Canadian side of the Arctic will likely be the last region to experience the elimination of year-round ice. First-year ice will reform in the winter months, limiting shipping to only those vessels that are ice-capable. The summer months will become increasingly ice-free but communication will remain difficult until additional communication and global positioning satellites are situated in orbits that accommodate the high latitudes. It is difficult to expect that the northern straits will be similar to all other straits in terms of accessibility, navigation, and communication. The great challenges to navigation well into this century will require different and more powerful forms of regulations and controls than any other waterway. It is clear that, in these cases, Canada must retain some form of control.

In addition to the challenges that Canada faces in its attempts to retain control over the Northwest Passage, it is also necessary to consider the unintended results of the American and European position on the Northwest Passage. If the Passage becomes an international strait, the security of the North American Arctic will be compromised in terms of air security and maritime security. Under international law, an international strait also accords the right of overflight to all states. This means that the Russians, who recently reinstituted their long-range Tu-95 (Bear) bomber air patrols in the Arctic, would have the right to overfly the passage if it was eventually determined to be an international strait. This overflight ability allows them to come much farther into North American airspace than ever before. Canada would also be denied the right to stop vessels that it may consider a security risk unless it could demonstrate that the vessel in question was breaking international rules and laws. The problem for the north is that given the widely unpopulated regions that exist, if a vessel was attempting to smuggle any illicit product into the country, it would only have to appear to be following international rules. Canada would not have the right to conduct mandatory inspections or to deny passage if it did not have solid evidence against the vessel.

In the future, countries that may not be friendly to the United States or Canada would also have the right of navigation without being required to ask the Canadian government for permission to transit. What would it mean for Canadian security to have a hostile navy sailing through the passage? Of course states such as Iran have to deal with hostile US and UK navies sailing through the Strait of Hormuz. Thus it is possible to argue that Canada will have to deal with a situation similar to Iran's. But if that is the case, then Canada and the United States will have to ensure that if and when that happens they can provide security for the North American Arctic. Maintaining North American Arctic security is both simple and effective if Canada is understood to have control over the waterway. The same cannot be said if the classification of the Passage changes. Thus it is somewhat troublesome to note that the policy positions of Canada's allies will increase the threat to Canadian Arctic security.

Strategic developments

What are the new strategic realities that are taking shape in the Arctic? What do these developments mean for Canada? It is difficult to fully delineate this issue as these new realities are only now starting to take shape. The Arctic states are beginning to rebuild their northern military capabilities. The major driving force is the recognition that new economic development in the Arctic is going to increase the activity level in the region, but no one can fully anticipate what this new economic activity will look like. It is expected to be substantial. As such, Arctic nations are beginning to prepare so that they are able to respond to new contingencies.

Concern is particularly rising among some Arctic states that Russia is beginning to militarily redeploy to the Arctic. But this concern has yet to translate into a fear that the Russians are an actual threat, especially as none of the Arctic states are willing to acknowledge this potential military threat. Instead, the concern is to ensure that, should Russian actions become more threatening, the Arctic states will have the ability to respond if necessary.

An equally nebulous concern is the impact that climate change is expected to have. Most Arctic states have issued statements that the increasingly accessible melting Arctic is expected to facilitate new economic activities. The full nature of these activities is not yet understood. As such the concern is to be sufficiently prepared. This desire for preparation focuses the attention of most decision makers—Canadian included—on surveillance and enforcement capabilities. Most officials want improved means of knowing what is happening in the Arctic and they want to have the ability to respond if unlawful action occurs.

These concerns are accompanied by the growing recognition that the Arctic remains a very expensive region to operate in. As the Arctic states prepare plans to revitalize their security abilities in the Arctic, most recognize that it remains a challenging operational environment. Given the lack of existing infrastructure, any effort to improve both surveillance and enforcement capabilities remains costly. The current economic crisis has only heightened concerns over how an improved Canadian Arctic capability is to be achieved.

A general agreement was reached at the end of the Cold War that the strategic significance of the Arctic had ended and that the need to be concerned about traditional security threats was eliminated. The Soviet northern fleet with its vast number of nuclear-powered attack and nuclear missile-carrying submarines (SSNs and SSBNs) were immediately retired. The collapse of the USSR was so total that the threat posed by these submarines changed overnight from a threat of nuclear war resulting in the destruction of North America (and even the world) to one of a potential Arctic environmental disaster as these vessels were left to rust in northern Russian harbours with the inherent risk of a massive radio-nuclear spill or accident. It took the direct intervention of the G8 and Norway to provide the Russians with both the funds and the technology to properly dispose of these submarines. The United States Navy also disposed of its older class of submarines, including the Sturgeon class, which was considered to be their best submarine for under-ice operations. Furthermore, the Seawolf class submarines, which were to be the new class of American SSNs, were scaled back to three vessels. A new and cheaper submarine, the Virginia class, was selected instead despite the fact that it was not given the same degree of under-ice capability as the Seawolf.[25] The other Arctic nations also reduced the northern element of their own forces. From 1989 to approximately 2002, the northern military capabilities of all the Arctic states were substantially reduced.

There were some important exceptions. One of the most important, which received little attention,

was the American decision to place one of two ballistic missile interceptor ground bases in Fort Greely, Alaska, in 2002. This base is now operational, meaning that missiles designed for interception are now in the ground and ready to engage incoming missiles. The location is presumed to be well suited for a missile attack on the United States from Asia. Currently, the Americans are supplementing their two bases with additional maritime mobile systems, such as placing anti-ballistic missiles onboard ships, and negotiating to place other interceptor sites in countries such as Poland. But with its secured silo placement, Fort Greely ensures that the Arctic will remain a strategic concern for the United States well into the future.

The Canadian effort to maintain military control over its Arctic ended almost as soon as the Cold War ended. Any meaningful military exercises were stopped and even the sovereignty patrols of the navy and air force were either stopped or reduced to only symbolic levels. The only current land force presence in Canada's Arctic is the Canadian Rangers Units. It was not until 1999 that members of the CF seriously reconsidered their role in the Arctic. This was to a certain degree the result of the initiative of individual officers who had become concerned about what they perceived to be a changing Arctic security environment.[26] These concerns led to the creation of an interdepartmental (federal and territorial) security work group named the Arctic Security Intergovernmental Working Group (ASIWG) as well as an internal Department of National Defence (DND) review of its Arctic capabilities. After the terrorist attacks of 11 September 2001, the entire Canadian government began to take security issues much more seriously. In 2002, Canada resumed military training operations in the north.

The short-lived Martin government sought to improve Canada's Arctic security. Its 2005 International Policy Statement, focusing on the expected rise of activity in the north, stated that '[t]he demands of sovereignty and security for the government could become even more pressing as activity in the North continues to rise',[27] meaning that Canada will need to increase its ability to act in the north. The Martin government was also developing a domestic policy statement that would provide a Government of Canada position on the north. This statement was an attempt to move away from the traditional approach of department specific policy and was further aimed to provide a Government of Canada Arctic policy. Referred to as the Northern Strategy, it was to be built on seven pillars or sub-sections, one of which was 'Reinforcing Sovereignty, National Security and Circumpolar Cooperation'.[28] However, the document was not finalized before the government's defeat in the 2006 federal election.

The Harper government has increasingly recognized the significance of maintaining a strong presence in the Arctic and has vigorously begun to improve Canada's northern abilities. Northern Watch is a research program dedicated to developing a Canadian-built and -designed system that will provide surveillance of the subsurface, surface, and airspace of the Arctic. It is not yet ready for operational status and is still being developed. Canadians scientists have also developed a more advanced program of satellite imagery systems designed to provide space-based surveillance of surface vessels in the Arctic. At the lower end of the technology spectrum, both the Martin and the Harper governments increased the size and the training of the Ranger units based in the north. The Rangers are a northern militia unit whose primary task is to provide surveillance in the north at the local level. They are volunteers comprised primarily of indigenous peoples, and are particularly skilled observers who can live off the land. All of these initiatives will enable the Canadian government to know who is in its Arctic region and what

they are doing, which is the first step in controlling activity in the Canadian north.

The Harper government has also made a series of promises to considerably expand Canada's northern capability, including: six to eight Arctic offshore patrol vessels that will be able to sail in first-year ice that is up to one metre thick; a replacement for the Coast Guard's largest and oldest icebreaker, the Louis St Laurent; the construction of a deep-water replenishment site at Nanisivik; new replenishment vessels that will have the capability to operate in first-year ice for the navy; new long-range patrol aircraft to replace the Aurora (CF-140); and the establishment of a northern military training base in Resolute Bay. The 2007 throne speech also emphasized the protection of Arctic sovereignty and security and promised to establish a world-class research station in the Canadian north.[29] If these promises are implemented, Canada will have significantly improved its ability to control activity in its Arctic. However, most of these commitments have not yet moved from promise to reality. There are now signs that the government is backtracking on some of its promises. The program to build the new replenishment vessels, for instance, has been postponed because domestic builders submitted bids that were too high for the government. What will happen with this program remains uncertain. Likewise there is little discussion of when construction of the Arctic Offshore Patrol Vessel or ice-breaker will begin.

Other Arctic nations are also reviving their military capabilities. From a strategic position, nuclear-powered submarines remain the principle weapon platform. In 2004 both the Russians and then the Americans took action to rebuild their under-ice capabilities.[30] The Russians have also begun to consider rebuilding their surface fleet capability. Recently the naval commander-in-chief announced the plan to build up their forces to six carrier battle-groups.[31] This announcement has also been accompanied by an increase in operations in the region. The Russian's Arctic sovereignty flights were suspended in 1992, but resumed in the summer of 2007.[32] Using its long range TU-95 (Bear) patrol and bomber aircraft, the Russians are now sending out patrols over the Arctic and as far as the Sea of Japan and Cuba. The Russians also resumed Arctic patrols of their surface naval vessels in 2008.[33] As a Russian navy official stated, '[t]he Russian Navy has restored the presence of combat ships of the Northern Fleet in the Arctic region, including in the region of Spitsbergen'.[34] The two vessels, the destroyer Severomorsk and cruiser Marshal Ustinov, also made a point of sailing through several regions that are the subject of ongoing diplomatic disputes between Russia and Norway.

Norway has refocused its entire defence policy on the north. In a series of recent statements, the Norwegian Defence Minister Anne-Grete Strøm-Erichsen has made it clear that Norway recognizes that resources and climate change are bringing new actors to the north. To this end, the most recent Norwegian Defence Policy Review makes it clear that 'the Armed Forces play an important role by virtue of their operational capabilities with the emphasis on maintaining a presence and upholding national sovereignty in the North'.[35] As a result Norway has been rebuilding its ability to operate in its Arctic region. It has a slightly easier task than the other Arctic states in that its Arctic waters seldom freeze because of the impact of the Gulf Stream. It is in the process of taking possession of five new frigates that are Aegis-capable (Aegis is an integrated weapons system used by the US navy) and also have a very sophisticated anti-submarine capability.[36] The Norwegians have also announced that they will be moving air assets to northern bases and increasing the defence budget. Lastly they have also signed a contract to buy 48 F-35 Joint Strike Fighter aircraft in November 2008.[37]

The American military, despite possessing the most vigorous Arctic security apparatus, has also rediscovered the Arctic. While it did decommission older nuclear-powered submarines, the United States maintained and added new submarines to its navy throughout the 1990s and 2000s. The American Coast Guard has been arguing that it needs to build new icebreakers. Right now, there are three icebreakers, but two of them are reaching the end of their operational lives.[38] The United States also maintains a very strong air wing in Alaska, with three wings of National Guard F-15 (22 aircraft/wing) as well as a number of AWACs (large aircraft that carry advance radar and electronic systems designed to give a very detailed surveillance picture of the region around the aircraft). They are now replacing the F-15 with the newer F-22 Raptors. To support these activities the numbers of serving personnel remained at about 26,000 in 2005.[39]

In an effort to come to terms with the changing Arctic, the Americans have been engaged in a policy development process since 2008. The US executive branch, led by the Department of State and National Security Council, reviewed its policies in the Arctic region. The core issues examined by this review were:

1)   national security and homeland security;
2)   international governance;
3)   extended continental shelf and boundary issues;
4)   international scientific co-operation;
5)   shipping;
6)   economic issues including energy; and
7)   environmental protection and conservation of natural resources.[40]

The Bush Administration released the above policy on 9 January 2009 as Presidential Directive 66. The document makes it clear that national security considerations are the first priority of the United States when it comes to the Arctic. This

Directive presents five points in its National Security and Homeland Security Interests in the Arctic:

1) The United States has broad and fundamental national security interests in the Arctic region and is prepared to operate either independently or in conjunction with other states to safeguard these interests.

2) The United States also has fundamental homeland security interests in preventing terrorist attacks and mitigating those criminal or hostile acts that could increase the United States' vulnerability to terrorism in the Arctic region.

3) The Arctic region is primarily a maritime domain; as such, existing policies and authorities relating to maritime areas continue to apply, including those relating to law enforcement. Human activity in the Arctic region is increasing and is projected to increase further in coming years. This requires the United States to assert a more active and influential national presence to protect its Arctic interests and to project sea power throughout the region.

4) The United States exercises authority in accordance with lawful claims of United States sovereignty, sovereign rights, and jurisdiction in the Arctic region, including sovereignty within the territorial sea, sovereign rights and jurisdiction within the United States' exclusive economic zone and on the continental shelf, and appropriate control in the United States contiguous zone.

5) Freedom of the seas is a top national priority. The Northwest Passage is a strait used for international navigation, and the Northern Sea Route includes straits used for international navigation.[41]

Where, then, does this leave Canada in regards to protecting its Arctic security? First, the strategic environment is in flux as Arctic states are improving their northern military capabilities. All of the main Arctic states contend that this is only being done to provide an ability to respond to the expected increase in activity in the Arctic. But it is interesting to note that both Norway and Russia are increasing their Arctic capabilities with weapon systems that are clearly designed to fight and not to act in a Coast Guard-type capability. The Americans are also looking to further develop the strategic nature of their forces. Canada does not face a direct military threat in the Arctic, but the indicators are becoming somewhat worrisome. Why would Canada's neighbours dedicate increasingly substantial resources for the harder edge of their security forces in the region unless they were beginning to see a need? Canada will need to maintain a careful watch on events as they unfold.

CONCLUSION

The Arctic is changing in so many different ways and with such complexity that it almost seems impossible to comment on how best to protect Canadian Arctic sovereignty and security. Clearly Canadian officials are going to have to make some hard decisions sooner rather than later if Canada will ensure that it can control its section of the Arctic for the protection of Canadian interests and values.

So how is this to be done? First it needs to be recognized that there is no one set solution to the problem. The rapid and complicated transformation of the Arctic is an ongoing process. Thus the government needs to be thinking in terms of process rather than result. The challenges of the Arctic require government action that transcends any one department. It is currently trendy to use terms such as 'whole of government' when talking about efforts to break down departmental silos. The Arctic definitely requires that such silos be broken down. But Canadian Arctic policy needs to go even beyond this. The territorial governments must also be included, as well as the various northern aboriginal peoples organizations. But perhaps most importantly, this process must have direct access to the prime minister. Canadian Arctic policy develops when the prime minister is interested. If not, other priorities quickly refocus the bureaucracy. Thus the creation of a Cabinet committee that is chaired by the prime minister would be one means to ensure that attention on the Arctic is maintained. There may be other means, but the main point is that the prime minister must be continually engaged in the process.

Once the attention of the Prime Minister is institutionalized, there are three major sets of actions that the Canadian government must follow in order to establish and then maintain control. To a certain degree, both the Martin and the Harper governments already began the process, but the critical point will be sustainability. Historically, Canadian governments have promised a wide array of policy actions only to renege on them when other political and economic issues have arisen. The issue then is developing a flexible long-term program that will be maintained. Ultimately this program needs to provide for the ability to:

1) know what is happening in the Canadian north;
2) enforce Canadian rules and laws
3) co-operate with Canada's circumpolar neighbours

One of the greatest political challenges now is the artificial divide that seems to be developing between Liberal and Conservative Arctic policy. A disturbing trend is emerging whereby the Conservatives are focusing on providing Canada with enforcement and surveillance capabilities while the Liberals have traditionally focused on diplomatic initiatives. In keeping with their policy position, the Conservatives eliminated the position of Circumpolar Ambassador and have contentedly followed the diplomatic initiatives of the other Arctic states. Throughout the entire Chrétien era no discussion was ever undertaken regarding building up Canadian Arctic capabilities. This debate is being increasingly cast in unilateral versus multilateral terms. In addition, the Conservatives are perceived as focusing on Canada's military while the Liberals are viewed as focusing on the diplomatic requirements for establishing control. The reality is that both sets of actions are required. Canada needs to have strong surveillance and enforcement capabilities to control the new activities that will increasingly being taking place in the Arctic. These capabilities will primarily be the responsibility of the DND, but it also requires the involvement of the Coast Guard and Royal Canadian Mounted Police.

At the same time, Canada cannot act in isolation in the Arctic. It needs to work with its Arctic neighbours in order to develop the international frameworks that will provide both the international rules necessary to protect the Arctic as well as a spirit of co-operation in the region. The new accessibility of the Arctic will bring new actors and activities to the region and it will therefore be necessary to develop a regional set of rules and arrangements for these new activities. These include a co-ordinated approach to search and rescue, as well as pollution response for environmental accidents that will inevitably occur. It would also be beneficial for the entire region if agreements were reached on future economic activity. A regional approach to the expanding Arctic fisheries would head off differences before they arise over the issue of fishing new stocks as they move north. Likewise, a regional approach could be a means of avoiding the sovereignty challenges surrounding the issue of international shipping. If the Arctic nations could agree on the standards for ship construction, operation, and crew requirements in Arctic waters, then Canada could possibly achieve the control it seeks over the expected shipping in Canadian northern waters.

The greatest international challenge facing Canada may be the reality that two of its Arctic neighbours are the United States and Russia. The United States is Canada's most important trading partner and ally, and the former USSR, at various times throughout Canada's recent history, was both an important ally and a most dangerous enemy. Throughout the Cold War period, both the United States' and Russia's importance and significance to Canada was amplified by their geographic location as Arctic neighbours. Now that the Arctic is warming and becoming more accessible, the dynamics of this relationship are about to become even more important.

Canada must work with both the United States and Russia in the region, but the problem is that they have very different Arctic visions. The Russians see the Arctic as the key to their future economic prosperity, understanding that the undeveloped oil and gas resources in their Arctic region will provide them with the economic capability to regain their great power status. They are also aware that, from a strategic perspective, the north is their primary access to the world's oceans. During the past few years, the Russians have clearly become more assertive in their foreign policy, including their policy in the Arctic. This does not mean a return to the Cold War, but it does signify that the period of complete co-operation of the 1990s has ended. Canada can still expect to work with the Russians, but this needs to be tempered by a more realistic framework. The Russians will not co-operate simply for the benefit of co-operation. Rather, it will be increasingly necessary for Canada to show the Russians why co-operation is in their interest. At the same time, when Canadian interests do not intersect with Russian interests, the Canadian government needs to be prepared for an increasingly assertive Russian response. Such an incident would occur if Canada

decides to claim any part of the Arctic continental shelf that has been claimed by the Russians. If this happens, the Russian government's reaction will set the tone for future Canadian-Russian relations. If the reaction is tempered and diplomatic, Canada should seize the moment by trying to further engage the Russians in other means of co-operation. If the reaction is more belligerent, then Canada may need to garner support from its other Arctic neighbours in order to maintain its claim.

Canada's Arctic relationship with the United States will also continue to develop. The Americans are increasingly aware of the transformations that will increase the Arctic's importance. Canada's key challenge will be to minimize, if not resolve, the various disputes over boundaries and sovereignty in the North American Arctic. The issues of control of international shipping through the Northwest Passage and the division of the Beaufort Sea are challenging. However, the two states must find ways to prevent these issues from contaminating future co-operation. Ultimately, the two states must find ways to co-operate in the Arctic since it is in their mutual interest to do so. Both states need to ensure that the new activities in the Arctic are controlled in such a manner that environmental protection remains a core requirement. At the same time, it is also in the interests of both states to ensure that those who call the north home benefit fully from the forthcoming activities.

Thus Canada needs to pay special attention to its relationship with Russia and the United States. While many of the issues can be addressed in a bilateral fashion, the time has arrived for Canada to renew its efforts to strengthen the multilateral forums in the region. The Arctic Council, which Canada will soon chair, is at the centre of this. Canada can serve the interests of the region and itself by dedicating its time as chair to strengthening the Council. First, Canada needs to avoid directly undermining the Council. For example, the Ilulissat meeting in May 2008 of the five Arctic continental shelf claimant states should have taken place within the Arctic Council. While Iceland, Sweden, and Finland do not have claims, each state will be affected by what happens within the areas claimed by others. Likewise, the permanent participants also have interests in these regions. Yet these members of the Council were excluded from this very important meeting. Second, Canada should lead the way in creating a more powerful support system for the Council. Relying on each member state to simply volunteer support is not working. Canada should establish some form of a permanent support body. Third, Canada should also take the initiative to work out a series of regional agreements to deal with issues such as standards for international shipping, fishing,

tourism, environmental protection, and so on. Canadian interests are best served by the creation of such agreements now and not later when many other competing interests will seek to be included.

Ultimately, Canada needs to recognize what it wants its Arctic to look like in the emerging future. The time when lip service could be paid to the north is over. The forces of transformation are creating a new era in which the world will be coming to the entire Arctic region. Canada can choose to simply react to the new changes or it can take the lead and recognize that there are both dangers and opportunities. The dangers can be mitigated by thoughtful preparation. The opportunities can best be taken advantage of by allocating the necessary resources to promote and protect Canadian interests and values.

Key Terms

Climate Change
Human Security
International Law of the Sea

Security
Sovereignty

Notes

1. James Allan, *Sovereign Statehood* (London: Allen and Unwin, 1986).
2. R.R. Churchill and A.V. Lowe, *The Law of the Sea,* 3rd edition (Manchester: Manchester University Press, 2002).
3. For the best collection of articles that addresses the entire discussion on the nature of security see: *Strategy in the Contemporary World,* 2nd edition, eds. John Baylis, James Wirtz, Colin Gray and Eliot Cohen (Oxford: Oxford University Press, 2007); and *Contemporary Security Studies,* ed. Allan Collins (Oxford: Oxford University Press, 2007).
4. *Human Security and the New Diplomacy: Protecting People, Promoting Peace,* ed. McRae and Don Hubert (Montreal and Kingston: McGill-Queen's University Press, 2001).
5. Thomas Homer-Dixon, *Environment, Security and Violence* (Princeton: Princeton University Press, 1999).
6. *Northern Lights against POPs: Combating Toxic Threats in the Arctic,* ed. David Downie and Terry Fenge (Montreal and Kingston: McGill-Queen's University Press, 2003).

7. The story of their association with the Hell's Angels and drugs are alleged activities since they were never proven to have engaged in such actions. CBC, '"Wild Vikings" Land in Cambridge Bay Jail', *CBC News.* August 30, 2007, Accessed June 5, 2009, www.cbc.ca/canada/north/story/ 2007/08/30/cambay-vikings.html.
8. See Arctic Climate Impact Assessment (ACIA), *Impacts of a Warming Arctic: Arctic Climate Impact Assessment* (Cambridge: Cambridge University Press, 2004), Accessed June 5, 2009, www.acia.uaf.edu/ and Rheal Seguin, 'Scientists predict seasonal ice-free by 2015', *Globe and Mail,* December 12, 2008.
9. ACIA, *Impacts,* 1011.
10. Anne Casselman, 'Will the Opening of the Northwest Passage Transform Global Shipping Anytime soon?' *Scientific American,* November 10, 2008. Accessed June 5, 2009, www. sciam.com/article.cfm?id=opening-of-northwest-passage.
11. Kenneth J. Bird et al., 'Circum-Arctic resource appraisal; estimates of undiscovered oil and gas north of the Arctic

Circle', *U.S. Geological Survey Fact Sheet* 2008–3049 (2008), Accessed June 5, 2009, http://pubs.usgs.gov/fs/2008/3049/.

12. For a more complete history of the development of Canadian policy see: Rob Huebert, 'Canada and the Changing International Arctic: At the Crossroads of Cooperation and Conflict' in *Northern Exposure: Peoples, Powers and Prospects for Canada's North*, ed. Frances Abele et al. (Montreal: IRPP, 2009). Accessed June 5, 2009, www.irpp.org/books/archive/AOTS4/huebert.pdf.

13. 'The Ilulissat Declaration'. Arctic Ocean Conference. Ilulissat, Greenland, May 27–29 2008. Accessed June 5, 2009, www.oceanlaw.org/downloads/arctic/Ilulissat_Declaration.pdf.

14. UN Oceans and Law of the Sea, Division for Ocean Affairs and Law of the Sea, 'Chronological lists of ratifications of, accessions and successions to the Convention and the related Agreements as at 31 December 2008', Updated December 31, 2008, www.un.org/Depts/los/reference_files/chronological_lists_of_ratifications.htm.

15. Barents Observer, 'Russia sends Naval vessels to Spitsbergen', July 15, 2007. Accessed June 5, 2009, www.barentsobserver.com/russia-sends-navy-vessels-to-spitsbergen.4497720-58932.html.

16. Doug Struck, 'Russia's Deep-Sea Flag-Planting at North Pole Strikes a Chill in Canada', *Washington Post*. August 7, 2007. Accessed June 5, 2009, www.washingtonpost.com/wp-dyn/content/article/2007/08/06/AR2007080601369.html.

17. Donat Pharand, *Canada's Arctic Waters in International Law* (Cambridge: Cambridge University Press, 1988).

18. 'The Ilulissat Declaration'.

19. Associated Foreign Press, 'US "committed" to ratifying Law of Sea Convention: Clinton'. April 6 2009. Accessed June 5, 2009, www.google.com/hostednews/afp/article/ALeqM5gB1OPzPfiju89sybtB66q9Sq4f6A.

20. Donat Pharand, 'The Arctic Waters and the Northwest Passage: a Final Revisit', *Ocean Development and International Law* 38 no. 1–2 (January 2007).

21. Brian Flemming, Canada–US Relations in the Arctic: A Neighborly Proposal (Calgary: Canadian Defence and Foreign Affairs Institute, December 2008); Don McRae, 'Arctic Sovereignty? What Is at Stake', *Behind the Headlines* 64 (January 2007).

22. The White House, National Security Presidential Directive/NSPD 66 Homeland Security Presidential Directive/HSPD 25—Arctic Region Policy. January 9, 2009.

23. Commission of the European Communities, Communication from the Commission to the European Parliament and the Council. *The European Union and the Arctic Region*. (Brussels, COM (2008) 763).

24. Commission of the European Communities, *The European Union and the Arctic Region*, 9.

25. Rob Huebert, 'Renaissance in Canadian Arctic Security', *Canadian Military Journal* 6, no. 4 (2005–6): 17–29.

26. Department of National Defence, *Canada's International Policy Statement: A Role of Pride and Influence in the World—Defence* (Ottawa: 2005): 17.

27. Canadian Arctic Resource Committee (CARC), Northern Perspective 30, no.1 (Winter 2006): 2. Accessed June 5, 2009, www.carc.org/pubs/v30no1/CARC_Northrn_Perspctves_Winter_2006.pdf.

28. Government of Canada, 'Protecting Canada's Future', Speech from the Throne. October 16, 2007. Accessed June 5, 2009, www.sft-ddt.gc.ca/eng/media.asp?id=1364.

29. 'SSN-774 Virginia-class New Attack Submarine [NSSN] Centurion', Globalsecurity.org. September 5, 2008. Accessed June 5, 2009, www.globalsecurity.org/military/systems/ship/ssn-774.htm.

30. 'Russian Navy Promised new Nuclear subs with new strategic missiles', Bellona, October 6, 2008. Accessed June 5, 2009, www.bellona.org/news/news_2008/new_nuke_subs.

31. Defence Update, 'Russia Plans to Deploy 6 Carrier Battlegroups by 2025', 2007. Accessed June 5, 2009, http://defenseupdate.com/newscast/0707/news/150707_russian_Navy.htm.

32. BBC, 'Russia restarts Cold War Patrols', BBC News, August 17, 2007, June 5, 2009, http://news.bbc.co.uk/2/hi/europe/6950986.stm.

33. The Russian Federal Ministry of Defence, 'Russian Navy Resumes Presence in Arctic Area', News Details, July 14, 2008, Accessed June 5, 2009, www.mil.ru/eng/1866/12078/details/index.shtml?id=47433.

34. Associated Foreign Press, 'Russian Navy Boasts Combat Presence in Arctic', Canada.com. July 14, 2008. Accessed June 5, 2009, www.canada.com/topics/news/world/story.html?id=3572ff95-9a88-4dd8-944f-58af497c3fa6.

35. Norwegian Ministry of Defence, Norwegian Defence 2008 (Oslo: 2008). Accessed June 5, 2009, www.regjeringen.no/upload/FD/Dokumenter/Fakta2008_eng.pdf.

36. Endre Lund, 'Norway's New Nansen Class Frigates: Capabilities and Controversies', Defence Daily Industries. June 7, 2008. Accessed June 5, 2009, www.defenseindustrydaily.com/norways-new-nansen-class-frigates-capabilities-and-controversies-02329/.

37. Doug Mellgreen, 'Norway picks US fighter to replace aging fleet', Foxnews.com. November 20, 2008, www.foxnews.com/printer_friendly_wires/2008Nov20/0,4675,EUNorwayJointStrikeFighter,00.html.

38. These numbers were provided directly to the author by a senior American Military official in an open briefing in Alaska on March 10, 2005.

39. Ronald O'Rourke, *Coast Guard Icebreaker Modernization: Background, Issues, and Options for Congress*—CRS Report for Congress RL 34391(Washington: Congressional Research Service, September 11, 2008). Accessed June 5, 2009, http://fas.org/sgp/crs/weapons/RL34391.pdf; and Committee on the Assessment of U.S. Coast Guard Polar

Icebreaker Roles and Future Needs, National Research Council, *Polar Icebreakers in a Changing World: An Assessment in a Changing World* (Washington DC: The National Academics Press, 2007). Accessed June 5, 2009, http://books.nap.edu/catalog.php?record_id=11753.

40. Margaret F. Hayes, Director of Office of Oceans Affairs, Department of State, 'Arctic Policy—Speech to Arctic Parliamentarians on Aspects of U.S. Arctic Policy', Fairbanks, Alaska, August 13, 2008.

41. White House, National Security Presidential Directive 66/Homeland Security Presidential Directive 25—Arctic Region Policy. January 9, 2009, 2–3.

SELECTED BIBLIOGRAPHY

Axworthy, Lloyd. 1997. 'Canada and Human Security: The Need for Leadership', *International Journal* 52, 2 (Spring): 183–96.

Barry, Donald and Duane Bratt. 2008. 'Defense Against Help: Explaining Canada–US Security Relations', *The American Review of Canadian Studies* 38, 1 (Spring): 63–89.

Bell, Stewart. 2004. *Cold Terror: How Canada Nurtures and Exports Terrorism Around the World.* Toronto: Wiley.

Bland, Douglas L., ed. 2004. *Canada Without Armed Forces?* Montreal and Kingston: McGill-Queen's University Press.

——— and Sean M. Maloney. 2004. *Campaigns for International Security: Canada's Defence Policy at the Turn of the Century.* Montreal and Kingston: McGill-Queen's University Press.

Bratt, Duane. 2006. *The Politics of CANDU Exports.* Toronto: University of Toronto Press.

———. 1999. 'Nice-Making and Canadian Peacekeeping', *Canadian Foreign Policy* 6, 3 (Spring): 73–84.

Buckley, Brian. 2000. *Canada's Early Nuclear Policy: Fate, Chance, and Character.* Montreal and Kingston: McGill-Queen's University Press.

Cameron, Maxwell A., Robert J. Lawson, and Brian W. Tomlin, eds. 1998. *To Walk Without Fear: The Global Movement to Ban Landmines.* Don Mills, ON: Oxford University Press.

Carroll, Michael K. 2009. *Pearson's Peacekeepers: Canada and the United Nations Emergency Force, 1956–67.* Vancouver: UBC Press.

Clearwater, John. 1998. *Canadian Nuclear Weapons: The Untold Story of Canada's Cold War Arsenal.* Toronto: Dundurn.

Coates, Ken S., P. Whitney Lackenbauer, William R. Morrison, and Greg Poelzer. 2008. *Arctic Front: Defending Canada in the Far North.* Toronto: Thomas Allen.

Dallaire, Romeo. 2003. *Shake Hands with the Devil: The Failure of Humanity in Rwanda.* Toronto: Random House.

Dawson, Grant. 2007. *'Here Is Hell': Canada's Engagement in Somalia.* Vancouver: UBC Press.

Dewitt, David B., and David Leyton-Brown, eds. 1995. *Canada's International Security Policy.* Scarborough: Prentice-Hall.

Edgar, Alistair D., and David G. Haglund. 1995. *The Canadian Defence Industry in the New Global Environment.* Montreal and Kingston: McGill-Queen's University Press.

English, Allan D. 2004. *Understanding Military Culture: A Canadian Perspective.* Montreal and Kingston: McGill-Queen's University Press.

Ehrhart, Hans-Georg and Charles C. Pentland, eds. 2009. *The Afghanistan Challenge: Hard Realities and Strategic Choices.* Montreal and Kingston: McGill-Queen's University Press.

Gammer, Nicholas. 2001. *From Peacekeeping to Peacemaking: Canada's Response to the Yugoslav Crisis.* Montreal and Kingston: McGill-Queen's University Press.

Granatstein, J.L. 2007. *Whose War Is It? How Canada Can Survive in the Post-9/11 World.* Toronto: HarperCollins.

———. 2004. *Who Killed the Canadian Military?* Toronto: HarperCollins.

Granatstein, J.L., and David Stafford. 1990. *Spy Wars: Espionage and Canada from Gouzenko to Glasnost*. Toronto: Key Porter Books.

Hayes, Geoffrey and Mark Sedra. 2008. *Afghanistan: Transition under Threat*. Waterloo, ON: Wilfrid Laurier University Press.

Hillier, Rick. 2009. *A Soldier First: Bullets, Bureaucrats and the Politics of War*. Toronto: HarperCollins.

Jockel, Joseph T. 1999. *The Canadian Forces: Hard Choices, Soft Power*. Toronto: Canadian Institute of Strategic Studies.

———. 1994. *Canada and International Peacekeeping*. Washington: Center for Strategic and International Studies.

Laxer, James. 2008. *Mission of Folly: Canada and Afghanistan*. Toronto: Between the Lines.

Legault, Albert. 1999. *Canada and Peacekeeping: Three Major Debates*. Clementsport: Canadian Peacekeeping Press.

Legault, Albert, and Michel Fortmann. 1992. *A Diplomacy of Hope: Canada and Disarmament, 1945–1988*, trans. Derek Ellington. Montreal and Kingston: McGill-Queen's University Press.

Mackenzie, Lewis. 1993. *Peacekeeper: The Road to Sarajevo*. Vancouver: Douglas & McIntyre.

Morrison, Alex, ed. 1992. *A Continuing Commitment: Canada and North Atlantic Security*. Toronto: Canadian Institute of Strategic Studies.

Morton, Desmond. 2003. *Understanding Canadian Defence*. Toronto: Penguin.

———. 1999. *A Military History of Canada: From Champlain to Kosovo*. Toronto: McClelland and Stewart.

Nossal, Kim Richard. 1994. *Rain Dancing: Sanctions in Canadian & Australian Foreign Policy*. Toronto: University of Toronto Press.

Plamondon, Aaron. 2009. *The Politics of Procurement: Military Acquisitions in Canada and the Sea King Helicopter*. Vancouver: UBC Press.

Rempel, Roy. 2006. *Dreamland: How Canada's Pretend Foreign Policy Has Undermined Sovereignty*. Toronto: Dundurn.

Roach, Kent. 2003. *September 11: Consequences for Canada*. Montreal and Kingston: McGill-Queen's University Press.

Sloan, Elinor C. 2005. *Security and Defence in the Terrorist Era: Canada and North America*. Montreal and Kingston: McGill-Queen's University Press.

Spooner, Kevin A. 2009. *Canada, the Congo Crisis, and UN Peacekeeping, 1960–1964*. Vancouver: UBC Press.

Stein, Janice Gross and Eugene Lang. 2007. *The Unexpected War: Canada in Kandahar*. Toronto: Viking.

Windsor, Lee and David Charters. 2010. *Kandahar Tour: The Turning Point in Canada's Afghan Mission*. Toronto: Wiley and Sons.

PART V

TRADE AND OTHER ECONOMIC ISSUES

Until the last decade only a small number of academics focused on Canada's foreign trade and economic policy. The end of the Cold War, the negotiation of the Canada–United States Free Trade Agreement (FTA), the North American Free Trade Agreement (NAFTA), the creation of the World Trade Organization (WTO), the prominence of the G7/8, the launching of the Doha Round, and the failure of the Multilateral Agreement on Investment (MAI), all contributed to increased interest and awareness in this policy area. The nature of trade and investment also changed during this period. Specifically, Canada faced new challenges related to the relevance of non-traditional issues, such as services, subsidies, labour, and the environment. The increasing fluidity of financial capital and the intrusiveness of these commitments into areas of domestic policy space also made it increasingly difficult for federal and provincial officials to respond to these changes.

Recent events continue to highlight the need to better understand Canada's role in the global political economy. The ongoing global financial crisis, a seemingly inflated Canadian dollar, the pursuit of a comprehensive trade agreement with Europe, a failure to negotiate similar ties with Asian markets, and the recent US softwood lumber dispute, all make it clear that Canada is potentially vulnerable to international economic developments. In some cases, however, the Canadian government continues to assert its influence in response to these challenges. As John Kirton notes in Chapter 9, Canada has a long history of leadership in the G8 and G20 forums, and most recently hosted both summits in 2010. Ottawa also successfully negotiated a bilateral agreement with Washington to limit provincial exclusions under US 'Buy American' economic stimulus legislation. Three prominent authors with extensive background in trade and economic policy will address many of these issues in Part Five. Although there are notable omissions—namely Michael Hart, Gilbert Winham, Sylvia Ostry, Brian Tomlin, Grace Skogstad, Bruce Doern, and Thomas Courchene—these three chapters offer a range of perspectives to better understand Canadian foreign trade and economic policy.

Robert Wolfe's evaluation of Canada's role in the current Doha Round of WTO negotiations adopts the theme of 'clubland'. He highlights the tendency of Canada to 'belong to any club that will have us' in an attempt to influence foreign affairs. In the case of the WTO, a proliferation of clubs have emerged around various issue areas with 'banal and whimsical' names, such as the *Dirty Dozen* and the *Friends of Fish*. Although Canada is not a member of every prominent club, Wolfe notes that federal negotiators are active in several of these groups. As a result, Canada has managed to play an important role in the lengthy Doha negotiations. He is also optimistic of the importance of these clubs as the WTO moves into final, and highly technical, Green Room meetings.

Stephen McBride, on the other hand, questions Canada's handling of the global economic crisis. He begins by noting various academic perspectives of Canada in the international community and Ottawa's tendency to adopt both bilateral and multilateral approaches to economic policy. During the ongoing crisis, however, the federal government initially adopted a perspective of denial, which was soon followed by an attempt to minimize the significance of these developments for Canada. When Canada did act, it was to pursue bilateral solutions related to procurement and the automobile industry. As a result, McBride argues, the financial crisis highlighted Canada's limited options in matters of foreign economic policy, especially when dealing with the much stronger United States.

Finally, Elizabeth Smythe's discussion of Canada and the negotiation of WTO investment rules suggests that although the European Union was viewed as the main catalyst for including investment in the Doha Round, Canada also supported these negotiations. Unlike Wolfe, however, Smythe makes it clear that Canada was not able to influence this international economic regime to reflect its interests. This was due to negative public opinion related to NAFTA's Chapter 11 provisions and the potential limitations a WTO agreement would place on the ability of states to regulate in the public interest. Significant divergence between WTO members on the issue also contributed to its removal from the Doha agenda. As a result, Canada placed a stronger emphasis on regional and bilateral agreements, many with developing states. In conclusion, Smythe raises normative concerns related to the asymmetrical partnerships these agreements create.

21

CANADA'S ADVENTURES IN CLUBLAND: TRADE CLUBS AND POLITICAL INFLUENCE

Robert Wolfe

Unlike Groucho Marx, Canadians want to belong to any club that will have us as a member, and that turns out to be quite a few international clubs. It is axiomatic that a central objective of Canadian foreign policy is to *participate* in making decisions that affect the country directly, while having *influence* on decisions that affect the evolving structure of global governance. The political practice of multilateralism, however, is not an open-ended Athenian forum where every state can speak freely, expecting its views to be given serious consideration by all others. In the messy reality of global governance, Canada can only play a role by aggregating its efforts with other countries. The notion of 'clubs' is one way to think about how that process works. It is an especially useful idea when studying the World Trade Organization (WTO), where the current Doha Round of multilateral trade negotiations is characterized by a bewildering array of clubs with banal and whimsical names, from the G4 through the Dirty Dozen and the Friends of Fish to the G90. Canada is a great joiner, but many observers now wonder whether Canada is still a member of the best clubs in WTO 'clubland'.

It is common to see international organizations in themselves as 'clubs', meaning places where insiders (certain states and selected officials of those states) know the rules, and outsiders (citizens, other states) are not welcome (Keohane and Nye, 2001). Regional agreements can also be seen as clubs (Padoan, 1997), and particular treaties can be seen as providing 'club goods', in the sense of excludable goods available only to members of those clubs. Sometimes the term will be applied to a loosely structured body, like the Paris Club of creditor states, or to a set of countries with no structure at all, as in referring to the states possessing nuclear weapons as the nuclear club. There was a time when the WTO's predecessor, the General Agreement on Tariffs and Trade (GATT), could be seen as an exclusive club: only selected countries could be Contracting Parties, and only selected officials could penetrate its inner mysteries. The WTO, however, is no longer an exclusive club and Membership automatically implies participation in every formal WTO body.[1]

The Doha negotiations take place in Negotiating Groups for Agriculture, Services, Non-Agricultural

Market Access (NAMA), Rules, Trade Facilitation, Environment, and Trade-related Intellectual Property Rights (TRIPS), all under the supervision of the Trade Negotiations Committee. Only the largest WTO Members can monitor and participate in all the associated meetings in addition to the regular work in the roughly five dozen WTO bodies. The US does so easily. The 27 member states of the European Communities (the branch of the European Union that is a WTO Member) are represented by the European Commission. Perhaps less than half a dozen more Members have the capacity to participate actively across the board, notably Canada and Japan. Other leading developed and developing countries participate more actively in some areas than others. And all countries must find ways to aggregate their efforts with others in clubs. Members know they had best work with others to advance their interests, limit their losses, and counterbalance the perceived European Communities/United States dominance of past bargains.

CLUBS IN THE WTO

I define a 'club' as a group of nations united or associated for a particular purpose, a definition that purposely evokes a looser form of association than the common tendency to see informal groups of states working within international organizations as 'coalitions' (Odell, 2006). These clubs are voluntary—no Member of the WTO has to join a club, nor must a given club accept the participation of any Member.

Clubs provide their members with an opportunity to learn about issues with like-minded colleagues; to coordinate positions for WTO meetings, whether plenary or restricted group; to span the gaps between opposing clubs in Bridge clubs; and to debrief on past meetings. Clubs often speak as a group, allowing members to expand support for each other's preferred issues. Clubs also engage in

analytic burden-sharing in the preparation of common proposals. The most structured clubs require high-level recognition in capitals, especially for subordinating national strategy to joint negotiating positions. They have formal co-ordination/decision-making procedures, sometimes meet at the ministerial level, and sometimes have sophisticated analytical support. The least organized are loose consultative mechanisms at the technical or delegate level, often requiring authority from capitals, but they matter in the larger dynamics of building consensus and in solving substantive problems.

The many WTO clubs show differing patterns of membership because countries do not have a single preference schedule that can readily be aligned with those of other countries across all issues. In agriculture, for example, Canada's allies on issues affecting eastern dairy farmers are not the same as its otherwise closer allies on issues affecting western grain farmers. Clubs vary, therefore, on the extent to which members share a common agenda. In the Cairns Group, Canada and Australia agree on ending export subsidies but disagree on whether 'sensitive products' (usually understood to include sugar, dairy, and rice) should be exempted from liberalization obligations. Similar tensions are found in the G20, where India and Brazil do not agree on the extent to which some 'special products' (ones important for food security or rural development) should be exempt from new obligations. That club formed to advance their agriculture objectives; their divergent interests on industrial goods mean that in that area of the negotiations, only a rump is able to work together as the NAMA-11. In services, Canada is associated with 'collective requests' on many issues, but it is a target of other requests. Offensive and defensive concerns form a complex pattern for most Members.

Clubs in the WTO also differ on their procedural characteristics, as do similar groups in the International Monetary Fund (Woods and Lombardi,

2006). Some clubs will always be chaired by one Member but some will have a rotating chair. The influence of some clubs depends more on the institutional power discussed below than on its members share in world trade. Finally, the members of clubs will differ in their diplomatic and analytic capacity: some delegations have more, and better, resources in Geneva and in capitals than others, which affects the effectiveness and influence of their clubs.

The clubs that seem such an important part of the institutional design of the Doha Round have roots in earlier GATT rounds, indeed in long established multilateral practices going back to the League of Nations. The establishment of groups was part of the United Nations (UN) from the beginning and now voting blocs and clubs of all sorts are common (Smith, 2006: 50, 77ff). Unlike the UN system, electoral clubs as such do not play a role in the WTO, although some regional clubs do work together occasionally on political issues and in the process of reaching consensus on appointing the chairpersons of WTO bodies.

Three sorts of clubs are relevant for WTO negotiations. Clubs based on a broad *common characteristic* (e.g., region or level of development) can influence many issues, including the round as a whole, but only weakly.

Clubs based on a *common objective* (e.g., agricultural trade, like the G20 and the G33) can have a great deal of influence, but on a limited range of issues. These clubs were structured by the nature of the Doha Round agenda. The G33 (led by Indonesia) was formed to advance the interests of import-sensitive poor farmers because the Cairns Group (led by Australia) and the G20 (Brazil) were dominated by export interests. The G10 (led by Switzerland) defends exceptions to the formula for 'sensitive' products. The SVEs and RAMs also formed to defend the need for exceptions. The older ACP group ensured that the European Communities (EC) did not lose sight of the banana problem. The

possibility of an exception for a certain class of Members creates a NAMA club to lobby for the provision; the existence of clubs forces a Chairperson to be sure that something in the text responds to that group's concerns.

Bridge clubs can be essential for breaking deadlocks, or managing negotiations, often by building bridges between opposed positions. In the Law of the Sea negotiations in the 1970s, they were called 'compromise groups' (Buzan, 1980). In the UN such clubs are called 'contact groups', 'negotiating groupings' (Smith, 2006: 73–4) or 'Friends of the chair' when they are formed to help the Secretary General in his efforts to resolve a specific conflict (Prantl and Krasno, 2004). As will be seen in Table 21.1, they are also known under different names in the WTO.

I have not seen mention of clubs in histories of the first 15 years of the GATT, perhaps because the small number of Contracting Parties were sufficiently like-minded not to need the device. Inevitably the emergence of clubs in the GATT was a story about the slow pace of agricultural reform, and conflict between Europe and the United States.

Agriculture was effectively exempted from the GATT in the 1950s, and little progress was made in the Kennedy Round of the 1960s, whose main purpose had been to assimilate the then-new European Economic Community's Common Agricultural Policy (CAP) to the rules of the system, an objective that was not met. Some major deals in that round began life in small meetings of the most significant participants—the so-called 'bridge club' consisting of the United States, the European Community (EC, then with only six member states), the United Kingdom, Japan, and Canada (Winham, 1986: 65). I take my term for groups formed to break deadlocks from this early example. The US hoped that the Tokyo Round of the 1970s would achieve what the Kennedy Round had not, but the EC argued that agriculture should be negotiated separately from industrial products, whereas the US, seeking maximum liberalization, insisted on treating agriculture like any other sector (Winham, 1986: 95). The group that became known as the Quad (for Quadrilateral Group of Trade Ministers: US, EC, Japan, Canada) after the 1981 Ottawa G7 Summit had already made a contribution to bridging differences in the closing stages of the Tokyo Round.

As in the Tokyo Round, the US was the main proponent of liberalization in the Uruguay Round, but this time it was joined by the newly formed Cairns Group. A group of developing countries with preferential access to EC markets were concerned that they would lose market access and a group of mostly African countries was concerned that liberalization would increase world prices of key imported food products (Croome, 1995: 113). The EC and US retained their prominence in the negotiations, but a growing role was played by clubs, like the Quad, the Cairns Group, the de la Paix group (a north/south group that pushed for a broadly based agenda), the G10 (with Brazil and India in a blocking role) and the Invisibles group, a little-known Bridge club.

In the Doha Round, launched in 2001, clubs have proliferated. Part of the explanation is based on institutional design factors—the many developing country Members have discovered that clubs are essential in an organization that never takes votes (the consensus rule) and in which nothing is agreed until everything is agreed (the Single Undertaking). The clubs are influenced by the national characteristics of their members (Costantini et al., 2007), but they are also influenced by other clubs—the many new clubs formed around the time of the Cancún ministerial in 2003 had learned from the practices of the Cairns group, formed nearly two decades before. The list in Table 21.1 shows the common characteristic, common objective, and Bridge clubs as they existed in early 2007. Some domains might have fewer clubs because in the current negotiations the chair holds most meetings in informal plenary; it

may also be that clubs proliferate as more WTO Members take a more intense interest in a particular domain. The services clubs are a special case. The more active members have always organized themselves in 'Friends of' groups. These groups of experts do not include the WTO secretariat, and decide for themselves who can come to meetings. The list in Table 21.1 is based on the 'collective requests' submitted in early 2006 under the plurilateral approach introduced in paragraph 7 of Annex C of the Hong Kong declaration (WTO 2005).

DECISION-MAKING AND CRITICAL MASS

At most 40 delegations are significant players in the negotiations, a reality mentioned again and again by senior members of the secretariat and by ambassadors, including from developing countries.[2] Agriculture is the area followed most closely, but at most 15 delegations really play a significant part (and the principal ideas come from less than 10). And yet the reality of the WTO is that consensus and the Single Undertaking require every member to understand and feel engaged in the negotiations. Reaching a consensus with 153 Members is not easy. The institutional design issue becomes that of structuring a process where the key players can get on with it, without losing touch with the interests of all the rest, and doing it in a way that builds confidence in the process and the results. Clubs are part of the solution.

The systemic public good of an open liberal multilateral trading system does not require collective supply by all 153 Members of the WTO, as long as the non-discrimination norms are respected. If the largest markets are open, the system will be open. And the necessary intellectual work of negotiating new rules need not involve all Members all the time. But how many Members are needed to provide systemic 'critical mass'? The EC (now with

Table 21.1 WTO clubland in early 2007

Common characteristic clubs

    G-90†

        ACP†

        African Group†

        LDCs†

    ASEAN†

    CARICOM†

    Small and vulnerable economies (SVEs)

    Recently acceded members (RAMs)

    Small vulnerable coastal states (SVCSs)

Common purpose clubs

Agriculture

    Offensive coalitions

    Cotton-4†

    Tropical and Alternative Products Group

    Cairns Group (N/S)†

    G-20 (S/S)†

    Defensive coalitions

    G-10†

    G-33†

    RAMs, SVEs

Non-agricultural market access (NAMA)

    NAMA 11†

    Friends of MFN

    Friends of Ambition in NAMA

    Hotel d'Angleterre

    RAMs, SVEs

Rules

    SVCS

    Friends of fish

    Friends of antidumping negotiations (FANs)

TRIPS

    African group

    "Disclosure" group of developing countries

    Friends of geographical indications

    Friends against extension of geographical indications

Table 21.1 *continued*

Services

G-25

ASEAN-1 (Singapore)

African Group, ACP, LDCs, SVEs

Real Good Friends of GATS/Friends of Friends*

Friends of . . . (plurilateral expert) groups: Audiovisual, **legal; Architectural/ Engineering/Integrated Engineering***; **Computer and related services**; Postal/Courier including express delivery; **Telecommunications**; **Construction and Related Engineering**; distribution; education; **Environmental service**; **Financial services***; **Maritime transport**; Air transport; logistics; **energy**; Services related to Agriculture, Cross-border services (Mode 1/2), Mode 3, Mode 4, MFN exemptions

Trade Facilitation

Core Group/W142 group

Colorado Group/W137 group

Environment

Friends of environmental goods

Friends of the environment and sustainable development

Textiles

International Textiles and Clothing Bureau (ITCB)

Bridge clubs

Agriculture and NAMA (principal antagonists):

G-4 (US, EC, Brazil, India)†

G-6 (add Australia, Japan)†

Services

Enchilada Group

General (deadlock-breaking)

Oslo or Non-G-6

Quad

Dirty Dozen (Quad plus)

'Senior officials' (25–30)

Mini-ministerials† (25–30)

1. Canada belongs to groups in bold, and is the coordinator of *starred groups. † indicates groups that have met at ministerial level during the Doha Round.
2. For a glossary of agriculture groups, see WTO 2006. The list in this document is based both on self-identified groups and on sets of Members that have submitted joint proposals at various stages of the negotiations. The Five Interested Parties (FIPS) has ceased meeting in that form, as has, therefore, the FIPS Plus. The agriculture Quint does not seem to have met for some time.
3. The Enchilada Group incorporates Members who once met as the Core Group and then the G15.
4. Certain regional (common characteristic) groups apparently no longer actively coordinate in WTO except occasionally on electoral or political issues, such as observer status: ALADI, Andean Group, Arab Group, APEC, CEFTA, GRULAC, Islamic Group, Mercosur, OECS, SADC, SAPTA, SELA.
5. The once-prominent Like-Minded Group (LMG) has not been active for many years. The status of the 'informal group of developing countries' is not clear.

27 member states) and the US are necessary but not sufficient for a deal. The idea of critical mass implies that the relevant process is of a sufficient size to be self-sustaining, whether it is a nuclear reaction or the wide diffusion of a social norm. Many applications in social science derive from Mancur Olson's work on the provision of collective goods. Whereas Olson's work is pessimistic on the possibility of cooperation, other scholars explore the circumstances under which a group of sufficient size can be created to supply public goods (Oliver and Marwell, 2001).

Critical mass with respect to the WTO implies first that markets that represent a significant share of global production and consumption should help to supply the systemic public good, a form of *material power*. The public good of new rules also depends on acceptance by participants in the trading system that the rules themselves are appropriate and legitimate, which suggests that critical mass must have another dimension. The coercive power of the largest markets is limited now both by the emergence of other significant markets and by equally powerful symbolic and normative claims based on justice for developing countries, in general but especially for the poorest. In the Tokyo Round, developing countries could opt out of any aspect of the bargain, and their views could be ignored. But the WTO is now a Single Undertaking: once the shape of the package is agreed, final decisions are made on the package as a whole, not on the individual elements. Each participant must accept all the new obligations. That decision is inevitably made by consensus (meaning that nobody present objects). These two principles give every Member the ability to slow the process down, a form of *institutional power*, and developing countries are increasingly aware of that power in the WTO. They are also increasingly aware of the need to participate, because they will not be able to opt out of any of the new obligations, which has

put stress on the ability of the WTO process to remain effective while becoming more inclusive and transparent.

Critical mass in the WTO, therefore, has two dimensions. When all issues are lumped together, and any Member can block consensus, institutional power must be joined to compulsory power to reach a successful outcome in negotiations. A bargain must satisfy those Members whose market weight is sufficient to give effect to the deal, but it must also satisfy those Members whose acquiescence is sufficient to give the deal legitimacy. Most matters will be settled informally because consensus forces actors to find a compromise when a vote is not available as a means to decide a controversy.

It is not surprising, therefore, that the real work is done in informal meetings of the various negotiating groups, in restricted meetings organized by the chair, or in bilateral sessions. Members talk at the Ministerial Conference every two years, in regular committees that meet two or three times a year and in the Negotiating Groups that meet every four to six weeks. They talk in hundreds of formal on-the-record meetings every year, and they talk in many hundreds more informal meetings, including 'mini-ministerials' (Wolfe, 2004). No organization with 153 Members can find consensus on sensitive matters like agricultural reform if all discussions must be held in public, in large groups, with written records. All Members must be in the room when the deal is done, but assembling the requisite critical mass requires smaller meetings.

WTO insiders understand the process as a series of nested 'concentric circles'. In the outer ring are official WTO meetings (mandated by the treaty or the rules of procedure); these plenary meetings are held only for the record. In the next circle are informal plenary meetings of a regular body, under its regular chair, held mostly for transparency purposes. The real work is done when the chair meets with a limited number of technical experts, or when he or she invites a small group of key players to explore selected issues. When these discussions reach an impasse, the traditional GATT response to negotiating difficulties now carried over to the WTO has been meetings of a restricted group of Members, usually known by the colour of the Director-General's boardroom. The Green Room is therefore a real place, but the term also refers to a specific type of meeting, whether of ambassadors in Geneva or ministers at the biennial Ministerial Conference. The original Green Room practice reflected three negotiating realities: informality is vital; the largest Members, especially the US and the EC, must always be in the room; and other interested parties should be engaged in the search for consensus. Part of what the many clubs of Table 21.1 do is to create a claim that one of their number should represent them in the Green Room. Up to 30 Members often participate in Green Room meetings. At the July 2008 informal ministerial meeting, each participant was represented by two ministers or officials. While it is a large group for a negotiation, all key players plus all groups must be represented if it is to be *inclusive* and therefore legitimate. The members of the original Quad are always represented along with other leading traders, representatives of clubs, and coordinators of the regional groups. The process must also be *transparent* to other Members of the WTO. Representatives in the room must fairly articulate the views of their club, and must expeditiously and comprehensively report on the deliberations. Any results must also be fairly presented by the chairperson when he or she reports on the state of negotiations in plenary meetings, or when he or she drafts documents designed to attract consensus.

THE VALUE OF BRIDGE CLUBS

The approach of the end game for the Doha Round is exposing the weaknesses of the clubs, as anticipated in the negotiation analysis literature. They work well to make *distributive* demands, but badly to make *integrative* decisions. Common interest clubs are organized by negotiating group, and negotiating groups are partly organized along the lines of the bureaucratic homes of the negotiators—the officials responsible for agriculture, NAMA, and fish subsidies have different home ministries in capitals. No club, therefore, has a balanced view of the overall Single Undertaking.

Bridge clubs are intended to play a co-ordinating role, but they are located outside the WTO concentric circles, since they are not chaired by the chairperson of the regular body, and the secretariat is often not invited. The utility of all restricted Bridge clubs was questioned after the Doha negotiations were 'suspended' in July 2006. A representative Green Room or mini-ministerial may be too large to provide leadership, and the old Quad will never return, but some new grouping may be needed to conclude the round. Such a new grouping may need to change either the *level* of participation or the *Members* involved.

The first approach was to try to bump thorny issues up to heads of government. Former Canadian Prime Minister Paul Martin was convinced that an informal meeting of leaders could make a major difference on issues like agricultural trade reform (Martin, 2004). He received little support for the idea. Brazilian President Luiz Inacio Lula da Silva angled for months in 2005–6 to have a summit devoted solely to breaking the Doha logjam, but also received little support. In the event, on the margins of the St Petersburg summit in 2006, the G8 had a meeting with their five regular interlocutors (Brazil, India, China, Mexico and South Africa) but managed only to tell their trade ministers to get the job done. The ministers then failed. The similar injunctions delivered at subsequent meetings, including of the so-called G20 Summit, were no more useful. The effort to engage leaders is based on what people think they remember about the G7 Summit contributions to ending the Tokyo Round in 1978 and the Uruguay Round in 1993. In both cases, however, leaders did little more than ask the Quad trade ministers to meet in advance in order to present a report at the summit. Leaders can force coordination within their own government if the lack of such coordination is the obstacle to agreement, but leaders can not solve the agriculture problem from the top.

If changing the level does not help, changing the countries might. Part of the effort to re-start the round after the failed Cancún ministerial in 2003 was a process involving the principal antagonists on agriculture: the United States and the EC, who are opposed to each other; and Brazil and India who are opposed both to each other and to the US and the EC. These four tried to sort things out as a 'new Quad', (or G4) and failed. In 2004, they included Australia, representing the Cairns Group, in what became known as the 'five interested parties', or FIPs. They next included Japan, representing the G10 (agricultural importers), in what became known as the G6 that met frequently, without success. The group did not meet at the ministerial or senior official level for many months after its spectacular failure to resolve the modalities conundrum in the summer of 2006. Efforts by the G4 countries to find a compromise again failed at their June 2007 Postdam meeting—and their efforts were not seen as legitimate even by the developing countries that Brazil and India purport to represent because the process is not transparent and multilateral.

The G4/6 failed as a Bridge club because they could not advance a systemic interest. The club contains the principal antagonists, but they are all publicly committed to their positions which make compromises difficult. The old Quad was more effective because one participant, Canada, was not a principal antagonist. Having listened to all the others, Canada was able to put possible

compromises forward quietly among senior officials in a way that could advance the negotiations. Some negotiators thought it might help, therefore, to change countries as well as the level at which Members are represented.

Two Uruguay Round events are precedents for changing the countries. The first is the 'café au lait' process led by Switzerland and Columbia in 1986. Known as the de la Paix group after the hotel where they first met, this group advanced a compromise proposal on the arrangements and subjects for the Uruguay Round that was successful in part because the proponents shared not specific negotiating objectives but a commitment to the importance of the Round itself. The group was reconstituted in June 1988 with an informal proposal by seven countries (Australia, Canada, Hong Kong, Hungary, Korea, New Zealand, and Switzerland) that helped energize the process (Croome 1995). A group of six WTO Members (Canada, Chile, Indonesia, Kenya, New Zealand, and Norway) tried something similar. Senior officials (not ministers) met in Oslo in October 2006 to discuss key issues blocking progress in the negotiations. None of the six belonged to the G6, but they did represent many of the major clubs, north and south. The 'non-G6' or Oslo group also failed to be an effective Bridge.

WTO Clubland in July 2008

When Pascal Lamy, the Director-General, called selected WTO ministers to Geneva in July 2008 in an attempt to break the logjam in the Doha Round, Canadians ministers were there, but they had little to do. The dynamic of meetings with so many people in the room (each of the more than 30 Members invited could have at least two or more people at the table) is not conducive to real engagement. When the discussions proved sterile, the Director-General proposed that he hold 'consultations with a smaller group'. This little group of seven Members, or G7, was a 'friends of the chair' group constituted by the Director-General as Chairperson of the TNC. The seven in July 2008 were the EC, the US, and China, considered the big three of world trade, plus representatives of the agriculture clubs—Brazil for the G20, India for the G33, Japan for the G10, and Australia for the Cairns Group. It was an odd assortment, but they were some of the principal antagonists on the tough issues. Perhaps if they could agree, then other countries would too but this may have been an unrealistic assumption. They could not agree, as it turned out, and at the time of writing, the round remains stalled. (For an analysis of the July 2008 ministerial, see Wolfe, 2010.) The Canadian ambassador attended the G7 meetings, but in his capacity as the NAMA Chairperson. Canadian ministers were once involved in such meetings, but no longer.

Opinions are divided on whether the G7 was a useful device in July 2008. Some said that it was not useful because such agreement as was reached could have been reached without them, and they failed to bridge the remaining gaps. The positive answer recognizes that the Green Room was too big. Something like the G7 was necessary in this view, if not sufficient.

No one small group will ever represent all interests on all issues. The NAMA-11 hardliners were not represented. The US presentation of the agriculture exporters' position camouflaged the unhappiness of the many developing country exporters who had related views. Some people thought an African should have participated for cotton, and Indonesia for the developing country importers. Within the group, it seemed that the US, EC, and Japan often lined up against China, India, and Brazil, with an ineffectual Australia unable to play the middle-ground role that Canada is said to have played in the old Quad.

WHERE IS CANADA IN WTO CLUBLAND?

This picture of power and influence in the WTO is remarkably complex. Some old hands who compare it to the simpler days of the Tokyo and Uruguay Rounds think the Canadian role is diminished. It should be apparent from Table 21.1, however, that the only current club to which Canada might once have expected to belong is the G4. Is Canada's absence significant?

A minority government keeps Canadian ministers closer to home than some of their counterparts. Agriculture minister Gerry Ritz missed an important meeting of the Cairns Group of agricultural exporters in Indonesia in June 2009, ostensibly because the Official Opposition would not send an MP as a 'pair' as part of the delegation to mitigate the minister's absence in the case of a confidence vote in the House of Commons. The Liberals deny the charge. Minority government limits Canadian negotiators' public room to manoeuvre on sensitive issues like supply management, inhibiting any inclination to take an active role, but it is not the issue in itself that has marginalized Canadian ministers. Nevertheless, politicians are tied in knots by the farm lobbies, as in November 2005 when the House of Commons, after a full day of debate on agricultural trade policy, gave unanimous approval to a motion instructing negotiators at the WTO's Hong Kong ministerial to seek increased market access abroad for agricultural exports while offering none at home in order to protect the supply management system (Canada, 2005: 9960, 10017).[3]

All Canada's trading partners understand why, in a minority, government ministers will not risk even whispering that the likely Doha outcomes will be manageable for Canadian farmers, even if some adjustment will be needed (Gifford,

2005). But that limits Canadian ability to build bridges on 'sensitive products', as the trade minister admitted to a House of Commons committee (Wilson, 2007). As one Geneva ambassador said privately, 'Canadian ministers are not in the game.' If material power were the whole story, this claim would be silly, but anything that affects a negotiator's credibility can affect other forms of power. It was awkward in April 2007 when Canada could join its Cairns Group colleagues in submitting a non-paper on tropical and alternative products, but could not sign on to the submission on sensitive products. It is hard to exert influence in favour of compromise if others know that you have promised your own domestic interests that you yourself will not compromise. But the main reason that Canada is not in the smallest groups is because it is not a principal antagonist; Canada is not needed for a solution to the central blockage. On agriculture, other members only want Canada to reduce the restrictiveness of supply management and to end the export monopoly of the Wheat Board. Whatever the merits of those actions, they would make a trivial contribution to the overall Doha outcome. Similarly, on trade in goods, Canada does not bring a lot of new trade to the table in market access negotiations because the country has relatively low levels of remaining protection as a result of NAFTA and the Uruguay Round.

It is neither surprising nor especially significant, therefore, that Canada is not in the G4, G6, or G7. Of more importance, Canada is still a valued player in many clubs, as shown in Table 21.1. Canadian officials remain at the centre of things in Geneva. The previous ambassador chaired the negotiations on trade in Goods; the current ambassador chairs the Dispute Settlement Body. He is supported by a staff of eleven professionals in Geneva, one of whom, for example, coordinates the 'Friends of Friends' club in services which manages the 'collective requests' process. With its substantial number of trade policy professionals in Ottawa, Canada has been able, as the secretariat observed, to make contributions or proposals in a wide range of areas, including trade facilitation, agriculture, market access for non-agricultural goods, services, subsidies, anti-dumping, and countervailing duties and intellectual property—a total of 70 documents in the trade negotiations series ('TN') in the WTO Documents Online database between January 2003 and October 2006 (WTO 2007b: para 37; when less formal JOB documents are added, the number more than doubles—see WTO 2007c: Annex 1).[4] Few Members have made as substantial an analytic contribution to the negotiations. Canada is represented at all levels of the concentric circles in every area of the negotiations, from Green Room-type meetings (20–40 delegations) of ambassadors in Geneva and ministers at the Ministerial Conferences, through numerous mini-ministerials of trade and agriculture ministers, to things like the Fireside Chats held by the chair of the agriculture negotiations, Enchilada talks held by the services chair, and the NAMA caucus, which the previous Canadian ambassador chaired. With respect to Bridge clubs, Canada has played a leading role in the Oslo group. The old Quad that met regularly from the end of the Tokyo Round in the 1970s through the lengthy Uruguay Round negotiations to the early days of the WTO, has not met at ministerial level since 1999. However, it still meets informally among Geneva delegates where Canada is useful as an intermediary and for its analytic capacity.

The jury is still out on whether clubs have helped or hindered the Doha Round, which was still struggling when this chapter was written, but what we know is that decisions in any social context are taken, or at least shaped, by small groups. Fewer than 10 participants may be most efficient for decision-making, but effectiveness and legitimacy in the WTO often requires up to 30 Members in order to ensure that all perspectives are heard in the search for consensus. The list will differ by issue, but Canada is always present at that level in the concentric circles. However the round ends, and whatever form the next round takes, it is a safe assumption that decision-making will include some sort of Green Room-type meetings, and that clubs will be needed to ensure inclusive and transparent representation of all Members. Within the various domains of the WTO, it also seems probable that Members will find it easier to assemble the requisite critical mass by working together in clubs in an effort to manage the scale and complexity of the agenda. Finding a consensus on the management of a global trading system with 153 members, with more set to join, is not going to get easier, but maintaining the Single Undertaking is vital. Canadians will continue to use clubs to advance the country's interests in this complex environment, playing a traditional analytic and bridge-building role.

Key Terms

Club
Consensus in the WTO
Doha Round

Notes

1. I capitalize Member when referring to the WTO, and not when referring to members of a club.
2. The WTO has 150 Members in May 2007. Counting the EC-27 as one, if 40 are more or less effective, that implies that roughly 80 Members are to varying degrees content to follow a lead set by others.
3. The opposition Bloc Québecois moved:

   That, in the opinion of the House, the government should give its negotiators a mandate during the negotiations at the World Trade Organization so that, at the end of the current round of negotiations, Canada obtains results that ensure that the supply management sectors are subject to no reduction in over-quota tariffs and no increase in tariff quotas, so that these sectors can continue to provide producers with a fair and equitable income.

   The Conservatives (then in opposition in a minority parliament) moved:

   That the motion be amended by replacing all the words after "quotas" with "and also ensure an agreement that strengthens the market access of Canada's agricultural exporters so that all sectors can continue to provide producers with a fair and equitable income".

4. To give just one example, Canada led the effort to prepare quantitative simulations of reductions in domestic support for agriculture and helped a developing country group with analysis of the criteria for designation of "special products". Officials observe that many aspects of the current negotiating texts began as Canadian ideas, and reflect Canadian objectives. Few Members have made as substantial an analytic contribution to the negotiations. But ministers have been almost invisible for years (WTO 2006; WTO 2007a).

References

Buzan, Barry (1980). '"United We Stand . . .": Informal Negotiating Groups at UNCLOS III'. Marine Policy 4(3): 183–204.

Canada (2005). 'Official Report (Hansard)'. House of Commons Debates 140(155).

Croome, John (1995). Reshaping the World Trading System: A History of the Uruguay Round (Geneva: World Trade Organization).

Gifford, Mike (2005). 'Can Canada's Supply Managed Dairy Industry Survive the Doha Round?' Canadian Agricultural Trade Policy Research Network: Trade Policy Brief 2005–3. November 2005.

Keohane, Robert O., and Joseph S. Nye, Jr (2001). 'The Club Model of Multilateral Cooperation and Problems of Democratic Legitimacy'. In Roger B. Porter, Pierre Sauvé,

Arvind Subramanian, and Americo Bevigilia Zampetti, eds, *Efficiency, Equity, and Legitimacy: The Multilateral Trading System at the Millennium*, pp. 264–94 (Washington, DC: Brookings Institution Press).

Martin, Paul (2004). Prime Minister Paul Martin Speaks at the World Economic Forum On 'The Future of Global Interdependence'. 23 January 2004.

Odell, John S., ed. (2006). *Negotiating Trade: Developing Countries in the WTO and NAFTA* (Cambridge: Cambridge University Press).

Oliver, Pamela E., and Gerald Marwell (2001). 'Whatever Happened to Critical Mass Theory? A Retrospective and Assessment'. *Sociological Theory* 19(3): 292–311.

Padoan, Pier Carlo (1997). 'Regional Agreements as Clubs: The European Case'. In Edward D. Mansfield and Helen V. Milner, eds, *The Political Economy of Regionalism*. New York: Columbia University Press. 107–34.

Prantl, Jochen, and Jean Krasno (2004). 'Informal Groups of Member States'. In Jean E. Krasno, ed., *The United Nations: Confronting the Challenges of a Global Society*, pp. 311–57 (Boulder, CO, and London, UK: Lynne Rienner Publishers).

Smith, Courtney B. (2006). *Politics and Process at the United Nations: The Global Dance* (Boulder, CO, and London, UK: Lynne Rienner Publishers).

Wilson, Barry (2007). 'Minister Maintains Stance on Supply Management'. *Western Producer*, 8 March.

Winham, Gilbert R. (1986). *International Trade and the Tokyo Round Negotiation* (Princeton: Princeton University Press).

Wolfe, Robert (2004). 'Informal Political Engagement in the WTO: Are Mini-Ministerials a Good Idea?' In Dan Ciuriak and John M. Curtis, eds, *Trade Policy Research*, 2004, pp. 27–90 (Ottawa: Department of Foreign Affairs and International Trade).

——— (2010). 'Sprinting During a Marathon: Why the WTO Ministerial Failed in July 2008'. *Journal of World Trade* 44(1).

Woods, Ngaire, and Domenico Lombardi (2006). 'Uneven Patterns of Governance: How Developing Countries Are Represented in the IMF'. Review of International Political Economy 13(3): 480–515.

WTO (2005). 'Doha Work Programme'. World Trade Organization: Ministerial Conference, Sixth Session Hong Kong, 13–18 December 2005 WT/MIN(05)/W/3/Rev.2. 18 December 2005.

——— (2006). 'Agriculture Negotiations: Agriculture Domestic Support Simulations'. World Trade Organization, Committee on Agriculture, Special Session: paper circulated at the request of the Delegation of Canada—on behalf of Australia, Brazil, Canada, China, the European Communities, Egypt, India, Japan, Kenya, Malaysia, Norway and the United States JOB(06)/151. 22 May 2006.

——— (2007a). 'Draft Modalities for Agriculture'. World Trade Organization, Committee on Agriculture, Special Session: note by the Chairman JOB(07)/128. 17 July 2007.

——— (2007b). 'Trade Policy Review Canada: Report by the Secretariat'. Trade Policy Review Body, World Trade Organization: WT/TPR/S/179. 14 February 2007.

——— (2007c). 'Trade Policy Review: Report by Canada'. Trade Policy Review Body, World Trade Organization: WT/TPR/G/179. 14 February 2007.

22

CANADA AND THE GLOBAL ECONOMIC CRISIS

Stephen McBride

A. THE FOREIGN POLICY CONTEXT[1]

Descriptions of Canadian foreign policy during the Cold War period usually focused on three images: Canada as a 'middle power' (or 'honest broker'), a 'principal power', and a satellite of the United States (see Cooper, 1997). These different images highlighted some of the ambiguities in Canadian foreign policy. Canada made significant efforts to construct a role as a 'middle power'. Some analysts considered that over time Canada achieved this goal and actually made the transition to being, if not a great power, then at least a 'principal' power. Others detected a growing subservience to the United States that rendered those categories pure imagery. They saw the roots of Canadian subservience as lying in the close and growing integration of the Canadian and US economies.

Political factors, of course, also played a role. After the election of the Progressive Conservative government led by Brian Mulroney government in 1984, Canada pursued a strategy of close political alliance and closer economic integration with the United States. Under the previous Liberal governments of Pierre Trudeau, Canadian efforts to maintain a sense of distance from the United States had at least limited substance, expressed through initiatives like the Foreign Investment Review Agency, the Third Option, and the National Energy Program. The shift from Trudeau to Mulroney has been represented as a redefinition of Canada's middle-power role—from an approach partially exercised in a 'counter-consensus' direction to one that was 'limitationist', reflecting 'an orientation more in keeping with existing power and privilege in Canadian society and in the global order' (Neufeld 1995: 22). Another trend saw a heightened emphasis on economic priorities in Canada's foreign policy. This was symbolized by the addition of international trade to the external affairs ministry, and its renaming as the Department of Foreign Affairs and International Trade (DFAIT) (see Doern, Pal, and Tomlin, 1996b: ch. 10). In the general policy paradigm literature (see Hall 1993) such trends might reflect a shift in the overarching policy paradigm from one of Keynesianism, which had been more tolerant of national autonomy, to one of neo-liberalism, in which the focus was on global economic integration. It is clear that a distinct neo-liberal trajectory came to infuse not only foreign economic policy, but all of Canadian foreign policy.

For example, despite its long-standing reputation as a peacekeeper and a country committed to humanitarian efforts, Canada's record in this area has drawn sharp criticism from all sides of the political spectrum. Pointing to declining levels of official development assistance (ODA), unavailability of military resources for conducting peacekeeping operations, and a preference for pursuing trade over human rights concerns, critics have argued that Canada has changed its priorities. Similarly, Canada's record on international environmental negotiations over issues such as climate change has drawn widespread adverse comment.

The term 'middle power' has been applied to Canada in two related senses: first, as 'occupying the "middle" point in a range . . . usually measured by reference to such quantifiable attributes as area, population, size, complexity and strength of economy, military capability, and other comparable factors' (Cooper, Higgott, and Nossal, 1993: 17); and second, on the basis of function and behaviour in the international system. Canada, with countries such as Denmark, the Netherlands, Norway, and Sweden, gained a reputation for actively supporting the international community through the provision of more nationals to the international civil service, more military personnel to peace operations, and more funds to overseas development assistance through multilateral agencies than other countries. While Pratt claims that, overall, these states 'have both the capacity and the will to play an important role on the international scene' (Pratt, 1990: 14), the extent to which Canada still retains both the will and the capacity to assume this role has been seriously questioned in years (see Axworthy, 2003; Cohen, 2003).

Much of the discussion of Canada as a middle power has focused on the country's role in security and humanitarian contexts. But there are some common threads with discussions of Canada as an economic middle power. For example, considered as a middle power, Canada's greatest influence was exercised multilaterally through its membership in various international institutions and organizations. Its foreign policy was functionalist, in that it deliberately focused on those issues in which it has had the greatest potential to exert influence in the international system. Multilateralism and functionalism, therefore, often go together. As a middle power, Canada's interests and foreign policy objectives are said to have been based largely on its need for cooperation in the international system (Holmes, 1976: 13). The Canada 21 Council (1994: 12) concluded that Canada, which draws on a wide range of instruments and resources, must rely on its social, human, and intellectual capital to carve out an influential role for itself in the international arena. Andrew Cooper, Richard Higgott, and Kim Richard Nossal (1993: 13) considered that waning US hegemony had given way to alternative forms of leadership whereby 'games of skill' increasingly replaced 'tests of will'. Emphasis on technical and entrepreneurial leadership refers to what then Foreign Affairs Minister Lloyd Axworthy termed 'soft power', a concept that he argued must be cultivated and wielded by Canada if it were to emerge as an important and influential actor in the twenty-first century (Axworthy 1997: 192). The elimination of Cold War tensions should have expanded the terrain in which 'middle powers' could operate. But for Canada the end of the Cold War seemed to increase the contradictory nature of its foreign policy—participating in US-organized military ventures such as the Gulf War and Kosovo but declining to do so in the case of the later Iraq war; and campaigning to outlaw anti-personnel land mines, promoting the concept of human security, and advocating a UN-sponsored International Criminal Court (ICC).

In economic terms, the middle-power approach assumes that rules and norms have a significant impact on interstate relations and that, as a functioning middle power, Canada has the potential to play an important role in multilateral and bilateral arrangements. From this point of view, strong multilateral regimes become a means of enhancing economic welfare and peace in an interdependent global system and of reducing US domination of the economy. These goals are usually articulated by federal representatives extolling the benefits of Canada's membership in these regimes: 'Indeed, Canadian foreign policy officials stress that Canada has a strong interest in multilateralism and economic liberalization because this enhances economic welfare and Canadian influence in international affairs' (Cutler and Zacher, 1992a: 3).

Michael Hart (1985) and Frank Stone (1992), for example, cited the development of international economic regimes such as the General Agreement on Tariffs and Trade (GATT) and the Canada–United States Free Trade Agreement (FTA) as important mechanisms for managing systemic changes related to globalization. Stone (1992: 1) suggested that the GATT constituted 'a great advance in international co-operation over the anarchical conditions that characterized world trade relationships during the inter-war period, and indeed, represents one of the most successful efforts in international co-operation of the post-war period'. Tom Keating (1993: 13) also stressed the importance of multilateralism and suggests that Canadian policy-makers have repeatedly relied on both economic and security regimes in an attempt to fulfill a wide range of foreign policy objectives. For Canada to wield influence and authority, the most effective medium is a co-operative and rules-based system whereby Canada's strength is derived, it is said, not from traditional sources such as military

capabilities or economic status, but instead from its ability to generate ideas.

Yet Canada's traditional commitment to multilateralism and the establishment of regime-based norms has been questioned. Certainly Canada has pursued bilateral as well as multilateral agreements: 'The Canadian commitment to multilateralism and liberalization is an exaggerated one, and in some cases, an inaccurate portrayal of Canadian foreign economic policy.' (Cutler and Zacher, 1992a: 4; see also Cooper, 1997: ch. 2; Keenes, 1995). Thus one analysis of Canada's postwar international trade policy argued that the Canadian commitment to international economic regimes was never absolute (Finlayson and Bertasi 1992). Similarly, Christopher Thomas (1992) examined the establishment of a bilateral trade regime with the United States in terms of Canada's growing disillusionment with the GATT and the need to reinforce the economic relationship with its largest trading partner. Such initiatives mirrored a long history of 'creeping continentalism' from the wartime Hyde Park Declaration through the Defence Production Sharing Agreement of 1958 to the 1965 Auto Pact (Black and Sjolander, 1996: 14).

The emphasis in thinking about Canada as a middle power eventually spawned another interpretation: that Canada made the transition to being a 'foremost' (Eayrs, 1975), 'major' (Lyon and Tomlin 1979; Gotlieb, 1987), or 'principal' power (Dewitt and Kirton, 1983). John Kirton has argued that despite the apparent rise during the 1990s of the United States as the only superpower, the Asian financial crisis of 1997–99 affirmed Canada's position as a principal power. According to Kirton (1999: 607), 'In the diplomacy behind the Hong Kong reform package, Canada acted as an equal member of the G7 concert in which different members lead on specific issues and mutually adjust to create a new and effective consensus'. Thus Canada's diplomacy during that financial crisis called into question traditional interpretations of Canadian foreign policy. The crisis, Kirton argued, demonstrated that Canada was a global player, rather than one with a more restricted, niche-based, regional focus (624).

However, other commentators have made strong arguments to the contrary. For example, Michael Webb (1992) held that small and medium-sized countries were ineffective in multilateral settings, which is why Canada turned to a bilateral agreement with the United States—not from strength but rather from weakness. Others considered that the closing of the Cold War ended the conditions in which middle powers found space in which to act (David and Roussel, 1998).

Certainly, the economic crisis that became manifest in 2008 provides an opportunity to gauge Canada's current status in the global political economy.

In contrast to arguments suggesting middle- or principal-power status, there is an interpretation of Canada as a dependent, satellite state. In this view Canada's capacity for independent and autonomous action in international affairs had been much reduced by its successive membership in the British and US empires. Canada went from colony to nation to colony, so 'what for some marked the emergence of a middle power in world politics was, for others, merely a transfer of dependent orbit, with Canada consigned to the periphery—or at best the "semiperiphery" of the world economy' (Nossal, 1997: 60–61; see also Hawes, 1984; Clarkson, 1968; Lumsden, 1970).

David Dewitt and John Kirton (1983: 28), who have advanced the idea of Canada as a principal power, labelled this perspective as the 'peripheral-dependence' perspective because it stresses Canada's cultural, political, and economic dependence on a more powerful international actor. It also highlights the reliance of Canada on the US market for international trade, and the predominance of US investment in Canada.

Growing nationalism in the late 1960s and 1970s had led to a number of measures that suggested, even to supporters of the satellite interpretation, that this situation might be reversed. For example, the so-called Third Option represented a desire to 'lessen the vulnerability of the Canadian economy to external factors, in particular the impact of the United States' (Sharp, 1972). Despite the Third Option's lack of success, nationalist hopes were aroused periodically, as with the nationalist measures taken by the Trudeau government of 1980–84.

Indeed, it could be argued that by the 1970s Canada was close to achieving, or had achieved, middle-power status as measured by autonomy from the United States, but that later events returned the country to a satellite-like status. Clarkson (1991) considers that although the Canadian state had reached a point in history where it was at its most advanced stage of development, the federal government's decision on the Free Trade Agreement with the United States abdicated most of Canada's economic and cultural sovereignty. Efforts at greater autonomy, such as the attempt at a third national policy and the Third Option trade initiative, proved to have lasted only as long as the global balance of power was conducive to the more autonomous role. The arrival of President Reagan signalled a much more aggressive US stance, and the arrival of Prime Minister Mulroney signalled the end of any Canadian attempt to retain autonomy in the face of the new US stance. Clearly the rise of Reagan and Mulroney signalled the arrival of a neo-liberal era in many policy spheres.

Once this shift happened, the most important international agreements became the bilateral ones with the United States. Canada's involvement in multilateral economic regimes was primarily designed to support US preferences and policies— 'Multilateralism was always first and foremost a product of American hegemony' (Black and Sjolander, 1996: 27). In sum, Canada's multilateral involvement 'provides direct reinforcement for

United States foreign policy doctrines and limits [Canada's] dissent from US positions to marginal aspects. Bilaterally [Canada] assigns the highest importance to themes of harmony and commonality in the "special relationship" . . . and encourages a flow of transaction from the United States into Canada' (Dewitt and Kirton, 1983: 28). As we shall see, the theme of bilateralism has certainly been a feature of Canada's reaction to the 2008 economic crisis.⌉

B. CANADA IN NORTH AMERICA: TRIUMPH OF ECONOMISM

The policy record of the Mulroney years—the Canada–US Free Trade Agreement, the pursuit of deregulation, the elimination of some of the key elements of the welfare state, and the embrace of a more hawkish foreign policy—signalled to some that Mulroney had 'closed down the Canadian dream' of autonomy and independence (Martin, 1993: 272–73). Yet, even under Mulroney, it has been argued that there were examples of an independent course being followed—on the Strategic Arms Limitation Treaty, and on Central America, Cuba, and South Africa (Clarkson, 2002: 387–8).

Following Mulroney, foreign policy once again exhibited ambiguity and contradiction in which, however, economic considerations loomed largest. The Chrétien and Martin years were characterized by a concerted pursuit of export-led growth typified by large 'Team Canada' trade missions. Although much of Canada's trade liberalization agenda was in step with that of the US, particularly with respect to hemispheric free trade in the Americas, other aspects of Canadian foreign policy deviated from the 'US-friendly' version articulated by the Mulroney government.[2]

Of course, in the case of trade, Canada–US relations are not always harmonious. Though

many argue that Canada's heavy reliance on the US as an export market, combined with the CUFTA and NAFTA trade deals, put Canada in a vulnerable position vis-à-vis the US (Cohen, 2003: 38–9), Canada nonetheless has vigorously engaged in numerous trade disputes with the US through both the WTO and NAFTA. The ongoing softwood lumber dispute is perhaps the best known of these disputes (see Zhang, 2007) but many others have taken place in areas surrounding agriculture, steel, fisheries, and magazines. However, these are disputes over specific applications of the internationally agreed rules and in defence of specific private interests. On the need for a rules-based system and the content of those rules there are no significant differences between Canada and the US.

Proponents argue that the overall trading relationship between Canada and the US runs quite smoothly when one considers its size. As Andrew Cohen suggests, 'the commercial relationship is without acrimony, which is remarkable considering the exponential increase in volume of goods and services crossing the border in years' (Cohen, 2003: 39). According to the US Department of State, bilateral trade disputes between the two countries occur in about two per cent of total trade (US Department of State, 2008). Yet this ignores pressures which have been brought to bear since the Canada–US Free Trade Agreement and NAFTA were signed and which have led to some of the dispute settlement procedures of those agreements falling into disuse. Chapter 19 of both agreements allowed an appeal of US determinations on dumping and subsidy issues to a binding bi-national panel of trade experts. A report commissioned by the Canadian–American Business Council demonstrated that the US government had sought to delegitimize the Chapter 19 process, originally a feature of the Canada–US agreement, by a variety of means. These included changing the language of Chapter 19 when NAFTA was negotiated, underfunding the

US section of the NAFTA Secretariat, making political and protectionist appointments to the US roster of prospective NAFTA Chapter 19 panellists, delaying adjudication wherever possible, attacking the integrity of NAFTA panellists involved in adverse decisions,[3] rewriting US laws to escape adverse rulings, and adopting administrative practices, such as refusing to accept that practices ruled inadmissible in one case should not be used in other cases. The effect of this strategy is to deprive exporters of finality with respect to chapter 19 decisions, thus rendering the process unattractive to many (Baker and Hostetler, LLP, 2004: 1–5). So the absence of current disputes may reflect inadequate mechanisms to resolve them rather than an absence of grounds for them.

The lack of balance in the economic relationship with the US created vulnerability for Canada, especially in a post-September 11 environment where the Unites States' security concerns trumped trade. Canadian exports to the United States account for approximately 85 per cent of Canada's total exports while exports from the US to Canada represent only 25 per cent of US exports (Cohen, 2003: 38).

In a report issued by the 'Standing Committee on Foreign Affairs', Professor Gordon Mace, director of Inter-American Studies at the Institut québécois des hautes études internationales, told the committee that 'the FTA and NAFTA trade deals have fundamentally and inescapably altered the foreign policy landscape. Canada's increased economic vulnerability within the "new Economic management framework" . . . has "greatly decreased" Canada's leeway in bilateral relations with the United States' (House of Commons, 2002: 14). In order to mitigate the effect of this asymmetrical relationship, Mace argues that Canada needed to pursue an expanded relationship with Mexico and other states in the Americas (14–15). Similarly, in the early 2000s, long-time supporters of continental free trade made the case for trade diversification:

'However, it may now be necessary for Canada to consider a second policy direction, one that would attempt to confront the US export dependency that is at the root of the present uncertainties facing Ottawa. . . . The Canadian government should take a more proactive role in analyzing Canada's strengths and weaknesses in export trade, including the prospects for developing new overseas markets. In the past decade, exports from Canada and other countries were drawn into the United States due to the extraordinary vitality of the US economy. The current US slowdown may provide Canada [with] an opportunity to diversify export trade in a way that would strengthen the country's economy and, ultimately, its polity' (Winham and Ostry, 2003).

Those who argue that Canada has more influence in Washington than is commonly believed do so in a way that provides little reassurance for those concerned about Canadian sovereignty in the bilateral relationship. Christopher Sands, director of the Canada Project at the Center for Security and International Studies in Washington DC, considers that, '[t]hanks to deepening interdependence through economic integration, Canada is not a fading power in the United States. It is instead a rising power, more important to Americans and their prosperity today than ever before in US history' (Sands, 2002: 72). In order to be a 'rising power', however, Sands maintains that Canada will have to adopt a 'strong state strategy' which includes 'improving Canadian domestic security and implementing a creative counter-terrorism effort . . .' (71). A 'weak state strategy', on the other hand, would be one that treated 'the threat of international terrorism largely [as] a US concern, and [sought] to placate US pressure with minimum efforts while husbanding Canadian sovereignty and avoiding commitments to undertake new responsibilities with regard to the defence of North America' (71). The adoption of either a weak or strong state strategy, Sands claims, will have a 'decisive impact on its relationship with the United States', as the US will view a weak state strategy as 'an obstacle to progress towards greater security' (74). So in this view, while Canada may stand to gain some leverage due to its significant trade relationship, this leverage is contingent upon greater integration with the US both militarily and economically, and stands to be lost if greater integration does not occur.

Many argued that the events of 11 September 2001 necessitated some degree of greater integration with the US and that Canadian foreign policy must be articulated more within a 'North American' context. Organisations such as the C.D. Howe Institute and the Canadian Council of Chief Executives have promoted further policy integration between Canada and the US in both military and economic matters. In rather stark contrast to this US-oriented approach, others, such as the Council of Canadians, the Canadian Centre for Policy Alternatives, and the Polaris Institute were deeply skeptical of further integration in either area.

A parliamentary report (House of Commons, 2002) suggested that Canada must conduct cost–benefit analysis in order to determine in what areas 'more integrated policies make sense, as well as where Canadian policies—on foreign, defence, security, and trade issues, and in affected domestic fields—ought to be different from, or even at odds with, those of its North American partners' (14). However, the report went on to say that, 'this analysis must take into account cross-border effects, given how costly disruptions to established continental connections could be, potentially raising the 'price of difference' to unacceptable levels' (14).

The latter part of this recommendation was very much in keeping with the Canadian Government's trade-focused and pro-liberalization foreign policy trajectory, which either viewed the trade-off of some degree of sovereignty as an acceptable cost to securing open markets and unrestricted borders,

or insisted that these trade-offs were an 'expression of sovereignty'. Thus trade trumps other foreign policy objectives. Andrew Cohen argued, 'Today trade is the brightest face of Canada's internationalism. As a soldier, Canada is ill-equipped; as a donor, Canada is underfunded, and ineffective; as a diplomat, Canada is becoming less influential and less imaginative. As a trader though, Canada is a success, and getting stronger . . . ' (Cohen, 2003:109).

Canadian business was the chief architect of deep integration with the United States and tirelessly promoted the original free trade agreement with the US and its NAFTA successor. But the push for a new 'grand bargain' (Dobson, 2002) gave way, in the face of US indifference, to a more incremental approach.

C. THE CRISIS

Whatever the ultimate cause of the financial and economic crisis that became headline news in the fall of 2008, its immediate impact was felt in the US finance and banking sector. From there its effects spread to other banking systems which, it transpired, were either interlocked with the US system or had been similarly deregulated and exposed to high-risk investments. The impact of actual or threatened bank collapse and a consequent credit crunch were quickly transferred to the 'real' economy with resulting bankruptcies and layoffs.

The crisis was deep and global and it became a real issue whether the world was in for a repeat of the Great Depression of the 1930s or whether this could be averted by a coordinated policy response by the world's leading states. Two noted US economists have contributed a periodically updated column comparing the current crisis to its 1929 predecessor.[4] In the first version of their column (6 April 2009) they reported that the global decline in industrial production in the previous nine months had been at least as severe as in the nine months following the 1929 peak. Similarly, while the fall in the US stock market was roughly similar to that of 1929, global stock markets had fallen further. This was also true of the decline in the volume of world trade. The authors were careful to point out that it was too soon to predict whether the decline would continue as long as in the Great Depression (i.e., three years), and noted signs that the policy response was different. Specifically, central bank discount rates had fallen more quickly in the current crisis, money supply had continued to grow, unlike the post-1929 situation, and there was a much greater willingness to run budget deficits. Thus, they concluded that '[t]he world is currently undergoing an economic shock every bit as big at the Great Depression shock of 1929–30. . . . The good news is that the policy response is very different'.

The findings of the first update of the column (4 June 2009) were that:

- World industrial production continues to track closely the 1930s fall, with no clear signs of 'green shoots'.
- World stock markets have rebounded a bit since March, and world trade has stabilised, but these are still following paths far below the ones they followed in the Great Depression.
- There are new charts for individual nations' industrial output. The 'big four' EU nations divide north–south; today's German and British industrial output are closely tracking their rate of fall in the 1930s, while Italy and France are doing much worse.
- The North Americans (US and Canada) continue to see their industrial output fall approximately in line with what happened in the 1929 crisis, with no clear signs of a turnaround.
- Japan's industrial output in February was 25 percentage points lower than at the equivalent stage in the Great Depression. There was, however, a sharp rebound in March.

By the second update (1 September 2009) there were signs that global industrial production was recovering (a clear difference from the Great Depression where its decline continued for three years); global stock markets were also moving up (though the decline in total stock value remained higher than at a comparable stage in the earlier period); and global trade volumes had begun to increase (though their collapse remained significant in comparison to 1930).

Whatever the outcome of these encouraging signs, it is clear that the world economy experienced its most significant crisis since the 1930s and escaped, if it proves to have done so, because of major policy interventions falling well outside the box of the neo-liberal orthodoxy that has long informed economic policy-making and was arguably part of the reason for the crisis itself.

D. CANADA'S RESPONSE

Canada's response to the crisis can be analysed using a number of descriptors, some of which highlight its government's lack of speed and urgency, a feature that could be ascribed to the country's avoidance of the worst impact of the crisis and/or to its government's innate neo-liberalism and disinclination to interfere with the operation of market forces. Other categories focus attention on the importance of the bilateral relationship with the United States and the government's determination to fit Canada's response to emerging priorities in Washington. We can term these denial, minimalism, and bilateralism.

E. DENIAL

Many accounts of the crisis begin by noting the role of deregulation of banking and finance in the US. The reforms reduced state regulation to minimal levels and instead increasingly relied on self-regulation by the industry. These moves 'permitted banks and investment companies to overexpose themselves to risky mortgage-backed financial instruments . . . (and) . . . the expansion of unregulated mortgage-brokers with their subprime mortgages increased the fragility of the housing market' (Hudson, 2009: 57–8; see also Campbell 2009). It was, as many have noted, a crisis waiting to happen. The shocks in the US were severe. The five largest investment banks, Bear Stearns, Merrill Lynch, Lehman Brothers, Goldman Sachs, and Morgan Stanley were all hit hard, and either failed or were subject to government reorganization. The Washington Mutual Bank failed in September 2008, and other banks and insurance companies were on the verge of collapse. In response the US government introduced a $700 billion Troubled Asset Relief Program (TARP) to purchase bank equity and buy out bad loans. Other measures included the nationalization of Fannie May and Freddie Mac institutions, which held half of US mortgages, complemented by other initiatives to restore liquidity and provide assistance to financial institutions (see Loxley, 2009: 60–70). Similar measures were taken in other countries and world attention was focused on the developing crisis in the autumn of 2008.

But not in Canada. Or, at least, the government of Canada was not focused on the looming crisis. The first pattern in Canada's response to the crisis was one of official denial. In part, the denial rested on the argument that the Canadian banking system was better regulated and not as exposed to the meltdown as banks in many countries. There is obviously some truth to this claim, although deregulatory measures in the 2006 budget did bring a version of sub-prime mortgages to Canada until a policy reversal in 2008 banned the practice (McNish and McArthur, 2008). It is also true that the federal government has subsequently pumped very large sums into supporting financial

institutions and that a number of Canadian banks have had to write down billions of dollars in bad loans. But Canada has not had to nationalize banks as has been the case elsewhere (Loxley, 2009: 70–1).

Unsurprisingly, the prospect that Canada faced an economic crisis was downplayed by the ruling Conservatives during the federal election campaign, which concluded with the election of another minority Conservative government on 14 October 2008. On 4 October Prime Minister Stephen Harper followed his earlier (*Globe and Mail*, 15 September) opinion that '[i]f we were going to have some kind of crash or recession we would have had it by now' by criticizing the US Congress for 'panicking' after deciding on a $700 billion bailout package: ' I think if we don't panic here, we stick on course, we keep taking additional actions, make sure everything we do is affordable, we will emerge from this as strong as ever' (*CanWest News Service* 3 October 2008 p. A2). Perhaps more surprisingly, the government continued to deny the severity of the economic situation in the immediate post-election period. Indeed, when the government presented a fiscal and economic update to Parliament on 27 November it turned out to contain a series of provocations to the opposition parties—suspension of the right to strike for federal civil servants until 2011, suspension of the right of female federal employees to achieve remedies on pay equity issues, privatization of some crown assets, and elimination of subsidies to political parties. More importantly, in an international context in which many governments were engaged in drastic action to address the economic crisis, Finance Minister Jim Flaherty declined to introduce a stimulus program at that point and opted for a neo-liberal 'business as usual' approach consisting of low taxes and a prediction of a small budget surplus (Valpy, 2009: 9–10). The effect was to launch the country into a short but bitter constitutional crisis as a coalition of opposition parties representing a majority of seats in the House of Commons unsuccessfully attempted to oust the minority Conservative government (see Russell and Sossin, 2009).

In the course of the constitutional crisis the government demonstrated its determination to stay in power at all costs, and arguably did so as a result of a Governor General's decision which violated Canada's constitutional order in a number of respects (Heard, 2009). Notwithstanding the economic crisis, government leaders, including the prime minister, used rhetoric that inflamed traditional regional and linguistic–cultural divisions.

F. MINIMALISM

Early signs of a 'business as usual' approach on the part of the Canadian government included an emphasis on tax cuts rather than spending as a way of producing a stimulus. As late as 29 November these were defended as an adequate response to the crisis. Certainly the tax cuts were significant, amounting to 2 per cent of GDP (*Globe and Mail*, 29 November 2008, p. B6). Moreover, they were conceived as permanent, i.e., to remain in place after any recession had ended. Finance Minister Flaherty contrasted them with any temporary spending stimulus package that, in his view, gave only a transitory economic boost (*Globe and Mail*, 29 November 2008, p. B6). By 3 January 2009 he was contemplating further tax cuts plus infrastructure spending.

By the time of the 27 January 2009 budget, the federal government was prepared to admit that the global crisis had reached Canada and that the economy was in recession (albeit one that had come later and was shallower than elsewhere). In the budget the government claimed it would provide a stimulus of $30 billion or 1.9 per cent of GDP (Canada Department of Finance, 2009: 10). There were grounds for thinking the actual stimulus

might be less. For example, the figures assumed that provinces and municipalities would step forward with matching funds for infrastructure programs. To the extent that they did not, the stimulus could fall to 1.5 per cent (Canada Department of Finance, 2009: 30). Moreover, critics claimed that the government, in attempting to come close to the IMF, OECD, and other international recommendations of a stimulus of 2 per cent of GDP, had jumped ' through a variety of creative hoops . . . but the reality is that the proposed federal stimulus amounts to just 0.7 per cent of GDP in 2009–10' (Macdonald, 2009: 5). Moreover, almost 35 per cent of the stimulus came in the form of broad-based and corporate tax cuts, measures with poor stimulative multipliers compared to spending programs (Macdonald, 2009: 5). By the CCPA's calculations only 4 per cent of the budget tax cuts were directed to low-income Canadians, arguably the group most likely to spend any moneys received and thus help stimulate the broader economy (CCPA, 2009: 3). The spending component of the stimulus package was explicitly declared to be temporary in order to enable a quick return to balanced budgets (Canada Department of Finance, 2009: 12). Thus program spending, 13 per cent of GDP in 2007–8, was projected to rise to 14.7 per cent in 2009–10 before falling back to 13.1 per cent in 2013–14 (Canada Department of Finance, 2009: 29). Clearly the role of government in the economy was to revert to the status quo once the immediate crisis was over. Interesting, but beyond the scope of this chapter, is the fact that spending and tax cuts were dwarfed by up to $200 billion made available to fill gaps in credit markets and 'improve access to financing for Canadian households and businesses' (Canada Department of Finance, 2009: 15). The ultimate destination of these funds and their effect remain unclear.[5]

Just as Canada's early domestic stance on the crisis was minimalist, so too was its reaction in international circles. At the IMF meeting of finance ministers and central bank governors in October 2007, the conclusion was drawn that the private sector was responsible for developing solutions to rectify the credit crisis. Reportedly, Canada was one of the strongest advocates of leaving it to the private sector (Baragar, 2009: 88).

A year later, in advance of a G20 meeting of finance ministers and central bankers, the *National Post* reported that Canada was opposing efforts by European states to make significant reforms in the global financial architecture—crafting financial regulations to bind all countries and having them enforced by a stronger IMF. Canada, together with the US and Australia, emphasized domestic regulation and, according to John Kirton, was on 'the minimalist end of the spectrum and is probably even more minimalist than the United States' (Viera and Callan, 2008: FP1). The subsequent G20 leaders' summit adopted a compromise declaration that emphasized better international oversight of large financial institutions, greater transparency of financial products and monitoring of executive salaries (Montreal *Gazette,* 16 November: A4); a more detailed communiqué was issued after the London G20 in April 2009. Pending detailed research on these meetings, the role played by Canada is unclear. In a leaked report it was suggested that Canada was very much in a second-tier role as far as the priorities of the host country were concerned. Subsequently, the British government denied the reports. While this episode is hardly conclusive evidence, it is consistent with the pattern indicated on the public record of a country less engaged in responding to the crisis than some and one playing the role of a sometimes reluctant follower, rather than a middle power or principal power leader. Perhaps the subtitle of Hillmer and Molot's 2002 collection, 'A Fading Power', most aptly describes Canada's international role in the management of this crisis.

G. BILATERALISM AND THE PURSUIT OF SPECIAL STATUS

In considering Canada's role in NAFTA, Stephanie Golob (2008) has made the argument that just as Canada entered NAFTA to protect its already existing bilateral free trade agreement with the US, its conduct inside the agreement has continued to exhibit bilateralism rather than trilateralism. Although the formation of the Security and Prosperity Partnership (SPP) in March 2005 appeared to herald greater attention to trilateral relations, it has languished as Canada has continued a more traditional approach seeking to be viewed as an 'insider' in Washington whilst seeking to privilege Canadian over Mexican interests.

The approach was highlighted in an exchange of opinion pieces in the Toronto *Globe and Mail* in May 2009. Andrés Rosenthal, a former Deputy Foreign Minister of Mexico and Chairman of the Mexican Council on Foreign Relations, and Robert Pastor, Co-Director, Center for North American Studies at American University, penned an appeal for Canada 'to accept Mexico as a true partner. If it does, the North American concept will be reinvigorated and become an example of progressive co-operative integration, rather than a failed experiment to be disdained and discarded . . .' The current reality, they argued, was that 'the three countries of North America have reverted to two bilateral relationships—US–Canada and US–Mexico—rather than approaching our common challenges together' (Rosenthal and Pastor 2009). In response John Manley, former Finance Minister and Deputy Prime Minister of Canada and now President and CEO of the Canadian Council of Chief Executive Officers (CCCE), together with Gordon Giffin, former US ambassador to Canada, asserted the case for bilateralism: 'Our friends seem skeptical that Canada and the United States share a "special relationship". We assert that this is a unique bilateral relationship, a model in international relations built over many decades based upon similar values and democratic institutions and common heritage. . . . By contrast, the trilateral relationship began with NAFTA in 1994. It is an economic arrangement with none of the deep historical and other connotations of the Canada–US partnership. While the United States does have two borders, the similarity ends at that statement. . . . If the concept of a real North American Community is ever going to be realized, it will be because leadership has been shown by the northern partners' (Manley and Giffin, 2009). The tendency towards bilateralism can be seen at work in Canadian reactions to the 'Buy American' components of the US stimulus package and in the 'me too-ism' of the bailouts of the automobile industry.⌐

H. BUY AMERICA

The US stimulus package contained provisions barring foreign suppliers from participation in funded projects. As most of the money in question was to be spent by state and municipal governments, which are not part of either WTO or NAFTA government procurement provisions, US officials considered the measures compliant with trade agreements. Canadian politicians and officials reacted by pleading for exemptions or for President Obama to veto the legislation, or else Canada would take action under trade treaties (*Globe and Mail*, 9 April 2008). Business organizations worried that protectionist measures could spread and start a trade war on a 1930s scale. It soon became apparent that threatening action under trade treaties was an empty gesture since the US was correct that state and municipal procurement was excluded. The Canadian tactic then switched to calls for reciprocal procurement liberalization. Under these proposals Canadian companies would have access to procurement in the US, and Canadian provinces

and municipalities, some of which had adopted calls for retaliatory action against US companies, would be open to bids from US companies. There was broad provincial agreement and some support, too, from highly integrated companies with cross-border supply chains (CBC *News*, 29 September 2009). At the time of writing, a reciprocal deal was rumoured to be in place but few details were available (Whittington, 2009).

I. AUTO

The crisis of the tightly integrated North American auto industry meant that Canada had a strong interest in making sure it participated in any industry bailout lest a US package privilege auto production that country. With 12 per cent of manufacturing GDP and 150,000 direct jobs and another 340,000 in distribution and after-market activities (*Financial Post*, 11 November 2008, p. FP1) the sector was a high priority for Canada. Expressed willingness to participate does not obscure the fact that it was the US which devised the package, leaving Canadians as 'ultimately passive observers, who can only cross our fingers and hope that the Obama administration's plans save Canadian autoworkers' jobs' (Ibbitson, 2009: A19).

The negotiations between the US government and the auto industry were protracted. Over the course of 2008–9 a pattern gradually emerged. It was clear that Canada's contribution would be set by, because proportionate to, the package established by the US. Similarly, conditions attached to the deal in the US would resonate north of the border—reduced labour costs, amounting to $10 per hour, and changes in work organization were a prominent part of the US deal. Because of the integration of the industry and the North American auto market Canada would have little choice but to follow suit (Vieira and Van Praet, 2009). When the US had determined the size of the bailout to GM, for instance, the Canadian contribution ($10.5 billion, one third of which would be paid by Ontario) became clear. The deal was described by Prime Minister Harper as a 'regrettable but necessary step'. He went on to say, 'I wish there were an alternative but the alternative to what we are doing today would be vastly more costly and more risky'. As a result of its participation in the bailout, Canada acquired 12 per cent of the restructured GM (Whitehorse *Star* 17 June 2008: 8).

J. CONCLUSION

Canada seems to have played a limited role in handling the global economic crisis. It is possible that Canada's low profile reflects the lesser degree to which it was affected by the crisis. In any case, in terms of classic views of Canada as a middle or principal power there seems little to substantiate such roles. Indeed, as the G20 replaces the G7 or G8 as a key international forum, Canada may find its voice correspondingly lessened.

The trilogy of denial, minimalism, and bilateralism may also reflect the limited options available to a country that has increasingly prioritized economic factors in its foreign policy whilst having also emphasized, in practice if not in theory, bilateralism with a much stronger partner, rather than the multilateral approach traditionally favoured by Canadian governments. The choices made in the past, notably free trade and ever-tighter economic integration with the United States, may indeed, as Lawrence Martin commented about the Mulroney government, have foreclosed the possibility of Canadian autonomy and independence (Martin, 1993: 272–3), one that was never fully realised in any case. It is certainly difficult in conditions of neo-liberal globalization, augmented by continental integration, to imagine a Canadian government resorting to economic nationalist measures such as the National Energy Program, or imposing

controls or meaningful reviews of foreign investments. Of course, one of the explicit purposes of NAFTA was to end the possibility of this type of measure, and, as Bruce Doern and Brian Tomlin put it, for the Mulroney government this was a 'desirable loss of sovereignty' (Doern and Tomlin, 1991: 258).

The fact that Canada, for the past twenty-five years, has had neo-liberal governments reluctant to depart from pre-existing certainties about the superiority of market solutions only increases the difficulty of imagining alternatives and, more concretely, of estimating how many degrees of freedom a country like Canada would have in implementing them. Perhaps we will not really know until such time as Canada has a government prepared to at least examine whether the choices made in the neo-liberal period continue to serve the county's interests. For example, a future government might consider whether the collapse of the Chapter 19 process under NAFTA, the procedure that was supposed to guarantee Canadian exporters a fair hearing in the face of US protectionist pressures, means that the calculus of costs and benefits of that agreement should be revisited. It could be that NAFTA, the cost of which in terms of national autonomy in areas like energy is well known, no longer provides anything additional to what is available under the WTO, the autonomy costs of which are lower. A future government might revisit the climate change/environmental file and reach different conclusions than the Harper government has done; or might consider whether the Canadian military might be more usefully deployed in peacekeeping or conflict resolution situations rather than as a bit-player in US military operations; or it might re-evaluate the idea that one size fits all in free trade and investment agreements with developing countries; and so on. Were such initiatives to be attempted, or even seriously considered, we would get a better idea of the degree of autonomy the country retains.

Meanwhile, the argument that Canada is heavily constrained by global structural forces undoubtedly has some strength. But is also true that much Canadian policy, including its response of denial, minimalism, and bilateralism to the recent economic crisis, is self-imposed and seems driven by the application of abstract neo-liberal theory rather than by the honest analysis of problems and identification a range of potential solutions.

Key Terms

Keynesianism
Middle Power
Neo-Liberalism

Notes

1. The first two sections of this chapter consist of a revised version of material originally published in McBride 2005.
2. Most notable was Canada's refusal to contribute troops to the US-led war against Iraq and the adoption of its 'human security agenda', which once again espoused the virtues of multilateralism and the use of 'soft power'.
3. This was to such an extent that this was having a 'chilling effect' on the willingness of trade experts to serve (Herman 2005: 8–9, 9n).
4. Information in the following section is taken from Barry Eichengreen and Kevin H. O'Rourke, 'A Tale of Two Depressions' Sept 1, 2009. www.voxeu.org/index.php?q=node/3421.
5. For initial critical analysis see Rashi 2009; and da Silva 2009.

References

Axworthy, Lloyd. 1997. 'Canada and Human Security: The Need for Leadership.' *International Journal* 52, 2: 183–96.

Axworthy, Lloyd. 2003. *Navigating a New World: Canada's Global Future*. Toronto: Vintage Canada, 2004.

Baker and Hostetler LLP. 2004. *Duties and Dumping: What's Going Wrong with Chapter 19?* Washington, DC: Canadian–American Business Council and Center for Strategic and International Studies.

Baragar, Fletcher. 2009. 'Canada and the Crisis' in Guard and Antony, eds., 2009, 77–106.

Black, David, and Claire Turenne Sjolander. 1996. 'Multilateralism Re-constituted and the Discourse of Canadian Foreign Policy.' *Studies in Political Economy* (Spring): 7–36.

Bow, Brian and Patrick Lennox. eds. 2008. *In Independent Foreign Policy for Canada? Challenges and Choices for the Future*. Toronto: University of Toronto Press.

Canada. Department of Finance. 2009. *Canada's Economic Action Plan: Budget 2009*. Ottawa: Department of Finance.

Canada 21 Council. 1994. *Canada and Common Security in the Twenty-first Century*. Toronto: Centre for International Studies.

Canadian Centre for Policy Alternatives. *Federal Budget 2009: CCPA Analysis*. Ottawa: CCPA.

CanWest News Service 3 October 2008, www.canada.com/topics/news/features/decisioncanada/story.html?id=bc22b1f3-a93c-41b0-a97a-d05d4f3409eb.

Clarkson, Stephen (ed.). 1968. *An Independent Foreign Policy for Canada?* Toronto: McClelland & Stewart.

_____. 1991. 'Disjunctions: Free Trade and the Paradox of Canadian Development.' In D. Drache and M. S. Gertler (eds.). *The New Era of Global Competition: State Policy and Market Power*. Montreal and Kingston: McGill-Queens University Press: 103–26

_____. 2002. *Uncle Sam and US: Globalization, Neoconservatism, and the Canadian State*. Toronto: University of Toronto Press.

Cohen, Andrew. 2003. *While Canada Slept: How We Lost Our Place in the World*. Toronto: McClelland & Stewart

Cooper, Andrew F. 1997. *Canadian Foreign Policy*. Scarborough, Ont.: Prentice–Hall.

Cooper, Andrew, Richard Higgot and Kim Richard Nossal. 1993. *Relocating Middle Powers: Australia and Canada in a Changing World Order*. Vancouver: UBC Press.

Cutler, A. Claire, and Mark W. Zacher. 1992a. 'Introduction.' In Cutler and Zacher 1992b. (eds.). 1992b. *Canadian Foreign Policy and International Economic Regimes*. Vancouver: UBC Press: 3–16.

Da Silva, Steve. 2009. 'The Untold Story of Canada's $275 billion Financial Bailout', in Socialist Project. 2009. *Financial Meltdown: Canada, the Economic Crisis and Political Struggle,* 41–9.

David, Charles–Philippe, and Stephane Roussel. 1998. '"Middle Power Blues": Canadian Policy and International Security after the Cold War.' *American Review of Canadian Studies* (Spring and Summer), 131–56.

Dewitt, David, and John Kirton. 1983. *Canada as a Principal Power: A Study in Foreign Policy and International Relations.* Toronto: Wiley.

Dobson, Wendy. 2002. 'Shaping the Future of the North American Economic Space: A Framework for Action'. *The Border Papers.* C.D. Howe Institute No. 162, April.

Doern, G. Bruce and Brian W. Tomlin. 1991. *Faith and Fear: The Free Trade Story.* Toronto: Stoddart.

Doern G. Bruce, Leslie A. Pal and Brian W. Tomlin. 1996. *Border Crossings: The Internationalization of Canadian Public Policy.* Toronto: Oxford University Press.

Eayrs, James. 1975. 'Defining a New Place for Canada in the Hierarchy of World Powers'. *International Perspectives* May/June, 15–24.

Finlayson, Jack A., and Stefano Bertasi. 1992. 'Evolution of Canadian Post-War International Trade Policy.' In Cutler and Zacher, 1992b: 36–46.

Globe and Mail 15 September 2008. www.theglobeandmail.com/news/politics/article709599.ece.

Golob, Stephanie R.2008. 'The Return of the Quiet Canadian: Canada's Approach to Regional Integration after 9/11' in Bow and Lennox eds. *An independent Foreign Policy for Canada?: Challenges and Choices for the Future.* Toronto: University of Toronto Press: 83–100.

Gotlieb, Allan. 1987. 'Canada: A Nation Comes of Age.' *Globe and Mail* 29 October: A7.

Guard, Julie and Wayne Antony, eds. 2009. *Bankruptcies and Bailouts.* Halifax: Fernwood.

Hall, Peter A. 'Policy Paradigms, Social Learning, and the State: The Case of Economic Policymaking in Britain' *Comparative Politics,* 25, 3 (Apr., 1993), 275–96.

Hart, Michael M. 1985. *Canadian Economic Development and the International Trading System: Constraints and Opportunities.* Toronto: University of Toronto Press.

Hawes, Michael K. 1984. *Principal Power, Middle Power, or Satellite?* Toronto: York University Research Programme in Strategic Studies.

Heard, Andrew. 2009. 'The Governor General's Suspension of Parliament: Duty Done or a Perilous Precedent?' in Russell and Sossin, eds., 2009, 47–62.

Herman, Lawrence L. 2005. 'Making NAFTA Better: Comments on the Evolution of Chapter 19', Ottawa: Centre for Trade Policy and Law, Occasional Papers in International Trade Law and Policy, 57.

Hillmer, Norman and Maureen Appel Molot, eds. 2002. *Canada Among Nations: A Fading Power.* Toronto: McClelland and Stewart.

Holmes, John. 1967. 'Canada's Role in International Organizations.' *The Canadian Banker:* 74 (Spring): 115–30.

House of Commons. 2002. 'Partners in North America: Advancing Canada's Relations with the United States and Mexico' Report of the Standing Committee on Foreign Affairs and International Trade: Ottawa.

Hudson, Ian. 2009. 'From Deregulation to Crisis', in Guard and Antony, eds., 46–61.

Ibbitson, J. 2009. 'When it comes to the Canadian economy, Obama may as well be PM', *Globe and Mail* 20 May 2009, A19.

Keating, Tom. 1993. *Canada and the World Order: The Multilateralist Tradition in Canadian Foreign Policy.* Toronto: McClelland and Stewart.

Keenes, Ernie. 1995. 'The Myth of Multilateralism: Exception and Bilateralism in Canadian International Economic Relations.' *International Journal* 50, 4 (Autumn): 755–78.

Kirton, John. 1999. 'Canada as a Principal Power: G–7 and IMF Diplomacy in the Crisis of 1997–9.' *International Journal* 54, 4 (Autumn): 603–624.

Loxley, John. 2008. 'Financial Dimensions: Origins and State Responses' in Guard and Antony, eds., 2009, 62–76.

Lumsden, Ian (ed.). 1970. *Close the 49th Parallel, Etc: The Americanization of Canada.* Toronto: University of Toronto Press.

Lyon, Peyton, and Brian Tomlin. 1979. *Canada as an International Actor.* Toronto: Macmillan of Canada.

Macdonald, David. 2009. *To Little Too Late.* Ottawa: CCPA.

Manley, John and Gordon Giffin. 2009. 'A table for two, not three', *Globe and Mail,* 15 May.

Martin, Lawrence. 1993. *Pledge of Allegiance: The Americanization of Canada in the Mulroney Years.* Toronto: McClelland and Stewart.

McBride, Stephen. 2005. *Paradigm Shift: Globalization and the Canadian State,* 2nd ed. Halifax: Fernwood.

McNish, J. and G. McArthur. 2008. 'Special Investigation: How Mortgages Crept North'. *Globe and Mail* Friday, 12 December.

Neufeld, Mark.1995. 'Hegemony and Foreign Policy Analysis: The Case of Canada as a Middle Power' *Studies in Political Economy* 48 (Autumn): 7–29.

Nossal, Kim Richard. 1997. *The Politics of Canadian Foreign Policy.* Scarborough, On: Prentice–Hall.

Rashi, Roger. 2009. 'Canada's Big Five: Banking on the Crisis?' in Socialist Project. 2009. *Financial Meltdown: Canada, the Economic Crisis and Political Struggle,* 38–40. Toronto: SP.

Rozental, Andrés and Robert Pastor.2009. 'A case for the three amigos', *Globe and Mail* 1 May.

Russell, Peter and Lorne Sossin, eds. 2009. *Parliamentary Democracy in Crisis.* Toronto: University of Toronto Press.

Sands, Christopher. 2002. 'Fading Power or Rising Power: 11 September and the Lesson from the Section 110 experience' in Hillmer and Molot eds. Toronto: Oxford University Press: 49–73 .

Sharp, Mitchell. 1972. 'Canada–U.S. Relations: Options for the Future.' *International Perspectives* (Special Edition) 17 Oct: 1–24.

Stone, Frank. 1992. *Canada, the GATT, and the International Trade System.* 2nd ed. Montreal: Institute for Research on Public Policy.

Thomas, Christopher. 1992. 'Reflections on the Canada–US Free Trade Agreement in the Context of the Multilateral Trading System' in Cutler and Zacher, 47–61.

US Department of State. 2008. 'Diplomacy in Action' Background Notes: Canada: Bureau of Western Hemisphere Affairs. www.state.gov/r/pa/ei/bgn/2089.htm.

Valpy, Michael. 2009. 'The "Crisis": A Narrative' in Russell and Sossin 2009, 3–18.

Vieira, Paul and Eoin Callan. 2008. 'Canada set to fight Europe over financial cure' *Financial Post, November5, p. FP1.*

Vieira, Paul and Nicolas Van Praet. 2008. 'Canada Pushed to match U.S. Auto Aid' December 9. www.driving.ca/news/story.html?id=1052163.

Webb, Michael. 1992. 'Canada and the International Monetary Regime.' *In Canadian foreign Policy and International Economic Regimes,* ed: Cutler and Zacher, Vancouver: UBC Press: 153–85.

Whittington, Les. 2009. 'Deal close on "Buy USA"—with strings', *Toronto Star* December 4. www.thestar.com/mobile/news/canada/article/734439--deal-close-on-buy-usa-with-strings-attached.

Winham, Gilbert and Sylvia Ostry. 2003. 'The second trade crisis', *Globe and Mail.* 17 June.

Winnett, Robert. 2009. 'G20 summit: Foreign Office "relegates" countries'.

www.telegraph.co.uk/finance/financetopics/g20-summit/4983689/G20-summit-Foreign-Office-relegates-countries.html.

Zhang, Daowei. 2007. *The softwood lumber war: politics, economics, and the long U.S.–Canada trade dispute.* Washington, DC: Resources for the Future.

23

FRUSTRATED MULTILATERALISM: CANADA AND THE NEGOTIATION OF INTERNATIONAL INVESTMENT RULES

Elizabeth Smythe

INTRODUCTION

Foreign direct investment (FDI) and ownership have been sensitive issues for much of Canada's postwar history. Growing public concern often coincided with high profile takeovers of Canadian corporations by foreign (often US, but more recently Chinese) firms.[1] Like trade, investment has been tied to concerns about our sovereignty. Since the 1980s the landscape of Canadian policy on FDI and the negotiation of international rules on foreign investments have altered. Nowhere is this more clearly reflected than in Canada's failed effort to push the negotiation of a multilateral investment agreement onto the World Trade Organization (WTO) agenda. The WTO case reflects the evolving nature of Canadian international economic policy, especially changes in economic interests and official thinking about FDI and the challenges in pursuing these interests within the context of a changing WTO. It raises questions

about whose interests these efforts were intended to serve given how controversial and divisive the issue was at the WTO. It also helps in understanding recent efforts to secure Canadian investment interests through a more aggressive policy of negotiating bilateral and regional agreements.

Along with agriculture, divisions over the so-called 'Singapore issues', which include investment, are widely seen as having contributed to the failure of the WTO ministerial meeting in Cancún Mexico in 2003.[2] A proposal to launch negotiations on an investment agreement was so controversial that it was finally dropped altogether from the WTO agenda in July 2004; only one of the four Singapore issues, trade facilitation, went forward as part of the Doha Round. The European Commission, negotiator for the EU, is often blamed for pushing the Singapore issues, particularly investment.[3] With the EU identified as the main *demandeur*, little attention has been paid to Canada's role in trying to add the investment issue to the WTO negotiating agenda. In fact, Canada was one of the most active advocates of launching negotiations on investment rules at the WTO over the seven-year period of discussions.

Negotiating an investment agreement at the WTO made sense given Canada's support for multi-lateral institutions, trade rules, and the WTO, in par-ticular. As a net exporter of foreign direct investment since 1997, it is in Canada's interests to pursue international rules to enhance investors' access to foreign markets and protect them against arbitrary or discriminatory treatment by host states.[4] There are reasons, however, to question why Canada pur-sued these negotiations at the WTO. First, the issue was divisive as reflected in the compromise forged in Singapore in 1996 to launch a study of, but not negotiations for, an investment agreement. Second, the negotiations of the Multilateral Agreement on Investment (MAI), and the cases launched under the investment chapter (Chapter 11) of the North American Free Trade Agreement (NAFTA) had, by 1997, proven to be controversial. Even the need to maintain good relations with the United States did not necessitate pushing an investment agreement at the WTO since the US was not vigorously pursuing it at the multilateral level. At various points the United States either opposed the effort as a sinister EU plot to avoid movement on agriculture or saw the effort as laudable but unlikely to be successful.[5] Even Canadian business has waxed and waned about the priority placed on investment rules. Can-ada's continued support for negotiations even after a growing number of developing countries made their opposition known in the run up to Cancún is even more puzzling.[6]

This chapter examines why Canada pushed the negotiation of investment rules at the WTO and how it did so. It identifies Canadian interests in launch-ing investment negotiations and the ideas about the benefits of such rules that Canadian officials

employed to persuade WTO members. The case sheds light on the role of evolving ideas and argu-ments as a key element of the strategy employed to educate and persuade reluctant countries to negotiate, and on how Canada's interests altered depending on the negotiating forum and partners.

We begin with a discussion of how Canada's investment interests have been re-defined over time. This is followed by a description of Canada's role in the creation of the Working Group on Trade and Investment (WGTI) at the WTO in 1996 and Canadian activity in it up to the Doha Declara-tion in 2001. The third section examines intensi-fied efforts, post-Doha, to persuade WTO members to launch negotiations at Cancún in September 2003—an effort which ultimately failed. Two emerging trends are then discussed. The first is a domestic debate over the 'hollowing out' of cor-porate Canada and further revisions to FDI legisla-tion which has been attacked as selling the country out or as evidence of a new trend to investment protectionism.[7] The second is the shift in Can-adian foreign policy toward what has been called 'competitive liberalization' through bilateral and regional agreements designed to secure market access and greater protection for Canadian invest-ment abroad. The conclusion assesses Canada's policy on international investment agreements and the interests and ideas that have shaped it.

CANADA'S EVOLVING INVESTMENT INTERESTS: FROM SCREENING TO PROTECTING INVESTORS

Interests usually imply a material basis for action or policy related to the benefit or gain an actor will derive. In the case of policy on FDI and inter-national investment agreements, investment flows and the interests of powerful economic actors provide a key to understanding the source of Canadian negotiators' interest in investment rules.

For much of the postwar period, Canada was a major capital importer. This resulted in high levels of foreign (largely US-based) ownership in major sectors of the economy, a national debate about FDI, and a series of policies from the late 1960s to manage incoming FDI. Policy involved protecting a small number of sectors from foreign ownership, while managing incoming FDI, by providing conditional market access to investors in return for commitments ensuring local economic benefits and backward linkages to the domestic economy. From the mid-1970s to the mid-1980s the Foreign Investment Review Agency (FIRA) handled negotiations with investors.

Internal and external pressures in the 1980s combined to undermine this definition of Canada's investment interests. The US administration, and powerful American corporations, became increasingly hostile to Canadian FDI policies, even as Canada was becoming more dependent on the United States as an export market. Some provinces and Canadian business interests also became highly critical of the policy. Federal officials had concluded, even before a change of government in 1984, that bargaining with foreign investors in return for according them market access was no longer viable because it put secure access to the US market at risk and was necessary for economic growth. Screening put Canada at a disadvantage because international competition for investment, as many economies liberalized, was intensifying.[8] Continued high levels of foreign ownership and the persistence of a nationalist critique, however, meant that wholesale abandonment of the policies was also politically costly.

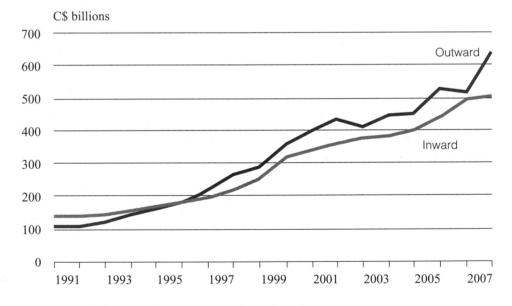

Figure 23.1 Canada's Inward and Outward Stocks of FDI

Source: DFAIT, State of Trade 2009

The changing pattern of investment flows was also significant in re-defining interests in investment rules. Inward and outward FDI increased rapidly in the late 1990s but the balance shifted as outward FDI began growing more rapidly. By 1997 Canada became a net capital exporter (see Figure 23.1). Initially the United States was the overwhelming destination for outward FDI, followed by other Organization of Economic Cooperation and Development (OECD) economies. At the same time Canada remains host to a large stock of FDI ($504.9 billion in 2008) of which about 58 per cent is US-based (down from 66 in the 1990s).[9] In its relationship with the United States, however, Canada has shifted from a capital importer to a net exporter by a small margin of $17.1 billion.

The destination of outward FDI has also changed. By 2008 $310 billion, just over one third of the $637.3 billion stock of Canadian FDI, was located in the United States, which, along with the rest of the OECD, accounts for about 74 per cent. As Figure 23.2 indicates, Canadian FDI in non-OECD countries, which was insignificant two decades ago, has rapidly grown.

Given the rapid growth of outward FDI, negotiating rules to protect Canadian investment appears to be in Canada's interests. At the same time, a large proportion of outward, and the majority of inward, FDI is with the United States. Clearly the complex nature of integrated global production today and the ebbs and flows of highly mobile capital, often sensitive to exchange and interest rates, require some way to attach meaning and significance to the changing flows. To understand how investment interests are defined, we need to look at both ideas about investment and the context in which negotiations take place. Canada's definition of its interests, and thus its

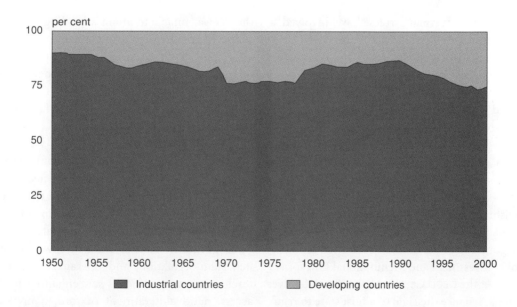

Figure 23.2 Canadian Direct Investment Abroad – Developed vc\s. Less Developed Countries
Source: State of Trade, 2005, 47.

Table 23.1 Top 15 non-OECD destinations for Canadian FDI, on average, 1999–2003

Country	CFDI (in millions of $)
Barbados	23,136
Bermuda	9,823
Bahamas	7,738
Cayman Islands	6,827
Hungary	6,807
Brazil	6,557
Chile	5,704
Argentina	4,924
Singapore	3,730
Indonesia	3,668
Mexico	3,293
Hong Kong	3,134
Peru	1,924
Thailand	918
South Korea	821

Source: DFAIT, State of Trade, 2005.

positions on investment rules, have involved a complex mix of what trade negotiators call offensive and defensive interests.[10]

In the 1970s Canada sought to preserve its ability to screen and regulate FDI in the face of rules designed to limit host state policy discretion. When developing countries called for a New International Economic Order at the United Nations (UN) in the early 1970s, including negotiations on a Code of Conduct for Transnational Corporations, the United States tried to counter it by establishing norms of national treatment and high levels of protection for foreign investors through the negotiation of the OECD's Declaration on International Investment and Multinational Enterprises in 1975. At the OECD Canada was on the defensive, seeking to balance the right of a host state to regulate incoming FDI with fair and non-discriminatory treatment of foreign investors; Canada fought hard to weaken the agreement or opt out.[11] While

the US was unable to attain a binding agreement at the OECD, the organization has since become an important institution in furthering norms of national treatment and transparency and delegitimizing host state regulation of FDI through its Committee on Investment and Multinational Enterprise.

Canadian officials in the 1980s viewed FDI inflows as necessary to ensure economic growth and competitiveness. No longer protected by high tariffs, Canada—as a host state—had to compete aggressively for FDI by providing an attractive investment climate. The 'right' climate was seen by corporate interests as one with low taxes, limited state regulation, and liberalized access for foreign investors. Officials saw enhanced market access, national treatment of foreign investors, and transparent regulation as important norms in the treatment of foreign investors; any deviations were considered necessary evils. Binding codes of corporate conduct, which implied an active regulatory role for states or international organizations, were not seen as legitimate. Instead, it was thought that states should encourage firms to develop voluntary conduct guidelines, similar to the OECD's Guidelines on Multinational Enterprises.

Investment flows were viewed as report cards on the Canadian economy, similar to the way in which the changing value of the Canadian dollar *vis-à-vis* the US dollar is perceived. Canada's share of global FDI inflows measured Canada's attractiveness as a location for FDI, an attractiveness which had to be promoted, while outward FDI was viewed negatively in terms of the country's attractiveness as an investment location. Protection of outward FDI was, therefore, not a priority.

Canada's policy of investment screening, although more limited by 1985, was still a target in bilateral trade negotiations, partly because of an American strategy of using bilateral agreements to establish norms that it wished to see embodied later in multilateral agreements. US demands reached their high-water mark with the negotiation of Chapter 11 of NAFTA in 1993.[12] Canada's NAFTA investment interests were driven not by a desire to protect the limited Canadian investments in Mexico but rather, as the trade minister indicated in 1992, 'to ensure that Canada remained an attractive location for investors wishing to serve the North American market'.[13]

Within multilateral organizations, the US sought to limit host state performance requirements imposed on foreign investors at the General Agreement on Tariffs and Trade (GATT), first by lodging a complaint against FIRA and then by the negotiation of Trade-Related Investment Measures (TRIMs) in the Uruguay Round. Opposition of a number of developing countries, and more pressing US priorities, yielded limited results. At the GATT, Canada was positioned between the two

sides and worked largely to ensure that any agreement did not impinge on existing investment policies. The US then set its sights on a NAFTA-like 'high standards' multilateral investment agreement that would afford foreign investors strong protection against host state regulations to be negotiated at the OECD—the ill-fated MAI.

As outflows of Canadian FDI increased in the 1990s they were viewed less negatively as necessary to maintaining Canada's competitiveness in increasingly globalized systems of production. Firms were part of 'global value chains' whereby whole processes of production are broken down and shared, either within a firm or among a number of firms.

Canadian negotiators became interested in protecting outward investment. The question was how and where to negotiate rules that would achieve this goal. Canada had been focused on bilateral negotiations to secure access to the US market and then trilaterally in NAFTA to preserve that access and ensure that Canada remained an attractive investment location on the continent. In both cases the US played the role of *demandeur* on investment rules. While Canadian foreign policy has traditionally been perceived as favouring multilateralism because the continental relationship is so asymmetrical, Canada's experience in the OECD in 1975 does not suggest that a multilateral organization in and of itself can offset continental asymmetries. More important is the nature of the organization's membership, the processes of decision-making, and the capacity, once rules are made, for them to be enforced. These aspects shaped Canada's preference about where rules on investment should be negotiated.

One option to protect non-OECD investment was to negotiate bilateral agreements following the pattern of the United States and Germany, major exporters of capital. In 1991 Canada began

Table 23.2 Foreign investment protection agreements

Country	Date Signed
Argentina	1991
Armenia	1997
Barbados	1996
Costa Rica	1998
Croatia	1997
Czech Rep.	1992 (amended 2009)
Ecuador	1996
Egypt	1996
El Salvador*	1999
Hungary	1993
Jordan*	2009
Latvia	1995
Lebanon	1997
Panama	1996
Peru	2006
Philippines	1995
Poland	1990
Romania	1996 (amended 2009)
Russia (USSR)	1991
South Africa*	1995
Thailand	1998
Trinidad and Tobago	1995
Ukraine	1994
Uruguay	1997
Venezuela	1998

*Agreements signed but not in force.

such a program with host developing economies and those in Eastern Europe to provide protection and legal recourse for Canadian investors abroad—a logical response given the growth of non-OECD outward investment. But the list of countries with which Canada signed FIPAs bore little relationship to the top 15 non-OECD destinations of Canadian FDI listed above. Only five of these countries, Barbados, Argentina, Hungary, Thailand, and most recently, Peru, have

investments covered under FIPAs while Mexico, Chile, and Costa Rica are covered under trade agreements with Canada. Despite efforts in 1998 to more clearly identify Canada's interests and priorities for FIPAs based on investment flows, future investment opportunities, and business demands, FIPAs are also driven by requests from partner countries seeking to show a welcoming face to foreign investors, assuage multilateral institutions such as the World Bank, or as a part of 'photo op' diplomacy and agreements for a visiting prime minister to sign.[14]

Canada's 2005 international market access priorities, outlined in *Opening Doors to the World*, included India, Brazil, and China—which has now replaced Japan as Canada's second largest bilateral trading partner. Canada has concluded negotiations with India and Madagascar on FIPAs and is negotiating with China, along with Bahrain, Kuwait, Indonesia, Mongolia, Tunisia, Tanzania, and Vietnam. Bilateral talks with Brazil are ongoing. Clearly there is no one-to-one relationship between the negotiation of agreements and investment patterns.[15] Instead, a complex mixture of economic and political interests play a role. The earlier FIPAs clearly cover a limited range of countries and were not broadly integrated with trade interests

As the following table indicates, a new pattern emerges in the post-2005 period in the aggressive negotiation of bilateral and regional trade agreements, many of which include chapters on investment.

In its continued negotiation of FTAs and FIPAs, Canada is following a trend that other countries had begun—a reflection of the diminishing prospects for concluding multilateral negotiations and the failed efforts over seven years to launch negotiations on investment rules at the WTO.[16] Why Canada's initial preferred strategy was to develop binding rules at the WTO is the subject to which I now turn.

CANADA AND THE WORKING GROUP ON TRADE AND INVESTMENT AT THE WTO

Efforts to launch investment negotiations at the WTO must be seen within the context of the US initiative to negotiate a binding MAI within the OECD. Canada had not supported the OECD[17] as the best venue to negotiate investment rules, as Canada's trade minister indicated at the OECD ministerial meeting in 1998:

> To be effective and beneficial any eventual investment agreement must be truly multilateral. Consequently, the MAI process at the OECD must remain open to non-members and, more importantly, the MAI's ultimate home should be the WTO.[18]

Table 23.3

FTAs being negotiated	FTAs signed
Andean Community	Chile
CARICOM	Colombia
Central America	Costa Rica
Dominican Republic	European Free Trade Association
European Union	Israel
India	Jordan
Korea	Peru
Morocco	
Panama	
Singapore	

Broader coverage of countries where Canadian FDI was growing, the WTO's credentials as a trade negotiating forum (Canadian officials saw trade and investment as tightly linked), and its strength-ened dispute resolution capacity made it the pre-ferred venue. However, Canada did not oppose the OECD effort, given its potential to be a model for a broader multilateral agreement, but continued to pursue the WTO option. Canada, along with the European Commission and Japan, worked to build a consensus to negotiate investment for the first WTO ministerial meeting in Singapore in December 1996 through informal discussions with WTO delegates in Geneva, public endorse-ment of the idea by EU Trade Commissioner Leon Brittan,[19] and a Canadian-hosted meeting with sixteen middle-sized countries.[20] The United States opposed WTO negotiations because the completion of an MAI at the OECD was its priority. Given the limits of the TRIMs negotiated in the Uruguay Round, the US was pessimistic about the prospects at the WTO. Despite US opposition, Canada, the EU, and Japan persisted.

Canada presented a proposal in April 1996 to begin an educative work program at the WTO that did not presuppose future negotiations, a recogni-tion that immediate attempts to launch negotia-tions were doomed to failure.[21] The US supported the proposal, largely for its educative value,[22] along with WTO Director-General Renato Ruggiero.

India spearheaded efforts to stop the inclusion of investment and a number of other new issues on the WTO agenda. A last-minute compromise reflected in the Singapore declaration established a working group to examine the relationship between trade and investment but said the work '[should] not prejudice whether negotiations will be initiated in the future'.[23] However, members' preferences for negotiations coloured their activ-ities within the group. The European Commis-sion, Japan, and Canada tried to use the working group to build consensus on the need to include investment in the agenda of a future round of negotiations. The US acquiesced to the extent that the process, as educative, allowed officials to proselytize on the benefits of investment and liberalization.

The WGTI began meeting in June 1997. Canada presented a written submission in December 1997 arguing the need to negotiate a new set of rules based on identified gaps in existing rules. It out-lined experiences with FIPAs and NAFTA, both of which included provisions not covered by the WTO, and provided 'guarantees of protection for our investors in their operations abroad and for for-eign investors coming into Canada'.[24] A particular source of pride was that 'investor–state dispute settlement mechanisms are also central elements of these agreements and, together with state-to-state dispute settlement, increase the effectiveness and enforceability of these agreements'. In contrast the WTO TRIMs agreement covered a limited range of trade-related performance requirements, while the General Agreement on Trade in Services (GATS) touched on investment as one of four modes for delivering services but provided no investor pro-tection for established firms. Canada argued a WTO focus on 'investment rights and obligations [to] deepen trade agreements' offered more consistent rules than bilateral investment treaties. At no time in the following six years did Canada outline any obligations of foreign investors in host countries beyond obeying domestic laws. Investor security was the priority.

The European Commission also focused on the growth and significance of FDI in the global economy, the growth of intra-firm trade, and the 'current patchwork of rules' and the need to 'level the playing field', so that small and medium enter-prises were more willing and able to undertake the risk of FDI. On the other side was India—a strong opponent of negotiations—supported by Pakistan,

Egypt, Morocco, Cuba, and the Association of Southeast Asian Nations (ASEAN) group. India reminded members of the purely educational and non-prejudicial role of the Working Group and argued that the 'development perspective should be all-pervasive'.[25] A list of elements for the focus of study was proposed, including 'the business practices and corporate strategies of transnational corporations, the interrelationship between mobility of capital and mobility of labour, and the impact of FDI on development'. Other opponents argued that many of them already had Bilateral Investment Treaties, which provided protection to foreign firms, once established, and which appeared to be operating well.

After eighteen months only a few areas of consensus in the WGTI had been identified, including the idea that FDI could provide benefits for economic development and that trade and investment were closely linked. There was no agreement on the need for new rules. Unable to reach consensus, the group left the matter to be decided by the WTO General Council while the WGTI continued to meet as a result of an extension of its mandate. External events had an impact on discussions, however.

The first was the growing controversy over, and then the collapse of, OECD negotiations on the MAI in December 1998. Canadian officials hoped the low-key talks of the WGTI at the WTO would allow them to dodge the 'flak', but the failure provided support to opponents of investment rules within the WTO. The MAI failure also meant that the trans-national coalition of critics of the MAI— which included a number of Canadian, labour, environmental, cultural, and other groups— would now turn their full attention to the WTO and the upcoming meeting in Seattle, which would attempt to launch a new round of negotiations including investment rules. The MAI also provided Canadian officials with a lesson on the need to consult more broadly domestically with groups

beyond traditional business and producer interests seen to have a stake in trade agreements.

Chapter 11 of NAFTA also provided critics of strong standards of investment protection with ammunition. By March 1999, US investors had filed four cases against the Canadian government under Chapter 11 of NAFTA. The Ethyl case was filed on 15 April 1997, when a Virginia-based company claimed compensation arguing that a Canadian law banning imports of the gasoline additive MMT, for environmental reasons, was tantamount to expropriation of their assets. Since that time, more cases have been filed against the NAFTA partners and have led to attempts by officials to address the problem. More pertinent is Chapter 11's impact on the proposals Canada put forward at the WTO and its negotiating position. As one developing country delegate indicated, by 1999 everyone knew about Chapter 11![26]

The failure of the December 1999 Seattle ministerial also had an impact on the WGTI and Canada's zeal for investment agreements. Post-Seattle, the WGTI largely 'spun its wheels' and Canadian officials took a low profile, providing no written submissions in 1999 and 2000. A similar situation prevailed outside the WTO. Despite having been enthusiastic about the inclusion of investment rules at the newly launched Free Trade Area of the Americas (FTAA) negotiations in 1998 and growing FDI in Latin America, Canada put forward no substantive proposals on investment until August 2001 and then only on the concept of 'Minimum Standard of Treatment'.[27]

At the WGTI the emphasis shifted to whether investment rules would limit developing country 'policy space' as a result of a presentation by the United Nations Conference on Trade and Development (UNCTAD) on the concept of 'policy space for development' and the need for flexibility, which opponents such as India picked up on. The *demandeurs* were going to have to make a case linking FDI rules and development if they hoped to persuade enough developing countries of the need to negotiate an investment agreement. First, proponents would have to show a positive relationship between investment rules that afforded investors security and an increased inflow of FDI. Second, they would need to address flexibility so that developing countries could sequence and pace the implementation of new obligations of market access or national treatment to meet their own unique development needs. Third, the reality that many developing countries lacked sufficient capacity to engage in ongoing negotiations on agriculture and services, never mind something as complex as investment rules, would need to be addressed.

The challenge to portray the demands for rules to protect investors in a more development-friendly way began with Canada's submission in March 2001 linking host-state regulation and investment flows.[28] To make the case that host-state regulation of foreign investors was discouraging FDI, Industry Canada and the Canadian Chamber of Commerce jointly funded a study and presented the results to the WGTI. Surveying 71 firms, it pointed to 110 specific restrictions affecting investment, primarily in non-OECD countries, and noted that in over 40 per cent of the cases restrictions had resulted in decisions to scale back or cancel investments. The EU followed with a submission in May that admitted that investment rules alone would not ensure FDI flows and that some developing countries would need assistance to develop both an enabling environment for FDI and a capacity to 'negotiate effectively'. It proposed an assessment of member needs and the development of technical assistance programs to be funded by WTO members.

On the issue of flexibility, Canada and other proponents recognized that the model of a 'top-down' NAFTA/MAI type of agreement, involving high-level broad commitments to standards of national treatment and market access, was unacceptable. Their alternative was the model of a bottom-up, positive list approach of the General Agreement on Trade in Services.

This re-focused effort to forge a consensus to negotiate also required firm timelines for a decision which, in turn, required isolating strong opponents and limiting their influence. The European Union played the leading role here, a role that turned out to be more costly than anticipated.

The November 2001 Ministerial meeting in Doha, Qatar involved many questionable and controversial decision-making procedures.[29] It included the arm-twisting of a number of developing-country delegates. With the aid of the United States, the EU was successful in isolating India and obtaining wording on the Singapore issues which reflected the position of the *demandeurs*. Paragraphs 20–22 indicate WTO members 'agree that negotiations will take place after the Fifth Session of the Ministerial Conference on the basis of a decision to be taken, *by explicit consensus*, at that Session on modalities of negotiation' and on the 'needs of developing and least-developed countries for enhanced support for technical assistance and capacity building'. Investment negotiations would be based on 'a GATS-type, positive list approach' and 'take due account of the development policies and objectives of host governments as well as their right to regulate in the public interest'.[30] Led by India, a group of developing countries requested language to ensure that a consensus would be required to launch negotiations and not merely to establish the modalities of negotiations. Members continued to dispute the meaning at the final session to the point that the chair, Qatar's Minister of Finance Yousef Hussain Kamal, had to further clarify it:

My understanding is that, at that session, a decision would indeed need to be taken by explicit consensus, before negotiations on trade and investment, and trade and competition policy . . . could proceed.[31]

The EU, Japan, and Canada interpreted the text to mean that agreement had been achieved and that negotiations would be launched in Cancún. Consensus was only required on trivial matters of procedure and timing. In contrast, opponents took the view that only after consensus on the broad parameters of the substance of the negotiations could the actual negotiations be launched.

The declaration led to a more focused effort in the working group and a major program of technical assistance for developing countries. The wording on an explicit consensus, however, reflected a growing unease among many developing country members with the whole process of WTO decision-making and its lack of transparency. The Declaration, including the text on investment, also clearly placed development, at least at the level of rhetoric, front and centre in the Doha Round. Thus proponents now had to show how negotiations could further development objectives.

FROM DOHA TO CANCÚN: WHEN DOES NO MEAN NO?

Post-Doha, WGTI activity intensified. In the 19-month period up until the last meeting of the WGTI in the spring of 2003 there were 56 written submissions, including nine from the European Union, eight from Canada—plus a joint one—and eight from Japan, reflecting the efforts of the *demandeurs* to persuade those still unsure. These were accompanied by a program of technical assistance financed by a trust fund from member contributions (including Canada's) and delivered by WTO and UNCTAD staff.[32] Forty-two investment training events were held in 2002–3 alone, either in Geneva or in developing countries.

While the proponents shared a strategy and overall goal, they did not agree on all issues. On the question of the scope and definition of investments to be covered by the agreement, Canada took the position that a very broad range of asset-based investments should be covered and argued that this reflected 'contemporary business dynamics associated with investing'.[33] While reflecting Canada's investment interests, in strategic terms it was not helpful in making its case since many developing countries were already nervous about the balance-of-payment issues resulting from the massive capital flight seen in the Asian financial crisis. UNCTAD officials made it clear that, in their view, such a broad definition of investment was a bad idea.

Canada's submissions also addressed flexibility, FDI flows, and technical assistance. Canada indicated openness to mechanisms in an agreement that would allow developing countries to use exceptions, or longer time periods, to phase in implementation. However, the experience of developing countries with special and differential treatment provisions at the WTO, the TRIMs, and the issue of HIV/AIDS and trade-related intellectual property (TRIPs), had created skepticism about such promises. Canada had not been especially accommodating of the special needs of developing countries in past agreements.

On the question of FDI flows, claims made about the link between investment agreements and increased FDI inflows to developing countries by the *demandeurs* were increasingly challenged even by researchers at the World Bank and UNCTAD. Canada's final written submission in June 2003—a joint submission with Korea and Costa Rica—had to acknowledge this reality and was vague on the benefits that would accrue from an agreement. For Canada, transparency was seen to be the 'central tenet' and bottom line of any agreement in creating a predictable and stable climate for investors. Finally, on the question of a NAFTA-like investor–state system of dispute resolution, Canada stated the obvious—that such a system would be 'inappropriate' and, it could be added, totally unacceptable. What had once been a model for an investment agreement in 1997 was now 'inappropriate'. The EU in its submissions called for 'a Multilateral Investment for Development Agreement' based on a GATS model.[34]

By the final meeting in 2003, no consensus among members to negotiate an investment agreement had emerged as Table 23.4 indicates.

Proponents were supported by a mixture of members, including some developing countries and states in transition. However, an equally large group of countries were opposed and some important developing countries, including China and Brazil, were on the fence. Brazil, as chair of the WGTI post-Doha, had not revealed its position, its strategy being based on a suspicion that the EU was using the Singapore issues to trade off, in the final hour, against agriculture. China had collaborated with opponents in a WGTI submission, arguing that

corporations also had obligations that an investment code should address. Proponents, including Canada, had not addressed the issue at all, beyond a 1999 EU paper that argued that existing weak and unenforceable guidelines for MNCs, such as the OECD's, were more than adequate to ensure corporate social responsibility. While many small and least-developed countries remained marginal to the process, opponents such as India worked hard in the summer of 2003 to organize their opposition in a series of meetings, which the *demandeurs* all but ignored.[35]

DECISION TIME: THE CANCÚN MINISTERIAL

The level of disagreement on the Singapore issues going into Cancún was reflected in the July 2003 General Council meeting, during which

Table 23.4 Country Positions

Demandeurs: in favour of negotiating an agreement	Friends of investment: support the idea but not necessarily the timing	Swing countries: might link to other issues or wait and see	Opponents of negotiations: very vocal
European Union	Argentina	Brazil	India
Japan	Chile	South Africa	Malaysia
Canada	Mexico	Philippines	Zimbabwe
South Korea	Turkey	Indonesia	Tanzania
Switzerland	Poland	Egypt	Zambia
Taiwan	Costa Rica	Cuba	Kenya
Norway	Hungary	Dominican Republic	Belize
	Columbia	Jamaica	Uganda
	New Zealand	Thailand	Sri Lanka
	Hong Kong	Bangladesh	CARICOM
	Singapore	Pakistan	
	Australia	Venezuela	
		China	
		Ecuador	

Source: Adapted from Luke Peterson, Oxfam, and WWF, May 2003.

opponents refuted proponents' insistence that the Doha declaration authorized the start of negotiations after Cancún as part of a single undertaking. They reminded delegates of the explicit consensus provision and concluded that further study and clarification of the issues, not negotiation, was required.[36]

The draft ministerial declaration discussed by the General Council in August seemed, at first, to fully capture divisions on investment.[37] However, the second part of the annex appeared to presuppose that negotiations would begin post-Cancún and laid out the modalities as they had been outlined in position papers of the EU and Japan, which had never been agreed to in the WGTI. Other concerns about the draft text were raised.[38] The chair refused to alter the text but was forced by members' protests to prepare a cover letter to accompany it that reflected the extent of disagreement.

The conflict then moved to Cancún. Following WTO practice, Mexico as host chaired the meetings and appointed facilitators to work through the issues and report back.[39] For the Singapore issues, Canadian trade minister Pierre Pettigrew was chosen as facilitator despite Canada having been an active proponent of negotiating investment rules and other Singapore issues. The disagreement on the Singapore issues became evident at smaller facilitator-led meetings, as did the link for a number of developing countries between these issues and real progress on agriculture. Agreement on the first was unlikely without the second.

On 12 September a group of 30 developing countries plus Bangladesh—representing the 30 least-developed countries—sent a letter to Pettigrew opposing negotiations on the Singapore issues and raising concerns about the capacity to both negotiate and implement potential commitments.[40] They complained about the process, reminded the Minister of the absence of an explicit consensus, and offered alternative wording on investment. The following day a second revised draft declaration text appeared. On a broad range of issues, especially agriculture and cotton, developing countries were disappointed. On investment, paragraph 14 of the draft read:

We agree:
- to convene the Working Group in Special Session to elaborate procedural and substantive modalities on the basis of paragraphs 20, 21, and 22 of the Doha Declaration.
- modalities that will allow negotiations on a multilateral investment framework to start shall be adopted by the General Council no later than [*date*]
- The date will coincide with the date for agreeing on modalities on agriculture and NAMA.[41]

The text approving negotiations, considering the level of opposition, was stunning. Tying the start of negotiation on investment to agreements in agriculture meant that many of the proponents of investment negotiations, such as the EU, Japan, and Korea, would have to give way there in order for talks to start. The Mexican foreign minister's strategy of first seeking a resolution of the impasse on the Singapore issues was criticized, as was the refusal of the EU to un-bundle the issues and drop investment and competition, as suggested by Pettigrew, until the eleventh hour. When a recess failed to breach the impasse and Botswana informed the chair that the African Union countries would not accept negotiation on *any* of the four issues and Korea (backed by Japan) insisted on all four, the chair called the meeting to an end, citing the impasse. The subsequent decision of the EU to drop all four, and the July 2004 WTO General Council decision to proceed only on trade facilitation, marked the end of the seven-year campaign on investment.

The failure at Cancún seemed to surprise only the Canadian officials. Despite extensive consultations with critics, evidence of well organized developing-country opposition, and critiques of mainstream economists that investment negotiations at the WTO were a bad idea,[42] Canadian officials persisted in seeing it as worthwhile. Before we address why Canada had undertaken this effort and why it failed, we must examine how foreign investment issues continued to pose challenges at home even as Canadian foreign policy tried to respond to the WTO failure.

HOLLOWING OUT AND NATIONAL SECURITY: PRESSURES ON INVESTMENT LIBERALIZATION

Despite the trend to liberalization in Canada, limitations on incoming investment in a small number of sectors and screening of a number of large takeovers remain in place, even though the latter process has provided few impediments to foreign investment. They reflect continued political sensitivity regarding foreign investment, especially takeovers, even as governments continued to vigorously promote Canada as an investment location. The issue of domestic screening came to the fore again in 2006 as the result of a number of economic forces, including commodity prices and exchange rates, which led to a wave of takeovers or attempted takeovers of iconic Canadian corporations including Hudson's Bay, Inco, Dofasco, and Falconbridge. These generated some public disquiet, media attention, and even concern among some corporate executives. Many referred to it as the 'hollowing out' of corporate Canada.

Yet the Conservative government's economic policy statement of 2006 reflected the continued negative view of state regulation, declaring that '[p]olicy restrictions on foreign investment in Canada have contributed to our economy's relative decline in foreign direct investment flows'.[43] While there is limited evidence of this, it nonetheless reflects the reluctance to, in any way, reverse the long-term trend to further liberalization of Canadian investment regulation. Yet pressures continued and the Conservative government was forced to respond, appointing a panel in November 2006 headed by a former BCE executive, Lynton (Red) Wilson, to review whether changes were needed to the Investment Canada Act. The report, entitled *Compete to Win*, was released in June 2008[44] and recommended an increased threshold for reviews of takeovers, changing the net benefit test to one where government must prove a takeover does not provide such benefit, and removing restrictions on FDI in certain sectors such as uranium mining. A number of these changes were adopted by the government and incorporated into amendments of the Investment Canada Act in March 2009, including increasing the threshold for review of foreign takeovers from $295 million to $1 billion, which eliminated an estimated two-thirds of the transactions reviewed.[45]

In addition to the high-profile takeovers of 2006, other deals involving foreign state-owned enterprises (from China, Norway, and the UAE) investing in resource sectors in Canada posed challenges, as have the high-profile attempted takeovers of technology-intensive or strategic corporations. These included the attempted takeover of Alliant Techsystems, owner of the Radarsat2 Satellite, by US-based Macdonald Detwiler. After a well coordinated public campaign and opposition outcry, the Conservative government was forced to intervene and stop the sale.

In 2007 the Conservative government also added amendments to the Investment Canada Act that included a national security review of takeovers. Some observers see this as adding a very open-ended set of criteria to the process which may reverse the liberalization trend or at least allow for the politicization of controversial transactions:

> Now, a proposed investment may be subject to national security review even if it does not exceed the threshold for the net benefit review, whether the investment is proposed or already implemented, and even in cases in which a minority interest is acquired in a Canadian business (*i.e.,* where there is no acquisition of control of a Canadian target). As in the case of other countries, there is no definition of what could be 'injurious to national security', and there is a distinct possibility that the test could be used to target certain types of sovereign investment.[46]

The government has articulated guidelines as part of its security assessment for state-owned enterprises which focus on transparency, disclosure, evidence of a Canadian presence in corporate management and governance, and distance from control of foreign governments—an effort clearly undertaken to address domestic concerns while reassuring potential foreign investors.

ALTERNATIVES TO THE WTO? BILATERALISM AND INVESTMENT PROTECTION

How have the interests of Canadian investors been addressed, given the failed effort to launch investment negotiations and the slowing momentum of multilateral trade negotiations? Canada's outward investment continued to increase, especially in regions of south and central America and Asia. In the absence of a comprehensive WTO agreement, Canada maintained its program of Foreign Investment Protection Agreements. In 2004, a new draft agreement, based on the NAFTA model, was developed despite Canada's assertion at the WTO

that aspects of its investor-state dispute process might not be appropriate for some developing countries. But the more recent wave of FIPAs and new bilateral trade agreements that cover investment reflect a much closer tie to the interests of investors and of regions where Canadian investment is growing.

Table 23.3 indicates that Canada is negotiating with a number of countries and has concluded trade agreements with several such as Peru and, more controversially, Colombia. It has also begun negotiations with the Caribbean Community (CARICOM) countries and the European Union. In each case, investor protection and market access are important elements. Agreements, such as Peru's, include variations on NAFTA permitting investors to sue governments in cases where state regulation has had an indirect impact that corporations could claim constitutes expropriation. Not all negotiations have gone smoothly. Some, such as those with Korea, have raised questions about the balance of benefits to Canada, while the agreement with Colombia involved concerns about human rights which held up a similar bilateral agreement in the US Congress. The table also reflects a clear emphasis on the Americas, where much of Canada's growing mining and financial investment is located.

These agreements suggest that Canada has joined a process that was already well underway by a number of other actors including the United States and the EU. In fact, a 2009 Canadian trade strategy document, *Seizing Global Advantage,* lays out the urgency of Canada joining the trend:

> [G]overnments are increasingly competing against one another to help their businesses and investors gain an edge in the race for market share, technological advantage, foreign investment and other global value chain opportunities. Canada must do the same.[47]

The primacy of commercial interests in the process of negotiations is clear. Although the Peru and other FTAs have side agreements on labour and the environment, they remain, as do Canada's, pronouncements on corporate social responsibility, limited largely to best efforts[48] with little capacity for enforcement, even as civil society groups in Canada and elsewhere continue to raise concerns about the behaviour of Canadian firms abroad, especially in extractive industries.

CONCLUSION

We began with the question of why Canada sought to launch negotiations on investment rules at the WTO in 1996 and persisted for seven years in that effort. Part of the answer lies in the growing importance of capital exports to non-OECD countries. Corporate interests in Canada, which were influential in trade policy, demanded higher levels of investment protection. But that does not fully explain the rationale behind seeking such rules at the WTO. Bilateral or regional agreements might have served that purpose. Moreover, why would the Canadian state go out of its way to facilitate outward investment? To understand Canada's interest in negotiating investment rules at the WTO, as this case indicates, we need to go further and look at ideas about both investment flows and the WTO. Second, we asked how Canada sought to create a consensus at the WTO that would be permissive of negotiations. Here the role of ideas was also important, particularly in the period after the Doha Development Declaration of 2001.

By the late 1990s, officials viewed capital exports as important to Canada's competitiveness and closely linked to trade. Moreover, international norms disseminated through organizations like the OECD, the International Monetary Fund (IMF), and the World Bank regarded state intervention to control entry of investment and

regulate it as illegitimate. Yet trade and investment policies have historically been sensitive issues in Canada, involving sovereignty and concerns over our bilateral relationship with the United States. Multilateral institutions like the WTO were viewed more positively because of their potential to offset bilateral asymmetry with the United States. In the case of investment, multilateral institutions might allow Canada to reconcile our mix of offensive and defensive interests. The WTO was also preferred because of its more universal membership, its dispute resolution system, and its experience in negotiating trade agreements. Given its large number of developing country members and its consensus decision processes, however, it would be necessary to persuade many of these members to negotiate.

Because this was not a negotiation but rather an exercise in persuasion, the process involved ideas that were linked strategically to the interests of proponents. Officials interested in protecting Canadian investors in developing countries had to couch these interests in the language and ideas of development, and make a compelling case that investment rules would facilitate development. This was necessary because states were being asked to accept limits to their domestic regulations in return for the hope that investment inflows would increase. Proponents, such as Canada, could offer little else because, as liberal states, governments do not control private capital flows.

Many of the states being asked to participate in negotiations were not capable of dealing with existing and growing demands of ongoing WTO negotiations and previous obligations. Nor had their experience with the Uruguay Round given them a lot of faith in promises of great benefits to come. To convince them, it was necessary to champion extensive technical assistance and promise that any agreement would allow for flexibility and a national right to regulate.

Canada's position was further shaped by the high levels of investment protection NAFTA accorded. In 1996 Canadian officials had embraced the NAFTA model and preached its virtues at both the OECD and the WTO. By 1999 it was clear that Canada itself faced conflicts between the high levels of protection afforded investors through recourse to investor-state dispute mechanisms and the right of host states to regulate in the public interest. The MAI experience exposed divisions among OECD members and led to more consultations on trade and investment agreements in Canada, thereby giving critics of these agreements more voice. The result was a scaling back of Canada's ambitions at the WTO and increasing controversy over the Singapore issues in 2003, which led many business organizations to drastically downgrade the negotiation of investment rules at the WTO as a priority.[49]

The failure at the WTO and the growing level of Canadian investment abroad resulted in a stronger emphasis on bilateral and regional agreements, first FIPAs and then FTAs. The shift from multilateralism to regional and bilateral agreements is a departure for Canada but is not new. Canada is following a broader trend that has been widely observed and raises concerns about the interests being served and the implications for multilateral trade rules, as well as questions of equity and fairness.

As Oxfam has indicated, the rate of growth of these agreements is daunting:

> During 2006, more than 100 developing countries were engaged in over 67 bilateral or regional trade negotiations, and signed over 60 bilateral investment treaties. More than 250 regional and bilateral trade agreements now govern more than 30 per cent of world trade, whilst an average of two bilateral investment treaties have been agreed every week over the last ten years. While driven largely by the US and the EU, other countries such as Canada and Australia are also busy negotiating such agreements. In many cases, as with the EPAs, these negotiations involve bilateral relationships that are profoundly asymmetrical.[50]

Just as investment regulation in Canada remains a sensitive issue, Canada's aggressive pursuit of bilateral trade agreements to secure a particular set of interests outside the WTO has raised concern within Canada about whose interests such agreements serve. As this case indicates, states' interests in international economic negotiations are not just a simple reflection of powerful economic trends or actors, but rather involve a complex, changing evolution of interests and contention within Canada and with an array of other international actors in multilateral institutions like the WTO.

Key Terms

Foreign Direct Investment
Investment Agreements

Investor-State Dispute Resolution
Investment Screening

Notes

1. The Chinese takeover bid for Noranda in early 2005 set off 'alarm bells' in Ottawa and led to amendments to the Investment Canada Act. See 'Security Concerns spur reviews on foreign investment', *Globe and Mail*, 18 June 2005, B5.

2. The four were trade facilitation, transparency in government procurement, competition policy, and investment. All four involve domestic regulation.

3. Larry Elliott. 'DTI Leak Blames Lamy for Cancún Failure', *The Guardian*, 23 October 2003.

4. Department of Foreign Affairs and International Trade, *State of Trade* (Ottawa: DFAIT, April 2005).

5. Elizabeth Smythe. 'Just Say No! The Negotiation of Investment Rules at the WTO', *International Journal of Political Economy* 33 (Winter 2003): 60–83.

6. Robert Wolfe. 'Informal Political Engagement in the WTO: Are Mini-Ministerials a Good Idea?' in John Curtis and Dan Ciuriak, eds., *Trade Policy Research* (Ottawa: DFAIT, 2004), 27–90. See also Pierre Sauve, 'Decrypting Cancún', Information Paper for the Session, Aftermath of the Fifth WTO Ministerial Conference: The State of Play and Implications for Developing Countries. Regional Policy Dialogue (Economic and Social Commission for Asia and the Pacific), Bangkok, 30–31 March 2004.

7. Karl Sauvant. *FDI Protectionism is on the Rise* Policy Research Working Paper No. 5052 Poverty Reduction and Economic Management Network, International Trade Department, The World Bank (September 2009). On the hollowing out debate see the six-part series, 'For Sale: Corporate Canada', *Globe and Mail* September 2006)

8. External Affairs Canada, *Trade Policy for the 1980s* (Ottawa: External Affairs, 1983).

9. Department of Foreign Affairs and International Trade, *State of Trade* (Ottawa: DFAIT, April 2005), Chapter 4, 45–47 and *State of Trade* (Ottawa: DFAIT, April, 2009), 70. A portion of the shift in the net investment position with the US is due to exchange value changes.

10. Analysts Torbjörn Fredriksson and Zbigniew Zimny, 'Foreign Direct Investment and Transnational Corporations' in *Beyond Conventional Wisdom in Development Policy: An Intellectual History of UNCTAD 1964–2004* (New York and Geneva: United Nations, 2004) have likened changing international views on investment issues to a swinging global pendulum.

11. For a discussion of Canada's role in the UN and OECD negotiations in the 1970s see Elizabeth Smythe, *Free to Choose: Globalization, Dependence and Canada's Changing Foreign Investment Regime,* (PhD dissertation, Carleton University, 1994), Chapter 6.

12. High levels of protection, despite the array of exceptions and reservations listed in the Annex of Chapter 11, were afforded in the agreement and set a new standard.

13. House of Commons, Standing Committee on External Affairs and International Trade, 'Statement of the Hon. Michael Wilson', 17 November 1992.

14. Andrea Bruce, *Assessing the Impact of Canada's Foreign Investment Promotion and Protection Agreements,* (MA thesis, Norman Paterson School of International Affairs, Carleton University, 1999).

15. A leaked memo to the Cabinet dated 22 October 2002, 'Memo to Canadian Cabinet Sets Out Proposed Changes to Canadian Foreign Investment Protection Agreements', *Investment Law and Sustainable Development Weekly News Bulletin,* (13 December 2002) claims that Canadian business had been lobbying hard for FIPAs with Brazil, India, and China. In other cases officials claim a number of developing countries, such as Peru, approached Canada to sign bilateral agreements. Often developing countries are seeking to attract new FDI and qualify for investment insurance from various export development agencies.

16. Department of Finance, *Advantage Canada* (Ottawa: Department of Finance, 2006), 85.

17. The case is based on interviews with Canadian officials, WTO officials, and delegates in 1998, 2002, and 2003, along with the documents of the WGTI, especially the Report of the Working Group on the Relationship Between Trade and Investment (WTO, December 2002) and Report of the Working Group on the Relationship Between Trade and Investment to the General Council, June 2003.

18. Hon. Sergio Marchi, Minister of Trade, Statement at the OECD Ministerial Meeting, 27 April 1998.

19. Sir Leon Brittan. 'Investment Liberalization: The Next Great Boost to the Global Economy', *Transnational Corporations* 4, 1 (April 1995): 1–10.

20. Elizabeth Smythe. 'Your Place or Mine? States, International Organizations and the Negotiation of Investment Rules', *Transnational Corporations* 7, 3 (December 1998): 85–120.

21. R.B. Ramaiah. 'Towards a Multilateral Framework on Investment?', *Transnational Corporations* 6, 1 (April 1997): 116–35.

22. At a Quad trade ministers meeting Canada, the EU, and Japan reaffirmed their support for the negotiation of the MAI at the OECD. *Inside US Trade* (1996), 28.

23. WTO Singapore Ministerial Declaration (Geneva: WTO, 1996), paragraph 20.

24. Submission from Canada to the Working Group on Trade and Investment, 11 December 1997 (WT/WGTI/W/19).

25. India, Submission to the WGTI, June 1997.

26. Comment by WTO delegate in Geneva to the author in 2003. There have been so many controversial cases that the Department of International Trade now has a section of its website devoted to them. Available at http:// www.dfait-maeci.gc.ca/tna-nac/NAFTA-en.asp.

27. The heavily bracketed leaked version of the FTAA investment chapter, which appeared on the Internet in 2001, was largely based on a US, NAFTA-like proposal.

28. Submission from Canada to the WGTI, March 2001, 'Foreign Investment Barriers: A Report by the Canadian Chamber of Commerce in Partnership with Industry Canada' (W/WGTI/W97).

29. Fatourama Jawara and Aileen Kwa. *Behind the Scenes at the WTO: The Real World of International Trade Negotiation Lessons from Cancun,* Updated edition (London: Zed Books, 2004).

30. WTO Doha Declaration (2001).

31. As quoted in Martin Khor, 'The Investment Issues in the WTO', *Seatini Bulletin,* 30 April 2003.

32. For a more detailed discussion of this program and its limitations see Elizabeth Smythe, 'What do You Know?' Paper presented at the International Studies Association Annual Meeting, Honolulu, Hawaii, 1 March 2005.

33. Communication from Canada to the WGTI, 'Scope and Definition', 11 April 2002, 2 (WT/WGTI/W/113).

34. European Community and Its Member States, Submission to the WGTI European community and its member states, 'Concept paper on Policy Space for Development', 3 April 2003 (WT/WGTI/W/1). Perhaps it was this sort of over-the-top rhetoric that made the EU the favoured target of NGOs, who, in the Spring of 2003, worked long and hard to challenge many of the EU's claims about an investment agreement. See Elizabeth Smythe, 'What Do You Know?'

35. Wolfe, 'Informal Political Engagement in the WTO', 27–90.

36. WTO General Council Comments on the EC Communication, 8 July 2003.

37. *Investment* 13. [Taking note of the work done by the Working Group on the Relationship between Trade and Investment **we decide to commence negotiations on the basis of the modalities set out in Annex D to this document.**] versus [We take note of the discussions that have taken place in the Working Group on the Relationship between Trade and Investment since the Fourth Ministerial Conference. The **situation does not provide a basis for the commencement of negotiations in this area**. Accordingly, we decide that further clarification of the issues be undertaken in the Working Group.]

38. This portion of the annex reads as follows:
Relationship between Trade and Investment
   1. The objective of the negotiations **shall be** to establish an agreement to secure transparent, stable and predictable conditions for [long term cross-border investment, particularly foreign direct investment], that will contribute to the expansion of trade, and the need for enhanced technical assistance and capacity-building in this area . . . and,
   3. The Chair of the Negotiating Group on Investment **shall** hold the Group's first meeting within one month from the date of this decision. The Chair of the Negotiating Group shall conduct the negotiations with a view to presenting a draft text by no later than [30 June 2004]. Draft Declaration, Cancún Ministerial, 24 August 2003.

39. Critics claim the facilitators are friendly to powerful members.

40. Seri Rafidah Aziz (Malaysia) and Arun Jaitley (India), *Letter to Hon. Pierre Pettigrew*, 12 September 2003.

41. World Trade Organization Preparations for the Fifth Session of the Ministerial Conference, Draft Cancún Ministerial Text, Second Revision, 13 September 2003.

42. Jagnish Bhagwati, *Financial Times*, 22 October 1998.

43. Department of Finance, *Advantage Canada,* (Ottawa, 2006).

44. Competition Policy Review Panel, *Compete to Win* (June. 2008).

45. Beltrane, Julian (2008) 'Allow more foreign investment, bank mergers in Canada: panel of experts says, *The Canadian Press*', June 26.

46. Karl Sauvant, (2009) *FDI Protectionism is on the Rise.* Policy Research Working Paper No. 5052, Poverty Reduction and Economic Management Network, International Trade Department, The World Bank (September), 11; see also Subrata Bhattacharjee, 'National Security with a Canadian Twist: The Investment Canada Act and the New National Security Review', *Columbia FDI Perspectives*, no. 10, (30 July 2009).

47. Department of Foreign Affairs and International Trade, *Seizing Global Advantage* (Ottawa: DFAIT, 2009), 3.

48. The government created the position of Corporate Social Responsibility Counsellor in 2008, reporting to the trade minister and equipped with limited powers of investigation.

49. Canadian Council of Chief Executives (CCE), 'Prosperity, Freedom, and Security: Renewing Canada's Commitment to Multilateral Trade Liberalization', 20 May 2003.

50. Oxfam, *Signing Away the Future: How trade and investment agreements between rich and poor countries undermine development* (2007).

SELECTED BIBLIOGRAPHY

Acheson, Keith, and Christopher Maule. 1999. *Much Ado About Culture: North American Trade Disputes*. Ann Arbor, MI: University of Michigan Press.

Anastakis, Dimitry. 2005. *Auto Pact: Creating a Borderless North American Auto Industry, 1960–1971*. Toronto: University of Toronto Press.

Anderson, Michael A., and Stephen L. Smith. 1999. 'Canadian Provinces in World Trade: Engagement and Detachment', *Canadian Journal of Economics* 32, 1 (February): 22–38.

Barry, Donald, and Ronald C. Keith, eds. 1999. *Regionalism, Multilateralism, and the Politics of Global Trade*. Vancouver: UBC Press.

Bratt, Duane. Forthcoming. *Canada and the Global Nuclear Revival*. Montreal and Kingston: McGill-Queen's University Press.

Brown, Douglas M., and Earl H. Fry, eds. 1993. *States and Provinces in the International Economy*. Berkeley: University of California Press; Kingston, ON: Queen's University Institute of Governmental Studies Press and Institute of Intergovernmental Relations.

Browne, Denis, ed. 1998. *The Culture/Trade Quandary: Canada's Policy Option*. Ottawa: Renouf Publishing/ Centre for Trade Policy and Law.

Cameron, Maxwell A., and Brian W. Tomlin. 2000. *The Making of NAFTA: How the Deal was Done*. Ithaca, NY: Cornell University Press.

Clarkson, Stephen. 2009. *A Perilous Imbalance: The Globalization of Canadian Law and Governance*. Vancouver: UBC Press.

———. 2008. *Does North America Exist? Governing the Continent after NAFTA and 9/11*. Toronto: University of Toronto Press.

Courchene, Thomas J., ed. 1999. *Room to Manoeuvre? Globalization and Policy Convergence*. Montreal and Kingston: McGill-Queen's University Press.

Cutler, A. Claire, and Mark W. Zacher. 1992. *Canadian Foreign Policy and International Economic Regimes*. Vancouver: UBC Press.

Doern, G. Bruce, and Brian W. Tomlin. 1991. *Faith and Fear: The Free Trade Story*. Toronto: Stoddart.

Doern, Bruce G., Leslie A. Pal, and Brian Tomlin, eds. 1996. *Border Crossings: The Internationalization of Canadian Public Policy*. Don Mills, ON: Oxford University Press.

Drache, Daniel. ed. 2008. *Big Picture Realities: Canada and Mexico at the Crossroads*. Waterloo: Wilfrid Laurier Press.

Froese, Marc D. 2010. *Canada at the WTO: Trade Litigation and the Future of Public Policy*. Toronto: University of Toronto Press.

Grinspun, Ricardo, and Yasmine Shamsi, eds. 2007. *Whose Canada? Continental Integration, Fortress North America and the Corporate Agenda*. Montreal and Kingston: McGill-Queen's University Press.

Halle, Mark, and Robert Wolfe, eds. 2007. *Process Matters: Sustainable Development and Domestic Trade Transparency*. Winnipeg: International Institute for Sustainable Development.

Hart, Michael. 2002. *A Trading Nation: Canadian Trade Policy from Colonialism to Globalization*. Vancouver: UBC Press.

———. 1995. *Decision at Midnight: Inside the Canada–US Free-Trade Negotiations*. Vancouver: UBC Press.

Hart, Michael, and William Dymond. 2001. *Common Borders, Shared Destinies: Canada, the United States and Deepening Integration*. Ottawa: Centre for Trade Policy and Law.

Helliwell, John F. 2002. *Globalization and Well-Being*. Vancouver: UBC Press.

———. 1998. *How Much Do National Borders Matter?* Washington: Brookings Institution Press.

Hoberg, George, ed. 2002. *Capacity for Choice: Canada in a New North America*. Toronto: University of Toronto Press.

Kaiser, Karl, John J. Kirton, and Joseph P. Daniels, eds. 2000. *Shaping a New International Financial System: Challenges of Governance in a Globalizing World*. Aldershot, UK: Ashgate Publishing.

Kirton, John J., and Virginia W. MacLaren, eds. 2002. *Linking Trade, Environment, and Social Cohesion: NAFTA Experiences, Global Challenges*. Aldershot, UK: Ashgate Publishing.

Kukucha, Christopher J. 2005. 'Lawyers, Trees and Money: British Columbia Forest Policy and the Convergence of International and Domestic Trade Considerations', *Canadian Public Administration* 48, 4 (Winter): 506–27.

McBride, Stephen. 2005. *Paradigm Shift: Globalization and the Canadian State*, 2nd ed. Halifax: Fernwood Publishing.

McDougall, John N. 2006. *Drifting Together: The Political Economy of Canada–US Integration*. Peterborough, ON: Broadview Press.

Madar, Daniel. 2000. *Deregulation, Trade and Transformation in North American Trucking*. Vancouver: UBC Press.

Muirhead, B.W. 1992. *The Development of Postwar Canadian Trade Policy: The Failure of the Anglo-European Option*. Montreal and Kingston: McGill-Queen's University Press.

Ostry, Sylvia. 1997. *The Post-Cold War Trading System: Who's on First*. Chicago: University of Chicago Press.

Plumptre, A.F.W. 1977. *Three Decades of Decision, Canada and the World Monetary System, 1944–75*. Toronto: McClelland and Stewart.

Schmitz, Andrew, ed. 2005. *Trade Negotiations in Agriculture: Case Studies in North America*. Calgary: University of Calgary Press.

Stairs, Denis, and Gilbert R. Winham, eds. 1985. *The Politics of Canada's Economic Relationship with the United States*. Toronto: University of Toronto Press.

Stone, Frank. 1992. *Canada, the GATT and the International Trade System*, 2nd ed. Montreal: Institute for Research on Public Policy.

Studer, Isabel and Carol Wise, eds. 2008. *Requiem or Revival? The Promise of North American Integration*. Washington: Brookings Institution Press.

Urmetzer, Peter. 2005. *Globalization Unplugged: Sovereignty and the Canadian State in the Twenty-First Century*. Toronto: University of Toronto Press.

Watson, William. 1998. *Globalization and the Meaning of Canadian Life*. Toronto: University of Toronto Press.

Winham, Gilbert. 1992. *The Evolution of International Trade Agreements*. Toronto: University of Toronto Press.

Wolfe, Robert. 1998. *Farm Wars: The Political Economy of Agriculture and the International Trade Regime*. New York: St Martin's Press.

PART VI

SOCIAL CONSIDERATIONS: THE NEED TO DO MORE?

National interests are usually narrowly defined to only two dimensions: 1) protecting a country's territorial integrity, physical security, and political independence; and 2) enhancing a country's economic prosperity. However, Canadian policy-makers have often added a third dimension: the promotion of Canadian values. This third dimension has been featured prominently in every comprehensive foreign policy announcement for the last four decades. The 1970 white paper identified six areas of national interest and three of them—social justice, quality of life, and a harmonious natural environment—are directly related to the promotion of Canadian values. The 1985 green paper similarly identified justice, democracy, and the integrity of the natural environment as key priorities of Canadian foreign policy. The 1995 white paper highlighted 'the projection of Canadian values and culture by promoting universal respect for human rights, the development of participatory government and stable institutions, the rule of law, sustainable development, the celebration of Canadian culture, and the promotion of Canadian cultural and educational industries abroad'. The 2005 International Policy Statement stated that Canada will make a difference globally by promoting sustainable development, respecting human rights, and building genuine development.[1]

This final section of *Readings in Canadian Foreign Policy* provides a greater analysis of Canada's efforts at promoting social dimensions in its foreign policy. Canada has a tendency, in order to differentiate itself from the American superpower, to see itself as a *moral* superpower. Typical of this sentiment is a report by Canada25, a non-partisan organization of politically active Canadians aged 20–35, entitled *From Middle to Model Power: Recharging Canada's Role in the World*.[2] This is neither a recent phenomenon, nor necessarily one that is appreciated by other countries. For instance, former US Secretary of State Dean Acheson once referred to Canada as the 'stern daughter of the voice of God'.[3] There are also prominent domestic critics of the idea of asserting a cultural role in Canadian foreign policy. For example, Denis Stairs has been skeptical of the idea that Canadian foreign policy is (or should be) driven by virtue instead of national interests. Attempting to project Canadian values, however defined, can lead to 'misunderstanding the true origins of their behaviour' and can cause 'significant damage to the effectiveness of their diplomacy'.[4]

Notwithstanding these critics, using foreign policy to promote Canadian values is widely supported by both policy-makers and the public. In Chapter 24, Nelson Michaud applies Joseph Nye's concept of 'soft power' to Canadian foreign policy.[5] By examining the inspiration and purpose of promoting Canadian cultural values abroad, he illustrates that there is not much of a difference between interests and values. Michaud argues that it is in 'Canada's interest to live in a world that shares what Canada stands for'. Therefore, values are 'on equal footing with economics and security' and 'are a vector, a force that influences the process as well as the content of Canadian foreign policy'.

Michaud's chapter provides the parameters of the debate over values and Canadian foreign policy. The remainder of the section focuses more narrowly on specific aspects of social considerations: environmental protection, foreign aid, African development, and human rights. The selected bibliography at the end of this section lists resources for students to more fully explore these areas plus others including democracy and good governance, immigration and refugees, and international law.

The problem of climate change caused by the emission of greenhouse gases into the atmosphere has been at the centre of Canada's international environmental policy. On 17 December 2002, Canada ratified the Kyoto Protocol and committed to reducing its greenhouse gas (GHG) emissions by six per cent of 1990 levels. Unfortunately for environmentalists who support action on climate change, Canada never even come close to meeting its Kyoto target. In December 2009 states met in Copenhagen, Denmark at the Fifteenth Conference of Parties Meeting. The hope had been that states would be able to negotiate commitments for the period beginning 2012. However, the conference resulted in a weak non-binding statement. Canada had been targeted in the press as a laggard and had been condemned broadly for its climate change policy. The Alberta oil sands, a major source of GHG emissions, but also a major source of wealth, has become a particular target of domestic and international opponents. Prime Minister Harper argued that Canada would align its climate change policy with that of the United States and in January 2010 notified the United Nations that the Canadian target for 2020 would be at 17 per cent reduction of emissions from a 2005 baseline 'aligned with the final economy-wide emissions target of the United States in enacted legislation', thus directly linking Canada's position with that of the United States.[6] In Chapter 25, Heather Smith uses the concept of internationalism to assess Canada's climate change diplomacy. She concludes that the Harper government has 'engaged in multilateralism but also engaged in activities that undermine key principles of the Kyoto Protocol and adopt[ed] diplomatic strategies that seek to divide the European Union and bully developing states into acting'.

Former Canadian Prime Minister Lester Pearson chaired the Pearson Commission on International Development in 1969. One of the commission's key recommendations was setting a target for developed countries of 0.7 per cent of their gross national product (GNP) to be set towards official development assistance (ODA). While several countries have consistently met that target (the Netherlands, Sweden, Denmark, and Norway), most developed countries have not come close. Canada is no exception.

While it did increase ODA throughout the 1970s and early 1980s, Canada never came close to the 0.7 per cent target. Additionally, in the last 20 years there has been a steady decline in Canada's level of foreign assistance. In 1986–7, Canada's ODA/GNP ratio was 0.5 per cent, but after years of sustained budget cuts by the Mulroney and Chrétien governments, it dropped to 0.23 per cent by 2003–4.[7] As Ottawa's financial situation improved, it began to reinvest in foreign assistance. Both the Martin and Harper governments gradually increased foreign aid. However, the 2008–9 recession, and the resulting large federal budget deficits, has sparked concerns that foreign aid, once again, will be slashed.

The debate over the size of the ODA/GNP ratio is an interesting one, but there other debates. For example, a basic question is why Canada gives between $2.5–3.5 billion a year in ODA? Many Canadians assume that foreign assistance is provided for altruistic reasons, such as helping the poorest people in the poorest countries. Cranford Pratt has argued that development assistance is a policy tool that combines all three of Canada's international objectives: physical security, economic prosperity, and the promotion of Canadian values.[8] This linkage remains a cornerstone of Canadian aid policy. The 2005 International Policy Statement asserts that 'failure to achieve significant political, economic, social and environmental progress in the developing world will have an impact on Canada in terms of both our long-term security and our prosperity'.[9] An additional debate, which Stephen Brown addresses in Chapter 26, is whether foreign aid is effective. After all, developed countries have spent hundreds of billions of dollars on foreign assistance for decades, and yet over a billion people remain in abject poverty. Brown notes that 'since Chrétien's final years in office, and increasingly so under Harper, the government has presented its policy initiatives as ways of improving the effectiveness of Canadian aid'. This has led to the 'the untying of aid, the questioning of impact and search for results, the issue of aid volume, the "focus on focus" (fewer recipient countries and economic sector), and the coherence between aid policy and policies in other areas'.

In Chapter 27, David Black conducts a case study of Canada's development policy by looking at Canadian–African relations. There have been political, security, and economic dimensions in Canada's relationship with Africa: the fights within the Commonwealth against South African apartheid that were led by John Diefenbaker and Brian Mulroney; the deployment of Canadian peacekeepers to the Congo, Rwanda, and Ethiopia-Eritrea; and the activities of Canadian mining and oil companies on the African continent. However, the major feature of the relationship has been Canadian development assistance to Africa. Some prominent examples include Canada's leadership on the New Partnership for African Development (NEPAD) at the 2002 G8 Summit in Kananaskis, and the efforts of Stephen Lewis as UN Special Envoy for HIV/AIDS in Africa.[10] Black argues that 'Canada's extraordinary engagement with Africa' has ended as the Harper government has disengaged from Africa. Its development focus has shifted away from Africa to Latin America, Canadian peacekeepers have abandoned Africa for the military conflict in Afghanistan, and diplomatically the continent has been forgotten.

A final social consideration in Canadian foreign policy is the promotion of human rights. In a brief introduction to Chapter 28, Bratt and Kukucha identify Canada's historical role in promoting human rights around the world. This supplies the context for Chapter 28, which is a first person account of Maher Arar's 'extraordinary rendition' by the United States (with Canadian complicity) to Syria. It is a Kafkaesque tale that includes sustained torture by Syrian officials for over a year. Eventually Arar was returned to Canada where his case launched a commission of inquiry that ended with a public apology from the RCMP and the Canadian government as well as a $10.5 million settlement. Arar's case highlights the intersection between human rights and security.

The Arar case also asks what is the responsibility that Canada has to its citizens abroad? Traditionally this has been viewed in terms of evacuating Canadians from natural disasters (like the 2010 earthquake in Haiti) or war zones (like the 2008 Lebanese–Israeli war), or consular services for Canadians accused of crimes in foreign lands (like William Sampson in Saudi Arabia). However, since 9/11 the issue has been expanded to human rights violations of Canadian citizens by foreign governments (especially the US and its allies) as part of the war on terror. For example, Omar Khadr was captured as a teenage 'unlawful combatant' by American forces in Afghanistan and currently resides at the US military prison in Guantanamo Bay.

Notes

1. Department of External Affairs, *Foreign Policy for Canadians* (Ottawa: Department of External Affairs, 1970), 14–16; Department of External Affairs, *Competitiveness and Security: Directions for Canada's International Relations* (Ottawa: Department of External Affairs, 1985), 3; Canada, *Canada in the World: Government Statement* (Ottawa: Canada Communications Group, 1995); Canada, *Canada's International Policy Statement: A Role of Pride and Influence in the World* (Ottawa: Government of Canada, 2005), 20.

2. Canada25, *From Middle to Model Power: Recharging Canada's Role in the World* (Toronto: Canada25, 2004). Available at: http://www.canada25.com/collateral/canada25_from_middle_to_model_power_en.pdf.

3. Dean Acheson, 'Canada: Stern Daughter of the Voice of God', in Livingston Merchant, ed., *Neighbours Taken for Granted* (Toronto: Burns and MacEachern, 1966), 134.

4. Denis Stairs, 'Myths, Morals, and Reality in Canadian Foreign Policy', *International Journal* 58, 2 (Spring 2003): 239.

5. Joseph Nye first coined the term 'soft power' in 1990 to describe American foreign policy. Joseph S. Nye, *Bound to Lead: The Changing Nature of American Power* (New York:

Basic Books, 1990). He elaborated further on the concept in Joseph S. Nye, *Soft Power: The Means to Success in World Politics* (New York: BBS Public Affairs, 2004).

6. Environment Canada, 'Canada's Submission to the UNFCCC of its Quantified Economy-Wide Emissions Target, (2010). Accessed 7 May 2010 at http://www.climatechange.gc.ca/cdp%2Dcop/default.asp?lang=En&n=C4BD2547-1#p4.

7. Canadian International Development Agency, *Statistical Report on Official Development Assistance: Fiscal Year 2003–2004* (Ottawa: CIDA, 2005), 1.

8. Cranford Pratt, 'Competing Rationales for Canadian Development Assistance', *International Journal* 54, 2 (Spring 1999), 306–23.

9. Canada, *Canada's International Policy Statement: A Role of Pride and Influence in the World*—DEVELOPMENT (Ottawa: CIDA, 2005), 6–7.

10. The 2002 G8 Summit is also discussed by John Kirton in Chapter 9. For Lewis's reflections on Africa, the UN, and HIV/AIDS see Stephen Lewis, *Race Against Time: The 2005 Massey Lectures* (Toronto: Anansi, 2005).

24

SOFT POWER AND CANADIAN FOREIGN POLICY-MAKING: THE ROLE OF VALUES

Nelson Michaud

ÉCOLE NATIONALE D'ADMINISTRATION PUBLIQUE

Canada's role and stance in the world cannot be explained by mainstream international relations theories that base a country's action on elements of power related to military might, population, territory and its resources, or economic strength. In fact, Canada's situation has fuelled a debate in academia and within the ranks of the foreign policy community, a discussion that aimed at finding the most appropriate description of its power: concepts such as middle power[1], intermediate power[2], satellite power[3] all found their defenders and detractors.[4] At the heart of the question is a practice of international relations that relies on what some authors call soft power, a concept that Joseph Nye coined in 1990.[5]

Soft power refers to 'the ability to get what you want through attraction rather than coercion or payments. It arises from the attractiveness of a country's culture, political ideals, and policies. When our policies are seen as legitimate in the eyes of others, our soft power is enhanced.'[6] This foreign policy tool is indeed quite appropriate for understanding Canada's foreign policy making. Even though Canada ranked among the most powerful nations at the end of World War II, its military capacity declined over the years. And if, at one point, Canada could be found among the top economic leaders of the world, the emergence of new actors—including the BRIC (Brazil, India, Russia, and China)—and the diversification of the world economy challenge the country's position. Although new spending and international commitments under the Martin and Harper governments allowed Canada to regain some clout in terms of military power, and even if Canada's economic structure helped the country to swiftly leave the 2008–9 financial world crisis, it would be hard to foresee a turn of events that would incite Canada to opt for a hard power approach as the basis for its future foreign policy. Figuring out how Canada uses soft power is therefore a key element in our reading and understanding of Canada's foreign policy past and future.

Soft power theorists identify the 'currency' or resources used in this context as values, culture, policies, and institutions. More specifically, in the realm of international relations, values are at the heart of how the other resources are used and shaped. For Nye, '(t)he resources that produce soft power arise in large part from the values an organization or a country expresses in its culture, in the examples it sets by its internal practices and policies and in the way it handles its relations with others'.[7] Constructing the analysis found in this chapter around the values to which Canada refers therefore makes sense.

This approach indeed clashes with the usual foreign policy analysis grid that put interests as the main motivation a country has to intervene on the international scene. Not that Canada avoids this aspect. Canada has interests and takes them into consideration in its foreign policy management. For instance, security objectives were highlighted following the 9/11 events, and Ottawa did successfully negotiate a 'smart border' agreement with the United States. The new context not only heightened security concerns, but it also challenged economic well-being; Canada responded by ensuring that trade flows across the Canada–US border were not disrupted.

However, we cannot neglect that Ottawa contextualized security issues. This was further demonstrated not once but twice, with both Jean Chrétien's and Paul Martin's reluctance to embrace American security choices related to the war in Iraq and the Anti-Ballistic Missile Defence System. Even more interesting is the fact that, in both instances, Canadian prime ministers have justified their rejection of the invitation by referring to 'Canadian values'.[8] Indeed, values are at the core of Canadian foreign policy. When one refers to the 1995 policy statement—which lasted over ten years as the cornerstone of Canadian foreign policy—the 'promotion of Canadian values' proudly stands as the 'third pillar' in the edification of Canada's international relations.[9] Under the leadership of Foreign Affairs ministers like Lloyd Axworthy,[10]

values gained even more importance. As well, in the *International Policy Statement* released by the Martin government in April 2005, values—though less prominent—are still very much present. And even if in practice the Harper government gave values a less prominent role, it was first elected on a value-based foreign policy platform. What are these values? Why are they so important? The need to study them is obvious.

The interest of this study is fuelled by the lack of unanimity regarding the role and definition of values in the formulation of Canadian foreign policy. Some have even openly questioned the need for a values-based foreign policy. The most common criticism is that the promotion of one's own values can be perceived as a lack of respect for values held by others; this can be interpreted as a form of imperialism, and as a consequence, foreign policy becomes much like that of the United States. Denis Stairs has also questioned the implementation of a hierarchy of values in Canadian foreign policy. Specifically, he has suggested that:

> Canadians have grown alarmingly smug, complacent, and self-deluded in their approach to international affairs. . . . More specifically, they have come to think of themselves not as others are, but as morally superior. They believe, in particular that they subscribe to a distinctive set of values—'Canadian' values—and that those values are special in the sense of being unusually virtuous.[11]

For his part, Jack Granatstein has also warned that '(m)oral earnestness and the loud preaching of our values will not suffice to protect us in this new century'.[12] Others, however, such as Jennifer Welsh, have argued for a greater role for values in Canadian foreign policy. She views values as a defining factor for Canada's international role in the twenty-first century. Notably, Welsh argues that as 'tempting as the interests-before-values mantra is, we cannot abandon a values-based agenda. We live in a democratic society, where the values and principles we stand for must form a critical part of our activities in the international arena'.[13]

Another way to look at things is to ask whether values are that far from interests. Isn't it in Canada's interests to live in a world that shares what Canada stands for? Indeed, Canada's power is not what it used to be and it is in its utmost interest to benefit from a context that will give a premium to behaviours based on similar values. The real discrepancy is then giving long-standing values an absolute priority and ignoring challenges that the new international context lays on Canada's doorstep.

Wherever we stand in these debates, it remains that values are an intrinsic part of the Canadian foreign policy landscape. There is no doubt that, in the Canadian context, they are considered on equal footing with economics and security. Therefore, values cannot be labelled merely as 'an element to be considered'; they are a vector, a force that influences the process as well as the content of Canadian foreign policy. Values are part of this image Canada projects and uses to garner support in defence of its interest. As Simonin underscored, 'The image can be expressed through general perception and reduced to a simple gestalt-like set of attitudes that trigger an overall positive or negative reaction.'[14]

The difficulty is that values in the Canadian context, although perennial, do not always match the challenges of a rapidly changing international system. As a result, it is necessary to evaluate the role of values in the formulation of Canada's foreign policy. It is also crucial to differentiate between two types of values—those perceived by the population and those advocated by the Canadian foreign policy apparatus. In doing so, it will become possible to consider whether values are a source from which a foreign policy that answers the call of a redefined world is crafted, or a stonewall that prevents Canada from updating a policy that needs to take new factors into consideration.

1. IDENTIFYING VALUES IN CANADIAN FOREIGN POLICY

The first question to be raised concerning values on which Canadian foreign policy is based refers to their uniqueness. Aren't they universal? Are they a mere image Canada wishes to project of itself or are they part of its identity? What is so distinctively Canadian about them? If values occupy such a major place in Canadian foreign policy, isn't this also the case in most countries?

To answer these questions, it is necessary to outline what the values represent and how they are articulated. This section of the chapter will offer us an analytical reading of what can be understood when we refer to 'Canadian values' in the foreign policy-making context. I will look at two potential issues that might influence this process. These are: what do people think, what do policy makers think, and what in fact lies out there?

1.1 Psycho-social Values

I have labelled the first set of sources 'psycho-social' values because they help craft Canada's 'social' self. Specifically, these are the values that Canadians claim to recognize in themselves as a society. Their importance lies in a factor suggested by Pico Yver: Canada is 'held together by shared values rather than shared roots'.[15] These values come from several sources. The key source that helps us identify these values is Steve Lee's article published in *Canadian Foreign Policy*.[16] In his paper, Lee reports on the conclusions reached at forums held by the Canadian Centre for Foreign Policy Development (CCFPD).[17] From these conclusions, general trends have emerged and Lee reports them as values that 'should guide the conduct of Canada's international relations'.[18]

The first of these values refers to respect for the environment. This does not come as a surprise given the importance Canadians give to environmental questions. This might not always be evident in their behaviour, but a country that is largely dependent on its natural resources cannot be insensitive to the issue. The relevance of this consideration is further evident in the support Canadians demonstrated for the Kyoto protocol and their reaction to political leaders who oppose it. This explains why Canadians expect their government to consider environment as an item to be discussed and acted upon at the international level.

A second value outlined by Lee is support for democracy and democratization. This approach includes not only the conduct of free and fair elections, but also principles of good governance. To a large extent, this is perceived as a sine qua non condition to any foreign relations Canada might entertain with other countries. In fact, it is this specific value that contributed to Canadians' support for intervention in Haiti at the height of the political crisis in 1990. This value is at the centre of Canadian foreign policy in the Americas and, to a large extent, in Africa.

In addition, Lee focuses on 'social equity', which emphasizes 'social and economic justice' and fairness. From a foreign policy point of view, this means that Canada should prioritize international relations that explicitly promote these considerations in as many domains as possible.

The fourth value is human rights and tolerance towards diversity. Canadians demonstrate the importance of this value by highlighting these issues during foreign visits by senior officials to countries where human rights are questioned—China being a prime example—and the absence of Prime Minister Harper at the Beijing Olympics is a witness to this sensitivity.[19] Conversely, Canadians do not understand when the issue is not put on the agenda. Although human rights are a very broad issue, Canadians extend their concerns to a higher level to include the concept of tolerance. This refers to the acceptance of differences, of individual expression, and of cultural or ethnic diversity. To many, this is perceived as an important feature that differentiates Canadian and American values.

Finally, one might not be surprised to find civil society involvement as a key value in a report produced by a group that has a clear mandate to promote such involvement. Moreover, this report refers to meetings where civil society representatives had an opportunity to voice their interest in being more involved. Keeping these possible biases in mind, it nevertheless remains that more and more Canadians want input into the policy process and, although issues are more complex than ever, citizens believe they should not be left in the hands of specialists. This is a growing trend in most domestic policy fields and foreign policy is no exception. This request adds to the alter-globalization movement's demands for a civil society in, for example, the conduct of world affairs.

In addition to Lee's analysis, other examples of psycho-social values are outlined in the May 2003 report of the House of Commons Standing Committee on Foreign Affairs and International Trade, entitled 'A Contribution to the Dialogue on Foreign Policy'. This report highlights values also reported by Lee such as democracy/good governance and human rights. It also sheds light on 'pluralism' as a 'particular Canadian strength',[20] a value that corresponds largely to Lee's tolerance.[21]

By initiating his 'dialogue on foreign policy' in the spring of 2003, then Foreign Affairs Minister Bill Graham offered Canadians an opportunity to express their views on Canadian foreign policy. In his Report to the Canadian Population,[22] he focussed on values similar to Lee's, including the environment, sustainable development, democracy, social and economic justice, human rights, and acceptance of diversity. Many of these themes were suggested in questions asked by the minister in the discussion paper released to initiate the dialogue.[23]

In studying people's perceptions, opinion polls could be useful, but they are effectively 'snapshots', often influenced by events that occurred at the moment they were conducted, which could distort the image they project. For instance, the values Lee presents in his paper are confirmed to some extent by an EKOS poll, released at the 'Canada in the World' conference held in Montreal in February 2005, in which Canadians viewed themselves as important actors in building a better world. At the same time, however, the promotion of values is also challenged as a foreign policy objective. This was clear in the release of polling data in conjunction with another conference, 'Defining National Interest: New Direction for Canadian Foreign Policy', held in Ottawa in November 2004. The Innovative Research data made public indicates that 79 per cent opposed the push of Canadian values abroad, thereby rejecting that 'third pillar'. Moreover, the 'quality of life' values Lee claims are at the centre of Canadians' perceptions of foreign policy were supported by only 41 per cent of those polled. Although a direct link cannot be made between these two images of Canada in the world, it seems difficult to completely ignore the gap that surfaces here. This is why I preferred to rely on other studies to define these values as only some of many to be considered.

1.2 Politico-operational Values

This next group of values is no less important as they are conceptualized and operationalized by foreign policy makers. Therefore, these values reflect both policy orientations and operational targets traditionally prioritized by officials, hence the label 'politico-operational'. These values can be traced throughout Canada's foreign policy history and are reflected in a series of official documents, including the 1995 white paper, *Canada in the World*; statements from government ministers and the Prime Minister, including Speeches from the Throne; press releases; and reports. Most of these values are well known and dear to most Canadians.

The first politico-operational value is the rule of law. In domestic politics, this refers to rules and norms conducted within a legal framework that includes a binding judicial system. In the Canadian case, however, the rule of law is also contrasted with the rule of power—that is, whenever a state has the means to impose its will, it will. Canada also extends these concepts of governance to the international level and supports the rule of law against the rule of power. In so doing, Canada does not advocate the end of the anarchical Westphalian system, but simply favours actions that are backed by a consensus within the community of nations and works toward the implementation of governance frameworks, including judicial and quasi-judicial institutions. In this, Canada clearly goes against the historical American approach to world affairs.

A related concept is multilateralism. First a practice, multilateralism is now perceived in many circles as a value that Canada should maintain. This principle has long dominated the conduct of Canada's foreign policy and Keating[24] sees in it Canada's distinctive signature. It influenced Robert Borden's participation in the Imperial war cabinet, guided Canada's role at both the San Francisco (UN) and Washington (NATO) conferences, and today remains a key principle tied to institution-building related to the environment, prohibited arms, or the war against terrorism. While the United States prefers to assert its supremacy on a one-on-one (bilateral) basis, Canada 'punches over its weight' in most settings by associating itself with other international actors who share similar concerns and attitudes.

A direct result of this internationalist approach is Lester B. Pearson's legacy to the world: peacekeeping, which today includes peacemaking and peacebuilding.[25] Although most Canadians still believe that Canada continues to rank first among UN peacekeeping contributors, it no longer plays such a prominent role. It might be true qualitywise, but in terms of effectives, as of January 2005, Canada ranked thirty-third[26] and has slipped to the fifty-sixth rank as of January 2010,[27] behind several African and Asian countries. In its defence, it must be noted that Canada is now involved in other multilateral operations, such as the ones undertaken under NATO's leadership. This is why it could be asserted that contributing to world safety is still seen as a major objective as well as a key value in Canadian foreign policy-making.

Of course, security does not have the same resonance in Canada as it does in the United States; nonetheless, it remains an important politico-operational variable. In the immediate aftermath of 9/11, institutionalist politicians easily agreed with offensive realist academics like John Mearsheimer[28]: security trumps economy. For a while, in Canada, the optics were reversed: economic well-being came first and security [was] a necessary ingredient to ensure prosperity. This value has deep roots in Canadian history given that trade has always played an integral role in Canada's development. This reality was made clear with enhanced security measures after 11 September: leaders had only to proclaim that Canada's economic health heavily depended on better security, and it was then possible to bring in tougher security measures.

A final value I will consider here is international development assistance. Aid is an integral part of Canadian foreign policy and, although Canadians do not heartily approve massive sums of tax money being routed out of the country, most are proud of what they perceive as Canada's leadership role—which of course is far from Canada's actual performance. For about 10 years, Canada's contributions have continuously diminished, reaching 0.25 per cent of Canadian GNP in 2000, far below the UN's 0.7 per cent target. According to an OECD report released in March 2009, Canada dedicated 0.32 per cent of its gross national revenue to aid, ranking sixteenth among 22 member countries.[29] In addition to this problem, CIDA's winter 2005 policy review also questioned Canada's dispersion of aid and the ongoing practice of tied aid, in which assistance is dependent on re-investment in the Canadian economy. Nevertheless, aid is a foreign policy value that gives Canadians the warm fuzzy feeling that Canada is a caring country.

Ultimately, politico-operational values, as promoted by policy-makers, benefit from a blurred knowledge of the international context and of Canada's true role in it. Building foreign policy on these values does have some short-term benefits. First, they have considerable support within this foreign policy community, which has conceptualized and socially constructed these Canadian 'assets' in terms of values. Second, these values promote a comforting sense of legitimacy for Canadian citizens, without the need for a significantly greater international contribution. These are two important factors in gaining popular support for foreign policy initiatives. At the same time, however, these politico-operational values often benefit from support that ignores important issues of context. Therefore, they represent a potential policy time bomb for actors who do not use them with great caution.

2. VALUES AT WORK

In order to understand the role of values in contemporary Canadian foreign policy, it is first necessary to explore examples of these considerations in

Canada's external relations. For this purpose, it is useful to return to 1947, when Canada was emerging as a full-fledged autonomous international actor. We will then review some more contemporary expressions of values under the Chrétien, Martin, and Harper governments.

2.1. Historical Perspective

Values were identified as a prominent feature of Canadian foreign policy as early as the Gray Lecture delivered by Louis St-Laurent, the first Canadian Secretary of State for External Affairs who did not hold the dual role of prime minister.[30] Specifically, in a speech that would become the cornerstone of Canadian foreign policy, St-Laurent continuously refers to Canadian psycho-social values and 'principles' such as generosity and openness, and uses them to lead his reflections.[31] For him, it is clear that '(n)o foreign policy is consistent nor coherent over a period of years unless it is based upon some conception of human values'. He also states that a 'policy of world affairs, to be truly effective, must have its foundations laid upon general principles which have been tested in the life of the nation and which have secured the broad support of large groups of the population'. We can see here the first traces of what Lee labelled equity, tolerance, and to some extent in considering the context of those days, civil society involvement. Finally, St-Laurent identifies 'basic principles' of foreign policy, including national unity, political liberty (read: democracy), the rule of law, and a willingness to accept international responsibilities, which could be linked to Lee's call for peacekeeping and support for international development. In this immediate postwar environment, St-Laurent concludes by stating that 'we must play a role in world affairs in keeping with the ideals and sacrifices of the young men of this University, and of this country, who went to war'. Without a doubt,

Canadian values are found throughout this seminal policy statement.

St-Laurent's stance was not without precedent. Canadian interests cannot be ignored, but it was also Canadian values and the country's perception of the world that motivated Canada's position in the formation of the United Nations and NATO. In the first instance, Canada was influential in the writing of the Charter.[32] Concerning NATO, Canada was influential in having Article 2 of the Charter—an article that opens the mandate of the organization to fields other than military security—adopted.[33] A final example of Canadian institutionalist values brought to the fore has been provided at the time of the Bretton Woods talks, which bore fruits known as the International Monetary Fund, the World Bank, and the GATT. Canada was invited to get involved and based its negotiating skills on its commitment towards multilateralism—a Canadian foreign policy core value, as we have seen. Of course, economic interests were undeniably present since the agreement was to be struck by Canada's two major trading partners. However, as Tom Keating analyses it, 'the formation of the Bretton Woods system was an important part of the Canadian effort to establish an international order that would be based on multilateral cooperation'.[34]

Among the main actors then involved were St-Laurent, of course, and most importantly, his deputy minister at the time, Lester Bowles Pearson. Along with a group of dedicated officials, they were to be key architects directly involved in the crafting of Canada's place in the world for the next twenty years. Such stability obviously helped to incarnate 'the government's commitment to "constructive international action" through international organization, based on the principles set forth by St-Laurent in the Gray Lecture'.[35] The inspiration and the values from which these first senior Foreign Affairs officers worked would last even longer, ultimately structuring what has been dubbed Canada's foreign policy's Golden Age, an epoch that has deeply influenced much of Canada's international actions up to the present day.

2.2 Values and the Chrétien Government

More recently, the role of values was highlighted in the 1995 white paper, *Canada in the World*. This document identified 'three pillars' on which Canada's foreign policy would rest: 'the promotion of prosperity'; 'the protection of security within a stable global framework'; and 'the projection of Canadian values and culture'. In terms of values, *Canada in the World* states that 'Canadian values, and their projection abroad, are key to the achievement of prosperity within Canada and to the protection of global security'.[36] In other words, although ranked third, this pillar is essential to meeting objectives that are more directly linked to economics and security. Moreover, it suggests the promotion of values should now be considered a foreign policy objective in and of itself. Obviously, this represents a new accent put on values, an emphasis that is not priceless, as we will see.

This new spotlight on values was largely the result of Lloyd Axworthy's efforts. First, as liberal foreign affairs critic in the 1980s and early 1990s, Axworthy was a prime actor in crafting the liberal foreign policy platform in view of the 1993 election,[37] which listed several value-related items. Once elected, the Liberals pursued their values-driven agenda. Among the engagements on which they followed up, one in particular helped to structure the use of values as an easily recognizable tool in the conduct of foreign policy, that is, the Canadian Centre for Foreign Policy Development to which I have already referred. In so doing, the Centre acted on two levels. First, it allowed citizens to engage with these issues and articulate

their thoughts and perceptions (in a word, their values). Second, the reports and papers published by the Centre advocated the importance of values as expressed by Canadians in CCFPD forums.[38] As a consequence, and in line with Lloyd Axworthy's policy choices, the third pillar became, under his tenure as Foreign Affairs minister, an unavoidable factor.

This was not the only value-oriented legacy Axworthy left. In fact, most of the actions for which he will be remembered as Foreign Affairs minister are along this line, and the promotion of the concept of human security falls squarely in this category. Human security is defined as 'a people-centred approach to foreign policy which recognizes that lasting stability cannot be achieved until people are protected from violent threats to their rights, safety or lives'.[39] The concept is clearly value-driven. Its importance has risen dramatically to the extent that Rob McRae does not hesitate to refer to a 'human security paradigm'.[40] Following this umbrella concept, better focussed initiatives were also part of Axworthy's legacy: the ban of anti-personnel landmines and the Ottawa protocol; the campaign to establish an International Criminal Court; and the fight against the use of child soldiers. These are probably the three best-known initiatives of the Axworthy years.[41] Clear links can be established between the values identified earlier and these foreign policy achievements.

Foreign Affairs ministers who followed in Axworthy's footsteps—namely John Manley and Bill Graham—did not espouse with the same fervour the importance given to values in Canadian foreign policy. In fact, after some frictions, including concurrent consultation processes held in the spring of 2003 by the CCFPD and by the Minister, Graham cut all funding to the Centre, which found itself with no other option but to fold. Nevertheless, the prominence of Canadian values in the Canadian public consciousness and among policy-makers was there to stay. It was no doubt present in the minds of most, on the morning of 11 September 2001.

2.3 Values and the Impact of 11 September

Although Canada was the lone partner ignored by President Bush as he thanked numerous countries from the rostrum in the House of the Representatives—it would take over three years before he officially acknowledged Canada's support in the immediate aftermath of 9/11—it is clear that Canada supported US interests in the hours and days during and after the terrorist attacks. To wit, Canada: harboured travellers stranded by the events of 9/11; it negotiated and, as we saw, implemented the 'smart border' accord; and it also tightened security measures including making major amendments to Canadian laws.

Why, then, did Chrétien and Martin give Washington negative answers regarding the war in Iraq and missile defence? It is important to keep in mind that, since the end of World War I, Canada has not accepted automatic involvement in any foreign conflicts. Ottawa has voiced these autonomist values towards Great Britain, starting with the Chanak crisis in 1925.[42] It also opposed the United States on the Vietnam War, a position made clear in Mike Pearson's speech at Temple University and which led to President Lyndon B. Johnson's cold reception of the Canadian leader the following day at Camp David.[43] Canada's autonomy and its unshakable belief in multilateralism have always been cornerstone values of Canadian foreign policy. This was most recently evident in Canada's military participation in Afghanistan, which occurred due to relevant United Nations resolutions.

Iraq, however, represented a different situation. Specifically, the United States' actions did not receive the support of a multilateral forum; hence, they were not endorsed by Canada. It is not that Canada was unsympathetic to the American position, even when the Canadian government was under considerable popular pressure to decline involvement. Notwithstanding this political stress, Canada tried to initiate a late proposal through the UN Security Council. Therefore, it is clear that Canadian multilateralist values were a major factor in Canada's policy toward Iraq.[44] As concerns missile defence, then Prime Minister Martin also insisted that militarization of space was contrary to Canadian values. This would not be the last time Martin would refer to values in his government's foreign policy.

2.4. Values and the IPS

In the spring of 2005, the Martin government tabled its *International Policy Statement*, a compound of 'White papers' covering all aspects of the foreign policy field: diplomacy, defence, development, and trade. The result was surprisingly different from the message carved in political platforms used in the June 2004 elections,[45] when most parties were sensitive to values, especially to the politico-operational component.

Scrutinizing the IPS, we see at once that all psycho-social values are mentioned and that four of the five that Lee indentified are met with favourable attention: respect for the environment, democracy and democratization, social equity, human rights, and tolerance. The only value that receives less attention is the inclusion of civil society in the foreign policy process. There are mentions of it as non-governmental input, but the perception we have from reading the Overview document is that it remains a minor actor in the foreign policy-making process: 'States remain the central actors on the global stage, but they are increasingly embedded in transnational linkages that diffuse power above to supranational frameworks and below to civil society. Individuals are playing a greater role in international affairs than ever before, with both positive and negative results.' This is, in fact, an evaluation that takes into account not only the potential contribution of civil society, but also problems that actors with individual interests (the states represent collective interests) can induce into the policy making process. This position no doubt also takes into account the breakage and violence that are sometimes associated with civil society protests (as in Seattle or Genoa), as well as the regalian power mentality that still impregnates some parts of the foreign policy making community.

One cannot ignore the fact that the final policy statement resulted from an effort to gather the thoughts of a number of departments; as a consequence, we could expect a dense presence of the politico-operational values in the IPS. This is indeed the case, since all identified values are present. The desire to see a 'rules-based and more predictable' international system agrees well with the promotion of the rule of law on the international scene and such a strong plea in favour of multilateralism hardly surprises. However, there are some innovations. For instance, peacekeeping, although present, is part of broader components, that is, democratization efforts and the review of the Canadian Armed Forces' mandates. As well, the value stating that Canada's security depends on the world's balance of power is now restricted to a continental dimension; the fact that security threats are now less related to large ideological plates that rub against each other, and are more associated with targeted acts of circumscribed origins, largely explains the new reading of a long-lasting value. This clearly shows that the government of Canada understood that it was necessary to adapt its foreign policy to a new environment—a challenge to which we will return soon. Similarly, one notes that the statement to the effect that security is a

necessary ingredient to warrant prosperity is still present, but, notably, priority is now given to security. Moreover, questions of security are not limited to traditional dimensions, but include other sectors such as health, information technology, and the environment. Lastly, international development is obviously present, but under a completely overhauled approach, in agreement with previous government-stated policies. We see that, although they are present, politico-operational values are unmistakably revamped, taking into consideration the new international environment.

Despite efforts to stay away from the 'promotion' approach, the presence of elements belonging to the two groups of values confirms to some extent that Canadian values always bear an important weight in Canadian foreign policy. The Overview document clearly states that they still guide Canada's international action.

2.5 Values and the Harper Government

The platform that brought the Harper government to power stated that 'Canada's foreign policy reflects true Canadian values and advances Canada's national interests'. It goes on, outlining the need for Canada to 'articulate [its] core values of freedom, democracy, the rule of law, human rights, free markets, and free trade—and compassion for the less fortunate—on the international stage'.[46] Once the Harper government was in power, however, the context was different: constant reports indicated Canadian foreign policy was determined in the Prime Minister's Office. Perhaps more importantly, Harper's primary interest in foreign policy, from his own admission,[47] is not high while the width of foreign policy topics in which he is interested and involved seems rather narrow.[48] It is also important to note that the relationship between the department of Foreign Affairs and the Prime Minister's

Office is perceived as not very harmonious. These are indications that there could be a break in the use of values as a basis for Canadian foreign policy.

There are few signs that emerged from political circles. Of course, we see in the Speech from the Throne of April 2006 that 'this Government is committed to supporting Canada's core values of freedom, democracy, the rule of law and human rights around the world'.[49] Values are also referred to when a specific value-related topic is discussed in the House or in Committees, and CIDA continues to promote democracy, human rights, gender equity, and preservation of the environment. But most of the statements issued by politicians—or even by government officials—refer to values much less often than their predecessors' did. This could be explained by the fact that the Harper government was served by rather weak foreign affairs ministers who did not articulate their own views as Axworthy or even Graham did under the Chrétien government, since their impact on the shaping of foreign policy seems to have been minimal.

A good example of the place given to values in the Harper government's foreign policy is found in the sole major foreign policy-related policy paper the Harper government issued in the four years following its first election. The *Canada First Defence Strategy*[50] is a logistics statement that presents an investment plan for the strengthening of the Canadian Armed Forces along three 'roles' (national, continental and international); six missions (daily domestic and continental operations, support to major international events in Canada, response to major terrorist attacks, support to civilian authorities during a crisis in Canada, major international operations for an extended period, response to crises elsewhere in the world for shorter periods); and four 'pillars' (personnel, equipment, readiness, and infrastructure). It is noted that the Canadian industry will benefit from this plan.

This description does not refer to values, however, but rather to material objectives or operational operations. It is not at odds with the statement itself since, with the notable exception of an implicit reference to multilateralism, no values are used to support or justify the policy. In the speech he delivered at the launch of the policy, Prime Minister Harper referred to history, portraying Canadian military achievements as 'great milestones of our nationhood'.[51] And when explaining Canada's third role, as identified in the policy, quick appeals are made to security, prosperity, and humanitarian interventions, a topic echoed by the Minister of National Defence in his own remarks.[52]

The fact that the Harper government seems to make a lesser use of values will need further research to establish whether this is a specific feature of a minority government more concerned with domestic politics; whether it is the expression of a departure from soft power to align more closely with an American-type, interest-driven foreign policy; whether it is the result of a weaker interest in these questions on the part of the Prime Minister; or whether it is a symptom of the reported rupture between foreign policy-makers in Pearson Building and the political apparatus at PMO. More importantly, it would be interesting to see, with the distance of time, whether we have witnessed a turning point in how Canadian foreign policy is thought of and shaped.

3. PLANNING FUTURE RESPONSES

These episodes are useful to demonstrate how these Canadian values can influence Canadian foreign policy. Politically, at times when domestic perceptions and domestic politics were of the utmost importance for the prime minister, it has been difficult to go against them. Moreover, Canadians were assured by Axworthy and CCFPD that their say in foreign policy-making was important. Going against this trend was not an option for Jean Chrétien, while Harper seems to make a more tentative use of values in his foreign policy-making approach.

A question remains though: although values generally seem solidly anchored in the Canadian foreign policy landscape, are they enough to carry Canada in a new environment, where actors are more numerous than ever and where consensus will probably more difficult to reach? I submit here that, should Canada wish to continue using or return to values as a core basis for its foreign policy, it will have to take into consideration a number of challenges that, if not met properly, could jeopardize the country's possibilities of success and influence on the international scene. These challenges have taken on a new meaning in the post-9/11 international system, which is not always consistent with 'traditional' Canadian foreign policy values. In this section, it will be argued that Canada must acknowledge, and work at taking into consideration, these new challenges related to the organization of foreign policy, the respect for Canadian autonomy, the priorities that need to be recognized, and the will to include new actors in the policy process.[53]

3.1 Organization

In terms of organization, there are four key[54] challenges that address two fundamental aspects of foreign policy organization: the identification of problems and policy priorities; and how to institutionally respond to these pressures. First, as already noted, there is a need for Canadian foreign policy to adapt itself to a rapidly evolving international environment. Specifically, this section will argue that the United States is not the neighbour it used to be; that peacekeeping has shifted from traditional Pearsonian values; that trade is now conducted in an increasingly neo-liberal rules-based

environment; and that international relations now include a wide range of international, transnational, and domestic non-governmental actors.

In itself, this new context poses the challenge of adaptability in general, but it also questions the advisability of operating from past foreign policy practices. Here, the first element that comes to mind is that Canada has to question its hallmark practice of multilateralism. Not that multilateralism is the only expression of Canadian foreign policy,[55] and not that multilateralism should be completely rejected, but Ottawa needs to focus greater attention on extended bilateralism in aid, diplomacy, security, and trade. As well, the ever-growing role of NGOs brings new actors to the international table and, if multilateralism is sometimes the right way to approach them, it cannot be considered the only way, due to the eclectic nature of this new family.

Together, these two elements create an additional organizational challenge: solving the heritage/innovation dilemma. Generally speaking, foreign policy is a world in which the importance of past practices as grounds for future action is a rule of thumb. Clearly, long-term policy is the standard. In Canada's case, such an attitude of carefulness and respect for established practices is increased tenfold by the aura that still surrounds this famous 'Golden Era' characterized by Pearsonian internationalism at its best. As I have outlined, however, a newly defined world calls for a new approach. Here, the challenge rests in the bureaucratic response that will be given to the new foreign policy endeavours upon which Canada must embark. In other words, bureaucratic political culture influences how Canada crafts its foreign policy, but this culture has to adapt to a new reality. Keeping with policies defined by past actions might be comforting, but it induces a lack of flexibility, and Canada requires the opposite. The challenge is to strike the right balance between successful practices dictated by bureaucratic political culture and innovation. This is what I call the innovation/heritage dilemma.

Some of these needed innovations could come from the involvement of other departments in the conduct of foreign affairs. Historically, when Wilfrid Laurier created a Foreign Affairs division within his government, it was to ensure cohesiveness among actions taken on the international scene by different ministries. We might soon come full circle since more and more issues 'belonging' to line departments are dealt with at the international level. As a result, most—if not all—departments in Ottawa house an international division. Therefore, there is a need to define the role these other departments will play in Canada's international relations, as well as a need to establish how to integrate their efforts into a genuine governmental—not a single department's—action. Since turf wars will no doubt characterize such harmonization, this, in itself, represents quite a challenge.

These first four challenges set the table for a better organized foreign policy community. Should they be met, they will provide Canada with adequate tools. The next group of challenges, those related to the respect Canada must re-earn in the international community, will bring an important complement in terms of the leverage Canadian foreign policy needs.

3.2 Respect

Evaluating respect is problematic.[56] By many accounts, Canada has gained its self-proclaimed 'middle power' status based on historical contributions to the international community. No longer a military power, Canada still plays an important role in the training of other countries' armed forces, including those of the United States, and its performance in theatres of operation, such as Afghanistan, is deemed to be nothing less than

remarkable. Despite economic challenges, Canada also remains a member of the G8, and uses its influence to steer key economic debates. Far from meeting internationally set targets, Canadian aid is appreciated not only because it is much needed, but because it comes from a country that has no imperialistic agendas associated with it. Regardless, Canada's status is based on past actions and if it wants to avoid being pushed to the sidelines, Canada must regain its worldwide credibility and respect. This can be achieved if Canada meets three specific, but related, challenges.

All three of these challenges are directly linked to Canada's relationship with the United States, a relationship most countries envy. As noted earlier, Canada has historically defended its interests, but for the most part it has maintained the respect of its southern neighbour. Despite periods of tension, Ottawa and Washington have a unique relationship. A specific example is Canada's role in NORAD, which is the only foreign defence institution in which the Canada and United States share command and control. Moreover, when Canada succeeds in motivating an American President to fight apartheid, as it did during the Mulroney era, other countries look at Canada as a credible broker in the world of international relations. Therefore, much of Canada's international influence depends on its relationship with the US. This is why the 'respect' factor, the one that gives Canada international 'political capital', depends in large part on the good health of this relationship.

The first challenge is linked to domestic pressures; many Canadians are ill at ease when Canada's choices mirror US policies too closely. The once-famous 'I am Canadian' beer ad might be an anecdotal evidence of such sensitivity, but it remains that Canada must establish a clear difference between its practices and US policies. As noted, this strategy poses an obvious challenge based on the historical and contemporary nature of the bilateral relationship. In this regard, multilateralism, with a focus on post-conflict resolution, the environment, and other policy areas, could provide a means by which Canada could differentiate itself from the United States. Not that Ottawa should be indifferent to Washington—no country should deliberately isolate such an important economic and political partner. Rather, quite the opposite situation should prevail.

Therefore, a second priority is to re-earn respect in Washington. Canada must do so if it ever wants to re-gain respect elsewhere in the world. For indeed, being different from the United States does not at all mean being indifferent to what is decided in Washington. In fact, the more often the United States is brought on board with Canadian initiatives, the better it is for Canada. And this will be done only when policy makers in the two capitals are on the same wavelength. Due to its middle power status and its soft power approach, Canada needs to solicit support and resources in order to reach its international goals. Succeeding in convincing the United States adds a lot of weight to one's side of the balance. And, put simply, the only way Canada can succeed in balancing independent policy choices and American support is if Canada earns 'respect' in Washington. In this regard, the too-numerous hesitations that preceded withdrawal of Canadian support for American proposals, such as the call to participate in the war in Iraq or in the anti-ballistic missile initiative, caused more damage than a simple, straightforward decline of the invitation received.

The Harper government, for its part, never showed any desire to be respected in Washington. It went to the other extreme, aligning itself very closely with George W. Bush's policies, even though the Prime Minister did not associate himself closely with the President. In contrast, during the Mulroney years, the leaders of both countries entertained an opened friendship, but Canada was never afraid to 'speak truth to power' when its values and interests were challenged by American positions. It remains to be seen what will characterize the Obama–Harper relationship. First indications are that Ottawa is not on the new Administration's priority list, while the Canadian Prime Minister has not openly expressed any specific interest in reframing his rapports with the new tenant of 1600 Pennsylvania Avenue.

When one refers to being 'respected' in Washington, the next question that comes to mind is: What about sovereignty? Sovereignty is at risk when exogenous pressures are exercised on a government's autonomy. As Stephen Krasner[57] has demonstrated, sovereignty is a multi-faceted concept. I had the opportunity to analyse elsewhere what aspects of Canadian sovereignty have been challenged in the aftermath of 9/11.[58] Historically, it is noticeable that whenever Canada has had a direct contact in the White House, Canadian sovereignty has not been in jeopardy. Why would the US threaten the sovereignty of such a good friend? Doing so would dramatically increase suspicion among other American allies. Conversely, when Canada ignores the US, why does the US pay attention to Canada? Oddly enough, it is when Canada keeps too much distance from its neighbour that its sovereignty is most at risk. The impact of this equation is clear: when Washington shows more respect for Canadian sovereignty Canada earns more respect in the world.

3.3 Prioritizing

Already, one has a sense of the tremendous task ahead. But from where should we start? In itself, this question centres on the issue of capacity. Recent history has seen Canada move from Jean Chrétien's leadership, where foreign policy was not always a priority, to that of Paul Martin, who considered most international commitments important: summits; the establishment of new institutions (namely, the L20); peacemaking in the Middle East, Haiti, Darfur, Libya, and Asia; and of course, a revamped relationship with the United States, which cooled after the government turned down participation in the SDI. The latest political developments in Canada brought to power a prime minister who shows minimal interest in world affairs. The problem is related to a prioritization of the issues to be tackled, but perhaps more importantly of the resources to be mustered. Already, Canada had altered its priorities for this reason and the severe cuts made by the Harper government exacerbated this reality, except perhaps in the military sector. In view of maintaining the prominence of Canadian values in the implementation of its foreign policy, Canada will need to take up this challenge, which is particularly difficult in times of budget constraints. If not, Canada runs the risk that, sooner rather than later, the whole of its foreign policy could be characterized as 'an inch thick, a mile wide'. As a consequence, Canada must prioritize its actions in the world and the resources that it will channel towards their achievement.

This being established, we must acknowledge that defining priorities is not an easy task. However, to ensure its ongoing relevance, Canada must define itself as a global actor. Specifically, it should more clearly define new or renewed foreign policy objectives. One area at issue is the North, with its economic potential and environmental sensitivity. There is also the Middle East, a region central to the pursuit of global stability, and in which Canada has a history of involvement (who does not remember Pearson's role in the Suez Crisis and peacekeeping on Golan Heights?). In addition, Canada should focus its attention on the economic and military power of Europe and Asia. Finally, there is Africa, a continent that Canada has pledged to support but that requires a strengthened commitment. Obviously, it is impossible to achieve all

of these goals and so Canada must be strategic in its global affairs. In doing so, it will provide the Canadian government with a better orientation for its foreign policy.

3.4 Inclusiveness

After considering all these factors, only one remains and it is found closer to home. It is related to endogenous pressures that complement the exogenous pressures previously discussed. In both cases, the government's autonomy is challenged. This time, though, the challenge comes from national actors seeking to influence the federal government in the conduct of international relations and in the framing of its foreign policy. These actors come primarily from three fields: civil society with its collective need to be heard and welcomed by recent liberal governments; corporate interests—both from the business world and specific NGOs—who lobby for having their pet projects put on the government's priority list; and provinces who see, day after day, the impact of globalization assail their constitutional fields of responsibility.[59] Due to the increasing complexity of international developments, the Canadian government should establish working partnerships with these new actors. However, inclusiveness is not something natural in the foreign policy-maker's chasse gardée. Pooling these domestic resources towards common foreign policy objectives is a challenge that cannot be left for future consideration. The price for neglecting these interests is high: a foreign policy lacking in transparency, accountability, and legitimacy. Here, the last of Lee's psycho-social values, that is civil society involvement, takes its full meaning.

This list of challenges is impressive. It covers most aspects of foreign policy-making and gives a good idea of the scope of Canada's priorities, especially in terms of its interests and values. The most important element to be retained, though, is not the length of the road leading to Canada's recovery of its former stance in the world. It is more the intricacy of the situation that stands out. This is due in large part to the close, interdependent relationship that binds the challenges. In order to face a world redefined after the events of 9/11, Canada needs the tools, the leverage, the political capital, and the appropriate orientations, as well as adequate partnerships. All these elements are represented in the challenges identified here. Will these prevail in the minds of those who will influence and shape future foreign policymaking in Canada?

CONCLUSION

This chapter started by positioning Canada's foreign policy within the parameters associated with the use of soft power, and more precisely with one of the currencies that is characteristics of soft power: values. We first defined what could be included in this realm, in terms of both psychosocial and politico-organizational values. We then explored through history and more recent times the place that values have taken in the shaping of Canadian foreign policy, before considering a few contemporary challenges Canada must address in order to retain values as an important contributor to the country's international stance.

A first conclusion that can be drawn is that values are present during most of the period this analysis covers. Of course, they vary in intensity depending on the context and on the importance a prime minister gives to each of them. We may say, for example, that the impact of values on foreign policy has been less evident since the coming to power of the Harper government (after a slight decline in importance during the formulation of the IPS), compared to the impact they had ten years earlier in the *Canada in the World* policy paper. Is this a trend or is it strictly related to

individuals, an important factor that other studies have revealed?[60]

A second set of questions is inspired by the observation that it is under Martin and Harper that changes occurred in the importance given to values in the foreign policy discourse. Chrétien was first elected in 1963 under the leadership of Pearson. Although Martin's father was Pearson's Secretary of State for External Affairs, Martin himself did not have a direct relationship with actors of the Golden Age. Does this mean that the use of values is a generational practice that faded out with the last political actors who were personally involved in the construction of Pearsonian internationalism? This in turn brings up the question of values as a soft power currency: as Canada apparently gives a lesser weight to values in its foreign policy advocacy, are we witnessing a departure from the use of soft power by Canada or will Canada rely on other 'currencies' such as culture, institutions, or policies?

Finally, is the fact that both Martin and Harper, for different reasons and with different objectives in mind, were more inclined to reinforce the relationship Canada entertains with its southern neighbour, an indication that Canada is also aligning its foreign policy to match Washington's? In this regard, how will Canada take into account the numerous challenges outlined here while keeping its specificity as an international actor? And as a result, will this help Canada regain part of its clout and prestige on the world scene?

As we can see, this study has brought some answers, but has also inspired several questions that will find their solutions in further research. One thing is clear, however; if the government acknowledges that there is a definite need to give values the importance they use to have, it would be wise to draw on them to help Canada to look straight ahead towards the world in which it evolves, rather than backwards towards comforting past glories.

Key Terms

Politico-Operational Values
Psycho-Social Values
Soft Power

Notes

1. About this concept, see John Holmes, *Canada: A Middle-Aged Power* (Toronto: McClelland and Stewart, 1976).

2. An idea brought by James Eayers in 'Definig a New Place for Canada in the Hierarchy of World Power', *International Perspectives*, May–June (1975): 15–24; it was developed by David Dewitt and John Kirton in their book *Canada as a Principal Power* (Toronto: John Wiley, 1983).

3. Stephen Clarkson; *An Independent Foreign Policy for Canada?* (Toronto: McClelland and Stewart, 1968).

4. This debate is analyzed in John Kirton, *Canadian Foreign Policy in a Changing World*, (Toronto: Nelson Education, 2007, Appendix 1); and in Michael K. Hawes, *Principal Power, Middle Power, or Satellite? Competing Perspectives in the Study of Canadian Foreign Policy* (Toronto: York Research Programme in Strategic Studies, 1984).

5. Joseph S. Nye, *Bound to Lead: The Changing Nature of American Power* (New York: Basic Books, 1990).

6. Joseph S. Nye, *Soft Power. The Means to Success in World Politics* (New York: BBS Public Affairs, 2004), x.

7. Joseph S. Nye (2004), 8.

8. House of Commons, *Debates* (Ottawa, 2003b); *Debates* (Ottawa, 2005).

9. Department of Foreign Affairs and International Trade, *Canada in the World* (1995), http//www.dfait-maeci.gc.ca/foreign_policy/cnd-world.

10. Lloyd Axworthy, *Navigating a New World: Canada's Global Future* (Toronto: Knopf Canada, 2003).

11. Denis Stairs, 'Myths, Morals and Reality in Canadian Foreign Policy', *International Journal*, vol. 58, no 2 (2003): 239–56.

12. Jack L Granatstein, 'The Importance of Being Earnest: Promoting Canada's National Interests through Tighter Ties with the US' *Benefactors Lecture 2003*. (C.D. Howe Institute: 2003, 19), http://www.cdhowe.org/pdf/benefactors_lecture_2003.pdf.

13. Jennifer Welsh, *At Home in the World: Canada's Global Vision for the 21st Century* (Toronto: Harper Collins, 2004, 203, emphasis in the original text).

14. Bernard L. Simonin, 'Nation Branding and Public diplomacy: Challenges and Opportunities', *The Fletcher Forum of World Affairs*, vol. 32 no 3 (2008): 21.

15. Pico Iyer, 'Canada: Global Citizen' in *Canadian Geographic*, Special 75th Anniversary Issue, (2004): 62–9.

16. Steve Lee, 'Canadian values in Canadian foreign policy' in *Canadian Foreign Policy/La Politique étrangère du Canada* 10, 1 (2002): 1–9.

17. The Center was conceived as a think thank to be housed in the foreign affairs building and its key mandate was to consult Canadians from all walks of life in an attempt to 'democratize' the foreign policy process. It was former Foreign Affairs minister Lloyd Axworthy who implemented this initiative. Steve Lee was its director.

18. Ibid, Steve Lee, (2002, 1).

19. Officially, a conflict in the agenda was evocated, but as Radio-Canada reported: 'Même s'il a rappelé plusieurs fois qu'il n'assistait pas aux Jeux pour des raisons de calendrier et non pour des raisons politiques, Stephen Harper est très critique du bilan des droits de l'homme en Chine'. Radio-Canada.ca, Agence France Presse, Associated Press, and Reuters, *Harper brille par son absence*. August 8, 2008. http://www.radio-canada.ca/nouvelles/International/2008/08/07/012-pekin-harper-emerson.shtml.

20. House of Commons, *A Contribution To The Foreign Policy Dialogue* (Report of The Standing Committee On Foreign Affairs And International Trade, 2003a, 12), http://www.parl.gc.ca/InfoComDoc/37/2/FAIT/Studies/Reports/fairp06/faitrp06-e.pdf.

21. They also add foreign aid as a value and spend most of the section on values considering its aspects. I have not retained aid in the psycho-social values for, as the parliamentary committee's report demonstrates, it is a value that origins from the government spokespeople they heard. It will then be considered under the next section.

22. Department of Foreign Affairs and International Trade, *A Dialogue on Foreign Policy: Report to Canadians* (2003b, 12), http://www.dfait-maeci.gc.ca/cip-pic/participate/Final Report.pdf.

23. Department of Foreign Affairs and International Trade, *A dialogue on Foreign Policy. Consultation Paper* (2003a), http://www.dfait-maeci.gc.ca/cip-pic/participate/fpd-en.asp.

24. Tom Keating, *Canada And World Order: The Multilateralist Tradition In Canadian Foreign Policy* (Toronto: Oxford University Press, 2002).

25. The distinction between the three concepts is explained in other chapters of this book.

26. United Nations, *Ranking of Military and Civilian Police Contributions to UN Operations* (2005), http://www.un.org/Depts/dpko/dpko/contributors/2005/January2005_2.pdf.

27. http://www.operationspaix.net/IMG/pdf/CanadaUNPKOF.pdf ; Canada reached its lowest point (61st) in 2007, but was among the leading counties making a contribution to UN peace operations, in 1992–3.

28. John J. Mearsheimer, *The Tragedy of Great Power Politics* (New York: Norton, 2001).

29. *L'aide au développement en 2008 à son plus haut niveau.* http://www.oecd.org/document/35/0,3343,fr_2649_34487_42461389_1_1_1_1,00.html.

30. Since the creation of the department in 1909, only two men (Charles Murphy, 1909–11 in the Laurier Government,and William James Roche,1911–12 in the Borden government) held the portfolio while not being prime minister at the same time. It is important to note, however, that this was in the early beginnings of the department, when Canada had no autonomous international role; as soon as Prime Minister Borden saw an opportunity to get Canada involved internationally, he made sure the Prime Minister was the actor involved. Such an arrangement continued until an aging Mackenzie King—he was to resign two years later after 24 years at the helm—shared the task with Louis St-Laurent in 1946.

31. Department of External Affairs, *Statements and Speeches* (Microform, 1947).

32. On this, see John Hilliker, Le ministère des affaires extérieures du Canada, vol. 1: 'Les années de formation 1909–1946' (Québec: Presses de l'Université Laval and Institut d'administration publique du Canada, 1990, 359–62).

33. This article reads: 'The Parties will contribute toward the further development of peaceful and friendly international relations by strengthening their free institutions, by bringing about a better understanding of the principles upon which these institutions are founded, and by promoting conditions of stability and well-being. They will seek to eliminate conflict in their international economic policies and will encourage economic collaboration between any or all of them.' http://www.nato.int/docu/basictxt/treaty.htm.

34. Tom Keating (2002, 44). Keating's excellent analysis provides an enlightening reading on the basis on which Canadian diplomacy then operated.

35. Don Barry and John Hilliker, 'The Department of External Affairs in the Post-War Years, 1946–1968' in *The Canadian Foreign Service in Transition*, ed., Donald C. Story (Toronto: Canadian Scholars' Press, 1993), 11.

36. Ibid.

37. A preliminary document had been prepared by Axworthy, then Chair of the Liberal caucus committee of foreign affairs and national defence and his vice-chair, Christine Stewart: the *Liberal Foreign Policy Handbook.*

For the platform itself, see: Liberal Party of Canada, *Pour la création d'emplois et la relance de l'économie. Le plan d'action libéral pour le Canada* (Ottawa: Liberal Party, 1993).

38. These forums were organized from coast to coast, between 1996 and 2001, under specific themes: communications, Asia-Pacific relations, circumpolar relations, peacebuilding, the UN, Africa, the Americas, etc. According the CCFPD chair, their objective was to contribute public advice to the long-term development of Canadian foreign policy.

39. Department of Foreign Affairs, http://www.humansecurity.gc.ca/menu-en.asp.

40. Rob McCrae, 'La sécurité humaine dans le contexte de la mondialisation', in *Sécurité humaine et nouvelle diplomatie: protection des personnes, promotion de la paix*, eds., Rob McCrae and Don Hubert (Montréal and Kingston: McGill-Queens University Press, 2001).

41. For a better understanding of Lloyd Axworthy's legacy, see Fen Osler Hampson, Norman Hillmer and Maureen Apel Molot, *Canada Among Nations 2001: The Axworthy Legacy* (Toronto: Oxford University Press).

42. Nelson Michaud, *L'énigme du Sphinx: regards sur la vie politique d'un nationaliste (1910–1926)* (Sainte-Foy: Les Presses de l'Université Laval, 1998).

43. Greg Donaghy, *Tolerant Allies: Canada & the United States 1963–1968* (Montreal and Kingston: McGill Queen's University Press, 2002).

44. In fact, however, Canada was involved, keeping operational vessels in the Persian Gulf. This aspect was reported, but nobody really paid attention to it. All that mattered to Canada was to portray itself as adhering, defending, and acting according to strongly held values. This was at the heart of the Canadian argumentation against participation.

45. Nelson Michaud, 'The Canadian Response to 9-11: Answering the American Call or Calling for Canadian Values?' (paper presented at the International Studies Association, Honolulu, 2005).

46. Conservative Party of Canada, *Stand up for Canada: Conservative Party of Canada Federal Election Platform 2006.* (Ottawa, 2006), 45.

47. John J. Noble, 'PMO/PCO/DFAIT: Serving the Prime Minister's Foreign policy Agenda' in Jean Dandelin and Daniel Schwanen, ed., *Canada Among Nations 2007: What Room for Manoeuvre?* (Montreal and Kingston: McGill Queen's University Press, 2008: 45).

48. Nelson Michaud, *Reading between the (Blue) Lines: How Can One Anticipate the Future of Canadian Foreign Policy under the Harper Government?* Paper presented at the International Studies Association Convention, New York, February 2009.

49. Government of Canada, *Speech from the Throne*, April 4, 2006. http://pm.gc.ca/eng/media.asp?id=1087.

50. Department of National Defence, *Canada First* Defense Strategy, http://www.forces.gc.ca/site/pri/first-premier/June18_0910_CFDS_english_low-res.pdf , May 2008.

51. Prime Minister's Office, 'PM unveils Canada First Defence Strategy', Speech delivered in Halifax, May 12, 2008. http://www.pm.gc.ca/eng/media.asp?id=2098.

52. Minister of National Defense, 'The Canada First Defence Strategy: Excellence at Home and Leadership Abroad'. Speech delivered in Halifax, May 12, 2008. http://www.forces.gc.ca/site/news-nouvelles/news-nouvelles-eng.asp?cat=15&id=2652.

53. I have identified the following ten challenges first, from a reading of the general situation, that is, the world political and economic trends and Canada's degree of preparation to deal with them. I also took into consideration the many opinions and analyses that have been voiced over the last few years, by analyst, observers, practitioners, and academics. Finally, I relied on scholarly presentations published in venues such as the *International Journal*, *Canadian Foreign Policy*, or the series *Canada Among Nations*, as well as recent academic published books.

54. Not that the other elements are of a lesser importance, but these first four items, need to be addressed before any further action is taken.

55. Historically, the Canada–UK relationship and now the one with the US are notable exceptions.

56. Respect is a difficult concept to measure. However, it can de said that in the international community, when a country's action is not opposed by a mighty partner, when a country's leader can pull its weight when participating in international talks, when the more powerful state signals to other international actors that this country matters, one can conclude that this country has earned respect from the more powerful one.

57. Stephen D. Krasner, *Sovereignty: Organized Hypocrisy* (Princeton: Princeton University Press, 1999).

58. Nelson Michaud, 'Souveraineté et sécurité: Le dilemme de la politique étrangère canadienne dans l'après 11 septembre', *Études internationales*, vol. 33, no 4, (2002): 647–65.

59. Nelson Michaud, 'Le Québec dans le monde: faut-il redessiner les fondements de son action?' in *L'État québécois au XXIème siècle*, ed., Robert Bernier (Québec: Presses de l'Université du Québec, 2004b, 125–68).

60. On this, see Nelson Michaud, 'The Prime Minister, PMO and PCO: Makers of Canadian Foreign Policy?', in *Handbook of Canadian Foreign Policy*, ed., Michaud, Nelson, James, Patrick and O'Reilly, Marc J. (Lanham: Lexington Books, 2006: 21–48); Adam Chapnick, 'A Question of Degree: The Prime Minister, Political Leadership, and Canadian Foreign Policy', in *The World in Canada: Diaspora, Demography, and Domestic Politics*, ed., David Carment and David Bercuson (Montreal and Kingston: McGill Queen's University Press, 2008: 16–30); Nelson Michaud, *Setting the Canadian Foreign Policy Agenda 1984–2009: Prime Ministers as Prime Actors?* Paper presented at the conference 'Serving the National Interest: Canada's Department of Foreign Affairs and International Trade 1909–2009', University of Calgary, January 29, 2009, under revision to be published.

25

UNWILLING INTERNATIONALISM OR STRATEGIC INTERNATIONALISM? CANADIAN CLIMATE POLICY UNDER THE CONSERVATIVE GOVERNMENT

Heather A. Smith

A. INTRODUCTION

In May of 2009, Prime Minister Harper, speaking in Afghanistan stated:

> As part of the family of civilized nations, we have a national obligation to do our part to contribute to our peace and security. As a prosperous and free country, we have the moral duty to share our good fortune, our freedoms and our opportunities with the citizens of the world who have too long had to endure violence, oppression and privation. (Office of the Prime Minister, 2009)

In the same month, Environment Minister Jim Prentice, in reference to ongoing international negotiations on climate change, stated, 'it is time to get serious—to make tangible progress through principled pragmatism that

will move the real toward the ideal' (Environment Canada, 2009d: 2).

These comments on Canada in the world and on Canadian climate change diplomacy can be held in contrast to comments made by Prime Minister Harper in 2007, when he likened Canada to a wolverine—'fierce about protecting our territory' (Office of the Prime Minister, 2007a)—and to acerbic statements made by Rona Ambrose in 2006 (Environment Canada, 2006b) who, as Environment Minister, claimed shock at the 'territoriality . . . driven by self-serving politics and self-righteousness' related to the Kyoto Protocol that she had observed.

What do we do with all these competing images of Canada? Is Canada now to be understood as a wolverine—snapping at others about territoriality? Or is Canada to be understood as a force for positive change? Does the invocation of obligations to others and pragmatism in international negotiations—ideas consistent with conceptions of internationalism—mean that internationalism is relevant to our understanding of Canadian foreign policy during the Harper era? More specifically, is internationalism relevant to our understanding of Canadian climate change diplomacy since 2006?

As is too often the case, relevance, like beauty, is in the eye of the beholder. As odd as this observation may appear, it is nonetheless appropriate. As will be seen, if we adopt a minimalist liberal and state-centric interpretation of internationalism it is possible to argue that, in the case of climate change, the Harper government is an unwilling internationalist. However, if we problematize internationalism as defined in Kim Richard Nossal's 'Pinchpenny Diplomacy' and consider it through the lens of critical theory, we find that behind Conservative claims of consensus building and so-called commitments to multilateral processes are practices and policies that are self-interested, divisive, and anthropocentric. From a critical perspective, Canada uses the internationalist lexicon for strategic purposes to reflect attention away from the true nature of Canadian climate change diplomacy.

B. STARTING POINT(S)

Prior to engaging in the analysis of internationalism and the Harper government's climate change policy, two fundamental assumptions that inform this article must be articulated. First, climate change policy is a foreign policy issue and, as such, is an appropriate case by which to examine the currency of internationalism. While climate change is difficult to pigeonhole into either domestic or international spheres, an examination of Canadian climate change diplomacy is relevant to our understanding of how Canada operates internationally. Since the late 1980s, with the emergence of climate change on the international political agenda, climate change has demanded time, resources, and

attention of numerous federal departments and agencies including Foreign Affairs, Environment Canada, Natural Resources Canada, the Privy Council Office, and the Prime Minister's Office. Canadian political leaders have articulated visions of Canada as a key actor in the international climate change regime but these visions too often have not been matched by appropriate action. The visions and the actions require our scrutiny. Our governments must be kept accountable for their contribution to the success or failure of efforts to combat climate change. Moreover, climate change is an issue that is having an impact on our lives— now. It is not far away and distant, something that will happen in fifty years. For these reasons, climate change merits examination.

Second, it is beyond the scope of this article to provide extensive background on Canadian climate change policy prior to the Harper government, but there is a substantive body of information available to those interested in pre-2006 Canadian climate change policy (see Bernstein, 2003; Broadhead, 2001; Harrison, 2007; Jaccard et al., 2006; MacDonald and Smith, 1999–2000; May, 2002; Simpson, Jaccard, and Rivers, 2007; Smith, 2002; 2008; 2008–9). The absence of an in-depth analysis of the Chrétien and Martin governments, in particular, does not mean that the Liberal governments were somehow more 'internationalist' than the Harper government. During the Chrétien era, ministers and negotiators behaved like bullies in international fora, placed economics before the environment, and never genuinely engaged in domestic emissions reductions at home. While the respective Liberal governments did try to cover themselves in the cloak of green internationalism, their self-interested diplomatic activities and domestic inaction belied claims that the Canadian government believed that climate change was a threat to humanity, and that Canadians were leaders on climate change (see Environment Canada,

2001, and Environment Canada, 2002a; Environment Canada, 2002b; Environment Canada, 2002c; Smith, 2008–9). The Liberal rhetoric was empty, but what about the current Conservative government? Does internationalism have any relevance to the current government? To respond to this question we first need to define internationalism.

C. DEFINING INTERNATIONALISM?

Defining internationalism and its constituent parts is easier said than done. Scholars from various perspectives have engaged in debates about both the definition of internationalism and the relevance of internationalism (see Munton, 2002–3; Kirton, 2007; Pratt, 1990; Neufeld, 1995; and Smith, 2003, 2008–9). To add another layer, assessments of internationalism are often linked to the vast literature on Canada's role and status (see, for example, Black, and Smith, 1993; Hawes, 1984; Kirton, 2007; Molot, 1990; Nossal, Roussel, and Paquin, 2010). As well, articles that define a particular diplomatic style such as pulpit diplomacy (Hampson and Oliver, 1998) or niche diplomacy (Cooper, 1995; Potter, 1996–7; Smith, 2000) have embedded and sometimes explicit assumptions about the characteristics of Canadian diplomatic practice. Simply put, there is no consensus on the elements or the purpose of internationalism and we should not take internationalism as a given. With that in mind, I now turn to the conceptualization of internationalism that informs this analysis.

As suggested above, I begin with the definition of internationalism provided by Kim Richard Nossal in his seminal article, 'Pinchpenny Diplomacy' (Nossal, 1998–9). In that article he defines internationalism as having four characteristics. First, he makes reference to multilateralism as a component of internationalism, although it is not given as much attention as his latter three components:

community, good international citizenship, and voluntarism. On community, Nossal writes, 'internationalism is, at bottom, directed towards creating, maintaining, and managing community at a global level' (Nossal, 1998–9: 98). Good international citizenship 'suggests that a country's diplomacy can be directed toward ameliorating the 'common weal' by taking actions explicitly designed to achieve that end' (Nossal, 1998–99: 99). Good international citizenship is designed to 'convince others to alter their behaviour and join in what ideally becomes a bandwagon effect' (Nossal, 1998–9: 100). Finally, internationalism is understood to be a 'voluntaristic form of diplomacy. . . . [I]t is an entirely optional form of statecraft—in the sense that one could get by without engaging in it' (Nossal, 1998–99: 100).

The definition of internationalism in the 'Pinchpenny Diplomacy' article is different from the one used in both Nossal's 1997 edition of *The Politics of Canadian Foreign Policy* and the forthcoming *International Policy and Politics in Canada*, authored by Kim Nossal, Stephane Roussel, and Stephane Paquin (2010).

In the 1997 edition of *The Politics of Canadian Foreign Policy*, internationalism is defined as having four elements, the first of which is responsibility. We are told that 'the notion of responsibility is the hallmark of internationalist statecraft: each state that has an interest in avoiding war is responsible for playing a constructive part in the management of conflict' (Nossal, 1997: 155). The second element, multilateralism, requires that, rather than acting unilaterally, states act in the 'larger interests of establishing and maintaining order within the community of states' (Nossal, 1997: 155). Third, internationalism involves a 'commitment to international institutions' (Nossal, 1997: 155), and fourth, 'support for institutions must be given concrete expression by a willingness to enter into prior commitments to use natural resources for the system as a whole' (Nossal, 1997: 155).

In *International Policy and Politics in Canada,* Nossal, Roussel, and Paquin offer a slightly modified definition of internationalism. For them, internationalism has five elements, four of which are almost identical to the four noted above. They add a fifth element which is 'the reinforcement of, and respect for, international law' (Nossal, Roussel, and Paquin, 2010: 24).

My preference is for the definition of internationalism in the 1998 'Pinchpenny Diplomacy' article. While all three definitions are state-centric and liberal interpretations of internationalism, the definition of internationalism in the 1998 article does not focus explicitly on the interests of states in avoiding war that is integral to the Nossal (1997) and Nossal, Roussel, and Paquin (2010) elements of responsibility. Consequently, the 1998 version of internationalism is more broadly applicable to issues outside the bounds of traditional conceptions of war and peace—such as climate change. Moreover, the definition in 'Pinchpenny Diplomacy' includes the concept of good international citizenship, which is not included as an element per se in either of the other two definitions. The obligation to others that infuses the notion of good international citizenship merits a central position in our analysis. Finally, Nossal (1998, 89) argued that under the Chrétien Liberals we witnessed a 'progressive retreat from internationalism'. He concluded that 'although the government remains concerned about community at a global level, there is no longer any great enthusiasm for voluntary acts of "good international citizenship"' (Nossal, 1998–9: 103). Nossal, Roussel, and Paquin (2010: 38–9) further suggest that we may be moving toward regionalism but the authors qualify this observation by noting, 'it is not clear that it [continentalism] has supplanted internationalism as the dominant idea of the early twenty-first century' (ibid, 42). The question of the currency of internationalism under the Harper government then remains open for examination.

It is also necessary to note that my work is informed by a critical perspective. I believe we can adopt the pinchpenny diplomacy version of internationalism and still engage in theorizing from a critical perspective that includes several elements. Related to the environment broadly, and climate change specifically, a critical perspective requires that we be suspicious about global environmental governance. Lorraine Elliott (2002: 58) reminds us that global environmental governance is about power relations and not just about international environmental institutions. She also (Elliott, 2002: 63) argues that while there is an increase in state-based negotiation on environmental issues, these negotiations are neither altogether global nor have they 'improved the state of the environment'. The critical theory approach to international environmental issues is also skeptical of assumptions that the market has the ability to respond to the problems and that sustainable development provides for the necessary environment–development balance (Broadhead, 2002: 23). More broadly, when we recall Robert Cox's statement (Cox, and Sinclair, 1996: 87) 'theory is always for someone and for some purpose' we are encouraged us to ask for whom? For whom is the policy discourse? Who has constructed it and what interests does it protect and promote? Who is included or excluded? By asking these questions, we can examine 'the many ways in which the prevailing order maintains its control of the debate by masking dangerous practices and packaging the debate in ways that obscure the destructive forces at work in the system' (Broadhead, 2002: 20).

These assumptions inform the analysis of Canadian climate change policy under the Harper government. We begin our analysis asking questions broadly consistent with the pinchpenny diplomacy version of internationalism and then we can ask questions consistent with a critical environmental approach. As will be seen, adopting a minimalist state-centric interpretation of internationalism provides for the possibility of considering the Harper climate change diplomacy to be internationalist, albeit unwillingly, while the critical perspective challenges us to think in different directions about the strategic purposes of an internationalist discourse.

D. CANADIAN CLIMATE CHANGE DIPLOMACY AND THE HARPER GOVERNMENT

In 2002 the Chrétien government ratified the Kyoto Protocol, thus committing Canada to meet a target of six per cent reductions of greenhouse gases from 1990 levels by 2008–2012. When the Harper government came into office in 2006, Canada was approximately 35 per cent over the Kyoto target (Environment Canada, 2006c) and there was concern that the Harper government would take Canada out of the Kyoto Protocol. After all, during the ratification debate in 2002, Stephen Harper had been critical of the imposition that 'made in Japan' (Smith, 2008–9: 53) commitments had had on Canada and he had referred to Kyoto, in a letter to Alliance Party members, as 'a socialist scheme to suck money out of rich countries' (Smith, 2008–9: 57). The Alliance Party (of which Harper was the leader) and other Kyoto critics had expressed concern about the economic cost of meeting Kyoto commitments, worried about being out of step with the United States, and rejected the idea that Canada had a historic responsibility to reduce emissions.

Yet, the Harper government stayed in the Kyoto Protocol. One explanation for this is that the Conservatives were a minority government and courting Quebec (a province consistently in support of Kyoto). Jeffrey Simpson, Mark Jaccard, and Nic Rivers (2007: 98) imply that public awareness of the climate change issue was a factor that impelled the Conservative government to stay in the Kyoto Protocol. And while the Conservatives did stay in Kyoto, they publicly rejected the Kyoto reductions commitment and blamed the Liberals for their inability to meet those commitments (See Environment Canada, 2006c).

In contrast to the Liberals, who embraced green internationalist rhetoric and engaged in numerous practices that undermined the Kyoto regime, the Harper government's early statements on climate change laid bare the Liberal's internationalist rhetoric and sought to shame the Liberal Party. For example, casting the Conservatives as honest truth-tellers, Environment Minister Ambrose implied that the Liberals were disingenuous in their commitments, and that the Conservative approach—to say that they could not meet the Kyoto targets—was the right thing to do (See Environment Canada, 2006d). John Baird, when he was Environment Minister, continued the anti-Liberal refrain likening Kyoto to a marathon and suggested that 'when the starting pistol of that marathon went off, Canada began to run in the opposite direction under the previous government' (Environment Canada, 2007a). Baird also attacked Stephane Dion and the Liberal Party in 2007, arguing that the Liberals only paid lid-service to the issue of climate change and said 'fighting climate change takes more than naming your dog Kyoto' (Baird, 2007).

There was also an element in the anti-Liberal discourse that was anti-Liberal internationalism. Ambrose declared that Canada had not earned its boy scout badges (Environment Canada, 2006a: 2) while the prime minister, in a speech not dedicated to climate change, stated that the new government represented a fundamental break with the past and that Canadians had 'a clear choice between a foreign policy that actively stands up for our national interests and values, versus a "soft power" approach that relegates Canada to the sidelines of the international arena' (Office of the Prime Minister,

2007a). One may not want to accept that soft power is internationalist, but the point by the prime minister is clear—climate change policy, like foreign policy, will not be like it was under the Liberals. There is a sense that the Conservatives would have a 'harder' foreign policy in contrast to the impotent soft power of the Liberals.

And while the Harper government has rejected ideas associated with the Liberal Party, Prime Minister Harper has invoked the traditional language of Canada as a middle power, as a state with obligations and duties to the greater international community. In September 2007, he stated: 'So success, in this global environment, requires concerted effort among capable, committed, like-minded nations. Success requires middle powers who can step up to the plate to do their part. Success demands governments who are willing to assume responsibilities, seek practical, do-able solutions to problems and who have a voice and influence in global affairs because they lead, not by lecturing, but by example' (Office of the Prime Minister, 2007d).

Similar language was used by Rona Ambrose when she stated that 'we will not deny the obvious, nor disrespect our international obligations by paying them mere lip service with no substance. We will confront the reality of previous governments' inaction' (Environment Canada, 2006d). More recently, the current Minister of Environment, Jim Prentice, emphasized Canada's commitment to being a constructive player in the ongoing international negotiations on climate change and claimed that climate change is one of the most significant public policy issues of our time (Environment Canada, 2009g). At the World Business Summit on Climate Change in May 2009, Prentice invoked intergenerational responsibility as a motivation for success at the forthcoming Conference of Parties meeting in Copenhagen (Environment Canada, 2009f).

The Conservative government has been extremely derogatory of Liberal incantations of internationalism. At the same time, the Conservatives have not entirely recreated the foreign policy lexicon—they speak of obligations to others, responsibilities to the global community, and role modeling for others, and even invoke intergenerational responsibility. Does this make the Conservatives . . . internationalist? Let us examine this question further by turning to the elements of internationalism draw from the 'Pinchpenny Diplomacy' definition.

Multilateralism

The first element of internationalism provided by Nossal is multilateralism. What Nossal means by multilateralism is not obvious; nonetheless, we can begin by asking, is Canada involved in multilateral activities related to climate change? The answer, quite simply, is yes. Canada is involved in discussions about climate change in numerous fora such as the G8, the United Nations, the Asia Pacific Partnership and the Major Economies Forum on Energy and Climate.

According to John Kirton, the G8 is central to the current Canadian government's climate change strategy, especially in light of his view that the United Nations 'Kyoto approach was fundamentally flawed' (Kirton, 2008–9: 161). In spite of Kirton's assessment, Canada has participated in the United Nations' climate change-related negotiations since 1990 and Canadian bureaucrats were key architects of the United Nations Framework Convention on Climate Change, which preceded the 1997 Kyoto Protocol. The Harper government continues to participate in these international efforts to combat climate change. It also joined the Asia Pacific Partnership (APP) on Clean Development and Climate in 2007. Created in 2005, the APP currently includes seven member states: Australia,

Canada, China, India, Japan, Korea, and the United States (Asia Pacific Partnership on Clean Development and Climate, 2009a). The APP is committed to working together 'to create new investment opportunities, build local capacity, and remove barriers to the introduction of clean, more efficient technologies' (US Department of State, 2009). Finally, Canada is also involved in the Major Economies Forum on Energy and Climate, established by US President Barack Obama in March 2009. The Major Economies Forum includes seventeen member states, led by the United States and including the other members of the G8, plus larger emitters such as China and India. Among other things, 'the Forum is intended to facilitate a candid dialogue among major developed and developing economies, [and] help generate the political leadership necessary to achieve a successful outcome at the December UN climate change conference in Copenhagen. . . '. (US Department of State, 2009).

So indeed, Canada is active multilaterally. If we simply use participation in multilateral fora as the measure of meeting this element of internationalism, then one would have to put a check mark in the multilateralism box. However, participation is not enough. As David Black and Claire Turenne Sjolander (1996: 9) have argued, '[W]hile the call to multilateral action may seem to reinforce the basis of traditional Canadian foreign policy, its evolving practice may well exacerbate the inequalities in the emerging world order, and undermine multilateralism itself'. We have to ask: multilateralism for whom? This question seems to fit neatly with the element of 'community', which is examined next.

Community

As noted above, for Nossal, 'internationalism is, at bottom, directed towards creating, maintaining, and managing community at a global level' (Nossal, 1998–9: 98). Typically, in the Canadian case,

the creation, maintenance, and management of community occurs in multilateral fora, a link that is made in Nossal, Roussel, and Paquin, (2010: 24).

So how, then, does the Harper government represent itself in the creation, maintenance, and management of community at a global level? For the purposes here, let us assume that 'global' relates to the Kyoto regime, for it is the most inclusive of the various multilateral endeavours in which Canada is active.

The Harper government appears to have sought to recreate or redefine the Kyoto processes. Early in the tenure of the 'new' Canadian government, they challenged member states in the United Nations negotiations on climate change. Rose Ambrose, when she became Minister of Environment, also became the President of the Conference of Parties. She used that platform to not only chastise the Liberals but to also take velvet-gloved jabs at the members of the Conference of Parties themselves. In early 2006 she noted there was a need for an 'effective' regime (See Environment Canada, 2006b) and in her November statement to the Conference of Parties delivered a more strongly worded statement: 'Our hope is that we truly find an inclusive approach as we move forward. That we include, and support and encourage, instead of exclude, isolate and criticize' (Environment Canada, 2006c). In the same speech she claimed Canada was not abandoning Kyoto because it publicly announced it could not meet its Kyoto targets. 'On the contrary, I would challenge each of us to recognize that we are abandoning our protocol obligations if we do not acknowledge that we must make improvements. Our debate needs to be one of constructive dialogue—centred on real policy discussions, not cynicism and political expediency. Ultimately we will not achieve success by denying the shortcomings of our past approach' (Environment Canada, 2006c). In making such statements Ambrose effectively called out many of the members of the Conference of Parties and she implied that dialogue has not been constructive and the processes have not been effective.

The need for an effective international climate change regime is a common refrain in other ministers' statements and in statements by the prime minister. Stephen Harper also called out European states for missing their targets, stating: 'Now, our country was not alone in failing to act. Many countries, including Kyoto's signatories in Europe, like Italy, Spain and Ireland, failed to achieve significant emissions reductions during the same period. In fact, for the most part the only countries that achieved serious reductions were those that suffered industrial downturns or transformations largely unrelated to any plan for emissions reduction' (Office of the Prime Minister, 2008).

Typically, the construction of 'effective' is linked to inclusive—and inclusive means including all large emitters. The prime minister made this point very clear in 2007 when he articulated the Canadian perspective on this matter: 'Canada believes we need a new international protocol that contains binding targets for all the world's major emitters, including the United States and China' (Office of the Prime Minister, 2007d; see also Environment Canada, 2007a; Environment Canada, 2008; Environment Canada, 2009a; Environment Canada, 2009b; Office of the Prime Minister, 2007c).

As a sign of Canada's commitment to an 'inclusive' climate change regime, and reflecting the fact that the global climate change community, in the Canadian construction, must include the United States, the Conservative government has been an advocate of finding ways to include the United States in international discussions on climate change. Rona Ambrose, for example, rejected the views of those who saw the United States as the enemy and said that chastising the Bush administration would not help to bring them back to the Kyoto fold. She continued by stating: '[O]ur partners within the Kyoto protocol have expressed their hope that Canada's unique relationship with the United States will be helpful to facilitate the dialogue between the key initiatives that are emerging to address climate change' (Environment Canada, 2006c). The prime minister has called for building a consensus on climate change and reminded audiences that the inclusion of developing states is necessary for any American government to take on emissions reductions commitments (Office of the Prime Minister, 2008). Canada, it would appear, is at least rhetorically, seeking to function as a bridge-builder, a conciliator—seeking to build a consensus among states divided.

Complementing the Canadian efforts to bring the United States 'back in' to international negotiations on climate change is a reinvigorated orientation toward a Canadian–American climate change and energy regulatory regime. The United States is and has always been a vital determinant of Canadian climate change policy. Our economies are intertwined and our geography shared. This said, the way in which we have interacted with and been influenced by the United States has varied over time (MacDonald, and Smith, 1999–2000; Smith, 2008–9).

Under the Harper government, there was a growing convergence of policies with the United States during the Bush Administration. Both government adopted greenhouse gas intensity targets (even though the Canadian government says it will move to an absolute target). Both governments included nuclear energy in their clean energy arsenals. Both governments called for the inclusion of larger emitters, often in tandem, at international meetings. Both federal governments lagged behind their subnational counterparts. Both governments engaged in multilateral fora to discuss climate change, external to the UN processes, and both acted in ways internationally that regularly got them called laggards and saboteurs.

Interestingly, with the election of Barack Obama, the Canadian tune seems more conciliatory internationally and the push is on to engage the United States in a broad-based regulatory regime. Minister Prentice expressed hope that the regime would be based on common principles and include a common target, similar to that of the European Union. Central to the proposed North American climate change regime, according to Prentice, would be the following elements: 'shared targets and shared timetables, a common carbon market and a price and standards and mandates that are based on science and upon common sense' (Environment Canada, 2009a).

The United States has agreed to a Canada–US Clean Energy Dialogue (Environment Canada, 2009c: 6), but there are suggestions that the Obama administration has been reluctant to focus on a North American climate pact as opposed to an energy dialogue (Amberts, 2009a). More significant for Canada than any dialogue is a recent bill put forward in the US Congress. The Waxman-Markey Bill proposes a series of initiatives to cut US emissions and included in the bill are fees applied to foreign manufacturers for the carbon content of their products. This bill has the Environment Minister up in arms with one report suggesting that Prentice said components of the bill would be a 'prescription for disaster for the global economy' (Amberts, 2009b). Interestingly, the impetus for Canadian emissions reductions, for energy efficiency, and for a low-carbon future could well come from the United States. The bilateral 'community' is largely being defined on American terms.

At first glance, we might say that Canada is adopting traditional community-building activities—calling on states to take responsibility for their actions, advocating a new way to bring together states that are now divided, and seeking to redesign a regime to make it more 'effective' and 'inclusive'. The use of evocative catch-phrases is impressive. However, there is also evidence to suggest that Canada's actions have been divisive and that the Conservative construction of the global is not entirely inclusive.

First, while the Conservative government sought to remake the global climate change regime, they also made it clear that there were other options for multilateral activity. That Kyoto is not the only game in town has been reiterated by Harper (Office of the Prime Minister, 2007d), Ambrose (Environment Canada, 2006b), and John Baird (Environment Canada, 2007a and Environment Canada, 2007c).

Given the intractability of climate change as a global issue, perhaps multilateral activities need not be isolated to United Nations negotiations. However, some of the alternative fora in which Canada is engaged have not exactly been 'effective' in the reduction of greenhouse gases. The Asia-Pacific Partnership, for example, is committed to working together to address issues of 'increased energy needs and the associated issues of air pollution, energy security and climate change' (Asia Pacific Partnership, 2009b). High on the agenda of this group are issues related to energy security; there are no targets or timetables for greenhouse gas emissions reductions. This organization is focused on energy security, not environmental well-being. Moreover, organizations such as the G8 and the Major Economies Forum focus on states with economic power and thereby exclude the voices of small island states who are facing extreme environmental change.

Second, in spite of Canada's claim that it is working for a more inclusive climate change regime, the Canadian position on large emitters including China and India is divisive and contrary to the norm of common but differentiated responsibilities. The problem with this position is that it may well violate articles in the Kyoto Protocol to which Canada is a party. Article 10 of the Kyoto

Protocol affirms the commitments of the Annex I states (such as Canada and the EU) and specifically rejects the requirement of commitments for developing states, invoking common but differentiated responsibilities (United Nations, 1997). If nothing else, the way that Canada is pushing the issue internationally violates the spirit of the notion of common but differentiated responsibilities. How can Canada claim that others must act when it rejects its targets?

One might argue that the United States has the same position—and indeed this is true. However, the Obama administration inherited its position on large emitters. In 1997, the US Senate passed the Byrd-Hagel resolution stating that it would not commit to an international protocol that did not require commitments of development countries and that did harm to the United States' economy (US Library of Congress, 2009). The current American administration continues to be bound by this resolution. Moreover, the United States is not currently a member of the Kyoto Protocol whereas Canada is a member. The Conservative government has chosen to adopt this position.

Finally, the Canadian position on emissions reductions is different from that of the United States. The Obama Administration has signalled that it will seek reductions of 1990 levels by 2020, with cuts of 80 per cent by 2050, while Canada has adopted a target of 20 per cent from 2006 levels by 2020 and by 60 to 70 per cent by 2050 (CBC News, 2009). Canada's baseline is sixteen years later than the American baseline and thus the cuts proposed by the American administration are deeper and signal a great willingness to act than do the Canadian targets. Both targets, however, are less than the Kyoto targets adopted by both nations in 1997.

There are also reports that Canada sought to divide the members of the European Union on the issue of large emitters. As reported in *Embassy*, the Conservative government 'devised a strategy that included trying to split European Union members and tying assistance to developing countries to binding emission reduction targets as part of a bid to influence international talks'(Berthiaume, 2009).

From a critical perspective, we need to go further than the actions of states. If global governance is about power relations, then we need to ask who is included and who is excluded and what does this say about power in the global climate change regime? In this instance we can consider the views and voices of indigenous peoples. Minister Prentice has made passing reference to Canadian indigenous peoples (Environment Canada, 2008), while Canadian negotiators have worked internationally to limit the rights of indigenous peoples. In discussions related to Kyoto on deforestation and forest degradation, Canada, Australia, New Zealand, and the United States rejected the concept of 'peoples' in favour of 'people' (Tebtebba Foundation, 2008). While the absence of the 's' may seem of little significance, the use of 'peoples' is understood to be a reference to collective rights and the right to self-determination, while the use of 'people' degrades the collective identities of indigenous peoples and could be seen as a violation of the UN Declaration on the Rights of Indigenous Peoples.

The community that Canada maintains is one that is state-centric and inclusive as long as you are a 'Major Economy'. For some observers this will be enough to meet the criteria of 'community' because their perspective privileges states as primary actors. However, from a critical perspective, Canada is seen as working to divide members of the community, while simultaneously marginalizing peoples and the environment.

Good International Citizenship

For Nossal, good international citizenship is equated with acts to support the common well being, acts that provide a demonstrable effect.

Included in his examples of such acts are 'contributing faithfully to development assistance programs; dispatching troops on a peacemaking mission to a country torn by civil war; [and] organizing a coalition of like-minded countries to pursue the liberalization of agricultural trade' (Nossal, 1998–9: 99). The use of resources in support of the 'common good' can be linked to this understanding of good international citizenship. The question is, how does this apply to the case of Canadian climate change policy?

Prime Minister Harper has stated that Canada must do its part and lead by example—ideas broadly consistent with Nossal's definition of good international citizenship. And there have been some resources committed internationally, thus perhaps meeting the requirement of acts matching words. In 2007, for example, Minister Baird announced funding to the Global Environment Facility's Special Climate Change Fund. The statement announcing the funding indicates that 'with this new $7.5 million contribution, Canada's total contribution to the Special Climate Fund is $13.5 million' (Environment Canada, 2007b). An additional $1.5 million was designated to the Clean Development Mechanism and in 2008 Prime Minister Harper earmarked $100 million for climate change adaptation. It is suspected that this $100 million was originally to go to the Canada Climate Change Development Fund that had been set up by the Chrétien government and housed in CIDA (Stefov, and Tomlinson, 2009: 9).

One could argue that, given the fact that climate change is both global and local, Canada could act as a role model for other states by taking actions at home that provide demonstrable effects and signal Canada's commitment by coming to the international negotiating table with its own house in order. To some extent, this is the angle the Conservative government has taken. In contrast to the Liberal governments, the Conservatives were going

to set realistic, achievable targets and meet their obligations. Or so they suggested.

Indeed, after rejecting the Kyoto target to which Canada had committed, the Conservative government has aimed to 'reduce total greenhouse gas emissions in Canada in 2020 by 20 per cent from a 2006 starting point, the so-called "minus 20 by 2020" approach' (Environment Canada, 2009a), with reductions to between 60 and 70 per cent by 2050, as noted above. To meet this target, Canada has announced the forthcoming regulation of fuel economy standards for vehicles, consistent with American standards, (Environment Canada, 2009e), set emissions targets for Canadian industry, produced preliminary plans for an offset systems that will allow firms to purchase credits toward their compliance obligations (Environment Canada, 2009; 2009h), and has funded activities across the country. For example, the federal government has committed $117.5 million over seven years for a biofuels project with Greenfield Ethanol in Johnstown, Ontario, and another $72.8 million to the same company for a project in Chatham, Ontario. Over seven years, $84.76 million has gone to a biofuels project with the Integrated Grain Processors Cooperative and another $23.2 million to an ethanol plant in Red Deer, Alberta (Environment Canada, 2009i). Funding has also been transferred to the provinces, for example $155.9 million to the province of Alberta for initiatives such as carbon capture and storage (Office of the Prime Minister, 2007b).

Do the commitments made by the Conservative government measure up to 'good international citizenship'? When we consider the fact that the Conservative government publicly rejected previously made international commitments and redesigned its Kyoto commitment, it does lend itself to questions of how it could possibly function as a role model for other states.

One could argue that Canada is now putting its money where its mouth is, when in the past it did not. The Chrétien government did provide funding for developing states, however, which shows that support for developing states, at least, is not new (See CIDA, 2009). Moreover, if the report from *Embassy* is accurate, the funding provided by Canada under the Conservatives to developing states was designed to act as leverage to force them to take on emissions reductions. The *Embassy* report is supported by Canadian government documents, submitted to the United Nations Framework Convention on Climate Change Secretariat, that indicated that Canada would not be able to commit to a financing scheme without knowing what commitments were going to be taken on by developing states (Demerse, 2009: 24). There is also the question of how much is enough? The Pembina Institute has calculated that Canada's fair share would be somewhere between $2.2 billion and $5.7 billion a year (Demerse, 2009: 28). By way of comparison, the same report shows that '[t]he low-end estimate (C$2.2B/year) is less than the C$2.7B that Canada spent on loans to bail out the auto sector in 2009 [and] the average estimate (C$4.0B/year) is less than the government's 1 per cent cut to the GST in the 2006 budget, which costs C$5.2B/year' (Demerse, 2009: 28). So maybe our international commitments are more about 'good enough international citizenship' (Black and Williams 2008, 3) than good international citizenship.

One could also point to the regulations being designed by the Conservative government as 'putting their money where their mouth is'. Indeed, there has been funding of clean energy initiatives and transfers to the provinces (not unlike those of the Liberals) and the Conservatives are seeking to use regulatory mechanisms to gain some emissions reductions. This said, critics have also noted that, for example, the offset system that is being designed is full of loopholes (Pembina Institute, 2009) that may indeed allow for companies to emit more—and ensure that Canada is now near its emissions targets. Finally, the vast amount of climate change-related funding is directed inwards, not outwards, forcing us to ponder whether our climate change policy is nationalist or internationalist. Rather than helping the most vulnerable outside of our borders, we are supporting Canadian companies.

Beyond the criteria of money and policies, what happens if we problematize the notion of good international citizenship? Tim Dunne (2008: 23), for example, in an analysis of good international citizenship, includes the criteria of harm avoidance. Canada has done harm to others. Through our denial of our historic emissions, our continued consumption, and policies that allow industry to pay for carbon credits rather than reduce their energy use, we contribute to climate change and to impacts that are already being felt around the world. We are also harming our indigenous peoples, who are feeling the effects of climate change now. Indeed, we are a small contributor to global concentrations of greenhouse gases, but the fact remains that through our own consumptive patterns, our divisive diplomacy, and our dismissal of international commitments, we are also harming other citizens and indeed ourselves. We are also harming future generations (See Dunne, 2008: 23). Given current impacts and projections from the lead scientific body on climate change, the Intergovernmental Panel on Climate Change, future generations are in for significant environmental changes. Regardless of any claims made by our current government that they are concerned about intergenerational equity, their actions suggest that they do not plan beyond the next election. The federal government is not entirely to blame as Canadians have not held their governments accountable. Canadians may claim that climate change is an issue, but do we want to pay for it? Do we want to forgo the luxuries of our everyday lives? And what of the environment?

Does common well-being include the environment? Our government tells us that they are seeking to balance the environment and the economy, and yet the environment continues to suffer.

Voluntarism

The final element in Nossal's definition of internationalism is voluntarism. Internationalism is a 'voluntaristic form of diplomacy. . . . [I]t is an entirely optional form of statecraft—in the sense that one could get by without engaging in it' (Nossal, 1998–9: 100). The acts in which Canada engages are not necessary—'you do it because you believe that acts of good international citizenship, a robust engagement in world politics, and contributing to a rules-based order will be in the general interest' (Nossal, 1998–9: 102). So, is Canadian climate change policy marked by voluntarism?

It is hard to argue that the Harper government's engagement in multilateral processes related to climate change is voluntaristic. This is a government that many assumed would pull out of the Kyoto Protocol but did not. Either because they were concerned about electoral viability or public opinion—or both—this government chose to stay in Kyoto when previous signals indicated that was not an option for them. Furthermore, this is not a party with a history of acceptance that climate change is a real issue, and so while Minister Prentice and Prime Minister Harper may now claim that climate change is a crucial public policy issue, one has to wonder if this is more a public relations play than a fundamental switch in beliefs. So the impetus is not for the 'general well being' or 'environmental well being'. Rather, once the decision was made to stay in Kyoto, the issue became how to make Kyoto suit Canadian interests. Thus we witness the calls for an inclusive and effective climate change regime.

Perhaps the most significant 'invariable' now driving Canadian climate change policy is the United States. Canada's change in tone and the appointment of a new Minister of Environment are oddly coincident with the election of Barack Obama. The Canadian government claims there are now opportunities to act in tandem with the United States when in the past there were not (CBC News 12, February 2009), but that is not supported as there is evidence of the Harper government acting in tandem with the Bush government. Rather, the Canadian government was watching the 2008 US elections during which both John McCain and Barack Obama had supported a cap-and-trade system. So regardless of which candidate won, it was possible that this regulatory regime was coming from the US. Canadian regulations on industrial emissions reductions did indeed precede the election of Barack Obama, but they were intensity targets and offered industry any number of loopholes to pay their way out of missing emissions reductions. The Canadian government may be seeking to pre-empt the American legislation, thus giving them more leverage in negotiations with the US by saying they already have their regulations in place, but do not underestimate the degree to which a level playing field for Canadian industry, in the continental sense, drives Canadian policy. Canadian policies are driven not by an interest in the greater global good, but rather Canadian–American economic interdependence.

From any perspective, it is hard to equate the climate change policy of the Harper government with voluntarism. Circumstance has forced our hand and the federal government has adapted to international circumstances in ways that seek the Canadian advantage. Canadian, or rather the Conservative Party's, self-interest would not be served by stepping away from the international climate change regime.

E. AND SO . . .

And so where does this leave us with the question of the relevance of internationalism to our understanding of Canadian climate change diplomacy under the Harper government?

Taking Nossal's 1998 definition of internationalism, it is seen above that we could argue that Canada is engaged in multilateral activities, seeking to recreate the international climate change community, while pushing for a Canada–US 'community', and engaging in acts that some may regard as good international citizenship. Declaring these acts as voluntary is a bit more difficult. Accepting this analysis, then, three of the four elements of internationalism are met. One could conclude then that the Harper government are essentially unwilling internationalists—seeking to make the best out of a bad situation.

However, it is also clear that if we push our understanding of internationalism beyond what is inferred of the Nossal definition, we get another picture of climate change policy under the Harper government. We find a state engaged in multilateralism but also engaged in activities that undermine key principles of the Kyoto Protocol as well as adopting diplomatic strategies that seek to divide the European Union and bully developing states into acting. The community that the Conservatives are trying to recreate is one that suits Canadian interests, first and foremost. Good international citizenship is really good enough international citizenship, with Canada contributing far less than its fair share. Moreover, state-based constructions of good international citizenship cannot account for questions related to harm, and exclude future generations and the environment. Voluntarism is challenged by the reality of circumstances that have forced Canadian government leaders to act in the face of changes coming from the south. From a critical perspective, claims of internationalism must be greeted with skepticism: internationalism, even unwilling internationalism, serves to mask dangerous and exclusionary practices.

That this article arrives at competing interpretations is of little surprise. The lens we adopt determines the way we see our subjects of study. Nonetheless, this analysis lends itself to valuable theoretical and practical conclusions. First, as noted above, we cannot assume what constitutes internationalism. Too often we use loaded words lightly, or assume a shared meaning where there is none. Second, internationalism, whether interpreted from a mainstream or critical perspective, requires more attention. There are rich bodies of literature available for us to craft more robust criteria for internationalism. Third and practically speaking, we must not linger on the early Harper government's rejection of the Liberal party variant of internationalism because there is evidence to suggest that traditional notions of Canada as a middle power, as a pragmatic international actor, as a bridge builder, are finding their way into the Conservative lexicon. This speaks to the durability of the ideas, as suggested by Nossal, Roussel, and Paquin (2010: 42) and is worth further exploration.

Fourth, given the very strategic nature of the Conservative government, we must assume that the invocation of traditional ideas of Canadian foreign policy serves a purpose. In the case of climate change, the adoption of more conciliatory language may be an attempt to score points with the Obama government, while simultaneously deflecting criticism of Canadian climate change policy by presenting ourselves as being on the side of angels—or at least of the immensely popular Barack Obama. But we must not be under any illusions because, just as the internationalism rhetoric of the Chrétien Liberals was an attempt to deflect

Canadian attention away from inaction, the use of the language of 'effective' and 'realistic' so common to the Harper government is designed to limit questions about how effective or realist issues are according to *whom*. Finally, we must move beyond a state-centric understanding of energy security and major economies in our analysis of climate change. Lost in such a perspective are peoples, the environment, small island states, and future generations. Surely they merit our attention as much as 'powerful' states?

Key Terms

Internationalism
Kyoto Protocol

References

Amberts, Sheldon. (2009a). 'US Climate Bill Could Sideswipe Oilsands' *Calgary Herald* 31, March from www.calgary herald.com/business/climate+change+bill+could+side swipe+oilsands/1449115/story.html.

Amberts, Sheldon. (2009b). 'US Climate Bill Would be Disaster', *National Post*, 14 May, from www.nationalpost.com/news/canada/story.html?id=1593753.

Asia Pacific Partnership on Clean Development and Climate. (2009a). 'Frequently Asked Questions' from www.asia pacificpartnership.org/english/faq.aspx.

Asia Pacific Partnership on Clean Development and Climate. (2009b). 'Factsheet' from www.asiapacificpartnership.org/pdf/translated_versions/Fact_Sheet_English.pdf.

Baird, John. (2007). 'Canada's Goals at Bali' *National Post*, 7 December, from: www.nationalpost.com/story.html?id=150888.

Bernstein, Steven. (2003). 'International Institutions and the Framing of Canada's Climate Change Policy: Mitigating or Masking the Integrity Gap' in Eugene Lee and Anthony Perl (eds.), *The Integrity Gap: Canada's Environmental Policy and Institutions*, (Vancouver: UBC Press,).

Black, David R. and Heather A. Smith. (1993). 'Notable Exceptions? New and Arrested Directions in Canadian Foreign Policy Literature', *Canadian Journal of Political Science*, 26 (December), 745–74.

Black, David and Claire Turenne Sjolander. (1996). 'Multilateralism Re-constituted and the Discourse of Canadian Foreign Policy' *Studies in Political Economy*, 49 (Spring), 7–35.

Black, David R. and Paul D. Williams. (2008). 'Darfur's Challenge to International Society' *Behind the Headlines* (Toronto: Canadian International Council).

Broadhead, Lee-Anne. (2001). 'Canada as a Rogue State: Its Shameful Performance on Climate Change' in *International Journal* (Summer), 461–80.

Broadhead, Lee-Anne. (2002). *International Environmental Politics: The Limits of Green Diplomacy*, (Boulder, Co: Lynne Rienner).

Berthiaume, Lee. (2009). 'Gov't Planned to Split EU on Climate Change Talks' *Embassy*, 17, June from: www.embassy mag.ca/page/view/climate_change_talks-6-17-2009).

CBC News. (2009). 'Canada to Stick Close to US on Environment Policy: Prentice' 12, February from: www.cbc.ca/canada/story/2009/02/12/environment-policy.html.

Canadian International Development Agency. (2009). Canada Climate Change Development Fund, www.acdi-cida.gc.ca/CIDAWEB/acdicida.nsf/En/JUD-4189500-J8U).

Cooper, Andrew F. (1995). 'In Search of Niches: Saying "Yes" and Saying "No" in Canada's International Relations', *Canadian Foreign Policy*, 3/3 (Winter 1995), 1–13.

Cox, Robert with Timothy Sinclair. (1996). *Approaches to World Order*, (Cambridge: Cambridge University Press).

Demerse, Claire. (2009). *Our Fair Share: Canada's Role in Supporting Global Climate Solutions* (Ottawa: Pembina Institute) from http://pubs.pembina.org/reports/our-fair-share-report.pdf.

Dunne, Tim. (2008) 'Good Citizen Europe' in *International Affairs*, 84: 113–28.

Elliott, Lorraine. (2002). 'Global Governance' in Rorden Wilkinson and Steve Hughes (eds.), *Global Governance: Critical Perspectives*, (London: Routledge).

Environment Canada. (2001). 'Notes for an Address by the Honourable David Anderson, Minister of Environment to the Canadian Institute of International Affairs, Ottawa' 27, October, from www.ec.gc.ca/media_archive/minister/speeches/2001/011031_s_e.htm.

Environment Canada. (2002a). 'Notes for an Address by the Honourable David Anderson P.C., M.P, Minister of Environment: Kyoto Speakers Circuit at the University of Calgary' 16, October, from www.ec.gc.ca/minister/speeches/2002/021016_s_e.htm, on 8/22/2003.

Environment Canada. (2002b). 'Notes for an Address by The Honourable David Anderson, P.C. M.P, Minister of Environment to Open the Parliamentary Debate on Ratification of the Kyoto Protocol', December 9, from www.ec.gc.ca/media_archive/minister/speeches/2002/021209_s_e.htm.

Environment Canada. (2002c). 'Notes for an address by The Honourable David Anderson, P.C., M.P., Minister of the Environment, on the occasion of the deposit of Canada's Instruments of Ratification for the Kyoto Protocol to the United Nations Framework Convention on Climate Change' New York, NY, December 17, from www.ec.gc.ca/media_archive/minister/speeches/2002/021217_s_e.htm.

Environment Canada. (2005). 'Carleton University: A Greener Canada; Speaking Notes for the Honourable Stephane Dion, P.C. M.P., Minister of Environment, Ottawa,' 15 February, from: www.ec.gc.ca/media_archive/minister/speeches/2005/050215_s_e.htm.

Environment Canada. (2006a). 'A Breath of Fresh Air: Made in Canada Solutions to Meet Canada's Environmental Challenges: Speaking Notes for an Address by the Honourable Rona Ambrose, Minister of Environment of Canada', 31 March, from www.ec.gc.ca/default.asp?lang=En&n=6F2DE1CA-1&news=4916CE91-6388-4532-8403-563A359EE167.

Environment Canada. (2006b). 'Speaking Notes for the Honourable Rona Ambrose, Minister of Environment on Clean Air at the Canadian Club', 7 June from www.ec.gc.ca/default.asp?lang=En&n=6F2DE1CA-1&news=147246F2-3675-4DFE-9D78-41A620D55D08.

Environment Canada. (2006c). 'Address to the United Nations Climate Change Conference', Nairobi, 15 November from, www.ec.gc.ca/default.asp?lang=En&n=6F2DE1CA-1&news=6158B437-52DC-46DB-9700-3BAFE008AC42.

Environment Canada. (2007a). 'Speech by the Honourable John Baird, Minister of Environment at the Economic Club of Toronto', 5 December, from www.ec.gc.ca/default.asp?lang=En&n=6F2DE1CA-1&news=B593A1B8-57D2-4080-85C8-542C6017EA0E.

Environment Canada. (2007b). 'News Release: Canada Takes Action to Help Developing Countries Fight Climate Change', 10 December, from www.ec.gc.ca/default.asp?lang=En&n=714D9AAE-1&news=323B0F50-9F66-424A-AF64-34EDBFB1A461.

Environment Canada. (2007c). 'Notes for an Address by the Honourable John Baird, P.C., M.P. Minister of Environment, United Nations Climate Change Conference, Nusa Dua, Bali, Indonesia', 13 December, from www.ec.gc.ca/default.asp?lang=En&n=6F2DE1CA-1&news=A3F93B01-2A5F-4FE1-9B42-C9836C56A870.

Environment Canada. (2008). 'Remarks for the Honourable Jim Prentice COP 14 National Statement', Poznon Poland,

December 11, from www.ec.gc.ca/default.asp?lang=En&n=6F2DE1CA-1&news=A59C4FA1-1776-4DC6-81BD-D64F8B59123C.

Environment Canada. (2009a). 'Notes for an Address by the Honourable Jim Prentice P.C., Q.C., M.P., Minister of the Environment to the Canadian Council of Chief Executives', 20 January, from www.ec.gc.ca/default.asp?lang=En&n=6F2DE1CA-1&news=E110AAE9-B810-4F07-ADEC-2A4C245D67D9.

Environment Canada. (2009b). 'Notes for an Address by the Honourable Jim Prentice P.C., Q.C., M.P, Minister of the Environment to the Institute of Corporate Directors', 6 March, from www.ec.gc.ca/default.asp?lang=En&n=6F2DE1CA-1&news=62019CBE-CD6C-4282-A9E9-AEE1754E9314.

Environment Canada. (2009c). 'Notes for an Address by the Honourable Jim Prentice P.C., Q.C., M.P, Minister of Environment to the Calgary Chamber of Commerce', 16 March, from www.ec.gc.ca/default.asp?lang=En&n=6F2DE1CA-1&news=B8CB2CC1-6F93-40E9-A911-338253A8BA0B.

Environment Canada. (2009d). 'Notes for an Address by the Honourable Jim Prentice, P.C., Q.C., M.P. Minister of the Environment during the 39th Conference of the Council of the Americas', 13 May, from www.ec.gc.ca/default.asp?lang=En&n=6F2DE1CA-1&news=9932B9CE-A306-47A7-B030-C403CF8E1A00.

Environment Canada. (2009e). 'Notes for an Address by the Honourable Jim Prentice P.C., Q.C., M.P. Minister of the Environment on New Regulations to Limit Greenhouse Gas Emissions' from www.ec.gc.ca/default.asp?lang=En&n=6F2DE1CA-1&news=D8C4903B-B406-4B70-8A4A-EDEF99B71D38.

Environment Canada. (2009f). 'Notes for an Address by the Honourable Jim Prentice P.C., Q.C., M.P. Minister of the Environment During the World Business Summit on Climate Change' from www.ec.gc.ca/default.asp?lang=En&n=6F2DE1CA-1&news=7A044947-22B0-406E-A066-687EC851ED94.

Environment Canada. (2009g). 'Notes for an Address by the Honourable Jim Prentice, P.C., Q.C., M.P. Minister of the Environment on Canada's Climate Change Plan', 4 June from www.ec.gc.ca/default.asp?lang=En&n=6F2DE1CA-1&news=400A4566-DA85-4A0C-B9F4-BABE2DF555C7.

Environment Canada. (2009h). 'Notes for an Address by the Honourable Jim Prentice, P.C., Q.C., M.P. Minister of the Environment on Canada's Offset System for Greenhouse Gases', 10 June, from www.ec.gc.ca/default.asp?lang=En&n=6F2DE1CA-1&news=B06CF8C3-A168-46FC-B456-7496E8E42A6E.

Environment Canada. (2009i). 'Green Initiatives' from www.ec.gc.ca/cc/default.asp?lang=En&n=0AF2FCE5-1).

Harrison, Kathryn. (2007). 'The Road Not Taken: Climate Change Policy in Canada and the United States' in *Global Environmental Politics,* 7:4, (November).

Hawes, Michael. (1984). *Principal Power, Middle Power or Satellite?* (Toronto: York Research Programme in Strategic Studies).

Hampson, Fen Osler and Dean Oliver. (1998). 'Pulpit Diplomacy: A Critical Assessment of the Axworthy Doctrine' *International Journal*, 53 (Summer 1998): 379–406.

Jaccard, Mark, et al. (2006). 'Burning Our Money to Warm the Planet: Canada's Ineffective Efforts to Reduce Greenhouse Gas Emissions', *C.D. Howe Institute: Commentary*, (CD Howe Institute).

Kirton, John. (2007). *Canadian Foreign Policy in a Changing World*, (Toronto: Thomson-Nelson).

———. (2008–9). 'Consequences of the 2008 US Elections for America's Climate Change Policy, Canada, and the World' *International Journal*, LXIV, (Winter): 153–62.

May, Elizabeth. (2002). 'From Montreal to Kyoto, How We Got From Here to There—Or Not', *Policy Options*, 55, 1 (December 2002–January 2003).

MacDonald, Doug and Heather A. Smith. (1999–2000). 'Promises Made, Promises Broken: Questioning Canada's Commitments to Climate Change', *International Journal*, (Winter), pp. 107–24.

Molot, Maureen Appel. (1990). 'Where Do We, or Should We, or Can We Sit? A Review of Canadian Foreign Policy Literature', *International Journal of Canadian Studies*. 1–2, (Spring/Fall), 77–96.

Munton, Don. (2002–2003). 'Whither Internationalism?', *International Journal*, 53, 8 (Winter), 155–80.

Neufeld, Mark. (1995). 'Hegemony and Foreign Policy Analysis: The Case of Canada as Middle Power', *Studies in Political Economy*, 48 (Autumn), 7–29.

Nossal, Kim Richard. (1997). *The Politics of Canadian Foreign Policy*. 3rd ed., Scarborough: Prentice-Hall.

Nossal, Kim Richard. (1998–99). 'Pinchpenny Diplomacy: The Decline of Good International Citizenship in Canadian Foreign Policy' *International Journal*, 54, 1 (Winter), 88–105.

Nossal, Kim Richard, Stéphane Roussel, and Stéphane Paquin. (2010). *International Policy and Politics in Canada* (Toronto: Pearson Education).

Office of the Prime Minister. (2007a). 'Prime Minister Outlines Agenda for a Stronger, Safer, Better Canada', 6 February, from http://pm.gc.ca/eng/media.asp?category=2&id=1522.

Office of the Prime Minister. (2007b). 'News Release: Prime Minister Announces ecoTrust Funding for Alberta', 8 March from www.ecoaction.gc.ca/news-nouvelles/20070308-2-eng.cfm.

Office of the Prime Minister. (2007c). 'Prime Minister Addresses Australian Parliament in Canberra, Australia', 11 September, from http://pm.gc.ca/eng/media.asp?category=2&id=1818.

Office of the Prime Minister. (2007d). 'PM Addresses the Council on Foreign Relations', 25 September, from http://pm.gc.ca/eng/media.asp?category=2&id=1830.Office of the Prime Minister. (2008). 'Prime Minister Harper

addresses the Canada–U.K. Chamber of Commerce in London', 29 May, from http://pm.gc.ca/eng/media.asp?category=2&id=2131.

Office of the Prime Minister. (2009). 'Prime Minister's Address in Kandahar', 7 May, from http://www.pm.gc.ca/eng/media.asp?id=2569Potter, Evan H. (1996–7). 'Niche Diplomacy as Canadian Foreign Policy', *International Journal*, LLI (Winter): 25–38.

Pembina Institute. (2009). *Reform Proposed Federal Offset System* (Ottawa: Pembina Institute) from http://pubs.pembina.org/reports/offset-system-proposal-letter.pdf.

Pratt, Cranford. (1990). *Middle Power Internationalism: The North–South Dimension*, (Montreal and Kingston: McGill-Queen's University Press).

Simpson, Jeffrey, Mark Jaccard, and Nic Rivers. (2007). *Hot Air: Meeting Canada's Climate Change Challenge*, (Toronto: McClelland and Stewart).

Smith, Heather A. (2000). 'Niche Diplomacy and Mission-Oriented Diplomatic Behaviour: A Critical Assessment' in Andrew F. Cooper and Geoffrey Hayes (eds.), *Worthwhile Initiatives? Canadian Mission-Oriented Diplomacy*, (Toronto: Irwin): 13–22.

———. (2002). 'Dollar Discourse: The Devaluation of Canada's Natural Capital in Canadian Climate Change Policy' in Deborah L VanNijnatten and Robert Boardman (eds.), *Canadian Environmental Policy: Context and Cases*, 2nd ed., (Toronto: OUP, 2002), 286–98;

———. (2003). 'Disrupting Internationalism and Finding the Others' in Claire Turenne Sjolander, Heather A. Smith, and Deborah Stienstra (eds.), *Feminist Perspectives on Canadian Foreign Policy* (Toronto: OUP), 24–39.

———. (2008). 'Canada and Kyoto: Independence or Indifference?' in Bow and Patrick Lennox, eds., *An Independent Foreign Policy for Canada?: Challenges and Choices for the Future* (Toronto: University of Toronto Press).

———. (2008–9). 'Political Parties and Canadian Climate Change Policy' *International Journal*, 64, 1 (Winter), 47–66.

Stefov, Dana and Brian Tomlinson. (2009). *Financing for Climate Change Adaptation: A Discussion Paper*, (Ottawa: Canadian Council for International Co-operation).

Tebtebba Foundation. (2008). Indigenous peoples, local communities and NGOs outraged at the removal of rights from UNFCCC decision on REDD www.tebtebba.org/index.php?option=com_docman&task=doc_download&gid=309&Itemid=27.

United Nations. *Kyoto Protocol to the United Nations Framework Convention on Climate Change*, 1997, Art. 3.3.

US Department of State. (2009). 'Major Economics Forum on Energy and Climate' from www.state.gov/g/oes/climate/mem/.

US Library of Congress. (2009). Byrd-Hagel Resolution, http://thomas.loc.gov/cgi-bin/query/D?c105:1:./temp/~c105fblnfe.

26

AID EFFECTIVENESS AND THE FRAMING OF NEW CANADIAN AID INITIATIVES

Stephen Brown

At the end of the twentieth century, foreign aid appeared to be in almost terminal decline, both in Canada and in other Western countries. During the 1990s, Canada's official development assistance (ODA) dropped from $3.0 billion in 1990–1 to $2.6 billion in 2000–1. Relative to the size of the Canadian economy, the decline was even more dramatic. The government cut aid disbursements almost in half during this same period, from 0.45 per cent to 0.25 per cent of gross national income (GNI) (Canada, 2009: 10). The optimism that accompanied the end of the Cold War quickly evanesced, while the widely heralded 'peace dividend' failed to materialize.[1] Disillusioned with the lack of tangible results, and as part of deficit-cutting strategies, Canada and most other donors slashed their aid budgets, turning their backs on longstanding commitments to reaching 0.7 per cent of GNI. After 30 years of growth, it felt like the end of an era. Across the world, a new term gained currency: aid fatigue. Imbued with *fin de siècle* pessimism, analysts used expressions such as an 'ebb tide' and an 'uncertain future' in the titles for their publications on Canadian development assistance (Morrison, 1998; 2000).

The new century ushered in a radical reversal of this trend. The Millennium Development Goals (MDGs), adopted at the United Nations in 2000, epitomized the new thinking. Donors recognized that massive efforts were required to reduce poverty drastically over a 15-year period, including increased spending to improve access to health and education. At the beginning of the twenty-first century, at UN conferences and G8 summits, Western donors renewed and reiterated their commitments to providing higher levels of aid, targeting poverty reduction, and focussing especially on Africa, the continent where needs are the greatest. They also sought to improve aid effectiveness, so as to provide not only more but also better aid. Canada participated enthusiastically in this, at least for the first few years. By 2008, however, Canadian ODA disbursements had bounced back to 0.32 per cent of GNI (OECD, 2009), though this remained less than half the international target.

A year after the adoption of the Millennium Development Goals (MDGs), another event was to shape profoundly the context in which foreign aid operated: the al-Qaeda terrorist attacks of

11 September 2001. The new mindset of the 'war on terror', as well as the US-led invasions of Iraq and Afghanistan, recast how Canada and other donors framed and oriented their aid programs. Almost overnight, security concerns gained a central importance, often eclipsing the focus on the MDGs. Within the context of these contradictory trends at the international level, Canada began to rethink its place in the world and especially its relationship with the United States.

Successive Canadian prime ministers each brought a new direction to foreign aid, usually building on his predecessor's achievements. For instance, Jean Chrétien reversed the decline in aid flows and designated Africa a priority. Paul Martin integrated aid more closely with other foreign policy 'instruments' (known as the 'whole-of-government approach') and took steps to focus on a smaller number of countries. Stephen Harper sought to concentrate and integrate aid even further, notably focusing resources on Afghanistan, but also replacing Africa with the Americas as the priority region for aid.

This chapter analyzes the main trends in Canadian development assistance policy since 2000–1, the pivotal 'international moment' that pulled ODA simultaneously in two new directions: a preoccupation with the immediate and medium-term needs of the poor, embodied in the MDGs' and the donor countries' own security concerns in the post-9/11 era.[2] It argues that shifts in Canadian aid policy reflect the government's broader foreign policy concerns, especially a preoccupation with prestige (the quest for a personal legacy under Chrétien and for Canada's place among peers and in the post-9/11 world under Martin and Harper) and most recently commercial self-interest, with the new geographical focus on Latin America and the Caribbean. Though these forms of self-interest are not new or unique to Canada, the language used usually frames the changes as improvements in aid effectiveness and thus as being for the benefit of poor countries, rhetorically reflecting the growing international concern with improving the quality of aid. With the notable exception of the gradual untying of aid, however, most of the initiatives' impact on effectiveness would be unclear or even detrimental. Through these changes, couched in aid effectiveness terms, the Canadian government is increasingly seeking to instrumentalize CIDA and its aid programs, including through a cross-departmental policy coherence mechanism known as the 'whole-of-government approach', to reflect non–development-related interests.

This chapter is organized as follows. Its first section analyzes the politics of aid effectiveness by examining in turn the main components in the effectiveness discussions that have been part of Canadian aid policy initiatives in recent years: the untying of aid, the questioning of impact and search for results, the issue of aid volume, the 'focus on focus' (fewer recipient countries and economic sectors), and the coherence between aid policy and policies in other areas. It then explores the motivations that underpin recent Canadian aid policy initiatives. The conclusion summarizes the main argument and speculates on the effect of global changes on Canadian foreign aid in the years to come.

THE POLITICS OF AID EFFECTIVENESS

Virtually every time the Canadian government announces changes in aid policy, it evokes the need for aid to have greater impact, regardless of who is in power.[3] At first blush, it might appear impossible for this to be anything but a good thing. After all, it would be hard to oppose effectiveness. Upon further examination, however, the concept's malleability permits its use to justify any new initiative, preventing it from having any fixed connotations.

'Effectiveness' becomes a substitute for 'good policy', which in turn is really the government's preferred policy, but with an aura of supposed objectivity and benevolence, underpinned by cost-effectiveness and international legitimacy.

'Aid effectiveness' is currently one of the most important buzzwords in aid circles. In recent years, the term has acquired two distinct meanings. First, in the late 1990s, the World Bank published an influential report entitled *Assessing Aid: What Works, What Doesn't, and Why* (World Bank, 1998). It argued that, based on econometric analysis, aid produces growth only in countries with a 'good' policy environment and 'sound' fiscal, monetary, and trade policies, without which, it inferred, aid is wasted (further argued in Burnside and Dollar, 2000). Though the methodology and reasoning were roundly criticized (Lensink and White, 2000), this strand of aid effectiveness came to signify the ability to produce economic growth (notably not a synonym of development) when combined with the 'right' policies in recipient countries.

Simultaneously, a different meaning emerged in a consensus among Western donors, more specifically the 22 member countries of the Development Assistance Committee of the Organisation for Economic Co-operation and Development (OECD/DAC), where Western donors discuss and try to coordinate aid policy. Concerned not only with policies in recipient countries, as the World Bank had been, they considered how *donor* aid policies could improve the effectiveness of their contributions. The 1996 report, *Shaping the 21st Century*, began to lay out basic principles, including not just recipient responsibilities but also important ones for donors: a sustained commitment from donors, improved coordination among them, increased support for 'locally-owned development strategies' and greater coherence among donor aid and non-aid policies (OECD, 1996: 2). These principles evolved into the 2005 Paris Declaration on Aid

Effectiveness, supplemented by the 2008 Accra Agenda for Action, which formalized as basic principles the centrality of the harmonization among donors, alignment with recipient country ownership, and the predictability of aid flows, among others. In other words, aid's effectiveness depended not on the 'correct' neoliberal policy environment in recipient countries, but rather on enhanced commitment and cooperation of donors amongst themselves and with recipient countries.[4]

As a member of the DAC and part of the DAC-led process in defining the principles of aid effectiveness, the Canadian government often invoked these principles to outline the basic philosophy of Canadian assistance. However, it continued to use the World Bank's approach and present its neoliberal justifications in its policy documents for directing aid to certain countries (Canada, 2002, 2005)—even after donors as a whole had abandoned not only the logic behind that argument, but also that particular use of the term 'effectiveness'.[5] Lacking any robust empirical evidence to support this approach, Canada was embracing what was essentially a political or ideological preference for countries with minimal state intervention in their economy and great openness to international finance and investment (Killick, 2004).

More recently, however, the government and especially the Minister of International Cooperation (who is responsible for CIDA) have been invoking effectiveness to justify any changes the government makes, even if they contradict the basic consensus principles. Canada's version of aid effectiveness is clearly 'a distinct, more narrow version' of the internationally endorsed agenda that concentrates on internal organizational issues and accountability to Canadian taxpayers (Lalonde, 2009: 169; see also Brown, and Jackson, 2009). Some Canadian initiatives, such as completely untying aid (i.e., not requiring that funds be spent on Canadian products and services), are fully in line with aid effectiveness principles. Others are less so, such as frequently changing priority countries and sectors. This raises the question of effectiveness for what and for whom, to be further addressed below. Some have gone as far as to argue that a measure of aid effectiveness should include a consideration of the extent to which aid helps donors achieve their own non–aid-related goals (Gillmore, and Mosazai, 2007).

This chapter does not seek to assess Canada's progress in the actual implementation of the international 'aid effectiveness agenda'.[6] Rather, this chapter examines recent Canadian policy initiatives and the extent to which they can be justified by the aid effectiveness rationale, by which I mean whether they improve the quality of aid from the point of view of the beneficiaries in recipient countries. The rest of this section thus examines the recent evolution of the five main components of Canadian aid policy changes and their links to aid effectiveness: tied aid, impact and results, volume, focus, and policy coherence.

TIED AID: THE LONG GOODBYE

Tied aid is a practice that involves making ODA conditional on the purchase of goods and services from the donor country. Tied aid adds, on average, an extra 15 to 30 per cent to costs because it prevents the funds from being used to buy the best value for money in a competitive market (Jepma, 1991: 15). This benefits the donor country, but provides no benefit to the recipient. Tied aid is thus antithetical to the notion of aid effectiveness.

The most unambiguous advance in Canadian aid policy since 2000 is the progressive, albeit slow, untying of aid. In 2002, the government recognized that tied aid was 'at odds with trends towards trade liberalization and the dismantling of investment barriers' and that tying its aid benefited Canada rather than developing countries. At the time, Canada tied more of its ODA than the majority of

its peers. At least 50 per cent of aid to African and least-developed countries, and two-thirds of aid to other countries, had to be spent in Canada. No more than 10 per cent of the cost of emergency food aid could be used to purchase food in countries other than Canada. Under pressure from G8 and DAC partners, Canada initially agreed to untie certain categories of aid to least-developed countries only, but not food aid (Canada, 2002: 19–23).

After a tsunami devastated the coastal areas of many Asian countries in 2004, the Canadian response highlighted the shortcomings of tied food aid. Rather than buy rice available in nearby Asian countries, the government shipped Canadian surplus wheat, which cost more, took longer to arrive, and was less suited to local diets. The government responded to widespread criticism by reducing the tied component of food aid to 50 per cent.

In 2005, Canada signed the Paris Declaration on Aid Effectiveness, which committed the government to untying aid, though with no specific deadline for eliminating the practice altogether (OECD, 2005: 6, 9). In 2007, Canada remained one of the countries with the highest rate of tied aid: 25.4 per cent, compared to DAC average of 15.2 per cent. By then, several countries, including Ireland, Sweden, and the UK, had completely untied all assistance (OECD, 2008: Table 23). In 2008, the government announced its intention to untie fully all aid by 2012–13 (CIDA, 2008). This will eliminate the ineffectiveness caused by tying procurement to the donor country and bring Canada in line with the international norm, though only slowly and rather belatedly.

Show me the impact! Criticisms of CIDA from within government

Outside actors raise a litany of criticisms against CIDA and Canadian foreign aid with great regularity. Commonly raised themes include CIDA's excessive bureaucratization and centralization; lack of both geographic and sectoral focus, leadership, and an overall vision or clearly articulated purpose; and failure to commit to a firm timetable for achieving the goal of disbursing 0.7 per cent of GNI on ODA (Chapnick, 2008; OECD, 2002, 2007; Goldfarb, and Tapp, 2006). On occasion, government bodies, such as Parliamentary committees, have published critical examinations of Canadian aid policy as well (for instance, Canada, 1987). A distinctive trend in recent years has been the number and, at times, vociferousness of attacks on CIDA from *within* government, as well as how drastic some of the remedies suggested are. Three government reports stand out on this regard, two from the Senate and one from a government-appointed panel, all of which lament in particular the lack of visible impact of Canadian aid. In addition, recent attacks on the agency by the minister responsible for CIDA can only be interpreted ominously.

In 2007, the Canadian Senate threw CIDA a one-two punch. First, the Standing Senate Committee on National Security and Defence complained about the lack of visibility of CIDA's efforts in Kandahar, the province of Afghanistan where Canada is playing a central role, and recommended that CIDA turn $20 million per year over to the Canadian Forces for them to use for development projects (Canada, 2007a: 9, 26). Second, the Standing Senate Committee on Foreign Affairs and International Trade deplored CIDA's '40 years of failure' in Africa and raised the possibility that the agency be abolished and its functions taken over by the Department of Foreign Affairs and International Trade (DFAIT). Among other things, it recommended focusing aid on the private sector and economic growth, at the expense of social spending and fighting poverty directly, which it considered unproductive welfare spending (Canada, 2007b). The media seized upon the moot possibility of abolishing CIDA, which was actually not the Senate committee's first preference.

Despite being very poorly argued and justified (for a detailed analysis, see Brown, 2007b), some of these recommendations squared well with pre-existing government beliefs and intentions, including the rationale for increased support to the private sector. The tenor of the report also supported the shift of focus away from Africa, first announced a few months after the report's publication. The government did not act on other recommendations, such as promoting trade with and investment in African countries or increasing support for UN peace operations in Africa.

In 2008, the government-appointed Independent Panel on Canada's Future Role in Afghanistan expressed its concern that more than 85 per cent of Canadian aid was being channelled through the Afghan government or multilateral institutions, with little left for 'quick-action' local projects or for initiatives that could be recognized as Canadian contributions. It recommended that CIDA fund at least one 'signature' project that would ensure that Canada achieved visibility, status, and gratitude for its development contributions (Canada, 2008: 25–6, 36). This resonated with public demands for demonstrable results for the hundreds of millions of dollars being poured into what had quickly become Canada's top foreign aid recipient.

Within a few months, the Canadian government announced three signature projects in Afghanistan: repairing the Dahla Dam and the connected irrigation system in Kandahar province, supporting the education sector, and eliminating polio. Results to date, however, have proved disappointing. More than a year later, as of September 2009, Canadian company SNC-Lavalin had not yet begun its work on the Dahla Dam because a key access road and bridge had not yet been completed, and only about 200 of the promised 10,000 jobs for Afghans had actually been created. Construction or repair work had been completed on only five of the promised 50 schools, with another

28 underway. During this period, violence forced the closure of 180, or roughly half, of the schools in Kandahar, suggesting that security should be a higher priority than new schools. The security situation also hindered immunization and the number of new cases of polio actually increased (A. Woods, 2009).

The Senate reports brought high-profile attention to CIDA's shortcomings, real and imagined, and placed the agency in a more vulnerable position. In 2009, an unprecedented event occurred: CIDA's own minister, Bev Oda, after spending her first two years in office talking up CIDA and its achievements, rather suddenly went on the attack and criticized the agency for its lack of technical expertise and its focus on inputs rather than results (Berthiaume, 2009). The patent unfairness of her criticisms further eroded morale among CIDA employees and raised the spectre that the government was laying the groundwork for future budget cuts (Brown, 2009).

These critiques all centred on the apparent lack of impact of Canadian aid. However, a fixation on immediately visible results has had a negative effect on effectiveness.

An unhealthy obsession with results

Since around 2007, CIDA has demonstrated an increased preoccupation with demonstrable results. The need to focus on results has long been a concern for the DAC (see OECD, 1996) and for CIDA itself (reflected in its use of 'results-based management' tools since the 1990s). The new fixation, bordering on obsession, is linked to both the Conservative leitmotif of accountability, and the need to justify massive expenditures in Afghanistan, which rapidly became by far the largest recipient of Canadian aid. It also reflects the scepticism of the Conservative Party and an important

part of its constituency towards the actual desirability of foreign aid, as well as the party's desire to demonstrate to taxpayers that their money is being well spent.

Unfortunately for donor governments seeking to claim credit, development assistance results are not always tangible or quick. For instance, 'qualitative changes in gender relations' are difficult to monitor and measure (Edwards, and Hulme, 1996: 968). Likewise, aid to the governance sector cannot be immediately assessed by quantifiable indicators—or if it can, only some components of results can be captured. Others can take a generation to bear fruit with any certainty. Even then, causality is difficult to establish. Long-term development successes are not attributable to a single source, especially when donors work closely with each other or a recipient government. As a growing proportion of aid funds are channelled to development programs and even sector-wide initiatives, rather than to individual projects (in line with current thinking on aid effectiveness), the task of attributing results becomes more difficult (Brown, and Morton, 2008: 3–4). Moreover, foreign aid is but one contribution to the development process in a given country. Others include domestic policies and planning, national and international investment, international trade policies, and resource endowments.[7]

As a result, CIDA has trouble identifying what it has accomplished. On its website, for instance, under the heading 'What are CIDA's achievements?', it mentions the global reduction in poverty levels, the increase in primary school enrolment, and the decline in infant mortality (CIDA, 2009b). No evidence, however, indicates that these accomplishments are the direct result of Canadian foreign aid, rather than other donors' assistance or in fact the policies of recipient governments themselves.

The inability to claim direct credit leaves CIDA vulnerable to unfair accusations of failure, epitomized by the Senate report on Africa, which concluded that Canadian aid had failed miserably because committee members could not find signs that CIDA's efforts had made a significant difference on a continental scale. It is not clear what kind of visible impact senators expected from an annual Canadian contribution that averaged only about 35 cents per African (Brown, 2007b). The lack of demonstrable results imputable to Canada does not mean, however, that Canadian aid was wasted.

By embracing the fetishization of immediately visible results, Canada biases its assistance towards short-term, stand-alone project assistance in sectors where results can be tangible and quick, exemplified by Canada's signature projects in Afghanistan. This can easily backfire when the high-profile projects fall behind schedule or fail to meet their targets, as is currently the case, further discrediting CIDA. Moreover, this type of assistance is at odds with the principles of the aid effectiveness agenda, which emphasizes the long-term integration of development efforts with recipient government institutions, based on recipient needs and strategies, rather than scoring quick points for individual donors. It also contradicts the state-building objectives that underpin assistance to 'fragile states' such as Afghanistan, whose future depends far more on its own government gaining legitimacy among Afghans than the Canadian government doing so. In sum, a fixation on short-term visible results emphasizes 'accountancy' more than it does actual 'accountability', which requires a longer time horizon (Edwards and Hulme, 1996: 968).

A more productive approach would also acknowledge the inherent uncertainties in development assistance, especially in conflict zones, and adopt aid modalities that try to mitigate these problems over the medium-to-long term. Rather than pandering to public pressure and aiming for 'quick wins' for Canada, the government could educate the Canadian public about the challenges of development, the importance of strengthening local institutions, and the real principles of effectiveness in the longer term—in Afghanistan and in other recipient countries.

Low volume, low impact

Though the question of the quantity of ODA can be considered independently of its quality, the volume of a country's aid program is strongly related to its impact. A country delivering a very small amount of highly effective aid is making a very limited contribution, no matter how effective it might be. For that reason, the volume of Canadian assistance is important to consider under the rubric of the effectiveness of Canada's aid. Moreover, when a country such as Canada contributes only limited resources, it will have difficulty claiming a leadership role among donors, an attempt that Denis Stairs (2003: 252) derides as the 'value-imperialism of the weak'.

In 2008, of the 22 OECD/DAC members, Canada was only the tenth largest donor and, in terms of generosity (as measured by the ODA/GNI ratio), it ranked sixteenth (OECD, 2009: 1).[8] Although Canada has become more generous since 2000, its global ranking has not improved. Other countries' aid programs, especially European ones, have grown faster and Canada's position may in fact slip further in coming years if this trend continues. This is consistent with Canada's historical decline in importance as a donor. Whereas in 1975, when Canadian ODA represented 0.54 per cent of GNI, Canada provided approximately 6 per cent of global ODA; in 2008 the figures had dropped to 0.32 per cent and about 4 per cent.[9] With the Obama Administration's planned massive increase of US aid expenditure, the rise of philanthro-capitalism (best illustrated by the Bill and Melinda Gates Foundation) and the increased importance of China and other non-OECD donors (Marten, and Witte, 2008; N. Woods, 2008), Canada will be further marginalized on the global aid scene, even if it increases its aid budget modestly every year.

In 2002, Chrétien announced that Canadian foreign aid would grow by eight per cent annually and that aid to Africa would double by 2009. Martin subsequently reaffirmed these two commitments and the Conservatives honoured them.[10] However, the Harper government was the first to abandon the commitment to eventually allocating 0.7 per cent of GNI to ODA, in line with the Conservatives' doubts about the value of foreign aid. Even while the Chrétien government was cutting expenditures in the 1990s, it always reiterated its commitment to the goal set in 1970 at the United Nations and in fact proposed by Canadian political icon Lester B. Pearson. The 2006 Conservative election platform, however, stated that it would 'increase spending on Overseas Development Assistance beyond the currently projected level and move towards the OECD average level' (Conservative Party of Canada, 2006: 46). It is worth noting that 'moving towards' is not the same as 'reaching' and that it is not clear whether the 'OECD average level' refers to the average DAC country effort, which was 0.47 per cent in 2008, or to the average for the entire DAC, which was 0.30 per cent, a ratio that Canada has already exceeded (OECD, 2009: 1).

Also unclear is what is to happen after 2010. The government has given no concrete indication that ODA levels will continue to increase or even be maintained. Though no official policy announcement has been made on this issue, Minister Oda stated in an interview that there will be 'no new major injections of funding until she is satisfied the agency is working properly' (Berthiaume, 2009). Likewise, now that aid to Africa has doubled but is no longer Canada's top priority region, it could well remain stagnant or be cut, possibly even dramatically.

Given Canada's relatively paltry generosity when compared to its peers and its lack of commitment to increasing aid flows substantially, it is logical that the government prefers instead to emphasize improving effectiveness, increasing Canada's prestige and the benefits that accrue to Canada, all discussed below. As part of its effectiveness mantra, the government constantly repeats the word 'focus'.

Focus, focus, focus

Increasing focus is the cornerstone of most aid policy announcements. Greater focus, both geographical and thematic, is assumed but never demonstrated to improve effectiveness. The constant shifting in priority countries, continents, and sectors, however, unambiguously decreases effectiveness.

Canadian aid has been very widely dispersed since the early 1970s (Morrison, 2000: 26). Canada is the only donor country to belong to the Commonwealth, the Francophonie, and the Organization of American States. Membership has its privileges, but also its obligations—or at least an interest in providing assistance to developing country members in Asia, francophone and anglophone Africa, Latin America, and the Caribbean. Aid is also dispersed in a broad range of sectors. The donor consensus, however, underlines the need to focus on a smaller number of both countries and sectors in order to increase effectiveness. Canada's donor peers, like its domestic critics, have often criticized CIDA programming for being excessively scattered (OECD, 2002, 2007). Successive Canadian governments have taken steps to concentrate not only on a subset of countries, but also on a handful of sectors.

In 2002, the Chrétien government announced its intention to enhance its relationship with 'a limited number of the world's poorest countries', emphasizing how this would improve the impact of Canadian ODA (Canada, 2002: 11).[11] Of the nine countries selected for 'enhanced partnerships', two-thirds were in Sub-Saharan Africa.[12] Unable to achieve this degree of concentration, the Martin government announced in 2005 that Canada would increase the impact of its aid by dedicating two-thirds of its bilateral aid to 25 'development partners' (Canada, 2005).[13] To the existing nine countries, it added eight Sub-Saharan African ones, two Latin American ones, five Asian ones, and one European one.[14] In 2009, the Harper government radically redrew the list, retaining the original core of nine, adding the West Bank/Gaza and four new countries in the Americas, while dropping 12 of the 16 additions from 2005, including all eight African ones.[15] Since only four years had elapsed, it was too soon to see results in the countries added in 2005, as CIDA projects take an average of three-and-a-half years just to be to be approved (Auditor General of Canada, 2009: 27).

Successive governments also announced a focus on a limited number of sectors. In 2001, CIDA adopted social development priorities in health and nutrition, basic education, HIV/AIDS, and protecting children, all of which were meant to include the promotion of gender equality. These aligned well with Canada's commitment to the Millennium Development Goals. In the 2002 development policy statement, the minister added rural development and agriculture, as well as the private sector (Canada, 2002: 14–16). In Martin's 2005 policy statement, the list was redrawn to focus on good governance, health, basic education, private sector development, and environmental sustainability, again with gender as a cross-cutting theme (Canada, 2005: 11). In 2009, the government announced three 'priority themes': increasing food security, stimulating sustainable economic growth, and securing the future of children and youth. This unexpected announcement created confusion in the Canadian development community, as 'themes' are not quite the same as sectors and could in fact encompass numerous sectors. For instance, the

future of children and youth would certainly include health and education, but arguably also a variety of efforts in technical training, job creation, and peacebuilding, to name but a few. The press release that announced the three themes also named a few specific sectors that will be strengthened via the themes, including the environment, gender equality, human rights, and governance (CIDA, 2009), further muddying the waters as to what was to be included and, more to the point, excluded.[16]

Though one could endlessly debate the merits of individual country recipients and sectors, two points put into perspective the question of focus. First, despite the consensus among donors on the need to focus on fewer recipients and sectors, the theoretical argument that it actually increases aid effectiveness has serious weaknesses, and claims to that effect lack empirical evidence (Munro, 2005). If all donors adopt such focus without coordinating their efforts, this also creates new risks, including the possibility of 'aid orphans', countries that donors have abandoned. Furthermore, a decision by a donor to focus only on certain sectors or themes contradicts its commitment—in previous aid policy statements (Canada, 2002; 2005) and under the Paris Declaration—to recipients' ownership of their development strategy and donor alignment with recipients' national priorities. Moreover, when a donor government seeks to pick specific sectors in which it has a comparative advantage, it reintroduces a more subtle form of tied aid through the back door.

Second, even if increased focus were in fact beneficial, radically changing the list of priority countries and sectors every few years—even in the name of effectiveness—increases aid volatility and thus actually reduces aid effectiveness. According to the latest report of the Auditor General of Canada (2009: 21), 'the lack of clear direction', in large part due to frequently changing priorities and senior staff, including presidents and ministers, 'has confused CIDA staff, recipient governments, and other donors, effectively undermining the Agency's long-term predictability'. The designation of priority sectors also contradicts other fundamental principles of aid effectiveness, notably the national ownership of development planning and donors' alignment with recipient countries' priorities, which Canada endorsed when it signed the Paris Declaration in 2005.[17] 'Focusing on focus', rather than on more substantive issues of the origins of and solutions to poverty and inequality, serves as a convenient justification for a given government's own preferences, while providing a veneer of selflessness and assuaging peer pressure.

Nevertheless, focus is not the only major donor preoccupation that often emphasizes form over content. Another is the question of policy coherence, to which this chapter now turns.

The quest for policy coherence

The question of coherence among different government departments and policies has been on the donor agenda for over a decade (OECD, 1996; Pratt, 1999). The Chrétien government mentioned it in its 2002 development policy statement (Canada, 2002: 17–18), but it was under Paul Martin that it became an important practice. Initially known as the '3-D approach' (referring to diplomacy, defence, and development), it was later expanded to include commerce and other areas and rebaptized the 'whole-of-government approach', which featured prominently in the Martin government's international policy statement.

Though in principle, coherence and consistency (much like aid effectiveness) can only be seen as a good thing, their impact on development goals is not necessarily positive. In essence, it depends on what becomes the overriding concern. If other departments, such as foreign affairs,

international trade, and defence, were to line up behind development goals, this could help a donor government achieve aid objectives. Notably, the interests of developing countries themselves could be better reflected in donor policies, at home and at the international level. For example, the lowering or elimination of tariff barriers and other protectionist measures would promote developing country exports and could raise incomes more than foreign aid does. Likewise, the use of donor troops to stabilize countries emerging from civil war could improve the impact of aid.

In practice, however, evidence from other donor countries suggests that policy integration leads to the subordination of development objectives to donors' foreign policy and defence priorities, not the other way around (Smillie, 2004: 15), which reduces rather than increases aid effectiveness. For many donors, the 'war on terror' has profoundly influenced their aid disbursements with the goal of enhancing their own security, in a global trend towards the increased 'securitization' of foreign aid (N. Woods, 2005). Such is clearly the case for Canada's involvement in Afghanistan, which commands a disproportionate amount of CIDA's attention and resources. Canadian ODA to that country ballooned from a paltry US$7 million in 2000 to US$345 million in 2007, representing about 8.5 per cent of total Canadian ODA.[18] The government presented Afghanistan as a 'laboratory' for a new way of carrying out foreign policy. In spite the unprecedentedly high expenditures, it is becoming increasingly but unsurprisingly clear that aid effectiveness is especially difficult in a war zone like Kandahar.[19] In 2007, CIDA President Robert Greenhill actually indicated that in the future Canada would focus less on 'failed and fragile states' such as Afghanistan and Haiti and more on countries where 'we've actually seen real results' (Berthiaume, 2007), suggesting that the 'lab experiment' had failed. In spite of the attempts to link

Canadian defence, diplomatic, and development initiatives in Afghanistan (Gillmore, and Mosazai, 2007; Simpson, 2007), none of the three Ds appears to be producing any clear progress, be it the defeat of the Taliban insurgency in Kandahar province, the strengthening of the Afghan state with a legitimate government, or the improvement of the lives of millions of impoverished Afghans.

Without this form of policy coherence, CIDA would be able to function with greater autonomy (Brown, 2008a) and have a greater impact on development by spending its funds in countries where they could be used more effectively, rather than being used—and ineffectually at that—to shore up Canadian and other donors' strategic priorities in Afghanistan and other countries engulfed in the war on terror, as is increasingly the case in Pakistan. It might nonetheless be too early to call for the end of the whole-of-government approach, as it might prove more effective for promoting development in countries in the midst of complex crises unrelated to the war on terror, such as Haiti (Baranyi, 2009). Much will depend on the mix of motivations that underpin donor policy coherence in such cases, addressed in the next section of this chapter.

MORPHING MOTIVATIONS

States are not monolithic unitary actors and it is generally not possible to discern clear, overarching motivations. As Ilan Kapoor (2008: 78) points out, one should avoid 'presupposing a homogeneous nation-state and fully rational and controlled policy-making'. Just as individuals can have mixed motives, so too can states. Moreover, different actors within government (CIDA, DFAIT, the Prime Minister's Office) or within a government department or agency (CIDA President's Office, Policy Branch, country desk officers) can differ widely in their approaches to ODA.

Analysts have long recognized that the simultaneous pursuit of political, commercial, and development objectives hampers aid efficiency (Canada, 1987: 7; Morrison, 2000: 15). The recent aid policy changes discussed above illustrate shifts in the government's thinking about ODA and the motivations that underpin them, even if the initiatives do not necessarily have a large impact on the actual day-to-day implementation of Canadian aid outside Afghanistan, especially not in the short term. Most CIDA employees try to keep their heads down and carry on with their jobs as before, regardless of new policy initiatives. In other words, though self-interested motivations characterize recent Canadian aid policy *changes*, one should not infer that those motives underlie Canadian foreign aid as a whole.

Traditionally, the motivation debate has been set up as a tug-of-war between self-interest ('realism', epitomized by Morgenthau, 1962) and selflessness ('humane internationalism', such as Lumsdaine, 1993). Though self-interest has become more important (Brown, 2007a; Pratt, 2000), the desire for prestige (as suggested by Nossal, 1988), in particular Canada's international reputation, better explains most recent changes than do more tangible commercial or even national security interests—including the emphasis placed on Afghanistan.

Throughout the 1990s, under Prime Minister Jean Chrétien, Canada's ODA declined steadily. Assistance to Africa was especially hard hit: It was cut from US$601 million in 1992 to $270 million in 2000, corresponding to a drop from 31 per cent of total Canadian aid to 19 per cent (Brown, 2008b: 272). It is thus a particularly noteworthy achievement—and compelling evidence of Canadians' capacity for collective amnesia—that Chrétien managed to reinvent himself in the early 2000s as a vociferous proponent of development assistance in general and aid to Africa in particular. Chrétien's sudden about-face in the final years of his mandate, including the renewal of aid itself and increased attention to Africa, were closely linked to his own concerns for personal legacy, a generous imprint he could make in Canada and on the global stage—though he was more successful at home than internationally (Brown, 2008b; Black, 2005, 2006).

Chrétien's successor, Paul Martin, focused less on personal credit than trying to improve Canada's global presence, notably mending its relations with the United States, which had suffered under Chrétien, most recently because of Canada's refusal to take part in the US-led invasion of Iraq. Martin's international policy statement was tellingly titled *A Role of Pride and Influence in the World*, which played to both the domestic and international audience. The priority the Liberals and later the Conservatives accorded to Afghanistan reflected a concern with proving that Canada could make important contributions to the NATO alliance, including by sending Canadian soldiers, assuming lead responsibility in Kandahar province, and making Afghanistan a top-priority recipient of Canadian ODA.

The Conservative government, in power since 2006, has not yet released any official documents outlining its approach to foreign aid. Despite the brevity of the section on international assistance, the federal budget is often the most detailed statement of the government's aid policies and priorities in any given year. For that reason, any analysis of aid policy initiatives is only slightly better than reading tea leaves. One must glean information from relatively brief press releases and vague public statements made by politicians, none of which has provided any in-depth rationale or justification for changes. As such, aid policymaking under Prime Minister Stephen Harper has been made 'by stealth' and is being drip-fed to Parliament, CIDA employees, and the Canadian public.

Still, some statements by top officials strongly suggest that international prestige has been a crucial consideration for the Conservative government

as well. For example, in 2007, the government indicated that Canada would concentrate efforts in countries where it could be among the top five donors, showing a clear desire to have a place at the table with the major donors (Canada, 2007c: 262)—assuming of course that there are actually five seats at the metaphoric and literal table. At the time, International Cooperation Minister Josée Verner noted that in some cases increasing expenditures only slightly would place Canada there, suggesting that the government was more interested in impressing voters and donor peers than it was in actual impact (Brown, 2008a).

After Bev Oda replaced Verner as CIDA minister in 2007, prestige abroad became less central—though it still characterized the desire for signature projects in Afghanistan. As Kapoor (2008: 87) notes, 'Nationalist symbols permit donors to be identified, thanked, or envied; they also enable it to stake its territory, and perhaps to gloat'. Signature projects mark Canada's international presence and enhance its national credibility, but they also contradict widely held principles of aid effectiveness. For that reason, they can actually detract from Canada's reputation among other donors and development workers in Canada and abroad. According to Nilima Gulrajani (2009: A13), '[i]n the world of international aid, Canada is reputed as a money-grubbing flag planter rather than effectively and selflessly serving the world's poor'. A discredited Canada makes it harder for the Canadian government and individual Canadian officials to influence donor debates within the OECD/DAC and in donor coordination groups on the ground in recipient countries. If the government ceases to increase or even fails to maintain aid budgets, its international reputation will suffer further.

With the shift in focus from Africa to the Americas, first announced by Harper at the 2007 G8 summit, the government's motivation ostensibly started to move away from rather symbolic prestige concerns and towards more concrete economic and more specifically commercial self-interest. The new list of 20 'core countries' released in 2009 operationalized this new regional priority when, as mentioned above, it dropped many poor African countries and added wealthier ones in Latin America and the Caribbean, notably ones of particular trade interest to Canada.[20] Soon after, CIDA President Margaret Biggs listed for the first time Canada's foreign policy considerations as an explicit official criterion for selecting core recipients (Lupick, 2009).

A concern for personal or national prestige, however, should not be overemphasized in the analysis of policy shifts.[21] Pressure from the donor community, notably within the OECD/DAC, plays an important but under-recognized part in shaping Canadian aid policy, as was the case with Canada's renewed emphasis on Africa in 2001–2 (Black, 2006). Chrétien and Martin generally followed the donor consensus, at times contributing to it. Harper, on the other hand, seemed at times to relish breaking with it and distancing himself from global norms (and Liberal priorities), especially eschewing the focus on Africa in favour of the Americas. Oda recognized this departure when outlining the government's new orientation in 2009, noting that it was 'not something that aims to please Irish rock stars', again framing it as beneficial for aid effectiveness (York, 2009: F7) when in fact it might be more beneficial for Canada than for the poor.

In this tale, one notable effort sought to push the Canadian government in the opposite direction. The ODA Accountability Act (Bill C-293) was passed by Parliament in 2008 as a private member's bill. It aimed to ensure that all Canadian aid would contribute directly to poverty reduction, take into account the perspectives of the poor, and be consistent with international human rights standards. However, its provisions lack teeth. According to the government's interpretation, Canadian ODA is

already in compliance with the new law, even if one can only at best expect a very indirect, long-term contribution of certain aid activities to poverty reduction. The new law may thus have no discernable effect on aid (Halifax Initiative, 2009) and the government would prefer to ignore its attempt to reorient aid, much to the consternation of Canadian development NGOs. Tellingly, none of the government's announcements since the law was passed have made any reference to the Act as providing any guidance on aid policy.

CONCLUSION: WHAT WOULD LESTER DO?

Prior to 2001, observers such as Pratt (2000) noted with concern that the government was increasingly justifying Canadian aid on the basis of global security, rather than the need to fight poverty and inequality. Most lamented the decline of Pearsonian idealism and a global justice imperative. This trend amplified after al-Qaeda attacks on the United States in 2001, impelling the government to focus on specifically Canadian security, rather than global security (Brown, 2007a; Simpson, 2007). As mentioned above, Canada is not exceptional in the 'securitization' of its foreign aid and the increased focus on self-interest, rather than poverty eradication (N. Woods, 2005).

At the same time, since 2000, a counter-trend has been emerging in the global aid regime. Epitomized by the MDGs' underlining of the urgency of the fight against poverty, emerging donor norms dictated increased aid volumes, especially to Sub-Saharan Africa, and much greater attention to social spending. This new trend also underscored the importance not only of policies in recipient countries but also highlighted ways that Canada and other donors themselves could improve their aid delivery, embodied in the Paris Declaration on Aid Effectiveness.

Since Chrétien's final years in office, and increasingly so under Harper, the government has presented its policy initiatives as ways of improving the effectiveness of Canadian aid. Some efforts, notably the untying of aid, were clear contributions to that goal, even if Canada was one of the last holdouts in this area. Similarly, Canada lags behind most of its peers in terms of the relative generosity of its aid. Other efforts, such as concentrating aid in fewer countries and sectors, have not been demonstrated to have a positive or negative effect on aid effectiveness—and raise some concerns and potential new risks for developing countries. Moreover, the frequency of changes in priority countries and sectors have in themselves undermined CIDA's aid effectiveness, as has the rapid turnover of senior officials. Other policies and practices, notably the emphasis on signature projects in Afghanistan and the redefining of core sectors and countries every few years, are political decisions and preferences, which directly or indirectly contradict stated Canadian policies on local ownership, the predictability of aid flows, the centrality of long-term relationships with recipients, and other internationally accepted principles of aid effectiveness. The continuing heavy concentration of Canadian ODA in Afghanistan, despite the severe security-related impediments to effective aid, epitomizes politically motivated aid priorities. Finally, the adoption of a whole-of-government approach to foreign policy could theoretically enhance aid effectiveness. However, to date, policy coherence has instead been undermining it by generally subjecting development priorities to donor self-interest, rather than the other way around.

Throughout this period, new Canadian policies and priorities usually reflected the desire for prestige: personal prestige in Chrétien's final years as prime minister, but more often Canada's international prestige, especially under Martin and in the early Harper years, which sought to use aid to bolster Canada's place in the world, including improving its relationship with the United States. The size and nature of Canada's involvement in Afghanistan best illustrates the government desire for the US and other Western allies to consider it a team player. The relative feebleness of Canada's renewal of aid, however, ensured that Canadians, rather than other donor countries, would be these efforts' main audience. By 2009, notwithstanding continued involvement in Afghanistan, it appeared that the Harper government was less interested in using foreign aid to redefine Canada's place in the world and gain international prestige. It has failed to make any commitment to increasing or even maintaining aid flows after 2010, it ended Africa's privileged position as the continent that most urgently needed aid, and it embraced instead the open use of ODA for Canadian commercial self-interest in Latin America and the Caribbean.

It should be noted, however, that self-interest and international prestige-seeking need not be incompatible with development efforts, depending on how national interest is constructed. If Canada were to seek prominence, through renewed Pearsonian internationalism, by becoming a leader in generous, innovative, poverty-fighting foreign aid, it could gain respect in the eyes of its donor peers and the developing world. Canada has brought new perspectives to donors' discussions in the past, including the importance of gender issues and NGOs (Morrison, 1998; 2000). Spearheading a similar issue in the future, such as human rights-based approaches to development, could help provide a platform for global leadership and enhance Canada's influence, for instance helping it obtain a non-permanent seat at the UN Security Council. The question of aid policy thus encompasses not only the volume of aid and the underlying objective of Canadian assistance, but also the kind of country Canada wants to be, Canada's place in the world, and the kind of world Canada envisions.[22]

The coming years will pose additional challenges to the aid regime in general and to Canadian policies in particular. In the short term, Canada and other donors are likely to cut aid expenditure due to the global economic crisis, despite the even greater effect of the crisis on poor countries. Over the medium and long term, climate change will increase the developing world's need for international assistance, notably due to more frequent and severe natural disasters, lower crop yields, food scarcity, and higher food prices (Ayers, and Huq, 2009). Alongside this process, Canada's place among donors is waning, as its share of global aid flow decreases, accelerated by the rise of non-traditional donors such as China and non-state donors. The G20, where Canada's influence is limited, is supplanting the G8, in which Canada sits among a select few. Canada could respond by further concentrating on narrowly defined self-interest, thereby sealing its fate as a minor player on the world stage, or it could radically rethink how and to whom it provides assistance and try to make niche contributions that would actually contribute to aid effectiveness on the ground.

Acknowledgements

For helpful comments and suggestions, I thank Chris Brown, Molly den Heyer, Brigette Depape, Tristen Naylor, Rosalind Raddatz, Arne Rückert, Jennifer Salahub, Liam Swiss, and two CIDA employees who prefer to remain anonymous. All remaining deficiencies are strictly my own. I am also grateful to the Social Sciences and Humanities Research Council of Canada and the University of Ottawa for funding that made this research possible.

Key Terms

Aid Effectiveness
Millennium Development Goals
Official Development Assistance

Policy Coherence
Tied Aid

Notes

1. Lumsdaine (1993) epitomizes the short-lived initial optimism of the post–Cold War period, celebrating the constant increase in aid budgets, an increased focus on humanitarian and egalitarian goals, greater emphasis on very poor countries and very poor people within those countries, the untying of aid, and the replacement of loans with grants.

2. It is worth underlining that this chapter focuses its analysis on changes at the policy level and does not examine the concrete impact of new initiatives on the ground, which may not yet be discernable and are only beginning to be studied in depth.

3. For instance: 'CIDA will reorient its programming in the poorest countries towards new approaches that are based on the principles of effective development' (Canada, 2002: 7); 'In order to increase the effectiveness of the development cooperation program, we will focus our efforts in a few priority sectors and in a small group of countries and will engage in value-added, selective partnerships with Canadians and with the most effective multilateral institutions' (Canada, 2005: 31); 'By fully untying Canada's aid, the Government is delivering on its commitment in the 2006 Speech from the Throne to support "a more effective use of aid dollars" and the 2007 Budget's promise not only to increase the amount of Canada's international assistance envelope, but also "to make our existing resources work more effectively"' (CIDA, 2008: 1); and 'With greater efficiency, focus, and accountability, our Government's new approach to Canadian aid will be even more effective' (CIDA, 2009a: 1).

4. I don't mean to accept uncritically the principles of the Paris Declaration (see Hyden 2008). Still, it represents the standing consensus on what constitutes aid effectiveness, to which Canada has subscribed and against which Canada's policies and practices can be assessed.

5. A notable exception is the United States, which embraced the concept of the presence of the 'right' policy environment as the basis for selecting recipients by its new bilateral development agency, the Millennium Challenge Corporation.

6. This is analyzed in Lalonde (2009), with a focus on the harmonization component.

7. As a result, the concept of *development* effectiveness is emerging as an alternative to *aid* effectiveness. Its meaning, however, has yet to be clearly defined and the term is used in many different ways (Kindornay, and Morton, 2009).

8. By way of comparison, Canada was the fifth largest OECD donor in the mid-1980s. Measured as a ratio of GNI, Canada's place slipped even further: it was the sixth most generous country as recently as 1994 (Morrison, 2000: 21).

9. OECD International Development Statistics, Internet, www.oecd.org/dac/stats/idsonline, accessed 27 September 2009.

10. Because its Africa expenditures for the baseline year of 2003–04 were lower than expected, the Harper government was able to cut $700 million from its targeted expenditure of $2.8 billion and still claim to have kept its promise.

11. As the policy document's title suggests, *Canada Making a Difference in the World: A Policy Statement on Strengthening Aid Effectiveness*, it emphasized better aid, rather than just more aid. Much of the thinking on effectiveness reflected, belatedly, the principles of OECD/DAC's 1996 document, *Shaping the 21st Century: The Contribution of Development Assistance* (OECD, 1996), which Canada had endorsed six years earlier. It also reflected a concern with orienting Canadian assistance in support of the MDGs.

12. Namely Ghana, Ethiopia, Mali, Mozambique, Senegal, and Tanzania. The others were Honduras, Bolivia, and Bangladesh.

13. As Stairs (2005) pointed out, two-thirds of bilateral aid were already going to 25 countries—though not the same 25. This new policy would therefore not necessarily achieve any greater concentration.

14. Benin, Burkina Faso, Cameroon, Kenya, Malawi, Niger Rwanda, and Zambia; Guyana and Nicaragua; Cambodia, Indonesia, Pakistan, Sri Lanka, and Vietnam; and Ukraine.

15. The other additions to the list in the Americas were Colombia, Haiti, Peru, and the Caribbean regional program. The other countries dropped were the two Latin American countries added in 2005 (Guyana and Nicaragua) and two newly added Asian ones (Cambodia and Sri Lanka).

16. The confusion was exacerbated in late 2009, when CIDA Minister Bev Oda unexpectedly rejected a grant application by KAIROS, an NGO affiliated with Canada's main Christian denominations. Though the NGO had developed the proposal in close cooperation with CIDA officials and it focused on human rights, good governance and environmental sustainability, which were all listed as priority areas on the latest policy press release, Oda's spokesperson stated that the 'project does not meet CIDA's current priorities' (Payton, 2009). The decision was widely interpreted as retaliation for the NGO's criticism of some Harper government policies.

17. As CIDA itself has recognized, 'Long-term development requires a predictable and stable source of funding to be effective' and 'effective international assistance involves long-term relationships with development partners' (Canada, 2005: 10).

18. OECD International Development Statistics, Internet, www.oecd.org/dac/stats/idsonline, accessed 28 December 2009.

19. This commonsensical fact explains why donors are currently providing only humanitarian assistance to Darfur. Before attempting to achieve longer-term development, they are waiting for security to be re-established.

20. Though ODA to Latin America can legitimately fight poverty and inequality (Cameron, 2007), the new list notably included comparatively well-off countries (the English-speaking Caribbean) and ones where Canada was actively pursuing free-trade agreements (Colombia and Peru).

21. Prestige-seeking and compliance with norms are not incompatible. As Lumsdaine (1993: 67) argues, 'doing something costly and right but doing it out of desire for approbation' is evidence of the strength of peer pressure and norms.

22. For a critique of this national(ist) framework for situating the aid relationship, see Kapoor (2008).

References

Auditor General of Canada. (2009). 'Chapter 8. Strengthening Aid Effectiveness—Canadian International Development Agency'. *Report of the Auditor General of Canada to the House of Commons*. Ottawa: Office of the Auditor General of Canada.

Ayers, Jessica M., and Saleemul Huq. (2009). 'Supporting Adaptation to Climate Change: What Role for Official Development Assistance?', *Development Policy Review* 27, 6: 675–92.

Baranyi, Stephen. (2009). 'Canada and the "Travail" of Partnership in Haiti' in Andrew Thompson and Jorge Heine, eds., *Haiti's Governance Challenges and the International Community* (draft).

Berthiaume, Lee. (2007). 'CIDA Boss Hints at Shift to Stable Nations'. *Embassy*, 27 June.

Berthiaume, Lee. (2009). 'CIDA Consultations on the Way, Minister Reassures'. *Embassy*, 27 May.

Black, David R. (2005). 'From Kananaskis to Gleneagles: assessing Canadian "leadership" on Africa'. *Behind the Headlines* 62, 3: 1–17.

Black, David R. (2006). 'Canadian Aid to Africa: Assessing "Reform"', -pp. 318–19 in Andrew F. Cooper and Dane Rowlands, eds., *Canada Among Nations 2006: Minorities and Priorities*. Montreal and Kingston: McGill-Queen's University Press.

Brown, Chris, and Edward T. Jackson. (2009). 'Could the Senate be Right? Should CIDA be Abolished?', pp. 151–74 in Allan M. Maslove, ed., *How Ottawa Spends, 2009–2010: Economic Upheaval and Political Dysfunction*. Montreal and Kingston: McGill-Queen's University Press.

Brown, Stephen. (2007a). 'Creating the World's Best Development Agency'? Confusion and Contradictions in CIDA's New Policy Blueprint', *Canadian Journal of Development Studies* 28, 2: 213–28.

Brown, Stephen. (2007b). 'Le Rapport du Sénat sur l'aide canadienne à l'Afrique : une analyse à rejeter', *Le Multilatéral* 1, 3: 1, 6–7.

Brown, Stephen. (2008a). 'CIDA under the Gun'. Pp. 91–107 in Jean Daudelin and Daniel Schwanen, eds., *Canada Among Nations 2007: What Room for Manoeuvre?* Montreal and Kingston: McGill-Queen's University Press.

Brown, Stephen. (2008b). 'L'aide publique canadienne à l'Afrique : vers un nouvel âge d'or ?'. Pp. 267–90 in François Audet, Marie-Eve Desrosiers, and Stéphane Roussel, eds., *L'aide canadienne au développement : bilan, défis et perspectives*. Montreal: Presses de l'Université de Montréal.

Brown, Stephen. (2009). 'CIDA under attack (from its own minister)'. *The Mark*, 23 June.

Brown, Stephen, and Bill Morton. (2008). 'Reforming aid and development cooperation: Accra, Doha and beyond'. Policy Note. Ottawa: North-South Institute.

Burnside, Craig, and David Dollar. (2000). 'Aid, Policies, and Growth', *American Economic Review* 90, 4: 847–68.

Cameron, John. (2007). 'CIDA in the Americas: New Directions and Warning Signs for Canadian Development Policy', *Canadian Journal of Development Studies* 28, 2: 229–47.

Canada. (1987). *For Whose Benefit? Report on Canada's Official Development Assistance Policies and Programs*. Ottawa: House of Commons Standing Committee on External Affairs and International Trade.

Canada. (2002). *Canada Making a Difference in the World: A Policy Statement on Strengthening Aid Effectiveness*. Hull, QC: Canadian International Development Agency.

Canada. (2005). *Canada's International Policy Statement: A Role of Pride and Influence in the World; Development*. Gatineau, QC: Canadian International Development Agency.

Canada. (2007a). *Canadian Troops in Afghanistan: Taking a Hard Look at a Hard Mission*. Ottawa: Senate of Canada, Standing Senate Committee on National Security and Defence.

Canada. (2007b). *Overcoming 40 Years of Failure: A New Road Map for Sub-Saharan Africa*. Ottawa: Senate of Canada, Standing Senate Committee on Foreign Affairs and International Trade.

Canada. (2007c). *Budget Plan 2007*. Ottawa: Department of Finance.

Canada. (2008). *Report of the Independent Panel on Canada's Future Role in Afghanistan*. Ottawa: Manley Commission.

Canada. 2009. *Statistical Report on International Assistance, Fiscal Year 2006–2007*. Gatineau, QC: Canadian International Development Agency.

Chapnick, Adam. (2008). 'Canada's Aid Program: Still Struggling After Sixty Years', *Behind the Headlines* 65, 3: 1–28.

CIDA. (2008). 'Canada Fully Unties its Development Aid' (5 September). Internet, www.acdi-cida.gc.ca/acdi-cida/ACDI-CIDA.nsf/eng/NAT-9583229-GQC, last accessed 28 September 2009.

CIDA. (2009a). 'Canada Introduces a New Effective Approach to its International Assistance' (20 May). Internet, www.acdi-cida.gc.ca/acdi-cida/ACDI-CIDA.nsf/eng/NAT-5208514-G7B, last accessed 27 September 2009.

CIDA. (2009b). 'CIDA in Brief' (5 August). Internet, www.acdi-cida.gc.ca/acdi-cida/ACDI-CIDA.nsf/eng/JUD-829101441-JQC, last accessed 27 September 2009.

Conservative Party of Canada. (2006). *Stand Up for Canada, Conservative Party of Canada: Federal Election Platform 2006*.

Edwards, Michael, and David Hulme. (1996). 'Too Close for Comfort? The Impact of Official Aid on Nongovernmental Organizations', *World Development* 24, 6: 961–73.

Gillmore, Scott, and Janan Mosazai. (2007). 'Defence, Development, and Diplomacy: The Case of Afghanistan, 2001–2005', pp. 143–67 in Jennifer Welsh and Ngaire Woods, eds., *Exporting Good Governance: Temptations and Challenges in Canada's Aid Program*. Waterloo: Wilfred Laurier University Press.

Goldfarb, Danielle, and Stephen Tapp. (2006). *How Canada Can Improve Its Development Aid: Lessons from Other Aid Agencies*. Commentary No. 232. Toronto: C.D. Howe Institute.

Gulrajani, Nilima. (2009). 'How politicization has been silently killing CIDA's effectiveness'. *Globe and Mail*, 8 June, A13.

Halifax Initiative. (2009). 'Official interpretations of the "ODA Accountability Act" one year later'. Issue Brief. Ottawa: Halifax Initiative.

Hyden, Goran. (2008). 'After the Paris Declaration: Taking on the Issue of Power', *Development Policy Review* 26, 3: 259–74.

Jepma, Catrinus J. (1991). *The Tying of Aid*. Paris: Organisation for Economic Co-operation and Development.

Kapoor, Ilan. *The Postcolonial Politics of Development*. London and New York: Routledge, 2008.

Killick, Tony. (2004). 'Politics, Evidence and the New Aid Agenda', *Development Policy Review* 22, 1: 5–29.

Kindornay, Shannon, and Bill Morton. (2009). 'Development effectiveness: towards new understandings'. Issues brief. Ottawa: North-South Institute.

Lalonde, Jennifer. (2009). *Harmony and Discord: International Aid Harmonization and Donor State Domestic Influence. The Case of Canada and the Canadian International Development Agency*. PhD. dissertation. Baltimore: Johns Hopkins University.

Lensink, Robert, and Howard White. (2000). 'Assessing Aid: A Manifesto for Aid in the 21st Century?' *Oxford Development Studies* 28, 1: 5–17.

Lumsdaine, David Halloran. (1993). *Moral Vision in International Politics: The Foreign Aid Regime, 1949–89*. Princeton, NJ: Princeton University Press.

Lupick, Travis. (2009). 'CIDA refocused international aid with foreign policy in mind'. *Georgia Straight* (21 May).

Marten, Robert, and Jan Martin Witte. (2008). 'Transforming Development? The role of philanthropic foundations in international development cooperation', GPPi Research Paper Series No. 10, Berlin.

Munro, Lauchlan T. (2005). 'Focus-Pocus? Thinking Critically about Whether Aid Organizations Should Do Fewer Things in Fewer Countries', *Development and Change* 36, 3: 425–47.

Morgenthau, Hans. (1962). 'A Political Theory of Foreign Aid', *American Political Science Review* 56, 2: 301–9.

Morrison, David R. (1998). *Aid and Ebb Tide: A History of CIDA and Canadian Development Assistance*. Waterloo: Wilfred Laurier University Press.

———. (2000). 'Canadian Aid: A Mixed Record and an Uncertain Future', pp. 15–36 in Jim Freedman, ed., *Transforming Development: Foreign Aid for a Changing World*. Toronto, Buffalo, and London: University of Toronto Press.

Nossal, Kim R. (1988). 'Mixed Motives Revisited: Canada's Interest in Development Assistance'. *Canadian Journal of Political Science* 21, 1: 35–56.

OECD. (1996). *Shaping the 21st Century: The Contribution of Development* Cooperation. Paris: Development Assistance Committee, Organisation for Economic Co-operation and Development.

OECD. (2002). 'Development Co-operation Review: Canada'. Paris: Development Assistance Committee, Organisation for Economic Co-operation and Development.

OECD. (2005). 'Paris Declaration on Aid Effectiveness'. Internet, www.oecd.org/dataoecd/11/41/34428351.pdf, last accessed September 28, 2009.

OECD. (2007). 'Canada: Development Assistance Committee (DAC) Peer Review'. Paris: Organisation for Economic Co-operation and Development, Development Assistance Committee.

OECD. (2008). 'Statistical Annex of the 2009 Development Co-operation Report'. Tables updated on 5 December 2008. Internet, www.oecd.org/dac/stats/dac/dcrannex, last accessed 28 September 2009.

OECD. (2009). 'Net Official Development Assistance in 2008'. Paris: Organisation for Economic Co-operation and Development. Internet, www.oecd.org/dataoecd/48/34/42459170.pdf, last accessed 20 September 2009.

Payton, Laura. (2009). 'KAIROS funding cuts chill community'. *Embassy*, 9 December.

Pratt, Cranford. (1999). 'Greater Policy Coherence, a Mixed Blessing: The Case of Canada'. Pp. 78–103 in Jacques Forster and Olav Stokke, eds., *Policy Coherence in Development Co-operation*. London and Portland, OR: Frank Cass.

Pratt, Cranford. (2000). 'Alleviating Global Poverty or Enhancing Security: Competing Rationales for Canadian Development Assistance'. Pp. 37–59 in Jim Freedman, ed., *Transforming Development: Foreign Aid for a Changing World*. Toronto, Buffalo, and London: University of Toronto Press.

Simpson, Erin. (2007). 'From Inter-dependence to Conflation: Security and Development in the Post-9/11 Era', *Canadian Journal of Development Studies* 28, 2: 263–75.

Smillie, Ian. (2004). 'ODA: Options and Challenges for Canada'. Ottawa: Canadian Council for International Co-operation.

Stairs, Denis. (2003). 'Myths, Morals, and Reality in Canadian Foreign Policy'. *International Journal* 58, 2: 239–56.

Stairs, Denis. (2005). 'Confusing the Innocent with Numbers and Categories: The International Policy Statement and the Concentration of Development Assistance'. Calgary: Canadian Defence and Foreign Affairs Institute.

Woods, Allan. (2009). 'Polio defeats Canada's pet project'. *Toronto Star*, 16 September.

Woods, Ngaire. (2005). 'The shifting politics of foreign aid', *International Affairs* 81, 2: 393–409.

Woods, Ngaire. (2008). 'Whose aid? Whose influence? China, emerging donors and the silent revolution in development assistance', *International Affairs* 84, 6: 1205–21.

World Bank. (1998). *Assessing Aid: What Works, What Doesn't, and Why*. New York: Oxford University Press.

York, Geoffrey. (2009). 'Banned aid'. *Globe and Mail*, 30 May, pp. F1, F6–7.

27

CANADA, THE G8, AND AFRICA: THE RISE AND DECLINE OF A HEGEMONIC PROJECT?

David Black

In 2001–2, the Canadian government, led by then-Prime Minister Jean Chrétien, seized the opening towards Africa created at the 2001 Genoa G8 Summit, and through a sustained and sophisticated diplomatic effort ensured that Africa took centre stage at the 2002 Kananaskis Summit in Calgary. The resulting G8 Africa Action Plan, itself a response to the New Partnership for Africa's Development (NEPAD) championed by several of the continent's then new leaders, effectively set this concert of the world's wealthiest capitalist countries onto a path of sustained engagement with the challenges of the world's poorest and least secure continent. Canada itself, having made 'Africa' a G8 focus, appeared set to build on its lead through ongoing commitments in aid, security, and investment. Yet by the Gleneagles Summit in 2005—an event that effectively overshadowed previous G8 initiatives toward Africa—there were indications that the ardour of the Canadian government was faltering, at least for the plans framed by Tony Blair's UK government. And by the Heiligendamm Summit in 2007, the

new Conservative Prime Minister, Stephen Harper, was signalling a shift in priority from Africa to the Americas (Freeman, 8/6/2007). Much subsequent critique has targeted the Conservatives for their ostensible (though overstated) 'abandonment' of Africa (see Ignatieff, 2009).

How are we to make sense of this trajectory, theoretically and historically? What does it reveal about the intra-hegemonic politics of Africa's erstwhile 'new partnership' with the G8, and the possibility of consistent, thoughtful engagement? What, more particularly, does it reveal about the nature and limits of Canada's role as a 'middle' or 'secondary power' in the world's wealthiest club? I will argue that Canada's extraordinary engagement with African issues in the early part of the decade can be understood as 'hegemonic work' in two senses: attempting to foster a broadly supported consensus on how to more fully integrate the continent that 'globalization left behind' into the dominant world order; and in so doing, reinforcing key legitimizing myths concerning the

Canadian state domestically. However, the 'success' and sustainability of this work has been compromised by the shallowness and inconstancy of Canadian interest(s) in Africa. While some resurgence, albeit limited, of Canadian concern with the continent can be seen in the run-up to the 2010 G8 (and now G20) Summit, to be hosted by Canada, it will be difficult to rebuild the credibility and connections that were disrupted in the second half of the decade, even if the will to do so can be mobilized.

The paper begins with an elaboration of Africa policy as 'hegemonic work'. It then focuses on what was, and was not, achieved at the 2002 Kananaskis Summit and its aftermath; on Canada's ambivalent role in the context of the 2005 Gleneagles Summit, anchoring 'the year of Africa'; and on the subsequent de-emphasis on the continent under the Harper Conservatives. Finally, it considers what can be anticipated as Canada prepares to host the G8 (and G20) once again in 2010, and the implications of this analysis for African governments and organizations.

AFRICA AS HEGEMONIC WORK[1]:

The G8's sustained engagement with Africa over the course of the 2000s can be understood as an attempt to forge a hegemonic project, in the neo-Gramscian sense popularized by Robert Cox, of fostering a relatively stable and widely accepted order based on an 'inter-subjective sharing of behavioural expectations' (Cox, 1989: 829; see also see Cox with Sinclair, 1996). This is particularly challenging, if important, in the face of vast inequalities of wealth and power, such as those that had deepened between the members of the G8 and the governments and peoples of Africa during the previous two decades of neoliberal globalization. In short, a continent that had been relatively

(and in some respects absolutely) diminished, in material and security terms, by its limited and frequently pathological encounters with globalization (see Ferguson, 2007: 25–49) posed a particularly acute challenge to the governments that had been the principal carriers and beneficiaries of that order. The need to be seen as responding to this challenge had been heightened at the start of the new millennium by the increasing scale and intensity of the anti-globalization protests that had overshadowed G8 and related meetings at Genoa, Seattle, Quebec City, and beyond.[2]

In the face of this challenge, an attractive assemblage of Africa's most prominent leaders, including Presidents Mbeki of South Africa, Obasanjo of Nigeria, and Wade of Senegal, brought forward a proposal for a 'New Africa Initiative' at the Genoa G8 Summit in 2001 as the basis for a comprehensive new 'partnership'. G8 governments, led by Canada's Chrétien, the UK's Blair, and France's Chirac, responded quickly and positively, agreeing to the appointment of African Personal Representatives to craft a concerted G8 response to what evolved on the African side into the NEPAD. The overture was attractive not only because of the considerations noted above, but because a central premise of the African plan was an acceptance by African governments of their primary responsibility for the challenges they faced, and the solutions to them. This suggested to G8 leaders the basis for a more attractive 'bargain' than had been possible in the past, including implied absolution for their own historic role(s) in the continent's trials. The assessment of Sir Nicholas Bayne reflects this understanding: 'This time, Mbeki, Obasanjo, Wade and their colleagues have accepted that Africans are themselves to blame for their problems and that they must take responsibility for their own recovery' (Bayne, 2003: 6). Whatever the historical and analytical shortcomings of this understanding, its political appeal for G8 leaders was clear.

Substantively, both the relatively spare Africa Action Plan (AAP, 2002) that emerged at Kananaskis, and the massive report of the Commission for Africa (2005) that controversially anchored the G8's next 'big push' on Africa at Gleneagles in 2005, reflected and reinforced a set of assumptions about the challenges facing the continent and the prescriptions to deal with them. These assumptions rested firmly within the dominant 'post-Washington Consensus' (see Brown, 2006; Williams, 2005; Sandbrook, 2005). These assumptions represented an elaboration beyond, and softening of, the draconian Market-oriented structural adjustment reforms that had been imposed across the continent since the early 1980s. They included a new emphasis on governance, security, social development, water, agriculture, and 'aid effectiveness', without altering the marketizing and growth-oriented core of the earlier approach. In this sense, they represented the extension of 'Third Way' logic to the global level, assuming a pragmatic, post-ideological consensus on the way forward that effectively denied, or at least obfuscated, the possibility of structural conflict or contradiction (see Coulter, 2009). The AAP explicitly took its lead from elements of the NEPAD, and in this way reinforced the sense that this was a new and genuine 'partnership'. It also sought to institutionalize positive reinforcement and create incentives for prescribed reforms by rewarding governments that conformed to the 'NEPAD vision'. It aimed to do so through an emphasis on support for 'Enhanced Partnership Countries' that could serve as 'a beacon of "best practices"' for other governments that 'still do not understand or accept what must be done to help themselves' (Fowler, 2003: 236).

Taking up this project was compelling to the Canadian government for several reasons. First, the consensus that was being advocated and advanced reflected the dominant ideological and policy assumptions of the Chrétien government—very much a Third Way government in practice if less self-consciously so in principle. Second, and of greater interest theoretically, is that this role fit firmly within what Cox, following the Canadian scholar-practitioner John Holmes, has characterized as internationalist 'middlerpowermanship' (Cox, 1989: 823–836). This role, for which middle-ranking capabilities are a necessary but not sufficient condition, is one that seeks to foster, sustain, and expand the zones of world order. Since the polities that have played this role, in current and previous historical contexts, generally lack the ability to impose a coherent, order-building vision, their approach has tended to be more pragmatic and process-oriented rather than architectural (though a certain amount of 'norm entrepreneurship' has often been involved). Cox follows Holmes in characterizing this role as 'lapidary' in the sense of building from the bottom up, stone upon stone, a structure that grows out of the landscape, not imposing from above some architectonic grand design' (Cox, 1989: 827).

This is a role which post-World War II Canadian governments had played with some regularity, albeit uneven—or consistent inconsistency. It was attractive to a relatively wealthy but 'secondary' state and its elites, insofar as it was understood to serve Canadian interests in a relatively secure, rules-based, and economically liberal order. In the specific context of a G8 response/overture to Africa, moreover, it can be argued that the Canadian government was uniquely well placed to orchestrate this effort. As a leading member of both the Commonwealth and *la francophonie*, it had developed relatively long-standing and comfortable relationships with Africa's post-colonial governments, free from the direct imperial legacies and baggage of the UK and France. Despite Canada's status as a charter member of the NATO alliance, it was perceived as having little strategic interest in Africa, and few means to pursue it. This, combined with its limited trade and investment role on the continent,[3] meant that Canada enjoyed a relatively benign image that enhanced its ability to serve as an interlocutor between G8 and African governments. Yet its relatively sophisticated and well-resourced diplomatic and aid resources[4] gave it the necessary means to help lead and 'sell' such an intensive diplomatic effort, at least in short bursts. The broader point is that, understood in neo-Gramscian terms, efforts to foster relatively consensual hegemonic arrangements often involve, and may even require, the skills and characteristics of secondary or 'middle' powers such as Canada.

This effort was also 'hegemonic work' for the Canadian government in another, related sense. To be sure, an order-building role that aspired to 'humanize' and stabilize globalization by seeking to incorporate Africa served elite interests, in a relatively diffuse sense at least. In addition, however, it also helped re-inscribe and stabilize a hegemonic order domestically, by reprising a couple of favoured roles and self-images.[5] On the one hand, a perceived leadership role in addressing African poverty, insecurity, and marginality strongly conformed with and reinforced a 'humane internationalist' (or 'liberal internationalist') self-image that has enjoyed substantial and long-standing appeal amongst the Canadian public and Canadian elites (see Pratt, 1989; Munton, 2003). Even though—indeed because—this image has often been contradicted in practice, such apparently enlightened initiatives enjoy considerable popularity and even a measure of collective relief when they are reprised, as if Canadian foreign policy is reverting to its 'natural' or at least its better impulses.[6]

On the other hand, and reflective at least in part of a more 'hard-nosed' or pragmatic variant of Canadian internationalism, Canada's status and participation in the G7/G8 has also enjoyed considerable popularity (see Kirton, 2007). While the constraining effects of Summit membership on Canada's international role have elicited some

academic controversy, the desirability of this status has become both an article of faith and a source of anxiety among Canadian political and bureaucratic elites and attentive publics. Our status as the 'smallest of the great' (with the world's eleventh-largest GDP in a club of 8; see Potter, 2009) simultaneously affirms our importance in the world, while also prompting insecurity about the possibility of decline and 'demotion'. Thus, an initiative such as that taken at Kananaskis, in which the Canadian government could be seen not only to have fully participated in, but in some real sense *led*, the G8 towards a more generous and enlightened engagement with Africa, was doubly compelling. The fact that Prime Minister Chrétien was in the final, 'legacy-minding' years of his long political career firmly reinforced this logic.

Leaving aside the question of the viability and desirability of the collective vision for African renewal developed in the AAP, however, this case also illustrates some core problems and limitations of such hegemonic work. First, as we shall see, the potential for sustained concertation is undermined by the corrosive effects of intra-hegemonic differences of approach and 'one-upmanship'. Second, participants in such initiatives have extraordinary difficulty sustaining the focus, commitment, and resources necessary to see such initiatives through to their logical ends. In this case, as we shall see, a Canada that had apparently set great store in its G8 leadership on this issue had, within five years, signalled a retreat—both rhetorically and, to a more limited extent, in practice. How did this occur, and what are its implications for Canada's and the G8's erstwhile African 'partners'?

THE 'CONJUNCTURAL MOMENT' OF KANANASKIS

One conclusion regarding the Kananaskis conjuncture is undeniable: the various factors noted above combined to produce a focus on Africa without precedent in the nearly thirty years of Summit history. The long shadow cast by the Gleneagles Summit should not obscure the degree to which it emerged out of a process that was 'locked in' at the 2002 Summit.

The Canadian government, and particularly its prime minister, worked very hard to achieve this focus. As Robert Fowler, Prime Minister Chrétien's chief 'Sherpa' for the Summit and Personal Representative for Africa, has somewhat hyperbolically put it:

> From Genoa, in July 2001, it was crystal clear that Prime Minister Chrétien would insist that the Canadian Summit he would host in 2002 would feature an all-encompassing effort to end Africa's exclusion from the rest of the world and reverse the downward-spiralling trend in the quality of life of the vast majority of Africans (Fowler, 2003: 223).[7]

Chrétien, whose previous political success had been far more the result of pragmatism and 'street smarts' than of statesmanship, was strongly supported in this effort at global leadership by Tony Blair of Britain and Jacques Chirac of France. What unfolded was a concerted, year-long diplomatic effort involving wide-ranging consultations with G7 governments, African leaders and NEPAD architects. The result was that a full day of the two-day Summit (shortened from the three-day format of previous years) was devoted to discussions concerning Africa, and that for the first time non-G8 leaders, specifically from Africa, were direct participants in Summit deliberations. The Summit resulted in the adoption of the AAP, incorporating 'more than 100 specific commitments' reflecting G8 consensus on where and how they should 'respond to NEPAD's promise' (Fowler, 2003: 228). These commitments spanned the areas of Resource Mobilization, Peace and Security, Governance, Trade and Investment, Health, Agriculture, Water, and Human Resources. As noted above, the AAP placed particular emphasis on channelling support to 'Enhanced Partnership Countries' that 'demonstrate a political and financial commitment to good governance and the rule of law, investing in their people and pursuing policies that spur economic growth and alleviate poverty' (see Fowler, 2003: 239).

How are we to assess the implications of these commitments? In part, such an assessment depends on whether one thinks that G8 Summits, and the documents they issue, have been more than talking shops and empty rhetoric (for contrasting views, see Kirton, 2002, and Elliot, 2003). In part, it depends on one's interpretation of both the AAP and the NEPAD, which Fowler characterized as a 'realistic' plan 'aimed at making African nations full and equal partners in the global economic and trading system and, above all, at attracting significant levels of foreign investment to that continent' (Fowler, 2003: 226; see also Taylor, 2005). Particularly when inflected by the new emphasis on rewards to 'Enhanced Partnership Countries', this is a scheme that, whatever its specific provisions and strengths, strongly reflected Western hegemonic preferences concerning the political and economic organization of both African countries and world affairs.

For our purposes, however, the evaluation can perhaps be reduced to a triple bottom line. First, the governments of the richest countries of the world gave more, and more sympathetic, attention to the challenges and opportunities confronting Africa than ever before. For this, the determined efforts of Jean Chrétien and his government deserve much of the credit. Second however, the AAP, for all its 'specific commitments', produced virtually no new resources for Africa beyond those already announced at the Monterrey Conference on

Financing for Development several months previously. In sum, it produced a qualified commitment to devote half (roughly USD $6 billion) of the USD $12 billion in new development funding committed to Africa at Monterrey—far short of the USD $64 billion that the NEPAD document estimated the Program required. This explains the verdict of most NGO and editorial opinion, reflected in such phrases as, 'they're offering peanuts to Africa—and recycled peanuts at that', and 'Africa let down by the rich' (*Guardian Weekly*, 4–10/7/2002). Thus, Canada's best efforts could not bring its G8 partners around to substantially 'putting their money where their mouths were'. The net result indicates the ability of Canadian policy-makers to shape agendas concerning Africa, on the one hand, but their sharply limited ability to shape outcomes, on the other.

Nevertheless, the third bottom line is that Kananaskis initiated a process of G8 engagement with African issues that proved surprisingly durable. The process leading up to, and following on from, the adoption of the AAP was firmly reinforced by the institutionalization of Personal Representatives of Heads of Government for Africa (APRs), which ensured a measure of follow-up and accountability. At the Evian Summit in 2003, this dynamic was deepened by the creation of the African Partnership Forum (APF), including APRs of 'G8 partners, 11 additional Organization for Economic Cooperation and Development donors heavily engaged in Africa, the members of the NEPAD Implementation Committee, and selected African and international organizations. . . .' Since then, the APF has met twice annually, with the stated objective of serving 'as a catalyst for cooperation in support of NEPAD and as a forum for information sharing and mutual accountability . . . ' (CIDA, 2004: 13). At Sea Island in 2004, the American hosts, who as usual had been relatively unwilling to engage in concerted efforts, nevertheless contributed significantly to the momentum of the G8 process by orchestrating a more precise and expansive commitment to helping Africa build its capacity for peace and security, including the training and equipping of 75,000 peacekeepers, mostly African, by 2010 (see Williams, 2008: 316). Beyond Gleneagles (addressed below), there was widespread concern that with the St Petersburg Summit in 2006, focus and momentum would be lost. Yet to the surprise of some in the German African Studies community (author interviews, May 2007), Chancellor Angela Merkel restored the focus on Africa at the Heiligendamm Summit, and the Japanese and Italian hosts retained it in 2008 and 2009. In short, a focus on Africa was institutionalized.

The impacts of this process are analytically complex. Counter-factually, it is reasonable to speculate that considerably *less* would have been done in response to NEPAD, and on shared policy priorities related to governance, aid, security, and trade for example, in the absence of this ongoing focus and the opportunities for accountability it has generated (see, for example, DATA Report, 2009). This is, at one level, a profoundly discouraging assessment, given that the main Summit 'story line' since 2005 has typically been the looming failure of G8 governments to live up to their aid commitments, and that G8 activities on security and trade negotiations, for example, have been unsuccessful in moving prospects in these areas decisively forward.[8] In another sense, however, the fact that African governments and organizations continue to invest in this process, anchored by annual G8 Summits, with a degree of legitimacy and credibility, as if it will or at least *could* produce important improvements, suggests that it has had some success as a hegemonic project of fostering a plausible political consensus on the way forward for the continent.

For its part, in the years immediately following Kananaskis the Canadian government spent considerable time and effort both bringing its policies toward Africa into line with the G8 consensus, and reporting assiduously about its progress in doing so (see CIDA, 2004). On aid, following up on the Monterrey and Kananaskis commitments of 2002, the government's 2005 *International Policy Statement* (IPS) confirmed its intent to double aid to Africa between 2003–4 and 2008–9—slightly more quickly than the doubling of the aid programme as a whole by 2010. Moreover, in the context of Prime Minister Chrétien's pre-Kananaskis diplomacy, the government had previously announced a CDN $500 million 'Canada Fund for Africa' in its December 2001 budget, which the Canadian International Development Agency (CIDA) candidly described as 'a showcase for Canadian leadership in pursuit of effective development through a series of large-scale, flagship initiatives in support of NEPAD and the G8 Africa Action Plan' (CIDA, 2002: 26; see CIDA, 2003 for details). In terms of aid practices and priorities, the government committed to bringing its programme into line with the emerging consensus on 'Aid Effectiveness' in the international aid regime, involving harmonization with other donors, aligning with recipient country priorities, and respecting developing country 'ownership' (see Lalonde, 2009; Black, 2006). Finally, and after at least one false start, it moved to focus on 'Enhanced Partnership Countries' by announcing, in the context of the 2005 IPS, a decision to focus two-thirds of its bilateral aid in 25 priority 'partners', 14 of which were to be African.[9]

In terms of trade and investment, even as Canada's presence in African extractive industries grew dramatically and often controversially (see Black, and Savage, 2010), the government supplemented its regular trade and investment development windows, such as the Export Development Corporation, with a CDN $100 million contribution to a 'Canada Investment Fund for Africa' (CIFA) drawn from the Canada Fund for Africa, to be co-funded with and managed by private sector investors.[10] CIFA eventually invested in 15 African projects,

although these were heavily concentrated in pockets of relative continental prosperity in South Africa (4), Nigeria (4), and North Africa (3), and were therefore of questionable developmental impact in nurturing 'pro-poor growth' where it is most urgently needed.

Finally, in terms of peace and security, the Canadian government made a modest contribution (CDN $19 million) through the Canada Fund for Africa to capacity-building in West Africa (CDN $15 million) and at the African Union (CDN $4 million). Even more modest contributions have been sustained through the Military Training Assistance Program (MTAP) of the Department of National Defence. A considerably larger contribution was eventually made, as international attention to the crisis in Darfur mounted, to the functionality of the African Union Mission in Sudan (AMIS; see Black, 2010). Yet given the inadequacy of this force to meet the challenge with which it was faced, there is a sense in which the Canadian (along with other G8 contribution[s]) did little more than sustain a veneer of respectability for an overmatched force, while diffusing and obfuscating responsibility for dealing with the crisis (see Black and Williams, 2008; Nossal, 2005).

In short, Canada's follow-up to its conspicuous role surrounding the Kananaskis Summit can be interpreted as a case of 'good *enough* international citizenship' (Black, and Williams, 2008)—good enough, that is, to retain credibility in the eyes of its G8 partners and their African interlocutors, but little more. In fact, the record since Gleneagles in 2005 has been one of relatively quiet retreat from the expectations generated in 2001–2.

GLENEAGLES AND BEYOND

Prior to the 2005 Summit at Gleneagles, the governments of Canada and the UK had been the two most consistent and concerted proponents of the

G8's engagement with Africa. It is not surprising, therefore, that Canadian Finance Minister Ralph Goodale was asked to join Tony Blair's hand-picked, 17-member Commission for Africa (CFA), whose massive 461-page report, *Our Common Future*, was designed to give focus and urgency to Summit deliberations. Nevertheless, the CFA and Gleneagles processes revealed some significant differences between these two governments and, beyond them, other G8 members. These had ambiguous but corrosive implications for their collective approach.

As noted above, the 'year of Africa' orchestrated by the British government of Tony Blair, and highlighted by the Gleneagles Summit in July 2005, effectively overshadowed previous Summit efforts and was widely seen, notably by Western 'civil societies', as the new benchmark for G8 efforts. Indeed, the broad sense periodically expressed by British officials that, in the words of Tony Blair, 'I think the (Gleneagles) G8 last year was the first time Africa has come to centre stage for the G8 Summit' (cited in Vines, and Cargill, 2006) was both symptomatic and a predictable irritant for other governments. Nevertheless, there is no gainsaying the scale of the effort and the extraordinary political theatre it generated. The Gleneagles Declaration was preceded by the year-long effort of the British-sponsored CFA, whose report noted that Africa was falling badly behind on progress towards the Millennium Development Goals (MDGs), including halving the number of people living on less than a dollar a day by 2015, to the extent that, given current trends, it would achieve the MDGs 135 years late. The Commission's analysis called for a doubling of aid to Africa by the end of the decade, entailing a $25 billion increase, and the allocation of another $25 billion by 2015 (Commission for Africa, 2005). Prodded by the sustained efforts of British leaders Tony Blair and Gordon Brown, in effective alliance with the celebrity activists associated with

the 'Live8' concerts and the Make Poverty History campaign, the G8 did produce some relatively substantial and 'firm' commitments at Gleneagles. These included commitments to double aid to the continent, write off debts of the poorest 18 African countries, and take new steps towards trade liberalization and support for peace and security and governance reforms[11] (see G8, 2005; 'What the G8 leaders', 2005).

Of course, as subsequent Summits have shown, there was good reason to be skeptical about the extent of delivery on these commitments. There were also concerns about the shallowness of the CFA's (and UK government's) analysis of African governance (e.g., Sandbrook, 2005; Williams, 2005; Brown 2006); about whether the prescriptions would therefore deliver sustainable and equitable development; and about how Africa and its people were portrayed, namely as passive and impoverished victims, in the frenzied run-up to the Summit (see Bunting, 8–14/7/2005). Nevertheless, the British government was able to deliver a significantly more robust and ambitious package than the Canadian government had mooted even three years before. In contrast, Canada was widely portrayed as an also-ran or even a laggard on account of its refusal to join the European G8 members in committing to a firm timetable for reaching the long-standing aid objective, set by the Pearson Commission on International Development in 1969, of 0.7% of GDP (e.g., Elliott, 15–21/7/2005).

For its part, the Canadian government was almost certainly feeling put out by the implicit and explicit discounting of its own role in G8 efforts to date, but also revealed a difference of perspective on the importance of aid as a vehicle for promoting African development. In short, Canada's commitment to development assistance, despite the increases announced at Monterrey and Kananaskis, had become increasingly ambivalent as compared to many European governments, and the UK government in particular. It was also skeptical of what it perceived as commitments that were unlikely to be fulfilled. This was reflected in the comment of a former senior diplomat, noting the 'voodoo arithmetic' required to arrive at 'the $50 billion quantum' of aid advocated in the CFA report and incorporated in the Gleneagles Declaration (confidential interview, March 2007). Finally, the Canadian government shared with some G8 counterparts (notably the Germans) a sense that the Blair government, in orchestrating its *own* process for framing the issue and the response, had ignored and undermined collective G8 processes and modalities set in motion at Kananaskis. One can be deeply skeptical about what was likely to be achieved through these processes and modalities, and still acknowledge that the tensions, differences, and frustrations surrounding the Gleneagles process revealed the challenges of sustaining an effective hegemonic coalition. Paradoxically, the Gleneagles outcome weakened the G8 effort from a political and procedural standpoint, even as it successfully enhanced some of the G8's material commitments.

THE HEILIGENDAMM WATERSHED

If the Gleneagles Summit fractured the axis on Africa that had effectively linked the Canadian and British governments prior to that time, the 2007 Heiligendamm Summit marked a clear course change in Ottawa concerning the political effort and resources the government was willing to commit to the G8's 'Africa project'. This argument needs to be made carefully. In some respects, very little changed in terms of Canada's Africa policies; indeed, at the l'Aquila Summit in 2009 the government was able to claim that it had become the first G8 government to meet the objective of doubling its aid to Africa between 2003–4 and 2008–9 (a claim that, while

technically valid, requires some parsing as discussed below). Yet from 2007 on, it became clear in a number of ways that Africa had been 'demoted' as a political and foreign policy priority.

A key turning point occurred in January 2006 when the Liberal government of Paul Martin, who had succeeded fellow Liberal Jean Chrétien as prime minister, was replaced by a Conservative Minority government led by Stephen Harper. The new prime minister was not experienced in international affairs,[12] and his inclinations were economically conservative and politically 'realist' and pro-Western (see Flanagan, 2009; Black, 2009). His economic conservatism, rooted in his training as a neo-classical economist, made him deeply skeptical of the utility of foreign aid. He and his government were also intensely partisan—even by 'normal' political standards—and he was suspicious of both non-governmental organizations and 'celebrity diplomats'.

Initially, Harper's government had little to say on foreign affairs beyond a strong commitment to the NATO operation in Afghanistan, combining a major combat role with a large infusion of aid (a 'whole of government' approach in the current parlance[13]), as well as other features such as a decidedly pro-Israel tilt in the Middle East and a cooling of relations with China. On Africa there was mostly silence, and policy drift. Thus, when the Heiligendamm Summit again shone a spotlight on G8 commitments to Africa, there was much uncertainty and speculation concerning the position Harper would take.

In the event, several noteworthy developments occurred. First, unlike his predecessor and other world leaders, Harper was 'too busy' to meet celebrity diplomats Bono and Bob Geldof. Trivial in itself, this could also be seen as a signal that he was not interested in their agenda of expanded aid and debt relief for Africa. Both subsequently accused Harper of working to block specific wording in the Communiqué on clear targets to meet

G8 governments' Gleneagles commitments (see 'Geldof calls', 2007)—a charge he denied. Then, a controversy erupted over the value of Canada's Gleneagles commitment to double aid to Africa between 2003–4 and 2008–9. Whereas the 2005 federal budget tabled by the Liberals had projected this increase to run from the estimated expenditures of CDN $1.38 billion in 2003/4 to CDN $2.76 billion in 2008–9, the new government argued that since the *actual* aid expenditures in Africa in 2003–4 had turned out to be only CDN $1.05 billion, the doubling of aid would bring it to only CDN $2.1 billion. This accounting adjustment thus effectively reduced the value of Canada's commitment by some CDN $700 million. Finally, as the Summit concluded, Harper signalled a new emphasis on the Americas, noting that while Canada will 'remain engaged' and 'will meet our targets' in Africa, 'a focus of our new government is the Americas' ('Harper signals', 2007).

It was not until nearly two years later that some specific policy developments emerged to support this rhetorical shift. Nevertheless, some clear signals were sent—for example, the relative lack of high-level Ministerial travel to Africa versus the Americas or Afghanistan (see Clark, 2007), and the appointment of a high-profile former journalist (Peter Kent) as Minister of State for the Americas, with no analogous appointment for Africa or for Asia. Then, in February 2009, the Minister for International Cooperation announced (with minimal consultation) a new, streamlined list of 20 priority countries for bilateral aid. This list cut in half the number of African priority countries, to seven from 14, while increasing the number of priority recipients in the Americas and Asia (Afghanistan had already emerged as the largest bilateral aid programme in Canadian history, at CDN $280 million in FY 2007–8, with Haiti becoming the second largest. See CCIC, 2009). Among those 'dropped' were long-standing Commonwealth and

francophonie partner governments, including Cameroon, Kenya, Malawi, Niger, Rwanda, and Zambia. This was the clearest signal to date of a shift in priorities, and cast into doubt the trajectory for Canadian aid on the continent beyond the 2008–9 target date for doubling aid to Africa; it also seemed to signal the end of expenditures associated with the Canada Fund for Africa. Indeed, while at l'Aquila in 2009, Canada was credited with being the first G8 government to meet its doubling target (as noted above);. Total aid spending remained very modest, and considerably below the OECD Development Assistance Committee (DAC) average, with a projected figure of no more than 0.31% of GNI by 2010 (Tomlinson, 2008: 279). These developments in aid programming were accompanied by the closing of several diplomatic missions on the continent, leaving Canada with fewer diplomatic missions in Africa than any G8 government other than Japan. Similarly, as a result of cuts to its trade-related presence on the continent, Canada was left with only 25 Trade Commissioners for Africa's 47 countries by 2009, compared with 68 Trade Commissioners for Latin America, with 13 countries and fewer than half as many inhabitants (CCA, 2009).

The government's diminished interest in Africa, and in initiatives of particular relevance to the continent, can be tracked in other ways as well. In the security domain, Canada's 'boots on the ground' in UN-led peace operations in Africa totalled less than 50 in 2008, compared with some 2,500 in Afghanistan. Similarly, the 'Responsibility to Protect', which had been a hallmark of Canadian foreign policy since 2001 and which has more—albeit controversial—relevance for Africa than for any other continent (see Williams, 2009), was virtually dropped from the lexicon of Canadian foreign policy. And, notwithstanding ongoing investments in health through CIDA programming, the landmark 2003 legislation ('Canada's Access to

Medicines Regime'), which had been intended to greatly increase the availability of inexpensive generic AIDS medication for Africans, has proven to be an almost completely dead letter, with the government showing no interest in amending it to make it more effective (Caplan, 2009).

In short, while it would be a mistake to overstate the degree of change in Canada's approach to Africa as measured in *actual* resource allocations, there was considerable evidence of declining political interest in various ways, both tangible and intangible, by mid-2009. How can we account for this striking trend?

'REGIME SPECIFIC' VS. CYCLICAL DYNAMICS

A full explanation for the Harper government's shift of focus away from Africa (and towards Latin America) is beyond the scope of this paper.[14] What needs to be highlighted in this context is the difficulty of sorting out the degree to which this trajectory represents a durable long-term shift, or merely the latest phase in an ongoing pattern of intensifying and then receding interest in 'Canada's African vocation'.

There are ways in which the Harper government's approach to Africa, and indeed its approach to foreign policy more broadly, appears to represent a qualitative departure from the dominant patterns of post-World War II Canadian foreign policy. Some of these are alluded to above. Beyond the government's relative inexperience in international affairs, the ideas and attitudes that have shaped its approach seem much closer than any of its predecessors, of either dominant party, to American conservative predilections concerning multilateralism and foreign aid on the one hand (i.e., relatively unsympathetic to both), and to a hard-nosed, realist view of the importance of military capabilities and alliances on the other.

The latter is manifested, most obviously, in its enthusiastic commitment to the NATO-led mission in Afghanistan, contrasted with its minimalist approach to UN-led operations in Africa (Sudan partially excepted). Similarly, the Harper government has demonstrated little enthusiasm for those old manifestations of active internationalism and bicultural identity—the Commonwealth and *la francophonie*—both of which led previous Canadian governments to be much more engaged in African countries and issues than they would have otherwise been.

The logic of a 'tilt' towards Latin America has been reinforced by similar, rational-utility maximizing and pro-American predispositions: towards the superior commercial opportunities of the Americas and a closer and more sympathetic engagement in a regional zone of particular, historic American interest (see Healy, and Katz, 2008). Finally, the Harper Conservatives' unusually intense brand of partisanship has arguably impelled them towards a Latin American tilt as a means of 'brand differentiation' from the ostensibly Africa-fixated Liberals (Owen, and Eaves, 2007).

If one accepts that the seeds of a more durable shift have indeed been sown, two supplementary questions become important, though speculative. First, what could be expected from a Harper majority government, versus a Michael Ignatieff-led Liberal government (minority or majority)? Would a new party in power substantially undo the steps the Harper government has taken in this issue area?[15] And second, what is the likelihood that the imperatives of Canada's international role, as embodied in both the expectations and legitimating myths of Canadians and in the external pressures and opportunities associated with its multilateral commitments,[16] will mitigate or even reverse such an emergent shift? This latter question will be revisited in the concluding reflections on the prospects for Africa in the context of the 2010 Summit(s).

On the other hand, there is another way of reading the current recession of interest in Africa. For it is not only the current Conservatives who have periodically sought to 'rebalance' Canadian foreign policy away from Africa. It was, after all, the Chrétien Liberal government that, in the mid-1990s, presided over the deepest cuts to the Canadian aid programme in its history, with disproportionate damage done to Africa (see NSI, 2003: 78). More broadly, various government leaders and permanent officials, particularly in the Departments of National Defence and Foreign Affairs, have more or less continuously taken the view that, given Africa's relatively marginality to Canada's 'core' economic and strategic interests, prudence demands that resource commitments and political exposure be limited (see Matthews, 1976; Dawson, 2009). From this perspective, the latest shift in emphasis reflects something less permanent yet more persistent: the chronic 'yin and yang' of Canadian foreign policy between its more 'liberal' or 'humane internationalist' impulses, and a more pragmatic or 'conservative internationalist' tendency (see Munton, 2003). Either way, the implications for Canada's 'African partners' are sobering—a point to which I will return.

CONCLUSION: PROSPECTS FOR HUNTSVILLE, 2010

There is, in fact, some evidence that a partial correction towards a stronger emphasis on development and, by implication, Africa is underway. Whereas Prime Minister Harper's articulation of Canada's priorities for the 2010 Summit in June, 2008 had noted three priorities—open markets, global warming, and democracy, human rights, and the rule of law—one year later (in June 2009) development had been added as a fourth priority theme (see Kirton, 2009: 4). This is interpreted by

Summit scholar John Kirton as a reflection of the need to take account of the developmental fallout from the global financial crisis. Still, while Canadian officials used Canada's early fulfillment of its commitment to double aid to Africa as a basis for stressing the need for strengthened G8 accountability, there was no explicit mention of Africa in the prime minister's articulation of Summit priorities (see Harper, 2009). In September 2009, in the context of the Pittsburgh G20 Summit, the government took another significant step by announcing that it would make CDN $2.8 billion temporarily available to the African Development Bank (AfDB) in the form of 'callable' capital, thereby enabling the Bank to significantly increase its lending capacity in the face of the global financial crisis. This was billed as 'a further demonstration of Canada's commitment to Africa' (PMO, 24/9/2009). And in January 2010, at the World Economic Forum in Davis, Switzerland, the prime minister announced that a 'major initiative to improve the health of women and children in the world's most vulnerable regions' would be a centrepiece of its G8 agenda (Harper, 2010). This initiative, if seriously acted upon, could be expected to benefit to the women and children of Africa—though how it relates to the broader contexts of poverty, inequality, and underdevelopment that underpin the poor health outcomes of these especially 'vulnerable groups' in Africa (and elsewhere) was not addressed (see York, 30/1/2010).

An additional consideration that could lead to some rebalancing toward Africa is Canada's current, somewhat belated campaign for a nonpermanent seat on the UN Security Council (UNSC). Since the founding of the UN, the pattern and now expectation in this country has been that Canada will serve a two-year term on the Security Council once each decade. Since our last term on the Security Council was in 1999–2000, the current government has launched a vigorous campaign for election for the two-year period beginning in January 2011. In the past, support from African governments has been pivotal to the success of these campaigns. There are signs that it has now dawned on the Harper government that it must reach out to this traditional base of support (and in so doing rebuild some damaged bridges) if its current campaign is to be successful. One such sign is the prime minister's appointment of one of the country's more able diplomats, and Robert Fowler's former 'right hand' at the UNSC and in the negotiations for the Africa Action Plan, as his new Personal Representative for Africa (APR). David Angell has reportedly been dispatched regularly to Africa to press governments on their support for Canada's Security Council candidacy (Edwards, 2009). This raises the question of what substantive basis (or 'campaign platform') the government is using to anchor its appeal for support?

Within Canada, there is some evidence of social mobilization, from business lobbies as well as civil society, for a course correction.[17] Whether the Harper government is sensitive to such mobilization is at best an open question. In contrast, as noted above, a Liberal government could be expected to embrace a fulsome course correction, rhetorically pitched as a 'return' to a global leadership and a more generous (or humane internationalist) foreign policy. This runs the risk of reinforcing the new pattern of partisan posturing over Africa policy.

Nevertheless, what the nearly completed Summit cycle, from 2002 to 2010, should teach us is that the Canadian government's interest in, and commitment to, Africa lacks depth and durability—a lesson that is reinforced by the inconstancy of Canadian support for Africa through the 1990s.

This pattern of inconstancy, in turn, erodes the base of knowledge, resources, and credibility on which an effective Africa policy depends. It will take some time for these foundations to be rebuilt, even if the social and political basis for doing so can be mobilized.

Finally, it is worth reconsidering the hegemonic possibilities of the G8's 'African project', as understood in neo-Gramscian terms and as discussed in the first part of this paper. What this case illustrates is that these possibilities are undermined not only by the policy limitations of the Summit's most powerful member states. They are also compromised by intra-hegemonic differences over tactics, strategy, and optics, as reflected in the politics surrounding the Gleneagles Summit; and by the political exigencies and course changes of 'lesser' or 'secondary' powers, such as Canada, that undermine the consistency and success of their hegemonic work. In this sense, the history of the AAP, and Canada's role in it, illustrates the instability and contingency of transnational efforts to build a new 'common sense' on the way forward for Africa. It remains to be seen how the changing institutional contours and normative frames of a post-Financial Crisis (and post-G8?) world will tackle this challenge. On the other hand, as a means for refreshing the hegemonic status of the Canadian state vis-à-vis its own society by reiterating its 'humane internationalist' credentials, Canada's unsustained leadership within the G8 may have served its purpose. In this sense, Canada's Africa policy and similar moments of ethical initiative serve as a basis for sustaining a favourable self-image domestically, even as the ostensible subjects of these initiatives fade from view.

Key Terms

Commission for Africa

Commonwealth

Hegemony

La Francophonie

Middle Power

Norm Entrepreneurship

Third Way

Notes

1. The language of 'hegemonic work' is borrowed from Coulter, 2009: 201.

2. The need to respond to these protests, not only in terms of logistics but of substance, was clearly in the minds of Summit planners. See, for example, Fowler, 2003: 225.

3. A point that must be qualified in light of the large and growing role of Canadian extractive companies in the controversial mining and energy sectors of many African countries. Canadian firms have collectively become among the largest investors in these sectors, with more than CDN 20 billion currently invested. See Black and Savage, 2010.

4. Another point that must be qualified given Canada's relatively limited and inconstant commitment to aid and diplomatic resources, as will be elaborated below.

5. For a Gramscian exploration of the interplay between transnational and domestic hegemonic work in Canadian 'middle power (or Pearsonian) internationalism', see Neufeld, 1995.

6. As reflected in the sub-title of Kananaskis Sherpa and African Personal Representative Robert Fowler's reflection on the Kananaskis process: 'Towards a Less Self-Centred Canadian Foreign Policy' (Fowler, 2003: 219).

7. Fowler was himself a periodic 'Africa hand', as reflected in his comment that 'as I approached the end of my career I would have another—this time unique—opportunity to assist Africa, a continent and a people that have held my fascination and deep affection for all of my adult and professional life' (Fowler, 2003: 221). He had already achieved considerable notoriety for his pivotal role, as Chair of the Angola Sanctions Committee while Canada's UN Ambassador in 1999/2000, in instigating the Council's creation of an unprecedented Panel of Experts to evaluate how sanctions against UNITA were being violated, and how they could be made more effective. The Panel's report caused a furor by 'naming names', but also highlighted key features of the Angolan war economy and produced recommendations that helped choke off UNITA's ability to sustain the conflict (see Mollander, 2009). Fowler's close association with the continent, and his notoriety, were further reinforced by his abduction and incarceration at the hands of al Qaeda linked rebels in West Africa for 130 days in the first half of 2009, while on a UN mission in Niger.

8. As reflected, for example, in the collapse of the 'Doha Development Round' of trade negotiations, and the ongoing insecurity in pivotal African conflict areas—most notably the Sudan and the Democratic Republic of the Congo (DRC)—to which the G8 AAP formally committed its collective efforts.

9. The proposed African Development Partners were: Benin, Burkina Faso, Cameroon, Ethiopia, Ghana, Kenya, Malawi, Mali, Mozambique, Niger, Rwanda, Senegal, Tanzania, and Zambia.

10. Cordiant of Montreal and Actis of London.

11. Though as noted above, the trade liberalization commitments, in particular, proved illusory.

12. Harper's first trip to Africa was for the Commonwealth Heads of Government Meeting in Kampala in November of 2007.

13. Canada's combat role in Kandahar province has become the country's costliest since the Korean War, in both human and material terms. Similarly, CIDA's bilateral aid programme in Afghanistan has quickly become its largest ever. On the 'integrated' character of the mission, see Travers and Owen, 2008.

14. For an extended analysis, see Black, 2009.

15. It is noteworthy that in his most substantial speech on foreign policy since becoming Liberal leader, Ignatieff explicitly castigated the Conservatives for 'abandoning' and 'deserting' Africa. See Ignatieff, 2009.

16. For example, as host of back-to-back G8 and G20 Summits in 2010 and as an aspirant to a regular, non-permanent seat on the UN Security Council.

17. As reflected, for example, in the business-oriented Canadian Council on Africa's organization of a broadly-based, high level conference on 'The New Africa: redrawing the blueprint for the Canada–Africa partnership' in October 2009. See www.ccafrica.ca/2009/new_africa/new_africa.php.

References

AAP—Africa Action Plan. (2002). Accessed at www.canada international.gc.ca/g8/summit-sommet/2002/index. aspx?lang=eng.

Bayne, Nicholas. (2003). 'The New Partnership for Africa's Development and the G8's Africa Action Plan: A Marshall Plan for Africa?' In M. Fratiani et al. (eds.), *Sustaining Global Growth and Development: G7 and IMF Governance.* Aldershot: Ashgate.

Black, David. (2004). Canada and Africa: Activist Aspirations in Straitened Circumstances. In Ian Taylor and Paul Williams (eds.), *Africa in International Politics* (pp. 136–54). London: Routledge Press.

Black, David. (2006). Canadian Aid to Africa: Assessing 'Reform'. In Andrew Cooper and Dane Rowlands (eds.), *Canada Among Nations 2006: Minorities and Priorities* (pp. 319–38). Montreal and Kingston: McGill-Queen's University Press.

Black, David. (2010). 'Canada'. In D. Black and P. Williams (eds.), *The International Politics of Mass Atrocities: The Case of Darfur.* London: Routledge Press.

Black, David. (2009). 'Out of Africa? The Harper government's new "tilt" in the Developing World'. *Canadian Foreign Policy*, 15 (2): 41–56.

Black, David and Williams, Paul. (2008). Darfur's Challenge to International Society. *Behind the Headlines*, 65 (6).

Black, David and Savage, Malcolm. (2010). 'Mainstreaming Investment: Foreign and Security Policy Implications of Canadian Extractive Industries in Africa'. In B. Charbonneau and W. Cox, eds., *Locating Global Order: American Power and Canadian Security after 9/11* (pp. 235–59). Vancouver: UBC Press.

Brown, William. 'The Commission for Africa: results and prospects for the West's Africa policy'. *Journal of Modern African Studies*, 44 (3): 349–74.

Bunting, M. (2005). 'Humiliated once more', *Guardian Weekly*, 8–14 July.

Caplan, G. (2009). 'Abandoning our responsibility'. *Globe and Mail*, 25 September.

CCA (Canadian Council on Africa). (2009). 'Presentation to the Standing Committee on Foreign Affairs and International Development of the Parliament of Canada', 3 June.

CCIC (Canadian Council for International Cooperation). (2009). 'A review of CIDA's Countries of Priorities: A CCIC Briefing Note'. February.

CIDA (Canadian International Development Agency). (2002). 'Canada Making a Difference in the World: A Policy Statement on Strengthening Aid Effectiveness'.

CIDA. (2003). 'New Vision, New Partnership: Canada Fund for Africa'.

CIDA. (2004). 'Canada and the G8 Africa Action Plan: Maintaining the Momentum'. Hull, QC, June.

Clark, Joe. (2007). Is Africa falling off Canada's map? Remarks to the National Capital Branch of the Canadian Institute of International Affairs, November 6.

Commission for Africa. (2005). *Our Common Future.* London: UK Government.

Coulter, Kendra. (2009). 'Deep Neoliberal Integration: The Production of Third Way Politics in Ontario'. *Studies in Political Economy*, 83: 191–208.

Cox, R. (1989). 'Middlepowermanship, Japan, and Future World Order'. *International Journal*, XLIV (4): 823–62.

Cox, R. with Sinclair, T. (1996). *Approaches to World Order.* Cambridge: Cambridge University Press.

DATA Report. (2009). www.one.org/c/international/hottopic/2816/.

Dawson, Grant. (2009). 'Contact Africa: Canadian foreign policy, the contact group, and southern Africa'. *International Journal*, LXIV (2): 521–36.

Edwards, Steven. (2009). 'Ottawa Manoeuvres for Spot on UN Security Council', *National Post*, 24 May.

Elliott, L. (5–11/6/2003) 'Do us all a favour—pull the plug on G8', *Guardian Weekly*.

Elliott, L. (15–21/7/2005). 'No Marshall Plan—but a start'. *Guardian Weekly*.

Ferguson, James. (2006). *Global Shadows: Africa in the neoliberal world order.* Durham: Duke University Press.

Flanagan, Tom. (2009). 'Do we have the means to match our will?' *Globe and Mail*, 22 September.

Fowler, R. (2003) 'Canadian Leadership and the Kananaskis G-8 Summit: Towards a Less Self-Centred Foreign Policy', in D. Carment et al. (eds.), *Canada Among Nations 2003: Coping with the American Colossus* (Don Mills: Oxford University Press), 219–41.

Freeman, Alan. (8/6 /2007). 'Harper signals shift from Africa to Americas'. *Globe and Mail.*

G8 Agreement on Africa. (2005). Gleneagles, Scotland, 8 July www.number-10.gov.uk/output/Page7880/asp, retrieved 9 July 2005.

'Geldof calls Canada obstructionist'. (2007). *Globe and Mail*, 5 June.

Guardian Weekly. (4–10/7/2002). '"Africa let down by the rich", and "Africa betrayed: the aid workers" verdict'.

Harper, Stephen. (2009). 'The 2010 Muskoka Summit'. In J. Kirton and M. Koch (eds.), *G8 2009: From La Maddalena to L'Aquila.* London: Newsdesk Communications Ltd.

Harper, Stephen. (2010). 'Statement by the Prime Minister of Canada'. World Economic Forum, Davos Switzerland, 28 January.

Healy, Teresa, and Sheila, Katz. (2008). Big and Little Brother Bilateralism: Security, Prosperity, and Canada's Deal with Colombia. *Studies in Political Economy* 82, 35–60.

Ignatieff, Michael. (2009). 'Speech to the Canadian Club of Ottawa: Canada's place in a changing world'. Ottawa, 14 September.

Kirton, J. (2002). 'Canada as a Principal Summit Power: G-7/8 Concert Diplomacy from Halifax 1995 to Kananaskis 2002', in N. Hillmer and M. Molot (eds.), *Canada Among Nations 2002: A Fading Power*, (Don Mills: Oxford University Press), 209–32.

Kirton, John J. (2007). *Canadian Foreign Policy in a Changing World*. Toronto: Nelson.

Kirton, John J. (2009). 'Prospects for the 2010 Muskoka G8 Summit'. G8 Information Centre. www.g8.utoronto.ca/evaluations/2010muskoka/2010prospects090702.html

Lalonde, Jennifer. (2009). *Harmony and Discord: International Aid Harmonization and Donor State Domestic Influence. The Case of Canada and the Canadian International Development Agency*. Unpublished Doctoral Dissertation, Johns Hopkins University.

Matthews, Robert. (1976). Canada and Anglophone Africa. In P. Lyon and T. Ismael (eds.), *Canada and the Third World* (pp. 60–132). Toronto: Macmillan of Canada.

Mollander, Anders. (2009). UN *Angola Sanctions—A Committee Success Revisited*. Uppsala University: Department of Peace and Conflict Research.

Morrison, D. (1998). *Aid and Ebb Tide: A History of CIDA and Canadian Development Assistance*. Waterloo: Wilfrid Laurier University Press.

Munton, Don. (2002/3). 'Whither Internationalism?' *International Journal*, LVII (1): 155–180.

Neufeld, Mark. (1995). Hegemony and Foreign Policy Analysis: The Case of Canada as a Middle Power. *Studies in Political Economy* 48, 7–29.

NSI (North-South Institute). (2003). *Canadian Development Report 2003*. Ottawa: North-South Institute.

Nossal, K. (2005). 'Ear Candy: Canadian policy toward humanitarian intervention and atrocity crimes in Darfur'. *International Journal*, 60 (4), 1017–32.

Owen, T. and D. Eaves. (2007). Africa is not a Liberal idea. *Embassy*, 3 October.

Payne, Anthony. (2006). 'Blair, Brown and the Gleneagles agenda: making poverty history, or confronting the global politics of unequal development?' *International Affairs*, 82 (5): 917–35.

Potter, Mitch. (2009). 'What next for G8. . . and Canada?' *The Toronto Star*, 26 September.

PMO (Office of the Prime Minister of Canada). (2009). 'Backgrounder: Canada's Capital Investment in the African Development Bank'. www.pm.gc.ca/eng/media.asp?id=2847].

Pratt, Cranford. (1989). 'Canada: A Limited and Eroding Internationalism'. In C. Pratt (ed.), *Internationalism Under Strain: The North-South Policies of Canada, the Netherlands, Norway, and Sweden*. Toronto: University of Toronto Press.

Sandbrook, Richard. (2005). 'Africa's Great Transformation?' *The Journal of Development Studies*, 41 (6): 1118–1125.

Taylor, Ian. (2005). *Nepad: Towards Africa's Development or Another False Start?* Boulder: Lynne Rienner.

Tomlinson, Brian. 2008. 'Canada: Overview: Unmet promises and no plans to increase Canadian ODA'. In The Reality of Aid Management Commmittee (eds.), *The Reality of Aid 2008*. Quezon City: IBON Books.

Travers, P. and Owen, T. (2008). 'Between metaphor and strategy: Canada's integrated approach to peacebuilding in Afghanistan'. *International Journal*, LXIII (3): pp. 685–702.

Vines, A. and T. Cargill. (2006). '"The world must judge us on Africa"—Prime Minister Blair's Africa Legacy'. *Politique Africaine*, April.

'What the G8 leaders were able to achieve'. (2005). *Globe and Mail* (Editorial), 9 July.

Williams, Paul. (2005). 'Blair's Commission for Africa: Problems and Prospects for UK Policy'. *The Political Quarterly*: 529–39.

Williams, P. (2008). 'Keeping the Peace in Africa: Why "African" Solutions Are Not Enough'. *Ethics and International Affairs*, 309–29.

Williams, Paul. (2009). 'The "Responsibility to Protect", Norm Localisation, and African International Society'. *Global Responsibility to Protect*, 1: 392–416.

York, Geoffrey. (30/1/2009). "Why has it taken so long?" *Globe and Mail*.

Introduction to 28

CANADIAN FOREIGN POLICY AND THE PROMOTION OF HUMAN RIGHTS

Duane Bratt and Christopher J. Kukucha

The international promotion of human rights has been a broad foreign policy goal of successive Canadian governments. This is because 'Canadians expect their government to be a leader in the human rights field by reflecting and promoting Canadian values, including respect for diversity, on the international stage'.[1] Canada's human rights efforts began in the immediate aftermath of World War II as a direct consequence of the horrors of the Holocaust. Canada participated in the Nuremburg Tribunals, which tried Nazi officials who had been charged with war crimes. In addition, Canada was an original signatory to the Universal Declaration of Human Rights and it was a Canadian, John Humphrey, who was the principal drafter of that Declaration. Canada also signed and ratified many of the subsequent United Nations–sponsored protocols. Despite this initial flurry of activity, however, 'it was not until the mid-1970s', as a major study on human rights and Canadian foreign policy concluded, 'that Canada was prepared to assign staff and resources to the task of promoting international respect for human rights'.[2] Kim Nossal similarly has noted that this commitment to human rights was 'neither sustained nor widespread. But there has been a historical empathy with those whose human rights have been violated and a desire to give expression to these symbolic interests'.[3]

Since the mid-1970s, Ottawa's rhetoric, both at home and abroad, was increasingly used to promote human rights. In 1977, External Affairs Minister Don Jamieson stated that 'Canada will continue to uphold internationally the course of human rights, in the legitimate hope that we can eventually ameliorate the conditions of our fellow man'.[4] Parliament's Special Joint Committee on Canada's International Relations declared in 1986 that 'the international promotion of human rights is a fundamental and integral part of Canadian foreign policy'.[5] The Mulroney government, following in the footsteps of John Diefenbaker in 1960–1, took a leadership position on the opposition to South African apartheid. Mulroney even publicly challenged his core allies (Ronald Reagan in the United States and Margaret Thatcher in the United Kingdom) to use economic sanctions to generate change. The 1995 foreign policy review by the Jean Chrétien government proclaimed that human rights were a 'fundamental value' and 'a crucial element in the development of stable, democratic and prosperous societies at peace with each other'. It added that Canada would 'make effective use of all of the influence that our economic, trading and development assistance relationships give us to promote respect for human rights'.[6] During his tenure as Canada's Foreign Affairs Minister (1996–2000), Lloyd Axworthy made human rights a central plank in his human security agenda. Axworthy's work on human rights was reflected in, among other things, his initiatives on the protection of children in armed conflict, the Ottawa Process on landmines, and his support for the establishment of an International Criminal Court (ICC). The *International Policy Statement* (IPS) from the Paul Martin government identified 'promoting respect for human rights' as a key foreign policy priority.[7]

Ottawa has also tried to go beyond statements and speeches and attempted to institutionalize its promotion of human rights. Human rights offices in both the Department of Foreign Affairs and International Trade (DFAIT) and the Canadian International Development Agency (CIDA) were created and human rights training programmes were established for Canadian officials. Canadian embassies were required to submit reports on states' human rights records. Human rights also became one of CIDA's six programme priorities in making decisions on Canadian development assistance. Critics maintain, however, that the promotion of human rights remains secondary to Canada's security and economic concerns.

Axworthy's legacy was also clear in Canada's role in the development of the concept of the Responsibility to Protect (R2P). At the core of R2P was a need to re-evaluate concepts of state sovereignty and humanitarian intervention. Motivated by atrocities in Rwanda, Yugoslavia, and Kosovo, the 2001 International Commission on Intervention and State Sovereignty (ICISS) promoted a new approach, in which governments had an obligation to respect the sovereign rights of other states as well as a responsibility to protect their own citizens. The criteria for involvement, however, would exclude intervention based on political oppression or the removal of democratically elected governments. As such, the ICISS process was endorsed by numerous non-governmental interests, in Canada and internationally, concerned about the potential abuse of R2P for less altruistic foreign policy objectives. In the aftermath of 11 September and the subsequent American invasion of Iraq, Prime Minister Martin also made it clear at the 2005 World Summit that R2P did not exist as a tool for US unilateralism. Michael Ignatieff's prior academic reflections on R2P, including being a member of the ICISS, also suggest a commitment to these principles if Liberal governments are elected in the future under his leadership.[8]

Canada's foreign policy has also highlighted questions of human rights in China. For the most part Canada has attempted to address these issues using 'quiet' or 'soft' diplomacy. Pierre Trudeau, for example, recognized the communist People's Republic of China in 1970, and famously met with Mao Zedong during a state visit, but was reluctant to raise questions concerning human rights. In contrast, Brian Mulroney's China Policy was extremely critical of Deng Xiaoping's violent response to student protesters in Tiananmen Square in 1989. The Chrétien government, on the other hand, took a more subdued approach on human rights in China, despite its commitment to Axworthy's human security objectives. This was due to Chrétien's efforts to increase Sino-Canadian trade and investment through several Team Canada Trade missions to China in the 1990s. The Chrétien government also failed to co-sponsor a UN resolution on China's human rights record during this period; instead, it established the Canada–China Bilateral Human Rights Dialogue in 1997. In a series of nine annual meetings, Chinese and Canadian officials discussed a wide range of human rights issues. During this period China signed the International Covenant on Civil and Political Rights (ICCPR) and the International Covenant on Economic, Social, and Cultural Rights (ICESCR). The current Harper government, on the other hand, has taken a noticeably tougher stance on human rights in China, especially on Tibet. Harper also waited five years to officially visit China and has continually rejected any attempts to link trade and human rights.

Historically, human rights have received considerable attention in Canada's foreign relations. This is not to suggest, however, that Canadian policies in this issue area are beyond reproach. Critics, for example, have highlighted the selective and economically marginal sanctions that Canada ultimately adopted against South Africa. Axworthy, despite his many successes, was often criticized as opportunistic and willing to capitalize on the work of other state and non-governmental interests, most notably the ICC and landmine initiatives. The Martin government also struggled with its

commitment to R2P, especially its failure to take a strong stand against atrocities committed by *janjaweed* militias against the Fur people in Sudan. Although the current Harper minority deserves credit for its action in Haiti, concerns have also been raised regarding the treatment of Afghan detainees and significant cuts to official development assistance.

A related issue in recent years is the question of Canadian citizens detained abroad. In September 2002 Maher Arar was arrested at New York's JFK airport and subsequently deported to Syria, where he was imprisoned and tortured until his release in October 2003. As the following excerpt suggests, Canada was criticized for its failure to aggressively pursue Arar's release or ensure his safety while in Syrian custody. It is important to note, however, that Arar is not an isolated example. William Sampson also languished in a Saudi Arabian prison for three years during this same period. The ongoing saga of Omar Khadr continues to raise similar questions regarding Canada's human rights rhetoric and its actual policies.

Key Terms

Responsibility to Protect

Notes

1. Department of Foreign Affairs and International Trade, 'Canada's International Human Rights Policy', (21 December 2009). Accessed on 1 April 2010 at www.international.gc.ca/rights-droits/policy-politique.aspx.

2. Robert O. Matthews and Cranford Pratt, 'Conclusion: Questions and Prospects', in Matthews and Pratt, eds., *Human Rights in Canadian Foreign Policy* (University of Toronto Press: Toronto, 1988), 294.

3. Kim Richard Nossal, *The Politics of Canadian Foreign Policy* 3rd Edition (Prentice-Hall: Toronto 1997), 114.

4. Canada, External Affairs Minister Don Jamieson, 'Human Rights: One of the Most Complex Foreign Policy Issues', *Statements and Speeches* (March 16, 1977), 7.

5. DFAIT, Human Rights and Canadian Foreign Policy (September 1998).

6. DFAIT, *Canada in the World: Canadian Foreign Policy Review* (1995).

7. DFAIT, Canada's *International Policy Statement: A Role of Pride and Influence in the World* (2005).

8. Brian W. Tomlin, Norman Hillmer, and Fen Osler Hampson, *Canada's International Policies: Agendas, Alternatives, and Politics* (Toronto: Oxford University Press, 2008), 249–61.

28

CHRONOLOGY OF EVENTS, 26 SEPTEMBER 2002 TO 5 OCTOBER 2003

Maher Arar

The following is an edited chronology of events as told by Maher Arar. It begins with his arrival at John F. Kennedy Airport in New York on September 26, 2002, and ends with his October 5, 2003, release from a Syrian prison.

26 SEPTEMBER 2002

Arar boards an American Airlines flight from Zurich to JFK airport in New York, en route to Montreal. He arrives in New York at 2:00 p.m., and lines up at the immigration counter. When his name is entered into the computer he is pulled aside. Two hours later he is fingerprinted and photographed. He is told this is regular procedure. Airport police search his bag and wallet and photocopy his passport. They refuse to answer any of Arar's questions, and will not let him make a phone call. Officials from the New York Police Department and the Federal Bureau of Investigation (FBI) say they will question him and then let him catch his connecting flight to Montreal. Arar asks for a lawyer,

but is told he has no right to a lawyer because he is not an American citizen. An intense interrogation continues until midnight. Arar is questioned about his work, his salary, his travel in the US, and about different people. He is questioned in particular about Abdullah Almalki. Arar tells them that he only knows him very casually, but that he worked with his brother Nazih at two high tech firms in Ottawa and Hull. He tells them that the Almalki family came from Syria about the same time as his, so the families know of each other. Arar does not know why they are questioning him so much about Abdullah. He tells them he has seen Abdullah a few times and he describes, in detail, the times he can remember. Arar is shocked when they show him the rental lease he signed when he moved to Ottawa in 1997. It was witnessed by Abdullah Almalki. Arar remembers this and explains he had asked Nazih to sign it, but that Nazih was busy and sent his brother instead. Arar describes the questioning as intense, and says he was pressured to answer all questions quickly. He says the American authorities were humiliating and rude. He tells them he has nothing to hide and tells them everything he knows. He asks repeatedly for a lawyer, but the request is ignored. Arar's wrists and ankles are chained, and he is taken in a van to a nearby building where others are being held and put in a cell.

27 SEPTEMBER 2002

At 9:00 a.m. Maher is taken for more questioning. He has not eaten or slept since he was on the flight from Zurich. He is interrogated for eight hours and is asked many questions including what he thinks about Osama Bin Laden, Palestine, and Iraq. He is also asked about the mosques he prays in, his bank accounts, his email addresses, and his relatives. An Immigration and Naturalization Service (INS) official informs him that they would like him to voluntarily return to Syria. Arar says no, he wants to return to Canada. He asks again for a lawyer but is again refused. Arar is asked to sign an immigration form, but they do not show him the contents; Arar, sleep-deprived, signs the form. At about 8:00 p.m. he is shackled and put in a van and driven to the Metropolitan Detention Centre (MDC). Arar continues to ask why this is happening, and they continue to refuse to answer him or tell him where he is being taken. He is strip searched and asked to sign more forms for a doctor and is vaccinated. He asks what the vaccine is, but they will not tell him. Arar continues to ask for a lawyer and a phone call and is ignored.

28 SEPTEMBER TO 7 OCTOBER 2002

Arar is not able to sleep until early in the morning and wakes up at 11:00 a.m. on 28 September. This is the first time he has slept since leaving Zurich two days earlier. Arar notices he is being treated differently from other prisoners at the MDC—for example, guards will not give him toothpaste, a toothbrush, or newspapers. On the second or third day at the MDC, Arar is given a document saying that he is inadmissible to the United States under Section 235C of the Immigration and Nationality Act because he is not is not a citizen of the United States; because he is a native of Syria, and is a citizen of Syria and Canada; because he arrived in the United States on 26 September 2002 and applied for admission as a non-immigrant in transit through the United States, destined to Canada; and because he is a member of an organization that has been designated by the secretary of state as a Foreign Terrorist Organization, to wit Al Qaeda a.k.a. Al Qa'ida. Arar continues to ask for a lawyer and phone call, and his requests are denied until 2 October when he is permitted to make a two-minute telephone call to his mother-in-law in Ottawa. He tells her that he is frightened and he might be deported to Syria. Arar asks her to get him a lawyer. On 3 or 4 October, Arar is asked to fill out a form asking where he would like to be deported to. He writes that he chooses to be sent to Canada and that he has no concerns about going there. He signs the document. On 4 October Arar receives a visit from Canadian consul Maureen Girvan. Arar shows her the document he has been given, and she notes the contents. He tells her he is frightened of being deported to Syria, and she reassures him that this will not happen. On 5 October Arar is visited by lawyer Amal Oummih. They talk for 30 minutes, and he relates his fears to her and asks her to help. She advises him not to sign anything without her being present.

6 OCTOBER 2002

At 9:00 p.m. on Sunday night, guards come to take Arar from his cell, saying that his attorney is there to see him. Arar is taken to a room where about seven officials are waiting. His attorney is not there.

He is told that they contacted his attorney and that 'he' refused to come (this is strange because Arar's lawyer is a woman). They ask why Arar does not want to go to Syria, and he tells them that he is afraid of being tortured there. He says he did not do his military service before leaving Syria and that he is a Sunni Muslim and that his mother's cousin was accused of being part of the Muslim Brotherhood and imprisoned. They ask him to sign a document and he refuses. This interrogation session continues until 3:00 a.m., when he is taken back to his cell.

8 OCTOBER 2002

Arar is woken at 3:00 a.m. and is told he is leaving. He is given food and then taken from his cell. A woman reads to him from a document, saying that based on classified information that they could not reveal to him, and because he knows a number of men—including Abdullah Almalki, Nazih Almalki, and Ahmad Abou-el-Maati—the INS director has decided to deport him to Syria. Arar protests and says that he will be tortured there. He is ignored. He is chained, taken to a waiting car, and driven to an airport in New Jersey. Arar is placed on a private jet. He is the only passenger. They fly to Washington, and the people with him disembark and a new team gets on the plane. Arar overhears the men talking on the phone saying that Syria is refusing to take him directly, but Jordan will take him. They fly to Portland, Maine, to Rome, and then to Amman, Jordan. On the trip to Amman, Arar is given a sweater and jeans to wear. He does not know then that he will wear these clothes until the end of December.

9 OCTOBER 2002

The jet lands in Amman, Jordan, at 3:00 a.m. There are six or seven Jordanians waiting for him. Arar is blindfolded, chained, and put into a van. He is forced to bend his head down in the back seat. He is beaten intensely every time he tries to move or talk. Thirty minutes later they arrive at a building where they remove his blindfold and ask him some routine questions before taking him to a cell. In the afternoon they take his fingerprints and photographs, and he is blindfolded and put in another van. He is told he is going back to Montreal. About 45 minutes later, they stop and he is put in a different car. He is forced to keep his head down, and he is beaten again. Over an hour later they arrive at what Arar believes is the Syrian border. He is handed over to a new team of men and put in a new car which travels for another three hours to Damascus. At about 6:00 p.m. he is taken into a building which he later finds out is the 'Far Falestin' or the Palestine Branch of the Syrian military intelligence. He is taken into a room for interrogation. There are three men in the room. Arar later learns that one of the men is a colonel. They put him on a chair and the colonel begins the interrogation. Arar is asked about his family and why they left Syria. Arar answers the questions but is threatened with a metal chair in the corner. He later learns that this chair is used to torture people. Arar decides he will confess to anything they want in order to stop the questioning. The interrogation lasts for four hours without any violence—only the threat of violence is used.

10 OCTOBER 2002

Early in the morning on 10 October, Arar is taken downstairs to a basement. The guard opens the door and Arar sees for the first time the cell he will live in for the next ten months and ten days. Arar calls the cell a 'grave'. It is three feet wide, six feet deep, and seven feet high. It has a metal door, with a small opening which does not let in light because of a piece of metal on the outside for sliding things into the cell. There is a one-by-two-foot opening in the ceiling with iron bars. This opening is below another ceiling and lets in just a tiny shaft of light. Cats urinate through the ceiling traps of these cells, often onto the prisoners. Rats wander there too. There is no light source in the cell. The only things in the cell are two blankets, two plastic bowls, and two bottles. Arar later uses two small empty boxes—one as a toilet, when he is not allowed to go to the washroom, and one for prayer water.

11 TO 16 OCTOBER 2002

Early the next morning Arar is taken upstairs for intense interrogation. He is beaten on his palms, wrists, lower back, and hips with a shredded black electrical cable which is about two inches in diameter. He is threatened with the metal chair, electric shocks, and with the tire, into which prisoners are stuffed, immobilized, and beaten. The next day Arar is interrogated and beaten on and off for 18 hours. Arar begs them to stop. He is asked if he received military training in Afghanistan, and he falsely confesses and says yes. This is the first time Arar is ever questioned about Afghanistan. They ask at which camp and provide him with a list, and he picks one of the camps listed. Arar urinated on himself twice during the interrogation. Throughout this period of intense interrogation Arar was not taken back to his cell but to a waiting room where he could hear other prisoners being tortured and screaming. One time, he heard them repeatedly slam a man's head on a desk really hard.

17 TO 22 OCTOBER 2002

During the second week of the interrogation, Arar is forced into a car tire so he is immobilized. This is done to scare him, but he is not beaten while in the tire, as was done with other prisoners. The

intensity of the beating and interrogation subsides after 17 October. Interrogators start using a new tactic. They take Arar into a room blindfolded so he can hear people talking about him: 'He knows lots of people who are terrorists.' 'We will get their numbers.' 'He is a liar.' 'He has been out of the country.' They occasionally slap him on the face.

23 OCTOBER 2002

Arar is taken from his cell and his beard is shaved. He is taken to another building where his interrogators and other investigators are waiting for him. They all seem nervous. Arar is warned not to say he has been beaten and is then taken into a room where he meets with a Canadian consul. He is accompanied by his interrogator, a colonel, and two other Syrian officials at all times. The meeting lasts for ten minutes with Arar crying throughout.

29 OCTOBER 2002

Arar receives his second visit from a Canadian consul and again is accompanied by Syrian officials and his interrogator throughout the meeting.

EARLY NOVEMBER, 2002

In early November 2002, Arar is taken from his cell to sign and place his thumbprint on every page of a handwritten document about seven pages long. He is not allowed to read it. He is shown another document about three pages long, with questions: Who are your friends? How long have you been out of the country? The last question is followed by empty lines. The first questions have already been answered by his captors, but Arar is made to answer the last in his own handwriting as they dictate to him. He is told to write that he has been to Afghanistan. He is forced to sign and place his thumbprint on the last page of that document.

12 NOVEMBER 2002

Arar receives his third visit from a Canadian consul and is again accompanied by Syrian officials and his interrogator throughout the meeting. Arar asks for money so he can purchase clothing and supplies. After the meeting, his captors are angry that he made that request, but he is not beaten.

10 DECEMBER 2002

Arar receives his fourth visit from Canadian consul and is again accompanied by Syrian officials and his interrogator throughout the meeting. The consul delivers money and, two weeks after the meeting, Arar is able to change his clothes for the first time since the flight from the US.

DECEMBER 2002

Sometime in December, Arar experiences a nervous breakdown. His mind is crowded with memories, and he loses control and starts screaming. This happens three times. The second time a guard notices and takes him to wash his face.

7 JANUARY 2003

Arar receives his fifth visit from Canadian consul and is again accompanied by Syrian officials and his interrogator throughout the meeting.

18 FEBRUARY 2003

Arar receives his sixth visit from Canadian consul, and is again accompanied by Syrian officials and his interrogator throughout the meeting. During the visit, the Syrian officials ask why consular visits are necessary. They say that they will take care of Arar.

EARLY APRIL, 2003

Arar is taken from his cell and placed in an outdoor court. This is the first time he has seen sunlight in six months.

23 APRIL 2002

Arar is taken from his cell and his beard is shaved. He is told to comb his hair and wash his face. He is taken outside, put in a car, and driven to another building. Once in the new building, Arar is given some tea. The Syrian officials seem very agitated and nervous. Arar is taken into a room to meet with Canada's Ambassador to Syria, Franco Pillarello, and two Canadian MPs, Marlene Catterall and Sarkis Assadourian. As usual, Arar is accompanied by his interrogator and other Syrian officials throughout the meeting. After he is taken from the room he overhears Syrian officials talking about media coverage of his case.

JUNE 2003

Arar is taken outside into the sunshine twice in June. He asks to meet with an investigator and his request is eventually granted. Arar also asks to be moved to a cell fit for human beings but is told that they are very busy because of the situation in Iraq and order him back to his cell.

JULY 2003

Arar asks again for a meeting with an investigator and, this time, his request is granted. Arar tells him he has nothing to do with Al Qaeda. The Syrian official asks Arar why he is accused of this, why they sent a delegation, and why these people hate him so much. Arar says he does not know. Arar notices his skin is turning yellow and feels he is at the brink of a nervous breakdown.

JULY 2003

Arar is taken from his cell and questioned about William Sampson [a Canadian in a Saudi Arabia jail]. He does not know who this is and says he does not. After the questioning Arar wonders if this is a journalist.

14 AUGUST 2003

Arar receives his seventh visit from the Canadian consul and is again accompanied by Syrian officials and his interrogator. However, this time, the head Syrian military intelligence is also present. Arar has decided he cannot survive living in these conditions anymore and that it is worth risking more physical torture to stop the ongoing psychological torture of remaining in the 'grave'. He bursts and tells the Canadian consul, in English, in front of the Syrian officials, about his cell and the conditions he is living in. The consul asks if he has been tortured, and Arar replies yes, of course—at the beginning. After the meeting, Arar can see that his captors are very angry, and he is terrified that he will be physically tortured again, but he is not.

19 AUGUST 2003

Arar is taken upstairs and made to sit on the floor. He is given a piece of paper to write on. He is told to write, among other things, that he went to a training camp in Afghanistan. The official kicks him every time he objects and also threatens to put Arar in the tire. Arar is forced to sign and put his thumbprint on the last page. Arar is then taken to the Investigation Branch and placed in a collective cell, which is about six by four metres in size. There are about 46 people crammed into the space—the door is difficult to open because of the crowding. The prisoners ask him who he is and where he

has been, and they are shocked to learn he has been in the 'grave' for so long. Arar spends that night there.

20 AUGUST 2003

Arar is blindfolded, put in a vehicle, and driven to Sednaya prison. Once again Syrian officials will not tell him where he is going. He has heard from the other prisoners at the Investigation Branch that prisoners are tortured when they arrive there, so he tells officials there he had been recently visited by a Canadian consular official. This seems to have an impact—Arar is not tortured when he arrives at Sednaya prison. He is placed in a collective cell and is able to talk with other prisoners and move around. Arar says this was like heaven compared to where he was at the Palestine Branch.

19 OR 20 SEPTEMBER 2003

Arar is teaching English to some other prisoners in his cell when he hears others saying that another Canadian has arrived. He looks up and sees a thin man with a shaved head looking very weak. After some time he realizes this is Abdullah Almalki. Almalki tells Arar he has also been at the Palestine Branch and that he was in a cell like Arar's for even longer. He tells Arar he has been severely tortured—with the tire and the cable. He says he was also hung upside down. Almalki also says he was tortured at Sednaya prison just weeks before.

28 SEPTEMBER TO 4 OCTOBER 2003

Arar is called from his cell and told to collect his things. He is blindfolded, put in a van, and driven back to the Palestine Branch. He is put in one of the interrogation waiting rooms and kept there for seven days. The entire time, he hears prisoners screaming while being tortured. Arar is devastated and does not know what is happening to him. At 9:00 p.m. on Saturday, 4 October he is told that he will be going to Canada. Arar does not believe this.

5 OCTOBER 2003

On Sunday morning Arar is told by the colonel to wash his face. The colonel seems very unhappy. They put chains on his wrists and legs and put him in a car. He is driven to a court. Arar still does not believe he is going to Canada. He is taken to meet with a prosecutor and asks again for a lawyer. He is told that he will not need one. The prosecutor reads from Arar's confession and Arar tries to protest, saying he was beaten and forced to say he went to Afghanistan. The prosecutor ignores him and tells him he must sign and put his fingerprint on the document. Arar does as he is told. He is not permitted to see the document. The prosecutor does not lay out any charges and tells him that he will be released. Arar is taken outside, put in a car and driven back to the Palestine Branch where he meets with the head of the Syrian Military Intelligence and officials from the Canadian embassy. Arar believes, at last, that he is being released. The colonel escorts them out of the building into a waiting embassy car. Arar is driven to the Canadian embassy and later taken to the Canadian Consul's home for a shower before taking his flight out of Syria.

Key Terms

Consular Services
Rendition

SELECTED BIBLIOGRAPHY

Adams, Michael. 2003. *Fire and Ice: The United States, Canada and the Myth of Converging Values.* Toronto: Penguin.

Breecher, Irving, ed. 1989. *Human Rights, Development, and Foreign Policy: Canadian Perspectives.* Halifax: Institute for Research on Public Policy.

Carment, David and David Bercuson. 2008. *The World in Canada: Diaspora, Demography, and Domestic Politics.* Montreal and Kingston: McGill-Queen's University Press.

Carty, Robert, and Virginia Smith. 1981. *Perpetuating Poverty: The Political Economy of Canada's Foreign Aid.* Toronto: Between the Lines.

Charlton, Mark W. 1992. *The Making of Canadian Food Aid Policy.* Montreal and Kingston: McGill-Queen's University Press.

Cooper, Andrew F., and Geoffrey Hayes, eds. 2000. *Worthwhile Initiatives? Canadian Mission-Oriented Diplomacy.* Toronto: Irwin.

Donaghy, Greg. 2003. 'All God's Children: Lloyd Axworthy, Human Security and Canadian Foreign Policy, 1996–2000', *Canadian Foreign Policy 10, 2* (Winter): 39–58.

Franceschet, Antonio, and W. Andy Knight. 2001. 'International(ist) Citizenship: Canada and the International Criminal Court', *Canadian Foreign Policy 8, 2* (Winter): 51–74.

Freeman, Linda. 1997. *The Ambiguous Champion: Canada and South Africa in the Trudeau and Mulroney Years.* Toronto: University of Toronto Press.

Gecelovsky, Paul, and T.A. Keenleyside. 1995. 'Canada's International Human Rights Policy in Practice: Tiananmen Square', *International Journal 50, 3* (Summer): 564–93.

Hampson, Fen Osler, and Dean F. Oliver. 1998. 'Pulpit Diplomacy: A Critical Assessment of the Axworthy Doctrine', *International Journal 58, 3* (Summer): 379–406.

Irwin, Rosalind, ed. 2001. *Ethics and Security in Canadian Foreign Policy.* Vancouver: UBC Press.

Kelley, Ninette and Michael Trebilcock. 1998. *Making of the Mosiac: A History of Canadian Immigration Policy.* Toronto: University of Toronto Press.

Knox, Paul. 1995. 'Trade, Investment and Human Rights', *Canadian Foreign Policy 3, 2* (Winter): 87–95.

MacDonald, Douglas and Heather A. Smith. 1999–2000. 'Promises Made, Promises Broken: Questioning Canada's Commitments to Climate Change', *International Journal 55, 1* (Winter): 107–24.

Matthews, Robert O., and Cranford Pratt, eds. 1988. *Human Rights in Canadian Foreign Policy.* Toronto: University of Toronto Press.

Morrison, David. 1998. *Aid and Ebb Tide: A History of CIDA and Canadian Development Assistance.* Waterloo: Wilfrid Laurier University Press.

Nossal, Kim Richard. 1998. 'Pinchpenny Diplomacy: The Decline of Good International Citizenship in Canadian Foreign Policy', *International Journal 54, 1* (Winter): 88–105.

———. 1988. 'Mixed Motives Revisited: Canada's Interest in Development Assistance', *Canadian Journal of Political Science 21, 1* (March): 35–56.

Pratt, Cranford. 2000–01. 'Ethical Values and Canadian Foreign Policy', *International Journal 56, 1* (Winter): 37–53.

———. 1999. 'Competing Rationales for Canadian Development Assistance', *International Journal 54, 2* (Spring): 306–23.

———, ed. 1996. *Canadian International Development Assistance Policies: An Appraisal.* Montreal and Kingston: McGill-Queen's University Press.

Potter, Evan. 2009. *Branding Canada: Projecting Canada's Soft Power through Public Diplomacy.* Montreal and Kingston: McGill-Queen's University Press.

Scharfe, Sharon. 1996. *Complicity: Human Rights and Canadian Foreign Policy.* Montreal: Black Rose Books.

Simpson, Jeffrey, Mark Jaccard, and Nic Rivers. 2007. *Hot Air: Meeting Canada's Climate Change Challenge.* Toronto: McClelland and Stewart.

Spicer, Keith. 1966. *A Samaritan State? External Aid in Canada's Foreign Policy.* Toronto: University of Toronto Press.

Stairs, Denis. 2003. 'Myths, Morals, and Reality in Canadian Foreign Policy', *International Journal 58, 2* (Spring): 239–56.

———. 1982. 'The Political Culture of Canadian Foreign Policy', *Canadian Journal of Political Science 15, 4* (December): 667–90.

Stoffman, Daniel. 2002. *Who Gets In: What's Wrong with Canada's Immigration Program—and How to Fix It.* Toronto: Macfarlane Walter and Ross.

KEY TERMS IN CANADIAN FOREIGN POLICY

1992 Vienna Conference on Human Rights: A major dispute occurred between Canadian indigenous groups and the federal government over the term indigenous 'peoples'. Canadian diplomats wanted this changed to 'people', as the former implied the acceptance of self-determination.

Aid Effectiveness: There is no consensus on the meaning of aid effectiveness. For some, especially economists, it refers to aid's capacity to promote economic growth. Others reject the conflation of growth and development, suggesting that aid effectiveness should refer to its capacity to reduce poverty and inequality. For some, it could even refer to the extent to which aid has contributed to other donor objectives, such as stability or security. Currently, discussions on aid effectiveness at international fora concentrate mainly on basic principles, such as the recipient country's role in formulating a development strategy and the need for donors to coordinate their assistance and align it with the recipient's strategy.

'Atlanticist' Unity: NATO is the institution that binds western civilization. There were threats to Atlanticist Unity during the Cold War, but these have become more pronounced since 9/11. This is a result of US unilateralism in Iraq and differing attitudes towards the Afghanistan mission between, principally, the North American and European members.

Autonomy: Although all political communities pursue specific objectives, none is able to consistently exercise complete autonomy due to internal and external demands and constraints. Autonomy can be minimal, partial, or significant.

Big Idea: An integrated approach to economic and physical safety in Canada–US relations, with Canada meeting American defence and security requirements in order to protect its access to the US market.

Border Security: A country's efforts to screen people and goods entering and leaving the country.

Buy American: An aspect of the 2008 American economic stimulus program that required recipients to use government funds to purchase American goods and services.

Canadian Centre for Foreign Policy Development: The Centre was established in 1994 to facilitate public engagement on foreign policy issues. Participants, such as non-governmental organizations, labour groups, the media, and business representatives, were engaged in ad hoc meetings and an annual National Forum on Canada's International Relations. The Centre was integrated into the formal structure of DFAIT in 2001.

Capacity: An organization's ability to deliver on its mandate. In the case of the public sector, this typically means a government department's ability to anticipate and prepare for events and trends, generate policy advice, and provide services.

Climate Change: The climate of a place or region is changed if, over an extended period (typically decades or longer), there is a statistically significant change in measurements of either the mean state or variability of the climate for that place or region.

Club: A group of nations united or associated for a particular purpose, a definition that purposely evokes a looser form of association than the common tendency to see informal groups of states working within international organizations as 'coalitions'.

Commission for Africa: The 17-member Commission struck by the British government of Prime Minister Tony Blair, and chaired by Blair, to formulate a blueprint for achieving African prosperity and security. It was created in anticipation of the 2005 Gleneagles Summit of the G8, with the intention of influencing summit decision-making. It produced a 460-page report, *Our Common Interest.* Just over half, or nine of the commissioners, were African.

Committee on Foreign Affairs and International Trade: Historically, the parliamentary committee established to study Canada's foreign policy. Sub-committees were also common, focusing on specific issues such as trade, Canada–US relations, and human rights.

Commonwealth: The 54-member international organization made up primarily of countries that were formerly part of the British Empire. Canada has long been a leading member.

Complex Neo-Realist Perspective: Focuses on the role of hegemonic powers in ensuring, defining, and extending international order in a system in which universal values remain secondary, in which a common security calculus and interest in balance provide no substitute, and in which leadership is required to transform convergent interests into stable order.

Consensus in the WTO: Means that nobody present objects; in practice it requires the active support of a critical mass of the most important players on any given issue.

Consular Services: Help and advice provided by the diplomatic agents of a country to citizens of that country who are living or traveling overseas.

Continentalists: People who advocate closer ties between Canada and the United States. They also argue that Canada should refrain from publicly criticizing the United States for fear of retaliation.

Cooperative Security: Emphasizes protecting the safety and human rights of individuals, the preventive use of international peacekeeping and peacebuilding efforts, greater attention to environmental and economic drivers of conflict, and collaborative institution-building, with a view of enhancing measures for conflict prevention, not just conflict resolution.

'Diplomacy of Concert': An international relations model that explains how countries are able to function cooperatively. Based on the Concert of Europe of the early nineteenth century, the model was developed by John J. Kirton to explain the successes of the G8. There are six factors considered by the concert diplomacy model when analyzing an international coalition: a shock to the prevailing order which induces mutual vulnerability; failure of other multilateral organizations; effectively equal and collectively predominant capabilities within the group; common core principles among members; controlled group participation; and domestic political capital.

Doha Round: WTO multilateral trade negotiations, formally known as the Doha Development Agenda, were launched in 2001 with the aim of ensuring that trade served the needs of development. As of early 2010, the negotiations remained stalled, although a substantial outcome remained within reach on agriculture and trade in goods and services.

Dual Bilateralism: Term referring to the separate development of cross-border relations and policies (US–Canada, US–Mexico) to accommodate differences in bilateral relationships and the often varied policy preferences of Canadian and Mexican governments in dealing with the United States.

Economic Policy: Includes all matters related to economic growth and fiscal and monetary issues.

Foreign Direct Investment: Usually defined by economic organizations as investment that allows the investor from one country (host or capital exporting country) to have a significant influence in the managing of an enterprise operating outside the investor's own country. This is usually set at ownership of 10 per cent or more of the ordinary shares or voting power. Investors may acquire this influence by establishing a new firm (a 'greenfield' investment) in a foreign (host or capital importing) country or by acquiring an interest in an existing foreign firm (i.e., via a takeover or merger)

Foreign Policy: The specific international goals of government officials and the values and mechanisms used to pursue these objectives.

Foreign Relations: A broader term, referring to functional issues and other non-controversial international activities.

'Fragmegration': Term coined to describe the simultaneous interaction of integrating and fragmenting forces at multiple levels of political, economic, or societal activity and policy development.

La Francophonie: An international organization of polities and governments with French as the mother or customary language, wherein a significant proportion of people are francophones or where there is a notable affiliation with the French language or culture. The organization currently has 56 member states and governments. Canada is a leading member, while the provinces of Quebec and New Brunswick are officially 'participating governments'.

Functional Principle: A post–World War II doctrine enunciated by the King government stating that non-great powers (like Canada) could make their most significant difference in world affairs when engaged in issues in which they had pre-existing expertise and active participation.

The Golden Age of Canadian Foreign Policy: The period generally understood to have begun shortly after the end of the Second World War and lasting until the late 1950s.

Good International Citizen: The myth that Canada is above all an enlightened middle power, more concerned with helping others on the world stage than with its own self-interest. Central to this national narrative or myth is the idea that multilateralism is the proper instrument of the middle power, that Canadians are the inventors of peacekeeping, and that Canada is the world's foremost peacekeeping nation.

The Gray Lecture: A speech by Secretary of State for External Affairs Louis St Laurent in January 1947 which outlined Canada's five international priorities: national unity, political liberty, the promotion of the rule of law in international affairs, global humanitarianism, and international activism.

Hegemony: A theoretical concept with both realist and critical meanings. As derived from the work of Italian Marxist Antonio Gramsci, and popularized by Canadian political economist Robert Cox, it is a form of dominance of one social group over another, i.e., the ruling class over all other classes, featuring a high level of consent on the part of the ruled. The ideas of the ruling class come to be seen as the norm; they are seen as universal ideologies, or a common sense, perceived to benefit everyone while in reality principally benefiting the ruling class. Cox has extended this thinking to the transnational level, arguing that transnational 'hegemonic orders' are pursued and sustained by transnational coalitions of elite groups.

Heiligendamm Process: The Heiligendamm Process was a specific G8 initiative that started at the 2007 G8 summit in Heiligendamm, Germany. The process itself was an official two-year dialogue in which the members of the G8 countries met with the Outreach Five countries (Brazil, China, India, Mexico, and South Africa) to discuss relevant issues.

Helpful Fixer: A depiction of Canada's middle power role in which it helps to solve some of the world's problems.

Human Security: This is a concept that transcends traditional military-centred notions of security to include additional threats. The United Nations Human Development report identifies seven aspects: economic security, food security, health security, environmental security, personal security, community security, and political security.

Idiosyncratic Variable: The extent or degree to which a prime minister seeks to distinguish the international behaviour of his/her government from other administrations; the way a prime minister uses the power of the office to achieve his/her goals.

Independent Diplomacy: An approach that uses exposure and public pressure in dealing with another country.

Independent Foreign Policy: An approach that seeks to differentiate Canadian foreign policy from that of the United States. The simplest—and most common—way of thinking about this is in terms of Canada's ability to pursue policies that the US opposes, without being forced to back down. But we could also think about independence in terms of autonomy more generally, in the context of a much wider variety of indirect pressures and structural constraints.

Indigenous Diplomacy: International initiatives by Aboriginal groups from a wide range of nation-states. In Canada, self-determination is an often-stated goal, but other efforts focus on matters of equality and fairness within Canadian federalism.

Inside/Outside: A binary division, developed by R.B.J. Walker, that underwrites most understandings of contemporary world politics. Those 'inside' the state are the proper focus of efforts to provide citizens with security and well-being, but those 'outside' the state are unambiguously defined as the 'Other' and thus beyond the definition of altruism, to be assisted and defended only if it is in the state's interests to do so.

'Intermestic': Term coined to capture the progressive interweaving of domestic and international factors in policy-making.

International Centre for Human Rights and Democratic Development: A non-partisan organization, created by an Act of Parliament in 1988, that promotes and supports principles of democracy, especially those codified in the International Bill of Human Rights.

International Law of the Sea: A branch of international law, largely codified in the United Nations Convention on the Law of the Sea, which is concerned with territorial waters, sea lanes, and ocean resources.

Internationalism: A central concept in the study and practice of Canadian foreign policy. Internationalism is also a contested concept, subject to multiple definitions and interpretations. Drawing off the work of Kim Richard Nossal, the idea commonly includes elements of multilateralism, good international citizenship, community, and volunteerism.

Investment Agreements: Bilateral or multilateral agreements between states that address aspects of the foreign investment relationship, including market access of foreign investors to host economies; national treatment, that is, non-discriminatory treatment of foreign firms once they have been established in a host country; and rules requiring host states to follow certain procedures if they expropriate the assets of foreign firms in their country, either directly or indirectly.

Investor-State Dispute Resolution: Refers to provisions in an investment or trade agreement that allow foreign firms to challenge host state actions that may be tantamount (or equivalent) to expropriation of their assets, often resulting from changes in host state laws or regulation. Traditionally such disputes have been handled between states that were party to the agreement. Chapter 11 of the North American Free Trade Agreement has investor-state provisions and is seen to afford a high level of protection to foreign investors.

Investment Screening: A process by which host states bargain with foreign investors and require them to undertake certain commitments prior to affording them permission to invest in the host economy. Commitments may involve using a certain amount of local inputs in production and other activities that benefit the host economy.

Isolationism: A general opposition to military commitments abroad.

Keynesianism: A policy paradigm, influential in the postwar period, that recommended state management of the economy, by deficit financing if necessary, to ensure there was sufficient demand in the economy to produce full, or very high, levels of employment. Often associated with the construction of a comprehensive welfare state.

Kyoto Protocol: The Kyoto Protocol to the United Nations Framework Convention on Climate Change was negotiated in December 1997 and came into force in February 2005. Developed states with commitments to the Kyoto Protocol have struggled to meet their commitments. The United States withdrew from the Kyoto Protocol in 2001 and Canada has not met its commitments.

Mandate Letters: A two- or three-page note given to a minister at the outset of his/her tenure outlining those issues and areas of importance on which the minister is to focus. The letter is written by the Privy Council Office, after consultation with the Prime Minister's Office and the deputy minister(s) affected by the change.

Middle Power: A country, like Canada, that was not as big as the great powers, but more important than small powers. This allowed Canada to make a significant contribution to international affairs but without the influence or obligations of the great powers.

Millennium Development Goals: Eight goals adopted in 2000 by all member states of the United Nations and two dozen international organizations. They set targets to be achieved by 2015 in several areas, including extreme poverty and hunger, primary education, gender equality and women's empowerment, child mortality, maternal health, and environmental sustainability.

Multilateralism: Working with other countries, usually in international organizations, to achieve its foreign policy goals.

Multi-level Governance: The formal and informal interactions and processes between various levels of government at the domestic and international levels for policy development and implementation.

NATO Transformation: After the end of the Cold War, NATO decided not to disband, but rather to transform itself in two ways: 1) enlargement, by adding new members from central and eastern Europe; and 2) adding new functions like participating in peacekeeping operations in the former Yugoslavia and Afghanistan.

Nationalists: People who advocate an independent foreign policy for Canada in its relations with the United States. Measures should be taken to prevent economic dependence on the United States and to distance itself from American security preoccupations.

Neoliberalism: A policy paradigm, influential since the 1970s, premised on a reduced role for the state and an enhanced one for markets. Protection of property rights and value of money are key goals. Domestically, the paradigm recommends spending cuts to ensure balanced budgets, deregulation, and privatization; and internationally, capital mobility and free trade.

New Multilateralism: Challenges traditional notions of multilateralism by envisaging a more interventionist set of international institutions as well as the possibility of moving beyond these institutions to intervene if and when the institutions fail to act.

Norm Entrepreneurship: The process by which new norms are promoted and popularized so that a broad consensus is built around them, leading to their eventual socialization and institutionalization among a wide range of governments. The process requires 'norm entrepreneurs' who actively seek to build support for the norms in question. Canada has sometimes been thought of as a norm entrepreneur, notably in relation to ideas such as human security or the Responsibility to Protect.

Official Development Assistance: Aid provided by donor countries primarily to promote economic development and welfare in developing countries. Contributions from individuals, foundations, or private corporations do not count as ODA, nor do military assistance or export credits meant primarily to promote the sale of goods from the donor country.

Pacifist Quebec: A belief that English and French-Canadians hold differing views on security and defence issues, with French-Canadians being more dovish, isolationist, and antimilitary than their Anglophone counterparts.

Partnership Paradigm: The framework for Canada–US relations during the Cold War, which saw the United States give Canada favourable economic treatment in return for Canada's willingness to maintain an open investment climate and contribute to continental and North Atlantic defence.

Peacekeeping: The deployment of a United Nations force involving military, police personnel, and civilians to preserve the peace.

Policy Coherence: The degree to which the different donor country policies are complementary, rather than working at cross-purposes (for instance, when a country's trade or defence policies contradict its aid policies). Ideally, a country achieves policy coherence through a 'whole-of-government approach', whereby its different departments cooperate around a common objective.

Policy Parallelism: Policy processes reflecting unilateral decisions by governments to adopt the broad outlines of initiatives taken by their counterparts while attempting to retain some discretion to respond to domestic political, economic, or socio-cultural conditions.

Politico-Operational Values: These are values and priorities emphasized by political officials. In Canadian foreign policy these traditionally include the rule of law, multilateralism, peacekeeping, and international development assistance. The priority placed on these values has shifted dramatically over time.

Principal Powers: These have three characteristics: 1) they stand at the top of the international status ranking, collectively possessing decisive capability and differentiated from lower-ranking powers by both objective and subjective criteria; 2) they act as principals in their international activities and associations, rather than as agents for other states or groupings or as mediators between principals; and 3) they have a principal role in establishing, specifying, and enforcing international order.

Protector: The myth that Canada is a 'protector'. In the specific case of the Afghanistan mission, Canada, through its soldiers on the battlefield, is presented as the protector of weak, notably Afghan, civilians (and most particularly, women and children). This narrative constructs Canada as an international citizen with a particular moral compass against which it is difficult to express criticism or express opposition: to do so means that the critic is content to let women and children suffer.

Provincial Reconstruction Team: A combination of civilian and military forces to provide security and reconstruction in an unstable state.

Psycho-Social Values: These values, recognized within Canadian society, include, respect for the environment, democracy and democratization, social equity, and human rights and tolerance.

Québécois: The French-speaking population living in the territory of the province of Quebec.

Quiet Diplomacy: An approach in which the parties tacitly agree to negotiate in confidence, refrain from criticizing one another in public, and, more generally, avoid 'politicizing' the issues by talking to the media or stirring up the general public. In the Canada–US context, it is often used more broadly to refer to a general commitment to seek influence in Washington, by going out of one's way to work closely with the US.

Quiet Revolution: A period of rapid change in 1960s Québec, including secularization, economic reforms, attitudes towards military institutions, level of education within the population, and an increase in national identity.

Realism: A school of international relations that is state-centric and prioritizes national interest and security, rather than ideals, social reconstructions, or ethics.

Realm: Connotes a sphere or domain that is both a political space and an ideational construct of political identity and community that goes beyond the state as it is usually defined in international relations.

Rendition: The handing over of prisoners to countries where torture is allowed.

Responsibility to Protect: Governments have a responsibility to protect their own citizens. The concept also justifies humanitarian intervention based on political oppression or the removal of democratically elected governments.

Role or Positional Variable: The constitutional powers of the office, or the range of authority that any person occupying the position would possess. The four constitutional powers of the office of the prime minister, of relevance to our discussion regarding foreign policy-making, are: (1) power of appointment; (2) design of administrative structures; (3) design of decision-making processes; and, (4) plenipotentiary authority.

Satellite: Canada is a peripheral-dependent/satellite country that moved seamlessly from existing as a British colonial dependency to being pulled into the orbit of the American empire.

Security: The military ability of a state to either defend itself against the military actions of other states or to enforce its will on another state.

Sherpa: The sherpa is a head of state's personal representative for the G8 summits. The sherpa prepares the way for the summit meetings by communicating with high-ranking government officials of other countries. Generally several sherpa meetings are held prior to the summit in which the ground work for the discussions and communiqués are laid out, ensuring that the summits themselves are efficient and productive.

Soft Power: According to Joseph Nye, soft power is defined by the culture of a country or organization, and by how these values define internal policies and practices, as well as external relations. In contrast, hard power is based on material resources, especially those tied to military end economic power.

Sovereignty: There are three main elements of sovereignty: a defined territory; an existing governance system and a people within the defined territory.

Special Relationship: Canadian and American political leaders have long maintained that there is a special relationship between the two countries, but there is room for debate about whether that is so, and what it might mean. Usually the phrase is used to refer to the idea that the US treats Canada differently than other, similar allies or trade partners, in being more attentive to Canadian concerns and/or more forgiving of Canadian provocations.

Standing Committee on Foreign Affairs and International Development: One of two House of Commons committees established during the 40th session of Parliament by the minority government of Stephen Harper. The FAAE's work included Afghanistan, corporate social responsibility, and energy.

Standing Committee on International Trade: Was the second House of Commons committee established by the Harper government. It evaluated various trade negotiations, the United States, and NAFTA's Chapter 11. The CIIT also aggressively supported the protection of Quebec's protectionist supply management system in ongoing WTO negotiations.

Strategic Culture: A set of ideas (concepts, metaphors, images, symbols, etc.) shared by a given community, forming a coherent and persistent whole and helping to shape the group's attitude toward the use of force and the role of military institutions. Because a strategic culture is formed primarily by historical experience, it tends to remain stable over time.

Summit: A meeting of heads of government.

Third Way: A pragmatic, centrist political approach that espoused a combination of growth, entrepreneurship, enterprise, and wealth creation along with greater social justice. It sees the state playing a major role in bringing this about. In the words of one of its leading proponents, Anthony Giddens, the Third Way rejects both top-down socialism and traditional neo-liberalism. It was most vigorously championed by the 'New Labour' government of British Prime Minister Tony Blair, but was supported by other centrist governments including those of Bill Clinton of the United States, Gerhard Schroeder of Germany, and Jean Chrétien of Canada.

Tied Aid: Development assistance that must be used to purchase good and services from the donor country. This usually adds an estimated 15 to 30 per cent of the cost, since the same goods and services are usually available elsewhere for a lower price.

Trade Policy: Focuses on the exchange of goods and services and the negotiation and implementation of international (and domestic) trade commitments that often fluctuate between protectionism and liberalization.

Trade Promotion: The expansion of export markets for domestic goods, and in some cases the pursuit of investment.

Transgovernmental Relations: Formal and informal relations and processes between legislative, executive, regulatory, and judicial officials outside formal diplomatic channels.

Undersecretary of State: In Canada, the highest ranking executives in the bureaucracy are typically referred to as deputy ministers, but in the Department of External Affairs, the DM is still often referred to as the undersecretary of state, because his 'minister' was the secretary of state for external affairs. The use of the elegant term still persists, but most government documents now refer to a deputy minister of external affairs and a deputy minister of international trade.

UN Permanent Forum: An institutionalized mechanism within the United Nations allowing an 'entrenched site' for indigenous diplomats.

Variable Geometry: Regional policy processes characterized by the willingness of some countries (or, in a North American context, interests in specific industries or policy sectors) to undertake deeper integration independently of the unwillingness of other members (or sectors) to do the same.

KEY DATES IN CANADIAN FOREIGN POLICY

BEFORE CONFEDERATION

19 June 1812	Start of the War of 1812 between the United Kingdom/Canada and the United States.
24 December 1814	Treaty of Ghent is signed, ending the War of 1812.
29 April 1817	Rush-Bagot Treaty is signed, restricting warships in the Great Lakes.
20 October 1818	Anglo-American Convention of 1818 is signed, fixing the British North America and United States border along the 49th parallel from the Lake of the Woods to the Rocky Mountains.
6 June 1854	Reciprocity Treaty is signed, creating a free trade agreement between British North America and the United States.
17 March 1866	Reciprocity Treaty is abrogated by the United States in retaliation for British support of the Confederacy.
April–June 1866	Fenian raids from the United States into British North America.

THE IMPERIAL ERA

1 July 1867	The British North America Act unifies the British colonies in Ontario (Canada West), Québec (Canada East), New Brunswick, and Nova Scotia into the Dominion of Canada.
23 May 1870	Rupert's Land and the Northwestern Territory Order is signed, transferring these lands from the Hudson's Bay Company to Canada.
15 July 1870	Manitoba enters Confederation.
8 May 1871	Treaty of Washington is signed with the United States, laying out fishing and trading rights on the Great Lakes.
20 July 1871	British Columbia enters Confederation.
1 July 1873	Prince Edward Island enters Confederation.
10 June 1880	Canada appoints its first diplomat, Sir Alexander Galt, as High Commissioner to Britain.
9 October 1880	Arctic islands ceded to Canada by Britain.
12 July 1882	Canada appoints a commissioner to France.
18 March 1885	Northwest Rebellion under the leadership of Louis Riel begins.
4 October 1899	Canadian troops depart to assist the British in the Boer War.
1 September 1905	Alberta and Saskatchewan enter Confederation.
1908	Ontario opens a commercial office in Britain.
11 January 1909	Boundary Waters Treaty signed with the United States, creating the International Joint Commission (ICJ).
19 May 1909	Department of External Affairs is created.
4 May 1910	Royal Canadian Navy is created.
1911	Québec opens a commercial office in Britain.
21 September 1911	Federal election sees Prime Minister Wilfrid Laurier defeated and replaced by Robert Borden. As a result, the negotiated reciprocity (free trade) agreement with the United States does not get ratified.

FIRST WORLD WAR (1914–18)

4 August 1914	Great War begins: Britain declares war on Germany and all parts of the Empire (including Canada) are automatically at war.
3 October 1914	First Canadian troops leave for Europe.
2 March 1917	First meeting of the Imperial War Cabinet in London.
9 April 1917	Canadian troops fight as a distinct national corps as the Battle of Vimy Ridge begins.
29 August 1917	Conscription (military draft) becomes law.
17 December 1917	Federal election, with conscription as the major election issue, sees Borden re-elected, but without any seats in francophone Canada.
1 April 1918	Anti-conscription riot in Québec City results in four deaths.
1 October 1918	Canadian forces arrive in northern Russia to assist in civil war against the Bolsheviks.
11 November 1918	Armistice brings First World War to an end.

INTERWAR PERIOD (1919–39)

28 June 1919	Canada signs the Versailles Peace Treaty, officially ending the First World War.
10 January 1920	The League of Nations is established with Canada as a founding member.
2 March 1923	Canada signs its first international treaty—the Halibut Treaty with the United States.
1 July 1923	Chinese Immigration Act is proclaimed, barring Chinese from entering Canada.
14 September 1926	Federal election has Mackenzie King win a majority government after the 'King-Byng' affair'.
October 1926	Imperial Conference (October 27–November 19) agrees to grant Canada and the other dominions full autonomy in domestic and international affairs.
18 February 1927	Canada's first diplomatic mission—a legation in Washington—opens in Washington.
18 September 1929	Canada opens a diplomatic mission in Japan.
29 October 1929	New York Stock Exchange crash; beginning of the Great Depression.
17 June 1930	US adopts the Smoot-Hawley tariff on imported goods; most of the rest of world also raises tariffs.
11 December 1931	Statute of Westminster gives Canada and the other dominions full sovereignty.
20 July 1932	Imperial Economic Conference creates preferential trade within the British Empire.
1935	The 'Riddell Affair': Canada's Representative to the League of Nations, against the wishes of the King government, pushes for economic sanctions against Italy for its invasion of Ethiopia.
29 June 1937	Mackenzie King, visiting Germany, meets Hitler.
18 August 1938	US President Franklin D. Roosevelt visits Queen's University and issues the 'Kingston Dispensation.'

SECOND WORLD WAR (1939–1945)

1 September 1939	Nazi Germany attacks Poland, starting the Second World War.
10 September 1939	Canada declares war on Germany, seven days after Britain.
10 June 1940	Canada declares war on Italy.
18 August 1940	Ogdensburg Agreement on defence is signed with the United States.
7 December 1941	Japan attacks Pearl Harbour; United States declares war on Japan; Canada declares war on Japan.

25 December 1941	Allied troops in Hong Kong surrender after being overrun by Japanese forces; 2000 Canadians are killed or captured.
1 January 1942	In Washington, 26 states (including Canada) sign the Declaration by United Nations pledging cooperation in the defeat of Germany and Japan.
27 April 1942	Referendum on conscription reveals strong support in English Canada and equally strong rejection in Québec.
19 August 1942	Dieppe Raid leads to 3367 Canadian casualties in its first European battle of the war.
9 July 1943	Mackenzie King sets forth in the House of Commons the 'functional principle' for representation in international institutions.
10 July 1943	Beginning of the Italian campaign: British, Canadian, and American troops land in Sicily.
1–16 May 1944	First Commonwealth Prime Ministers' Meeting in London.
6 June 1944	D-Day: American, British, and Canadian troops land at Normandy.
1–22 July 1944	Canada participates in the UN Monetary and Financial Conference at Bretton Woods, New Hampshire.
23 November 1944	Mackenzie King decides to implement conscription.
8 May 1945	Germany surrenders, ending the war in Europe.
25 June 1945	UN Charter is signed in San Francisco.
15 August 1945	Japan surrenders, ending the war in the Pacific.

THE COLD WAR ERA (1945–90)

5 September 1945	Igor Gouzenko, a clerk at the Soviet embassy in Ottawa, defects with evidence of a Soviet spy ring.
13 January 1947	Louis St Laurent, Canada's Secretary of State for External Affairs, delivers the Gray Lecture which outlines the principles of Canadian foreign policy.
12 March 1947	US President Harry Truman announces the policy of containment (Truman Doctrine) that becomes the basic principle of US policy towards the USSR.
5 June 1947	The Marshall Plan of US economic aid to Europe is announced.
9 July 1947	Brooke Claxton presents *Canada's Defence*, the first white paper on defence.
30 October 1947	The General Agreement on Tariffs and Trade (GATT) is signed at Geneva.
16 June 1948	Blockage of Berlin by Soviet Union begins (ends May 12, 1949).
31 March 1949	Newfoundland enters Confederation.
4 April 1949	North Atlantic Treaty, creating NATO, is signed in Washington.
23 May 1949	Federal Republic of Germany (West Germany) established; German Democratic Republic (East Germany) created October 7, 1949.
1 June 1949	Apartheid is instituted by the ruling Nationalist Party of South Africa.
1 October 1949	People's Republic of China, led by Mao Zedong, is proclaimed; Kuomintang (Nationalist) government under Chiang Kai-shek moves to Taiwan.
13 January 1950	Commonwealth foreign ministers meet in Colombo to establish the Colombo Plan for aid in South and Southeast Asia.
25 June 1950	Korean War begins; Canada sends destroyers and ground combat troops to serve with US-led UN force.
26 November 1950	China enters the Korean War and drives UN forces back.
31 January 1951	Canada deploys air and ground forces to Europe as part of its NATO commitment.
18 April 1951	European Coal and Steel Community is formed.

18 February 1952	Greece and Turkey join NATO
27 July 1953	Armistice agreement ends the Korean War.
30 June 1954	Canada approves the installation of the Distant Early Warning (DEW) radar line.
21 July 1954	French colonial rule in Indochina ends; Vietnam is divided into North and South at 17th parallel.
6 May 1955	West Germany joins NATO; Warsaw Pact formed in response (May 14, 1955).
26 July 1956	Egypt nationalizes the Suez Canal; precipitating the Suez crisis.
29 October 1956	Egypt, French, and Israeli forces attack Egypt; Lester Pearson proposes a UN peacekeeping force to intervene.
1 November 1956	Soviet Union invades Hungary
25 March 1957	Treaty of Rome establishes the European Economic Community (EEC)
26 August 1957	Soviet Union launches first intercontinental ballistic missile (ICBM).
4 October 1957	Soviet Union launches Sputnik, first satellite.
14 October 1957	Pearson awarded Nobel Peace Prize.
12 May 1958	NORAD agreement between Canada and the United States is signed.
1 January 1959	Fidel Castro's revolution overthrows the Cuban government.
20 February 1959	Prime Minister John Diefenbaker announces the cancellation of the Avro Arrow, a Canadian-developed jet fighter.
26 June 1959	The St Lawrence Seaway, a joint Canada–United States project, opens.
29 March 1960	Defence Minister George R. Pearkes announces that Canadian troops in Europe will acquire US 'Honest John' rocket systems equipped with nuclear warheads.
22 June 1960	Jean Lesage and the Liberals win the Québec election; the 'Quiet Revolution' begins.
17 January 1961	Columbia River Treaty on the use and control of the Columbia River basin is signed between Canada and the United States.
2 February 1961	First Sino-Canadian grain sale announced.
8–17 March 1961	South Africa leaves the Commonwealth, during a Prime Ministers' Meeting in London, over the issue of Apartheid.
12 June 1961	Canada acquires US F-101B (Voodoo) fighter aircraft, which is nuclear equipped, for North American defence.
12 August 1961	Construction of the Berlin Wall begins.
16–28 October 1962	Cuban Missile Crisis.
7 August 1964	Following naval incident in the Gulf of Tonkin, US Congress passes Gulf of Tonkin resolution, giving President Lyndon Johnson the power to deploy US forces for the defence of allies (primarily in Vietnam).
16 January 1965	Canada–US Automotive Agreement (Auto Pact) signed by Pearson and Johnson.
27 February 1965	Québec–France Entente in education.
8 March 1965	US combat troops are sent to Vietnam.
2 April 1965	Pearson gives a speech at Temple University where, in part, he criticizes US military activity in Vietnam.
12 April 1965	Paul Gérin-Lajoie, Quebec's minister of education, gives a speech articulating doctrine of Quebec's competence in international affairs.
1 July 1966	France withdraws from integrated military command of NATO, but remains a signatory to the North Atlantic Treaty.
1 May 1967	The Nigerian civil war begins as the province of Biafra declares secession.

5–10 June 1967	Arab-Israeli war (Six-Day War).
30 June 1967	Kennedy Round of GATT trade negotiations is signed.
24 July 1967	French President Charles de Gaulle gives his 'Vive le Québec libre' speech in Montréal, which appears to endorse the Québec separatist movement.
30 January 1968	The Tet offensive is launched by communist forces in Vietnam.
5 February 1968	Québec, on invitation from Gabon, participates in the Conference of Educational Ministers from francophone countries; Canada suspends diplomatic relations with Gabon on March 4, 1968.
29 May 1968	Pierre Trudeau, in his 'Canada in the World' statement, announces that Canada will move to recognize the People's Republic of China and will support its membership in the United Nations.
11 July 1968	The Nuclear Non-Proliferation Treaty is signed.
20 August 1968	Soviet and Warsaw Pact forces invade Czechoslovakia.
25 August 1969	First *Manhattan* voyage through the Northwest Passage.
16 September 1969	Defence Minister Léo Cadieux announces that Canada's NATO forces in Europe will be cut in half and that Canada will disengage from its nuclear role in Europe.
20 March 1970	Agence de coopération culturelle et technique (ACCT) created.
1 April 1970	Second *Manhattan* voyage; Parliament passes Arctic Waters Pollution Prevention Act (April 8).
25 June 1970	Trudeau government releases its foreign policy white paper: *Foreign Policy for Canadians*.
5 October 1970	The Front de Libération du Québec (FLQ) kidnaps British trade commissioner James Cross, starting the October Crisis; Quebec Cabinet minister Pierre Laporte is later kidnapped and murdered; War Measures Act is invoked October 16.
13 October 1970	Canada and China establish diplomatic relations.
14–22 January 1971	Commonwealth Heads of Government Meeting held in Singapore, first CHOGM held outside Britain.
24 April 1971	Defence Minister Donald S. MacDonald tables a defence white paper, *Defence in the 70s*.
15 August 1971	'Nixon Shocks:' US government imposes economic measures to stem balance of payments deficit, devalues the dollar, and abandons fixed exchange rates.
12 November 1971	Gray Report recommending a foreign investment screening agency is leaked.
16 December 1971	East Pakistan declares independence as Bangladesh following civil war and war between India and Pakistan.
22 January 1972	EEC expanded to include Britain, Denmark, Ireland, and Norway (Norwegians reject membership in a national referendum, September 1972).
21 February 1972	Nixon visits China.
15 April 1972	Great Lakes Water Quality Agreement between Canada and the United States is signed in Ottawa.
27 January 1973	Vietnam ceasefire agreement signed in Paris; last US troops leave Vietnam (March 29); last US prisoners of war released (April 1).
11 September 1973	Coup d'état in Chile; President Salvador Allende commits suicide and is replaced by General Augusto Pinochet.
12 September 1973	Tokyo Round of GATT negotiations begin (concludes April 1979).
6–24 October 1973	Arab-Israeli war (Yom Kippur war).

19 October 1973	Oil embargo imposed by OPEC against the United States, later extended to Japan and Europe; oil prices rise rapidly.
18 May 1974	India, using Canadian technology, explodes nuclear device; Canada ends all nuclear cooperation.
1 August 1975	The Agreement on Security and Co-operation in Europe (Helsinki Accord) is signed by 35 countries including Canada.
15–17 November 1975	The leaders of France, the United States, the United Kingdom, Germany, Italy, and Japan meet at Rambouillet, France, at the first Group of Seven summit; Canada attends the 1976 summit in Puerto Rico.
16 June 1976	The Soweto uprising results in the worst racial violence in South Africa's history.
15 November 1976	The Parti Québécois, under René Lévesque, wins the Québec election.
8–15 June 1977	Gleneagles Declaration of apartheid in sport agreed to by Commonwealth leaders in London.
3 November 1977	French President Giscard Valèry d'Estaing publicly affirms his support for self-determination in Québec.
September 1978	Camp David Accord marks Egypt's recognition of Israel and peace negotiations begin between the two countries.
25 December 1978	Vietnam invades Cambodia; thousands of 'boat people' begin to flee Vietnam.
16 January 1979	Iranian revolution; Shah Mohamed Reza Pahlavi abdicates and leaves Iran; he is replaced by the Ayatollah Ruhollah Khomeini.
5 June 1979	Prime Minister Joe Clark announces that the government will proceed to move its embassy from Tel Aviv to Jerusalem; decision is reversed, pending the settlement of the status of Jerusalem, on October 29.
4 November 1979	US embassy personnel in Tehran seized as 'hostages' by Iran; Canada's Ambassador to Iran, Ken Taylor, secretly helps six members of the US embassy to escape disguised as Canadians; remaining Americans released January 1981.
24 December 1979	Soviet Union invades Afghanistan.
22 April 1980	Canada joins boycott of 1980 Moscow Olympics.
22 May 1980	Québec referendum on sovereignty-association is defeated.
22 September 1980	Iraq invades Iran, beginning eight-year war.
7 June 1981	Israeli aircraft bomb a nuclear reactor in Iraq.
20–21 June 1981	Canada hosts G7 summit at Montebello, Québec.
21–23 October 1981	International Meeting on Cooperation and Development, Cancún, Mexico, chaired by Trudeau and Mexican President José Lopéz Portillo.
12 January 1982	Department of External Affairs reorganized to incorporate Trade and Commerce.
2 April 1982	Argentina invades the Falklands Islands.
17 April 1982	Elizabeth II signs Constitution Act in Ottawa.
1 September 1983	Korean Air Lines Flight 007 shot down by Soviet fighters.
25 October 1983	United States invades Grenada.
27 October 1983	Trudeau launches his 'peace imitative.'
November 1984	External Affairs Minister Joe Clark arrives in Ethiopia and announces an emergency food aid programme to address Ethiopia's famine.
17-18 March 1985	'Shamrock Summit' between Mulroney and Reagan in Québec City.
14 May 1985	Government green paper on foreign policy, *Competitiveness and Security,* is published.

23 May 1985	Air India bombing is linked to Sikhs in British Columbia.
10 July 1985	French intelligence agents bomb the Greenpeace ship *Rainbow Warrior* in Auckland harbour, killing one person.
21 July 1985	South Africa government imposes a state of emergency.
1 October 1985	Canada formally requests free trade negotiations with the United States.
16 October 1985	At the Commonwealth Heads of Government Meeting in Nassau, the Mulroney government states that it is committed to keeping the issue of economic sanctions against South Africa on the agenda, despite British opposition.
22 February 1986	First Francophone summit, Paris.
25 September 1986	Uruguay Round of GATT negotiations launched (completed December 1993).
1 May 1987	The House of Commons Standing Committee on External Affairs and International Trade releases *For Whose Benefit*, a report evaluating official Canadian development assistance efforts.
5 June 1987	Defence white paper, *Challenge and Commitment: A Defence Policy for Canada,* is released.
2–4 September 1987	Canada hosts francophone summit for the first time at Québec City.
2 January 1988	The Canada–US Free Trade Agreement is signed by Mulroney and Reagan.
19–21 June 1988	Canada hosts G7 summit at Toronto.
29 September 1988	UN peacekeepers win Nobel Peace Prize.
4 June 1989	Tiananmen Square massacre in Beijing.
5 November 1989	First meeting of Asia–Pacific Economic Cooperation forum at Canberra.
9 November 1989	Berlin Wall is breached.
13 November 1989	Canada joins the Organization of American States.
20 December 1989	United States invades Panama.
10 February 1990	South African black leader Nelson Mandela is released from prison.
2 August 1990	Iraq invades Kuwait.
3 October 1990	Germany is reunited.
19–21 November 1990	Second CSCE summit at Paris marks the formal end of the Cold War.

POST–COLD WAR ERA (1990–2001)

29 November 1990	The United Nations Security Council authorizes military action if Iraq does not withdraw from Kuwait by January 15, 1991.
16 January 1991	A US-led coalition launches air attacks on Iraq.
24 February 1991	A US-led coalition launches a ground offensive against Iraq.
27 February 1991	Iraq withdraws from Kuwait; the military offensive against Iraq ends.
13 March 1991	Mulroney and George H.W. Bush sign the first Canada–US Air Quality Accord, committing both countries to reducing emissions causing acid rain.
25 June 1991	Croatia declares independence; civil war breaks out in Yugoslavia.
30 September 1991	Coup d'état in Haiti overthrows President Jean-Bertrand Aristide.
25 December 1991	Soviet Union formally dissolves.
21 February 1992	UN Security Council approves the deployment of a peacekeeping force for Yugoslavia (UNPROFOR).
24 April 1992	UN Security Council creates the first peacekeeping mission for Somalia (UNOSOM).
3–14 June 1992	UN Conference on Environment and Development (Earth Summit), Rio de Janeiro.

8 December 1992	US troops land in Somalia, beginning Operation Restore Hope; Canadian troops arrive December 14–15.
17 December 1992	NAFTA is signed by Mexico, Canada, and the United States.
26 February 1993	Islamists detonate a truck bomb in the North Tower of the World Trade Center, New York.
March 1993	Somalia affair: members of the Canadian Forces kill Somali civilians caught stealing from Canadian base in Belet Huen.
14–25 June 1993	World Conference on Human Rights, Vienna.
1 November 1993	Maastrict Treaty comes into force; European Community becomes the European Union.
5 November 1993	External Affairs and International Trade Canada is renamed the Department of Foreign Affairs and International Trade (DFAIT).
11 January 1994	Canadian General Roméo Dallaire sends a fax to the United Nations regarding the need for more troops in Rwanda.
22 February 1994	Jean Chrétien's first budget includes a decrease in official development assistance spending.
6 April 1994	Plane carrying presidents of Rwanda and Burundi is shot down; ethnic violence and genocide erupt in Rwanda, leaving 800,000 dead in 100 days.
26–28 May 1994	Nelson Mandela elected first black President of South Africa.
19 September 1994	After US invasion embarks for Haiti, military agrees to restore Aristide to power.
1 December 1994	National Defence Minister David Collenette releases *1994 Defence White Paper*.
1 January 1995	World Trade Organization is inaugurated.
7 February 1995	Foreign policy white paper, *Canada in the World*, is released.
23–24 February 1995	'Turbot War': Canada arrests the Spanish fishing vessel *Estai* in international waters for overfishing.
15–17 June 1995	Canada hosts G7 summit, Halifax.
4–15 September 1995	Fourth UN World Conference on Women, Beijing.
30 October 1995	Second referendum on Québec sovereignty is narrowly defeated.
21 November 1995	Dayton General Framework Agreement for Peace in Bosnia and Herzegovina is negotiated.
14 May 1997	International currency speculators assault Thai baht, marking the start of the Asian financial crisis.
20 June 1997	At the G7 summit in Denver, Russia joins as a full member (making it the G8).
1 July 1997	Hong Kong returns to Chinese sovereignty.
5 July 1997	Canada concludes a bilateral free trade agreement with Chile.
21–25 November 1997	Canada hosts APEC summit, Vancouver.
3 December 1997	Convention on the Prohibition of the Use, Stockpiling, Production and Transfer of Anti-Personnel Mines and on their Destruction (Ottawa Treaty) is signed by 125 countries.
11 December 1997	Kyoto Protocol to the UN Framework Convention on Climate Change is adopted.
May 1998	India tests five nuclear bombs and Pakistan responds with six nuclear tests.
17 July 1998	Rome Statue of the International Criminal Court is signed.
7 August 1998	Al Qaeda bombs US embassies in Kenya and Tanzania.
2 December 1998	La Francophonie creates Organisation international de La Francophonie (OIF).
1 January 1999	Euro becomes the official currency of the EU.
16 March 1999	Czech Republic, Hungary, and Poland all join NATO.
24 March 1999	NATO commences bombing of Serbia over Kosovo; Canadian CF-18s bomb Serb targets.

20 September 1999	Security Council-authorized INTERFET forces intervene in East Timor to expel Indonesian militias; Canada's contribution (Operation Toucan) arrives by October 15.
14 December 1999	Ahmed Ressam arrested entering the United States with materials for a bomb he was planning to detonate at Los Angeles International Airport on New Year's Eve.
15 December 1999	First meeting of the G20 finance ministers and central bank governors is chaired by Paul Martin, Jr., in Berlin.
20–22 April 2001	Summit of the Americas, Québec City.
23 April 2001	Canada concludes a bilateral free trade agreement with Costa Rica.

POST–9/11 ERA (2001–PRESENT)

11 September 2001	Al Qaeda hijacks four airliners and flies two into the World Trade Center towers and one into the Pentagon; a fourth airliner crashes into a Pennsylvania field.
13 September 2001	NATO invokes Article 5, its collective security provision, for the first time in response to the 9/11 attacks.
7 October 2001	US attacks Afghanistan where Al Qaeda is headquartered; Canada contributes troops.
9 November 2001	Doha Development Round of WTO trade negotiations begins.
10 November 2001	China joins the WTO.
27 November 2001	The Bonn Summit discusses the future in post-Taliban Afghanistan.
11 December 2001	The United Nations War Crimes Tribunal charges former Serbian president Slobodan Milosevic with genocide.
12 December 2001	Canada and the US issue a 'smart border' declaration.
12 December 2001	Battle of Tora Bora forces last Taliban units in Afghanistan into Pakistan.
13 December 2001	The US withdraws from the 1972 Antiballistic Missile Treaty.
20 December 2001	UN Security Council creates International Security Assistance Force (ISAF) for Kabul.
30 January 2002	During his State of the Union speech, US President George W. Bush declares that Iraq, Iran, and North Korea represent an 'axis of evil'.
15 March 2002	The UN Conference on Financing for Development is held in Monterrey, Mexico.
18 April 2002	American fighters accidently bomb Canadian soldiers outside Kandahar, killing four.
26–8 June 2002	Canada hosts G8 at Kananaskis.
1 July 2002	International Criminal Court at The Hague enters into force.
26 September 2002	Maher Arar, a Canadian citizen of Syrian origin, is arrested at New York's airport and is renditioned to Syria where he is tortured; he is released to Canada on October 3, 2003.
12 October 2002	Jemaah Islamiyah terrorist attacks in Bali, Indonesia, kill 202 and injure 209.
17 December 2002	Canada ratifies the Kyoto Protocol.
12 February 2003	Canada announces that it will send 2000 soldiers to Afghanistan as part of ISAF in Kabul.
17 March 2003	Chrétien announces that Canada will not join the US-led 'coalition of the willing' in using force against Iraq.
19 March 2003	The US-led war against Iraq begins (called Operation Iraqi Freedom).
1 May 2003	George W. Bush announces that major combat operations are over in Iraq.
20 May 2003	An Alberta cow is found to have bovine spongiform encephalopathy (BSE), or mad cow disease, causing the United States and Japan to halt their imports of Canadian beef.
7 December 2003	Zimbabwe leaves the Commonwealth.
12 March 2004	Canadian forces begin deployment to Haiti.

2 April 2004	Bulgaria, Estonia, Latvia, Lithuania, Romania, Slovakia, and Slovenia all join NATO.
1–3 September 2004	Chechen militants take 1000 children hostage at an elementary school in Beslan, Russia; 344 people are killed, more than half of whom are children.
26 December 2004	Indian Ocean tsunami; Canada deploys its Disaster Assistance Response Team (DART) to Sri Lanka.
22 February 2005	Martin government announces it will not participate in Ballistic Missile Defence plan with the United States.
25 March 2005	Martin, Bush, and Mexican President Vicente Fox sign the Security and Prosperity Partnership.
19 April 2005	Martin government tables its *International Policy Statement* in Parliament.
7 July 2005	Islamist suicide bombers attack London transport system ('7/7' attack).
16 August 2005	Canada assumes command of provincial reconstruction team in Kandahar City.
14–16 September 2005	The United Nations World Summit is held in New York; its outcome document endorses the Responsibility to Protect principle.
27 April 2006	Harper government announces that Canada and the United States have reached an agreement on softwood lumber.
5 May 2006	Québec given permanent representation at UNESCO within the Canadian delegation.
6 May 2006	Harper government announces an increase in defence spending of $5.3 billion over five years.
2 June 2006	Police arrest 17 Muslim men in Toronto, alleging a plot to detonate truck bombs against targets in Ottawa and Toronto and to decapitate Harper; eighteenth member of the 'Toronto 18' arrested August 3.
12 July 2006	War between Israel and Hezbollah in southern Lebanon; Canadian government evacuates some of the 30,000 Canadian citizens in Lebanon.
13 March 2008	House of Commons passes motion to extend Afghanistan mission to 2011.
7–16 August 2008	South Ossetian war between Russia and Georgia.
September 2008	Global financial crisis.
1 April 2009	Albania and Croatia join NATO.
7–18 December 2009	UN Climate Change conference, Copenhagen.
12 January 2010	Massive earthquake hits Haiti; Canada deploys DART.
12–13 April 2010	Nuclear Security Summit brings world leaders to Washington to discuss measures towards safeguarding nuclear materials.
26–7 June 2010	Canada hosts G8 and G20 summits, Huntsville and Toronto.